THE INSIDERS' GUIDE TO
Madison

THE INSIDERS' GUIDE TO Madison

by
Genie Campbell
and
Chris Martell

Co-published and marketed by:
Madison Newspapers, Inc.
1901 Fish Hatchery Road
P.O. Box 8056
Madison, WI 53708
(608) 252-6200

Co-published and distributed by:
Insiders' Publishing
105 Budleigh St.
P.O. Box 2057
Manteo, NC 27954
(252) 473-6100
www.insiders.com

Sales and Marketing:
Falcon Publishing
P.O. Box 1718
Helena, MT 59624
(800) 582-2665
www.falconguide.com

•

2nd EDITION
1st printing

•

Copyright ©1998
by Madison Newspapers, Inc.

•

Printed in the United States
of America

•

All rights reserved. No part of this book may be reproduced in any form without permission, in writing, from the publisher, except by a reviewer who wishes to quote brief passages in connection with a review in a magazine or newspaper.

Publications from The Insiders' Guide® series are available at special discounts for bulk purchases for sales promotions, premiums or fundraisings. Special editions, including personalized covers, can be created in large quantities for special needs. For more information, please write to Karen Bachman, Insiders' Publishing, P.O. Box 2057, Manteo, NC 27954, or call (800) 765-2665 Ext. 241.

ISBN 1-57380-083-X

Madison Newspapers, Inc. publishers of Wisconsin State Journal and The Capital Times

Project and Editorial Manager
Gwen Evans

Sales Executive
Lisa Maly

Advertising Art Manager
Sharon Schroeder

Editorial Assistant
Julie Cline

Insiders' Publishing

Publisher/Editor-in-Chief
Beth P. Storie

Vice President/
New Business Development
Michael McOwen

Creative Services Director
Deborah Carlen

Art Director
David Haynes

Managing Editor
Dave McCarter

Project Editor
Eileen Myers

Project Artist
Andrew Smith

Insiders' Publishing
An imprint of Falcon Publishing Inc.
A Landmark Communications company.

Preface

Madison is at an especially interesting moment in its history. Almost daily, you can see evidence that this quiet university town is becoming a big city. As more people move here in search of a better life, longtime residents who love the city are faced with a challenge of, on the one hand, welcoming a growing and diverse population and, on the other hand, guarding the things that make Madison special: its green space, its schools, its unhurried lifestyle.

Madison's longstanding reputation as a tolerant city is being put to the test. Nowhere are the rapid changes in Madison more noticeable than Downtown. Not more than a decade ago, like many urban centers, Madison's Downtown lost its retail vigor. Retailers that had been on the Capitol Square since the turn of the century fled the Square for outlying malls.

City leaders came up with a Master Plan called Downtown 2000 in 1989. It aimed to keep the Downtown as the center of government, business, finance, education and culture. It would make the central city as vibrant as it once was and persuade people to live near the Square once again. And they aimed to add something new to Madison's distinctive persona: It was to be a tourist and convention mecca.

The plan worked, better than anyone dared to dream. You will hear the word renaissance used a lot when people discuss the central city these days. Its Downtown business district has new upscale office buildings, enough new restaurants to ensure that dining out in Madison will never be dull, and a growing residential neighborhood made up of young and old alike. Handsome new condos and apartments have been built, most of them skillfully blending in with buildings that have been here for most of the century.

The megavitamin that Madison took was the opening of the Frank Lloyd Wright-inspired Monona Terrace in the summer of 1997, followed shortly afterward by the opening of the Kohl Center, where UW sports events and major concerts are held. At long last, Madison, despite always having been beautifully located on an isthmus between two lakes, became something it never was before: a tourist haven.

In this book, we hope to give you a feel for the Madison that has been around for as long as anyone can remember, as well as the Madison that is on the fast track into the next millennium.

About the Authors

Genie Campbell

Genie Campbell feels like a Madison native even if she truly isn't one. Genie moved here in the fall of '77 to join the staff of the *Wisconsin State Journal*. But she first became acquainted with the city while living in Chicago and covering the arts scene for Paddock Publications, a chain of suburban newspapers. Accompanied by her roommate, who was originally from Stoughton, a small community just south of Madison, Genie enjoyed driving to the Capital City on football Saturdays to watch the UW Badgers play (back in the days when winning wasn't everything).

Genie earned a bachelor's degree in journalism and psychology from Indiana University. Before coming to Madison, she lived in four different states — all in the Midwest.

As features editor of the *State Journal*, she oversaw a half-dozen lifestyles sections and spearheaded other special projects for Madison's morning newspaper. A weekly dining review column she initiated — "Diner's Scorecard" — is still going strong after almost 20 years.

Today, as a freelancer, Genie writes on a variety of topics for area and national publications. Many of her travel stories — whether to nearby Spring Green or overseas — have been published by the *State Journal*, which also carries Genie's Sunday retail business column, "Shop Talk."

During the summer when Genie isn't facing a deadline, she's likely to be on the golf course trying to break 100. She managed to nail her first hole-in-one while putting the finishing touches on the first edition of this book. She also enjoys dining out, theater and traveling just about anywhere. Genie met her husband, Tom Rostad, an attorney and Madison business owner, while cross-country skiing at one of the many beautiful outdoor recreational areas she writes about in *The Insiders' Guide® to Madison*.

Genie and Tom live on the near West Side of Madison, within 10 minutes of the Capitol, with their two teenage daughters, Berit and Mollie, two gerbils, two birds and a German shorthaired pointer.

Chris Martell

Chris Martell owes her existence to Madison, since her parents met there as college students after World War II. Her family has roots in the state that date back to the late 1800s, and Chris was raised in the Milwaukee suburb of Elm Grove. Summers were spent at the family cottage on Lake Winnebago, about two hours north of Madison, where her grandfather bought property in the 1920s so he could fish.

Chris graduated from the University of Wisconsin in fine arts and journalism, and began her career as a radio and television reporter in Madison and Milwaukee. She covered the State Capitol, city and county government and police beats during those years. In 1985 she began working for the *Wisconsin State Journal* as a regional reporter. The experience introduced her to many parts of Wisconsin that she'd never seen before, and hundreds of interesting people.

Since the birth of her daughters Julie and Sara, who are now 12 and 10, she has been working in the features department of the *State Journal* because it is one of the few places in a daily newspaper that offers a regular schedule. In addition to writing general features, she is a restaurant reviewer for the paper. Madison has become something of a dining mecca in the last few years. Being a feature writer has meant concentrating on the happier aspects of life, and getting to know a side of Madison that has nothing to do with politicians and bureaucrats. It is a city full of constant surprises and intriguing people.

Chris still spends as much time as possible in the summer at Lake Winnebago, in a cottage 10 doors down from the one her grandfather built and her parents now own. Chris' husband of 16 years is Jim Jerving, an editor at *Cuna*.

Acknowledgments

Chris . . .

I often tell my two daughters, Julie and Sara, how lucky they are to be growing up in a city like Madison. They agree. It's a great thing to thoroughly enjoy the community you have chosen to be your home, and I don't think it is all that common.

As a reporter in this city for many years, I thought I knew just about everything about Madison. Working on this book showed me all sorts of nooks and crannies that I wasn't aware of before, and ways to make living here even more interesting than it has been. Now that this book is finished I plan to spend the summer doing many of them — as soon as I clean up the mess in my home office.

I'd like to thank many of my colleagues at the *Wisconsin State Journal* for sharing their expertise with me. Librarian Ron Larson was always the picture of good-humored patience, no matter how bizarre the questions I brought him. Entertainment reporter Natasha Kassulke graciously helped me figure out what clubs and live arts deserve mention in this book. Sports editor Greg Sprout guided me through the many changes in local sports in the last year, and higher education reporter Jennifer Galloway had valuable insights about the UW-Madison. Liz Beyler, at the UW news service, was also a big help.

I'd also like to thank my neighbor and federal highway engineer, Bill Bremer, for sharing his knowledge of the roadways with me — a person who still manages to occasionally get lost on streets I've driven hundreds of times. Julie Maryott Walsh was kind enough to help me figure out the Madison bus system.

It has been a great pleasure working on this book with my longtime friend and former editor at the WSJ, Genie Campbell. And although Eileen Myers, the editor of this book, lives on the East Coast and we know each other only through email messages, her observations and questions contributed greatly to this book.

I thank my girls and my husband, Jim, for being good sports when work on this book resulted in their feeling ignored, and way too many frozen pizzas. I also thank my parents, Betty and Don Martell, for bringing me to Madison, where they met while attending the UW, for Badger games and walks through the campus when I was a girl. They gave me an appreciation for this city that has never waned.

Genie . . .

This book represents for me a bigger-than-life jigsaw puzzle: finding the pieces, then deciding which ones best fit together. The painstakingly detailed process of sifting and winnowing is made more difficult because, as any of you who reside here know, nothing is ever a given in Madison. But, if I appreciated Madison before, after so much fact finding I'm simply in awe of the diverse opportunities the city offers and, at the same time, more cognizant of the pressing challenges ahead as the Capital City and surrounding communities continue to grow and spread.

I'm certainly indebted to the trail blazers ahead of me. I'm thinking of Ron Seely of the *Wisconsin State Journal*, whose book *Madison & Dane County* perfectly captures the spirit of this glorious locale; Susanne Voeltz, a communications guru who wrote the handy *Downtown Guide* that is now out-of-print but richly deserves to be republished; and Frances W. Hurst, whose love of outdoor art in Madison, captured in *Common Joy II*, smoothed out some of the wrinkles in the Attractions chapter. In very short supply — but, oh, so very helpful — were the Madison Heritage booklets published by the Madison Landmarks Commission and the Madison Trust for Historic Preservation. Thanks Gary Tipler for tracking them down and for your own contribution on "Mansion Hill." And, of course, the all-inclusive *Madison, A History of the Formative Years* by David Mollenhoff was invaluable in providing solid background information.

Many thanks, too, to Lynne Eich, executive director of the Dane County Cultural Affairs Commission. It's always nice to do business with you, Lynne. The Dane County Cultural Resources Directory is superb, as always. For cross reference, I'm also indebted to the Madison dailies's annual *Answer Book*, edited by Rick Uhlmann and Gary Neuenschwander, and the *Isthmus Annual Manual*.

For this book, I literally talked to hundreds of people, some of whom were not only kind enough to offer pearls of wisdom, but also gathered relevant information for me. While I can't name them all, they include Ken Chraca, coordinator of the Arts Consortium on the UW-Madison campus; Bob Brennan, longtime president of the Madison Chamber of Commerce; Deb Archer, president of The Greater Madison Convention & Visitors Bureau; Robert D'Angelo, director of the Madison Civic Center; George Hagenauer, assistant director of Community Coordinated Child Care Inc.; Sandy Kallio, assistant features editor of the *Wisconsin State Journal*; and Madison Newspapers librarians Ron Larson, Dennis McCormick and Carol Schmitt. A highlight of writing this book was receiving a private tour of Frank Lloyd Wright's Taliesin estate. Thanks for taking the time, Beth.

When it came to fitting the physical pieces of this book together, I'm obliged to ace photographer Roger Turner; to WSJ religion writer Bill Wineke and Faith Community Baptist Church organist George Rogers; to editors Eileen Myers (in North Carolina) and Gwen Evans (in Madison); my "personal" advisors, Jean Petersen and Anita Clark; and co-author, Chris Martell, a former colleague of mine. Where would I be without my longtime "Trifemirate" partners, Anita and Sunny Schubert: Our shared camaraderie and adventures all these years served me well — as fodder for many of these entries. And what would I have done without frequent words of encouragement from friend Gayle Galston and soul mate/fellow writer Mary B. Good! (Yes, that's her real name.)

I realize I'm not up for an Academy Award — Pulitzer Prize would be even better — but indulge me as I acknowledge the support of my better (did I say that?) half, Tom Rostad; my teenage daughters, Mollie and Berit; and the biggest fans any writer could have, my parents, Olive and Guy Campbell, who thoroughly enjoy Madison whenever they come to visit.

Finally, it's important to recognize two people no longer associated with this project who were instrumental in producing the first edition of *The Insiders' Guide To Madison*®: co-author Shari Hamilton and editor Margo O'Brien Hokanson. I know what you're thinking, but it really wasn't the workload that chased them away.

Table of Contents

History 1
Area Overview 9
Politics and Perspectives 19
Getting Here, Getting Around 27
Restaurants 39
Nightlife 83
Brewpubs, Wine Bars and Cigar Bars 105
Hotels and Motels 113
Bed & Breakfast Inns 127
Festivals and Annual Events 135
Kidstuff 157
The Arts 173
Attractions 193
The Literary Scene 215
Shopping 227
Sports 257
Parks and Recreation 265
Daytrips 297
Wisconsin Dells 311
Real Estate 325
Neighborhoods 337
Child Care 359
Schools 365
Higher Education 377
Healthcare 387
Retirement and Senior Services 401
Media 415
Worship 427
Index of Advertisers 432
Index 433

Directory of Maps

Madison and Surrounding Areas x
Madison xi
Downtown Madison xii
University of Wisconsin/Madison xiii

Madison & Surrounding Areas

Madison

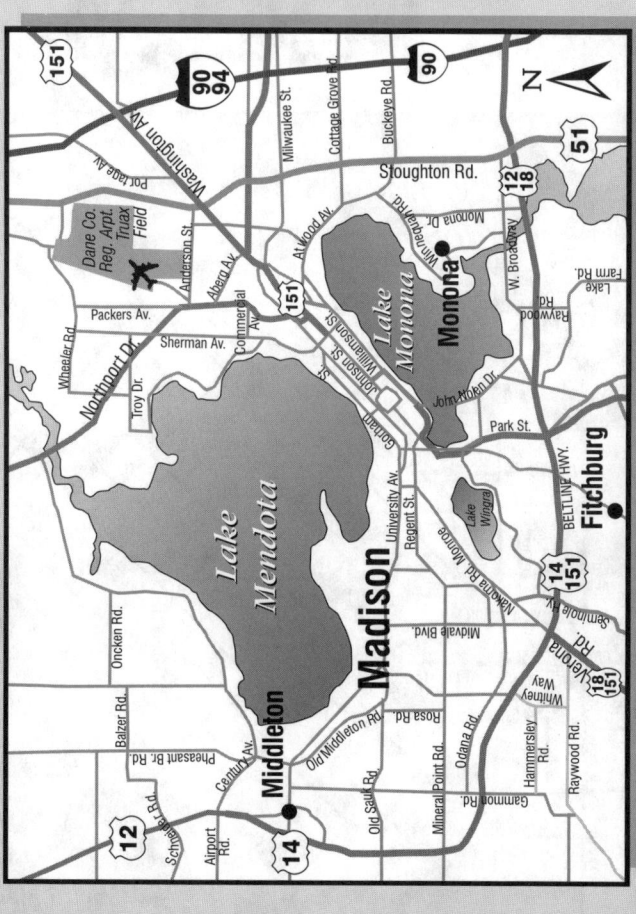

Downtown Madison

University of Wisconsin/ Madison

1. Lowell Hall (Wisconsin Center Guest House)
2. Campus Assistance Center
3. Memorial Union
4. Elvehjem Museum of Art
5. Geology Museum
6. Union South
7. Observatory Hill and Drive
8. Babcock Hall Dairy Plant
9. Camp Randall Sports Complex
10. Picnic Point
11. UW Hospital and Clinics
12. Kohl Center

How to Use This Book

There are many ways to organize a book. Our goal in writing *The Insiders' Guide® to Madison* is to allow you, the reader, to map your own approach for gleaning information. You could make this one long, entertaining read or just use the book as a quick reference guide. Either way, we suspect you'll use this guide repeatedly, not read once and forgotten.

This is a book for all ages, with answers for all kinds of questions. From Kidstuff to Retirement and Senior Services, we've researched topics and put together information to help you quickly find the answers you want to take advantage of all that Madison and surrounding communities offer. Whether you're looking for a good restaurant, a place to buy a new suit before a big meeting, activities for your kids to do or help in caring for an aging parent, you'll find information to help you within *The Insiders' Guide® to Madison*.

One of our biggest challenges in writing this book has been to simplify geographical boundaries. Even some people who live in Madison will call the UW-Madison campus "Downtown" part of the time, then later describe the campus as part of the Isthmus. (Since some people never leave the boundaries of the campus — making it a city within a city — we decided to separate it out.) People also draw uneven lines between what is southeast and northeast, southwest and northwest. That's Mother Nature's fault, really. With our unusual topography, it's difficult to dissect Madison into nice even grids. For brevity, therefore, we have divided informational listings into just five categories: Isthmus, Campus, West Side, East Side and Outlying Area. The latter category includes the towns of Stoughton, Monona, Middleton, Sun Prairie, Oregon, Fitchburg, Verona, Cottage Grove, DeForest, Waunakee and, every once in awhile, Cross Plains (see our Neighborhoods chapter et al). If you have access to an automobile, the entire city is at your doorstep. A trip across town takes less than 30 minutes (excluding rush hour).

Be advised that you may come across listings for some places in more than one part of the book. We have cross-listed items in some places to make it easier for those who are using the book as a quick reference and who are pressed for time. For instance, you'll find some eateries listed in the Restaurants and Nightlife chapters as well as in the Brewpubs, Wine Bars and Cigar Bars chapter. When we list places more than once, you'll find we added chapter-specific information.

For hotels and motels, we increased the number of geographical categories to help you get to your destination faster when you are tired of traveling and just want to relax.

We include pricing information in the Accommodations, Bed and Breakfast Inns and Restaurant chapters. Some chapters such as the Restaurants, Nightlife and Kidstuff are broken out by category — not just geographically — so you can quickly find your favorite style of dining or fun.

If you're new to Madison, we suggest you start your voyage of discovery with the Getting Around chapter. It will help you understand the eclectic nature of our city's layout.

Thinking of staying in Madison for awhile? If you'd like to buy or build a house here, check out the Real Estate and Neighborhoods chap-

ters for hints and resources. The History and Politics and Perspectives chapters will key you into Madison past with such tidbits as a recounting of the days when live pigs were kept in the Capitol basement, and legislators would poke the pigs to make them squeal to drown out their opponents' arguments.

Be advised that the most common area code used for places listed in this book is 608 although it is not usually necessary to dial it for local calls. There are some exceptions, described in the Daytrips and Wisconsin Dells chapters. For instance, from Madison, it is necessary to first dial 1 and then the area code, 608, to reach the Wisconsin Dells. Communities of Jefferson and Fort Atkinson, along with most of Jefferson and Dodge counties, switched their area code from 608 to 920 in the fall of 1997. More changes are bound to occur as cellular phones eat up available phone num-

bers. For convenience sake, whenever we list a telephone number, we include the area code.

With all of Madison's resources, we regret that we could not include every option in every category. We have, however, provided you with a sturdy platform from which to start. Since Madison's most interesting resource is its people, we hope you'll talk to local residents when you have further questions. As a last resort, there's always the Yellow Pages.

We've made every effort to ensure accuracy in this book and to include the best of Madison. We are human, however, and Madison tends to change at an amazing pace. So if your reality in using this book differs from what we've stated, we'd like to hear your comments along with your suggestions for improving future editions. Direct your letters to Insiders' Publishing, P.O. Box 2057, Manteo, North Carolina 27954.

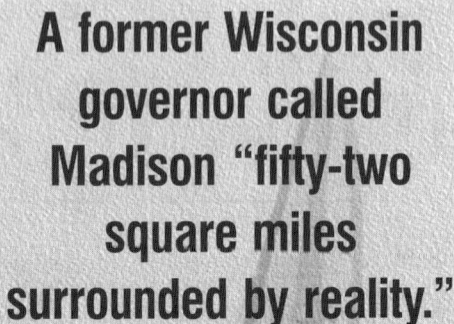

A former Wisconsin governor called Madison "fifty-two square miles surrounded by reality."

History

Wisconsin celebrated 150 years of statehood in 1998 with a yearlong series of events that examined its past.

The sesquicentennial was kicked off by Gov. Tommy Thompson and state lawmakers, dressed in vintage clothing, traveling by horse-drawn carriage to the remote town of Belmont. There, they held a legislative session in the drafty clapboard building that was once the capital of the Wisconsin Territory.

It was in Belmont, in 1836, that Madison's future was determined. Madison beat out a long list of other locations for the grand prize of being chosen as Wisconsin's permanent capital.

Some argued that other places would make much better capitals. Fond du Lac, Milwaukee and Green Bay were among the contenders. Madison's chief drawback was that it was landlocked. It couldn't be reached via the Mississippi River, on the state's western border, or Lake Michigan, to the east. There was also the fact that much of it was a swamp. On the positive side, it was in the center of the state, and it was strikingly beautiful, with four glacial lakes and rolling prairies.

Madison won only because of a persistent land speculator named James Doty, who offered free land on the isthmus to the lawmakers — plus buffalo robes to keep them warm as they debated. Doty's plan squeaked through the legislature at Belmont, and the isthmus' destiny was sealed. In 1836 it was named Madison City, after U.S. President James Madison, who had died earlier that year.

Madison's rough-hewn founding fathers were by no means the first to occupy the isthmus. The first humans arrived 11,000 years ago. Among the early inhabitants were mound builders, who left at least 1,000 effigy mounds in Madison. But by 1832, the United States militia had banished the remaining Native Americans from the area, and the stage was set for the birth of Madison.

It grew into a city that has often been called the "Athens of the Midwest" and makes frequent appearances on lists of best places to live in the nation. A former governor also called Madison "seventy-eight square miles surrounded by reality."

The State Capitol

The first capitol wasn't finished by the time lawmakers arrived in 1838. What the state eventually got for $60,000 was a building with a leaky roof, so drafty that in winter the ink in lawmakers' pens froze. Pigs lived in the basement, and the oinking sometimes got so loud that speakers in the legislative chambers were drowned out. After enduring such indignities for a while, the legislature tried again, this time earmarking $500,000 for a second capitol. It was used for 12 years until it was gutted by fire in 1904.

The building that replaced it has been described as the most beautiful state capitol in the United States. Patterned after the Capitol in Washington, D.C., the $7 million building was completed in 1917. Its dome — the only one in the nation that's made of granite — is the second highest in the United States and just 17 inches shorter than the dome in Washington.

It contains 43 types of stone quarried all over the world. There are distinguished murals, bronze railings and andirons, hand-carved Italian marble fireplaces, marble statues, columns and mosaics. It is now undergoing a massive renovation. Early estimates were that $65 million would ultimately be spent on the restoration — but those are now considered optimistic.

Government business is just part of what goes on in the 460,000-square-foot Capitol. It is a place where people go to the rotunda to watch the lighting of the holiday tree, watch school children or dance groups perform, and listen to oratory. Some just like to stand and stare up at the luminous dome and its amazing murals. The grounds are famously well-groomed, with thick beds of tulips in the spring, annuals in the summer and ancient shade trees. It's at the heart of the city, its lawn a communal picnic ground in summer.

The University

The legislature's second priceless gift to the young city of Madison was the creation of the University of Wisconsin in 1848. The first graduating class in 1854 had two members. But by the time Madison was granted a city charter in 1856, the university was flourishing along with it.

In 1863 the university, which now has one of the most respected women's studies programs in the United States, admitted its first females. They were not, however, allowed to take regular courses in mathematics, languages and philosophy, according to guidelines set by then-president Paul Chadbourne. In a bit of posthumous revenge, a women's dormitory was eventually named Chadbourne Hall, after a man who was so ambivalent about educating females.

The university began to spread out on some of Madison's prime real estate, much of it on the shores of Lake Mendota, its largest lake. Lovely brick and sandstone buildings began to appear on campus, and many of them still stand. The most treasured landmark among them is Bascom Hall, set on a steep hill of the same name. A statue of a seated Abraham Lincoln was eventually placed in front of Bascom Hall, and the setting is the campus' most familiar and photographed setting. Skirting the edge of Bascom Hill is Observatory Drive, which has become a popular hiking and running path, with one of the city's most magnificent views of the sunset. Two other historic brick campus buildings, Science Hall and the Red Gym, which resembles a medieval fortress, are also among the landmarks of the university's fledgling period. Another is the Washburn Observatory, where the public can look at the sky through its telescopes.

Student life expanded when intercollegiate sports were introduced in 1890 and the Red Gym added in 1894. Since the campus was on Lake Mendota, rowing became one of the university's first sports. Football and track soon followed. In modern times, hockey and women's basketball have become prominent and well-attended sports. The football Badgers of UW-Madison won the Rose Bowl in 1994.

UW-Madison became the birthplace of WHA radio in 1917. It is today the oldest continually running radio station in the world. The UW was also the first to offer correspondence courses. And it drew to the city people who would make major discoveries in human nutrition, medicine, genetics, agriculture, chemistry and wildlife management.

Satellite schools were eventually built throughout Wisconsin, but UW-Madison has remained its core, in a state where educating the young is taken very seriously.

And so Madison, as the center of government and the university system, gained its reputation for being recession-proof. Ordinary businesses may come and go, but government and academics are presumably here to stay.

Development of the Economy

After fur trading, Wisconsin's earliest economy was based on mining. The lead miners gave the state its nickname, "The Badger State" — not the creature that now serves as state mascot. Early miners didn't have homes, so they often holed up in abandoned hillside mines and wound up with the moniker "badgers." Some of those early badger holes can still be seen in the nearby Mineral Point area.

For most of Wisconsin's history, dairy farming has been the base of the economy. The first milk cows were imported to the area from England in the 1830s. The first cheese factory in what is now "America's Dairyland" was built

HISTORY • 3

A wagon train across the state commemorated Wisconsin's 150th birthday in 1998.

in Fond du Lac (almost two hours north of Madison on the state's largest inland lake, Lake Winnebago) in 1864.

Wisconsin is still one of the nation's top dairy producers, second only to California. Dane County, where Madison is located, produced more than $208 million in dairy products in 1993 (the last year the federal government kept individual county statistics). There are still rambling farmsteads right outside Madison's city limits. There are still about 3,000 farms in the area surrounding Madison — most of them about 190 acres — but urban sprawl continues to eat away at them. Even so, Wisconsin residents still consider themselves cheeseheads — anyone who watched the recent Super Bowls couldn't help but notice the Packer fans with the foam cheese hats on their heads and bare bellies painted yellow and green.

Despite its rural surrounding areas, Madison wound up considerably more cosmopolitan than most of Wisconsin. Beyond the influences of the government and university, that happened because of entrepreneurs like Leonard Farwell. He bought much of the land in the isthmus and spurred construction of canals and roads. Farwell is credited with naming Madison's lakes Mendota and Monona. Even before Wisconsin was officially a state, stagecoaches began running every weekday between Madison and Milwaukee, and inns were built to accommodate the often rowdy travelers. Several of those early stagecoach inns still stand in Madison; a few are open today as bed and breakfasts.

Farwell's aggressive boosterism paid off. By 1850, just three years after he began to promote Madison, the city's population had doubled and there were about 100 buildings. The face of the city was changing quickly. The humble frame buildings that once huddled in the shadow of the Capitol were being torn down, or dragged by horses to less valuable land farther from the city's center. Madison got its first elite neighborhoods, around the Square and closer to Lake Mendota, on what would be called Big Bug Hill, Society Hill, or more recently, Mansion Hill. Some magnificent examples of architecture from that period still stand (see our Attractions chapter for details).

The Civil War Years

Wisconsin was known for its abolitionist leanings and its active Underground Railroad, which helped runaway slaves make their way to Canada. The state Legislature adopted a resolution opposing federal fugitive slave laws, and many Wisconsin residents thwarted the efforts of slave hunters. Wisconsin had sev-

HISTORY

The Black Hawk War

The word "Wisconsin" comes from a Native American term meaning "gathering of the waters." Although Native Americans lived throughout Wisconsin, many were drawn to the peace and solitude of the Four Lakes, or Taychoperah, as the Winnebagos called it. The tribes grew corn and harvested wild rice, nuts, berries, roots and maple sap. They hunted game and fished. Their homes, set along the lakeshores, were lodges made of bark and skins.

Native Americans, specifically the Sauk, Winnebago (now called Ho Chunk) and Fox tribes, held the Four Lakes territory until 1825, when they sold their rights to all lands east of Mississippi.

The first white settler in the Four Lakes area was a prospector named Col. Ebeneezer Brigham. Awed by the oasis of unspoiled natural beauty, Brigham declared that one day this would be the site of a state capital.

It took a while for his prophecy to come true.

Although a treaty said that the Native Americans could remain on the land until it was settled, frequent clashes between whites and Indians became more common.

In 1832 a proud and stubborn man, Black Hawk, the elderly chief of the Sauk and Fox tribes, rallied his people to defy a government order to abandon the tribes long-held land in northern Illinois, near the Mississippi. By age 62, Black Hawk had a reputation as an uncommonly fierce and heartless warrior.

In April 1832 Black Hawk led his band back from Iowa to their traditional summer camp in Illinois with the intent of planting corn. Food was scarce at the Indians' site in Iowa, and members of the group were starving.

Soldiers intercepted the returning tribal members. Black Hawk tried to surrender, but despite that, the poorly trained militiamen attacked. An Indian was killed, and the Sauks avenged the death. The Black Hawk War had begun.

Before the 118-day battle was over, 3,000 U.S. militiamen pursued Black Hawk and his followers — about 500 braves with 500 women, children and elders — across northern Illinois and southern Wisconsin.

For weeks, Black Hawk's people escaped direct confrontations with the troops by traveling through wetlands and marshes. Many Indians, however, were weakened by the poor diet available on the run.

To save his starving followers, Black Hawk decided to head for the Mississippi River and Iowa. The militia caught up with some of Black Hawk's stragglers on July 21 at Four Lakes. Black Hawk led his tribe through the dense growth of the Four Lakes' isthmus, where soldiers could not detect them.

Chief Black Hawk and his followers were pursued by 3,000 U.S. militiamen across northern Illinois and southern Wisconsin.

Illustration: Indian Tribes of North America, 1836-1844

— continued on next page

On the night of July 22, 1832, Black Hawk crept to a tree near the soldiers' camp, climbed it and yelled loudly into the night "Friends, we will fight no more." He used the language of the Winnebagos because members of that tribe had on occasion traveled with the troops. But on that night, no Winnebago were in the camp, and his second attempt at surrender went unheeded.

With the militiamen about a day behind him, Black Hawk pushed forward toward Iowa. The chief was leading his people into the Mississippi when he was intercepted by a steamer carrying soldiers from Fort Crawford. Black Hawk tried, for a third time, to surrender by waving a stick tied with white cloth. But the soldiers did not understand the gesture. They fired a cannon at the Indians, who scrambled back up the river banks, some returning fire with muskets. Two hours into the siege, when the steamer ran out of fuel and retreated, 23 braves lay dead.

Black Hawk led his people north along the Wisconsin side of the river. The next day, the Indians were caught between the military-chartered steamer in the bloody Battle of Bad Axe. Records say 950 Sauk were massacred.

Somehow Black Hawk escaped. It was Winnebagos who eventually captured him and in August of 1832 turned him over to a Fort Crawford Indian agent Col. Zachery Taylor, who would one day be president of the United States.

Jefferson Davis, a young lieutenant who was Taylor's prospective son-in-law and, 30 years later, president of Confederate States of America, was entrusted with moving Black Hawk to an army barracks in St. Louis.

A treaty with the Sauk and Fox, signed the next month at Rock island, marked the official end of war. Black Hawk lived out his days in Iowa.

eral communities founded by freed or escaped slaves, including Pleasant Ridge, in Grant County. Pleasant Ridge no longer exists, but it is being recreated at Wisconsin's outdoor ethnic museum, Old World Wisconsin, in Eagle, an hour east of Madison just off Interstate 90/94 (see our Attractions chapter). Some of those freed slaves served Wisconsin during the Civil War. And many of their descendants eventually moved to Madison.

Wisconsin's governor during the Civil War, Alexander Randall, was an ardent abolitionist and a Republican supporter of President Lincoln. Randall pushed to form Wisconsin regiments to join the war effort. When Fort Sumter fell to the Confederates, Madison's 157 enlisted men rushed into the fray. Gov. Randall quickly transformed the 10,000-acre State Agricultural Fairgrounds in Madison into a military camp. During the Civil War, 70,000 of Wisconsin's 91,000 Union soldiers trained at Camp Randall. At first the soldiers lived there in tents. Later, barracks were built. Eventually the site became Camp Randall Stadium, where the home football games and major rock concerts, including a Rolling Stones show, are played.

Madison has a poignant reminder of the Civil War in its shady, parklike Forest Hill Cemetery. It has the northernmost Confederate burial ground. Nearby are the graves of Union soldiers. There are also tiny white stone markers for the war orphans who died in Madison.

The 20th Century

Madison's big break, in terms of jobs and industry, came in 1919 when three Bavarian brothers from Chicago decided to expand their specialty meat business here. Their names were Gottfried, Max and Oscar Mayer. The Mayers' Old World Sausages and Wesphalian hams were a hit, and the Madison plant quickly turned a profit. Eventually Madison became the site of the company headquarters.

Oscar Mayer introduced its first Wienermobile in 1936. It was a 13-foot-long hot dog on wheels that carried Little Oscar, the World's Smallest Chef. The distinctive vehicle has never stopped drawing stares — even in Madison — and shows up at events like the

HISTORY

The Oscar Mayer Wienermobile celebrated its 60th anniversary in 1996. An old dog can learn new tricks.

Super Bowl. The Wienermobile planned for the year 2000 is a 27-foot-long General Motors vehicle with state-of-the-art video equipment, a big-screen TV and a hot dog-shaped dashboard. Look for vanity plates like YUMMY and WEENR.

Another Madison business that took off at the turn of the century was the French Battery and Carbon Company, founded in 1907. It's Rayovac now, with annual revenues of $570 million and Michael Jordan as its pitchman.

Madison also became the site of headquarters of the national and international credit union movement. The Credit Union National Association (CUNA) was formed in 1936. Madison was chosen because of its proximity to both coasts and Canada. The World Council of Credit Unions was formed in 1970 as its international counterpart. Among CUNA's offshoots are Cuna Mutual Group, which sells insurance to credit union members and has more than 3,000 employees in Madison. American Family Insurance is another major employer. And more recently biotechnology companies have been attracted to Madison because of its highly educated work force (see our Overview chapter for more about the city's economic climate).

In the 1930s, Wisconsin also acquired its share of gangster lore. Al Capone had a hideaway in the Northwoods, and on his way up north, he and his hoodlum cronies often stopped in the Madison area. One of their favorite haunts was the Wonderbar, (still standing) which has specially designed machine-gun ports. Capone also stayed frequently at a cottage on Lake Kegonsa, in nearby Stoughton.

Madison's greatest notoriety, though, came during the years of the Vietnam War. It was a center of the protest movement, and wrenching battles erupted between protesters, most of them UW students, and police. Tear gassing on campus was routine, and a campus grocery store was burned during the riots. The Mifflin Street block parties, which also pitted young people against police, were born in those years.

The greatest tragedy of those years, and the event that is generally considered the denouement of the antiwar movement, was the bombing of Sterling Hall on campus, in the middle of a late summer night in 1970. A young researcher working late was killed (see our Politics and Perspectives chapter). The blast was felt well beyond Madison's city limits. Two of the Sterling Hall bombers, Madison-born brothers Karleton and Dwight Armstrong, spent time in prison for their role in the bombing. Karleton, who has been selling juice from a cart on campus for many years, has expressed profound remorse for the death of Robert Fassnecht. A third bomber, Leo Burt, vanished and has become the subject of local mythology. There was even widespread speculation in Madison that Burt was the Unabomber. The Academy Award-nominated documentary *The War at Home* tells the story of Madison's antiwar movement. Paul Soglin, a student activist at the time, went on to become a respected and long-standing Madison mayor. He resigned in 1997.

Many of the youthful student war protesters, now in their 40s and 50s, have stayed on in Madison and the nearby areas. Vestiges of the 1960s counterculture can still be found here in the food and housing cooperatives.

Madison in the 1970s had as much building fever as disco fever. The driving force behind the civic construction mania was the realization that the downtown business district, once the hub of the city, had begun to wither. There were, for the first time, empty storefronts on the Capitol Square. Malls that kept popping up on the edges of the city were draining the downtown of its vitality. There were jokes about how prostitutes were very nearly the only people with successful businesses on the east side of the Square during that period. The first significant efforts to bring the dying downtown back to life was the building of the Civic Center and the construction of the Capitol Concourse and the State Street Mall (a pedestrian mall between the Capitol and Bascom Hill). Fountains, kiosks, beautiful street lights and bus shelters were built. The malls attracted food carts, with an impressive range of ethnic food, and the phenomenally successful Dane County Farmers' Market and the Concerts on the Square (see our Attractions and Annual Events chapters).

Despite those positive changes, it wasn't until the Frank Lloyd Wright-designed Monona Terrace Convention Center opened in 1997 (see the related Close-up in our Attractions chapter) that the long-awaited renaissance in downtown Madison really got underway full throttle. Since then there has been an unprecedented rush to open restaurants, bars and other businesses in the isthmus.

No yardstick exists that can accurately measure Madison's most palatable, endearing trait: Its ability to harmonize nature with urban sophistication.

Area Overview

For a number of years, the national press has been singling out Madison (and the rest of Dane County) for one reason or another — "Top 10 Canoe Towns" and "Top 20 Counties for Economic Strength" to name two distinctions on seemingly opposite sides of the fence. But it wasn't until July 1996 that Madison got the nod many residents felt it so richly deserved.

In '97, Madison remained on *Money's* top-10 list of the 300 largest U.S. metropolitan areas, in seventh place. The magazine changed its format for singling out cities in '98. Still, Madison was ranked No. 1 of all mid-size cities in the Midwest.

The city has often been singled out by *Money* because, as one reporter noted, "someone forgot to tell the folks in Madison that life is supposed to be full of trade-offs."

Within weeks of *Money's* initial tribute, the floodgates opened, so to speak. Even *Cosmopolitan* magazine got into the act, calling Madison "one of the 10 hottest places to live if you're a woman." (Many of our single, female friends sure wouldn't say that, but who are we to turn down a compliment!)

The *Ladies' Home Journal* in 1997 chose Madison as the best city in the nation for women to live. The article ranked America's 200 largest cities on the qualities women care most about, including health care, education, day care, violent crime, divorce rate, the ratio of single men and weather conditions that create bad hair days.

Indeed, public reaction to all these accolades has been mixed.

"I told you so," some people say knowingly. While it's true that few metropolitan areas can duplicate Madison's beautiful isthmus setting and/or quality of life, longtime residents of the county sometimes wish all the "outsiders" lauding this region would go away. Too much attention, they believe, even if well deserved, can ruin a good thing.

References to Madison and Dane County in National Magazines

July 1998: No. 1 Mid-size City in the Midwest —*Money*

October 1997: "Fourth Best City for Cycling in North America" —*Bicycling*

July 1997 and July 1996: "Best Places to Live in America," No. 7 and No. 1, respectively —*Money*

June 1997: "Ninth Best City to Live and Work in America" —*Employment Review*

May 1997: "Third Best Pace to Raise a Family" —*Parenting*

January 1997: "No. 1 Healthiest City for Women to Live" —*American Health For Women*

October 1996: "Third Best City To Start A Small Business" —*Entrepreneur*

May 1996: "One of the 10 Best Cities for Working Moms" —*Redbook*

January 1996: "Ninth in the nation in survey of America's safest cities" —*Money*

October 1995: "Top 10 Canoe Towns in the U.S." —*Paddler*

Demographics

Madison, with an estimated 1998 population of just more than 201,786, encompasses about 67.5 square miles. While many liberties have been taken with that number, the feeling continues to ring true. Yet, counting adjacent villages of Shorewood and Maple Bluff, the town of Madison, Middleton, Monona and Fitchburg, the greater metropolitan area is home to more than a quarter-million people.

Eighty miles west of Milwaukee and 142 miles northwest of Chicago, the Capital City is the second-largest city in the state. (Milwaukee is the largest.) Based on the latest official census figures (1990), Madison alone has a minority population of 10.5 percent, with the fastest growing segment being Asian. From 1980 to 1990, the percentage of Asian residents more than doubled, from 1.6 percent to 3.9 percent. Yet, much of this city's cosmopolitan attitude can be directly attributed to the UW-Madison. There are about 4,000 foreign students on campus representing 126 different countries.

Dane County encompasses 1,283 square miles with a population of 402,988 that is almost exclusively white if you subtract metropolitan Madison. Dane County is the second fastest-growing county in the state in absolute numbers, but percentage-wise, from 1990 to '98, it ranked 10th.

Madison is well known for being the home of state government and the UW-Madison, which has a total student body of about 40,000 students. Yet, in addition, because of Dane County's agricultural strength — a sixth of all farms in Wisconsin are here — Madison is also a leading center for the world dairy industry. Dane County is ranked among the top 10 counties in the nation in value of farm products including corn, alfalfa, hogs, cattle and, of course, dairy products. When you think of Wisconsin and Dane County, you automatically say "cheese."

Natural Beauty

No other city boasts a landscape quite as unique as Madison's. The Downtown is built on a half-mile-wide isthmus between two glacial lakes — Monona and Mendota. A walk around the Capitol Square offers glimpses of both lakes. But that only tells half the story.

It was the Winnebago Indian tribe that first recognized the supreme beauty of the area, naming it "Taychoperah," meaning "Four Lakes City," after the four glacial lakes connected by the Yahara River that now provide a wealth of recreational activity for visitors and residents alike. Early settlers borrowed Algonquin Indian names for these lakes: Mendota ("great"), Monona ("spirit" or "beautiful"), Kegonsa ("fish") and Waubesa ("swan"). A fifth, small spring-fed lake is on the near West Side of Madison. Named Wingra, its shores are easily accessible from an adjacent park of the same name (see our Kidstuff and Parks and Recreation chapters) and the UW Arboretum (see Attractions).

While lakefront property is prime real estate in Madison (about $4,000 per frontage foot on Mendota, $3,000 on Monona), you don't have to live on a lake to feel close to water. It's all around Madison, wherever you walk, bike or drive. Sometimes that means taking the long way around to reach a destination. But nobody living here would have it any other way.

Some of Madison's many attributes — excellent healthcare, high scholastic achievement of its elementary and secondary school students and low unemployment — are easy to quantify. Yet, no yardstick exists that can accurately measure Madison's most palatable, endearing trait: its ability to harmonize nature with urban sophistication. Especially for its size and locale, Madison revolves around a wide variety of ethnic restaurants, performing arts and outdoor leisure activities. The city boasts nearly 200 parks, 13 area beaches and four city golf courses. It offers miles of trails, many of which encircle the lakes, for cyclists, in-line skaters, joggers and hikers.

Yet, like frosting adds flavor to a cake, it's the ambiance at Madison's doorstep that truly sets this city apart. Where else can you dine on superb Eastern Mediterranean cuisine for lunch Downtown, then drive 15 minutes in any direction and be in America's heartland, in Wisconsin's rolling countryside dotted with picturesque farms and charming, small communities? In South-Central Wisconsin, with interstate highways whisking motorists from home to work and back again every day, it's still easy and extremely pleasurable to get lost in a rural setting of winding trout streams, hardwood forests and deep ravines. It's a rec-

---

www.insiders.com

See this and many other **Insiders' Guide®** destinations online — in their entirety.

Visit us today!

We take cheese very seriously — it's not just for breakfast anymore.

reational paradise affording a plethora of activities including downhill skiing, hunting and fishing. And it's all to be found within a matter of miles.

In his book *Madison & Dane County*, *Wisconsin State Journal* writer Ron Seely talks lovingly about a "sense of place" and how Madison's "special landscape — its splendid lakes and green hills — works its way so deeply into peoples' lives." Although there are perhaps more famous scenic spots to visit in this country, few places exact as much commitment and pride from their residents as does Dane County.

Booming Economy

A UW-Madison graduate who rose within the ranks to become a high-ranking editor at *The New York Times* was envied by aspiring members of the local press when he returned for a visit.

"Wait a minute," he said, attacking success from a different direction. "You're the ones who did it right ... landing a job and being able to work in Madison."

Many graduates of the UW who move to Madison and fall in love with the city often take any job just to remain here. Today, it's easier than ever to do that. Within the last couple of years, the unemployment rate in Dane County has consistently remained one of the lowest in the country, hovering between 1.4 and 2 percent. In certain fields, including high-tech, job hunting can be very rewarding.

It's true, however, that too low an unemployment rate can come back to haunt a city by strangling its economic growth and stability. But Madison isn't like most cities. Its academic-driven, entrepreneurial spirit is foreign to all but the most progressive communities.

"The available work force dictates what gets developed," says Bob Brennan, president of the Greater Madison Chamber of Commerce. "Madison is geared to more of a high-tech center than a Chevrolet body plant. You live with what your talents are."

INSIDERS' TIP

The Greater Madison Chamber of Commerce, 615 E. Washington Avenue, (608) 256-8348, can provide a wealth of background material about Madison.

That's why Cognetics Inc., an economic research firm in Cambridge, Massachusetts, in 1993 called Madison an "Entrepreneurial Hot Spot, one of the best places to start and grow a company." Its assessment was an early harbinger of things to come.

In 1996, *Entrepreneur* magazine ranked Madison the "third best city for starting a small business." In '97, *Employment Review* magazine selected the city as one of the "10 Best Places to Live and Work." *Kiplinger's Personal Finance* magazine, upon learning that 250 technology companies had sprung up in Dane County since 1980, dubbed it "a Midwestern Silicon Valley."

Kiplinger also wrote in January 1997:

Madison's labor supply is so tight that it has difficulty attracting manufacturing firms from outside the region. Instead it grows its own entrepreneurs. The community sponsors venture-capital fairs, offers classes to high school students on starting their own businesses and helps local businesses get access to technology developed at the university ... the biggest challenge for companies is finding and holding on to good employees.

These new high-tech businesses, whose services range from biomedical research to designing computer software and serve not only South-Central Wisconsin, but also a global marketplace, now employ 6 percent of the labor force in Greater Madison.

They include firms such as Agracetus, a Middleton-based company specializing in genetic engineering; Promega Corp. of Fitchburg, a world leader in molecular-biology research; and entrepreneurs such as Jan Eddy, who developed and sold one software company and now is on her second, Wingra Technologies.

Building Bridges

Brennan, who helped launch the venture-capital fairs 10 years ago in Madison to match financiers with promising new ideas, credits a good working relationship between business (noted for its conservative approach) and the university (a more liberal voice) for Madison's successful entrepreneurial spirit.

"One of our strengths is the ability for the right and left factions to sit down together," says Brennan.

While that doesn't always occur without turmoil and debate, the fact that the two entities appreciate what each can bring to the table is an important component of the Madison way. Brennan acknowledges his phone is ringing off the hook from officials in other college cities eager to learn how two very different factions can work for the common good.

While high-tech is an increasingly important employment outlet for Greater Madison, the biggest employer is the government. About a third of the work force — about 66,000 residents — is employed in local, state and federal government. The UW alone provides more than 21,000 of those jobs.

In light manufacturing, Madison is the site of world headquarters for Rayovac Corporation, Ohmeda and Nicolet Instrument Corporation. Sub-Zero Freezer Co., maker of top-of-the-line, built-in refrigerators, is also based in Madison. Next door in Middleton is the Pleasant Company (acquired in the summer of 1998 by Mattel), creator of the American Girls Collection; the Springs Window Fashions Division of Graber Industries; and Wintersilks, which specializes in silk clothing.

Madison is also home base for many of the country's largest insurance companies, including American Family Insurance, CUNA Mutual Insurance Group and General Casualty.

The Oscar Mayer meat-processing plant (now part of Kraft Foods, owned by the Philip Morris Companies) that opened in Madison in 1919 was for many years the city's largest private employer. (American Family now has that distinction.) Yet, though Oscar Mayer

---

INSIDERS' TIP

To appreciate Madison's diversity, pick up a copy of *The Directory*, a listing of gay-owned and/or gay-oriented businesses and organizations in the area, from Outreach, 14 W. Mifflin Street.

Find your...

...new hobby

...new pen pal

...new wheels

...next career

...new best friend

Find it all
IN THE CLASSIFIEDS

The Capital Times
WISCONSIN STATE JOURNAL

To **subscribe** call 252-6363 or 1-800-362-8333

Weather

Believe it or not, we know somebody who moved to Madison from Honolulu and says he actually prefers the weather here. Of course, he wasn't talking about those bone-chilling days when a high of 20 degrees is a welcome relief. No, he was referring to the changing of the seasons; but in Dane County, one can't be enjoyed without the other.

Says *Money* magazine in ranking Madison as one of the best places to live in America in spite of its weather: "If residents of the Wisconsin capital have any major complaint, it might be about the weather. The average winter high is a mere 20 degrees, and April snow-showers sometimes usher in late May flowers. But Madisonians will tell you that's the price to pay for the sublime spring, summer and fall weather."

Perhaps that's why Madisonians do their darnedest to make every day of sunshine (the annual average is 190) count. In mid-January, they may complain of chapped lips and dry skin, but it doesn't keep them inside very long. Winter has its own appeal — downhill and cross-country skiing, ice-skating and even sledding.

There is something exhilarating about not being able to control — or sometimes even predict — the weather. Fifty degrees and showers can be followed in a matter of hours by a raging snowstorm. We've had Thanksgiving days when it was below freezing; others when the golf courses were filled.

Madison's year-round average temperature is 45.2 F. But that doesn't begin to tell the story. In spring and fall, the average temperature is close to that — 44.8 and 48.1 respectively; in summer, the temperature is a very comfortable 68.8. That leaves winter at 19.4 degrees.

— continued on next page

You can skip the gym on the days you shovel snow — it's a great workout.

Just so you know, the lowest temperature ever recorded in Madison was 37 degrees below zero on January 30, 1951. Nobody even knows what the windchill was that day! But at 1 AM on January 19, 1982, we sure do. With a wind speed of 28 mph, the minus 19-degree temperature really felt like minus 76 degrees. But, hey, that's really unusual.

In the upper Midwest, snow is often welcomed, except when it comes all at once, like on December 3, 1990, when 17.3 inches fell within a 24-hour period. The kids loved it. School was called off for two days. Normally, Madison averages about 40 inches of snow per year, although many people remember the winter of 1978-79, when the city received a record 76.1 inches. Generally, snow doesn't fall until November, but once it begins, ground sometimes is not seen again until early spring. (The earliest measurable snowfall was 1.5 inches on September 26, 1942.) If you're an ice-fishing enthusiast — there are many in Madison — cold weather is greatly anticipated. Lake Monona usually freezes over a few days before Lake Mendota — around December 15. But the warming winds of El Nino changed all that for winter 1997-98. Area lakes didn't freeze until January 11, and even then, the ice was very thin and dangerous to be on. In fact, the 1997-98 winter (December through February) tied for the fourth-warmest in Madison history with an average temperature of 28.4 degrees.

Spring, although often late, is for many the most anticipated season of all. It's ushered in with balmy breezes, the smell of lilacs and sailboats on the lake. Fall's colorful panorama of foliage is stunning. Summer is nice for boating, swimming, camping and hiking, as long as rainfall is moderate. The wettest year on record is 1881, when 56.1 inches of precipitation fell; the driest is 1895, with 13.6 inches. (In June 1996 the Madison area experienced flooding at near-record levels, especially after 4.5 inches of rain fell on June 17. That almost beat a 1906 record, when 4.96 inches of rain fell in a single day in August.)

The highest temperature ever recorded in Madison is 107 degrees, on July 14, 1936. Thankfully, the thermometer hardly ever climbs above 100, although high humidity sometimes makes it feel that way. A week of above-normal temperatures in July 1995 cleared out every air-conditioner from every store in town.

Talking about the weather in Dane County, whatever the season, constitutes more than small talk around here — it's a way of life.

Foods has been a pillar of the community for decades, heavy industry was never particularly wooed by the genteel Madison establishment for fear that smokestacks would mar Madison's beautiful landscape. In hindsight, it was a wise decision. A white-collar city from its inception, Madison has remained relatively recession-proof .

Madison's smaller neighbors also are benefitting from the area's vigorous economy.

The largest employer in Waunakee is Marshall Erdman & Associates, a building company that, besides introducing other innovative concepts, is a national leader in high-quality, ready-to-assemble particleboard furniture. Techline was developed by the late Marshall Erdman, a visionary architect who worked alongside Frank Lloyd Wright in constructing Madison's Unitarian Meeting House and a number of prefabricated homes statewide.

Although Stoughton is most widely recognized for its historic shopping district and Nor-

INSIDERS' TIP

Including faculty and students, the University of Wisconsin-Madison, were it a city, would be the state's eighth-largest community.

wegian heritage, it's also site of the world headquarters of Nelson Industries, maker of exhaust mufflers and industrial machine silencers. Nelson, employing about 2,400 people worldwide, was recently purchased by Cummins Engines Company. Semitrailers, seen on highways across the nation, are built at Stoughton Trailers.

On the Cutting Edge

It's no surprise that many new high-tech companies get their start in Madison. Research is one of the UW's strongest suits, spanning a wide variety of fields including genetic engineering, robotics, highway planning, zoology, agriculture and dairy science. In annual college rankings for research-and-development expenditures by the National Science Foundation, the UW consistently ranks fourth or higher in the nation. Founded in 1940, McArdle Laboratory for Cancer Research was the first basic cancer research center established within a university setting in the United States.

Medical research and healthcare are important industries for Madison and add to its quality of life. University Hospital has one of the most successful transplant programs in the nation, and promising new research for halting the progression of Alzheimer's disease was recently introduced by two professors at the UW — one in chemistry and the other in engineering.

In January 1997, *American Health* ranked Madison as the "healthiest city to live [in]" if you're a woman. Excellent healthcare also helped push Madison over the top when *Ladies Home Journal* named the city No. 1 for Women in the nation.

In driving home the notion that Madison is very much on the cutting edge in a variety of fields, here are some other interesting tidbits.

Madison is home to the U.S. Forest Products Laboratory, the only federal government lab engaged in wood research; a U.S. Fish and Wildlife Laboratory; the Space Science and Engineering Center; the Waisman Center on Mental Retardation and Human Development; the Air Pollution Lab; and the U.S. Department of Agriculture Research Service.

Lively Spirit

The aging of the baby boomers is having an effect on every corner of the world; Madison is no exception. Its nickname, "Mad City," continues to underline its lively spirit, although the city's tendency to embrace liberal causes has somewhat softened over the years in the face of home mortgages and retirement portfolios. That's an Insider's view. From the outside looking in, Madison remains a stronghold for liberal thinking, a hotbed of political correctness, which, depending upon your outlook, comes off either very bold and refreshing or pretentious and overbearing.

Yet, beneath it all, Madison remains a tolerant community, open to alternative lifestyles and new ideas. There are almost 100 organizations in Dane County, ranging from purely social groups to advocacy agencies that serve the gay, lesbian and bisexual population. A Madison ordinance allows same-sex city employees to register as domestic partners to take advantage of health insurance and other benefits.

Another constant for Dane County is the ability of its citizenry, both urban and rural, to "fight the good fight." It doesn't make a difference what opinions you have — as long as you have them. Most residents not only do, but also feel compelled to act upon them occasionally. Madisonians are notorious for making sure their individual voices get heard.

INSIDERS' TIP

Here's one record Dane County isn't particularly fond of: During the last several years there were more deer-and-vehicle collisions (1,287 in '97) here than in any other county in Wisconsin. It's not surprising that the worst month was November, the height of deer hunting and mating seasons. The best way to avoid hitting deer is by being an alert driver.

The fact is, anybody who has lived here for any length of time isn't surprised that it took 50 years to build a Frank Lloyd Wright-designed convention center, but that, with so much discourse and discord, it got built at all.

Madison's citizenry likes to be consulted. Call it government by committee if you will. There is an organization for everything, and it takes a consensus of many groups to move something forward. The process is frustrating, especially for civic leaders, but it's never, ever boring. And things do get done, obviously. Otherwise, Madison wouldn't be the toast of Metropolitan U.S.A.

Best of Times and Most Challenging of Times

With accolades rolling in, a healthy economy and two new buildings — the Frank Lloyd Wright-inspired convention center and the Kohl Center university sports arena — garnering a great deal of attention, many people feel this is the best of times for Madison.

Indeed, these are exciting times, says Brennan, who has headed the chamber of commerce for 25 years. Yet, they are also the most challenging of times. Madison and Dane County can't afford to sit back on their laurels.

While Wisconsin ranks as one of the safest states in the United States, safety continues to be an important issue as long as a single assault or break-in is reported on the evening news. Madison had only 3.9 violent crimes per 1,000 people in 1996 while almost 150 other cities with populations between 100,000 and 250,000 averaged 8.8 violent crimes per 1,000. Another big concern is affordable housing. The rising population of poor families (4.8 percent of all families in Dane County according to the '90 census) goes hand-in-hand with the growing number of at-risk children in public schools. And anyone who lives in the great recreational state of Wisconsin can't ignore such pressing issues as water quality and land usage.

In winter 1996-97, the county introduced the first draft of its Vision 2020 plan for controlled growth to preserve the county's quality of life while accommodating an expected influx of 100,000 people over the next 20-plus years. Key proposals include a $2 million study of transportation options, namely light and commuter rail. While recent transplants from both coasts laugh off Madison's version of rush hour, traffic flow is a big concern to city planners.

The county executive and mayor, both of whom happen to be women (as are the fire chief and district attorney), must grapple over how best to manage new and greatly expanded convention center space at Monona Terrace and the Expo Center and maintain the area's record for quality public services in the face of welfare reform and state-mandated property-tax relief. Wisconsin is noted for having some of the highest state and local taxes in the nation. That's no surprise when you consider the high quality of services here.

It all depends upon your expectations. Especially in Dane County, those expectations have always run very high.

FREE Madison Visitors Guide

Call **1-800-373-6376**

*The official guide of the
Greater Madison Convention & Visitors Bureau*

http://www.visitmadison.com

Politics and Perspectives

The eyes of the nation have been on Wisconsin as it plunges into the untested waters of welfare reform. Republican Governor Tommy Thompson's W-2 program, which dismantled programs like Aid for Families with Dependent Children, is now sending able-bodied mothers — willingly or not — into the workplace, some of them for the first time. A lifetime cap on the amount of time a person can receive benefits also was implemented.

Thompson presented his reforms as a chance to end the habit of dependency that was passed from generation to generation and made Wisconsin, long known for its generous entitlements, a "welfare magnet." All that has changed. New programs help W-2 participants find and keep jobs and even provide them with new clothing as they enter the work force.

The safety net that has been in place since President Roosevelt's New Deal reforms has been abruptly pulled away. Critics of W-2 say the big losers are children, who will sink into poverty and/or poor-quality day care. Almost immediately after W-2 took effect, sharp declines in welfare rolls were seen. Are the former welfare recipients, as the governor promised, on their way to being productive taxpayers? Or are they, as many fear, being shoved into a dark nook of poverty? Even the strongest supporters of W-2 admit there is much fine-tuning to be done. It's a debate that is certain to be raging in Madison for years to come. Stay tuned.

Women in Public Office

After the April 1997 elections, the headline "Dame County" was splashed across the front page of *The Capital Times*, Madison's afternoon daily newspaper. Not everyone appreciated the use of the word "dame." But even so, it captured the mood of elation that was felt, especially among women, when Madison elected its first female mayor, Sue Bauman, and Dane County voted in its first county executive, Kathleen Falk.

Bauman has been a labor attorney, 12-year Madison City Council member, former middle school teacher and teacher's union president.

The election of Falk, a former assistant state attorney general, meanwhile, has been heralded as a boost for progressive politics and environmental issues. Bauman and Falk have pledged to bring new levels of cooperation between city and county governments.

In 1998 another woman lawyer, Diane Nicks, became the first Dane County District Attorney when Bill Foust resigned to become a judge. The rise of women to such powerful positions has made it clear that the glass ceiling, at least within the confines of Dane County, has been broken. Women also hold seats on the Wisconsin Supreme Court and top posts in the 26-campus University of Wisconsin System, the Madison Fire Department and at Madi-

---

INSIDERS' TIP

Some of Madison's Downtown streets are named after signers of the U.S. Constitution.

20 • POLITICS AND PERSPECTIVES

son Area Technical College, the state's largest technical college.

The recent rise of women to power in Dane County isn't really surprising — the Madison area has had an active women's movement for many years. One of the founders of the National Organization for Women, the late Kathryn Clarenbach, lived in Madison. And U.S. Health and Human Services Secretary Donna Shalala was formerly the chancellor at UW-Madison.

Madison's Love Affair with Politics

The State Capitol is just across the street from the City of Madison and the Dane County government offices. So it's no surprise that conversations you overhear in bars and restaurants are often about politics. People here get involved in the public schools, in land-use questions and in fights about historic preservation. Even when it's a question of whether dogs should be allowed in certain parks, you can be sure the City Council will get lots of advice from the public. The tendency in Madison to debate things to death is not popular with land developers, but it has protected natural resources and historic landmarks much of the time. Madison has a long-standing reputation for being politically liberal, or more derisively, "politically correct." But the fact is, Madison citizens and politicians are all over the ideological spectrum. Voter turnout here is usually high, and allegiance to political parties is low. It is the individual that Madison voters tend to scrutinize, not his or her political affiliation. In the last 50 years Democrats and Republicans have shared the governor's office equally. In 1995, residents contributed three times as much to national Republican candidates and organizations than to Democrats.

Madison's reputation for progressive politics stems from a set of reforms that date back to the early 1900s and became known as "the Wisconsin Idea" — a mix of concern for social welfare, an appreciation for small business, belief in equal opportunity and support of individual freedoms.

In 1903 the progressive arm of the Republican party took control of the state Legislature and over the next decade produced sweeping reforms in politics, the workplace, transportation and social services. One of the reforms, the "direct primary" law, changed election history when Wisconsin became the first state in which residents directly selected candidates who would appear on the general election ballot. Before direct primaries, powerful business leaders controlled political parties and influenced which candidates would be placed on election ballots. Those political bosses could weight the legislature with pro-business puppets who could ignore the rights of workers without jeopardy. From that point on, ordinary Wisconsin citizens had a far greater voice in the governance of the state.

The star of the Progressive Movement was "Fighting Bob" La Follette, who became a legendary governor, and his wife, Belle, who was active in women's suffrage, racial equality, child labor laws, workplace reforms for women and world peace. She was a teacher in the neighboring communities of Spring Green and Baraboo, and was often regarded as more radical than her husband. When they were married in 1881, she had the word "obey" removed from her vows — something common now, but shocking at the time. Not long after the birth of the couple's daughter, Belle became the first woman to earn a law degree

---

INSIDERS' TIP

When the U.S. flag is flying over the south wing of the Capitol, the state Senate is in session. When the flag is over the west wing, the Assembly is in session.

The Miss Forward statue stands proudly vigilant before the State Capitol.

from UW-Madison. The red brick house the La Follettes lived in is still a local landmark.

During the La Follette era, close bonds were established between government and the university. Experts in academe were called in often to help shape legislation. It became a popular practice that still flourishes. After three terms as governor, La Follette moved on to the United States Senate.

Fighting Bob died in 1925, and government moved in the opposite direction with the election of businessman Walter Kohler, founder of the plumbing empire, to governor. During the Depression, Kohler continued to insist that the economy could correct itself without government intervention.

When that didn't happen, the public again turned to a La Follette, Fighting Bob's son Phillip. But unlike his popular parents, Phillip was autocratic and lasted just six years in office. His contributions, though, included acquiring a $100 million grant to put Wisconsin men idled by the Depression to work on soil conservation, wildlife management, reforestation, highway construction and urban renewal. He championed the unemployment compensation bill, and in 1932 Wisconsin was the first state in the nation to pass it. Within three years, every state followed suit. The first check was paid in Madison for $15.

Another legacy of the Progressive Movement was the development of the nation's most

INSIDERS' TIP

Wisconsin's former U.S. Senator Gaylord Nelson started Earth Day.

Monona Terrace Convention Center

The Monona Terrace Convention Center has been compared to half a wedding cake, a parking lot for UFOs and, on a foggy days, a ghost rising from Lake Monona. The state Capitol, after decades of dominating Madison's skyline, finally has a rival landmark.

The story of Monona Terrace is as complicated as its architecture. It was designed 1938 by Frank Lloyd Wright, who lived in Madison as a youth and designed 32 buildings for the city. But his scandalous personal life, which included running off with a client's wife, his arrogance and a tendency not to pay his bills made him an unpopular figure in Madison back then. The design for Monona Terrace was on Wright's drafting table when he died in 1959.

By the 1980s, the public had apparently forgiven his philandering, and he was generally regarded as the greatest architect in American history. So in the 1980s, it seemed to some Madison civic leaders that Wright's blueprint should be taken out of mothballs and given another look. Construction of the center, like many public projects in Madison, moved forward in fits and starts, having been abandoned and revived a dizzying number of times. World War II got in the way, as did repeated lawsuits and arguments about a site. It may have taken longer to build than any other public building in modern history.

But in the summer of 1997, the grand opening of the $67 million Monona Terrace was an orgy of public celebration. It was described as "a party that was 60 years in the making." It immediately became a premier site for weddings, galas and conventions — despite an undercurrent of grumbling about high drink prices, miniscule food portions, and not enough parking.

Monona Terrace is a short walk down a wide promenade from the Capitol. With its rooftop garden, it weds Lake Monona with the Capitol, just as Wright intended. He also intended for Monona Terrace to echo the Capitol's classical architecture in its rounded forms and white color.

— continued on next page

The Monona Terrace Convention Center is a jewel on Madison's lakeshore.

If Monona Terrace had been built during Frank Lloyd Wright's lifetime, it would have been a very different building. Technology has only recently caught up with the flamboyant architect's design. It was too sophisticated for materials that were available in the 1930s.

The structure would almost certainly have had a leaky roof, a chronic complaint about Wright buildings. Monona Terrace's builders and engineers took extreme pains to make sure history wouldn't repeat itself in this building. The roof consists of a metal deck of its trusses, plus 6 inches of concrete sloped in all directions into rooftop drains. The layers include waterproof membranes, a filter fabric and insulation. Then there are adjustable pedestals set every 2 feet to hold up thousands of paving bricks, most of them are inscribed with names of donors.

Modern technology also made it possible to use lighter, thinner insulated precast concrete forms. The structure's wide, low design forced the use of long and heavy trusses that had to be hoisted straight up, rather than brought in from the sides.

Even now, with all the engineering and technological progress made since Wright's time, Monona Terrace required constant innovation. It began with 1,730 steel pilings sunk up to 90 feet into an old Lake Monona landfill. Each pile is capable of holding 320 tons and withstanding tornadoes, which are not uncommon in Wisconsin. Workers drove the piles through ice in winter and worked on floating piers in warmer weather.

Because the bottom of the lake (and the old landfill) was being disturbed during construction, a slit was cut in the ice of Lake Monona the length of the building, and a weighted 1,500-foot-long silt curtain was dropped to the bottom to stop pollutants from being stirred during the pile driving.

Monona Terrace, set on stilts capped with concrete, juts 90 feet over the lake. Very few buildings of this magnitude have ever been cantilevered over water. A giant net was installed under the building to keep people from swimming underneath it and debris from collecting there.

One of Monona Terrace's happy surprises, at least for people who like to fish, is that the grotto beneath it has become a haven for bluegill, crappies, perch, walleye, northern pike, bass and even an occasional muskie.

Monona Terrace has taken its place beside other Frank Lloyd Wright buildings in the stream of books and retrospectives that keep appearing. There are those who will never accept it as "authentic" because it was built after Wright's death and its interior uses were changed (the project's lead architect was Wright protege Tony Puttnam, of Taliesin Architects).

With its use of arcades, ellipses and concrete, Monona Terrace shares structural concepts with the Marin County Civic Center in California, the Guggenheim Museum in New York, the Greek Church near Milwaukee, and the Johnson Wax building in Racine, Wisconsin, all of which are based on rounded forms. The Madison building is a Wright style seldom seen in this part of his home state.

For all its glistening white grace during the day, it's at night that Monona Terrace becomes an almost magical presence. Illuminated beehive domes and 20-foot spires of light sparkle on the 68,000-square-foot terrace garden, and its trees are underlit with green light. The building's broad arches are outlined against the night sky, and reflections from the lake move across its facade.

UW-Madison art history professor Jim Dennis, of Madison, who lives in a Usonian house that Wright designed as an experiment in affordable housing, described Monona Terrace as "one of the dream-like projects he did in the late part of his career that had such different geometry than his earlier work. This building is like an ornament the city wears around its neck."

comprehensive road system. By 1917 the state had the ground-breaking State Trunk Highway Act, which set the stage for the massive state highway system that would eventually connect every community of 5,000 or more residents.

By 1923 Wisconsin had 10,000 miles of road in its highway system, and one of the first road sign programs to warn travelers of hazards and mark roads. Again, other states followed suit. When Wisconsin set up a system to number roads, it was so successful that the idea was copied by foreign countries as well as other states. Wisconsin's first concrete road was poured in 1913.

The darkest figure in Wisconsin politics was Senator Joseph McCarthy, from Appleton. The bellicose McCarthy questioned the loyalty of many Americans, including many in show business. Being blacklisted ruined many careers.

The whole world was watching UW-Madison in the 1960s, when it was one of the most turbulent campuses in the nation. Students had almost daily demonstrations — sit-ins, pickets, riots, mock burials. For a time classes were shut down, and students worried if they would be able to graduate. In 1967, a demonstration against Dow Chemical, producer of Agent Orange, escalated into a violent confrontation between students and authorities that resulted in the National Guard being called in.

In August 1970, a van filled with fuel, fertilizer and blasting caps was parked outside Sterling Hall, the army research center on the UW campus. It exploded. The blast killed a researcher there, and many historians believe the bombing of Sterling Hall was the incident that shattered the national antiwar movement (see our History chapter).

After the intensity of the 1960s and early 1970s, the UW student body was ready for buffoonery. The Pail and Shovel Party took over student government, and their accomplishments included covering Bascom Hill with plastic pink flamingos and erecting a model of the Statue of Liberty that looked like it was surfacing from the ice of Lake Mendota. The climate on campus ever since has been relatively tranquil.

Books on Madison Politics, History and Reference

Madison, a History of the Formative Years, by David V. Mollenhoff

Madison & Dane County, by Ron Seely

Greater Madison: Meeting the 21st Century, by Doug Moe

Wisconsin Women: a gifted heritage, a project of the Wisconsin State Division AAUW

Wisconsin: The Story of the Badger State, by Norman K. Risjord

Cultural Map of Wisconsin: A Cartographic Portrait of the State, by David Woodward, Robert Ostergren, Onno Brouwer, Steven Hoelscher and Joshua Hane

Wisconsin Land and Life: A Portrait of the State, by Robert Ostergren and Thomas Vale

Frank Lloyd Wright's Monona Terrace: The Power of an Enduring Civic Vision, by David Mollenhoff and Mary Jane Hamilton (available summer 1998)

The History of Wisconsin Series, by Paul Haas and Jack Holzhueter

Wisconsin in the Civil War: The Home Front and the Battle Front, 1861-1865, by Frank Klement

Madison's Conservation Ethic

Developers who consider profits before the environment might not wind up tarred and feathered in Madison, but sometimes they

INSIDERS' TIP

Tom Loftus, former speaker of the Wisconsin State Assembly, is now U.S. Ambassador to Norway.

come pretty close. Dane County is filled with ardent environmentalists. In the 1990s a plan to build a modern glass and steel business complex on Lake Monona caused such a ruckus that the local corporation that proposed it quickly withdrew its proposal and moved elsewhere. The city bought the property for parkland.

Voters also rejected a referendum to build a municipal swimming pool in that same neighborhood because of potential harm to the lake and the park.

Madison's efforts to keep its environment beautiful began early. In 1908 the city hired famed landscape architect John Nolen to make a plan for the city. He recommended that buildings near the Capitol have a height limit so nothing would ruin the view of its magnificent dome. He urged the city to buy key lakefront property, and to widen and improve State Street, which connects the Capitol with Bascom Hill, on campus. Nolen suggested that the city control the park system and provide neighborhood playgrounds as well as plant and maintain trees along the streets.

Nolen was asking a lot, but his advice was taken. His namesake boulevard, John Nolen Drive (see Getting Here, Getting Around), takes motorists over the causeway and into the heart of Downtown Madison. It traverses Madison's isthmus and is a favorite spot from which to photograph the Madison skyline. Parks, greenways and trees punctuate Madison, just as he planned.

Nolen's efforts meshed with those of John Olin, the father of the Madison Park System. Beginning in 1894, Olin was the first president of the Madison Park and Pleasure Drive Association. At that time, the city had a grand total of 3.5 acres of parkland. By 1909 the association controlled 269 acres of Madison parkland, and Olin had persuaded the city to donate $250,000 to buy, develop and maintain parkland. The latest count is 5,800 acres of public land offered by the city for public recreation, along with 150 miles of hiking trails in the county. And since it opened in 1911, the Henry Vilas Zoo (see Attractions) has become one of the finest in the region — and admission is free.

The university also contributes its share of greenspace to Madison. Its arboretum has walking trails, and regular conservation programs are held there. Picnic Point, a spit of land that extends into Lake Mendota, is one of the most popular places for leisurely walks in all of Madison. Madison's lakes are used year round for sailing, fishing, swimming, boating, wind sailing and water skiing. In winter, skaters and ice shanties dot the frozen lakes.

Much of Madison is enclosed by a Beltline with exits leading to major landmarks and attractions. With several highways, including two interstates, traffic usually moves smoothly.

Getting Here, Getting Around

Madison is the hub of South-Central Wisconsin. As the seat of government and home to a major university and a research center, it is usually awash with out-of-towners. But the maze-like street patterns, including many one-way streets, are rarely the favorite part of Madison for newcomers. The topography of the land, along with the city's many waterways, tends to make even those streets that are carefully gridded out seem less organized than they really are. In this chapter, we hope to take some of the mystery out of maneuvering through Madison.

Once you get your bearings, you'll find Madison is a reasonably easy place to navigate. Much of the city is enclosed by a Beltline with exits leading to major landmarks and attractions. With several highways, including two interstates, traffic usually moves smoothly. Even the most distant suburbs can be reached within 25 to 30 minutes of leaving Downtown. What we call "rush hour" is in reality rush minutes. The busiest times on the Beltline are usually between 7:15 and 8:30 AM, with the evening rush starting up just after 4 PM.

Since Madison is so close to Chicago, commuters and business professionals often take advantage of frequent bus trips and commuter flights to ease their travels (and allow them to squeeze in some extra minutes of paperwork.) Express buses leave Madison 10 times a day for Chicago's O'Hare International Airport. Because many Madison residents are concerned about the environment, discussion about the development of a light rail system continues.

To best get around Madison in a timely fashion these days, you need a set of wheels. Whether you prefer to travel by bus, bike or car, you'll find our city has plenty of user-friendly routes.

Traveling by Car

If you're coming into the city from Chicago or Milwaukee, you will find that two major interstates converge on the east edge of Madison — **Interstate 94** and **Interstate 90**. The interstates join together in Madison and continue on to the state's playground, Wisconsin Dells. When the interstates split, travel on I-90 to La Crosse or I-94 to Minneapolis (about 4½ hours from Madison). Traveling eastbound I-90 will lead you first to the smaller city of Janesville (home of Palmer Park with its unique, mega-size wood play structure) and then to metropolitan Chicago (about 2½ hours from Madison depending on traffic, weather and other conditions). I-94 eastbound leads to the historic city of Milwaukee, home of the Milwaukee Brewers baseball team.

INSIDERS' TIP

On several Saturday mornings from late April to October the Capitol Square is blocked off to traffic to accommodate special events on the Square.

28 • **GETTING AROUND**

Madison's "red bikes" is a free bicycle system — when you're done riding, leave it for the next person to use.

• **U.S. Highway 51** runs directly through Madison; in town it's known as Stoughton Road. This north-south road will take you south to the Mardi Gras in New Orleans or north for skiing and snowmobiling in Big Snow Country (Hurley, Wisconsin, and Ironwood, Michigan), about five hours north of Madison on the shores of Lake Superior (see *The Insiders' Guide® to the Lake Superior Region* for details).

• **U.S. highways 12 and 18** run together to form the south side of the Madison Beltline, our expressway. Beyond the city, this road becomes a twisting two-lane stretch through bucolic countryside between Madison and Cambridge. It has earned a reputation as a killer. In fact, to drive Highway 12/18 through the drumlins of eastern Dane County is to feel like you're on a roller coaster. In response to numerous traffic fatalities, construction has begun on a new four-lane highway between I-90 and Highway N and two straighter and wider lanes from there east to Cambridge. Completion is expected by late 1998. Unfortunately, the road project has already begun to claim many historic farmsteads that give this part of Wisconsin its character, an issue that raised a long and fierce debate between those who sought to preserve the structures and those who felt safety was more important.

• **U.S. Highway 151** enters Madison on the northeast side (E. Washington Avenue), travels through Downtown and south on Park Street, then joins with the Beltline until the Verona Road Exit, where U.S. 151 and U.S. 18 head southwest toward Verona, Dodgeville and sites beyond. **U.S. Highway 14** enters the city from the southeast, dovetails with the Beltline, then exits the city to the west, carrying travelers to La Crosse. U.S. 12 provides an alternate route to Wisconsin Dells.

GRAY LINE

Not just sight-seeing!

- Narrated Tours of Madison, WI Dells, House on the Rock & more!
- Charters.
- Convention Services - Attendee / Spousal tours.
- Step on Guide Service.
- Airport Transfers/shuttles.
- Bilingual Guides

GRAY LINE MADISON

Call
608-257-8983
800-256-6820

Surface Streets

A bonus to driving in Madison is that several of the main arteries of the city's street system have names that indicate cities on their paths. For example if you want to get to Stoughton, Verona, Cottage Grove, Mineral Point or Monona, just jump on the street by that name and follow the signs to your destination.

Here are some descriptions of Madison's main arteries and where they can take you.

•**E. Washington Avenue** (U.S. Highway 151) is the gateway to the Capitol from the East Side. Exiting from I-90/94, you will travel past clusters of hotels and motels, East Towne Mall and a lot of fast-food and full-service restaurants. Along the route are numerous strip malls and specialty stores, including those selling computer equipment, sporting goods and fabrics. As you get closer to the Capitol, moving west, you will pass East High School, some of Madison's long-established residential neighborhoods and the Madison Chamber of Commerce (615 E. Washington Avenue). The street ends at the Capitol Square.

•**Wis. Highway 30** is the city's main entrance when traveling west (from Milwaukee) on I-94. The interchange is somewhat confusing since the "exit" off of I-94 onto Wis. 30 (and to the Dane County Regional Airport) is actually straight ahead, and to continue westbound on I-94 you must use the right lane off-ramp to connect with I-90. (That's one way the State Department of Transportation contributes to getting travelers to visit the Mad City!) Continuing on Wis. 30, you will intersect with Stoughton Road (U.S. 51) and E. Washington Avenue (U.S. 151), where the highway ends, but the road continues on as Aberg Avenue to Packers Avenue, the location of Oscar Mayer's headquarters. All of this occurs in about 3 miles. If you continue north on Packers Avenue, you will intersect International Lane, which will take you to the Dane County Regional Airport.

•**U.S. Highway 12/18** is commonly known as the Beltline after crossing under I-90, just east of Madison's city limits. The Beltline is a limited-access road so you don't have to worry about traffic lights. Train tracks cross the Beltline between Fish Hatchery Road and Todd Drive.

The following thoroughfares (described in the order they exit the Beltline) will take you into the heart of Madison:

•**Stoughton Road** is the local name for north-south U.S. Highway 51. Traveling north on Stoughton Road will take you through the east end of Madison, where you will find several furniture stores, a fast-food outlet and Farm and Fleet, among other businesses along the frontage roads on each side. The Milwaukee Street interchange is one of the city's busiest and has been recently revamped. In the block west of the Stoughton Road-Milwaukee Street juncture, you can find a full-service grocery and liquor store (Woodman's) and the central Madison Post Office. Fast-food restaurants are within a block of the intersection traveling either east or west. Traveling south on Stoughton Road will take you through the community of McFarland, with its diverse selection of shops and restaurants, then on to Stoughton, a community currently celebrating 150 years of Norwegian-American heritage.

• **Monona Drive** provides access to Monona, an island city often overshadowed by its faster-growing metropolitan neighbor. Monona offers a variety of shopping venues, restaurants, a few motels and some very nice parks.

• **South Towne Drive** can take you to several discount stores, South Towne Mall, theaters and a handful of restaurants.

• **John Nolen Drive** is one of Madison's most scenic parkways, providing access to the Dane County Coliseum, the Expo Center, the Monona Terrace Community and Convention Center, State Street and the Capitol. Turning left onto Olin Avenue (just past the Coliseum and Expo Center) will take you to Park Street and the UW-Madison campus. John Nolen Drive passes through an isthmus between Lake Monona and Monona Bay (with parks and lakes on both sides) and eventually turns into Law Park Drive, which leads to Monona Terrace. Turning left onto Broom Street will take you to W. Washington Avenue and eventually to State Street and the UW-Madison campus. Make a right on W. Washington Avenue and you will be only a few blocks from the Capitol.

• **Rimrock Road** leads primarily to residential neighborhoods and outlying communities.

• **Park Street** leads you to the heart of the UW-Madison campus, providing access along the way to Meriter Hospital and numerous medical clinics. Travel south on Park Street under the Beltline to the Oregon community. Park Street intersects with W. Washington Avenue to lead you directly to the Capitol Square.

• **Fish Hatchery Road** heading south goes to (what else?) a state fish hatchery. Also south, Fish Hatchery Road brings you to several restaurants and the community of Fitchburg. Drive north on Fish Hatchery Road to reach the Henry Vilas Zoo (turn left at the Wingra Drive intersection). However, left turns aren't allowed during peak traffic hours so you'll have to go up a few blocks and double back. Continuing in to the city on Fish Hatchery Road, you will intersect with Park Street and head toward the UW campus.

• **Todd Drive** provides frontage-road access to several retail stores and restaurants.

• **Seminole Drive** is the route to the UW Arboretum, Nakoma Golf Course and Monroe Street, home of some of the city's most interesting shops and the Edgewood College campus.

• **Verona Road** and **Midvale Boulevard** (Midvale Boulevard turns into Verona Road at the Beltline) pass through major shopping and residential areas. Travel south to Verona, past Nakoma Shopping Center, sports facilities, grocery, shopping and restaurants. Travel north through residential areas and school zones (slow down!). Hilldale Shopping Center — home of Madison's only Marshall Field's — is at the intersection of Midvale Boulevard and University Avenue. If you take a right (going east), you will soon see the UW Hospital and Clinics on your left. University Avenue becomes Campus Drive and then becomes Johnson Street as it traverses the UW campus and heads toward State Street and the isthmus.

• **Odana Road** is a main thoroughfare from east to west ending at West Towne Mall. Its many curves, intersections and commercial driveways make it a contender for the worst place to drive in Madison during peak traffic times.

• **Whitney Way** (north) at Odana Road leads you to Westgate Mall and cinemas, shopping and dining. Several blocks across from Westgate on Whitney Way are also lined with stores and restaurants. It is one of the most

---

INSIDERS' TIP

Monroe Street, one of Madison's most charming shopping areas, is best traveled on foot.

Many Madison and area commuters rely on Madison's Metro Bus system to take them anywhere in the city.

dangerous and congested intersections in the city.

• **Gammon Road** travelers going north will find West Towne Mall to the left and a large number of stores and eateries to the right. Turn left on Mineral Point Road for more shopping and dining entertainment. This is another high-traffic area where fender benders are common.

• **Mineral Point Road** leads you back into the city's West Side. Once again, here's a good place to find interesting shops and good places to eat.

• **Old Sauk Road** and **Greenway Boulevard** provide access to hotels, restaurants and clinics.

• **University Avenue** introduces you to the charming city of Middleton. Travel east to find the main street, shops, restaurants and, ultimately, the University of Wisconsin campus. (See the previous Verona Road and Midvale Boulevard note.)

• **Century Avenue** passes through Middleton to County Highway M for a scenic trip from the far West Side to the far East Side of Madison around the north side of Lake Mendota. County M intersects Wis. Highway 113 (turning right, this road becomes Madison's Northport Drive) and then becomes Packers Avenue. Exiting onto Aberg Avenue eastbound, the road passes under E. Washington Avenue, becoming Wis. Highway 30, and eventually brings you to intersections with I-90 (to Chicago and La Crosse) and I-94 (to Milwaukee and Minneapolis).

Parking

Downtown

Madison operates 13 parking ramps and lots that provide 4,130 spaces. Most lots are metered, and meter charges range from 30¢ to 75¢ an hour depending on the lot. Some lots offer monthly parking. Another, the Brayton Lot, uses a self-service payment method, and the charge is 70¢ an hour.

There are six city-operated ramps in Madison. Most have cashiers and no meters. Only the State Street Capitol ramp has both. Four of the six offer monthly rental parking.

INSIDERS' TIP

To drive around the Capitol Square you need to navigate in a counterclockwise pattern.

Questions about parking? Call the Parking Division of the Madison Department of Transportation, (608) 266-4761, between 7:30 AM to 4:15 PM weekdays.

At the University

The UW-Madison operates about 100 ramps and parking lots on campus. Due to high demand from faculty, university staff and students, however, you can still have an extremely difficult time finding a spot to park, even for a short time. It's possible to obtain half-day or full-day visitor parking permits for central campus lots at rates of $2.50 or $5 respectively. Call (608) 263-6666 for information about visitor parking permits and special-events parking. Parking at the Kohl Center has been a headache, so call for updates before you attend an event there.

Metered visitor stalls are available in some campus lots for periods ranging from 25 minutes to 10 hours. The 25-minute meters will give you 10 minutes of free time if you turn the parking meter handle before inserting any coins. Meter rates are 60¢ an hour.

Do not leave your car in any lot without first checking parking lot signs to make sure you can park without a permit. Parking limits are strongly enforced throughout the campus and the city. For information on obtaining a visitor's parking pass or on longer-term parking, contact the Director of Transportation Services, Room 124 WARF, 610 N. Walnut Street, (608) 263-6666.

Traveling By Air

Dane County Regional Airport
4000 International Ln., Madison
• **(608) 246-3380**

On a normal day, the airport does a respectable if not bustling amount of business. One of the joys about living in or visiting Madison is this airport. It's small enough that more often than not, you can easily arrive 45 minutes before your flight and complete your check-in without fighting crowds or long lines.

Each year, about 1 million passengers arrive and depart from Dane County Regional Airport. Eight commercial airlines — offering a total of 83 flights daily — can accommodate up to 6,000 people a day. Private planes and military craft account for most of the airport's daily use.

The airport recently completed renovations to the food-service and news and gifts areas. In spring 1997, work began on a new runway — estimated to cost more than $17 million. That project is expected to take two to three years to complete and is designed to reduce noise in nearby neighborhoods.

Long-term and short-term parking is available in the airport parking ramp or a surface lot at maximum daily rates of $6 and $4 respectively. The first 15 minutes of parking are free.

Major carriers at Dane County Regional include Midwest Express, (800) 452-2022; Northwest, (800) 225-2525; and United, (800) 241-6522. Regional commuter service is offered by United Express, (800) 241-6522; American Eagle, (800) 433-7300; COMAIR, (800) 221-1212; Skyway, (800) 452-2022; and Trans World Express, (800) 221-2000.

Morey Airplane Co.
8300 Airport Rd., Middleton
• **(608) 836-1711**

This private airport accepts private and rental air traffic and provides fuel and tie-down services ($4 per night, one free night with fuel purchase; $44 per month). This airfield includes one paved and two grass runways; landing fees are $4. You also may charter one of the company's three airplanes to take you just about anywhere in the continental United States, or take instruction to earn a private or commercial pilot's license. Air-traffic control is handled through Dane County Regional Airport (Unicom

---

INSIDERS' TIP

If you use the bicycle lane on the north side of the heavily trafficked University Avenue, be forewarned that you'll share tight quarters with buses and cars. There's lots of potential for crossing paths — so be careful.

Madison's Dane County Regional Airport provides commercial, private and military air service.

frequency 123.0). Car rental is available on site through Avis. Airport Road is 1 mile west of U.S. Highway 12.

Rental Cars

Most major rental car agencies are available in Madison and provide services to clients using Dane County Regional Airport. Here's a sampling with some local numbers: **Avis**, (608) 242-0600; **Budget**, (608) 249-5544; **Enterprise**, (608) 242-5000; **Hertz**, (608) 241-3803; **National**, (608) 249-1614; and **Thrifty**, (608) 251-1717.

Mass Transit

Commuter Buses

Metro Transit System
(608) 266-4466 or (608) 267-1143 (TDD)

The Madison Metro Transit System provides bus service throughout much of the city. Buses are clean, drivers are friendly, and you can feel comfortable choosing this mode of travel. The buses arrive and depart pretty much right on schedule. For information about fixed routes and paratransit service, call the Customer Service Center number listed above between 6:15 AM and 6 PM weekdays, 8 AM and 4:30 PM Saturdays, and 12:30 to 4:30 PM Sundays.

You can purchase a monthly unlimited ride pass for $35. A monthly commuter pass (unlimited rides Monday through Friday) costs $31. Metro also offers unlimited ride passes for youth and college students. Children younger than 5 always ride free. If you are riding a bus, you must have the exact fare; however, buses do accept dollar bills. The base fare is $1.25 for adults, 85˙¢ for youth and 60¢ for disabled individuals and senior citizens 65 and older. The Metro Visitor Pass allows unlimited fixed-route bus rides for $3 per day.

A "FREE FARE ZONE" is in effect 10 AM to 3 PM Monday through Saturday allowing travelers in the campus and State Street areas to hop a bus without charge.

Bus Lines and Tours

Alco-VanGalder Bus Lines and Van Galder Tour & Travel
(800) 747-0994

This company's Chicago routes are very popular. Buses depart for downtown Chicago three times daily — at 5 and 7 AM and 2 PM — for passengers boarding at the UW Memorial Union. Departures from the Dutch Mill Park and Ride are 15 minutes later. The 4¼-hour bus ride costs $18, and tickets may be purchased from the driver.

Van Galder buses run back and forth between Madison and O'Hare International Airport, downtown Chicago or the Amtrak Station 10 times daily. The ride takes just more than three hours, and tickets cost $18 each. If you're lucky, you'll get one of the luxury party buses for no extra cost.

Van Galder Tour & Travel offers a variety of scheduled vacations tours: Branson, Missouri; Packer Nostalgia & Mississippi Golf Coast Fun; Holland, Michigan, at tulip time; and trips to New York, Philadelphia, Canada and other spots.

Badger Coaches
200 Beltline, Madison • (608) 255-1511

This company offers charters throughout the United States and Canada.

Badger Bus Depot
Madison Bus Depot, 2 S. Bedford St., Madison • (608) 255-6771

Greyhound Bus Lines
Madison Bus Depot, 2 S. Bedford St., Madison• (608) 257-3050, (800) 231-2222

You can catch either a Badger Coach or Greyhound Bus from the Madison Bus Depot, which is just west of the Capitol. Badger Coaches provide 90-minute express service between Milwaukee and Madison. Buses leave Madison eight times daily. Greyhound buses depart from Madison 17 times a day.

Charlie's Charters
(608) 873-9172

This touring company specializes in casino and bingo hall runs.

Evergreen Transport Corp.
6502 Grand Teton Plaza, Madison • (608) 833-1005

Evergreen provides regular charter bus service for groups. It also transports the elderly and disabled in Dane County individually and in groups.

Gray Line Madison
3 S. Pinckney St., Madison
• (608) 257-8983, (800) 256-6820

Gray Line Madison offers bus day tours from Madison to The House on the Rock, Wisconsin Dells, Baraboo and Taliesin in Spring Green. (See our Wisconsin Dells and Daytrips chapters for details about these destinations.) Buses will pick up passengers from the Gray Line office or from any major hotel in Madison.

Visitors can also sign up for a three-hour sightseeing tour showcasing the best of what Madison has to offer — sweeping vistas of both lakes, the UW-Madison campus, historic Mansion Hill and the Governor's Mansion. With the recent opening of the Monona Terrace Convention Center, whose design was heavily influenced by Frank Lloyd Wright, the bus company has added a drive-by tour of homes and buildings in Madison designed by the celebrated architect. This trip can be combined with one to Taliesin, Wright's estate.

Coming to town with a group? Gray Line can tailor a sightseeing package to suit special interests and needs. Also, inquire about sightseeing/hotel packages.

Laidlaw Transit Inc.
200 W. North St., DeForest
• (608) 846-3939

Laidlaw charters school buses for tours and trips.

Metro Ride of Wisconsin Inc.
4605 Pflaum Rd., Madison
• (608) 223-0610

Metro Ride features luxury motor coach and school bus charters, including trips to casino gambling venues and nationwide tours.

Rite-Way Leasing/Safe-Way Coach and Equipment
4212 Robertson Rd., Madison
• (608) 249-6462

This company leases buses and equipment for in-state charters.

Verona Bus Service
219 Paoli St., Verona • (608) 845-8516

Verona Bus Service runs charters from five locations and charters school buses for group activities anywhere in Wisconsin.

Trains

Amtrak
(800) 872-7245

Amtrak does not travel through or stop in Madison. To access national rail service, passengers from the Madison area must travel to Amtrak stations in Portage or Columbus (approximately 45 minutes north), or travel to Milwaukee (90 minutes east) or Chicago (2½ hours south).

Taxis and Other Ride Services

Madison taxis usually don't cruise for fares, so you'll have to call. To arrange for a taxi, contact one of the following companies: **Badger Cab**, (608) 256-5566; **Madison Taxi**, (608) 255-TAXI; **Union Cab Cooperative**, (608) 242-4000; and **University Cab**, (608) 278-0000.

The **Women's Transit Authority** is Madison's nighttime rape-prevention ride service for women traveling in the campus area. The WTA operates from 9 PM to 1 AM nightly. Call (608) 256-SAFE to arrange a free ride or for more information.

Next to the Wienermobile, the white limo with the hot tub on its rear end is the most famous vehicle in Madison. Most limo services require a two-hour minimum rental. Hourly rental rates start at around $60. The more hours you rent, the less you pay per hour. Several limo companies do business in Madison: **Day and Night Limo Service**, (800) 679-3865; **D. Royal Limousine**, (608) 845-3211; **Gallant Knight**, (608) 825-7000; **Sir Michael's**, (608) 255-1311; and **Sunlife "Cloud 9" Limousine**, (608) 833-4444.

A carriage ride: What better way to get some private time with someone you love! Horse-drawn carriages offer a memorable and leisurely way to enjoy the excitement of Downtown. Many bridal couples spend time between their ceremony and reception on such a ride, and many proposals are made here. Carriage stops are set up at the Concourse Hotel, State Street and the Convention Center. Rates vary by length of rental time and number of passengers. Call **Cobblestone Carriages**, (608) 251-3030, for specific rate information and reservations.

Motorless Motion

Biking

Madison is a city filled with bicycle commuters. The number of bike paths is growing constantly. There's even a bicycle path right through a terrace at the Monona Terrace Convention Center. Business professionals, students, faculty, retired people and just about anyone else you name in the Madison area owns and uses his or her bike.

While many people store their bikes during winter's worst weather, it is not uncommon in Madison to be driving along in a snowstorm and see some brave soul pedaling through the elements. The city maintains more than 100 miles of bike paths, covering every part of the city. Routes are marked by easy-to-follow green and white "bike route" signs. Routes vary from on-street types to separate bike paths.

It's illegal to ride on the sidewalk, and the law says pedestrians always have the right of way. Since the city has so many bicycles, enforcement of bike safety rules is a priority. If you run a red light while riding a bicycle, don't be surprised if you get a ticket. Bicyclists are expected to follow the same rules as cars. The city has a number of bike cops who keep active during warm weather.

All bicycles are required to be licensed, and this is your best insurance policy for seeing your bike again if it is stolen. You may pick up a four-year license for $8 from any police station, many bike shops, the UW Memorial Union or the City Treasurer's Office, Room 107 in the City-County Building on Martin Luther King Jr. Boulevard. All bikes should be licensed within 10 days of purchase or moving to the city. As bicycle thefts are common, UW officials encourage new students to buy less showy models. Investing in a good U-shaped lock and using it along with a thick cable can help you hang on to your wheels. Most public places have bike racks, but you can lock your bike just about anywhere. Don't lock your bike to a tree, though; it's illegal.

The Monona Terrace Convention Center forms the backdrop for a quick game of hockey.

Free Bikes and Bike Rentals

A free bicycle system operates on campus. These "red bikes" (named for their bright color) are older, unlocked bikes designed to help students who lack bikes to traverse the sprawling UW campus and State Street area. When you are done with the bike, leave it for the next rider as the free bike system won't work if the bikes disappear. Anyone who locks up a free bike or takes it home faces fines.

If you left your bike at home or haven't purchased one yet, you might want to consider renting a bike. Three shops in town rent bicycles by the day, week or month: **Budget Bicycle Center**, 1202 Regent Street, (608) 251-8413; **Williamson Bicycle Works**, 601 Williamson Street, (608) 255-5292; and **Yellow Jersey**, 419 State Street, (608) 257-4737.

Bike rentals begin at $7 per day for touring bikes and $9.50 for mountain bikes. Some rental packages include bike locks and helmets. Tandem bicycles may also be rented.

Bicycling Resources

For a copy of the *Madison Bicycling Resource Guide and Bus Map*, write to the Madison Department of Transportation, 215 Martin Luther King Jr. Boulevard, Madison, WI 53202. Call (608) 266-4761 to have a map mailed to you. City and county maps are also free at area bike shops.

Best Wisconsin Bike Trips, a guide to more than 30 one-day bike trips, is available for $12.95 plus shipping and handling from Wisconsin Trails Inc., P.O. Box 5650, Madison, WI 53705, (608) 231-2444 or (800) 877-5280.

Bike Clubs

Bike clubs offer a great way to exercise and meet new friends. The **Bombay Bicycle**

Club, (608) 833-3335, is the biggest bike club in town and puts together rides from April through November. Madison has several United States Cycling Federation clubs (check with bike shops for current contacts).

Walking

Last but not least, walking is a terrific way to get around the city. It's also the only way you can really experience the State Street pedestrian mall. Take some time to stroll down State Street, sit by the fountain on Library Mall, then walk over to the Memorial Union Terrace for a cold drink or ice cream cone.

There are also a number of excellent walking tour brochures to some of Madison's historic neighborhoods. To get the guides call the city's historic preservation office at (608) 266-6552, or check the local library.

Many walkers like to walk the scenic route over John Nolen Drive, along Lake Monona, where they can enjoy one of the best views in the city of Monona Terrace and are well-protected from traffic. There's a lot of natural beauty to be enjoyed in this city, and walking allows you to pause and take it all in.

Go For It!

Now that you've got some idea of where you are going, grab your gear and hit the trail. There's plenty of natural and city life waiting for you to explore. If you get lost, don't sweat it. It's usually not hard to find an agreeable Madison resident to point you in the right direction.

Stone House

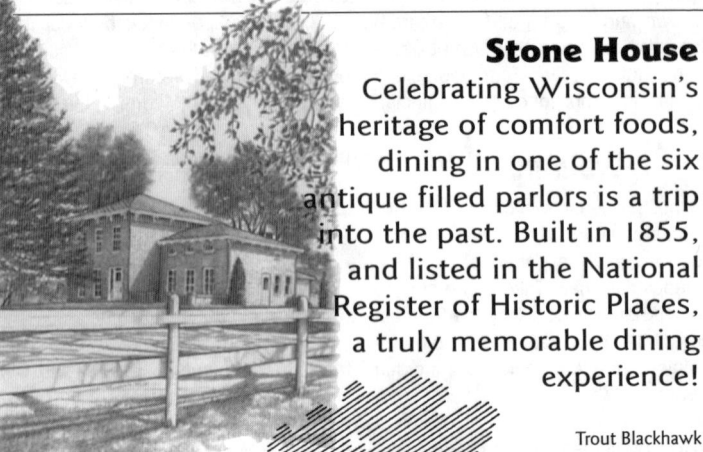

Celebrating Wisconsin's heritage of comfort foods, dining in one of the six antique filled parlors is a trip into the past. Built in 1855, and listed in the National Register of Historic Places, a truly memorable dining experience!

Trout Blackhawk
Pork Hanerville
Daleyville Duck
Schurz Schnitzl
Sterling Beef
Roxbury Ribs
Lamb Doty
Walleye Smith
Chicken Verona
Popover Glover
Middleton Perch
Chicken Fairchild
Vegetable Leopold
Whitefish Van Slyke

Where locals take out of town guests.

QUIVEY'S GROVE

6261 Nesbitt Rd. • 273-4900
*Verona Road (Hwy. 151)
exit at PD, left on Nesbitt*
VISA & MC ACCEPTED
www.madisondining.com/quiveys

Stable Grill

Connected by tunnel is the restored horse stable, featuring Wisconsin Micro tap beers, Wisconsin wines, full bar, and casual dining in the hay lofts. Friday fish fry and Saturday prime rib. Entertainment on weekends.

"Other restaurants are in Wisconsin, Quivey's Grove *Is* Wisconsin"

Restaurants

People living and working in Madison often brag that our city has more restaurants per capita than any other city in the United States. That's a tall claim — San Francisco and Myrtle Beach typically vie for that distinction — that we weren't able to verify factually. Even so, it's probably not far from the truth.

By sheer number alone — well into the hundreds — Madison should come out very near the top. Add the variety of ethnic eateries available, and we doubt any city Madison's size could measure up. There are dozens of Oriental restaurants specializing in Chinese, Thai, Japanese and Vietnamese cuisine. Coming on strong are those specializing in Mediterranean and Middle Eastern cuisine: traditional dishes of Turkey, Iran, Egypt and Morocco. Mexican fare is well represented, as is French and Italian. Madison even has a restaurant specializing in Russian cuisine — the Russian House (see subsequent entry). Although Madison diners enjoy eating around the world, they never forget their roots. A number of restaurants feature the best of Midwestern cuisine and change their menus almost nightly to take advantage of fresh, regional food products such as poultry, fish and berries. And nowhere else but in Wisconsin do you have so many places offering a Friday night fish fry; we've noted many restaurants that do.

There are some people here — oh, let's just call them snobs — who believe truly fine dining has to originate out of a thriving metropolis like Chicago or New York. Who are they kidding. Restaurants like Louisianne's, La Paella and L'Etoile, whose owner, Odessa Piper, has single-handedly trained many of Madison's top chefs, prove you can enjoy fine dining here and, might we add smugly, for quite a bit less money. Visitors are amazed at the incredible choice and food value in Madison.

Across the board, service usually is efficient and very friendly. And that is difficult to maintain in a city like Madison that, despite the presence of a large student population, has one of the lowest unemployment rates in the country. It means that wait staff, especially at places that have withstood the test of time, are loyal and committed.

In this chapter, we've concentrated on listing a wide selection of independent restaurants (those you won't find anywhere else), first by category and then by location. It's wise to look over all the listings, however, to know what's available. Take seafood, for instance. While we offer a separate category of "Steak and Seafood," many other restaurants, especially those under "European and Fine Dining," consider seafood one of their specialties. If you're looking for a restaurant near a Downtown hotel, don't overlook the Campus area. The walking distance can be insignificant.

Of course, Madison also has its share of fast-food chains and franchise restaurants that do very well, too. They include Chili's, The Olive Garden, Applebee's, Houlihan's, Mountain Jack's, the Outback Steakhouse and every kind of bagel place imaginable. Damon's, on the far West Side, serves ribs, steak, seafood and chicken as diners watch big-screen TV and try their hand at sports trivia. Even Hooters has made it to Madison.

There are two things you should know about Madison restaurants. First, most are very kid-friendly, and the few that don't have separate children's menus are usually more than willing to bring out something that will surely please: a side order of spaghetti, cottage cheese or baked potato. Let price be your guide. The less expensive the restaurant, the more likely kids will be in tow. Second, Madisonians don't worry about dressing down on Fridays because seldom does anybody dress up for dinner any day of the week. Thus, it's not unusual to see someone in jeans (nicely ironed, however) and a polo shirt dining next to someone in a three-piece suit. "Comfortable" is a good word to describe both the ambiance of many Madison restaurants and the way people dress when they come.

Since most places do take one or more major credit cards, we only point out the ones that don't. The same thing goes for wheelchair accessibility; if we think you might have problems accessing restaurants in some of the older buildings, we let you know. In addition, we've indicated when reservations are appropriate or when a wait might be necessary because a restaurant doesn't accept them. Also, be advised that all restaurants in Madison and Middleton are designated by city ordinances as no-smoking establishments. While that doesn't hold true for taverns or bars, compared to other parts of the country, you'll notice fewer people lighting up in and around Madison. This is a health-conscious community, remember?

Price-Code Key

Preceding the address and telephone number for each listing, we've added a dollar-sign code indicating what you can expect to pay for a dinner for two. Keep in mind, the amount excludes appetizers, cocktails, tip, tax and any extras, so if you enjoy a glass of wine with dinner, the bill will be slightly higher.

$	Less than $20
$$	$20 to $40
$$$	$40 to $60
$$$$	More than $60

Please give this chapter a good read. Become familiar with all the categories and helpful tips. It will make dining all the more pleasurable.

American

Isthmus

Angelic Brewing Company
$-$$ • 322 W. Johnson St., Madison
• (608) 257-2707

Featuring pub-style food with an emphasis on pastas and hearty dinner fare, Angelic Brewing Company is a spacious, relaxing brewpub just a short walk from the Square (see our Brewpubs, Wine Bars and Cigar Bars chapter.) If an appetizer is all you're interested in, try the homemade artichoke dip — it's a house specialty. Angelic is open for lunch Thursday through Sunday and for dinner seven days a week. The bar closes at 2 AM. Parking always is available in an adjacent lot on the east side of the pub and Monday through Friday after 6 PM and Saturday and Sunday after noon on the west side.

Argus Food & Spirits
$ • 123 E. Main St., Madison
• (608) 256-4141

This restaurant/bar — a favorite gathering spot for politicians, bankers and lawyers — is a great place to stop for lunch where such American comfort food as pot roast and mashed potatoes, roast pork and spaghetti supplement a sandwich, soup and salad menu. The food is good, hearty and inexpensive. There are only 12 tables upstairs, but seating for more than 100 is available on the lower level, accessible by a staircase in the

INSIDERS' TIP

Restaurants offering good fish fries on Fridays are crowded, so a wait is not uncommon.

www.madison.com
Dining Guide

rear of the building. Outdoor seating is also available in the front of the restaurant (weather permitting).

The building in which Argus is housed is one of the oldest commercial structures still standing in Madison, having turned 150 years old in 1997. Originally, it was the home of the *Argus*, the first newspaper in Madison, hence the restaurant's name. Argus is only open for lunch Monday through Friday. It also offers catering and books special parties; call (608) 256-4226.

Cafe Montmartre
$ • 127 E. Mifflin St., Madison
• (608) 255-5900

This charming Downtown hideaway opens at 3 PM every day for late lunches and dinner with a menu featuring mostly light fare: soups, salads, sandwiches, individual gourmet pizzas, appetizers and desserts. When the weather cooperates, alfresco dining is available. Reservations are not accepted. (For more information, refer to the Cafe Montmartre entry in our Brewpubs, Wine Bars and Cigar Bars chapter.)

The Curve
$, no credit cards • 653 S. Park St., Madison • (608) 251-0311
The Curve II
$, no credit cards • 44 S. Fair Oaks Ave. S. (East Side), Madison • (608) 244-8899

This Madison institution makes the most of its "greasy spoon" image. It's open for breakfast and lunch seven days a week with breakfast food served all day. The Curve is noted for its cheap, good food such as ham and eggs served with American fries or a ham, egg and cheese sandwich. For lunch, Monday through Friday, specials for the "working man's appetite" include baked chicken, Swiss steak, pork cutlets or beef roast. While not right on the Isthmus, the Curve is only a short drive from Downtown Madison. Its newer sister operation, The Curve II, is on the East Side.

Dayton Street Cafe and Bakery
$ • 1 W. Dayton St., Madison
• (608) 257-6000 Ext. 1257

In the Madison Concourse Hotel, just a block off the Square, the Dayton Street Cafe serves breakfast and lunch plus a nice selection of bakery goods seven days a week. Especially popular is the cafe's 20-foot-long salad bar. Alcoholic beverages are available. A Sunday brunch is served from 9:30 AM to 1:30 PM.

Dotty Dumpling's Dowry
$ • 116 N. Frances St., Madison
• (608) 255-3175

In business for more than 20 years, Dotty Dumpling's has racked up one award after another for its 5-ounce thick burger including "Best in the State" from *Wisconsin Trails* magazine and "Best in the Big 10" from *USA Today*. If you've never tried one, you're missing out. But Dotty's also serves a wide selection of sandwiches, hearty soups and pies baked from scratch. The casual cafe, decorated in antique Wisconsin, features live jazz every Thursday evening. There are 18 beers on tap from all over the world. Dotty Dumpling's, just off the Square, is open for lunch and dinner every day of the week.

The Great Dane Pub and Brewing Co.
$-$$ • 123 E. Doty St., Madison
• (608) 284-0000

Housed in a historic building just off the Square, The Great Dane specializes in traditional English pub food for lunch and dinner every day of the week. The menu is extensive with a wide selection of hot sandwiches and appetizers including a house favorite: artichoke and cheese dip. This is where you'll find fish and chips and North Woods Cottage Pie, prepared much like shepherd's pie, only with lamb. Reservations are accepted only for parties of eight or more, except on Fridays and Saturdays. But the place is large, so the wait is seldom long. On a nice day, the outdoor courtyard is a nice place to be. (See the entry in our Brewpubs, Wine Bars and Cigar Bars chapter for more information.)

Heartland Grill
$$ • 706 John Nolen Dr., Madison
• (608) 258-9505

A couple of miles south of Downtown in the Sheraton Inn, which is directly across

Sugar and Spice Is Nice . . .
If You Don't Count Calories

It seems that almost every time you turn around in Madison, there's an opportunity to indulge your sweet tooth. Of the many excellent bakeries in the area, we've singled out three that have become integrally interwoven into the personality of Wisconsin's capital city.

Lane's Bakery, 448 S. Park Street, has been doing a booming business since first opening its doors in 1954. Today, it's in a Swiss chalet-like building a couple miles from the Capitol Square. People don't just buy their bakery goods from Lane's — they hang out there too, especially the over-60 crowd. Because the dozen or so tables are at a premium, it's common to sit down with someone you don't know but are most likely to see again if you stop by the same time the following day. Yes, there are many regulars who start their morning at Lane's with a sweet roll or doughnut and cup of coffee. According to one employee, "it's hard to keep the doughnuts in the case."

The family-owned bakery covers the gamut of baked goods quite well but is especially noted for its braided egg bread, which is dyed multiple colors for Easter and Christmas; butter cookies; kringles (we always go for the raspberry); and specialty cakes. Lane's does a big business in wedding cakes, and brides-to-be are welcome to visit the gift shop upstairs, which has a number of bridal displays.

Lane's is open from 6 AM until 6 PM Monday through Friday and until 4 PM on Saturday. On Sunday, the bakery is open from 7 AM until 12:30 PM. Call (608) 256-6645.

One block west off U.S. Highway 12 in Middleton is the popular European baked-goods haven, **Clasen Bakery**, 7610 Donna Drive, noted for its more than 30 types of coffee cakes, chocolate novelties, petit fours, strudels, European tortes and German sourdough breads. In business for more than 35 years, this is the place to go for Marzipan animals and hot-cross buns at Easter and stollen and gingerbread houses at Christmas. In fact, during the winter holidays, Clasen's features a 10-foot-tall Gingerbread House in which children can frolic; at Easter, there's something similar. (In fact, there's a house for children to explore any time of the year — only it's made of wood, not candy, as it is during the holidays.) To keep small fingers from pulling off pieces they can't seem to resist (could you?), Clasen's offers free candy samples during the holidays. Also, free coffee and cake is available every day to patrons.

Clasen Bakery is open from 7:30 AM

Chuck Lane, owner of Lane's Bakery, a popular gathering spot for the over-60 crowd, shows off some of his creations from the height of last season's Super Bowl frenzy.

Photo: Wisconsin State Journal/The Capital Times

— continued on next page

until 5:30 PM Monday through Friday and 7:30 AM until 5 PM on Saturday. It's closed on Sunday. Call (608) 831-2032.

The **Greenbush Bakery**, 1305 Regent Street, is one of the best kept secrets in Madison and the only place in town where you can buy Kosher-certified doughnuts. Catering to primarily a university crowd, co-owner Marvin Miller has learned to accommodate his clientele. So, unlike most bakeries, he's open and baking when the students are hungry — from 5 PM until 3 AM weekend nights, until midnight or 1 AM other nights. You'll usually find him around most afternoons, too, although it's early evening when hot doughnuts start rolling out. Beginning in the fall of '98, Miller frequently also offers cream puffs and eclairs. Call (608) 257-1151.

---

from the Dane County Expo Center, the Heartland Grill specializes in Midwestern cuisine, showcasing a rotisserie in the dining room. Salads, sandwiches and daily specials are featured at lunch, and a wide selection of fresh fish, rotisserie dishes, pasta and grilled meats are available for dinner. Signature dishes are chicken pot pie and the Heartland Salad (smoked chicken with bleu cheese and red and white poached apples served over leaf lettuce and topped with dried Door County cherries). The prairie-style design of the room reflects Madison's renewed interest in Frank Lloyd Wright. The full-service bar provides an ample selection of wines by the glass or bottle, a selection of microbrews, cognacs and cordials. The Heartland Grill is open for breakfast, lunch and dinner every day of the week and for brunch on Sunday. Reservations are always a good idea, especially for brunch and parties of six or more.

Heinemann's...Too
$ • Firstar Plaza, 1 S. Pinckney St., Madison • (608) 251-1300

This is a convenient spot by the Capitol Square for breakfast and lunch on weekdays. Take-out is another option for downtown workers. The dining room is attractively furnished, and service is cafeteria style. For anyone seriously pressed for time, there's a good selection of packaged to-go items to take back to your desk. Lunch includes hot and cold sandwiches, salads, soups and a changing selection of hot entrees. For something sweet after lunch you can have cookies, brownies and pies. Breakfast selections include eggs and grilled coffee cake.

Plaza Tavern and Grill
$, no credit cards • 319 N. Henry St., Madison • (608) 255-6592

In existence since Prohibition was repealed, this lively downtown grill, operated for more than 30 years by the same family, is especially famous for its quarter-pound burger served with a special sour cream/mayonnaise sauce that tastes like ranch dressing but isn't. Anybody who has lived in Madison very long and has never tasted a Plaza Burger is deprived, by our standards. Second on the list of favorite sandwiches is the grilled tuna and cheese. The Plaza has a full bar and serves the same menu from 10:45 AM to 11:45 PM Monday through Saturday.

Stillwaters
$-$$ • 250 State St., Madison • (608) 256-0596

Stillwaters, which celebrated its 20th anniversary in 1997, is noted for a menu encompassing small bites to daily dinner specials. Open for lunch and dinner seven days a week, the restaurant features a prime-rib sandwich on Monday, Mexican cuisine on Tuesday and pasta on Wednesday. On Saturday night, the special is beer-battered jumbo shrimp. Stillwaters, which has a separate bar and features both a (hot) winter drink list and (cool) summer one, looks out on State Street and is practically across the street from the Madison Civic Center. In warmer months, outdoor seating is available. Check out the homemade soups and desserts on the menu; they're very good. Reservations are only accepted for groups of six or more.

Wilson Street Grill

$$ • 217 S. Hamilton St., Madison
• (608) 251-3500

Serving contemporary American food, the Wilson Street Grill changes its menu daily to take advantage of the freshest seasonal produce. Sample entrees include apple-smoked pork chop with field greens and Wisconsin blue cheese and cranberry spinach salad with crispy beets and onions. The individualized, homemade gourmet pizzas are very popular for lunch, and one Milwaukee food critic said the bread "rivaled anything I've had in France"; it *is* wonderful.

Two-tiered seating creates intimate dining in a modern, airy environment enhanced by fine art and flowers on the table. A sister operation to Kennedy Manor, the Wilson Street Grill has a full bar with an impressive American wine list and three Wisconsin microbrews on tap. Open for lunch and dinner every day of the week, the Wilson Street Grill is frequented by those who live and work Downtown. After 4 PM, free underground parking is available adjacent to the restaurant. The restaurant is proud to have a committed, diverse staff; one-third of the crew is disabled.

Campus

Marsh Shapiro's Nitty Gritty

$ • 223 N. Frances St., Madison
• (608) 251-2521

You don't have to be celebrating your birthday to have lunch or dinner at this Madison institution, going strong since '68. But if you do happen by on your personal holiday, the Nitty Gritty, "Madison's Official Birthday Bar and Restaurant," will give you a glass memento mug of your very own from which you can drink either free beer or soda the entire time you're there.

While a lot of college students hang out at the Nitty Gritty, it's also a gathering spot for families with small children, who are given balloons, crayons and coloring sheets to keep them busy. The atmosphere is very informal and relaxed; there are several dining areas broken up with large booths and tables. The cartoon-like menu features a wide variety of sandwiches, salads, soups and appetizers including onion rings, deep-fried potato wedges, Marsh's Mexican cheese spread, jalapeno poppers and hot spinach dip. The specialty of the house, however, is the Gritty Burger — more than 5-ounces of ground chuck chargrilled and bathed in a special house sauce.

The Nitty Gritty is open seven days a week for lunch and dinner, except during the summer months when dinner only is served on Sundays. When the weather is nice, seating is available on an outdoor patio. The Nitty Gritty is the closest restaurant/bar to the Kohl Center. But be advised that reservations are never accepted. So, if you're planning to eat there before an event, arrive early.

Mickies Dairy Bar

$, no credit cards • 1511 Monroe St., Madison • (608) 256-9476

This old-fashioned eatery, which celebrated its silver anniversary in '97, draws a varied clientele — from high school and college students to middle-age professionals — all of whom are attracted by the down-home atmosphere and servings of inexpensive comfort food. This is a great place for bacon and eggs, a malt, BLT or slice of pie. It's like time is standing still here. Mickies is open for breakfast and lunch every day of the week except Monday. It caters to the early riser, with doors opening at 6 AM Monday through Saturday and at 7 AM on Sunday. You don't need a reservation here, though sometimes you'll wish you had one.

Oakcrest Tavern

$-$$, no credit cards • 1421 Regent St., Madison • (608) 250-8989
$-$$, no credit cards • 5371 Old Middleton Rd. (West Side), Madison • (608) 233-1243

The original Oakcrest on Old Middleton Road has been a popular neighborhood fixture since the '50s; the one a block from Camp Randall Stadium opened just prior to the first Badgers football game in '96. Though perhaps a bit more sophisticated, it too would rather be known as a neighborhood tavern than a campus hangout. Menus, with some shrimp and steak specials, are almost the same at both places. Oakcrest has received a slew of "Best Of Madison" awards over the years for its burgers and fish fry (Wednesday and Friday) featuring lake perch. During football Saturdays, the parking lot of Oakcrest on Regent is roped off and made into a beer garden.

Wild Iris Cafe
$-$$ • 1225 Regent St., Madison
• (608) 257-4747

One of our favorite places for lunch or dinner, the Wild Iris Cafe serves an eclectic mix of new American cuisine in an old narrow storefront that only seats between 35 to 40 at a time. Though tables are pushed close together, the atmosphere is very warm and relaxed. Main entrees for which the Wild Iris is especially noted include Cajun items like etouffe, gumbo and lightly-breaded catfish. Lemon pasta is always a good choice as is a peasant or vegetarian muffuletta sandwich (available for lunch).

Don't fill up on the delicious sourdough bread or you won't have room for a home-baked dessert. The cafe is open for lunch Monday through Friday, dinner every day of the week and brunch on Saturday and Sunday. Reservations are accepted for all meals and are advised, especially on weekends, though some space is always saved for walk-ins. Beer and wine are served along with limited cocktails.

West Side

Bailiwick's
$$ • 6617 Odana Rd., Madison
• (608) 833-0110

In the Radisson Inn, Bailiwick's is open for breakfast, lunch and dinner seven days a week. Serving selections from five regions of the United States, including Southwestern, Southern and Northeastern favorites, the restaurant is especially proud of its prime rib, which is not only on the dinner menu, but also part of the Sunday brunch (when ordering off the regular menu is unavailable). The contemporary decor is very classy, offset with rich wood trim and deep, earthy shades. It's a comfortable setting for any occasion, casual or more formal. Reservations are advised, especially for Sunday and holiday brunches, which fill up fast. Bailiwick's also features a separate bar and lounge area.

Bluephies
$ • Knickerbocker Place, 2701 Monroe St., Madison • (608) 231-FOOD

A favorite spot for breakfast, Bluephies is one of the few places in Madison that serves grits (but only on Saturday and Sunday) with your eggs. French toast made with cinnamon-swirl bread and mile-high pancakes are also excellent choices. Open for breakfast, lunch and dinner seven days a week, Bluephies is a casual, contemporary diner with a high-tech feel, featuring a midday and evening menu of gourmet sandwiches, homemade soups, salads, scrumptious desserts and a variety of daily specials. Bar service is available. Reservations are helpful.

Francie's Casual Cafe
$$ • Inntowner Hotel, 2424 University Ave., Madison • (608) 233-4080

In the Inntowner Hotel, Francie's is a comfortable spot serving many families and visitors to the UW-Madison. It's open for breakfast, lunch and dinner seven days a week including brunch on Sunday. The menu is primarily American, with an extensive seafood category and popular Friday-night fish fry. Also

---

INSIDERS' TIP

Friday night fish fries are a Wisconsin tradition. We think they began out of the Roman Catholic restriction on eating meat on Friday. The feast includes huge platters of fried fish — usually cod or perch — nestled amid a heap of french fries, served with mountains of cole slaw. Many are "all you can eat," so bring a big appetite.

RESTAURANTS • 47

If you want a more exotic approach to dining out, try one of Madison's Middle Eastern-style restaurants, where you can enjoy your meal while reclining on pillows in a cozy booth. Of course, tables are also available.

featured are twilight meals (for the early but not-so-hungry diner) and a variety of sandwiches and salads for lighter eaters. If you like pot pie, then you must try the one served here. It's a hearty dish with a very delicate crust. A small, separate bar area is equipped with a television that is always tuned to the Badgers when their games are televised. Terrace seating is available during warmer months.

Irish Waters Restaurant and Tavern
$-$$ • 702 N. Whitney Way, Madison
• (608) 233-3398

Founded by the late Mike Campion on St. Patrick's Day 1979, the restaurant/tavern, designed with plenty of oak woodwork and brass, was built to reflect a turn-of-the-century Irish pub. He succeeded very well. At the corner of Whitney Way and University Avenue, Irish Waters serves a wide variety of homemade soups, salads, sandwiches and nightly specials, though it's probably most famous for its weekly "Irish Fest" on Wednesdays, at which time cream of potato soup, Irish stew, soda bread and traditional corned beef and cabbage take top billing, washed down with a pint of stout. While it's a lively place to visit any time, you can imagine the euphoria on St. Patrick's Day! The restaurant serves lunch and dinner every day of the week.

Ivy Inn Restaurant
$-$$ • 2355 University Ave., Madison
• **(608) 233-9717**

In the Ivy Inn on the edge of campus, this restaurant — open for breakfast, lunch and dinner Monday through Saturday and for brunch on Sunday — has built a reputation over the years for tasty, heart-healthy cooking spearheaded by a vegetarian brunch offered the first, third and fifth (if there is one) Sundays of every month. On the second and fourth Sundays of the month, "Passport" brunches are featured in which ethnic dishes from a different country each time are highlighted. Popular dinner entrees throughout the week include seafood lasagna and Cajun chicken pasta. All dishes are prepared with fresh, seasonal ingredients. On Fridays, fish dinners are a tradition. The restaurant also has a full bar with a wide selection of wine and beer.

JT Whitney's Brewpub
$-$$ • 674 S. Whitney Way, Madison
• **(608) 274-1776**

Offering American and pub fare, JT Whitney's features a fish fry on Wednesday and Friday, live music (no cover charge) on weekends and such specialties as jerk chicken, raspberry ribs and smoked rainbow trout. Pasta is also on the menu. The brewpub is open for lunch and dinner seven days a week. (For more information, refer to the Brewpubs, Wine Bars and Cigar Bars chapter.)

Old Town Pub
$ • 724 S. Gammon Rd., Madison
• **(608) 276-8589**

This neighborhood pub, in a strip mall in a rapidly expanding commercial and residential area on the far West Side, is a favorite stop for homemade soups, burgers and sandwiches. Specialties include shredded beef chili served year round, deep-fried crab busters and more than 60 kinds of imported and domestic beer, many of which are from microbreweries. While eating here, you can try your hand at darts or pinball or, on a Sunday afternoon, watch the Packers on a big-screen television set. But don't despair. The noise doesn't even approach that of a sports bar. What really sets apart the Old Town Pub, however, is the fact that all employees learn enough sign language to be able to communicate with the hearing-impaired. The pub is open for lunch and dinner every day of the week and brunch on Sunday.

Ovens of Brittany, Shorewood
$-$$ • Shorewood Hills Plaza, 3244 University Ave., Madison
• **(608) 233-7701**

The only remaining Ovens of four that once graced Madison, this restaurant/bakery is home of the famous chewy cinnamon roll, the Brittany Bun, that is now copied all over town. For dinner, the stir fries are always popular. Omelets are often ordered for breakfast or even lunch. Ovens, in the Shorewood Hills Plaza, offers casual dining with a full bar in a comfortable, con-

---

INSIDERS' TIP

Although Madison is situated between two lakes, few restaurants enjoy lakeside access. The nearest two places to the Square to "dine on the water" are the Union Terrace of the Wisconsin Memorial Union on the UW-Madison campus and the pier of the Edgewater Hotel. Other options involving a drive are the Nau-Ti-Gal, Captain Bill's and the Mariner's Inn, all included in the Restaurants chapter.

temporary setting. Left of the dining area is a complete bakery. The restaurant is open seven days a week, including brunch on Saturday and Sunday. Reservations always are accepted. Ovens also does catering. Call (608) 231-6858.

Sunprint Cafe
$-$$ • Heritage Square Shopping Center, 702 S. Whitney Way, Madison • (608) 274-7374

This is a contemporary American bistro with a foreign accent. Everything is made from scratch, from salad dressings to salsa, hearty soups, breads and desserts. There is not a deep fryer on the premises. The classy atmosphere and Big Band background music is set off by a 48-foot mural of the Manhattan skyline, circa 1930. Noted for its gourmet bakery and ethnic dishes with an emphasis on fresh vegetables, chicken and fish — charcoal burgers are the only beef dish served — Sunprint is open for breakfast, lunch and dinner seven days a week and serves a wide range of alcoholic beverages, including wine. Except for dinner, orders are placed at the counter. In Heritage Square Shopping Center, Sunprint is a great place for friends, family and business people to gather; it well represents Madison's casually sophisticated persona. Reservations are accepted for all meals, and a few tables are available outside during warmer months.

Sunporch Cafe and Art Gallery
$-$$ • 2701 University Ave., Madison • (608) 231-1111

This worldly little eatery on the West Side also doubles as an art gallery and features live music — from jazz to classical — every Sunday from 6 to 9 PM for a $2 cover charge. It's open for breakfast, lunch and dinner seven days a week, though there is only a wait staff for evening meals and Sunday brunch. Otherwise, orders are taken at the counter, which also doubles as a bakery. Everything is made from scratch here, and daily dinner specials feature meat, seafood and vegetarian dishes. Save room for the caramel pecan upside-down apple pie; it's a tradition here. Gallery shows, encompassing everything from wearable art to acrylic paintings and photographs, change about every six weeks. Sunporch offers a full bar and takes reservations for parties of five or more. Outdoor seating is available when the weather warms up.

East Side

The Avenue Bar
$-$$ • 1128 E. Washington Ave., Madison • (608) 257-6877

What started out as little more than a bar that served great steaks and featured a fish boil on Friday night has grown into a large but still very amicable, down-home restaurant serving lunch and dinner seven days a week and country-style breakfast Saturday and Sunday. Keeping pace with the growth and expansion of the restaurant has been the burgeoning array of antiques and memorabilia collected by owner Skip Zach.

The Avenue Bar is truly an original, catering to couples, families and politicians, many of whom have hung out there since the place opened in '70. Reservations are accepted, and they're greatly needed for the Friday night fish dinner featuring Icelandic cod. Prime rib, another favorite, is on the menu Monday, Tuesday, Thursday and Saturday. Ample parking is available in the rear of the restaurant.

Harmony Bar & Grill
$, no credit cards • 2201 Atwood Ave., Madison • (608) 249-4333

The Harmony may look and act like a bar, but the food here is definitely a step above what you'll find in other neighborhood taverns. In addition to burgers, homemade pizzas and such, the Harmony dishes out pasta salads and a different ethnic special made from scratch every night of the week. Need an example? How about pesto tomato quesadillas. All beers on tap are microbrews. A favorite hangout for couples, the after-work crowd and families, the Harmony's only drawback is that because it's a bar, smoking is allowed, though most people don't light up in the main dining room. The Harmony is also a popular place to go to hear live blues on a Friday or Saturday night; music begins at 9:45 PM. The Harmony is open for lunch and dinner seven days a week.

Monty's Blue Plate Diner
$ • 2089 Atwood Ave., Madison
• (608) 244-8505

No matter who you are or what your business is, you'll fall in love with Monty's Blue Plate Diner, offering such comfort foods as meat loaf, roast turkey with mashed potatoes and gravy, wonderful burgers and soups that stick to your ribs. Monty's — open for breakfast lunch and dinner seven days as week — is in an old gas station that has been lovingly converted into a spiffy, old-fashioned-looking diner with Formica counters, roomy booths and plenty of neon and chrome. You can get beer (domestics and microbrews) and wine, though it's the milk shakes and malts that get top billing here. Though Monty's doesn't take reservations, it's not unusual at all for couples and families living on the West Side to drive to the East Side to eat here.

Nau-Ti-Gal
$ • 5360 Westport Rd., Madison
• (608) 244-4464

Surprisingly, Madison doesn't have many restaurants with access to the water, which makes this American eatery perched on the Yahara River a fun place to be, especially during the summer months when fish boils, sand volleyball and just watching boaters go by are popular pastimes. About a 10-minute drive north of the Square, the Nau-Ti-Gal offers a festive, relaxed setting with plenty of patio seating and a full bar, highlighted by a whimsical nautical motif.

Especially popular are the Friday fish fry, Saturday prime-rib dinner and an all-you-can-eat buffet brunch on Sunday. Unique appetizers include shark and alligator, and a small portion of cookie dough is served practically with every meal — a big hit with the kids. The Nau-Ti-Gal is open every day of the week for lunch and dinner (brunch and dinner on Sunday). Reservations are accepted for dinner parties of five or more. And did we mention that parking is readily available for cars, boats and seaplanes?

Sophia's Bakery and Cafe
$, no credit cards • 831 E. Johnson St., Madison • (608) 259-1506

Dining at Sophia's Bakery and Cafe is like eating in someone's kitchen. There are only a half-dozen tables crowded together, and the kitchen, behind which owner/chef Sophia Barabas is usually hard at work, is just on the other side of the counter where you pay. But this small establishment that started out serving wonderful homemade muffins and sweets and hearty bowls of soup during the day has now graduated to dinner four nights a week, Tuesday through Friday. Dinner options are limited to three nightly specials that might include pasta, a fish entree and/or a vegetarian creation. You can't eat much better for less money. All dinners are served with a choice of house salad or soup and homemade bread. No liquor is served. Sophia's opens at 7 AM every morning except Monday. No matter the time of day, it's first-come, first-served.

Willalby's Cafe
$, no credit cards • 1351 Williamson St., Madison • (608) 256-6088

A friendly neighborhood diner that likes to call itself "Home of the Clean Plate," Willalby's specializes in breakfast foods and is especially noted for its cakes and omelets. Open every day of the week for breakfast and lunch, the diner also caters to night owls by also serving eggs and bacon from midnight until 4 AM Friday and Saturday.

Outlying Area

Cambridge Country Inn & Pub
$ • 206 W. Main St., Cambridge
• (608) 423-3275

Drive 20 minutes southeast of Madison on U.S. Highway 12/18 and you'll end up in the quaint little burg of Cambridge, where the Cambridge Country Inn & Pub perfectly reflects this town's warmth and charm. (For more information about Cambridge, refer to the Daytrips and Getaways chapter.)

Operated by a former school teacher, the English-style Country Inn has been greatly expanded over the years, but not to the detriment of the eatery, which is noted for generous portions of '50s-style meat-and-potatoes fare reminiscent of Sunday dinner at grandmother's. The original main building — more than 100 years old — contains

Photo: Bruce Craig

The ambiance is warm and inviting at this Madison restaurant. The city offers a variety of options, from elegant to casual.

a two-way brick fireplace that separates the main dining area into several, more intimate alcoves. An addition on the back of the pub consists of banquet facilities and a courtyard.

The house specialty is fork-tender roast beef, served along with other favorites: roast turkey and dressing, baked chicken and pot pies. Often, chicken dumpling soup is on the menu as are baked ham and creamy mashed potatoes — always a favorite of adults and children alike. On Friday nights, there's an all-you-can-eat beer-battered fish fry featuring cod.

Just inside the entrance of the restaurant is The Pantry, featuring a wide selection of gourmet food and gifts. Across the hall is The Crabtree Room filled with luxuriant toiletries, many of which carry the Crabtree and Evelyn label. The Country Inn and Pub also contains a small bakery and ice cream counter. So, if you don't have room for dessert, you might just want to carry out a homemade slice of coconut-cream pie. We endorse the homemade beer bread too.

The restaurant is open seven days a week serving breakfast, lunch and dinner. Reservations are accepted, but unless there's a special event going on, it's usually easy to get a table; the place is much bigger overall than it looks from the entrance.

Cinema 4 Pizza Cafe
$, no credit cards • 124 W. Main St., Stoughton • (608) 873-7484

While pizza parlors are plentiful, we can't resist singling out this family-owned operation — the only movie house/restaurant in South-Central Wisconsin. Pizza is the staple item, but the cafe also serves lasagna, salads and submarine sandwiches. Hours vary according to the season, though during the summer, weekends and school vacations, you can eat and enjoy a movie at the same time over both the lunch and dinner hours. Call in an hour before showtime, and a table will be reserved. No alcohol is served. Parking is readily available on the street or behind the theater.

Clay Market Cafe
$ • 157 Main St., Cambridge • (608) 423-9616

Housed in the front of the restored 1848 grist mill in downtown Cambridge, this small cafe with only 15 tables offers creative American cuisine with a twist of Italian. Featured are homemade breads, desserts, pasta dishes and many vegetarian options. It's open for lunch and dinner seven days a week, with brunch on Sunday. In keeping with its location, the Clay Market sets its tables with antique mismatched silverware and an eclectic mix of dinnerware from area pottery shops. Wine and beer are served, though mimosas, made with fresh-squeezed orange juice, are the alcoholic drinks of choice for brunch. Don't forget to fill out your comment card when you finish eating. The Clay Market will mail some of their more popular soup recipes to you if you do.

Grianan Bris Caife
$ • 5430 Century Ave., Middleton
• (608) 836-8791

Another great transformation of a service station, this spot on the far side of Lake Mendota has been home since '95 of a bright, airy cafe serving scrumptious "small bites" prepared from scratch — everything from scones, muffins, pies and cookies to breakfast foods, sandwiches prepared on a panini grill and, sometimes, Cornish pasties, too. But if all you want is a cup of fresh-brewed coffee, that's OK, too. The atmosphere is casual and very relaxing, with the morning sun (when it shines) streaming through the front windows. That's even more important in the winter than the summer, when outdoor seating is available. Appealing to commuters, families and seniors, Grianan Bris Caife — which is Gaelic for "Sun Break Coffee" — is open 6 AM to 3 PM weekdays, 7:30 AM to 3 PM Saturday and 7:30 AM until noon on Sunday. And did we mention? . . . Babcock ice cream from the UW-Madison is available here.

Herreman's
$$ • 109 W. Main St., Sun Prairie
• (608) 837-7355

There aren't many true supper clubs left in the Madison area. But Herreman's, in business since 1944, is one. The restaurant features steaks, seafood and prime rib, a Friday-night fish fry, brunch on Sunday, a cocktail lounge and a large salad bar. Herreman's is open for lunch Monday through Friday and for dinner seven days a week. Reservations are accepted.

O'Malley's & O'Malley's Sports Pub
$ • 403 W. Main St., Waunakee
• (608) 849-7401

A mainstay of Waunakee, O'Malley's was sold in '96 to a family intent on keeping the best of the former country atmosphere and homestyle breakfasts while expanding the nightly menu with more choices, including stir-fry and pasta dishes. Popular items are Irish stew and Mardi Gras chicken. There's an all-you-can-eat Italian buffet on Wednesday, a Texas-style barbecue buffet on Thursday and brunch on Sunday. Friday night is the all-you-can-eat fish fry.

A sports pub equipped with television sets, darts and a jukebox is in the rear of the large restaurant. O'Malley's features full bar service and is open for breakfast (beginning at 6 AM for the early risers), lunch and dinner seven days a week. The Sports Pub opens at 11 AM daily and stays open until 1 AM Friday and Saturday. (For a full listing of sports bars, see the Nightlife chapter.) The restaurant, itself, opens at 6 AM daily.

The Old Feed Mill
$$ • 114 Cramer St., Mazomanie
• (608) 795-4909

In downtown Mazomanie, about a 30-minute drive from the State Capitol, The Old Feed Mill offers American country cuisine within a rustic, old-Wisconsin atmosphere. This is a great place to go for chicken pot pie, maple-glazed smoked pork and bread pudding. Housed in a restored 1857 flour mill listed on the National Register of Historic Places, The Old Feed Mill also showcases an antique marble soda fountain, bakery and old-fashioned general store, the Millstone Mercantile. The restaurant opened in October 1995 following a four-year restoration process. It's open for lunch and dinner Tuesday through Saturday and for a family-style dinner, 11 AM until 3 PM on Sunday. Reservations are recommended for dinner, especially on weekends. (Note that when calling this establishment from Madison, you must first dial the 608 area code.)

Quivey's Grove Stable Grill
$-$$ • 6261 Nesbitt Rd., Fitchburg
• (608) 273-4900

Attached to the main dining house (see the subsequent Quivey's Grove Stone House entry under "Fine Dining") by a stone tunnel added in 1980, shortly after Joe Garton bought the 4-acre property, the Stable Grill building dates back to 1855. The grill offers inexpensive, hearty dining in a very relaxed setting. The bar also serves as a holding tank for those going to dine in the main house. The tunnel, which was built so patrons wouldn't have to brave the elements, no matter how short the distance, took nearly 50 tons of stone. Because horses had been living in the old barn for more than 130 years, a new wood floor had to be laid, though it was appropriately "aged" to look authentic by beating it with bicycle chains.

Now on the National Register of Historic Places, the Stable Grill offers a limited menu for dinner every day of the week and lunch Monday through Saturday. Staples include burgers, Reubens and bratwurst sandwiches. Specials consist of prime rib, a fish fry on Wednesday and Friday, beer-battered perch (always), marinated pork loin, grilled tenderloin and boneless trout fillets.

Stamm House At Pheasant Branch
$-$$ • 6625 Century Ave., Middleton
• (608) 831-5835

This personality-laden place, which serves more than 250 pounds of ocean redfish (like perch) in a single Friday night, is housed in what is believed to be the oldest existing tavern in Dane County. Originally, the historical stone building — it basically enjoys the same floor plan it had when constructed in 1847 — was in the town of Pheasant Branch, now a part of Middleton, hence the distinction. There is nothing fancy about this place; just the age of the building gives it character.

The Stamm House is especially noted for its all-you-can-eat fish fry on Wednesday and Friday and chicken and dumplings on Wednesday and Sunday. Because reservations are limited to six per half-hour to accommodate walk-in traffic on Friday, it's always easier to find a table any other day of the week, though the mood is not nearly as loud and festive. The restaurant consists of a large bar and cocktail lounge that always features several local beers on tap including Capitol Brewery's Garten Brau, a large dining room upstairs and a smaller one off the lounge. In addition to fish and chicken, other nightly specials include prime rib on Saturday, spaghetti and meatballs on Tuesday and New York Strip on Monday. The Stamm House is open for dinner seven days a week. Parking is almost always available in a large lot surrounding the restaurant. A wheelchair entrance is at the rear of the building.

Village Green
$, no credit cards • 7508 Hubbard Ave., Middleton • (608) 831-9962

If you like the atmosphere of a friendly, down-home Wisconsin tavern with good, substantial tavern fare, the Village Green is a great spot to stop for lunch or dinner. The menu includes hamburgers, spicy chili and a variety of sandwiches including roast beef, turkey, tuna and barbecued pork. Owner Ron Boyer, in business since 1976, is especially proud of his recipe for "hot" — as in spicy — buffalo wings, which he serves with celery sticks and sour cream dip. The tavern is open from 11 AM to 11 PM every day of the week except Sunday. The Friday night fish fry is especially popular, and Ron always keeps Middleton's own Garten Brau Beer on tap.

Village Inn Restaurant & Catering
$, no credit cards • 214 W. Cottage Grove Rd., Cottage Grove
• (608) 839-4141

This family-oriented establishment offers American homestyle cooking for breakfast and lunch Tuesday through Sunday and features a fish fry on Friday nights. It's noted for its homemade soups and fresh-baked pies including coconut cream, pecan and apple. But there's also "Better Than Sex" chocolate cake (you be the judge). The Village Inn is more than a small cafe; it acts as an extended family for the community.

Cajun/Creole

West Side

Creole Cafe
$-$$ • 2611 Monroe St., Madison
• (608) 233-6311

This is a great little eatery for basic Cajun and creole dishes including crawfish etouffe, jambalaya and chicken or sausage gumbo. Other seafood specials are available nightly. The cafe, open for lunch and dinner every day of the week except Sunday, is set in a converted 1915 storefront. Insiders know the Creole Cafe is a great place for takeout, too.

Insiders' Recipe

Quivey's Grove Heritage Cookbook, by Madison food writer Margaret Guthrie, shares favorite recipes used in both the Stone House and Stable Grill (see this chapter's entries in the "European and/or Fine Dining" and "American" sections respectively), both of which are on the 4-acre Quivey's Grove estate just south of Madison. Here's one popular recipe from the cookbook, which you can order by calling (608) 273-4900.

Quivey's Grove Raspberry Muffins

Ingredients:
    4½ cups flour
    1¼ cups sugar
    2 tsp. baking soda
    ½ tsp. salt
    ½ tsp. allspice
    2 eggs
    2 cups buttermilk
    ¼ lb. (1 stick) butter, melted
    2 cups fresh raspberries, washed and drained
    sugar to top muffins

Directions:
Grease 24 muffin tins or line them with paper cups. Sift together flour, sugar, baking soda, salt and allspice. In another bowl, beat eggs and buttermilk. Add melted butter to egg mixture and stir. Add half the dry ingredients to the egg and butter mixture; mix lightly. Add raspberries; mix lightly. Add remaining dry ingredients and mix just to moisten. Spoon into tins three-quarters full. Top with a sprinkle of sugar. Bake 18 to 22 minutes at 425 degrees.

Quivey's Grove is set inside a 19th-century Wisconsin farmhouse.

East Side

New Orleans Take-Out
$ • 1920 Fordem Ave., Madison
• (608) 241-6655

Hungry for a heaping helping of red beans and rice? See the subsequent entry for this favorite Madison spot in the "Takeout" section.

Outlying Area

Louisianne's Etc.
$$-$$$ • 7464 Hubbard Ave., Middleton
• (608) 831-1929

Though this restaurant specializes in many traditional Creole dishes, we feel it is best represented as a fine-dining establishment. Please look for it in the subsequent "European and/or Fine Dining" section.

Delicatessens

Isthmus

Ella's Kosher Deli & Ice Cream Parlor
$, no credit cards • 425 State St., Madison • (608) 257-8611

The oldest authentic deli in Madison, serving kosher food for breakfast, lunch and dinner, Ella's is a good place to go for a quick, inexpensive sandwich or hearty breakfast. The atmosphere is vintage '60s, low-key and very friendly. Bring the entire family; there is something for everybody on the menu. We can vouch for the Reuben, and the signature sundae — hot fudge served with ice cream over grilled pound cake — will set you back a few calories, we know, but it's worth every bite. Ella's serves no alcoholic beverages. If you're staying in a Downtown hotel, it's a leisurely walk down State Street.

West Side

Atlas Delicatessen
$ • 1923 Monroe St., Madison
• (608) 256-0606

A combination deli and gourmet food store, Atlas Delicatessen offers a wide selection of homemade pastas, 39 different sandwiches with hand-sliced breads and meats, a variety of salads and a brownie to die for made with French Valrhona chocolate (hooray, no nuts!). Atlas also features a wide variety of imported and Wisconsin products and has one of the most extensive collections of olive oils and vinegars in town. (Go next door and pick up a fresh loaf of bread from Breadsmith and you'll be set for life — or at least until you eat it all.) Atlas is open every day except Monday. The deli offers seating for about a dozen people inside the store and more seating in a garden terrace behind Atlas.

Delitalia
$, no credit cards • 7854 Mineral Point Rd., Madison • (608) 833-3354
$, no credit cards • 2850 University Ave., Madison • (608) 233-4800

Open from 10 AM until 9 PM every day of the week, Delitalia offers casual dining for people who can't wait long or who are on the run, though a large share of its business is take-out. Safe bets here are Italian favorites like lasagna and chicken Tetrazzini. Delitalia also sells a wide variety of salads and subs, both hot and cold.

INSIDERS' TIP

The Essen Haus German Restaurant opened in Downtown Madison in September '83 in a building that was originally part of the historic Germania Hotel (c. 1863). The hotel is believed to have offered quarters to German immigrants arriving in Madison. Today the high-spirited German flavor lives on.

Upstairs, Downstairs Restaurant and Deli
$ • Hilldale Shopping Center, 702 N. Midvale Blvd., Madison • (608) 238-8853

This deli, at the south entrance of the Hilldale Shopping Center, features a variety of soups, salads, kosher-meat sandwiches and daily specials. Serving breakfast, lunch and dinner every day of the week, Upstairs, Downstairs opens two hours before the shopping center does. Wine and beer are available to dining patrons. In addition to a full-service restaurant, there is a self-service counter where muffins, bagels and cookies are always available for a quick bite.

East Side

Ella's Kosher Deli & Ice Cream Parlor
$ • 2902 E. Washington Ave., Madison • (608) 241-5291

Though this Ella's is under separate ownership from the one downtown, deli sandwiches and ice cream also receive top priority here. The place is a kid's fantasy world come to life. Ella's is filled with wonderful figures and toys hung on walls and ceilings. (See the "Taking the Fuss Out Of Birthdays" Close-up in our Kidstuff chapter.) But receiving even more attention than mile-high ice cream concoctions is a beautifully restored working carousel outside the main entrance that can be ridden from April (weather permitting) through mid- to late October.

European and/or Fine Dining

Isthmus

The Admiralty Room of the Edgewater Hotel
$$$$ • 666 Wisconsin Ave., Madison • (608) 256-9071 Ext. 120, (800) 922-5512

The Admiralty Room not only has built a reputation for being one of the more expensive dining rooms in town (if not the most expensive), but also has thrived on that distinction for almost 50 years. Trends may come and go, but the Admiralty Room has remained true to what it provides best: stately, elegant dining. (A dozen years ago, even *Fortune* magazine steered all of its executive readers to the door of the restaurant.)

Whether the continental cuisine, often prepared tableside, lives up to such high billing (no pun intended) is a matter of taste, but certainly the overall experience — superb service; formal, well-appointed table settings; and one of the most beautiful panoramic views of Lake Mendota — is outstanding, which makes the Admiralty Room a coveted spot for celebrating a momentous event. This is one of the few places in Madison where you can't get away with wearing jeans.

The menu lists more than a dozen traditional dinner entrees including beef, rack of lamb, chicken, veal and seafood, with specialties including steak Diane, Caesar salad and flaming desserts. A full bar features single-malt Scotches and a wine list of 200 selections from 14 countries. Complimentary parking is available in the Edgewater Hotel's underground garage, and live entertainment is featured in the bar area from 8 to 11 PM Friday and Saturday.

During the summer, the outdoor pier is a favorite gathering spot to enjoy cocktails after work and dine on light fare. (Take the elevator down to Level 7.) The Admiralty Room is open for breakfast, lunch and dinner seven days a week and brunch on Sunday. Reservations are suggested for every meal except breakfast.

The Bistro
$-$$$ • W. Dayton St., Madison • (608) 257-6000 Ext. 1264

The upscale dining room of the Madison Concourse Hotel, The Bistro serves a continental menu featuring Black Angus steaks, seafood and chicken. Two excellent choices are the broiled salmon and the pesto pasta with prawns. Reservations are recommended for The Bistro, which is open every night of the week for dinner with full bar service. On Sunday a brunch is available from 9:30 AM to 1:30 PM. For lighter fare during the day, visit the hotel's Dayton Street Cafe and Bakery (see the related entry in the previous "American" section).

Deb & Lola's Restaurant & Lounge
$$-$$$ • 227 State St., Madison
• (608) 255-0820

A contemporary elegant spot to dine with a nice view of happenings on State Street, Deb & Lola's is an easy walk from the Square and next door to the Madison Civic Center. Specializing in fine dining utilizing traditional Mexican ingredients and techniques, the restaurant is noted for such entrees as smoked pork tenderloin with ancho chile jus and cornmeal-crusted catfish with cucumber salsa. It has a separate bar and, in addition to its extensive wine list, is also noted for specialty Margaritas and martinis.

Deb & Lola's is open every night of the week for dinner except Sunday. Reservations are suggested.

L'Etoile
$$$ • 25 N. Pinckney St., Madison
• (608) 251-0500

One of the premier restaurants in Madison for cuisine and service, L'Etoile utilizes European cooking methods to feature the finest and freshest products of regional vegetable growers, cheese makers and lamb and poultry producers. For a perfect example of the care given to food here, consider this specialty: slow-roasted duck in two courses, on a spiced rusk with red currants followed by a salad of curly endive and crisped pieces from the thigh and leg.

The decor is softly lighted, simply but elegantly appointed, with lots of polished copper and a view looking out on the State Capitol. A wine steward is on hand nightly to help diners choose from the restaurant's impressive wine list. L'Etoile, in business on the Square in Madison since 1976, has been featured in many nationally renowned culinary magazines including *Bon Apetit* and *Food and Wine*. Eating here is an event unto itself.

L'Etoile is open for dinner Monday through Saturday, and reservations always are advised. Parking is readily available in two city lots, each within a block of the restaurant, which is on the second floor and is not wheelchair-accessible.

Kennedy Manor Dining Room & Bar
$$ • 1 Langdon St., Madison
• (608) 256-5556

Singled out by *Madison Magazine* as one of the "most visually pleasing restaurants" in the city, the Kennedy Manor is a wonderful living testament to the '30s, when the apartment building that houses the restaurant was built. The elegant ambiance is established by the white linen on the tables, beautiful and stately light fixtures, black woodwork and banquettes. The black-and-white photographs of Madison photographer Glenn Trudel hang in the dining room; his color photographs, in the bar. Background music is jazz and blues from the '30s.

Featuring the European style of bistro cooking, with an emphasis on the French and Italian tradition of family cookery, the Kennedy Manor is noted for risotto, salmon with sorrel, oven-roasted beef tenderloin, fresh pasta, seasonal bruschetta and chocolate steamed pudding. The menu is a la carte; portions are generous. The wine list is moderately priced and features, for the most part, French wines. Reservations are encouraged, especially on weekends. Wheelchair access to the restaurant is possible with advance notice. The bathrooms, however, are not wheelchair-accessible.

A sister operation to The Wilson Street Grill, the Kennedy Manor is open for lunch Tuesday through Friday, dinner Tuesday through Saturday and brunch and special dinners on some holidays. Though the restaurant is in a congested residential area, parking is readily available after 4:30 PM in a parking lot across the street.

The Opera House Wine Bar and Restaurant
$$$ • 117 Martin Luther King Blvd., Madison • (608) 284-8466

An upscale dining establishment with an elegant, very contemporary and trendy decor that will appeal particularly to young professionals, The Opera House is in the lower level of an office building, just a block up the street from the new Monona Terrace Convention Center. Designed by a Chicago architectural firm, the restaurant is set off by an oval-shaped wine bar of green granite.

While regional and seasonal-inspired cuisine, including fish and lamb dishes, are

Monty's Blue Plate Diner is housed in an old gas station that has been converted into a retro-looking diner with Formica counters, neon and chrome.

spotlighted here, so is an extensive choice of fine wines. Four hundred different wines are available by the bottle, more than 50 by the glass. Open for lunch and dinner every night of the week except Monday, the wine bar and restaurant sometimes feature jazz on weekend nights. (See the Brewpubs, Wine Bars and Cigar Bars chapter for more information.)

Restaurant Magnus
$$$ • 120 W. Wilson St., Madison • (608) 258-8787

The decor of this restaurant has been described as a dazzling combination of old-fashioned bordello and contemporary pizzazz. The food is equally exciting. The South American-inspired cuisine includes a dozen or so tapas, which are interesting and ample enough to make a meal of. A lot of people do just that, as just hanging around in the large and beautiful bar with drinks and appetizers is a favorite way to end the work day for many downtown professionals. If you want to quickly get rid of your paycheck you can go for the beluga caviar ($110) and some of the better wines on the impressive wine list. On weekends there is live music, often jazz. For entrees, you will find dishes such as zarzuela de mariscos ($22), a mixture of steamed seafood tossed with leeks, fennel and onion served in a broth flavored with anisette, sherry, brandy and saffron. The seafood in this dish includes lobster, shrimp, mussels, clams and squid, all of it fresh. Desserts are another reason to stop by, for you will find sumptuous sweets such as bittersweet chocolate rum cake made with polenta accompanied by a sweet caramel syrup accented with coffee. The restaurant serves dinner from 5:30 to 9:30 PM every night, but tapas are served until 2 AM.

RESTAURANTS • 59

Top Of The Park
$$-$$$ • 22 S. Carroll St., Madison
• (608) 257-8831

This elegant dining room on the top floor of the Inn On The Park has one of the most spectacular views of the Square and State Capitol. It's big-city swank, with white linen tablecloths, excellent service and traditional American fare often prepared with an innovative twist. Favorite entrees include a pecan-crusted walleye or New York strip, peppercorn-seared and served with a whiskey-Dijon sauce. The Top Of The Park is quite affordable if you don't order many extras, though that's easier said than done. The view itself, deserves a toast.

But lunch is also a treat here. Menu items include sandwiches, salads and pasta dishes. Dinner is served Tuesday through Saturday night, and lunch is served Tuesday through Friday. Reservations are recommended.

White Horse Inn
$$-$$$ • 202 N. Henry St., Madison
• (608) 255-9933

Across from the back door of the Madison Civic Center, the White Horse Inn serves a wide variety of American cuisine including pasta, prime rib, seafood and chicken dishes. Especially popular are steak Diane and chicken Oscar. Decor is modern but comfortable, set off by a large, classy wood bar where you can get many specialized coffee and ice cream drinks. It's a favorite hangout before or after the theater. But then, so is the restaurant.

In operation since 1981, the White Horse Inn is now a Madison institution, serving lunch Monday through Friday, dinner seven nights a week and desserts, drinks and appetizers until midnight Monday through Saturday. The restaurant has banquet facilities and also does private catering. Parking is available around the corner in a city ramp.

East Side

Bon Appetit
$ • 805 Williamson St., Madison
• (608) 283-4266

This tiny, humble-looking restaurant offers one of the best food bargains in town. The proprietors ran the Mediterranean Lunch food cart off Capitol Square for several years before bringing their following of downtown workers into this eatery. They are known for giving fresh interpretations to Middle Eastern and southern European dishes. The lunch and dinner menu includes rice dishes, sandwiches and salads with the exotic stamps of one of the owner's Middle Eastern upbringing and Italian culinary training. You will find such fare as Moroccan beef, Italian-style chicken sandwich, gypsy stew and kofte.

Bon Appetit gift certificates are welcome gifts for those who know and love this spot. Bon Appetit is open for dinner every day of the week, and serves lunch Monday through Friday.

David's Restaurant
$$, no credit cards • 909 E. Broadway, Madison • (608) 222-0048

This hole-in-the-wall (literally, there is a hole in the knotty pine wall of this former tavern) restaurant has earned a reputation for producing some of the best cuisine in town. The idiosyncratic establishment has a long bar, and a room jammed with cheerfully mismatched overstuffed furniture where patrons can sip their drinks or wait for their tables. The chef is a local cheese carving champion. The Friday night fish fry is outstanding, and you'll enjoy the sourdough bread and oyster chowder. The blackened swordfish is another standout. A downside for nonsmokers is that smoking is permitted at the tables and ventilation is minimal.

David's is open for lunch Tuesday through Friday and dinner Tuesday through Saturday.

Coyote Capers
$$$ • 1201 Williamson St., Madison
• (608) 251-1313

In a restored, turn-of-the-century storefront decorated with handpainted faux marble walls and the original pressed tin ceiling, Coyote Capers is, as its name implies, a delightfully innovative restaurant featuring food of many cultures prepared in an elegant yet whimsical manner referred to as "eclectic-fusion cuisine." Singled out in local and national restaurant reviews, Coyote Capers is especially noted for its fresh fish specials, crab cakes, pecan chicken and New York Strip steak prepared with caramelized onions and shiitake mushrooms. The baked fresh salmon with cilantro cashew chutney was described as "brilliant" by one critic. Everything is made from scratch, including breads and pastries.

Open for dinner every night of the week and for brunch on Saturday and Sunday, the restaurant does not have a separate bar but does serve wine, microbrews and cocktails. Reservations are strongly recommended, especially for dinner on weekends.

Outlying Area

La Paella
$$ • 2784 S. Fish Hatchery Rd., Fitchburg • (608) 273-2666

Pretend you're on a beach in Barcelona, walking up to a small stucco Mediterranean restaurant highlighted by an exposed wine cellar just inside the door, hanging garlic and ceramic tiling. In Madison in December, you can skip the beach, but La Paella is the real thing — the only restaurant in Madison featuring authentic Spanish cuisine, tapas and a wine bar. (See our Brewpubs, Wine Bars and Cigar Bars chapter.)

A longtime restaurateur in Madison, Tomas Ballesta never tackles anything he doesn't do exceedingly well. His restaurant will appeal to anyone from the "fisherman's daughter to the king." Fresh seafood is prepared especially well here. One dish we're particularly fond of is salmon con pasta de Hojaldre — fillet of salmon stuffed with crabmeat, pine nuts and red onions, then topped with a puff pastry and served with a light cream dill sauce. In terms of value for the money — atmosphere, service and food — it doesn't get much better than La Paella.

The restaurant is about 5 miles south of the Capitol Square and is open for dinner every day of the week except Sunday. The Tapas Bar opens at 3:30 PM, and dinner is served beginning at 5:30 PM. Reservations for dinner are a good idea any night of the week, but especially on Friday and Saturday nights.

Louisianne's Etc.
$$-$$$ • 7464 Hubbard Ave., Middleton • (608) 831-1929

Open for dinner six days a week (closed on Sunday), Louisianne's offers a delectable assortment of steaks, chicken and fresh fish, much of it prepared in a traditional Creole style. The appetizers are hard to pass up, and the wine list is extensive — served by the bottle and glass. In the lower level of an old stone building in downtown Middleton, Louisianne's is a cozy retreat with exposed stone walls and lots of greenery. Live jazz entertainment is offered Tuesday through Saturday in the bar area. Reservations are highly recommended for any day of the week.

Quivey's Grove Stone House
$$ • 6261 Nesbitt Rd., Fitchburg • (608) 273-4900

A 10-minute drive from Downtown Madison will bring you to Fitchburg and Quivey's Grove, which truly represents the heart of Wisconsin, both of yesteryear and today. The 1855 Stone House, filled with beautiful antiques, contains six intimate dining rooms. Of those, probably the most celebrated is the "Valentine Room," where a number of marriage proposals have taken place and countless anniversaries celebrated. Behind the Stone House and connected by an underground tunnel is the more casual Stable Grill (see the previous listing in the "American" section).

Like the buildings themselves, the recipes served are tried-and-true to bring out the best of hearty Midwestern fare. Many entrees — selected for showcasing the best of locally raised meats (pork, lamb, chicken and duck), fish (Door County whitefish), vegetables and fruits — are named for prominent and not-so-prominent figures in Wisconsin history. For instance, Popover Glover (chicken, fresh mushrooms and a mild cream sauce in a popover served on a bed of rice with maple-glazed carrots) honors "black slave Joshua Glover whose capture and release in 1854 prompted Wisconsin's Supreme Court to challenge the Fugitive Slave Act." Speaking of popovers, Quivey's Grove is famous for them as well as muffins — apple, banana nut, orange cranberry and, best of all, raspberry (see the recipe in this chapter) to name just a few — all served warm at every table.

Full bar service includes 11 microbrews, mostly from Wisconsin, an extensive wine list including a nice selection from nearby Botham and Wollersheim wineries and nine different martinis. Quivey's Grove serves a great Bloody Mary, too.

The Stone House is open for dinner Tuesday through Saturday. Reservations are highly recommended. The 4-acre country estate is the site of many wedding receptions and banquets.

German/Swiss

Isthmus

Essen Haus German Restaurant
$$ • 514 E. Wilson St., Madison
• (608) 255-4674

With an authentic German atmosphere and decor, the Essen Haus promises "good times, good food and drink . . . always on tap." In fact, the restaurant offers nightly German music (polkas galore), 16 German beers on tap (in addition to 270 bottled varieties) and such German favorites as sauerbraten and Wiener schnitzel in addition to American standbys such as prime rib (Saturday and Thursday) and an "all-you-can-eat" fish fry on Friday nights. The Essen Haus is open for dinner Tuesday through Sunday. It's a popular place no matter the day of the week, so reservations are suggested. (See our Brewpubs, Wine Bars and Cigar Bars chapter for more information.)

Greek

Isthmus

Parthenon Gyros Restaurant
$ • 316 State St., Madison
• (608) 251-6311

Many a graduate of the UW-Madison heads right to the Parthenon upon a return visit for a whopping gyro sandwich or platter. The Parthenon, one of the first Greek restaurants to open in the State of Wisconsin, has been around since 1972. In '91 the building was almost totally rebuilt and a rooftop garden added. The restaurant, which serves alcoholic beverages, is open every day of the week. If it's a bright spring day, best arrive early to enjoy the rooftop garden because plenty of other people will have the same idea.

Italian

Isthmus

Antonio's
$-$$ • 1109 S. Park St., Madison
• (608) 251-1412

Southwest of Downtown, just a short drive or taxi ride from the Square, Antonio's is a very friendly, family-owned restaurant specializing in traditional Italian and Mediterranean cuisine. With a warm, cozy atmosphere, it's a good place to stop anytime — on the spur of the moment or for a more planned, intimate dinner. Two small dining rooms are separated by a horseshoe-shaped bar and lounge area where many of the city's journalists occasionally stop after work to shoot the breeze. Antonio's is noted for its Italian wines and dry martinis. Dinner specialties include spiedino, tenderloin Marsala and a wide range of pasta dishes. For dessert, you can't go wrong with the homemade cannoli. Antonio's is open for dinner Tuesday through Saturday. Reservations are appreciated.

Luigi's Diner
$ • 102 King St., Madison
• (608) 257-0790

The all-Italian menu includes pasta, pizza, sandwiches and salads. All the wines are Italian, and the beer is either locally brewed or imported from Italy. One of the most popular items in this small, casual dining establishment is the vegetarian pizza. Luigi's Diner is open for lunch and dinner Monday through Saturday, but only for dinner on Sunday.

Campus

Gino's
$ • 540 State St., Madison
• (608) 257-9022

One of the oldest Italian restaurants in Madison, Gino's is named after its owner, Gino Gargano. The restaurant serves food from 11 AM until midnight daily, with delivery service available until 12:30 AM. A varied menu includes reasonably priced pasta, chicken and veal dishes, sandwiches and salads, though Gino's stuffed pizza and homemade lasagna are two of the more popular items on the menu.

Greenbush Bar
$ • 914 Regent St., Madison
• (608) 257-2874

In the lower level of the Italian Workmen's Club, the Greenbush specializes in fine wines and single-malt Scotches, Italian pastas and individualized gourmet pizzas, including our favorite, pesto, made with ground fresh basil. Most everything here is made from scratch — pizza dough, sauces, bread and desserts. This is a wonderful spot to dine, especially for the price. A regal wraparound bar dominates the single room, and background music features jazz and blues. But be forewarned that the Greenbush is technically a bar, not a restaurant, so smoking is allowed. However, a large air-filtering machine seems to work quite well, and no one is allowed to light up a cigar. Food is served every night of the week until midnight. The Greenbush is not wheelchair-accessible.

Josie's Restaurant (3 Sisters)
$, no credit cards • 906 Regent St., Madison • (608) 256-5558

Part of the old Greenbush neighborhood, Josie's looks much as it did when it opened in 1964. And that's what makes it so unique. Italian specialties come first, but Josie's, now operated by the three daughters of the restaurant's namesake, also serves a fish fry on Friday and nightly American specials including (occasionally) chicken and dumplings. But if you like spaghetti and meat balls, the time to come is Monday, when the price is even less than other days of the week. Dive in. Josie's even supplies plastic bibs. There is a separate full bar that sometimes gets a little smoky, though the dining room is just fine. Parking is available along the side of the building. Josie's is open for dinner seven nights a week and lunch Monday through Saturday. Carry-outs are available.

Porta Bella
$$ • 425 N. Frances St., Madison
• (608) 256-3186

Because Porta Bella doesn't take reservations for Friday and Saturday, it's not unusual to be greeted by a two-hour wait when the university is in session. Patrons are invited to cool their heels in the bar adjacent to the lobby or downstairs in the wine cellar where appetizers and pizzas are available. (See the Brewpubs, Wine Bars and Cigar Bars chapter for more information.) The menu includes steaks and seafood, though homemade pasta — tomato basil or black-pepper, to name two varieties — is what's most popular here. So is the seating arrangement; it's all very private, with individual, padded booths. Etched and stained-glass windows in the entry, offset by plenty of rich wood trim, give the restaurant a unique, ornate glow. But dress remains casual. Porta Bella is open for lunch on Friday and dinner every day of the week.

Paisan's
$ • 80 University Sq., Madison
• (608) 257-3832

A sister operation to Porta Bella, Paisan's is equally popular and has a similar setup (save for one small dining alcove and a small outdoor patio) of individual booths, though these are wooden and arranged in long rows. Either way, privacy is insured. Paisan's is noted for its thin-crust pizza — the Bella, with a sloppy Joe-like sauce, is popular — lasagna and Garibaldi hot submarine sandwiches. It also serves many Porta salads, tossed with ham, salami, green peppers and garbanzo beans. Paisan's is open for dinner every night of the week and for lunch Monday through Friday. Reservations are taken only for larger parties during the week. Like Porta Bella, this place — also a campus favorite — often entertains a long wait.

The Taste of Madison is a toast to the city's diverse restaurants.

Tutto Pasta Trattoria Bar & Caffe
$ • 305 State St., Madison
• (608) 294-1000

Madison didn't necessarily need another Italian restaurant in March of 1998 when this restaurant opened in the heart of campus, but it proved to be a more than welcome addition, and its owner is a genuine Sicilian (how he got here is a long story). Anyhow, this modestly priced restaurant has an inventive and exhaustive menu of more than 40 authentic Italian entrees, plus wonderful bread. Especially good are the spaghetti ai frutti di mare and the tutto pasta. Food is served on three levels in an attractively restored historic building that offers cat-bird seats of the perpetual parade on State Street. There is a well-chosen list of modestly priced wines. The restaurant is open daily for lunch and dinner.

West Side

Granita Italian Restaurant
$$ • 5518 University Ave., Madison
• (608) 233-2200

Good, reasonably priced classic Italian food served in a warm, romantic setting, with spacious booths and a mural of an Italian fishing village along one wall, sets off this Mediterranean Italian restaurant owned and operated by longtime Madison chef Peppino Gargano. For the price and atmosphere, it is one of our favorite restaurants. Popular dishes include fresh fish, veal Florentine, tuna alla Mediterranean and fusilli alla Bolognese (cork screw-shaped pasta topped with a light meat sauce). A separate barroom is noted for its limoncello, a lemon liquor with a touch of lime served cold. Granita is open for dinner seven nights a week, and reservations, especially on weekends, are recommended. Parking is readily available behind the restaurant.

Lombardino's
$-$$ • 2500 University Ave., Madison
• (608) 238-1922

Lombardino's has been a family tradition in Madison since 1954 and, thankfully, new owners who took over in 1990 realized just how important it was to maintain the Old World flavor permeating this place. We love Lombardino's, not only for the food it serves, but also because of its wrought-iron decor, tile pictures and a replica of the famous Trevi

Fountain in Rome. Some people might call it tacky. We think it's charming, even romantic (unless you happen to arrive on a crowded Friday night or football Saturday). The extensive menu includes a variety of pasta dishes (popular choices are the lasagna and the fettuccine with white clam sauce), great pizza and other specialities of the house including chicken cacciatore. Lombardino's is open for dinner every night of the week except Monday. It has a large bar with stool seating only that's adjacent to the dining room. Reservations are highly recommended for Friday and Saturday.

East Side

Pasta Per Tutti
$$ • 2009 Atwood Ave., Madison
• (608) 242-1800

Serving regional gourmet Italian food, Pasta Per Tutti is a small, upscale eatery that bespeaks of what Madison is all about: casual sophistication. Specialties include fruita di mare, grilled chicken ravioli, shrimp crostino and potato-crusted salmon. If you like garlic, this is a good place to come. Pasta Per Tutti offers a full bar and extensive wine list. Reservations are recommended. The restaurant, which opened in '93, serves dinner seven nights a week.

Outlying Area

Fraboni's Italian Specialities & Delicatessen
$ • 108 Owen Dr., Monona
• (608) 222-6632

Everyone from high school students to bankers is likely to drop in for lunch or dinner at this combination deli and grocery store featuring a wide variety of fresh, homemade Italian food: mostaccioli with meatballs, lasagna and Italian porketta (boneless pork roast), a house specialty. There is seating for 45 indoors, with more outdoors in nice weather, though customers are as apt to carry-out dinner as they are to sit down. Monday through Friday, Fraboni's closes at 7 PM; Saturday, 6 PM; and Sunday, 5 PM. The store opens every day at 9 AM. Take-out is also available at a second location, 822 Regent Street, but seating is not.

Rossario's
$ • 6001 Monona Dr., Monona
• (608) 221-3940

While many people come here often just for spaghetti and meatballs, Rossario's has five signature dishes including seafood Alfredo with shrimp, crabmeat and clams, and carciofo, artichoke hearts prepared in a white wine sauce with scallions and whole tomatoes and served over ziti (tubular pasta). The Italian-American restaurant has been going strong since 1974 and is open for dinner every night of the week and for lunch every day except Saturday and Sunday. The decor is rustic Italian, with red-and-white checked tablecloths, candles on the tables and plenty of antiques on the walls. If you like Rossario's spaghetti sauce, you can take a jar home with you or buy it at more than 85 stores in the area.

Tony's
$-$$ • 637 W. North St., DeForest
• (608) 846-2755

Tony's is a casual, family-style restaurant offering an extensive menu of Italian favorites and gourmet, stuffed pizza, Chicago-style. Signature dishes include lasagne, fettuccine Alfredo, Italian beef and pesto pasta. Tuesday is all-you-cat-eat spaghetti night, and on Wednesday, kids eat free. A fish fry is featured on Friday. Full bar service is available as well as carry-out and delivery (within a 7-mile radius) service. The restaurant is open for lunch Tuesday through Saturday and for dinner every day except Monday.

Vin Santo
$$ • 7462 Hubbard Ave., Middleton
• (608) 836-1880

One of the owner's accents may be wrong — she's British, not Italian — but Clarissa and Gregg Edwardsen have the hospitality part of Italian dining right. Expect huge portions, great bread to dip in flavored olive oil, good salads and an interesting selection of Italian wines. We highly recommend the pollo alla Marsala with mushrooms and Italian ham and roasted potatoes. The dining room is small and unpretentious, but cozy and pleasant. Vin Santo is open Monday through Saturday for dinner.

Indian

West Side

Taste Of India
$-$$ • 6713 Odana Rd., Madison
• (608) 833-3113

This is one of the few restaurants in the area that specializes in authentic Indian food. Items range from pork and lamb vandaloo (highly spiced meat cooked with potatoes, green peppers and coconut milk in an herb sauce) to chicken, vegetable and seafood dishes such as shrimp Bengal served in a curry sauce. Taste of India, decorated with Indian wall hangings and other ethnic bric-a-brac, offers a full bar and features Indian beer and an all-you-can-eat Indian buffet for lunch every day except Monday when the restaurant is closed. It also serves dinner every night except Monday. Reservations are recommended, especially on Friday and Saturday nights.

Mexican/Southwestern

(Please note that Southwestern barbecue is listed with Southern cooking.)

Isthmus

Casa De Lara Authentic Mexican Restaurant
$ • 341 State St. (upper level), Madison
• (608) 251-7200

A family-operated business that opened in 1982, Casa De Lara is meant to look like a Mexican home, decorated with photos of the Mexican Revolution, sombreros, Mexican pottery and plants. The atmosphere is ethnic but simple. It's noted for staples such as burritos plus gourmet Mexican dishes such as nopalito con queso — cactus leaves, chicken and shrimp simmered with cheese. The restaurant has a full-service bar specializing in Mexican beer and Margaritas. Parking is available at nearby ramps. Frequented by students, families and couples, Casa De Lara is open for lunch and dinner every day except Sunday.

Taqueria Gila Monster
$, no credit cards • 106 King St., Madison • (608) 255-6425

This small taqueria just off the Square serves fast, inexpensive, authentic Mexican food — tacos, burritos, enchiladas, etc. — for lunch and dinner Monday through Saturday. Carry-out also is readily available. There are tables but no table service. The alcoholic beverages served include beer, Margaritas and sangria.

East Side

El Dorado Grill
$ • 744 Williamson St., Madison
• (608) 280-9378

The chef here hails from Austin, Texas, and came up with a menu of authentic Southwestern cuisine for this charming addition to the Willy Street dining scene. The El Dorado, which opened in May 1998, has some lively starters, including bacon-wrapped jalapenos stuffed with shrimp and cheese, corn soup livened up by fresh poblano peppers, pan-fried fish cakes, fish wrapped in a tortilla grilled and dressed with lime cream and three purees. A specialty is chile relleno stuffed with four cheese — feta, goat, cream and white cheddar — then fried in a light tempura batter. This is the latest restaurant owned by highly respected Madison restaurateur Monty Schiro.

West Side

Laredo's
$ • 694 S. Whitney Way, Madison
• (608) 278-0585

This restaurant is owned and operated by a man from Guadalajara, Mexico, and his love of his native cuisine is reflected in the generous portions of good food and gracious service, though the atmosphere is on the garishly bright side. It opened in 1998 and quickly attracted a following, including many families with children. The menu has about 24 dinner specials and 30 combination plates. There are also a half-dozen vegetarian plates, which is unusual for a Mexican restaurant. We can recommend the parilla, which is spicy grilled chicken served with Spanish rice, and the chicken enchiladas. For dessert you'll find sopapillas, and there is a good selection of Mexican beers. Laredo's is open for lunch and dinner daily.

Pasqual's Salsaria
$ • 2534 Monroe St., Madison
• (608) 238-4419
$ • 2098 Atwood Ave. (East Side), Madison • (608) 244-3142
$ • 6913 University Ave., Middleton
• (608) 836-6700

Starting out as a small hole-in-the-wall in 1985, Pasqual's now has three locations of ample size, all of which specialize in Northern New Mexican cuisine featuring burritos, tamales, quesadillas, three kinds of chili, 12 types of salsa, blue-corn enchiladas and, most recently, global-wrap burritos. The latter change weekly and might include jerk chicken wrap, Bombay wrap, red beans and rice wrap, Moroccan veggie, Mediterranean, pulled pork and more. There is no denying the authenticity of the food, as most of Pasqual's main ingredients are shipped from Santa Fe. Owner Tim Guilfoil teaches Southwestern cooking at several culinary schools in the area.

While orders are normally given at the counter and then delivered to your table, the Middleton location does have a wait staff and separate, full bar. Pasqual's specializes in Mexican and microbrewery beers, wine and real Margaritas made with Cuervo Gold tequila. The restaurants are open for lunch and dinner every day and for breakfast on Saturday and Sunday. Carry-outs are readily available.

Pedro's
$ • High Point Shopping Centre, 499 D'Onofrio Dr., Madison • (608) 833-9229
$ • 3555 E. Washington Ave. (East Side), Madison • (608) 241-8110

A gas-fired tortilla press in the center of the dining room is kept busy supplying diners with hot, soft tortillas (they're great lathered with butter) as they await their meals. These sister operations each include a large dining room and bar; an outdoor cantina is available at the West Side location. Specialties include grilled Caesar salads, chimichangas, burritos, fajitas, fried ice cream desserts and flavored Margaritas, the latter of which are half-price on Tuesday and Thursday. Reservations are taken only for parties of five or more, but a large barroom can accommodate anyone who does have to wait for a table.

Middle Eastern/ Mediterranean

Campus

Caspian Cafe
$, no credit cards • 17 University Sq., Madison • (608) 259-9009

This small campus cafe specializing in Persian food and vegetarian dishes is a wonderful little spot operated almost single-handedly by Mohila Nateghi who every morning prepares the day's menu items from scratch. The restaurant is open for lunch Monday through Saturday and dinner only on Friday and draws substantial business during those times. It's a popular take-out place because there isn't room for many people to sit down at one time. Kebabs are a specialty, as are stuffed green peppers, salads, heaping sandwiches on Caspian bread and such vegetarian offerings as eggplant stew. The restaurant serves beer.

Husnu's
$-$$ • 547 State St., Madison
• (608) 256-0900

Specializing in Turkish, Italian and Middle Eastern cuisine, Husnu's was immediately embraced by the university community when it opened in 1979; it's been going strong ever since. Open for lunch and dinner every day of the week, this small, ethnic restaurant is especially noted for fresh fish and kebabs. It serves beer and wine and offers outdoor seating on State Street during the warmer months.

Kabul Afghanistan and Mediterranean Restaurant
$-$$ • 541 State St., Madison
• (608) 256-6322

Since opening in '90, owner Ghafoor Zafari has established a solid reputation for preparing excellent Afghani and Mediterranean specialties in a dining room decorated with Middle Eastern and Afghani paintings, relics, antiques and pieces of ethnic embroidery. Entrees served here are prepared with lamb, chicken, seafood and a variety of vegetables. They have names like Murgh kabab, vegetarian couscous and Kofta Chalow. The latter is Afghani-style meatballs with a sauce of crushed tomatoes, yellow split peas and fresh herbs served with seasoned white rice. All are served with Kabul's signature side dishes: Mashawa soup (made with chick-peas, kidney beans, split peas, rice and meat) or salad and Afghani bread baked fresh daily (it's also available at select grocery stores in town).

Open for lunch and dinner seven days a week, Kabul offers some alcoholic drinks and more than 25 kinds of beer, including Turkish and Indian as well as Wisconsin microbrews. Reservations are suggested for dinner.

Saz
$ • 558 State St., Madison
• (608) 256-1917

This popular student hangout features exotic, inexpensive food such as pizza stuffed with spinach, feta cheese and olives. Sandwich varieties include artichoke, falafel, barbecue chicken and burgers. You'll also find a good selection of kebabs, salads and Mexican entrees. The daily specials are always a surprise — they might be borek quesadillas or tandoori chicken — and always a bargain, usually costing between $5 and $6. You can pay at the counter and have your food delivered curbside. Saz is a kid-friendly place that's open for lunch and dinner daily.

West Side

The Dardanelles
$$ • 1851 Monroe St., Madison
• (608) 256-8804

Specializing in food from southern France, Italy, Greece, Spain and Turkey, The Dardanelles, which opened in 1996, is a comfortable neighborhood restaurant drawing families, foreign students and lovers of Mediterranean cuisine. The appetizing menu is based on several old Turkish cookbooks specializing in the cuisine of the Ottoman Empire. Signature dishes include Iskender, grape-leaf salmon and roast leg of lamb.

The Dardanelles is open for lunch Monday through Saturday, breakfast Saturday and Sunday (including a brunch featuring jazz music on Sunday beginning at 11 AM) and dinner Monday through Saturday.

Lulu's Restaurant
$$ • 2524 University Ave., Madison
• (608) 233-2172

Lulu's opened in 1984, and while still operating out of the same space near campus it has grown tremendously over the years from a plain storefront and simple menu into one of Madison's more unique dining experiences. Open for lunch and dinner every day of the week except Sunday, Lulu's offers an extensive menu of grilled meats, vegetarian dishes including couscous, hummus, falafel, tabouleh and stuffed grape leaves prepared using traditional Middle Eastern methods. Floor seating is available for those who wish to eat in an authentic Middle Eastern setting. Lulu's serves beer and wine as well as a variety of tropical juices such as mango and guava. There is a Middle Eastern food store at the back of the restaurant, and carry-outs are always available.

Otto's Restaurant & Bar
$$ • 6405 Mineral Point Rd., Madison
• (608) 274-4044

Housed in a beautiful, renovated 1870s stone farmhouse, Otto's specializes in Mediterranean cuisine and also serves Black Angus steaks. It features a lower-level bar (the only part of the building that is wheelchair-accessible) and two dining levels separated by an oak staircase. The atmosphere is casually elegant with white tablecloths and jazz background music. On weekend nights during the warmer months, diners can sit outside under the shade of 100-year-old oaks and listen to live jazz. Interesting menu items include grilled salmon in grape leaves with lemon-currant sauce and pine nuts, and grilled sea bass with artichokes, shiitake mushrooms and capers.

Madison's Italian Food

One of the first things a food lover will notice about Madison is its abundance of Italian restaurants. Some of the best have deep roots in the community, in a place that exists only in memory, known as The Greenbush.

The "Bush" was the old immigrant neighborhood just west of the Isthmus. Among the immigrants was a close-knit group of Sicilians, some of whom ran taverns. You'd see wives and daughters lugging Nesco cookers filled with things like lasagna through the streets of the Bush to feed the tavern customers their lunch.

Close-up

The Bush was unfortunately leveled during an urban renewal effort in the 1960s. But luckily for us, its heritage of great food and hospitality lives on.

Many people insist that **Antonio's**, 1109 S. Park Street, is the best Italian restaurant in town. Owner Tony Schiavo is the son and grandson of Bush tavern owners. And the legacy goes on. Tony and Rose Marie Schiavo have a son, Nick, whose **Cafe Continental** opened in 1998 at 108 King Street.

You'll also hear a lot about Monty Schiro from Madison food fanatics. Schiro is

— continued on next page

Lombardino's has been a family tradition in Madison since 1954.

the force behind four of Madison's most popular newer restaurants: **Monty's Blue Plate Diner**, 2089 Atwood Avenue; **Pasta Per Tutti**, 2009 Atwood Avenue; **Luigi's Diner**, 102 King Street; and **El Dorado**, 744 Williamson Street. Schiro's grandfather owned a bar in the old neighborhood that, legend has it, served "the best Italian hamburgers you ever tasted."

Another well-regarded local restaurateur with roots in the Greenbush is Anna Alberici. Her **Greenbush Bar**, at 914 Regent Street, has interesting pizzas and appetizers, and her nearby **Wild Iris Cafe**, 1225 Regent Street, has Italian family recipes on its multi-ethnic menu.

Delitalia was founded by Joe Brusca, a former Greenbush butcher and store owner. There are now several Delitalia's in Madison. His son, Mike, is equally successful with his string of **Milan's** throughout the city.

The Greenbush Bar is located in the lower level of the Italian Workmen's Club.

The only original restaurant still standing at the edge of the old Greenbush is **Josie's Spaghetti House**, 906 Regent Street. In its Bush days it was known as Jimmie's Spaghetti House, but much of the charm remains. In it there's an old neighborhood bar and a dark, cozy traditional restaurant where you can find bargains such as ravioli lunch for $4.

You can still find spaghetti "on the board" — the way they served it in the Bush — at **Rossario's**, 6001 Monona Drive. The spaghetti is spread across a long wood table and everyone just digs in with their fork. No plates allowed, but a glass of red wine is. Owner Rossario Parisi is the son of Greenbush families. They now bottle their award-winning spaghetti sauce.

Yet another restaurant with Greenbush pedigree is **Lombardino's**, 2500 University Avenue. It is owned by Rick Vivianni, whose mother long ago operated a deli and catering service at the edge of the immigrant neighborhood. You will still see Sicilian artifacts brought to the United States by the late restaurateur, Matt Lombardino, who founded it.

A prominent Italian restaurant clan in Madison without a Greenbush lineage is the Garganos. **Granita Italian Restaurant**, 5518 University Avenue; **Gino's Italian Deli**, 4606 Verona Road and 2524 Allen Boulevard; and **Gino's Restaurant**, 540 State Street, are the Gargano's considerable contributions to the Sicilian dining scene.

Another pair of enduring Italian restaurant landmarks in Madison are **Paisan's**, at 80 University Square, and **Porta Bella**, 425 Frances Street. They were started by the Greenbush's Troia family, but ownership has changed hands.

Madison's passion for Italian food may have begun in the Greenbush, but it has taken off in many directions. For one thing, there's what the locals call designer pizza. Nobody in the old Bush put chicken, potatoes and gorgonzola cheese on the crust like they do at **The Urban Pizza Co.**, 1501 Monroe Street, across from the Field House, in late 1997. What it lacks in Sicilian authenticity it makes up for in surprise and great crust.

Sal's Pizzeria, 313 State Street, is another 1997 entry into the competition for Madison pizza dollars. Sal's quickly developed a following.

— continued on next page

Madison is also home to almost every national pizza chain, including **Pizza Hut**, dine-in locations and delivery. Pizza Hut offers a salad bar that is quite impressive for the price.

Having gotten its start in Madison and now prominent throughout the state is **Rocky Rococo**, which not only delivers pizza from most of its nine area restaurants but also serves pasta dishes and offers a salad bar — especially popular with the lunch crowd. Rocky's is noted for its pan-style, thick crusts (although "classic thin" is also available) by the slice or by the pie. The company does a booming business around Valentine's Day when it offers heart-shaped pizzas and balloons.

Rocky's Party Pizzeria, 7952 Tree Lane, on the West Side, offers two giant party rooms that can be rented out. Each contains a 200-inch television screen.

Another statewide pizza delivery franchise that originated in Madison is **Pizza Pit**, which now has about 40 outlets in the state, including at least a dozen in Madison and surrounding communities. While Pizza Pit covers all the toppings bases, its spicy pepperjack cheese pizza offers a decidedly tasty punch.

For pizza delivery to the Downtown and Campus areas, try **Supreme Pizza**, 912 E. Johnson Street, that specializes in lasagna (meat or vegetarian) in addition to pizza with a choice of white or 100 percent whole-wheat crust and more than 25 different toppings including unusual choice like tofu, pastrami, sauerkraut and avocado.

For more information about Madison's staggering wealth of pizza parlors, refer to the Yellow Pages. Among the other pizza notables are the following:

Extreme Pizza
605 E. Washington Ave. (Campus, Isthmus), Madison • (608) 259-1500
1207 N. Sherman Ave. (East Side, northern Madison), Madison • (608) 244-7700
2936 Fish Hatchery Rd. (south-central, southwestern locales), Madison
• (608) 278-1800

Extreme likes to bill itself as "Madison's No. 2 pizza . . . since everyone else says they're No. 1!" Available for carry-out or delivery (areas are noted in parentheses, above) are hand-tossed thin and stuffed pizzas, pasta dinners, salads, 12 kinds of submarine sandwiches and chicken wings with a choice of 10 varieties of sauce.

Buck's
5255 Midvale Blvd. (West Side), Madison • (608) 238-9166
219 Cottage Grove Rd. (East Side), Madison • (608) 222-8011

Buck's, around since 1961, has thin crust that practically melts in your mouth. It serves pizza for carry-out and delivery only.

Pizzeria Uno
State and Gorham Sts. (Campus), Madison • (608) 255-7722
7601 Mineral Point Rd. (West Side), Madison • (608) 833-7200

Specializing in deep-dish pizza, Pizzeria Uno is patterned off the original Chicago restaurant and offers a full menu of appetizers, sandwiches, salads, pasta dishes and other dinner specials in addition to pizza. But the deep-dish pizza (including several varieties topped with seafood) is the restaurant's calling card. The West Side Uno's is a delightful place to visit. It's in a refurbished, historically significant pre-Civil War house built on a hill that now overlooks massive West Side commercial development. There is seating on the main floor and upstairs in the former home, plus patio seating. Uno's offers delivery service within a limited area, full bar service and will take reservations every evening except Friday and Saturday. Call for the Downtown location or for the Uno's on the West Side (near West Towne Mall).

Otto's, open Monday through Saturday for dinner only, offers an extensive wine list and martini menu. Reservations are recommended on weekend nights.

The Shish Cafe
$$ • 5510 University Ave., Madison
• (608) 236-9006

Beef or shrimp kebabs marinated in Syrian spices and extra-virgin olive oil and served with a choice of basmati rice or hummus are favorite menu items here, as are falafel and tabouleh. This small, ethnic restaurant opened in 1996. There are Arabian artifacts and paintings on the walls and Middle Eastern music discernible in the background. Open for lunch and dinner every day of the week, this friendly eatery serves locally microbrewed beer, wine and Arak, a Syrian aperitif. Don't leave without sampling a cashew finger for dessert; it's great.

Oriental

Isthmus

China Moon
$ • 112 E. Mifflin St., Madison
• (608) 251-1002, (608) 251-1003

Just a half-block off the Square, this veteran Chinese restaurant (formerly known as the Golden Dragon) is offering new-wave Oriental dining by specializing in "little foods," or what best can be described as Chinese tapas. It's great if you're only interested in a bite or enjoy sampling a wide range of tastes. Of the 25 or so items offered, might we suggest goat cheese wontons, wok-seared salmon with burnt ginger or steamed mussels with ginger, garlic and black beans? China Moon also offers a traditional Chinese menu and has a very successful delivery service. (Most everything on the menu, except the tapas, is available for delivery.) Specialties of the bar are ginseng infusions, premium liquors mixed with ginseng. The restaurant is open for lunch Monday through Friday and dinner every day of the week.

Kitakuni Noodle House
$ • 437 W. Gorham St., Madison
• (608) 251-3377

A sister operation to Restaurant Ton-Ton (see next entry), Kitakuni Noodle House specializes in what its name infers: Japanese noodles. If you like ramen, you'll be in heaven here. About a dozen kinds are offered, including spare-rib ramen, chicken-wing ramen, Seafood Delight ramen and spicy beef or ground pork ramen. A popular stop for students, the restaurant also offers unusual Japanese appetizers and seafood delicacies that change day-to-day, but no sushi is served. Table and counter dining are available for lunch and dinner Monday through Saturday. Kitakuni offers a full bar, and reservations are accepted for large parties only.

Restaurant Ton-Ton
$-$$ • 122 State St., Madison
• (608) 251-2171

Restaurant Ton-Ton, one block off the Capitol Square, specializes in Japanese cuisine including tempura, teriyaki and sukiyaki beef, pork, chicken and fish in addition to sushi and a full bar serving beer, wine and cocktails. The restaurant, which opened in '85, is open for lunch Monday through Friday and dinner Monday through Saturday. The extensive sushi bar features more than 50 different items and remains open until 1:30 AM Thursday through Saturday, when karaoke is also available. Reservations are recommended only for large parties.

Wasabi Japanese Restaurant and Sushi Bar
$$ • 449 State St., Madison
• (608) 255-5020

This popular Japanese restaurant, open for dinner Tuesday through Sunday and lunch Tuesday through Saturday, specializes in a variety of Japanese cuisine including tempura, teriyaki, hibachi and sukiyaki. An extensive sushi menu is also available, as well as ubon and soba noodle dishes. Especially popular is the restaurant's Bento Box, which offers a wide sampling of different items. Beer, wine and saki are available. For dessert, we highly recommend the green tea ice cream. Wasabi does not take reservations. Plan to get there early on a Friday or Saturday night, or cool your heels people-watching on State Street. The restaurant is located on the second floor and while there is an elevator available, a key to use it must be picked up from the restaurant.

Campus

Hong Kong Cafe
$ • 2 S. Mills St., Madison
• (608) 259-1668

On a corner in a storefront near Meriter Hospital, this unpretentious Oriental restaurant does a brisk luncheon business attracting hospital personnel and UW students and faculty. For lunch you usually have a choice of a dozen express entrees, but the entire menu is quite extensive, covering all the bases of Cantonese, Hunan and Szechuan cooking. Two of the more popular items are spicy-hot Governor's Chicken and cashew chicken. The Hong Kong Cafe, in operation since 1991, is open for lunch and dinner every day of the week and offers a full-service bar.

Lao Laan-Xang
$ • 1146 Williamson St., Madison
• (608) 280-0104

This small Laotian restaurant is known for its prompt service and good food. Some of the most popular dishes are its moak pa (stuffed catfish wrapped in banana leaves and steamed, and heavily seasoned with lemon grass), and the tum som (green papaya with lime, shrimp paste, hot peppers, garlic and fish sauce served with grilled chicken and sticky rice). The menu at this unassuming eatery includes many other fascinating dishes. It is open for dinner Sunday through Thursday.

West Side

Bahn Thai
$-$$ • 2809 University Ave., Madison
• (608) 233-3900
$-$$ • 944 Williamson St. (East Side), Madison • (608) 256-0202

Specializing in Thai food, Bahn Thai is open Monday through Saturday for lunch and dinner and on Sunday for dinner only. Thai curry specialties include Pad Thai — fried rice noodles prepared with either ground pork, chicken or fresh shrimp with egg, tofu, ground peanut, chili and bean sprouts. Bar service is available.

China International Gourmet
$-$$ • 736 N. Midvale Blvd., Madison
• (608) 231-3588

An extensive menu features dishes from the four regions of Peking, Szechuan, Shanghai and Canton, though it's the huge Chinese buffet that brings hundreds of diners for daily lunch and dinner and Sunday brunch to this restaurant behind Hilldale Shopping Center. The buffet contains more than 60 items divided among three steam tables featuring salads, appetizers and main dishes. The feast includes some American food but mostly Chinese — from egg-drop and hot-and-sour soup to sweet-and-sour pork ribs, fried won tons, spring rolls and chicken, beef and shrimp prepared in a variety of fashions. China International also serves authentic Chinese banquets by reservation.

Sa-Bai Thong
$ • 2840 University Ave., Madison
• (608) 238-3100

Considered one of the best Thai restaurants in Madison, Sa-Bai Thong does an especially good job with curry dishes such as chicken Panang prepared with chili paste, peas, zucchini and peanut sauce. Of the peanut sauce, one Madison food critic wrote it "almost got a round of applause at the table." For appetizers, you can't go wrong with the Angel Wings (chicken wings stuffed with ground pork) or egg roll. The restaurant, which serves alcoholic beverages, is open for lunch Monday through Saturday and for dinner every day of the week.

Saigon Restaurant
$ • 6802 Odana Rd., Madison
• (608) 829-3727

If you visit the Saigon Restaurant, specializing in Vietnamese food, be sure to order an egg roll that won an award for "Best Appetizer" twice at the annual summertime

Taste of Madison event (see our Festivals and Annual Events chapter). Saigon is also noted for traditional Vietnamese noodle soups and its extensive 21-page menu. Open for lunch and dinner Tuesday through Saturday, the Saigon, which opened in 1984, offers an attractive setting filled with plants, both fresh and silk. Reservations are recommended when dining on weekends and during major holidays or when part of a large party (10 or more). The restaurant has a full bar serving a wide variety of imported beers, wines, exotic and mixed drinks. But it's particularly noted for its Vietnamese iced coffee.

East Side

Imperial Palace
$ • 1291 N. Sherman Ave., Madison • (608) 241-7708

Imperial Palace was recently rated one of the best Chinese restaurants for the price in terms of food and atmosphere by a local food critic for the *Wisconsin State Journal*. Two large fish tanks greet visitors at the door, and in the buffet dining area, an open pool is filled with koi. A full menu is available, but many people stop by for the buffet made up of salads, appetizers, soups and entrees such as sizzling scallops with beef, lo mein, sesame chicken and sometimes even pieces of teriyaki duck. There is a separate bar area. The buffet is available for lunch and dinner every day of the week except on Saturday, when it is only set up for dinner.

Lotus Chinese Restaurant
$-$$ • 3737 E. Washington Ave., Madison • (608) 249-1116

In operation since 1978, the Lotus offers a wide selection of Chinese food — more than 100 different items — along with some American entrees. More intimate and elegant than many Chinese restaurants in Madison, the Lotus will try to honor any special request. The Lotus Specialty is a favorite — prepared with seafood and assorted vegetables, Mongolian beef and fried rice. A full-service bar turns out a variety of Oriental cocktails. The Lotus, near many hotels on E. Washington Avenue, is open for lunch Monday through Friday and dinner every day of the week except Sunday.

Phoenix Garden Chinese Restaurant
$-$$ • 4802 E. Washington Ave., Madison • (608) 249-3188

This family-operated business serves traditional Hunan, Szechuan, Mandarin and Cantonese cuisine in a casual atmosphere. Several dishes prepared with chicken — the Phoenix, General Tso's and Szechuan — are considered house specialties. Other favorite entrees include orange beef and Shanghai shrimp. Between the Comfort Inn and Econo Lodge, the Phoenix is within easy walking distance of many hotels on the far East Side, though parking is also readily available. The restaurant, open for lunch and dinner seven days a week, features a full bar with such specialty drinks as Flaming Volcano, Blue Hawaii and Jade Phoenix. Reservations at least two hours in advance are recommended for parties of eight or more.

Red Pepper Chinese Restaurant & Bar
$-$$ • 1518 N. Stoughton Rd., Madison • (608) 249-1373

As you might guess, red permeates the interior of this Chinese restaurant featuring Hunan, Szechuan and Mandarin cuisine, and spicy dishes dominate the menu. But speak up; the cooks are glad to alter anything to taste. The separate bar is as large as the dining room. Specialities here include Marco Polo's Beef prepared with beef tenderloin and Kung Bao Four with shrimp, scallops, beef and chicken. The take-out menu even comes with a number of colored photos to make selection easier. Red Pepper is open for lunch and dinner seven days a week.

Outlying Area

Imperial Garden
$-$$ • 2039 Allen Blvd., Middleton • (608) 238-6445

Consistently voted one of the best Chinese restaurants in the Madison area, Imperial Garden, on the corner of Allen Boulevard and University Avenue, is also one of the largest Chinese restaurants in the Madison area, with four dining rooms attractively decorated with ornamental Asian prints and reproductions of period pieces. Even from the outside, there is no mistaking what kind of cuisine this restaurant serves, and during the warmer months, customers are invited to stroll through owner Henry Chen's flower garden. Favorite entrees include Sizzling Seafood, Spicy Governor's Chicken, Mongolian Beef and Crispy Duck along with lo mein, chow mein and sweet/sour dishes. All items are available for carry-out.

The Laughing Buddha welcomes diners to the cocktail lounge where a festive selection of drinks is concocted, including the Jade Monkey and Ginger Colada. The restaurant is open for lunch Monday through Friday and for dinner every day of the week. Reservations are recommended.

Russian

Isthmus

Russian House
$ • 320 W. Johnson St., Madison
• (608) 258-8448

Greatly adding to the ethnic variety of restaurants in Madison is the Russian House, the only restaurant we know of in the entire state that specializes in Russian cuisine. Family-owned and operated by recent immigrants to Madison, the restaurant serves appetizing, generous portions of such traditional entrees as sabzi (fresh lamb sauteed with spinach, mint and green onion and served over rice), golubtse (cabbage leaves stuffed with beef and rice) and vareniky (a Russian appetizer consisting of dumplings filled with cheese or potato). Beverages include beer, wine, Russian tea and vodka. The Russian House is open for lunch and dinner every day of the week except Monday. Reservations are appreciated.

Southern/Southwestern Barbecue

Campus

Buffalo Wild Wings & Weck
$ • 529 State St., Madison
• (608) 255-WING

Buffalo Wild Wings & Weck, or BW-3 as it is commonly known, is a State Street campus hangout that is especially noted for its Tex-Mex Buffalo chicken wings served with any one of 12 varieties of sauces. This is a place to come to relax. It has a multitude of television sets, including two giant screens for watching sporting events, and trivia games to play as you eat or sip a beer. The restaurant is especially famous for its 25¢ Tuesdays when buffalo wings are just a quarter apiece. BW-3 is open seven days a week for lunch and dinner beginning at 11 AM. Happy Hour starts at 3 PM.

West Side

Big Mama & Uncle Fats'
$-$$ • 6824 Odana Rd., Madison
• (608) 829-BMUF

Yes, there really is a Big Mama and an Uncle Fats — from Alabama — who are the grandmother and uncle, respectively, of one of the owners. It's Big Mama's tried-and-true

---

INSIDERS' TIP

Since 1985, the Nitty Gritty, "Madison's Official Birthday Bar," has helped more than 200,000 people celebrate their birthdays. The restaurant averages 1,500 birthdays a month. One time, two people who came to celebrate their birthdays on the same night, met, fell in love and later got married.

recipes for pulled pork and hickory-smoked ribs that have made this Southern barbecue joint so popular since opening in '94. This restaurant in the corner of a strip mall also offers fried catfish coated with a blend of cornmeal, flour and spices plus sweet potato fries, smoked corn, mustard and turnip greens, fried okra, hush puppies and barbecue beans, of course. There is a separate children's menu. BMUF is closed on Monday. It's open for dinner all other nights and for lunch Monday through Friday. Reservations are accepted, and the restaurant has a full-service bar.

Dry Bean Saloon & Smokehouse
$-$$ • 5264 Verona Rd., Madison
• (608) 274-2326

After you polish off a barbecued rib or chicken dinner at the Dry Bean, just walk across the entry way and work it off on the dance floor. Many a Madison-area resident has learned to line dance here. In addition to barbecue, Dry Bean serves steaks, smoked duck, prime rib and a Friday-night fish fry. The decor fits its name: very rustic and spacious. Open for lunch and dinner every day of the week, Dry Bean is a favorite hangout of the "mature" single crowd. Its brunch on Sunday is very popular. Reservations, especially for dinner on busy weekends, are a good idea. (Also see our Nightlife chapter for details about the Dry Bean after dark.)

East Side

Smoky Jon's No. 1 BBQ
$-$$, no credit cards • 2310 Packer's Ave., Madison • (608) 249-RIBS

In the world of Pro Barbecue Tour competition, Smoky Jon's consistently comes out on top for its pig roasting, wood-smoked pork loin, back ribs and delectable sauce. It's also been singled out for "Best of Madison" *Madison Magazine* awards several years running. In addition to ribs, Smoky Jon's serves barbecue chicken, smoked beef brisket, turkey and a spicy-hot New Orleans-style cod dinner. Side dishes include barbecue baked beans, tangy pasta salad and American potato salad. The restaurant is open daily, except Monday, for lunch and dinner. Take-outs include "family packages" that feed anywhere from four to 12 people. Or if all you want is a jar of sauce, you can buy that, too. On-site catering is also available.

Outlying Area

Fat Jack's Barbecue
$-$$ • 6320 University Ave., Middleton
• (608) 238-4767
$-$$ • 6207 Monona Dr., Monona
• (608) 221-4220

Fat Jack's serves great Southern-style pit barbecue, hickory-smoked ribs, chicken, beef and pork. Dinners are economically priced and served with two side dishes, including corn-on-the-cob and red beans and rice. The two locations, owned by separate but related families, basically serve the same menu. Beer and wine coolers are also available.

Fat Jack's got its start in Monona in '86. The Middleton location opened in '96. Open for lunch Tuesday through Friday (when barbecue beef and pork sandwiches take precedence) and dinner Tuesday through Sunday, Fat Jack's also does a brisk take-out business, has a popular Friday-night fish fry and provides on-site barbecue catering.

Holle Mackerl Southern Style Fish & Seafood
$ • 111 River Pl., Monona
• (608) 222-1500

New in 1997, Holle Mackerl specializes in fried catfish, ocean and lake perch, shrimp, clam strips and grilled salmon and tuna to eat in or carry out. Dinners are served with cole slaw and meatless spaghetti or fries. Side orders include hush puppies, corn bread and red beans and rice. For dessert, there's always sweet potato pie or peach cobbler. Holle Mackerl, which also does catering, is open for lunch and dinner Monday through Saturday. Beer and wine are available for dine-in customers. The restaurant is easy to find just off the Monona Drive Exit of the South Beltline.

Sports Bars

Campus

Babe's Grill & Bar
$-$$ • at the Depot, 640 W. Washington Ave., Madison • (608) 250-6411
$-$$ • 5614 Schroeder Rd. (West Side), Madison • (608) 274-7300

While the Babe's on the West Side came first and entertains large crowds every day of the week, the newer one in the Depot packs them in, too, especially since the Kohl Center, home of UW-Madison basketball and hockey, is only a short distance away. Like a typical sports bar, Babe's can become fairly loud at times. But don't let that dissuade you; this grill and bar offers an extensive menu and serves good food for lunch and dinner every day of the week. Extremely popular are Ring Side nachos (layered with a spicy beef and bean mixture among other accouterments) and Red Hot (that's true) chile poppers. For main entrees, the menu includes a wide variety of sandwiches, burgers, salads, pizza, chicken and fish.

West Side

Coaches Sports Bar & Grill
$-$$ • 439 Grand Canyon Dr., Madison • (608) 833-4485

Another popular sports bar in Madison, Coaches is equipped with 32 wall-mounted oversized television sets and, during the football season, an entire wall devoted to Packer and Badger memorabilia. If you can't be sitting in the stands, this is the next best thing. The menu includes a wide variety of salads, soups and sandwiches in addition to dinner specials. If you're looking for a booth before a big game, best get there early. Reservations aren't accepted. Coaches is open every day of the week for lunch and dinner.

East Side

Pooley's
$ • 5441 High Crossing Blvd., Madison • (608) 242-1888

Here's a place where you can eat and work off your meal in the same visit. Pooley's offers a bar and dining area in addition to a large game room — with pool, darts, pinball, shuffleboard and other games — and volleyball courts (two inside, one outside). The menu includes 20 varieties of sandwiches, four salads and pizza, though many patrons who come to watch a televised sporting event simply go for the nachos with "the works." Pooley's is open every day of the week most of the year; it's closed Sundays in summer.

Outlying Areas

O'Malley's Sports Pub
$ • 403 W. Main St., Waunakee • (608) 849-7401

Yes, this place is a sports bar, but it serves good food as well. (For details, see

---

INSIDERS' TIP

A great way to view Madison's skyline and the Executive Residence is by water. Bar and restaurant service is available to groups of up to 49 diners on the *Betty Lou* motor yacht that began operating the spring of 1998 by von Rutenberg Ventures, owner of The Mariner's Inn, Nau-Ti-Gal and Captain Bill's restaurants. Options include everything from appetizer buffets and full dinners to moonlight dessert and cocktail cruises. The 51-foot cruiser is named after the late Betty von Rutenberg, a successful Madison businesswoman and an avid promoter of Madison and its lakes. The boat is moored at one of the restaurants. For information, phone (608) 246-3136.

Regional cuisine is often offered in stylish surroundings.

Steak and Seafood

Isthmus

Blue Marlin
$$-$$$ • 101 N. Hamilton St., Madison
• (608) 255-2255

One of Madison's premier seafood restaurants, the Blue Marlin offers a set menu but emphasizes nightly specials featuring fresh fish including tuna steak with sauteed spinach in a lemon/mustard vinaigrette and seafood linguine with mussels, clams, shrimp and scallops. Do you like lobster and/or crab? This is a great place to come to enjoy either one. The Blue Marlin, a sister operation to the Tornado Steak House (see subsequent entry), is open for dinner Tuesday through Sunday and for lunch Tuesday through Friday. The restaurant is closed on Monday at which time it hosts corporate functions. Reservations, especially for dinner, are almost a must here.

Kosta's Restaurant
$$-$$$ • 117 State St., Madison
• (608) 255-6671

Originally a Greek restaurant that now specializes in steak and seafood, Kosta's is situated in a beautiful restored turn-of-the-century building. Aptly described once as a "fancy place to eat casual," Kosta's features a wide Gone-With-The-Wind staircase up to a mezzanine balcony where dining is also available. On the third floor is Madison's booming Funny Business Comedy Club, owned and operated by the Villacrez brothers who bought the restaurant in 1997. Dinner and show combinations are very popular. Kosta's is open for lunch and dinner Monday through Friday (and Saturday during the summer months) and for dinner every night of the week. Live jazz is featured Friday and Saturday evenings. Reservations are recommended, and full bar service is available. The Dayton Street parking ramp is a half-block from the restaurant.

Tornado Steak House
$$-$$$ • 116 S. Hamilton St., Madison
• (608) 256-3570

The Tornado is a classic-style, Wisconsin steakhouse that has been open only since '96 but is housed in a 1950s building that has enjoyed a colorful restaurant history. It's the only steakhouse in Downtown Madison and has all the trimmings: white linen tablecloths, a separate cocktail lounge (that stays open very late) and two intimate dining rooms. Specials include a 20-ounce tenderloin on the bone, fish on Friday nights, prime rib on Saturday and roasted chicken with mashed potatoes every Sunday, the latter costing only $10 per person. It's also a great spot to enjoy Alaskan King Crab legs — but they don't come cheap. Nightly specials always include a fresh seafood item and other delicacies such as rabbit, lamb, venison or duck. In addition to top steaks and other fine dining options, the Tornado is also noted for serving great wine and Bloody Marys.

The restaurant, open for dinner Tuesday through Sunday, is less than a block off the Square. Street parking sometimes is available; if not, you can park in a county ramp across Main, less than a half-block away. Diners in wheelchairs are advised to enter through a second Main Street door; restrooms in the Tornado are not easily accessible because the building is old. Reservations are recommended and on weekends usually needed.

West Side

Captain Bill's
$$ • 2701 Century Harbor Rd., Middleton
• (608) 831-SEAS

A rustic, casual Key West atmosphere distinguishes this restaurant, which offers dining inside or out seven nights a week. Though the menu specializes in seafood and boasts of having "the best clam chowder in the world," you can also order beef, chicken and pasta dishes. A favorite hangout of boaters, Captain Bill's specializes in "boat drinks" such as the Captain's Colada and what has generally been billed as one of the best Bloody

Marys in town. The most recent addition to the Von Rutenberg Ventures family of restaurants, Captain Bill's is named after Bill von Rutenberg Sr., longtime Madison-area restaurateur. Reservations are only taken for parties of five or more. The restaurant opens at 4:30 PM nightly.

Delaney's Charcoal Steaks
$$ • 449 Grand Canyon Dr., Madison
• (608) 833-7337

Diners treat Delaney's like an old friend. A family-owned and operated restaurant that's been in business since '73 and has managed to retain a staff of long-term, friendly employees, Delaney's specializes in charbroiled steaks cut on the premises. The restaurant is made up of several small, intimate dining rooms decorated with Tiffany-style lamps and photos of old Madison. The separate bar is usually lively and features automobile memorabilia including an antique gas pump. Open seven nights a week for dinner, Delaney's is near West Towne Mall and has an ample parking lot. But getting through the door for dinner on a football Saturday might be a problem. Many people will have the same idea, and they don't mind cooling their heels in the bar. Some reservations are taken; most of the tables are saved for walk-ins.

Smoky's Club
$$-$$$, no credit cards • 3005 University Ave., Madison • (608) 233-2120

This Madison treasure has been written up in national culinary magazines as one of the top steakhouses in the country. It's a place where visiting college coaches and even entire football teams eat — and eat well. If you like your filet mignon, large T-bone or New York strip sirloin rare, this is the place to come. Most people also go with the hash browns, and everyone is welcome to the ice cold, old-fashioned relish tray featuring, among several things, homemade beets. Going strong since '36, the restaurant was taken over in 1969 by the Schmocks, who have expanded the place four times since then. Smoky's is an original, filled with international kitsch that hangs a foot deep off the walls and from the ceiling.

The restaurant is open for dinner every night except Sunday, Tuesday and holidays. Unless you're there when the doors open — 5 PM most days — expect to wait at the bar. On a football Saturday, that wait has been known to be as long as two hours. Reservations are not accepted.

East Side

Fyfe's Corner Bistro
$-$$ • 1344 E. Washington Ave., Madison • (608) 251-8700

Specializing in steak, seafood and homemade California-style pastas, Fyfe's serves dinner every night of the week and lunch Monday through Friday. The atmosphere is casual but charming; the restaurant is in a 100-year-old-plus building — 10 blocks from the Capitol — with a cobblestone floor and brick walls. Next to the dining room is a large bar area where live music draws an audience on weekends (see our Nightlife chapter for details). Fyfe's features 25 kinds of wine by the glass. Reservations are recommended.

Mariner's Inn
$$ • 5339 Lighthouse Bay Dr., Madison
• (608) 246-3120

Specializing in steaks and seafood, the Mariner's Inn is the flagship restaurant of Von Rutenberg Ventures, which also operates the Nau-Ti-Gal and Captain Bill's (see previous entries), all of which are waterfront restaurants. The Mariner's Inn is a warm oasis, in summer or winter, accented with marine antiques. In times of modern change and upheaval, we like to think of it as a comfortable, old shoe. So would the late Betty von Rutenberg, a grand lady and jovial spirit who started the restaurant with husband Bill in 1966.

Menu favorites include steaks, shrimp and lobster often accompanied by the restaurant's legendary hash browns. Cap off a meal with a slice of homemade cheesecake topped with Door County cherries. Mariner's, now managed by von Rutenberg's sons, Bill and Jack, serves dinner every night of the week and accepts reservations for only parties of five or more, though it often helps to call ahead just as you're

RESTAURANTS

leaving. In the summer of 1998 the restaurant began offering chartered dinner cruises.

Take-Out

Here's a peek at the take-out scene, just in case you prefer the ambiance of your own dining room.

Looking for a delivery other than pizza or Chinese? Food from about 25 restaurants in the Madison area is available through the Take-out Taxi delivery service for an extra surcharge of about $4 per delivery. Minimum order must be $10 or more. Restaurants participating include Friday's, Chili's, Fat Jack's Red Lobster, Uno and Pedro's. For a brochure listing menu items from various eateries or for delivery, call (608) 273-9921.

Isthmus

Kitchen Hearth
$ • 114 E. Main St., Madison
• (608) 283-4202
$ • 6644 Mineral Point Rd. (West Side), Madison • (608) 833-1320

From main entrees to salads, bread and desserts, a wide selection of Midwestern comfort food made from scratch is turned out at both locations of Kitchen Hearth for people who are on the run. Although primarily a carry-out operation, there is limited seating in and outside the West Side location and in the main atrium area and outside the Tenney Building facing the Square (Downtown). The Downtown business also features a grill for made-to-order hamburgers, brats, etc. Rotating a wide selection of side dishes and main entrees, Kitchen Hearth always features a variety of sandwiches and substantial, main-course lettuce-based and pasta salads. Other popular entrees include veggie or meat lasagna and Greek lemon chicken made with chunks of chicken breast and fettuccine.

The Downtown location is open from 7 AM until 4 PM Monday through Friday, with extended hours during the summer, especially during Concerts on the Square (see the Arts chapter as well as our Festivals and Annual Events chapter). The West Side location is open from 10 AM until 7 PM Monday through Saturday. Catering, (608) 833-2363, is available practically 'round the clock.

Campus

Fraboni's Italian Specialties
$ • 822 Regent St., Madison
• (608) 256-0546

This is a great place for carry-out Italian food. For a description, refer to the Fraboni (in Monona) entry in the "Italian" section of this chapter.

West Side

Atlas Delicatessen
$ • 1923 Monroe St., Madison
• (608) 256-0606

This neighborhood food emporium sells regional and imported oils, vinegars, cheeses and meats, although it's the fresh homemade pasta, pasta salads and sauces for which it is best noted. Some seating available. (See the previous entry in the "Delicatessens" section for related information.)

Gino's Italian Deli
4606 Verona Rd., Madison
• (608) 273-1981
2524 Allen Blvd., Middleton
• (608) 827-0999

After enjoying lasagna from Gino's, you'll wonder why you bother making it from scratch anymore. It's great for a quick pick-up or or-

---

INSIDERS' TIP

No need to duck if the name "Food Fight" is mentioned in polite conversation. It's the parent company of five popular restaurants in Madison. They are Pasta Per Tutti, Bluephies, Monty's Blue Plate Diner, Luigi's and the El Dorado Grill. A sixth is expected to open in Middleton in 1999.

dered ahead for a large party. This Italian deli is noted for a variety of main and side dishes including submarine sandwiches as long as 6 feet and salads (Greek pasta and Cajun chicken are two tasty examples). Many gourmet condiments are also available. Gino's is open 9 AM to 8 PM Monday through Friday, until 7 PM Saturday and from noon until 5 PM Sunday. The Middleton location offers some seating.

East Side

New Orleans Take-Out
$, no credit cards • 1920 Fordem Ave., Madison • (608) 241-6655

Owner John Roussos maintains the food he serves is even "more authentic and better" than what you'll find in New Orleans. And judging by the number of newspaper write-ups and testimonials he's received from creole lovers everywhere, including Louisiana-born-and-bred Brett Favre of the Green Bay Packers, no doubt he's right. Although there are several bar stools for those who can't wait to eat, Roussos is committed to remaining a take-out entity, pouring his energies instead into the food. All dishes are made from scratch with fresh ingredients. On the menu is shrimp creole, seafood gumbo and jambalaya. New Orleans Take-Out is particularly famous for its red beans and rice (prepared with and without sausage) and shrimp po' boys. For dessert, save room for sweet potato pecan pie. A former chef at Antoine's in New Orleans, Roussos opened New Orleans Take-Out in 1985. It's open 11 AM to 9 PM every day except Sunday.

Vegetarian

Isthmus

Canterbury Cafe
$ • Canterbury Inn, 315 W. Gorham St., Madison • (608) 258-8899

Open 10 AM to 11 PM Sunday through Thursday and 11 AM until midnight Friday and Saturday, the Canterbury Cafe has a bakery and also serves light fare including soups, sandwiches and salads. Wine and beer are available. Reservations are not necessary, although if you're with a party of eight or more, it's helpful to call ahead. The Cafe is part of Canterbury Inn (see our Hotels and Motels chapter for details).

Noodles & Co.
$ • 232 State St., Madison
• (608) 257-6393
$ • 7050 Mineral Point Rd., Madison
• (608) 829-0202

Noodles, noodles and more noodles. This restaurant, which originated in Denver and now has two outlets in Madison (one Downtown and the other on the far West Side), serves a variety of noodle dishes including Thai noodles with chicken and shrimp, tomato basil penne, Indonesian noodles with a spicy sauce and creamy macaroni and cheese. Picky eaters can even order a plate of buttered noodles; tofu can be substituted for any meat item. Noodles & Co. is self-service, open for lunch and dinner. Beer and wine are available.

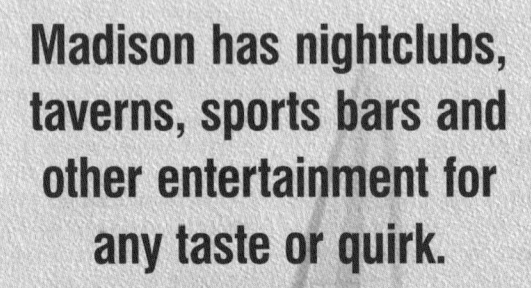

Madison has nightclubs, taverns, sports bars and other entertainment for any taste or quirk.

Nightlife

Madison has long had a reputation for being a place that is beautiful and interesting by day, but goes to bed snoring in flannel pajamas after the evening news. All that has changed. Madison's nights are no longer the exclusive domain of college students.

The number and caliber of major acts that come to Madison has improved drastically in the last decade. The number of restaurants has skyrocketed in the past few years. And live music, from classical piano to techno-berserk garage bands, seems to be going on everywhere: in little coffeehouses, on the Capitol Square, at countless local bars.

This chapter is intended to steer you in the direction you may want to go. There are nightclubs, taverns, sports bars and other entertainment for any taste or quirk. (See our Brewpubs, Wine Bars and Cigar Bars chapter for additional nightlife information.) For an up-to-the-minute listing of bands and entertainers, check out the current edition of *Rhythm*, published each Thursday in *The Capital Times* and *Wisconsin State Journal*.

A Few Words About Drunk Driving

Madison's reputation as a party town dates back to its earliest days. Problems with binge drinking, especially among students, prompted the state to raise the legal drinking age to 21 and enact some pretty tough drunk-driving laws. That said, it's always a good idea to designate a driver to ensure that you get home safely after your evening out.

If you are arrested for drunk driving, you will be handcuffed, fingerprinted, put in jail and will lose your driver's license — at least for a while. That's not likely to be a cherished memory of your time in Madison. If in the past you've driven while intoxicated and not had problems, don't be so sure your good luck will continue. Seventy-eight percent of the approximately 33,000 people convicted in Wisconsin annually for operating a motor vehicle while under the influence (OWI) of alcohol or controlled substances are first-time offenders.

If you refuse to take a test for intoxication, you will lose your license for one year. If you take the test and are found to have a .10 percent blood-alcohol content, you will have your license suspended for at least six months and be fined about $690. If you are younger than 19, you are not allowed to have any alcohol in your system when driving. If you do, you'll face a $92 fine and lose your license for three months. If underage drinkers are found driving while legally intoxicated, they are subject to the same fines and penalties as their over-21 counterparts.

Negotiating Nightlife

Unless otherwise noted, all of the clubs and taverns listed in this chapter are open every day. Last call usually comes around 2 AM. Madison bars must be empty of all patrons at 2:30 AM. They allow both cigar and cigarette smoking. If they usually have a cover charge, we'll let you know what that is. Otherwise, you can expect to get in free unless there's some special activity. It's a good idea to call ahead to check ticket availability for some shows.

This chapter is divided not only by geographical boundaries but also by types of entertainment. We give you the inside scoop only on nightspots unique to Madison, but bear in mind that we also have plenty of national chains here, including such popular spots as T.G.I. Fridays, Houlihan's and Damon's, to name a few. (Many of these establishments that are as noted for their food as their bars, are also written up in the Restaurants chapter.)

Comedy Clubs: Laughing With the Pros

ComedySportz
449 State St., Madison • (608) 255-8888

How many comedy clubs have you been to where you could take your 7-year-old, a 16-year-old and your mom and everybody (especially you) would have a good time? ComedySportz pits two teams of improvisational comedians against each other in a sports-like setting. Each team must score enough points to win. Members of the audience offer constant input, providing suggestions and participating in skits. Lewd, crude and obscene behavior — and puns — are not allowed, even from the audience. Ridiculous situations, speed trials and physical comedy make a night at ComedySportz memorable. The comedy teams play two matches per night Friday and Saturday — at 7:30 and 10 PM. Admission is $5 for students and $7 for the rest of the public. At "halftime," you can buy soda, popcorn and candy at bargain prices. (Because ComedySportz's seating is in bleachers and wood chairs, you might want to bring along a stadium cushion.)

Funny Business Comedy Club
117 State St., Madison • (608) 256-0099

If you love stand-up comedy, plan to visit Funny Business, where some of the nation's best comedians, including the late Madison native Chris Farley and Drew Carey, have appeared in their pre-star years. The comics at Funny Business tend toward risque humor, so don't take the kids expecting a family night with Bozo the Clown. The usual crowd ranges in age from mid-20s to mid-40s. This is a very popular spot to go if you are celebrating something — your birthday, anniversary, divorce or pending nuptials. The usual admission to one of two nightly shows is between $6 and $10. There is a two-drink minimum, but you don't have to drink alcohol; soft drinks and nonalcoholic choices are available. On tap you'll find selections such as Miller Lite, Sam Adams, Killian's and Garten Brau. No smoking is allowed in the comedy showroom on Saturday nights.

Dancing the Night Away

Isthmus

Cardinal Bar and Dance Club
418 E. Wilson St., Madison
• (608) 251-0080

Of all the bars in Madison, the historic Cardinal Bar has changed the least in appearance since it was built at the turn of the century. It has lots of beautiful dark wood, a mosaic tile floor, a gorgeous back bar and plenty of charm. The Cardinal has a loyal gay clientele among the regulars and is often the setting for political events, fund-raisers and election-night parties. It's within walking distance of Monona Terrace Convention Center, and people often make a stop at the Cardinal after a more formal affair.

The club features a live DJ every night (except Mondays, when it's closed), playing contemporary adult music for a crowd of college students and young professionals. You'll hear everything from Brazilian salsa and merengue to retro disco, new wave, industrial classics and electric underground. It's usually $3 to get in the door. On tap you'll find Berghoff, Sprecher, Garten Brau and New Castle among the beer selections. Sunday night is Cigar Lover Night, and you can learn Latin dances on Saturday evenings.

Mango Grill
56 University Square, Madison
• (608) 259-9955

The Mango Grill is quickly earning a reputation as one of the hottest live music venues in town, bringing in rock, blues, jazz, reggae and other acts from Wednesday through Saturday each week. In the daytime it is a restaurant serving grilled items and its famous mashed potatoes. When the band takes over, it becomes a nightclub (though you can still order food until bar time and even a little later). It is tiny, just 1,500 square feet, so only 100 or so music lovers can squeeze it. But when a reggae band takes over, everyone somehow finds enough space to dance. The cover charge is usually about $4. It caters primarily to the campus crowd.

O'Cayz Corral
504 E. Wilson St., Madison
- **(608) 256-1348**

You'll find live music — from hard-core rock to laid-back blues — nightly at O'Cayz Corral, which caters to the 21- to 45-year-old crowd. The usual cover charge ranges from $3 to $6 nightly. O'Cayz has a wide selection of microbrew beers including Berghoff Lager, Berghoff Dark, Sprecher and Summit. Chips and other munchies are available at the bar, and you can play pool or darts.

West Side

Flashbacks
Marriott Madison-West, 1313 John Q. Hammons Dr., Madison • (608) 831-8202

Flashbacks typically draws a young, high-energy crowd that's geared up for drinking and dancing. The nightclub has a DJ spinning tunes Tuesday through Saturday, beginning at 5 PM. Pitchers of beer sell for $3.50 from 8 to 10 PM Tuesday through Friday. If you're celebrating a birthday, come to Flashbacks on the Thursday of your birthday week and drink free all night. Try the "Friday Feeding Frenzy," a happy hour on Friday from 5 to 7 PM.

East Side

Anchor Inn
1970 Atwood Ave., Madison
- **(608) 244-6095**

This relatively small neighborhood bar hosts popular acoustic jams Thursdays and blues jams Sundays. Cover charges usually are $2 to $3. On tap you'll find Bud, Rolling Rock and New Glarus, among others. The Anchor Inn can accommodate up to 80 customers.

Barrymore Theatre
2090 Atwood Ave., Madison
- **(608) 241-2345**

This historic Madison theater now hosts a wide variety of nationally known entertainers, such as John Prine, Ben Harper and many other artists whose music you can dance to. Ticket prices range from around $10 to $24 or more, depending on the band or performer. The box office opens 1½ hours before showtime. Call the listed number for a calendar of events. All tickets are general admission, and if it's a dancing show, you are not guaranteed a place to sit. Advance tickets are sold next door at Green Earth, among other places.

Crystal Corner Bar
1302 Williamson St., Madison
- **(608) 256-2953**

This landmark neighborhood bar breaks the boundaries when it comes to live, terrific blues and rock music. Bands at the Crystal usually get started about 9:45 PM, and cover charges range from $5 to $12. Brew-on-tap options include Point, Berghoff, Old Style, Sam Adams and Red Hook. The Crystal Corner Bar does not serve food, but packaged munchies are available.

Harmony Bar and Grill
2201 Atwood Ave., Madison
- **(608) 249-4333**

If you love progressive blues, roots music and microbrews, then check out the Harmony Bar on Friday or Saturday nights. This neighborhood bar draws a diverse crowd. Cover charges vary according to the band; an average cover is $6. The Harmony is also a worthy dining destination for such fare as burgers, Cajun and Mexican specials, pastas, soups and homemade pizza. Cigar smoking is not allowed.

The Inferno
1718 Commercial Ave., Madison
- **(608) 245-9583**

This huge club can handle 475 patrons. It was built in 1939 and has changed hands many times since then, but the old Spanish arches are still in place. It's dimly lit except for chandeliers. There are two bars and three levels, with an elevated lounge that has couches and round tables and a stage. This club features nearly every type of music: industrial, swing, electro-industrial-gothic, psychedelic-acid-gothic, 1960s surfer-rock, rockabilly, psychobilly, ska, 1980s dance music, lounge acts and others. There is a regular "Torture Garden" interactive bondage show (it's all legal). Regular swing dance lessons are also offered. There is often a DJ. Cover charges usually range from $2 to $11.50.

Sergio's Niteclub
1753 Thierer Rd., Madison
• (608) 246-2690

There's almost always something going on at Sergio's, but the big focus here most nights is music. You can dance while a DJ works the buttons Monday through Saturday, beginning at 7 PM. There is no cover charge. Happy hour runs from 4 to 7 PM weekdays with $1 taps and $1.50 rail drinks, domestic bottled beers and regular Margaritas. Jumbo Margaritas cost $3 each. Chomp on free chips and salsa and play pool for free on one of the nightclub's three back-room tables. Mondays are dedicated to celebrating birthdays. Come in any Monday during your birthday month and get a free bucket of beer. You can also join the Friday Fan Club and receive 52 free drinks. (Like the lottery, this is paid out over time — one free drink each Friday for a year.) Sergio's has Foosball, darts, virtual motorcycles and sponsors plenty of fun events like the make-your-own-swimsuit contest where any material — except fabric — is permissible. One winner wore a snake.

Pearl's Nightclub
Crowne Plaza, 4402 E. Washington Ave., Madison • (608) 244-4703

You'll find a DJ at Pearl's every night of the week except Sunday. The CDs start spinning at 8 PM in this hotel dance lounge that's popular with older college students and young professionals. You might even meet some interesting people from out of town who are staying at the hotel.

Real and Virtual Entertainment

West Side

Challenger's Pub
6722 Odana Rd., Madison
• (608) 827-6070

Challenger's Pub is Madison's version of virtual reality. Try out the soccer, football and baseball virtual reality games for free. Challenger's also draws large number of golfers, particularly during winter months, to keep up their games with virtual golf for $18 an hour. If you ski, you'll love the virtual skier. Pick your course and ability level, and you'll be zipping down a slope faster than you can yell "snow bunny." The ski machine costs just $1 to play. And the friendly staff will even give you hints and encouragement on your games if you appear receptive. There are pool tables and Foosball tables in the back room. Challenger's has an excellent and very reasonably priced grill menu. (The Black Forest sandwiches are particularly tasty.) Challenger's serves crowds of all ages, especially active sports enthusiasts. The pub has a huge selection of foreign and domestic beers. Happy hour is 4 to 6 PM Monday through Thursday.

Jazz Lovers Unite

Isthmus

The Bar
The Madison Concourse Hotel, 1 W. Dayton St., Madison • (608) 257-6000

You won't find a cover at The Bar, but you will find good jazz. Entertainers perform

---

INSIDERS' TIP

Buck's Madison Square Garden Tavern at 113 N. Hamilton Street, just off the Capitol Square, is famous for having some of the strongest drinks in Madison and patrons with some of the best — as well as many of the lamest — pickup lines around.

Madison knows how to throw a party — fabulous fireworks, spectacular skylines and we're happy.

most weekends in this upscale, low-key lounge in the prestigious Madison Concourse Hotel (see our Accommodations chapter). Six beers are on tap, including Guinness, Ex Light and Sam Adams. Drafts cost from $1.50 (a glass) to $4 (a pint). House wines are $2.25 a glass. The Bar serves hotel guests as well as members of the general public.

La Provenzale
540 State St., Madison • (608) 257-9022

Upstairs from Gino's Restaurant, La Provenzale is a small, elegant lounge with a handful of tables for two and a tiny bar. La Provenzale's decor features lots of ornamental wrought iron. On Fridays and Saturdays, the bar usually features jazz. The lounge opens at 5 PM Tuesday through Saturday.

Restaurant Magnus
120 W. Wilson St., Madison
• (608) 258-8787

This is, foremost, an excellent restaurant. But the seductive modernistic red decor and huge, beautiful bar area make it a popular place to stop for a drink, nibble on South American-inspired tapas and on the weekends listen to live jazz. See our Restaurants chapter for more about the cuisine.

East Side

Fyfe's Corner Bistro
1344 E. Washington Ave., Madison
• (608) 251-8700

You can relax to the sounds of jazz at Fyfe's most weekends, but even when there isn't live music, this is an excellent place to get together with friends for an evening. You'll find some of Madison's most comfortable chairs in the large lounge and plenty of drink choices to keep you amused. When there's entertainment, you'll be asked to pay a cover charge, usually about $4.

Craving Karaoke?

Campus

Karaoke Kid
614 University Ave., Madison
• (608) 294-1997

Are you convinced you sing better than anyone with a multimillion dollar recording contract? Here's a place to go to prove it. Against recorded accompaniment meant to enhance your voice, you can sing any one of hundreds of songs, from Broadway show tunes to country and rock, not only in English, but Spanish, Korean and Japanese, too. The cost of each song is $1. Although the bar is not very large, two small rooms have been carved out of the space available so you and a few friends can sing in complete privacy if you so prefer. But relax. Everybody always offers a round of applause!

East Side

Farm Tavern
1701 Moorland Rd., Madison
• (608) 221-1646

The Farm Tavern has karaoke on Wednesday nights and country music or a rock band on Saturday nights. There isn't a cover, but when there's a band, drink prices go up 25¢. Genuine Draft and other Miller products as well as Budweiser brews are on tap. During happy hour — 3 to 7 PM Monday through Friday — bottles of Coors and Old Style are $1, and you can get a six-pack of shorties in a bucket for $6. The Farm Tavern has pool, video golf, darts and Foosball.

West Side

Hanna's 77
77 Sirloin Strip, Madison
• (608) 251-7733

This restaurant and lounge is perched on a hill over the Beltline Highway, one of the highest elevations in Madison — all the better to carry the sounds of your voice through the night sky as you retreat after dinner to the popular karaoke lounge here. There's a nice deck to take in the breeze after your exertions.

Adult Entertainment

East Side

Visions Night Club
3554 E. Washington Ave., Madison
• (608) 244-9771

Dane County's only burlesque nightclub, Vision's is a popular spot for bachelor parties. The club has a DJ and 12 female dancers nightly. The cover charge for afternoons is $3. At night, the cover charge is $5 to $6. On Sundays, amateurs take the stage. Visions has monthly male dance reviews. The bar serves free pretzels, popcorn and chips.

Bars with Gifted Grills

Isthmus

The Argus
123 E. Main St., Madison
• (608) 256-4226

Politicos and professionals mix at The Argus, in a 150-year-old building just a block from the Capitol Square and two blocks from the Monona Terrace Convention Center. The Argus offers inside and outside seating during summer months and Saturday brunches on the patio (see our Restaurants chapter for details). Twelve brews rotate through the taps. The Argus grill serves lunch from 11 AM to 2 PM daily. Patrons often play euchre and cribbage on Fridays and Saturdays.

Ken's Bar and Grill
117 S. Butler St., Madison
• (608) 257-1176

Ken's Bar, open for 30 years, consistently attracts a professional gang, ranging in age from 23 to 55. On Wednesdays, Ken's has bluegrass, and on Thursdays, live blues. You won't have to pay a cover, but please donate when they pass the hat. Berghoff, Garten Brau and Special Export are on tap, and you can dine on burgers, brats and other sandwiches.

Campus

Marsh Shapiro's Nitty Gritty
223 N. Frances St., Madison
• (608) 251-2521

This is the destination for 50 to 60 birthday boys and girls of all ages every day. Maybe it's the free commemorative glass that you can have refilled all day and all night with free soda or beer. Maybe it's because it's the one place someone is going to still play a jazzy "happy birthday" tune for you and make a

NIGHTLIFE • 89

little fuss. If you're a kid, maybe you like going to the Nitty Gritty to get a free helium balloon and choose your food off a special kiddie menu. Some people like going there just because of Marsh Shapiro himself, the retired sportscaster-turned-tavern owner who greets everyone at the door with a big smile and kind word.

Regardless of its patrons' reasons, the Nitty Gritty has celebrated 200,000 birthdays since 1985. It is consistently named one of Madison's top bar and grills and has been for years. The food is excellent (see our Restaurants chapter for details). Once you've tried a Gritty Burger, you'll never again be satisfied with fast food. The fried-chicken salad is another family favorite. With the new Kohl Sports Center just a half-block away, the Nitty Gritty is a great place before and after events at the center.

West Side

Irishman's Bay
7436 Mineral Point Rd., Madison
• (608) 833-4262

This popular bar, in a strip mall across the street from West Towne Mall, offers plenty of grilled choices and a good selection of brews — 10 beers on tap. The Irishman's Bay is also known for its Margaritas . . . go figure. Maybe the Irish ancestors made a detour on the way to America.

Irish Waters
702 N. Whitney Way, Madison
• (608) 233-3198

This is always the place to be on St. Pat's Day — and almost any night in between. Since 1979, good food and a friendly atmosphere have drawn customers back to Irish Waters, just south of the intersection of University Avenue and Whitney Way. The crowd ranges from the newly gainfully employed to experienced business folk. On tap, you'll find Guinness, Harp, Bass, Sam Adams, Killian's and Gray's — to name a few. When you're not visiting with friends or meeting new people, you can entertain yourself with pool, Foosball, an electronic golf game or trivia game. The happy hour with appetizers runs from 4 to 6 PM Monday through Friday (see our Restaurants chapter for food details).

Laurel Tavern
2505 Monroe St., Madison
• (608) 233-1043

The Laurel Tavern is almost a monument on Monroe Street. This friendly watering hole is a good place to sip a beer or eat one of its famous burgers while watching satellite TV. The Laurel has numerous beers on tap including Ex Light, Berghoff, Killian's, Sam Adams and Pete's Wicked Ale. You're likely to run into some of Madison's local celebrities such as TV sportscasters, meteorologists and politicians.

Tony Frank's Tavern
1612 Seminole Hwy., Madison
• (608) 271-2177

This is the home of the original Tony Frank's (there are now three). The bar and grill is famous for its grilled cheeseburgers, cooked with fried onions and served on dark seeded buns. There's no fancy dinnerware here — just plain, good grilled food served on waxed paper. Other Tony Frank's locations can be found at 2952 Fish Hatchery Road on the West Side and, on the East Side, at 3302 Packers Avenue. At night this comfortable tavern is a great place to get together with friends, watch a game and enjoy a brew.

Monkeyshines
6209 McKee Rd., Madison
• (608) 274-5339

Monkeyshines' gifted grill has attracted a steady following. The bar sponsors volleyball, pool and dart leagues and has sand volleyball courts in back. On tap you'll find — among others — Ex Light, Berghoff Red and Berghoff Honey Wheat.

Quivey's Grove Stable Grill
6261 Nesbitt Rd., Madison
• (608) 273-4900

Without a doubt, this is one of the most special places in town for a night out with friends. The Stable, like the stone house on the site (the two are connected by an underground tunnel with a wine cellar), is on the National Register of Historic Places and features — as you might expect — a rustic but extremely inviting atmosphere (see our Restaurants chapter for food and decor details; the stone house is also a restaurant). You'll discover 11 Wisconsin microbrews on tap, a martini menu, piano player and terrific wine selection. You'll also find a diverse menu with everything from light fare to hearty prime rib dinners and a Friday fish fry.

East Side

Caribbean Club Bar and Grill
1617 N. Stoughton Rd., Madison
• (608) 249-6539

An island paradise is not what you'd expect to find on this major thoroughfare. The Caribbean Club, with its Tiki Hut bar, palm trees and bamboo wall coverings, offers four frozen drinks on tap in three sizes, ranging from the $2.95 for a 10-ounce daiquiri to $4.95 for the 16-ounce version. You can also choose from a variety of delightful drink concoctions including Turbo Koolaid, a Hiram Walker concoction that tastes remarkably like the children's-favorite drink. The Caribbean Club also has a diverse menu. Try the grilled shrimp salad.

Favorite Cafes, Taverns and Lounges

Isthmus

Maduro
117 E. Main St., Madison
• (608) 294-9371

This striking new establishment, which opened its doors in early 1998, offers stogies (with ventilation) and an impressive bar with a huge selection of single-malt Scotches, wines by the glass, cordials, dessert wines and liqueurs. There are also a half-dozen or so interesting appetizers and several desserts.

West Side

Blue Moon Bar and Grill
2535 University Ave., Madison
• (608) 238-0519

This unique '40s-deco style neighborhood tavern serves 10 beers on tap daily including Garten Brau Amber, Leinie's Red, Red Hook ESB, Garten Brau Maibock and Blue Moon Belgian White. You can listen to tunes on the jukebox, play darts or pool, visit with friends or watch satellite TV on one of seven screens. The clientele spans ages 25 to 60.

Le Tigre Lounge
1328 S. Midvale Blvd., Madison
• (608) 274-0944

Watch the eye of the tiger as it watches you. This unique lounge transports you into the domain of a real tiger (albeit a stuffed specimen). You'll enjoy the owner's efforts to bring the tiger theme into every corner of the lounge. The vintage jukebox is filled with classics from the '40s to '60s, including Patsy Cline, the Animals and the Beatles. There are no tap beers at Le Tigre, but you can choose from a fine selection of bottled beers and liquor.

Campus

Second Story
508 State St., Madison • (608) 256-2434

The funky black and white decor welcoming you to the Second Story is your first hint that this place is not ordinary. This is a nice

---

INSIDERS' TIP

Is it political intrigue you're looking for? The best eavesdropping opportunities in town may be at Genna's Lounge, 105 W. Main Street, just off the Capitol Square. This is where legislative types tend to drink too much and get their names in local gossip columns. University faculty and students also get into the action here.

bar in which to share a bottle of wine and try out some delightful appetizers such as duck strudel ($6), shrimp bisque ($4.50) or a baguette stuffed with ratatouille ($4.25). Once a month the Second Story hosts a contemporary-music concert complete with a multimedia show. Call to find out the next date.

East Side

Jolly Bob's
1210 Williamson St., Madison
• (608) 251-3902

Choose from more than 60 wines and 40 rums at this tropical bar on Williamson Street. Jolly Bob's is known for its spicy Caribbean food and innovative appetizers. Occasionally the bar has live music. Outdoor seating is available.

Ballrooms

East Side

Sapphire Ballroom
Northgate Shopping Center, 1133 N. Sherman Ave., Madison • (608) 245-0627

You can find everyone from doctors to truck drivers gliding across Sapphire's huge, 5,000-square-foot dance floor. Depending on the night, a DJ might be spinning the tunes, or there might be a live band at the center of the action. The usual cover charge is $5, and the ballroom opens at 5 PM. If you haven't yet learned your dance steps, don't dismay. Ballroom-dancing lessons are $8 each (with a one-month minimum). Class is held Sundays at 5 PM, and you don't need to bring a partner. For those who care to drink while they dance, Miller and Leinenkugel are on tap. Smoking usually is not allowed.

Outlying Area

Park Ponderosa Ballroom and Supper Club
5100 Erling Ave., McFarland
• (608) 838-9527

All types of music for all types of music lovers is what you'll find at the Park Ponderosa Ballroom. In business for 27 years, the Park Ponderosa is the frequent setting for wedding receptions, banquets, rehearsal dinners and Big Band action. The usual cover charge is $5. The ballroom has live bands every Friday as well as some Saturdays and Sundays. Park Ponderosa is closed on Mondays. Wednesday night is Euchre Night. Miller Lite, Genuine Draft and Leinenkugel Red are on tap.

Country Music: Kicking Up Your Heels

West Side

Dry Bean Saloon and Smokehouse
5264 Verona Rd., Madison
• (608) 274-2326

If you want to strut your stuff, country-style, then the Dry Bean Saloon is the place for you, with live bands Wednesday through Saturday. Dance instructors take the floor Tuesday, Wednesday and Thursday nights, beginning at 6:30 PM. Lessons cost just $2 each, and in no time at all, you'll have what it takes to have a great time dancing. The Dry Bean also has a super bar with all kinds of choices, including nine tap beers. The full-service restaurant has some of the best ribs in town as well as chicken, seafood, Black Angus steaks, duck and buffalo (see our Restaurants chapter).

East Side

Country Corners
3737 County Hwy. AB, Madison
• (608) 222-2077

You can dance to live country music Thursday through Saturday at this bar on the far East Side near the intersection on County Highway AB and U.S. Highway 12/18. The average cover charge is $4. Country Corners has karaoke Wednesdays (there's no cover). If you're hungry you can choose from a variety of sandwiches. The grill opens daily at 11 AM.

Take Time to Listen: Jazz, Blues, Country, Rhythm and Blues and Rock 'n' Roll

When it comes to outdoor concerts in southern Wisconsin, Milwaukee's Summerfest on the shores of Lake Michigan is the big event. World class performers such as James Taylor and Tina Turner come to Summerfest stages, and so do Madison's top acts. Spectators wander past rows of stages that seem to go on forever. On them is a revolving parade of bands that play from morning until night for 11 days.

Close-up

National acts also make regular stops in Madison at such places as the Kohl Center, which has a capacity of up to 14,000 and during its short life has already drawn Aerosmith, Yanni, Lord of the Dance and the UW Varsity Band to its stage. Major acts also appear regularly at the Dane County Coliseum, the Madison Civic Center and the UW-Madison Field House.

There is also a lot of great music being produced here year round. Ben Sidran and his son Leo, the internationally known bassist Richard Davis, Rachelle and the Red Hot Rattlers, the Reptile Palace Orchestra, Clyde Stubblefield, Doc DeHaven, his daughter, Kelly DeHaven and the MisbeHaven Band, West Side Andy Linderman, Paul Black, and The Wizenheimers are just a few of the entertainers that keep Madison's nightlife exciting.

The alternative rock group Garbage, which released its second CD in 1998, was spawned in Madison as well. So, given the talent pool here, you may want to listen carefully when you pass a street musician in Madison, and there are many of them. You might be getting a preview of something special.

Jazz

Madison's jazz scene produced the internationally known jazz performer and producer **Ben Sidran**. Sidran, a regular contributor to National Public Radio, has teamed up with Van Morrison on occasion. The jazzman has an intense touring schedule that includes gigs in Europe and Japan. But, if you're lucky, you can catch him at Cafe Montmartre jamming with his drummer son Leo. Another world renowned jazz artist is bassist Richard Davis, a professor at UW-Madison.

Doc DeHaven is the king of the Madison jazz scene and a master of smooth Dixieland jazz. It's always a treat to hear Doc on his trumpet. In November 1996, Doc released his first CD in five years, a collection of a dozen songs in which he is accompanied by some old friends — 22 of the jazz musicians he has played with

Kelly DeHaven – pictured here with her husband, trumpeter Dave Cooper – is a prominent fixture in the Madison music scene.

Photo: Wisconsin State Journal/The Capital Times

— continued on next page

over the years. If you're lucky, you'll find DeHaven playing at one of the local clubs. (Check the newspapers' "Rhythm" section.)

Doc's daughter **Kelly DeHaven**, accompanied by her MisbeHaven Band, has carved her own niche in the Madison jazz scene as a premier vocalist. Together six years, the MisbeHaven Band's current repertoire is nearly half original work.

Funk and Blues

Blues is peaking in Madison. Like all types of music, its popularity ebbs and flows. But lately, the city has been full of world-class musicians, some of them home grown.

Madison legend **Clyde Stubblefield** is the drummer credited with creating the rhythm of funk music, is a frequent headliner at local clubs. Stubblefield toured with James Brown and the late Otis Redding. These days he works on his own productions, plays in many venues around Madison and mixes it up with Ben Sidran, Steve Miller, Phil Upchurch and others. **Mama Digdown's Brass Junction** is a New Orleans-style brass band with six horns and two drummers. The band has won kudos from Branford Marsalis and other music-industry giants. Mama Digdown's incorporates elements of R&B, hip-hop and jazz into the band's music. The band was part of the 1997 Summerfest lineup.

Stubblefield, even though he is revered internationally as the patron saint of the funk beat, has done a tremendous amount of mentoring to local blues talent.

Among the rising local talent is blues harmonica player **"West Side Andy" Linderman**. Linderman has been performing for more than 20 years, collaborating with legends such as Luther Allison and Charlie Musselwhite. His harp solos have been heard from Milwaukee's Summerfest to the Mississippi Valley Blues Festival, and the Kentuckiana Blues fest. He has recorded with local slide guitar master Paul "Blackie" Black. Black recently signed with the Private Music record.

The list of other notable blues musicians who have made their mark on Madison runs on: guitarists **Andy Ewen**, **Revend Dippermouth**, **Jim Schwall** and **John Davis**; pianist **John Chiames**; singer-keyboardist **Tracy Nelson**; singer **James "Earl" Tate**; harmonicist **Frankie Lee**; and acoustic bassist **Joel "Fats" Patterson**.

Some local blues musicians stick to the basics while others, like the **Bol Weavils**, push the form into unchartered waters, adding the flavors of psychedelia, jazz, country and zydeco.

Alternative Rock

Garbage, an alternative rock band, released its much-anticipated sophomore album, *Version 2.1*, in May 1998. The CD has much riding on it. The album follows the band's self-titled debut album, which spent 81 weeks on the Billboard 200 list and peaked at number 20 in August 1996. *Garbage* also sold 4 million copies worldwide and earned three Grammy nominations. Members of the group describes their music as electronica, pop, punk and even "organic."

Garbage was born in Madison when drummer Butch Vig, who had produced landmark rock albums for Nirvana and the Smashing Pumpkins, hooked up with Duke Erikson and Steve Marker who had done remixes for U2, nine inch nails and other groups. With the addition of vocalist Shirley Manson, the group's music first caught on in Europe, then began to gain attention in the United States. Garbage now has several releases and does national tours.

Rock

Voted the best of Madison in 1995, **The Wizenheimers**, a roots-rocking quartet, bubbles over with enthusiasm and energy. Probably nothing could have endeared the band more to Wisconsin fans than to create a song urging on the home team: "Go You

— continued on next page

Packers Go." The Wizenheimers perform in Milwaukee, Chicago and Minneapolis, but they always get a big Packer welcome when they return home to Madison.

Other Options

Another hot ticket in Madison is the **UW Marching Band**, which in spring of 1998 turned out a spectacular Varsity Band concert series at the Kohl Center. The director of the band, Mike Leckrone, is a flamboyant showman, known to do things like fly circus-style onto the stage. Add to that fireworks, a blimp, confetti, pompons and some of Madison's best guest performers like jazz trombonist Claude Cailliet and Leotha Stanley with Three J's (Jackie Colbert, Jonathan Overby and Jan Wheaton)ˆ.

You'll also want to keep an eye on local club postings for such groups as **Rachelle the Red Hot Rattlers**, considered one of the state's best country acts. The group took first-place honors in the summer of 1996 at the state country band contest in Rhinelander.

Filling another very different musical niche is the **Reptile Palace Orchestra**, one of the area's best ethnic-international groups. It's hard to peg their music, but it is often described as gypsy-lounge-funk.

Second Homes for Sports Fans

Isthmus

Babe's Grill & Bar
At the Depot, 640 W. Washington Ave., Madison • (608) 250-6411
5614 Schroeder Rd., Madison (West) • (608) 274-7300

The large and popular West Side Babe's (seating capacity 472 plus TVs, darts and video games) opened a second location on the Isthmus in 1996. Babe's at the Depot is housed in one of Madison's most spectacular historic buildings, a train depot with high ceilings and an expansive dining room. It's perfectly situated for a stop before or after an event at the Kohl Center. Patrons can watch one of many televisions in the immense dining room and enjoy Miller, Special Export, Gray's Honey Ale and Pete's Wicked Ale, to name a few. (See our Restaurants chapter for food-related information about Babe's.)

Jingle's Coliseum Bar and Restaurant
232 E. Olin Ave., Madison
• (608) 251-2434

Whether you're a party of one or a banquet of 350 people, you can find a friendly welcome at Jingle's. (Call ahead for the banquet.) Jingle's enjoys a large clientele, drawing many people who work Downtown. On Badger and Monster hockey nights (see our Sports chapter) or during other Coliseum events, this is the place to be to get in the team spirit, celebrate a big win or bemoan a defeat. If you want to go to a hockey game and don't have tickets, you might find some available here just before game time. (Remember, scalping is illegal, but you can buy tickets for face value or less.) Jingle's menu covers just about the whole spectrum of American fare — from salads to grilled sandwiches to complete dinners.

INSIDERS' TIP

If you're going out on the town and are enrolled in college, be sure to bring along your student ID. Many clubs and theaters offer students discounts on admission.

Campus

Big Ten Pub
1330 Regent St., Madison
* **(608) 251-6375**

The University of Wisconsin is a gem in the Big Ten Conference, and this popular sports pub plays tribute to the Badgers with its Wisconsin-theme decor. On football Saturdays, you can find the Big Ten Pub's beer garden overflowing with Badger fans. The bar has three satellite dishes to provide sports fans with the latest coverage of favorite teams. The Big Ten Pub is within walking distance of the Camp Randall Stadium, Fieldhouse and Union South. Eight beers are on tap — Miller Genuine Draft, Miller Lite, Michelob, Lienie's Red, Black Hook and Ex Light, to name a handful. The Big Ten Pub has a full sandwich and appetizer menu and serves a Friday fish fry.

Copper Grid
1509 Monroe St., Madison
* **(608) 256-3811**

Marked with a large red "W," this bar is an old-time favorite hangout before and after Badger football games, due to its proximity to Camp Randall Stadium. This is a typical '50s-style bar; the walls are lined with commemorative beer cans. Patrons can play darts, air hockey or video games. If you're ready to sit a spell and enjoy a pint, you'll find Pete's Wicked Ale, Berghoff, Spaten and Budweiser on tap.

Oakcrest Tavern at the Stadium
1421 Regent St., Madison
* **(608) 250-8989**

This tavern caters to the Badger crowd with special events and parties before and after Badger games. The Stadium-area Oakcrest is an offshoot of the popular West Side Oakcrest tavern at 5371 Old Middleton Road. The bar has darts and pool. On weekends the Oakcrest sometimes has a live band — '50s rock 'n' roll on up. The owners keep the cover charges to $3 or less. Happy hour is 4 to 6 PM Monday through Friday.

Regent Street Retreat
1206 Regent St., Madison
* **(608) 256-7750**

This huge bar, just off the UW campus, is the "Home of the Hoover" — a potent concoction of vodka, rum, papaya juice and orange juice — which sells for $3 and comes with two straws so you can share (the hangover?). The Regent Street Retreat caters to an energetic young crowd of college students and young professionals. There's plenty to do here, with numerous big TVs (including a 150-inch sports TV), live contemporary music on Saturday and Sunday, and pre-, post- and mid-game parties for Badger sporting events. Four pool tables, electronic dart boards, Foosball, air hockey and video games add to the atmosphere of perpetual motion. You also can drink microbrews, domestics and imports on tap here. Try one of the grilled sandwiches, a homemade pizza or a salad.

The Stadium Bar
1419 Monroe St., Madison
* **(608) 256-2544**

Formerly Jingles, this renovated bar changed ownership in January 1997. The Stadium Bar is a favorite stop for sports fans for pre-football game parties. You'll find Miller and Leinenkugel products on tap. The bar opens daily at 11 AM and serves a lunch menu of sandwiches. The campus bar has two outdoor sand volleyball courts.

INSIDERS' TIP

The gay scene in Madison suffered a huge setback several years ago when the historic Hotel Washington, which housed several popular gay clubs, was destroyed by an accidental fire. Since then, places like Manoeuvres at 150 S. Blair Street, Geraldine's Tavern at 3052 E. Washington Avenue and The Shamrock Bar at 117 W. Main Street have become popular gathering spots for the gay community.

Wando's Tavern
602 University Ave., Madison
- **(608) 256-5204**

Wanna meet a Badger? This is where the UW football players tend to hang — when not in training, of course. The corner college bar has Sam Adams, Bass Ale, Devil Mountain and Pete's Wicked Ale. Wando's serves a fruity $10 drink called the Fishbowl, suitable for sharing. (Don't try to drink it alone unless you have a designated driver, liver donor and/or medic standing by.) Wando's has TV and a CD jukebox for additional entertainment.

West Side

Coaches Bar and Grill
439 Grand Canyon Dr., Madison
- **(608) 833-4485**

Hope you like TV sports! Coaches has 32 televisions including two big-screen TVs, bringing you the latest and greatest sports action. You can try the bar's signature drink, a "Coach's Cooler," for $3.50. (It's a mixture of vodka, Malibu, peach Schnapps and pineapple juice.) Or play it safe and go for one of the tap beers — Gray's, Special Export, Special Export Light, Sprecher's or Leinie's. Coaches has darts, an electronic golf game and Friday fish fry. Happy hour is 4 to 7 PM Monday through Friday, featuring reduced prices on domestic and premium bottled beers and mixed drinks, along with half-price appetizers.

Pitcher's Pub
323 W. Beltline Hwy., Madison
- **(608) 271-9702**

You'll find eight televisions, including three big-screens, at Pitcher's Pub, behind Nedrebo's Formal Wear. Bud, Bud Light, Ice House, Miller Lite, Red Hook and Gray's Honey Ale grace the taps. During happy hour (2 to 6 PM Monday through Saturday), pitchers are $3.75 to $5, reduced from the usual pitcher charges of $5 to $7.50. Pitcher's has 10 pool tables and eight dart games.

East Side

Pooley's
5441 High Crossing Blvd., Madison
- **(608) 242-1888**

Pooley's is a sports-fan nirvana with indoor and outdoor sand volleyball courts, an indoor basketball court and 18 televisions with satellite hookups, including one 10-foot screen. This huge, far East Side bar has a full food menu, too (see the Restaurants chapter). In addition, Pooley's invites you to drop by for happy hour from 3 to 6:30 PM weekdays. Tap beers include Miller and Budweiser products and Gray's Honey Ale.

Water Tower Pub
5914 Monona Dr., Madison
- **(608) 221-9400**

This cozy, well-lighted bar is a fun place to kick back and relax. The Water Tower Pub has plenty of private booths so you can talk undisturbed, numerous TVs, two sand volleyball courts out back and darts inside. Water Tower Pub frequently has karaoke, usually on Monday and Saturday nights.

World Famous Buckeye Inn
4420 E. Buckeye Rd., Madison
- **(608) 222-8366**

This friendly neighborhood bar and grill has been a landmark on the East Side for more than 20 years. Just off U.S. Highway 51 at Buckeye, the inn usually has about 11 domestic and imported beers on tap. The Buckeye has big-screen televisions for watching your favorite sports and other events, pool, darts and Foosball.

INSIDERS' TIP

Some of Madison's best nightlife is found along State Street: In addition to a diverse selection of bars and live entertainment, you can find street musicians, jugglers and other performers.

Outlying Area

The Club Tavern & Grille
1915 Branch St., Middleton
• (608) 836-3773

If you're 8 years old or 80, you'll find fun at the Club Tavern, housed in a historic, 150-year-old building. In warm weather the sand volleyball courts create lots of enthusiasm. Patrons also enjoy live music, darts, pinball leagues and lots of hearty American dishes. Gray's, Bass, Guinness and Rolling Rock are on tap. Cover charges vary depending on the type of entertainment.

Neighborhood Pubs

Isthmus

Cay's Comic Strip
502 E. Wilson St., Madison
• (608) 256-7110

Not a traditional comedy club by any means, Cay's Comic Strip relies on its customers for the entertainment and advertises "live characters performing nightly" (their patrons). The bar — open for 25 years now — caters to a raucous, local crowd ranging in age from about 21 to 70. Beer is just $1.25 a bottle all the time, and the jukebox plays 10 songs for $1. Mondays are euchre (a popular card game in Wisconsin) night, Tuesdays you can join in bingo, and on some Fridays, the place goes Hawaiian.

Come Back In
508 E. Wilson St., Madison
• (608) 258-8619

If you like trying new beers, you'll like the Come Back In, right next door to another beer-lover's paradise (see the Essen Haus description in the Serious Beer Lovers section), just blocks from the State Capitol and the Convention Center. CBI has 16 microbrews and imports on tap. Happy hour is 3 to 6 PM every day; at other times, draft beers will run you between $2 and $3.75. Wine usually sells for $2.50 a glass. Foodwise, CBI serves just about everything — from breakfast items to sandwiches.

Campus

The Greenbush Bar
914 Regent St., Madison
• (608) 257-2874

The Greenbush Bar has a good selection of wine, beer and liquor and some of the best old-style Italian pizza in town (see our Restaurants chapter). The bar is in what used to be a large Italian neighborhood, and the owner is a granddaughter of "Bush" immigrants. Now the area is perched between the University of Wisconsin and numerous medical clinics. The Greenbush has low ceilings so cigar smoking is not allowed.

East Side

The Avenue Bar
1128 E. Washington Ave., Madison
• (608) 257-6877

The Avenue Bar, famous for its Friday fish fry and potent drinks, is a popular East Side hangout for politicians and business people. On tap you'll find Berghoff, Leinie's, Norski Honey Bock, Badger Red Ale, Honker's Ale and Export Light. The Avenue Bar has a large room available for private parties and occasionally features live bands.

Caribou Tavern
703 E. Johnson St., Madison
• (608) 257-5993

You can play darts and pinball at the Caribou Tavern. You'll find Sam Adams and Special Export on tap.

Packer Inn
300 Cottage Grove Rd., Madison
• (608) 222-9984

With a name like the Packer Inn, you know most of Wisconsin is going to love this place and its patriotic green and gold accents. On Fridays the Packer Inn has live musical entertainment ranging from pop to rock to blues.

Wilson's Bar
2144 Atwood Ave., Madison
• (608) 241-2226

Wilson's Bar has five pool tables, eight satellite TVs and four dart boards. There are lots of brews to choose from here, including Miller, White Tail, Garten Brau, Sam Adams and Miller Genuine Draft. Feeling hungry? Try the Wilson Burger.

Outlying Area

Rusty's Bar
6413 University Ave., Middleton
• (608) 836-1766

Rusty's has been attracting new customers for 24 years with budget-priced drinks, fun bartenders, a good jukebox and tasty grilled food. Rusty's has pool and dart leagues four nights a week. Customers vary by occupation and age (21 to 60) but share a common enthusiasm for sports.

Black Bear Inn
320 Cottage Grove Rd., Cottage Grove
• (608) 839-5222

Sand volleyball, euchre and good food are just a few reasons why locals and visitors keep coming back to this popular Cottage Grove nightspot. The Black Bear serves a variety of grilled sandwiches, has nightly dinner specials and is open for brunch on Saturdays and Sundays. The bar has sand volleyball courts and summer volleyball leagues.

Tripping Down Memory Lane

Campus

Memorial Union Terrace and Rathskeller
800 Langdon St., Madison
• (608) 262-2263

A Friday or Saturday night on the Union Terrace can attract as many as 2,500 people. That's because few things are nicer than listening to a band while sitting next to a lake, watching the sunset behind the boats and drinking wine or a beer. Summer concerts begin Memorial Day weekend and run through August. A student music committee selects performers. On the Terrace and inside the Union at the Rathskeller, you can hear bands of all types including bluegrass, reggae, jazz, jump-swing, rock and pop. You must have a valid University of Wisconsin ID or a Union membership card to buy alcohol, but just hanging around, eating an ice cream or a sandwich and feeding the ducks is for everyone. Annual union memberships are $30 to $50, depending on where you live.

State Street, in Downtown Madison, is a hotspot for nightlife, especially because of its close proximity to the UW campus.

Other Popular University Hangouts

Campus

Brothers
704 University Ave., Madison
• (608) 251-9550

Beer lovers can choose their favorite libation from among 19 taps including Blue Moon, Heineken, Bass, Harp, Sam Adams Honey Porter and Guinness. Drafts range from $1.50

to $3 at this college bar. Wines are $2.50 a glass. Brothers is open for lunch from 11 AM to 3 PM, with grilled and fried items on the menu. Patrons can play pool, darts or electronic golf; sip beer, wine or frozen drinks while listening to Brothers' extensive list of classic and alternative rock CDs; or visit with friends.

Bull Feathers
303 N. Henry St., Madison
- **(608) 257-6444**

This sports pub is a favorite with the older college crowd. You can play darts or pool, cheer on your favorite team during a televised ballgame or just hang out. Tap beers include Ex Light, Ice House, Killian's, Blue Moon, Wood Chuck and Garten Brau. The bar and grill also serves salads and seafood. Occasionally, Bull Feathers has live bands.

Bullwinkle's Pub
624 University Ave., Madison
- **(608) 257-1122**

The ever-popular Bullwinkle's features a big-screen TV, dancing with a DJ and multiple bars. The bar, which attracts young singles, usually opens at 9 PM, and you might have to wait in line to get in. There's no cover except on Wednesday night, College Dance Night, when the club is open to those 18 and older and is alcohol-free. The Wednesday night cover is $3. Thursday night is retro-night, when *Saturday Night Fever*-era music is played.

Madhatter's
3 University Sq., Madison
- **(608) 251-0802**

Just a hop and a skip from campus — if you feel like hopping and skipping — this college bar offers nightly drink specials and $1 Jell-O shooters. Tappers include Rolling Rock, Ice House and Special Export. Madhatter's has a big-screen TV and numerous dart games.

State Street Brats
603 State St., Madison • (608) 255-5544

Occasionally, someone not from these parts will wonder why a bar would be named after obnoxious children. Brats — rhymes with tots — is short for bratwurst, the food of choice around here at summer picnics and year-round at sporting events. A recent renovation has just about doubled capacity at State Street Brats, where you can gobble a grilled bratwurst and savor a wide selection of bottled and tap beers, including Badger Porter, Ex Light, Miller, Woodchuck, Gray's, Sprecher and Point Amber. The signature drink here is The Rosebowl, a fruity blend that sells for $2.75 (except on Saturdays, when it's $2.25). No matter how much we begged, the bartender wouldn't tell us what's in it. But she did say it has similar ingredients to an Alabama Slammer. When you enter State Street Brats, you'll find yourself in a traditional, dimly lighted pub. The new upper deck is brighter and offers two satellite TVs with 8-foot screens. If it's a nice night, you just might want to find a spot in the outdoor seating area and people watch on State Street.

Stillwaters
250 State St., Madison • (608) 256-0596

This is another State Street landmark, where many a college kid has learned to drink Swampwaters, potent lime-flavored concoctions in the rustic wooden booths. Don't let the Kool-Aid appearance fool you. This is no kiddie drink. Stillwaters has indoor and outdoor seating, daily food specials and a selection of tasty burgers and melts.

The Kollege Klub
529 Lake St., Madison • (608) 257-3611

If you're looking to meet a Greek, come to the KK, as it's called — a long-standing bastion of fraternity and sorority members. On tap you'll find Miller and Leinenkugel products. Monday nights rock at the KK. Bring your own mug, and the bartender will fill it for $1.

The Living Room
529 University Ave., Madison
- **(608) 250-0700**

The Living Room is part of the campus scene. By day, it is a specialty coffee shop. Try a Keith Richards — four shots of espresso — for $3.50. As the daylight dims, patrons turn their attention to the bar's 14 tap beers, including Guinness, Bass, New Castle and Sierra Nevada. Happy hour is 4 to 7 PM daily, and beer sells for just $2.50 a pint. Wines are about $3 a glass. Cigarette smoking is allowed at The Living Room, but if you've got a good cigar, the staff prefers that you enjoy it on the patio. The Living Room's 200-disc player, jam-packed with blues and alternative rock music, sets the entertainment scene.

The Red Shed
406 N. Francis St., Madison
* **(608) 256-2214**

The Red Shed has been drawing college students since it first opened in 1969. You'll find 10 beers on tap including Miller products, Molson, Sprecher and Sam Adams. The Red Shed is famous for its Long Island Iced Teas, which come in two sizes: The "small" sells for $2.50; what the bartender calls a "real" Long Island Iced Tea — about a quart — sells for $4.50. A jukebox keeps things lively here. The bar also sponsors softball and volleyball teams.

For Serious Beer Lovers

Isthmus

Essen Haus
514 E. Wilson St., Madison
* **(608) 255-4674**

The Essen Haus supplies robust beer lovers with the largest selection of imported German beers in town. When you belly up to the bar at this traditional German pub, you can choose from 16 German tap beers and 270 bottled beers. You can even order beer by the boot from wait staff wearing lederhosen. Tap beer prices range from $2.50 to $3.50. The Essen Haus offers dancing to polka music every night, and you can dine on marvelous German dishes in the full-service restaurant (see our Restaurants chapter). The Essen Haus is a favorite of many folks, ranging in age from 21 to 85.

East Side

Wonder's Pub
1980 Atwood Ave., Madison
* **(608) 244-8563**

Enjoy a pint of Wood Chuck, Honker's Ale, Guinness or other brews while challenging your friends to bumper pool, darts or cribbage. Beer sells for $3 a pint or $8 a pitcher. This bar's great beer selection draws the weekly meetings of the Madison Homebrewers and Taster's Guild.

The Gist of Java

If you are one of the millions of Americans who can't really enjoy a day without at least one shot of caffeine, then let us introduce you to Madison's coffeehouse scene. Like bagel shops, it seems new coffee stores and coffeehouses are springing up everywhere overnight. And it's a far cry from the days when Mrs. Olsen ruled the coffee world.

In Madison, two retailers currently hold the key to the specialty coffee industry. **Steep and Brew** has four locations: 7 University Square, 544 State Street, 2871 University Avenue and 6656 Odana Road. **Victor Allen's Coffee & Tea** can be found at 1730 Fordem Avenue, 2623 Monroe Street, 5501 Odana Road, 401 State Street, 2858 University Avenue, 449 Yellowstone Drive and 410 D'Onofrio Drive.

But if you want more than milk with your espresso, we invite you to try one of Madison's unique coffeehouses. As social venues in a college town where the under-21 crowd can access good music and conversation, coffeehouses are extremely popular. You'll find them all over Madison — and don't expect them to just be filled with teens. Coffeehouses draw patrons of all ages and backgrounds.

The first Madison espresso coffeehouse, The Symptom, opened in 1959. It's 5 AM closing time encouraged jazz players to stop by and jam after bar time. A few other coffeehouses popped up in Madison over the years, but the trend really didn't take off until the 1980s. Here's a sample:

Isthmus

Cafe Assisi
254 W. Gilman St., Madison
* **(608) 255-1816**

This combination art gallery and coffeehouse offers patrons bright-colored armchairs in a well-lighted setting. You can lounge in the large room or find a quieter seat in one of two smaller rooms. Cafe Assisi is known for its great coffee, but don't forget to check out the juice bar. Thursdays is usually open-mike night at Cafe Assisi. The coffeehouse offers a variety of music, including rock and jazz. Regional and national names have appeared here, including memorable performances by Chip Taylor, who wrote "Wild Thing" (performed by The Trogs, Jimi Hendrix and others), and Bernie Larsen, a former member of Melissa Etheridge's band.

**Canterbury
Booksellers Coffeehouse
315 W. Gorham St., Madison
• (608) 258-9911**

Even New Yorkers have been known to say this is the most appealing coffeehouse they've ever been in. This coffeehouse, in the heart of the Canterbury bookstore, has (as you likely guessed) a strong literary bent. In addition to fine coffee, cappuccino and coffee shakes (in regular or flavors like caramel or vanilla), you can dine on salads, sandwiches, pastries and other light fare (see our Restaurants chapter), including vegetarian dinners and fish. You'll often find folk music performed here on Saturday evenings.

East Side

**Mother Fool's Coffeehouse
1101 Williamson St., Madison
• (608) 259-1301**

Mother Fool's combines nontraditional coffeehouse music, such as acoustic rock, worked into a season-long lineup of pop rock, jazz, bluegrass and country. The coffeehouse has put together its own locally distributed CD, "Live at Mother Fool's." Kick back on one of the couches and relax with a mocha espresso.

**Wild Hog in the
Woods Coffeehouse
Wil-Mar Center, 923 Jenifer St., Madison
• (608) 283-3464**

Sip a latte and listen to live entertainment — usually folk music — every Friday at the Wild Hog in the Woods Coffeehouse. There's a $2 cover charge on Fridays. The Wild Hog also produces monthly barn dances with live music and dance instruction.

The Movie Scene: Blockbusters to Budgets

With more than 60 screens in town, you're always close to a movie theater. Most cinemas begin showing their first films of the day between 12:30 and 2:30 PM on weekdays and about 11:30 AM on weekends. Since many of us tend to hit the movies later in the day, however, we've included this section in the Nightlife chapter.

Madison has two major cineplexes, Eastgate and Point cinemas, playing the latest and greatest first-run movies and blockbusters. In addition you'll find several theaters around town — most also playing first-run films, but a few with second-run movies at greatly discounted prices. Parking is not usually a problem at Madison-area theaters as most cinemas have large lots with plenty of free parking. You'll notice, however, that for the Campus and Isthmus theaters, we've added some parking hints.

To find out what's showing at most Madison theaters, call the Marcus Movie Hit Line at (608) 242-2100. Using a touch-tone phone, you'll be able to find out when and where your favorite movies are playing. The recordings also list running times for each movie so you'll know exactly when to pick up the kids if they go to a movie on their own. (Children younger than 6 are not admitted to movies with R ratings, even when accompanied by their parents.) You also can find daily movie listings in *The Capital Times* and *Wisconsin State Journal*. The usual ticket prices for first-run films are between $6 and $7; exceptions are noted.

Isthmus

**Orpheum Theatre
216 State St., Madison • (608) 255-6005**

This old-fashioned movie theater takes you back to the days when parents jammed all the kids into the family's only car and went to see a movie that Dad had picked out. Those days are gone now, for most of us. But this elegant theater is well worth a visit. The Orpheum plays first-run films on its two screens.

From the Beltline, take Park Street north to W. Washington Avenue. As you travel around the Capitol Square, you will see several city parking ramps. The Orpheum is just two blocks down from the Capitol building on State Street.

Majestic Theater
115 King St., Madison • (608) 255-6698

The oldest, continually operating theater in Madison (built in 1906), the Majestic also has the distinction of having the longest-running cult film in town. You can view the *Rocky Horror Picture Show* every Saturday at midnight. The Majestic has a single screen and typically shows independent and foreign films.

From the Beltline, take Park Street north to W. Washington Avenue. As you travel around the Capitol Square toward King Street, you will see several municipal parking ramps. Shows before 6 PM cost $4.50 per ticket; after 6 PM, $6.50.

Campus

Carmike Cinemas University Square Four
62 University Square Mall, Madison • (608) 257-7200

This campus theater caters to the taste of the college crowd on four screens playing either in Dolby stereo or in digital sound. This is a good place to see a thriller because if you scream, you're unlikely to be noticed.

From the Beltline, take the Park Street Exit to Johnson Street, then turn right. There's a small parking lot a half-block up on the left (next to the theater), or if you continue to the end of the block, you'll see a large parking ramp.

West Side

Point Cinemas
7825 Big Sky Dr., Madison • (608) 833-3980

At Point Cinemas, near the Beltline and Mineral Point Road, you'll find the latest in movie releases and first-run films. With 15 screens, you're likely to find a film of interest. Ticket prices are discounted for shows that begin before 5:30 PM, for children 12 and younger and for senior citizens. Children younger than 6 are not admitted to R-rated films. To find out which movies are playing, call the Marcus Theater Hit Line, (608) 242-2100.

West Towne Cinemas
7309 West Towne Way, Madison • (608) 833-3000

This three-screen theater was the only theater on the far West Side until the major cineplex on Mineral Point Road opened. West Towne Cinemas shows first-run films. Take the Gammon Road Exit off the West Beltline.

Westgate Cinemas
340 Westgate Mall, Whitney Way, Madison • (608) 271-4033

Westgate Cinemas offers three movie choices each night. Westgate recently drew attention for its 6½-month run of *The English Patient*, an unprecedented string of showings in local years among Madison theaters.

Market Square Theatres
6604 Odana Rd., Madison • (608) 833-1500

A favorite with families and college students, this budget theater shows second-run films on seven screens. Tickets cost just $1.75 each at all times for all ages. From the West Beltline, take the Whitney Way Exit north. The first light is Odana Road; turn left. You soon will see Market Square Theater on your right, shortly before the intersection with Yellowstone Drive.

Hilldale Theatre
Hilldale Shopping Center, 702 N. Midvale Blvd., Madison • (608) 238-0206

Although this older theater has just two screens, you're likely to find that at least one screen is reserved for a special first-run film engagement. To reach the theater, take the Midvale Boulevard Exit from the West Beltline and continue north until you see Hilldale Shopping Center on your left. The theater is behind the Sentry Foods Grocery

Store at the end of the mall closest to University Avenue.

South Towne Cinemas
South Towne Mall, 2305 W. Broadway, Madison • (608) 223-3456

First-run films at value prices: That's the motto at South Towne Cinema. Adults can attend matinees for just $3.50 each. Evening-show adult tickets are $5. Children and senior citizens get into all shows for $2.50 each. South Towne offers free refills on any size soft drink or popcorn. The theater has five screens.

You can reach South Towne Mall from the Beltline. Take the South Towne Drive Exit and travel north around a curve; you'll see the mall on your right.

East Side

Budget Cinemas
96 East Towne Mall, Madison • (608) 241-5959

With six screens to choose from and $1.75 movie tickets, this is a popular spot for East Side youth and budget-minded families. You'll find second-run films of all types. The theater is on the south end of the mall, just off E. Washington Avenue, about a mile from Interstate 90/94.

Eastgate Cinema
5202 High Crossing Blvd., Madison • (608) 242-2119

Take the Sun Prairie Exit (U.S. Highway 151) off Interstate 90/94, then turn right on Nelson Road to reach Eastgate Cinema. The popular theater usually has 14 films playing on any given night. Blockbusters usually run on two screens at staggered starting times. Pick a show that starts before 5:30 PM and you can get in for the discounted price of $4.50.

Outlying Area

Cinema Cafe
124 W. Main St., Stoughton • (608) 873-7484

If you're thinking about pizza and a movie, why not combine the two? Cinema Cafe has all types of Italian and American food (see our Restaurants chapter). You can call ahead and order your food so it arrives precisely when you want it — either before the movie, during the previews or in the midst of the movie itself. Cinema Cafe does not have traditional theater-style seating, but rather you sit at tables facing the screen. The theater pulls in first-run films and has three screens. Seniors and children (10 and younger) get in for $2 at any time of day. Before 6 PM, older youth and adults pay $2 a ticket; after 6 PM, adult tickets increase to $4 each.

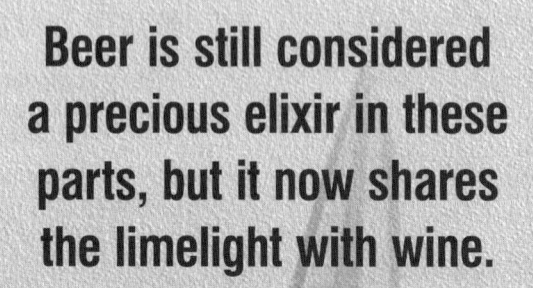

Beer is still considered a precious elixir in these parts, but it now shares the limelight with wine.

Brewpubs, Wine Bars and Cigar Bars

On the day prohibition ended in 1933, a crowd of 5,000 ecstatic people mobbed the street outside the Fauerbach Brewery on Madison's East Side, waiting for the beer barrels to start rolling once more. A lot of them were German, and they led the crowd in rousing beer hall songs. Others just cheered, and a few reportedly wept with joy. Wisconsin is as well known for its beer as its cheese.

Beer is still considered a precious elixir in these parts, but it now shares the limelight with wine.

Microbreweries, brewpubs, wine bars and cigar bars are opening in record numbers across the country, and Madison is no exception. Such specialty bars pride themselves on being different, on offering patrons choices they can't find anywhere else. Besides beverages, these establishments often offer menus that go well beyond the ordinary, giving diners a chance to try new things.

Of all Madison's specialty bars, brewpubs are probably the most family-oriented. Under Wisconsin law — unlike in some other states — it is permissible for children to be in bars when accompanied by their parents or legal guardians. That surprises — even shocks — some out-of-staters. But not to worry, our laws do not mean bars are the state's primary childcare establishments; they are not. The state legislature expects parents to use common sense, and peer pressure helps ensure that parents do not stay at the well overly long or neglect their children while imbibing.

The state also has strict drunk driving laws (see our Nightlife chapter) that encourage use of designated drivers. (Although it's legal, you probably don't want to take kids to the wine bars or cigar bars; these establishments cater almost exclusively to an adult crowd.)

A word on parking: After 5 PM, parking in downtown Madison is usually easy to find within two to three blocks of your destination. The city has 13 major parking ramps, and on-street metered parking is also available. Parking rates vary between 25¢ and 75¢ an hour, but some lots charge a flat rate of $1 for evening parking and weekend all-day parking. On weekdays before 5 PM, you'll have to look a little harder for a space, often pay a little more and walk a little farther. Specialty bars away from the city's hub offer lots with free parking. (Because many brewpubs and wine bars offer full menus, you'll also find many of these popular watering holes cross-referenced under appropriate headings in the Restaurants chapter.)

Brewpubs

Beer might be the brew that made Milwaukee famous, but some folks a little farther west — in Madison — are unleashing their passions for award-winning brew-making and gaining some flattering recognition. In a state where the beer-consumption rate is 415 beers per adult per year, you might guess that some Wisconsinites take their beer seriously. Even if you don't know your barley from your hops, you can have fun exploring one of Madison's friendly brewpubs. And you don't have to drink alcohol to have a good time. Several brewpubs produce their own versions of root beer, ginger ale and other soda.

If you're new to beer tasting, you'll find much of the same protocol for wine tasting holds true: You start with the pales and work up to the darks. Experts suggest you cleanse your palate with water and unsalted pretzels between samples.

Although Madison came into the brewpub scene later than some cities, residents are fast making up for their past inattention.

Isthmus

Angelic Brewing Company
322 W. Johnson St., Madison
- **(608) 257-2707**

Angelic won top national honors in 1996 for its Bacchanal Blonde Ale, a very light, golden ale, and its seasonal brew, Sinner's Stout, a mix of seven different malts. The blonde ale is Angelic's top-selling libation, brewed under the watchful eyes of head brew master Dean Coffey.

Angelic patrons unwind in an airy, spacious dining room resplendent with brass rails and other accents. You can people-watch from the bar, relax in a comfy booth, challenge a friend to a game of pool or enjoy a relaxing meal with friends and family. The menu at Angelic offers about eight types of pasta, several salads, a heavenly host of sandwiches and the usual hearty fare such as steaks and barbecue ribs. Sandwiches are priced in the $5 to $7 range. Dinners start at about $9. Although Angelic doesn't provide a kids' menu, the wait staff honors requests for sharing. Individual specialty pizzas, including "plain cheese," also present a happy choice for picky, young eaters.

The Great Dane Pub and Brewing Co.
123 E. Doty St., Madison
- **(608) 284-0000**

The Great Dane Pub and Brewing Company, housed in Madison's historic Fess Hotel (just off the Capitol Square), created Peck's Pilsner, the winner of a bronze medal at the 1996 Great American Beer Festival. The American Pale Ale is a crowd-pleaser at the Great Dane, which has also earned acclaim for its spiced pumpkin and nut brown ales.

The Great Dane is the largest — and probably the most colorful — of Madison's brewpubs; it has been described as four bars in one. Whether you're looking for a forum for casual dining with friends and family in a nonsmoking atmosphere, want to play billiards, yearn to sit back on a leather couch and puff on a select cigar, or just want to relax and grab a bite in the basement tavern, you will likely find the setting here to match your mood.

Chefs serve up a diverse menu, including some very popular vegetarian entrees and sides. For a tasty starter, try the Bruschetta Lombardi, made from sourdough bread and topped with veggies, basil and cheese. Hot and cold sandwiches are less than $6. Diners can choose from six salads including the delectable chicken salad Taliesin, named after Frank Lloyd Wright's home. Primary fare such as a Wisconsin twist on an all-time pub favorite — brats and mash — starts at $5.50. An entire rack of Dr. Tom's Soul Good Ribs costs $12.95. The Great Dane's children's menu offers fish, nachos, burgers, brats, chicken and pizza. Tour the brewery on Saturdays, from 1 to 4 PM, to find out the secrets of Great Dane brewing.

Essen Haus
514 E. Wilson St., Madison
- **(608) 255-4674**

Although it's not actually a brewpub, we had to include the Essen Haus here as it is widely recognized as the place in Madison to go for beer, due to its huge inventory. Essen Haus has the distinction of being the largest seller of German tap beers in the United States as well as home to an extensive menu of German food (see our Restaurants and Nightlife chapters). Fourteen German beers are on tap, or you can choose from 270 imports, all served in an Old World atmosphere where you can drink your beer from a glass boot or authentic German Stein to live oompah music. Closed Mondays, Essen House opens at 3 PM Tuesday through Sunday. The bar sponsors a very popular midsummer beer-tasting fest.

---

www.insiders.com

See this and many other **Insiders' Guide®** destinations online — in their entirety.

Visit us today!

BREW PUBS, WINE BARS AND CIGAR BARS • 107

The New Glarus Brewery offers a lineup of award-winning beers.

West Side

J.T. Whitney's Brewpub and Eatery
674 S. Whitney Way, Madison
• (608) 274-1776

J.T. Whitney's, found on Madison's near West, offers some traditional, but not typical, pub favorites. Here you can find a Scotch egg — a hard-boiled concoction, layered with sausage and breading, the tasty, albeit caloric, treat your Scottish grand mum would serve up (if you had one). J.T.'s "ugly potatoes" are a welcome respite from french fries; the baby red potatoes are mashed and mixed with onions, cheese and butter. It's rich enough to share. Some other specialties include the jerk chicken, J.T.'s distinctive raspberry ribs and the smoked rainbow trout. Dinners range from $7.95 for the Friday fish fry to $15.95 for surf and turf (three beer-battered shrimp and a filet). If you're desperately seeking a really good cheeseburger, then we dare you to splurge on the Cheesehead Burger — topped with cheddar, Swiss, mozzarella and pepper jack. You can dress up your burger with fried onions, sauerkraut, sauteed mushrooms or green peppers, bacon and Cajun spices.

J.T.'s also offers a variety of healthy salads that you can top with your choice of grilled chicken, tuna steak, shrimp or tenderloin. For lunch, the chef serves up four light-fare specials, three of which are priced at less than $4.

At barside or your table, if you are 21 or older, you can sample some of brew master Richard Becker's latest accomplishments, including Frozen Tundra Playoff Ale, which graced J.T. Whitney's rails just before the Green Bay Packers won the Super Bowl. J.T.'s classic German-style wheat beer, Heartland Weiss, is a flavorful favorite. Badger fans can sample J.T.'s Badger Red Ale, flavored with caramel and honey. J.T.'s offers four standard brews and has four seasonal ones on tap.

Outlying Area

Capital Brewery and Beer Garden
7734 Terrace Ave., Middleton
• (608) 836-7100

Considered one of the Midwest's finest microbreweries, Capital Brewery produces about 13,500 barrels annually, distributed in nine states. Brewmaster Kirby Nelson performs his magic in a former egg-processing plant that boasts walls up to 2 feet thick. Capital Brewery currently produces 13 flavorful beers — seven regular and six seasonal — under the Garten Brau label. Garten Brau beers have won numerous regional and national awards. Summer tours begin at 3:30 PM Wednesday through Friday and at 1 and 2:30 PM on Saturday. The outdoor Bier Garten is open Fridays from 4 to 8 PM and Saturdays from noon to 4 PM. Off-season tours are scheduled at 1 and 2:30 PM on Saturdays. You may sample some of the beers at the tour's end and visit the brewery's gift shop.

Wine Bars

The welcome reports on wine's health benefits have made it a popular choice for drinkers. Wine tastings have become regular events in Madison bars, restaurants and even liquor stores. You won't have to look too hard to find someone in Madison who will wax poetic about the raptures of having a glass of port wine in one hand and a hunk of Swiss chocolate in the other.

Isthmus

The Opera House
117 Martin Luther King Blvd., Madison
- **(608) 284-VINO**

The bartender here will lead you through a tasting of five wines taken from one of Madison's largest collections. Choose from approximately 100 foreign and domestic whites and reds.

The Opera House, named after Madison's first theater and opera house, reprints its wine list every two months to feature a particular grape or region. Beer lovers are not left out in the cold at this wine bar. Patrons, many of whom are professionals working in or near the State Capitol, find a small but significant collection of microbrews and imports.

The Opera House offers upscale, airy surroundings with white-aproned wait staff anticipating your desires. Alaskan halibut, salmon, walleye and trout tempt the taste buds of fish aficionados, while landlubbers feast on chicken, lamb and Angus beef dishes or sweet-potato strudel. Entrees range from $14.75 to $19.95. Lighter appetites may dine on "small courses" — salads, Spanish tapas including many vegetarian delights (the things they do with squash and beets our moms never knew) and other tasty sides — accented, of course, by a favorite libation.

The Opera House is open daily for lunch and dinner and serves a late-night light menu until 11:30 PM on weekends.

Cafe Montmartre
127 E. Mifflin St., Madison
- **(608) 255-5900**

If you love wine and oysters, this is the place for you. Blue points on the half-shell (a dozen for $13.50) are served Thursday through Saturday in this dimly lit wine bar in one of Madison's historic buildings.

Cafe Montmartre attracts a lively, young crowd. The bar is open for lunch and dinner. Here you will find a distinctive selection of domestic and foreign wines and champagnes — from California and Washington State favorites to a 1990 Chateau Palmer Bordeaux. Add to this top-shelf cognacs, Scotches and whiskeys, and most customers find Cafe Montmartre has what they need

---

INSIDERS' TIP

In the continuing rush to quench the microbrew-drinking public's thirst for new products, local brewers are turning to fruit. Cherries, raspberries, blueberries, peaches, elderberries and apples are pushing the boundaries of traditional beer-making, where hops was once the most popular beer flavoring. Among the local brews to win international honors is the New Glarus Brewing Co.'s cherry-flavored Belgian Red.

The Cheese Stands Alone

In Wisconsin, cheese isn't just a passion, it's a necessity. Take our word for it: Cheese is the perfect accompaniment to either a microbrew or special glass of wine.

Walk into any grocery store in these parts, and you're apt to come across cooler after cooler of cheese, glorious cheese. There's baby Swiss, cheddar, Colby, gorgonzola, gouda, gruyere, mozzarella, provolone, Muenster, Jack, Havarti dill . . . the list goes on and on. You could spend a lifetime becoming a cheese expert or just cherrypick your way through the dairy cases.

Wisconsin is the world's leading producer of cheese. The state's 27,000 milk-producing dairy farms generate more than 2 billion pounds of cheese annually, according to the state's Milk Marketing Board. Wisconsin cheesemakers produce an amazing 300-plus varieties, types and styles of cheese — far more than any other state. It's no wonder, then, that when Wisconsin children learn their ABCs, it's "American," "Brick" and "Cheddar."

In the Madison area, you'll find two major employers and cheese producers — the Wisconsin Cheeseman, in Sun Prairie, and Swiss Colony, in Madison and Monroe. Cheese production is an art, like fine winemaking or brewing. If you get a chance, stop off at one of the state's many cheese factories to get a firsthand peek at the process. Then nibble on a cheese curd, a uniquely Wisconsin delicacy, formed as part of the cheesemaking process. Raw curds, available by the bag, provide a burst of cheddar coupled with a slightly rubbery texture. Fried cheese curds are frequently listed in the appetizer section of restaurant menus and compete with french fries as a side for grilled sandwiches.

Wisconsin's record for excellence in cheesemaking goes way back. A little-known fact is that Colby cheese was invented in the Wisconsin town of Colby in 1874. Wisconsin is the only U.S. producer of Limburger cheese — one of the world's most fragrant (in polite terms) cheeses. Even as you read this book, new strides are being made in dairy research. Carol Cehn, a UW-Madison researcher, recently announced development of a new "pizza cheese" that won't

— continued on next page

Cheesehead wannabes can't get enough of the real thing.

blister, burn or turn to greasy oil when it gets hot. Low-fat cheeses are fast becoming a standard on the food market.

If you're visiting Madison from a cheese-challenged state, don't go home without sampling some of our cheese delights. Madison has an absolute plethora of delicious cheeses. Stop in at one of our many grocery stores or visit the following: **Bavaria Sausage Kitchen Inc.**, 6317 Nesbitt Road, (800) 733-6695; **Ehlenbach's Cheese Chalet**, 4879 County Highway V, De Forest, 846-4791; **House of Wisconsin**, 107 State Street, 255-5204; or the **Wine & Hop Shop**, 434 State Street, 257-0099.

---

to be satisfied. Call ahead for information on live jazz performances.

The popular wine bar serves up seven specialty pizzas and a variety of salads and sandwiches on a menu that tops out at $10 (oysters aside). It can be a challenge to find a seat at Cafe Montmartre during peak times on Friday and Saturday nights.

Campus

Porta's Wine Cellar
425 N. Francis St., Madison
• **(608) 256-3186**

This underground wine bar boasts a rustic red-brick interior and laid-back atmosphere. There's even a big leather couch to sprawl on. The Wine Cellar offers a selection of more than 100 wines. Eighteen beers — mostly microbrews — are on tap. Barkeeps are eager to introduce you to the finer points of wine tasting. You may sample six wines for $10 from the featured vineyard of the week. Pizzas and other homemade Italian-style appetizers are available in the Wine Cellar, cooked upstairs in Madison's acclaimed Porta Bella restaurant. Customers may choose a table or settle themselves on couches in an intimate alcove.

Outlying Area

La Paella
2784 S. Fish Hatchery Rd., Fitchburg
• **(608) 273-2666**

At La Paella, you'll discover a wine bar set within one of the city's best Mediterranean restaurants. You can taste wines to your heart's content at La Paella, where 40-some labels are lined up nightly for your inspection. Tasting is free, and you may purchase bottles on site to take home. While at the wine bar, you can also mix and match Spanish appetizers (or tapas); 15 hot and 15 cold tapas are available for about $5 each. Several feature seafood including squid and octopus. The grilled salmon is excellent and a great value at $4.95. (Read more about La Paella in our Restaurants chapter.)

Cigar Bars

For the most part, smoking is considered politically incorrect in health-conscious Madison. Those attitudes relax as you move out of the city's hub and closer to farmlands, where tobacco is still, for some, a significant cash crop. Smoking is prohibited in virtually all restaurants and public buildings in Madison.

Bars and taverns, however, have gained exception to this restriction. In some places, smoking is not only accepted, it's encouraged. Read on.

Isthmus

Maduro
117 E. Main St., Madison
• **(608) 294-9371**

This gorgeous cigar bar has a large selection of premium smokes and libations. And for further indulgence, there are upscale appetizers and desserts. You can assemble a cheese plate of intriguing imported and domestic cheeses, which come with slices of French and rye bread, or pesto chevre. You can wash it down with a fine martini, single-malt Scotches, wines by the glass, cordials, dessert wines and liqueurs or vanilla-spiked Spanish liqueur. Not enough sugar? Try the flourless chocolate cake with creme anglaise. Want to pretend you're being health conscious? Try the seasonal fruits poached in Riesling, and topped with creme fraiche. The ventilation is good enough to leave you smelling as good as when you arrived, so you can feel free to linger on a comfortable leather couch by the sofa, or around one of the dozen or so tables.

The Madison Cigar Bar
222 E. Olin Ave., Madison
- **(608) 256-9430**

If you're a cigar buff planning an excursion to the Dane County Coliseum, you'll want to stop at the nearby Madison Cigar Bar. This cigar bar was recently opened at an established tavern site by the owner of a local tavern chain, Jingles. Weeknights tend to be quiet, but activity increases by Thursday evening. The bar is closed Sundays and Mondays.

The Madison Cigar Bar offers a good selection of hand-rolled smokes, for about $6 to $10 each, from the humidor behind the bar. The club also participates in a Cigar of the Month Club, giving you a chance to discover some new favorites. The cigar bar's nostalgic decor dates to a time when rumble seats were a common option in automobiles. In the 1930s, the brick building was a stopover for Chicago mobsters passing through the area.

The Madison Cigar Bar offers a good supply of top-shelf cognacs, Scotches and liqueurs. An extensive beer menu features local and regional microbrews, popular domestics and seven popular imports. In the back room, you will find darts and a pool table. The front lounge has a small, but well-stocked bar, several tables and an intimate alcove.

The Great Dane Pub and Brewing Co.
123 E. Doty St., Madison
- **(608) 284-0000**

Cigar enthusiasts can choose from one of more than 20 styles of smokes housed in the Great Dane's humidor (to the left of the main entrance), then sink into one of the pub's comfy leather couches to savor and enjoy it. Cigars are permitted in many areas of the Great Dane, including the basement tavern, but are barred from the main restaurant and bar. (See the previous "Brewpubs" section for more details about The Great Dane.)

Staying Power

Whether it's the 360 beautiful guest rooms,
the award-winning restaurants, live entertainment

playing

nightly, an elegant new ballroom,
over 25,000 sq. ft. of meeting space

or working

out in our fitness center and pool –
you'll find our true hallmark to be premiere service and hospitality.
The Madison Concourse Hotel – within easy walking distance
of the campus, lakes, State Street, shopping,
restaurants, arts, theatre and

Capitol.

THE MADISON CONCOURSE HOTEL
and Governor's Club

1 West Dayton Street
608-257-6000
TTY: 608-257-2980

Madison, WI 53703
800-356-8293
www.concoursehotel.com

Hotels and Motels

There may be too much room in Madison's hotel market these days. Its overall room occupancy rate last year was 61.6 percent. Even so, another 327 rooms are expected to be built in the next year or so — and that's before you count the yet-to-be-built Monona Terrace Convention Center hotel and a 150-room DoubleTree Club hotel near the Kohl Center. Madison's hotel industry is going through a boom period of expansion, repositioning and upgrades that echoes changes in the industry nationwide.

What this means for Madison visitors is that you can find some great bargains. The average daily room rate in 1997 was $62.

It also means lodging establishments are vying with each other to provide better service and amenities. Visitors to Madison find themselves indulged. You can find reasonably priced rooms in the city to meet just about any need or desire. Lodging establishments are seeking out niches. Several hotels cater almost exclusively to traveling business professionals, and more of these are scheduled to open in 1998.

Spurred on by the Americans with Disabilities Act, hotels and motels are going further than just making buildings accessible; they're consulting people with disabilities to really identify what it is that make accommodations user-friendly. Most of the properties listed have handicapped access; however, at some sites the number of specially designed rooms are limited. It's probably wise to call in advance to make sure you will find what you need on arrival. (We've listed toll-free numbers whenever possible.)

Most hotels in Madison have reserved about half or more of their rooms for nonsmoking guests. We're beginning to see more "green" rooms, that is, hotel rooms that use low-flow spigots and shower heads, water filters and other environmentally friendly devices.

As more travelers trek across the country with lap-top computers in hand, hotels are meeting the demands of patrons by adding data ports to telephones; several offer 24-hour access to fax machines, PCs, printers and other technology.

Many places accept pets, but some do not. If no information is listed regarding pets, call the motel and ask. Several places have no set policy and allow pets only on a case-by-case basis.

This chapter includes an extensive listing of hotels in the Madison area; however, it is only a partial listing. Each hotel's listing includes a dollar-sign code indicating an average price range for a midweek one-night stay (see the following gray box).

Price-Code Key

The following price code is based on the average room rate for double occupancy during peak season. Please note that prices are subject to change without notice.

$	$50 and less
$$	$50 to $100
$$$	$100 to $150
$$$$	$150 and more

Pricing information contained within this book has been provided by the hotels and may vary. Rates are often higher during peak-demand times such as during UW Badger football games, World Dairy Expo and other events. Prices can drop, however, during off-peak times. Since the hotels in the city tend to be clumped together, once you identify the part of the city you'd like to stay in, it can be to your advantage to shop around and find the best deal for you. Many hotels offer discounts for government employees, seniors and business travelers and reduced room rates for those belonging to AARP, AAA and other groups.

All hotels accept major credit cards unless otherwise noted. Room taxes within the city of Madison average 13 percent (including city sales tax).

We've expanded our geographical headings in this chapter to include "South Side" and "Southeast," so you can have a clear picture as to where each hotel is located and what attractions are within easy access before you make reservations.

Isthmus

Best Western Inn on the Park
$$$ • 22 S. Carroll St., Madison
• (608) 257-8811, (800) 279-8811

Downtown is the place to be in Madison if you are looking for unique restaurants and shopping. The Inn on the Park is one of Madison's top-rated hotels in terms of amenities, service and location. At the Best Western Inn on the Park, across the street from the Wisconsin Capitol, guests can stroll past colorful gardens and beautiful fountains in the summer months and be the first ones to sample goodies at the Saturday morning Farmers' Markets. Year round, this inn provides easy access to State Street, the museum mile, Downtown businesses and a variety of casual and fine dining. The Top of the Park restaurant is a favorite setting for a multitude of celebrations; it's a place where legislators and lobbyists come to meet and greet.

The Inn on the Park has 213 fully appointed rooms (including suites), two lounges and an indoor pool. Eighteen meeting rooms provide accommodations for numerous conferences and receptions. Valet parking and airport and campus shuttle service help ease the transportation concerns that are sometimes associated with the Downtown.

The Edgewater Hotel
$$$ • 666 Wisconsin Ave., Madison
• (608) 256-9071, (800) 528-1234

Treat yourself to luxury lodging on Lake Mendota. The Edgewater has enjoyed a long reputation for excellence. Guests are pampered with limousine service from the airport, indoor parking, health-club passes, voice mail and nightly turndown. In summer months, enjoy watching the lake and the many beautiful sailboats on it from your room. Or better yet, order a cool drink from the cabana crew on the pier, then sit back and savor a splendid Lake Mendota sunset.

The Edgewater offers fine dining in a formal setting in its Admiralty Room. The hotel also provides a referral service for child care.

The Edgewater accommodates all types of business meetings and offers full-service conference facilities for up to 900.

The Madison Concourse Hotel and Governor's Club
$$$ • 1 W. Dayton St., Madison
• (608) 257-6000, (800) 356-8293

Madison's acclaimed Concourse Hotel offers 360 guest rooms, live nightly entertainment (including a jazz bar) and prime dining, all in the heart of the city. Just a block off the Capitol Square and State Street, the hotel places guests within easy walking distance of the Civic Center, museums, shopping and the lakes. Restaurants in the Concourse are top-notch; the extensive midday soup and salad bar is one of the best deals on our "Capitol Hill." The Concourse added a new pool and fitness center to the hotel in 1996, and many rooms and common areas, such as the hallways, have recently been refurbished.

The exclusive Governor's Club provides a great way for business professionals and others to get away from it all and bask in the comforts of thoughtful concierge service, terry-cloth robes and turndown service. Complimentary cocktails, delectable appetizers and breakfast are served in the Governor's Club's comfortable private lounge.

The Concourse has more than 25,000 square feet of meeting space and is the frequent choice for conventions, receptions and meetings.

Mansion Hill Inn

Elegance abounds in our eleven exquisite rooms. In-room marble fireplaces, sumptuous baths with whirlpool tubs and complimentary breakfast in your room are just a few of the luxurious amenities you'll enjoy.

Madison's only
Four Diamond
accommodations.

Four Diamond Award

Please write or call for a brochure.
424 N. Pinckney St., Madison, WI 53703
1-800-798-9070 • Fax (608) 255-2217
www.mansionhillinn.com

Campus

Best Western Inntowner
$$ • 2424 University Ave., Madison
• (608) 233-8778, (800) 528-1234

Whether you're looking for a place to set up a banquet or just a quiet, comfortable spot to lay your head, this upscale, full-service Best Western hotel is ready to heed your call with 180 guest rooms (including 19 special-needs rooms), a pool, whirlpool and fitness center. You can dine in Francie's Restaurant on site or venture to one of several nearby eating establishments. The four-story Inntowner is close to UW Hospital and Clinics, the UW campus and Camp Randall Stadium, and it's a quick cab ride to State Street or Hilldale Shopping Center. Shuttle service is available to the airport, hospitals and the campus. Meeting facilities serve up to 275. Pets are not allowed.

Howard Johnson Plaza Hotel
$$ • 525 W. Johnson St., Madison
• (608) 251-5511, (800) GO-HOJO

This hotel offers one of the most convenient locations for visitors to the UW-Madison campus. It's just blocks from Memorial Union, University Square shopping and cinemas, along with State Street shopping and dining. A restaurant is available on site. Guests can relax in the lounge, whirlpool and heated pool or watch ESPN or HBO. Most rooms feature queen-size beds, but luxury suites are available. The hotel's free

---

INSIDERS' TIP

One of the best places to watch the sunset with a cocktail is the pier at the Edgewater Hotel.

parking is definitely an asset in this part of the city. Howard Johnson Plaza Hotel also offers complimentary shuttle service based on availability. Pets are not accepted.

Ivy Inn
$$ • 2355 University Ave., Madison • (608) 233-9717

This unique Colonial country inn has a full-service restaurant. A welcoming fire often greets guests as they enter the lobby of the Ivy Inn. Its 57 guest rooms are elegant and spacious, tastefully decorated in hunter green with floral accents. You can choose from double, queen or king beds; suites with living rooms also are available. Free shuttle service is provided to the nearby UW Hospital and Clinics and UW campus.

Monthly and weekly rates are options if you're planning an extended stay. The restaurant at the Ivy Inn is best known for its fascinating brunches. Two Sundays a month it serves a vegetarian brunch, which alternates with "Passport" brunches that emphasize a foreign cuisine (see our Restaurants chapter).

Madison Inn
$$ • 601 Langdon St., Madison • (608) 257-4391

Smack-dab in the Downtown on the campus's famed fraternity row, this hotel is just a stone's skip from Lake Mendota walkways, bike paths and beaches. An on-site restaurant and lounge serves sandwiches, or guests may walk to nearby State Street to sample some of Madison's best dining. Rooms at the Madison Inn come in two sizes. You can choose a smaller room with one double bed or a larger guest room (400 square feet) with a king-size bed, two queens or a queen-size bed and a sofa. Rooms are decorated in blue with carpeting to match and floral bedspreads.

University Inn Hotel
$$ • 441 N. Frances St., Madison • (608) 257-4881, (800) 279-4881

You're within walking distance of almost every point on the UW-Madison campus if you stay at this hotel, the only one with side windows on colorful State Street. Guests can use the fitness center at an associate hotel seven blocks away or just spend time exploring the many wonders of State Street, the UW Memorial Union, museums, ethnic restaurants and nightlife.

West Side

Best Western West Towne Suites
$$ • 650 Grand Canyon Dr., Madison • (608) 833-4200

After a night in one of this hotel's comfortable suites, enjoy a complimentary cooked-to-order breakfast. Guests have quick access to shopping, restaurants and movies from this far West Side location. The hotel's 101 spacious rooms have sofas, refrigerators and tables to accommodate extended stays. Pets are allowed in guest rooms.

Budgetel Inn — BudgetDome
$$ • 8102 Excelsior Dr., Madison • (608) 831-7711

After enjoying a complimentary breakfast, guests can work it all off in the hotel's beautiful dome complete with indoor pool, whirlpool, game room, sauna and fitness center. The Budgetel allows pets and has 130 well-kept rooms, many with recliners. Two-room suites and whirlpool suites are available. The hotel also has a nice meeting room with lots of natural light that would be highly suitable for board- and executive-style meetings. Guests can call for the free airport shuttle.

Comfort Suites
$$ • 1253 John Q. Hammons Dr., Madison • (608) 836-3033

This 95-room, all-suite hotel on the city's far West Side offers friendly staff, a daily newspaper, complimentary continental breakfasts and cocktails. Bring the pets 'cause the staff says, "Pets are family." Human guests can unwind in the huge pool, whirlpool, fitness center or game room after a tough day of traveling, work or sightseeing. Each suite includes a microwave, refrigerator and pullout sofa. Ten two-story suites with double whirlpools are available. Com-

RAMADA INN *I-90*
CAPITOL CONFERENCE CENTER

We Have It All

- Golf packages
  (minutes away from 5 golf courses)
- 187 comfortable guest rooms
- Suites... whirlpool, fireplace
- Large indoor pool & sauna
- Computer, copier & fax services
- 8 miles from downtown
- Banquet/meeting facilities for up to 950 people
- Casual dining at *Suzan's* Restaurant

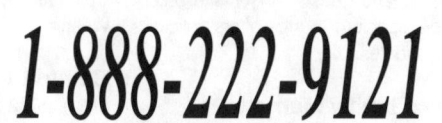

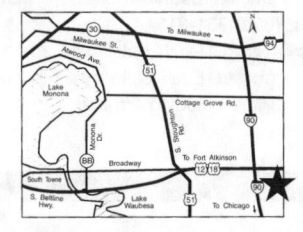

◆ ◆ ◆

1-888-222-9121

Interstate 90 • Exit 142B
3902 Evan Acres Rd.
Madison, WI 53704

fort Suites offers conference facilities for up to 100.

Hampton Inn
$$ • 516 Grand Canyon Dr., Madison
• (608) 833-3511, (800) HAMPTON

This Hampton Inn, just off the west Beltline, provides guests easy access to West Towne Mall, specialty shopping and myriad restaurants. Hotel amenities include an indoor pool, whirlpool and fitness room. The Hampton Inn unconditionally guarantees your satisfaction. Guests may choose from 45 doubles, 44 kings, 18 king rooms with sofa sleepers, seven specially equipped handicapped-accessible rooms and one hospitality suite. Some rooms have personal fitness equipment, and each room has an iron and ironing board. You can't bring your pet, but you can sleep under a down comforter.

Radisson Inn
$$$ • 517 Grand Canyon Dr., Madison
• (608) 833-0100, (800) 333-3333

With 153 guest rooms and suites, this Radisson has recently undergone a major renovation. The hotel now has 62 "business class" rooms with recliners, coffee makers, irons/boards, hair dryers and data ports. Hotel patrons can't bring their pets, but they can receive a daily discount at a nearby fitness center. The hotel has two- and three-room suites and 8,100 square feet of banquet facilities for up to 250 guests. An on-site eatery with a large, spacious lounge offers delicious American favorites.

Residence Inn by Marriott
$$ • 501 D'Onofrio Dr., Madison
• (608) 833-8333, (800) 331-3131

The Residence Inn is an all-suite hotel that caters to long-term guests. Each suite has complete kitchen facilities including a microwave and dishware. Rates are based on length of stay. The hotel has an outdoor pool, small fitness center and on-site washer and dryer. Guests are treated to a complimentary continental breakfast daily and light dinner Monday through Thursday. Pets are allowed with damage deposits.

Road Star
$ • 6900 Seybold Rd., Madison
• (608) 274-6900, (800) 445-4667

The Road Star, just off the Beltline (Wis. highways 12 and 18) at the Gammon Road Exit, is a clean, budget-priced motel with 95 rooms. About half the rooms have data ports. The Road Star serves a complimentary continental breakfast. The inn is close to grocery shopping, fast-food restaurants and West Towne Mall. Pets are allowed, but you will need to put down a $50 refundable deposit.

East Side

Budget Host Aloha Inn
$ • 3177 E. Washington Ave., Madison
• (608) 249-7667, (800) 825-6420

From the outside, it might not look like you're in Hawaii, but if you close your eyes in this motel's quiet, secluded whirlpool, you can imagine you're in paradise. The Aloha Inn has 39 clean, comfortable rooms — many with a warm, rustic look — and one suite. The Inn, which also has a pool, is about halfway up E. Washington Avenue toward the Capitol.

Comfort Inn
$$$ • 4822 E. Washington Ave., Madison
• (608) 244-6265, (800) 228-5150

A deluxe continental breakfast buffet, in-room movies, an indoor pool and whirlpool, a fitness center and guest laundry facilities are among the "comforts" you will find to enhance

---

INSIDERS' TIP

The best view of the dome of the Capitol is from the bar and restaurant at the Best Western Inn on the Park, on the Capitol Square. It's at its most spectacular in winter, when the huge trees around the dome are bare and lights from the Capitol are reflected in the snow.

your stay at this newly remodeled, 152-room Comfort Inn. The motel has 14 whirlpool suites and several special guest rooms outfitted with exercise equipment. Complimentary coffee, tea and fresh fruit are available 24 hours a day. Nearly 80 percent of rooms are for non-smoking guests. No pets are allowed. The hotel is 4 miles from the airport, and free shuttle service is provided.

Crowne Plaza Madison
$$$ • 4402 E. Washington Ave., Madison
• (608) 244-4703

With 227 rooms and suites spread over six floors, this newly renovated Crowne Suite hotel is aiming to draw in those looking for a full-service hotel on the city's East Side. Guest rooms have voice mail, coffee makers, irons/boards, free local calls and newspapers, data ports and turndown service. Twenty-five executive and four whirlpool suites are available. The Crown Club floor offers concierge service, mini-bars and complimentary breakfast and cocktails in a hospitality lounge. The hotel has a full-service restaurant, pub and a lobby bar with a piano player Tuesday through Friday. A gift shop, rental-car service, an indoor pool, whirlpool and exercise area round out guest services. The Crown Plaza has 6,800 square feet of conference space including five meeting rooms and three board-style rooms.

East Towne Suites
$$$ • 4801 Annamark Dr., Madison
• (608) 244-2020, (800) 950-1919

Set amid shopping (East Towne Mall and numerous other stores) and restaurants, East Towne Suites is in a terrific location, just off I-90. The price of each room includes a huge hot breakfast buffet served in the on-site breakfast cafe. Rooms are available in all sizes, with four two-room suites equipped with microwaves and wet bars and three double-size Jacuzzi suites topping the hotel's list of offerings. All rooms have computer lines and mini-refrigerators. East Towne Suites has a fitness center, whirlpool and indoor pool. In summer, guests can compete on the volleyball court.

INSIDERS' TIP

Out of the 570 hotels in the Howard Johnson chain, the Howard Johnson Plaza Hotel, at 525 W. Johnson Street, was chosen as the top in the country in 1998.

Visitors to Madison can stay anywhere from large, upscale hotels to restored, historic bed and breakfast inns.

Econo Lodge
$ • 4726 E. Washington Ave., Madison
• (608) 241-4171, (800) 55-ECONO

Across from East Towne Mall, this 99-room hotel offers easy access to shopping, I-90/94 and many restaurants. Guests receive a complimentary continental breakfast. This hotel offers especially nice "senior friendly" rooms with big-button telephones, large display clocks and grab bars in the bathroom.

Exel Inn
$ • 4202 East Towne Blvd., Madison
• (608) 241-3861, (800) 356-8013

Are you ready to shop until you drop? This Exel Inn is a great place for out-of-town shoppers who want to visit East Towne Mall or any of the many East Side restaurants. This clean and tidy budget hotel, which opened in 1973, does not have a pool, but guests can use the nearby Princeton Club (see our Parks and Recreation chapter) — one of Madison's largest health clubs — for just $2 per person per day. Rooms have TVs with free HBO and ESPN.

Fairfield Inn by Marriott
$ • 4765 Hayes Rd., Madison
• (608) 249-5300, (800) 228-2800

This newer motel has 54 double, 67 king and 13 single rooms. Up to 10 people can meet in the conference room. Guest amenities include an outdoor pool, in-room music system, free local calls and a complimentary continental breakfast. The inn is right off I-90/94 and close to East Towne Mall and restaurants. Seventy percent of rooms are reserved for nonsmoking guests. The Fairfield Inn does not allow pets.

Hampton Inn Madison East
$$ • 4820 Hayes Rd., Madison
• (608) 244-9400

This newly renovated hotel's amenities include an indoor pool, whirlpool, fitness

The Madison Inn

Leave your car in our parking lot
You won't need it here.

Lowell Hall, The Pyle Center, State Street shopping and dining, the Capitol, the Kohl Center, Madison Civic Center and Camp Randall Stadium all within walking distance. Plus a complementary breakfast.

On the UW Campus
601 Langdon Street
Madison, WI 53703
(608) 257-4391 FAX 257-2832
E-mail: madisoninn@travelbase.com
Website: www.travelbase.com/destinations/madison/madison-inn

---

center, continental breakfast buffet, dry cleaning service, pay movies, a small meeting room and Nintendo. As is this chain's policy, your 100 percent satisfaction is guaranteed. Numerous restaurants are in the vicinity. Three-quarters of the rooms are reserved for nonsmoking guests, and pets are not allowed.

Holiday Inn-Madison East
$$ • 3841 E. Washington Ave., Madison
• (608) 244-2481

This hotel recently changed hands and underwent an $8.5 million face-lift. The 197-room full-service hotel reopened in June 1998. The former Ramada Limited is a full-service, mid-tier hotel — more than a Holiday Inn Express but without all the amenities of a Crowne Plaza (Holiday Inn's first-class line of hotels). It has a 60-foot-by-120-foot indoor pool that is the largest hotel pool in Madison. The pool is adjacent to a courtyard in the middle of the hotel, and a game room adjoins the pool. A fitness center is next to the game room.

The complex also includes the Northwoods Bar and Grill, which serves three meals a day. All the guest rooms have been completely redone and have coffee makers, hair dryers and data port access for computers. Meeting rooms accommodate up to 250 people.

Motel 6
$ • 1754 Thierer Rd., Madison
• (608) 241-8101, (800) 466-8356

This 91-unit budget property offers quick access to I-90/94 and shopping and is about 10 minutes from the Capitol Square and State Street. The hotel has air-conditioned rooms, an indoor pool, free local calls, HBO and ESPN and complimentary morning coffee. One small pet is allowed per room, but you cannot leave it unattended.

Residence Inn by Marriott
$$$ • 4862 Hayes Rd., Madison
• (608) 244-5047, (800) 331-3131

The Residence Inn by Marriott gives you all the comforts of home to help make your extended stay in Madison memorable and comfortable. The average guest stay here is 28 days. Choose one of 66 suites as your home base. Each suite comes equipped with a full-size refrigerator, microwave (even microwave popcorn), coffee maker, stove and oven. The staff will even fill your grocery order, so when you arrive back at your suite, you'll be able to prepare your favorite meals. If you don't want to cook, you may partake of the complimentary continental breakfast and hospitality-hour appetizers. Several restaurants are nearby, offering diverse dining choices.

For recreation, you can use the exercise room, heated pool, whirlpool, sports court, cable TV and pay-per-view movies. There's even a gas grill available for cookouts. Pets are allowed, but you should check with the management about pet deposits. Rates are based on length of stay and type of suite — studio, one-bedroom or two-bedroom. A guest laundry room is available.

Select Inn
$ • 4845 Hayes Rd., Madison
• (608) 249-1815

This budget property has an elegant and charming "honeymoon suite" for guests who want to feel pampered. The hotel offers double and king rooms, 18 executive kings, two apartments, three family suites and six theme rooms. Other amenities include a hot tub and complimentary continental breakfast. The hotel offers quick access to shopping and dining. Pets are allowed with a $25 refundable deposit.

Southeast Side

Country Inn and Suites
$$ • 400 River Pl., Madison
• (608) 221-0055, (800) 456-4000

New in May 1997, this inn's claim to fame includes 25-inch television sets, coffee makers and data ports in each room. The Country Inns and Suites has 65 standard rooms, 22 two-room suites and meeting space for up to 30 guests. Guests can help themselves to a complimentary continental breakfast in the morning after a dip in the 24-hour swimming pool. There's also a fitness center and whirlpool. You may bring your pet if it is well-trained; there's no deposit.

Days Inn
$$ • 4402 E. Broadway, Madison
• (608) 223-1800, (800) 329-7466

This Days Inn offers styles of rooms to suit just about any traveler. The hotel's king "business suites" are most versatile. A partitioned living area can serve as an office during the day and then double as an additional sleeping area with its pullout sofa and second television at night. Days Inn amenities include an indoor pool, whirlpool, HBO, movie service, free local telephone calls and a video game room. Complimentary continental breakfast is provided each morning. Ten whirlpool suites also are available. This hotel ranks in the top 1 percent for the Days Inn system for quality and cleanliness. If you bring your pet, you'll pay a $50 refundable deposit.

Edgewood Motel
$ • 101 W. Broadway, Madison
• (608) 222-8601

This friendly, well-kept, locally owned motel has 14 rooms, each with a microwave, refrigerator, 30-channel cable TV and at-your-door parking. Guests are treated to a complimentary continental breakfast and daily newspaper (except Sundays). The motel allows pets and is easily accessible from the Beltline or U.S. Highway 51. Rooms with one or two double beds are available, and smoking is allowed in all rooms.

South Side

Exel Grand Hotel
$$ • 722 John Nolen Dr., Madison
• (608) 255-7400, (800) 574-3935

Across from the Dane County Expo Center and Coliseum, this hotel offers a great home base for anyone attending a major Coliseum event or meetings Downtown. The Exel Grand, which opened in fall 1995, has a 24-hour pool, cocktail lounge, fitness center, free local calls and in-room coffee makers. Whirlpool and executive king rooms are available. Even if you've stayed in an Exel Inn before, you'll be pleasantly surprised. This hotel now offers a completely new, more upscale experience.

Sheraton Madison Hotel
$$$ • 706 John Nolen Dr., Madison
• (608) 251-2300, (800) 325-3535

The newly remodeled Sheraton Madison Hotel is one of Madison's finest accommodations and the frequent choice of visiting celebrities. Guests enjoy luxurious rooms decorated in soft hues of rose and green. Each of the 236 guest rooms has a variety of amenities, including in-room coffee makers, data ports and personal voice mail. On weekdays guests are treated to a complimentary continental breakfast. The Sheraton has a large indoor pool, whirlpool, sauna and fitness facilities.

The hotel is just across the street from the Dane County Coliseum and the Exposition Center, and it's just a couple miles from the Capitol, University of Wisconsin and Monona Terrace Convention Center. The Sheraton boasts one of Madison's best restaurants — the beautiful, Frank Lloyd Wright-inspired Heartland Grill — where diners can discover a variety of tasty, heart-healthy dishes. (See the write up under American category in the Restaurants chapter.) The Prairie Cafe and the Harvest Lounge are also in the hotel.

Super 8
$$ • **1602 W. Beltline Hwy., Madison**
• **(608) 258-8882, (800) 800-8000**

Set between Fish Hatchery Road and Todd Drive, this moderately priced motel serves both traveling professionals and vacationing families. Frequent updates ensure that the Super 8 has what travelers are looking for: nice, comfortable rooms (many with recliners), new carpeting, a clean and welcoming pool/whirlpool area and attractive lobby where you can enjoy a complimentary continental breakfast. Guests have free local calls and TVs with HBO. The motel also offers a computer for guest use and has in-room telephone data ports.

Southeast

Motel 6
$ • **6402 E. Broadway, Madison**
• **(608) 221-0415, (800) 466-8356**

Budget travelers can make free local calls from this clean motel, off I-90 and the Beltline. The Motel 6 has 40 single rooms and 78 double rooms. Other amenities include free coffee, HBO and ESPN and an outdoor pool that's closed in the winter — sorry, no polar bears allowed . . . but you could bring a small dog. Fax service is available at the front desk, and your kids can stay in your room at no extra charge.

Quality Inn South
$$ • **4916 E. Broadway, Madison**
• **(608) 222-5501, (800) 228-5151**

Swim in the pool or relax in the lounge at the Quality Inn South. This 156-room motel with an on-site restaurant has long been a popular spot for wedding receptions and can accommodate parties or meetings of up to 500. Guests can bring their pets to this hotel, conveniently just off the south Beltline, near a Park-N-Ride, several restaurants and South Towne Mall.

Wingate Inn
$$ • **3510 Mill Pond Rd., Madison**
• **(608) 224-1500, (800) 510-3510**

If you'll be working from your hotel room while in Madison, this place can fill the bill. The Wingate Inn offers a 24-hour business center with fax, PC, copier and typewriter. You can work out any stress in the fitness center, whirlpool or indoor pool. Each guest room comes equipped with a large desk and modem line. If you're in a hurry, you can pop a credit card into the automatic check-in machine and quickly receive your room key and directions to your room.

Guests find welcoming and comfortable oversize rooms. Each room is tastefully decorated with dark wood accents and has two telephones (one cordless). Nine whirlpool suites offer guests large, spacious rooms with a double Jacuzzi. Special rooms with light-signaling systems are available for hearing-impaired guests.

The Wingate is just off the junction of I-90 and the Beltline. The hotel offers an extensive complimentary breakfast buffet. Sorry, no pets are permitted.

INSIDERS' TIP

The bar at the Concourse Hotel is a favorite spot for people to rendezvous if they don't know the city. The Concourse is easy to find, within walking distance of Capitol Square, and the bar is comfortable and casual enough for a long wait.

Ramada Inn Capital Conference Center
$$ • 3902 Evan Acre Rd., Madison
• (608) 222-9121, (800) 2-RAMADA

This Ramada Inn is a frequent choice for conferences, wedding receptions and other large gatherings due to its large conference rooms and handy location, just off 1-90 and the Beltline. The Ramada can accommodate conferences for up to 950 guests, with rooms for break-out sessions. Two-room suites, special-needs suites and a fireplace suite are available. The newly renovated hotel has an on-site full-service restaurant, indoor pool and sauna, sports lounge, guest laundry and video area. The front desk handles fax and copy requests, and each guest room has a telephone data line. The hotel offers 187 newly remodeled rooms, including non smoking and special-needs accommodations.

Outlying Area

Chose Family Inn
$ • 1124 W. Main St., Stoughton
• (608) 873-0330, (800) 521-1581

Set on the Main Street of historic downtown Stoughton, this friendly, clean, budget-priced family inn has 53 rooms, an indoor pool, whirlpool and exercise room. Fax and copier services are available to guests. Spend the day shopping in Stoughton's historic district of specialty stores, visiting the museum or library, strolling along the Yahara River or just driving around eyeballing the city's terrific Victorian mansions.

Colonial Motel
$ • 3001 W. Beltline Hwy., Middleton
• (608) 836-1131

Clean, quiet rooms for budget-minded guests are the key to the success of this locally owned motel. The Colonial has an indoor pool and whirlpool and has equipped each of its guest rooms with microwaves and refrigerators. Several restaurants are nearby. Senior citizens get a 10 percent discount.

Country Inn and Suites
$$ • 904 E. Main St., Waunakee
• (608) 849-6900

This 4-year-old facility has a total of 38 rooms and suites. There are two "celebration" suites with king-size beds and whirlpools and a V.I.P. suite that has French doors leading to a separate bedroom and sitting room and a bath with whirlpool jets. Suites have microwave ovens and mini-refrigerators. There is no restaurant, but continental breakfast is served. All rooms have coffeemakers and receive complimentary morning newspapers. Pets of less than 25 pounds and children are welcome. Other features include meeting rooms, laundry facilities and an indoor pool. Smoking and nonsmoking rooms are segregated.

Fairfield Inn
$ • 8212 Greenway Blvd., Middleton
• (608) 831-1400

Consider the newly opened Fairfield Inn if you are seeking a budget hotel near Madison's West Side. Part of the Marriott hotel chain, the Fairfield Inn offers guests bright, clean rooms, complimentary continental breakfast and a nice pool and whirlpool. If you need to take care of business while at the Fairfield, you'll find in-room telephone data ports and fax service at the front desk for $1 per page. Coffee makers are available to guests by request.

Madison Marriott West
$$$ • 1313 John Q. Hammons Dr., Middleton • (608) 831-2000

Walk through the door into a beautiful 10-story garden atrium with glass elevators and a waterfall. Choose from one of the 292 guest rooms and suites including 27 Plaza Suites, 30 special-needs rooms and 17 executive king suites. Eight floors here are reserved for nonsmoking guests. The hotel has a full-service restaurant, concierge, lounge and on-site "classic rock" nightclub. There's an indoor pool, whirlpool and fitness center. In warm weather guests can lounge on a sun deck. Some small pets are accepted. There are extensive meeting, conference and trade show facilities. A new business center has fax, copier and computer equipment for guests to use. The price range here is wide, from $89 to $395.

McGovern's Motel
$ • 820 W. Main St., Sun Prairie
• (608) 837-7321

You'll find seven suites for long-term stays and 45 clean, moderately priced motel rooms

Many of Madison's accommodations enjoy sunset views.

at McGovern's Motel. The suites, often rented by business professionals transferring into the Madison area, include one bedroom with a queen bed, a large walk-in closet, a living room with television and a separate kitchen with breakfast bar, dishware and microwave. Monthly suite rates are $800. Pets are not allowed. The hotel is easy to find, close to shopping and dining and about a 10-minute drive to Madison's East Side.

At a bed and breakfast inn, you can experience life on a Wisconsin farm, complete with livestock and chores, or enjoy convenient access to the heart of Madison at others.

Bed & Breakfast Inns

The number of bed and breakfast inns in this area has grown dramatically in the past several years. Many of the most spectacular are historic buildings that have been beautifully restored. Some are contemporary residences, owned and operated by active young families.

You can experience life on a Wisconsin farm, complete with livestock and chores, at others. Some offer seclusion and scenic beauty while others provide convenient access to the heart of Madison. In this chapter we describe some of our favorites.

All inns described in this chapter have air-conditioned guest rooms and offer other modern amenities, even in the restored historic homes. Some are wheelchair-accessible (we note the exceptions). And most innkeepers accept major credit cards; we indicate the ones who don't. Smoking is not permitted in any of these inns. Pets and children create special cases: Some inns allow them, others do not, so we let you know which do not.

$	Less than $50
$$	$50 to $100
$$$	$100 to $150
$$$$	$150 and more

Price-Code Key

The price codes indicated by dollar signs in each write-up reflect the average room rate for double occupancy during the peak season. Prices are subject to change without notice. Expect to a pay higher rate for more luxurious accommodations or expanded services. Some inns, for example, may have room rates that vary from $79 to $179 depending on special features of the selected room or suite.

Isthmus

Canterbury Inn
$$ • 315 W. Gorham St., Madison
• (608) 258-8899, (800) 838-3850

Just upstairs from the Canterbury Bookstore (see our Literary Scene chapter), adventurous literary minds can travel through arched interior doorways into Chaucer's dream. Each of the six large guest rooms is tastefully decorated and features a colorful mural depicting a scene from the traveler's story. Four rooms have oversize whirlpools.

The unique, locally owned Canterbury Inn is housed in a former commercial building constructed in 1924. In the bookstore downstairs, you will find a lively coffeehouse with frequent author readings, lectures, live music and delectable dining. Step out the front door, turn right and walk to colorful State Street and its many attractions. Guests receive continental breakfast, and wine and cheese. Pets are not allowed.

Collins House Bed & Breakfast
$$ • 704 E. Gorham St., Madison
• (608) 255-4230

This family-owned bed and breakfast on Lake Mendota is built in the Frank Lloyd Wright-style of prairie architecture and is listed on the National Register of Historic Places. Work on the then-private home was commissioned in 1911. Five distinctive suites are furnished with antiques and handmade quilts (two have double whirlpool tubs.) Amenities include fireplaces and balconies. You know you will eat well here as the owners also run one of the best catering businesses in the city. Look for evening pastries, full gourmet breakfasts and signature chocolate truffles for guests.

Guests are within easy walking distance of the State Capitol and shopping on State Street. A nearby park and bus route are bonuses for those who want to get out and explore. There is no wheelchair access.

The Livingston
$$$$ • 752 E. Gorham St., Madison • (608) 257-1200

This 1856 Gothic Revival mansion is one of Madison's most treasured landmarks and is on the National Register of Historic Places. It has been home to early Madison mayors and others influential in city history. It also had the first indoor bathroom in Madison. The sandstone mansion has been extensively decorated with period antiques, some original to the house. It has four guest rooms and an English conservatory in the back where afternoon wine and hors d'oeuvres are served. Or, you can walk down to the patio, from which there is access to Lake Mendota, to watch the sunset.

Continental-plus breakfast is served in either the formal dining room or the guest's room. All rooms have fireplaces and full private baths. There is no wheelchair access, and smoking is not permitted. The rooms have televisions but no VCRs. Children age 12 and older are welcome, but pets are not.

Mansion Hill Inn
$$$$ • 424 N. Pickney St., Madison • (608) 255-3999, (800) 798-9070

This beautifully restored 1858 stone Romanesque Revival mansion has tall arched windows, ornate cornices and hand-carved marble. The mansion's foyer mosaic and spiral staircase leading to its cupola overlooking Madison make it one of the most architecturally renowned historic buildings in the Midwest. The 11 guest rooms are decorated in period antiques. Amenities include continental-plus breakfasts, afternoon refreshments, 24-hour valet service, fireplaces and private baths. Eight of the rooms have whirlpools and four have fireplaces. Children ages 13 and older are welcome, but pets are not. Smoking is not permitted, and there is no wheelchair access.

Campus

Stadium House
$$, no credit cards • 810 Oakland Ave., Madison • (608) 251-0674

Stadium House is near the UW-Madison stadium and Monroe Street. You'll find European-style bedrooms with a shared bath in this small, moderately priced inn. The Stadium House has two double rooms and a single. Guests can relax in a shared living area. This inn gives you quick access to many of Madison's events and attractions. Long-term rates are available. Children, pets and smoking are discouraged.

Most of the inn's three rooms with shared bathrooms are rented by parents visiting their children on campus. Children are allowed to stay under certain circumstances, but make sure to ask first. Pets are not allowed. The Stadium House is not wheelchair accessible. Breakfast is continental-plus, with scones often on the menu.

University Heights Bed and Breakfast
$$ • 1812 Van Hise Ave., Madison • (608) 233-3340

This circa 1923 inn near the UW campus is set in one of Madison's most colorful and elegant historic neighborhoods. It was built in the American Foursquare craftsman style with a sun porch and fireplace. Guests can choose from two rooms, each with a private bath and telephone, or a larger two-bedroom suite with whirl-

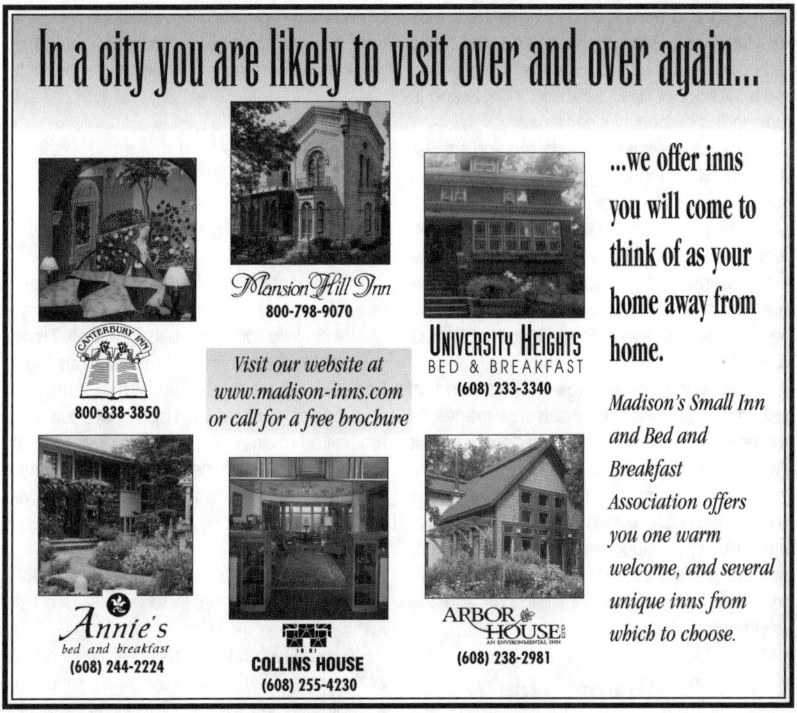

BED & BREAKFAST INNS • 129

In a city you are likely to visit over and over again...

Mansion Hill Inn
800-798-9070

Visit our website at
www.madison-inns.com
or call for a free brochure

800-838-3850

UNIVERSITY HEIGHTS
BED & BREAKFAST
(608) 233-3340

Annie's
bed and breakfast
(608) 244-2224

COLLINS HOUSE
(608) 255-4230

ARBOR HOUSE
(608) 238-2981

...we offer inns you will come to think of as your home away from home.

Madison's Small Inn and Bed and Breakfast Association offers you one warm welcome, and several unique inns from which to choose.

---

pool. Patrons also have access to a common area, exercise equipment, TV and VCR and a guest refrigerator, plus a full breakfast. Pets and children younger than 12 are not accepted.

West Side

Arbor House, an Environmental Inn
$$ • 3402 Monroe St., Madison
• (608) 238-2981

This environmentally friendly inn has attracted nationwide attention and won design awards as a model of urban ecology. The grounds are planted with native grasses and have mature trees. The 140-year-old Arbor House was constructed as a stage stop of dubious repute. Current owners John and Cathie Imes have expanded the inn, adding an annex built of natural and recycled materials. Each of the eight beautifully decorated guest rooms has a private bath, lots of natural light, hardwood floors and beautiful, unique furnishings. Guests can use a central business center.

Arbor House is across from the UW Arboretum (see our Attractions chapter). Guests can hike, use complimentary mountain bikes, bird watch or go canoeing on nearby Lake Wingra (late May through September). The inn is just a short walk from Monroe Street specialty shops and dining. Five of the rooms are air conditioned, and all have private bathrooms. Two have fireplaces, and five have whirlpools. Pets are not accepted, but children are welcome.

North Side

Annie's Bed and Breakfast
$$$ • 2117 Sheridan Dr., Madison
• (608) 244-2224

Since 1984, Annie's Bed and Breakfast has provided quiet luxury getaways for Madison visitors, including one recent guest who wrote about its charms in the *Chicago Tribune*. Overlooking the marsh and meadows of Warner Park (see our Parks and Recreation chapter), the rustic cedar shake and stucco craftsman-style house has a full floor of living space for guests and is surrounded by beautiful gardens.

Included are a master bedroom and smaller bedroom with connecting bath, a large pine paneled library with fireplace, and the lovely Woodland Whirlpool Room. Guests enjoy an indulgent homemade breakfast, served at their convenience in the dining room with its two-story windows and scenic views. The single, sprawling suite has its own bath, refrigerator, TV and VCR.

Trails lead guests to nearby Lake Mendota and the marsh, where they can view cranes, to the meadow where they can see deer or to visit tennis courts. Guests can also lounge in the gazebo or visit nearby golf courses. The library is stocked with CDs, books and magazines. Pets and children younger than 10 are not allowed, and the inn is not accessible by wheelchair. Annie's is six minutes from campus and the downtown area.

Southwest Side

Stoney Oaks
$$ • 4942 Raymond Rd., Madison
• (608) 278-1646

Children are welcome at this spacious contemporary bed and breakfast, but the owners request that you please leave your pets behind. The Grand Suite has a king bed, fireplace, TV with VCR, two-person Jacuzzi and personal refrigerator stocked with beverages. The Garden Suite has a four-poster bed and private living room. Guests can relax in the two-story great room and look out huge bay windows to 100-year-old white oaks.

The inn is close to shopping and golf courses and is a short drive from Madison's Downtown. On weekdays guests receive continental breakfast; a lavish gourmet breakfast is served on weekends. The inn is not wheelchair-accessible.

Outlying Area

BBB Farm
$$, no credit cards • 3883 Observatory Rd., Cross Plains • (608) 798-1123

This inn offers a taste of authentic Wisconsin farm life. It is set in the hills at the edge of the glacial driftless zone known as Pine Bluff, 7 miles west of Madison. Nearby is the famous Black Earth Creek trout stream. This farmhouse opened as a bed and breakfast in spring of 1998. Kids are invited to help owner "Uncle Joe" feed his chickens, cattle, rabbits and horses, or maybe even feed a calf with a bottle. Geese paddle about on a small pond. The land includes pasture, picnic areas and trails. The farm grows five types of berries, which you are invited to pick — and you can have them included in your breakfast.

A room with a king-sized bed has a private bath; a room with a queen bed and a room with a single bed share a bath. This inn is perfect for children, who are welcome here, but don't bring any more animals.

BBB is a working farm, with fields of corn, beans and hay. It's close to the Military Ridge Bicycle Trail. Uncle Joe whips up a breakfast fit for farm hands, with eggs, bacon, fruit, eggs, hashed browns and . . . crepes.

Beat Road Farm Bed and Breakfast
$$$ • 2401 Beat Rd., Verona
• (608) 437-6500, (800) ABA-RXRT

Just 15 minutes from Madison, this modern home offers comfortable accommodations in a country setting. The inn has four guest rooms. The master suite has a private bath. If you stay in one of the two queen rooms or a twin room,

---

INSIDERS' TIP

To get a free copy of the 1998 *Wisconsin Bed and Breakfast Directory*, call the Wisconsin Department of Tourism at (800) 432-TRIP. The directory lists 290 bed and breakfasts throughout Wisconsin that have met the requirements for membership in the Wisconsin Bed & Breakfast Association.

BEAT ROAD FARM INC.

*Bed & Breakfast...
Service & Friendliness
in the Country
Tradition*℠

Located on Highways 18/151 and Beat Road, 6 miles west of Verona and 5 miles east of Mount Horeb, Beat Road Farm Bed & Breakfast offers service and friendliness in the country tradition. Enjoy an exquisite night in the country surrounded in antique elegance.

For reservations: (608) 437-6500 or (800) ABA-RXRT

---

you'll share a bath. The family room has a fireplace and a big-screen satellite TV. Amenities include a spa, swimming pool, horse stables (but guests can't ride) and a player piano. Your hosts serve a full breakfast. Binoculars and books are available for bird watching. Pets are not allowed at the inn, but children are welcome. The inn is not wheelchair-accessible.

Cambridge House Bed and Breakfast
$$$ • 123 E. Main St., Cambridge
• (608) 423-7008

Set in a village about 30 minutes east of Madison that is filled with wonderful specialty shops, galleries and pottery stores, this 100-year-old home offers you the luxuries of the present with Old World charm. Choose from four luxurious suites, each with a private bathroom with a whirlpool. You can lay your head down on a four-poster rice bed, a king-size brass bed, an Italian sleigh bed or a patina-copper canopy bed. Expect a full breakfast in the morning. Hiking, biking, golfing and other activities are within easy reach. Pets are not permitted, and the inn is not wheelchair accessible.

Cameo Rose Bed & Breakfast
$$ • 1090 Severson Rd., Belleville
• (608) 424-6340

This sprawling Victorian-style inn was built recently on 120 acres of picturesque woodlands.

The home is immaculate and filled with antiques. Five elegant guest rooms feature comfortable beds, and one room has a double whirlpool. The inn offers a full formal breakfast, and leisure diversions include nearby hiking and skiing. The inn is halfway between Madison and New Glarus. Children 10 and older can visit, but pets aren't allowed. There is no wheelchair access.

Enchanted Valley Bed & Breakfast
$$ • 5554 Enchanted Valley Rd., Cross Plains • (608) 798-4554

This contemporary inn is set on 5 secluded acres with woods and a panoramic view. The grounds include flower, herb and vegetable gardens. The inn's common area is marked by a cathedral ceiling and fireplace. Guests also may use the hot tub, a comfort after a day of skiing on nearby slopes. Massage and herbal infusions are available. There are two guest rooms, one with a private bath and the other shared. Breakfast choices are gourmet and vegetarian. Enchanted Valley is close to Madison and Spring Green. Inquire about bringing pets and children. There is no wheelchair access.

Hawk's View Bed & Breakfast
$$ • E11344 Pochahantas Cir., Wisconsin Dells • (608) 254-2979

This chalet overlooking the Lower Dells has breathtaking views of the Wisconsin River and the sunset. A full breakfast is served on the deck overlooking the river when weather permits, and fireside when it doesn't. This is a great place for eagle watching. Hawk's View is near Cascade and Devil's Head ski areas. The inn has three bedrooms and one cottage, all with private baths. Children 12 and older may stay here, but pets are not allowed.

Historic Bennett House
$$, no credit cards • 825 Oak St., Wisconsin Dells • (608) 254-2500

This 1863 historic landmark home was once the residence of a renowned pioneer photographer who specialized in capturing the beauty of the Wisconsin Dells. The scenery is still magnificent, and you will enjoy full breakfasts by the fire. It has been recommended as a superior small lodging by *Midwest Living* and *Wisconsin Trails*. The inn offers three guest rooms, one with a private bathroom and two with shared bath facilities. Children and pets are not allowed, and there is no wheelchair access.

Jamieson House Inn
$$$ • 407 N. Franklin St., Poynette • (608) 635-2277

The former homes of local gentry Hugh Jamieson and his eldest son Hugh Pierce, erected in 1878 and 1883 respectively, now make up one of Wisconsin's finest country inns. The homes are set on 2 acres of patios, flowers and trees, and they are joined with an old schoolhouse. The three buildings make up the Jamieson House Inn. Decor is 19th-century style with antiques and reproductions, yet each building is centrally heated and air-conditioned. The inn has a fine European restaurant open to the public.

The 11 rooms and suites have private baths — five with double whirlpools. Some rooms have fireplaces, and a few have cable TV. (Most rooms do not have telephones or televisions, to encourage guests to relax in quiet.) The Jamieson House also hosts retreats, small conferences and meetings.

Guests receive a full breakfast. Ask before you arrive with children or pets. There is no wheelchair access.

Naeset-Roe Bed and Breakfast
$$$ • 126 E. Washington St., Stoughton • (608) 877-4150

This romantic Italianate-style brick home, built in 1879, has been painstakingly restored and is now on the National Register of Historic Places. All four guest rooms have private baths, and two have whirlpools. On weekends guests receive a full gourmet breakfast, and continental breakfast is served on weekdays. Located 15 miles south of Madison, the inn is a block from the Yahara River. Kids and pets are not allowed. There is no wheelchair access.

The Night Heron Bed & Breakfast
$$ • 315 E. Water St., Cambridge • (608) 423-4141, (800) 786-5669

This riverside inn set among flowering crab trees has an umbrella terrace, a hot tub, fireplace and art deco decor. Its three rooms have VCRs and one has a private bath. Leave your pets at home, but kids older than 12 can visit. There is no wheelchair access.

The Past and Present Inn
$$$ • 2034 Main St., Cross Plains • (608) 798-4441

A quaint restaurant and gift shop of the same name shares the site with this two-guest-room inn. The inn, which is 20 minutes from Madison, offers a full breakfast and a whirlpool suite. Both rooms have private baths and whirlpools. Pets are not allowed to stay, and the inn does not have wheelchair access.

Prairie Garden Bed & Breakfast
$$ • W13172 Highway 188, Lodi • (608) 592-5187

This inn is close to Lake Wisconsin and Mazomanie Beach, which is famous for its segment that features nude sunbathing. The inn

---

INSIDERS' TIP

Do you have any food or pet allergies? If you do, talk to prospective bed and breakfast inn owners before making arrangements.

The Livingston
A Victorian Inn

A 1857 Gothic Revival mansion in downtown Madison by lake Mendota. Offering Victorian Elegance and graciousness. Features include: nine fireplaces, antique furnishings, English conservatory, garden path to Lake Mendota, walking distance to downtown Madison, breakfast, wine and hors d'oeuvres. Excite your senses and relax.

752 E. GORHAM ST., MADISON, WI 53703
(608) 257-1200

---

features fluffy robes, fantastic breakfasts and a view of the Baraboo bluffs.

The inn has four bedrooms, one with a private bathroom and the others shared. One room has a whirlpool. There is wheelchair access.

Quiet Woods Bed & Breakfast
$$ ($60) • 10901 W. Hudson Rd., Mazomanie • (608) 795-4954

This newer home is set in rural solitude midway between Spring Green and Madison. It's a good place to watch birds and wildlife feed in the back yard. There are two guest rooms with private bathrooms. Pets are not welcome, but children generally are. There is no wheelchair access.

Victorian Treasure B&B Inn
$$$ • 115 Prairie, Lodi
• (608) 592-5199, reservations
(800) 859-5199

This eight-bedroom inn, consisting of two Queen Anne style homes, was featured on PBS' *Country Inn Cooking* program, which should tell you all you need to know about the kind of food you'll get here. The full breakfasts are memorable. The emphasis on the suites here is romance, with canopy beds, whirlpools and fireplaces. The inn is in the scenic Wisconsin River Valley between Madison and Devil's Lake/Baraboo.

The rooms have private baths and one has a whirlpool. There is wheelchair access.

In the warmer months, hardly a weekend goes by without something lively happening on the Capitol Square.

Festivals and Annual Events

To really feel the pulse of Madison and surrounding communities, glance over this list of annual festivals and events showcasing everything from ethnic celebrations and outdoor band concerts to farm and animal shows.

Because Madison is a very active, "fit" city, we've listed some of the major running events, including the Jingle Bell Run that takes place every December and attracts about 1,000 participants, no matter how cold a day it is.

Also, because it's a state capital and has many natural resources to offer, Madison attracts many large, regional trade shows devoted to fishing, hunting, boating, etc.

In the warmer months, hardly a weekend goes by without something lively happening on the Capitol Square. Setting the pace is the bountiful Farmers' Market each Saturday, but that's only the beginning. There are art and book fairs, weekends filled with live music and picnics on the Capitol grounds. Care to pet a cow? Why not. They're invited to come down to the State Capitol once a year, too. Few cities offer as many fun, free choices.

Before listing events in this chapter, we like to know they've stood the test of time. But four new "happenings" in Madison are very likely to be added soon to this growing calendar. One of the more exciting additions is the five-day Wisconsin Film Festival slated for the spring of '99 in Madison. Robert Redford has sent in his RSVP in anticipation of becoming the first recipient of the "Cheesehead Award" (he must have a wonderful sense of humor). February 12 through 14, 1999, the first Kites On Ice extravaganza will take place on Monona Lake in front of the Monona Terrace Convention Center. Kite flyers from all over the world are expected to participate.

A Downtown St. Patrick's Day parade is likely to be repeated for the second time in 1999, and a series of free concerts featuring various Madison musicians is expected to be renewed at the Monona Terrace Convention Center in fall and winter. When the weather is nice, the concerts are performed outdoors in the rooftop William T. Evjue Gardens. Call (608) 261-4000 for information.

While we've tried to narrow down the timing and hours of these annual events in the ensuing list, please either call the number provided for more information or check newspaper calendar listings closer to the event. This is by no means a definitive list, but rather a smorgasbord of the more popular and unusual activities here.

Admission fees, where applicable, may vary slightly from what we've listed. Use them only as a guideline. Another important item to note is that a separate parking fee, varying in amount, is charged for events taking place at the Dane County Expo Center. The few exceptions to that rule are subsequently noted.

Now, go have fun.

January

Winter Horse-drawn Vehicle Rally and Display
4718 Monona Dr., Monona
- **(608) 222-5783**

For two days, usually the weekend following New Year's Day, the Historic Blooming Grove Historical Society offers horse-drawn sleigh rides from 1 to 4 PM to raise money to continue restoring its home, a house dating back to 1856. Watch for scheduling information in Madison's daily newspapers. Often, the event is postponed because of weather (too cold or not enough snow), but the time and place is always the same. The cost is $2 for adults and $1 for children 13 and younger for a ride on one of two big bobsleds. For the smaller sleighs, it's $1 more. On Sunday, between 11:30 AM and 12:30 PM, contestants from the Dairyland Drivers Club compete in seven obstacle-course and race categories. The historical society serves Monona, southeast Madison and what's left of Blooming Grove.

Winter Concerts in the Gardens
Olbrich Botanical Gardens, 3330 Atwood Ave., Madison • (608) 246-4551

Free, one-hour concerts are performed beginning at 2 PM every Sunday, January through March, in the indoor commons area at Olbrich. Sponsored by the Olbrich Botanical Society and Madison Gas & Electric, the concerts feature a wide variety of music each week, including classical, folk, ethnic and swing.

The Wedding Planner and Guide Bridal Show
Exhibition Hall at Expo Center, 1919 Expo Way, Madison • (608) 233-7001

If you've just gotten engaged or are planning to soon, you might want to check out this wedding emporium, one of the biggest in the Midwest. Usually scheduled for the first or second weekend in January, this one-stop bridal extravaganza can tie up a ton of loose ends, from picking out a wedding gown to hiring a photographer. More than 135 exhibitors doing business in Greater Dane County participate annually. A highlight of the event is the fashion shows. Hours are 11 AM to 5 PM both days. Admission is $6 at the door.

Frostiball
Monona Terrace Convention Center, 1 John Nolen Dr., Madison • (608) 255-1008

A fund-raiser for Downtown Madison Inc., this elegant affair's guest list reads like a "Who's Who" of Madison. It usually takes place the third Saturday in January and attracts a sellout crowd of 1,200. You never know who you might end up dancing alongside — the mayor, university chancellor, football coach or even the governor. The event typically is held in the State Capitol, but it moved to Monona Terrace in '98 while renovation was being completed in the Capitol. As this book went to print, nothing had been decided yet for '99, except, of course, that it will take place.

The cost for an evening of live music, complimentary champagne and fancy hors d'oeuvres and desserts is about $75 per person or $100 with a reserved seat. Dress is formal. Most men (but certainly not all) wear tuxedos, and the majority of women sparkle. If you're planning to rent a limousine that night, best reserve one months in advance. Only prom weekends in Madison are as busy.

Madison Boat and Sportsmen's Show
Exhibition Hall at Expo Center, 1919 Expo Way, Madison • (612) 755-8111

The beginning of January is not too early to start thinking about fishing (and not through the ice, either), boating and hunting. About 100 exhibitors from all over the Midwest and Canada come to Madison to show off their equipment and/or help plan sporting vacations. The show opens on a Friday (noon to 9:30 PM) and continues on the weekend, 10 AM to 9:30 PM Saturday and 11 AM to 6 PM Sunday. Admission is around $5. The show is organized by Cenaiko Productions of Coon Rapids, Minnesota.

Remodeling Expo
Holiday Inn-Madison West, 1313 John Q. Hammonds Dr., Middleton • (608) 222-0670

If you're thinking about remodeling a bathroom or having a deck built, now is the time to plan it. Meet area remodelers and look for new ideas to spruce up your home at the Remodeling Expo in mid- to late January, sponsored by the local chapter of the National Associa-

FESTIVALS AND ANNUAL EVENTS • 137

Madison hosts many running races and events.

Photo: Wisconsin State Journal/The Capital Times

tion of the Remodeling Industry (NARI). Hours of the show are 3 to 9 PM Friday, 9 AM to 8 PM Saturday and 10 AM to 5 PM Sunday. Admission for the '98 Remodeling Expo was $4 for adults; children got in free.

February

Black History Month
Various locations

A number of educational and entertainment events occur throughout February to commemorate Black History Month. They include art exhibits, luncheons, jam sessions, lectures and seminars. A celebration always takes place at the South Madison Neighborhood Center, and an exhibit is featured for the entire month in the Truax campus lobby of Madison Area Technical College. For the best rundown of what's happening, refer to the special "Black History" section produced by *The Madison Times* or pick up the February issue of *Umoja* magazine.

Groundhog Day
Community Breakfast
The Round Table Restaurant, 1611 N. Bristol St., Sun Prairie • (608) 837-4547

We know a Madison attorney who sued Jimmy the Groundhog (but settled out of court for a round of golf) for incorrectly predicting an early spring one year. April showers quickly turned to snow ... lots of it. Yet, Jimmy is right 79 percent of the time, according to officials at the Sun Prairie Chamber of Commerce who annually sponsor this breakfast in his honor. The event takes place from 6 to 10 AM on February 2, Groundhog Day. Tickets are $4.50 in advance or $5 at the door. But please, if you decide to go, don't bring up the name of that East Coast "imposter," Punxsutawney Phil. It only makes Jimmy mad.

Dane County RV Dealers Show
Exhibition Hall at Expo Center, 1919 Expo Way, Madison • (608) 222-1507

If you're as fascinated as we are by all the modern amenities that go into recreational vehicles these days, you'll enjoy this show that takes place around the first weekend of February. Every area RV dealer, about 11 altogether, are represented. You'll see everything from small pop-up tent campers to deluxe motor coaches with price tags reaching $100,000. (That's camping in style!) Representatives from statewide campgrounds also set up booths, as do dealers simply interested in renting RVs. Price of admission runs around $6. Hours are noon to 8 PM Friday (admission for seniors that day is half-price), 10 AM to 8 PM Saturday and 10 AM to 5 PM Sunday.

Model Railroad Association Show
Exhibition Hall at Expo Center, 1919 Expo Way, Madison • (608) 273-1581

Everything to do with railroading, from the smallest model trains to railroad art and collectibles, is gathered under one roof for this two-day show usually held the third weekend in February. Attracting the most attention are about 30 operating layouts and another 20 exhibits. The show draws participants from all over Wisconsin, northern Illinois and southern Minnesota and features about 250 vendor tables. Hours are 10 AM to 5 PM both days. Admission has remained the same for a number of years: $5 for adults and $2 for children.

Garden Expo
Exhibition Hall at Expo Center, 1919 Expo Way, Madison • (608) 262-5255

Everything you'd want to know about gardening and sprucing up your backyard, from landscaping and lawn care to tending perennial beds and feeding the birds, is there for the asking at the two-day Garden Expo, sponsored annually the third week in February as a fund-raiser for Wisconsin Public Television (WHA-TV in Madison). UW Extension agents as well as commercial exhibitors staff the more than 120 booths. Educational seminars are scheduled both days. Hours are 9 AM to 5 PM Saturday and 10 AM to 4 PM on Sunday. Admission is $4 in advance for adults and $5 at the door. Children 12 and younger get in free.

Zor Shrine Circus
Memorial Coliseum at Expo Center, 1919 Expo Way, Madison • (608) 274-2260

Annually sponsored as a fund-raiser by Zor Temple in Madison (whose members also provide free camel rides at Henry Vilas Zoo Sundays during summer), this circus usually comes to town the third weekend of February for six performances Friday through Sunday. Admission is around $8, although every elementary school child in Dane County traditionally receives one free ticket. It's not the biggest circus to hit town, but it is one of the most affordable ones, and it arrives the same time every year. Money raised from ticket sales helps defray the operating costs of Zor Temple, 575 Zor Shrine Place on the far West Side.

Madison Fishing Expo
Exhibition Center at Expo Hall, 1919 Expo Way, Madison • (608) 245-1040

Started in '86, this show is organized by an all-volunteer staff of avid anglers who donate proceeds from the show to fund fishing-related projects throughout South-Central Wisconsin. In 1998, money raised went to helping restore 4 miles of Token Creek. More than 100 booths showcase fishing equipment, including boats, and experts are on hand to offer advice on any aspect of the sport. Trout Unlimited club members demonstrate fly casting throughout the weekend, and various seminars offer advice on how to catch Door County walleyes to trophy muskies. Options for youngsters include a six-hour boating safety class that requires advance registration and an extra fee. For pure fun, there's minnow racing. Hours are 4 to 9 PM on Friday, 9 AM to 7 PM on Saturday and 9 AM until 5 PM on Sunday. Admission is about $5 for adults, with children 12 and younger admitted free.

Madison Spelling Bee
At a Madison high school
• (608) 252-6111

Ranging in age from 9 to 14 years, Madison's top spellers, about 50 altogether from public and private schools, compete for the opportunity to represent the city in the Badger State Spelling Bee in April. The event, beginning at 9 AM, is annually sponsored by the *Wisconsin State Journal* and usually takes place the last weekend in February or the first Saturday in March. Admission is free.

March

International Children's Film Festival
Madison Civic Center, 211 State St., Madison • (608) 266-9055

At 11 AM and 1 PM on two Saturdays in March, Friends of the Madison Civic Center sponsor two free, G-rated movies in the Isthmus Playhouse that appeal to children pre-

Dane County Farmers' Market

If you asked people what they like best about Madison, the Dane County Farmers' Market would be mentioned over and over again. Consistently lauded by such publications as *USA Today* (selected the local market as the second best in the country in 1998), *Midwestern Living* and *Better Homes and Gardens*, the market is singled out for not only its wonderful array of fresh produce, but also its delightful setting. Even *National Geographic* has dropped by to sneak a peek and photograph.

During the height of the season, June through September, as many as 200 vendors show off their agricultural products (fresh-picked that morning) along shaded sidewalks encircling the Capitol. Hours are basically 7 AM until 2 PM. However, if you want the best selection, or for that matter, even the best view, it's wise to get down to the Square before 8:30. It can get pretty crowded between 9 and 11 AM. Total average attendance over the day is 18,000 people.

Mary Carpenter, school teacher, vendor and longtime manager of the market, may be biased when she describes the Saturday ritual as "simply gorgeous . . . a place where the city comes together." But we doubt anyone would find fault with that appraisal.

From the last weekend in April through the first weekend in November, the Farmers' Market is the place to be. There are plenty of stops for coffee (not associated with the market) and bakery goods to buy for breakfast on the run. The only Saturday the Farmers' Market isn't on the Square is during the Madison Art Fair on the Square, the second full weekend in July. Then, vendors graciously move over to State Street.

Rules for the Dane County Farmers' Market are strict. Vendors, representing 33 counties within the state, are licensed and only allowed to sell what they grow and produce within the state. A vendor who sells homemade jams and jellies, for instance, must have also grown the fruit. That makes it truly a Wisconsin market, although the

— continued on next page

The Dane County Farmers' Market wins high marks from all who attend.

selection of products seems endless. Depending upon the time of year, you might see bedding plants, berries, a wide range of fresh vegetables, frozen meats, German-style sausages, cheese, eggs, melons, apples of every variety, cider, dried herb arrangements, honey, pastries, breads and almost always, fresh-cut flowers. In recent years, Hmong truck farmers have contributed sweet, giant yellow Thai cucumbers, bok choy and other popular Asian vegetables.

It's hard to believe that the Farmers' Market was started in fall 1972 with 11 vendors. Today there are 350 members and more farmers on a waiting list.

But one thing that hasn't changed is the traffic pattern. If you go, walk counterclockwise. Why? Nobody knows. But you won't get very far trying to walk the other way. And, please leave your dog behind. They're not welcome at the Farmers' Market.

From 9 AM to 2 PM on Wednesdays, May through October, a smaller Farmers' Market takes place along Main Street on the Square. There's also a Holiday Farmers' Market usually held the first Saturday in December in the Crossroads lobby of the Madison Civic Center and sometimes the last weekend in November, too.

Parking is readily available Downtown in any one of the City of Madison's parking ramps — all day Saturday for just $1.

The market in the parking lot of Hilldale Shopping Center on the West Side is a separate operation, managed by the mall. It features 75 vendors, some of whom also have booths Downtown, and runs from the beginning of May through October. The Hilldale Market, open Saturday mornings from 7 AM to about 1 PM, might not have the ambiance of the one on the Square, but it's really convenient for a quick stop or for people who have trouble walking, because parking noses right up to the produce.

---

school-age and older. The films are award-winning endeavors from around the world, not Hollywood-produced. Watch for specific dates in Civic Center ads and schedules.

Dane County Kids Expo
Holiday Inn-Madison West, 1313 John Q. Hammonds Dr., Middleton
- **(608) 831-4303**

There are two good reasons for families to attend this free event that takes place on a Sunday in the beginning of March. First, there is plenty of entertainment — clowns, magicians and musicians, to name a few examples — for kids to enjoy; second, more than 100 exhibitors pass out information about children's programming. This expo is sponsored by the monthly publication *Dane County Kids*, and admission is free.

Home Products Show
Exhibition Hall at Expo Center, 1919 Expo Way, Madison • (608) 288-1133

Attracting people from all over South-Central Wisconsin, this show by the Madison Area Builders Association steers people in the right direction for anything about home building, including actual construction and picking out fixtures and window treatments. About 18,000 annually attend the show that's held during a three-day weekend in early March. Hours are 2 to 8 PM on Friday, 10 AM to 8 PM on Saturday and 10 AM to 5 PM on Sunday. Admission runs around $5 for adults ($4.50 in advance) and $2.50 for seniors. Children 12 and younger are admitted free. This show is strictly for consumers to get questions answered, make contacts and learn about new ideas in home building. Exhibitors are not permitted to sell.

Rutabaga's Canoecopia
Exhibition Hall at Expo Center, 1919 Expo Way, Madison • (608) 223-9300

Because South-Central Wisconsin is considered one of the prime canoeing spots in the country, it's not surprising that a show devoted to paddling sports occurs every year in Madison, usually over the second weekend in March. Most of the 100 exhibitors, representing outfitters, rental outlets, paddling schools and camps, are from the Midwest, although a few travel from as far away as overseas. The show is sponsored by Rutabaga, a Madison paddleboat outfitter. Hours of the show are 4 to 8 PM on Friday, 9 AM to 5 PM on Saturday and 10 AM to 5 PM on Sunday. Admission is $5 for adults; children younger than 16 get in free.

Spring Flower Show
Olbrich Botanical Gardens, 3330 Atwood Ave., Madison • (608) 246-4551

Mid-March in Madison, you're lucky to see a few crocuses peaking out of the soil, especially if snow still covers the ground. But spring arrives early in all its glory during this free, two-week show that showcases thousands of colorful flowers and bulbs in full bloom. Hours are 10 AM to 4 PM Monday through Saturday and 10 AM to 5 PM Sunday.

Electric Power Farm Equipment Show
Exhibition Hall at Expo Center, 1919 Expo Way, Madison • (608) 276-6700

In response to the growing mechanization needs of the progressive farmer, this show, sponsored by the Midwest Equipment Dealers Association and the oldest of its kind in the nation, was first held in 1960. Traditionally it takes place Wednesday through Friday in mid-March, and although the more than 300 exhibitors attract thousands of farmers, members of the general public often attend this show as well, just to view the enormous lineup of modern tractors, plows, cultivators, milking machines, etc. It's one of many Wisconsin traditions. Admission is free. Show hours are 9 AM to 4 PM Wednesday and Thursday and 9 AM to 3 PM on Friday.

(WIAA) State Basketball Girls and Boys Tournaments
Kohl Center, 601 W. Dayton St., Madison • (715) 344-8580

Held in UW-Madison's Kohl Center sports arena, these high school state basketball playoffs are commonly referred to as "March Madness." They take place two consecutive weekends (Thursday through Saturday) in mid-March and attract the top 20 girls' basketball teams and the top 20 boys' teams in the state. No matter the dates, usually on one weekend or the other, Madison experiences a bad snowstorm or equally inclement weather. You can bet spring on it. Tickets are $5 per session (two games). During the week of the tournaments, call the UW Athletic Ticket Office, (608) 262-1440, for tickets. Don't wait too long. The boys games always sell out, and the girls' games are becoming increasingly popular.

Madison Area Doll Club Show and Sale
Quality Inn South, 4916 E. Broadway Ave., Madison • (608) 836-6873

From cloth to porcelain, child-size to teenyweeny, antique to modern, the hundreds of dolls this annual show brings together are on view for one day only, usually the last Saturday in March, from 9 AM to 4 PM. There is no admission to the exhibit, but a donation is asked of people wishing to enter the sales rooms where vendors sell dolls, doll accessories, books and even some teddy bears.

Wisconsin Deer & Turkey Expo
Dane County Expo Center, 1919 Expo Way, Madison • (920) 242-3990

Attracting deer and turkey hunters from every county in Wisconsin and 25 different states, this show, produced by Target Communications in Mequon, features 450 booths. It takes place either the last weekend in March or first weekend in April, depending upon when Easter falls on the calendar. Participating in the show are manufacturers of hunting equipment and accessories, from bows and arrows and black-powder hunting rifles to clothing, tree stands, lures and calls. Also represented are resorts, guides, wildlife artists, publishers, video producers and food companies. It isn't unusual to witness a venison cooking demon-

---

INSIDERS' TIP

One thousand people, including 200 mayors, are expected to attend the U.S. Conference of Mayors' annual meeting in 2002 at the Monona Terrace Convention Center.

stration or two at this show. Hours of the show are 4 to 9 PM Friday, 9 AM to 7 PM Saturday and 9 AM to 5 PM Sunday. Admission is $7 per day or $12 for a two-day pass. Children 5 and younger are admitted free; youth ages 6 to 11 pay $3. On Friday night, children younger than 15 are admitted free with an adult.

Career Fair
Monona Terrace Convention Center, 1 John Nolen Dr., Madison
• (608) 252-6342

Looking for a job? This fair, sponsored by the *Wisconsin State Journal*, *The Capital Times* and WISC-TV and held at both the end of March and again at the beginning of September, attracts more than 100 employers with openings ranging from entry-level to executive positions. Hours are 10 AM to 7 PM. Speakers on a variety of employment issues are featured. Admission is free.

April

Badger State Spelling Bee
At a Madison-area high school
• (608) 252-6111

The 50 or so elementary and middle-school students who participate in the State Spelling Bee must master words such as "otalgia," "klinotaxis" and "lachrymose" to win prizes and vie for a chance to participate in the National Spelling Bee held the end of May in Washington, D.C. This 50-year tradition, sponsored by the *Wisconsin State Journal* and held at a different Madison area high school each year, begins at 1 PM and usually lasts four hours. Admission is free.

Midwest Horse Fair
Dane County Expo Center, 1919 Expo Way, Madison • (414) 623-4322

Sponsored by the Columbus-based Wisconsin State Horse Council Inc. and held during a three-day weekend, usually the third one in April, this show appeals to horse lovers of all ages. More than 450 horses of every shape, variety and size imaginable are brought to Madison for this entertaining and educational fair. The admission price of $8 a day (discounts are available for weekend packages, and children 9 and younger get in free) includes Friday and Saturday evening shows that vary widely, from country-and-western singing to full-fledged rodeos. Hours are 9 AM to 9 PM Friday and Saturday and 9 AM to 6 PM on Sunday.

Capital City Jazz Festival
Ramada Inn Capital Conference Center 3902 Evan Acres Rd., Madison
• (608) 877-4171

Calling all jazz lovers. Three five-hour sessions of New Orleans-style swing jazz make up the Capital City Jazz Festival that takes place annually either the last weekend in April or first weekend in May at the Ramada Inn, just off I-90. Tickets, about $18 in advance, are good for a single session featuring four different bands on Saturday afternoon or evening or on Sunday afternoon. A jazz brunch is available on Sunday for an additional cost. A "Friend of the Fest" reserved seat, good for the entire weekend (except the brunch), costs about $60.

Crazy Legs Run
Begins on the Capitol Square, Madison
• (608) 263-7894

Named for Elroy "Crazy Legs" Hirsch, a former UW football standout and gregarious athletic director of the university, this popular 5-mile run or 2-mile walk is usually scheduled the last weekend of April, which means you could be running in 70-degree weather or, perhaps, snow flurries. But the race, a fund-raiser for the UW Athletic Department, keeps growing in size, attracting more than 6,000 participants in recent years. Runners race around the Square, proceed down State Street and then up Bascom Hill. That's a killer, although the rest of the course is relatively flat. Registration in '98 was $15 in advance or $20 the morning of the race, which begins at 10:30 AM — a great time for people who like to sleep in.

Farmers' Market
Capitol Square, Madison
• (920) 563-5037

The Farmers' Market typically begins the last Saturday in April and runs through the first Saturday in November. (See this chapter's related Close-up.)

Only in Madison will you find a race that asks entrants to paddle a canoe and then run with it through Downtown streets.

May

WalkAmerica
320 Holtzman Rd., Madison
• **(608) 276-WALK**

Sponsored by the March of Dimes, this Madison version of the nationwide WalkAmerica usually takes place the first weekend of May and attracts as many as 2,500 participants. The walk begins and ends at the Capitol. All along the 20K route, walkers can partake of snacks and drinks. The pace is leisurely and very neighborly. In addition to the 20K walk, the event includes a 10K walk and a 2-mile "buggy brigade" for those pushing wee ones. Money raised from this event benefits prenatal-health research and advocacy for ensuring healthy births.

Meriter Nurses Run
Vilas Park, 1339 Vilas Park Dr., Madison
• **(608) 267-5620**

This event taking place the Thursday of the first full week in May — National Nurses Week — attracts an average of 3,900 runners and walkers, some of them pushing kids in strollers. It truly is a family event and the only race we know of where long-sleeve T-shirts are given out. You can sign up for any one of three events: a 5K or 10K run or 2-mile walk. Many children do the latter. All three begin at about 5:30 PM and end back in the park, where free sack lunches and sodas are handed out to all participants. Supper and a T-shirt for a registration fee of about $15 — a pretty good deal.

Badger Kennel Club Dog Show
Exhibition Hall at Expo Center, 1919 Expo Way, Madison • **(608) 221-1955**

This dog show, one of the biggest in the Midwest, usually occurs the first weekend in May. It's sponsored by the Janesville-Beloit Kennel Club and Badger Kennel Club in Madison. About 1,700 dogs representing about 120 breeds are featured in a variety of show-breed and obedience competitions, all of which are open to the public. The latest in doggy items, including beds, toys and treats, are available for sale. This show draws breeders and vendors from all over the country. Hours are 8 AM to 3 PM both days. Admission is about $4. Children younger than 12 get in free.

Gear Up Madison Bike Ride
158 Dixon St., Madison • (608) 241-3460

A popular noncompetitive event to promote bicycling and bicycling safety, Gear Up Madison attracts about 800 area bicyclists annually who are welcome to choose one of three rides: 6, 15 or 30 miles. The course winds through the Arboretum and along Seminole Highway. The longest ride goes to Paoli (where refreshments are available) and back. Cost of the ride, occurring mid- to late-May, is $11 to $15 depending upon when registration is made. T-shirts are given out to all who register. Even the longest route is relatively flat (though there are one or two killer hills). Participants are urged to bike at their own pace; helmets are required. Bikes should be in safe operating order though area bike shops are at the starting point (the Vilas Park Shelter) for free bike checks.

Race For The Cure
(608) 833-8892, (608) 273-3897

For the first time in '98, Madison presented its own edition of the Susan G. Komen Breast Cancer Foundation Race For The Cure that is annually held in almost 90 cities across the country. Money raised is used to help fund research to find a cure for breast cancer and promote early detection of the disease. Local honorary chairwoman is Sue Ann Thompson, wife of the governor who is a breast-cancer survivor. The event includes 5K all-men and all-women runs and a 1-mile family fun run/walk. All begin and end at the UW Soccer Field on University Bay Drive behind UW Hospital. Entry fee is about $15. The race is expected to occur annually mid- to late-May.

Mother's Day Concert
Olbrich Gardens, 3330 Atwood Ave., Madison • (608) 246-4551

After a nice Mother's Day brunch or trip out to the UW Arboretum to enjoy the lilacs, bring mom out for a stroll in the Olbrich Gardens, filled with blooming spring flowers including a dazzling array of tulips. A free concert begins at 2 PM, showcasing a variety of music, from Brahms to Dixieland. Coffee and iced cappuccino are for sale to benefit the Gardens. The Growing Gifts shop is also open Mother's Day from 10 AM to 4 PM and offers flower and plant-related gifts, including books, jewelry and unique garden ornaments.

Syttende Mai Folk Festival
Various sites throughout Stoughton • (608) 873-7912

One of the most popular ethnic festivals in South-Central Wisconsin, Syttende Mai is Norwegian for May 17, the date in 1814 on which the Norwegian Constitution was signed and Norway broke free from Denmark. The roots of this three-day festival, typically held the Friday through Sunday closest to May 17 (but never on Mother's Day), go back to 1897, although one of the more publicized events, the 20-mile Syttende Mai run from the Capitol Square to the middle of downtown Stoughton, didn't begin until the early 1970s. A walk was added in the '80s.

Activities begin on Friday night with a canoe race down the Yahara River and a street dance, usually held from 7 to 10 PM. Saturday overflows with a craft fair, Norwegian dancing, a rosemaling exhibit/competition and plenty of food. More of the same occurs on Sunday, with the highlight being a two-hour parade down Main Street beginning at 1:30 PM. Visit Stoughton on Syttende Mai weekend, and you'll think you've gone to Norway.

Now Hiring Job Fair
Exhibition Hall at Expo Center, 1919 Expo Way, Madison • (608) 831-4303

Sponsored by the regional publication *Now Hiring Employment Guide*, this fair is held on a designated Wednesday in May. About 100 potential employers in such diverse fields as service industries, retailing, banking and manufacturing are represented. Everything is free, including resume consultation and mini-seminars on how best to job search.

Madison Marathon
Begins on the Capitol Square, Madison • (608) 256-9922

Started in 1994, the Madison Marathon is attracting more than 3,000 participants from almost every U.S. state and a handful of foreign countries. The race begins at 7:30 AM on the Capitol Square and finishes 26.2 miles later at Olin-Turville Park. Don't worry if you're not in shape to run 20 miles, let alone more than 26. Other events include a half-marathon, 10K and 5K runs and a 5K walk. Registration fees vary, depending upon the event entered and date of registration. Participants are invited to register six months in advance.

Llama Market
Exhibition Hall at Expo Center, 1919 Expo Way, Madison • (608) 372-7877

Started in 1994 on a llama farm in Tomah, north of Madison, this show became so popular it was moved in '97 to the Dane County Expo Center in order to accommodate more llama ranchers and pique the interest of the general public. About 250 breeders, with about 400 llamas native to North America and Latin America, participate in a four-day conference the beginning of May. The public is invited to watch the fiber demonstration and view both the exhibits and animals from 8 AM to 5 PM Saturday and Sunday. An auction takes place Sunday at noon. The cost of admission is about $2.

June

Concerts in the Gardens
Olbrich Gardens, 3330 Atwood Ave., Madison • (608) 246-4551

Bring a lawn chair or blanket and enjoy concert band music amid fragrant flowers every Tuesday evening throughout the summer. Picnics are allowed in the gardens only on these nights. The free concerts, beginning at 7 PM, are moved inside in the event of rain.

Festa Italia
Expo Center grounds off Expo Way, Madison • (608) 258-1880

What began as a little neighborhood celebration to honor the Italian culture that thrived during the first half of the 20th century in Madison's old Greenbush neighborhood has turned into a lively three-day, citywide event usually taking place in early June. It attracts thousands of people, whether they have any Italian blood coursing through their veins or not. It was established by the Italian Workmen's Club, 914 Regent Street, founded in 1912 as a mutual-benefit organization and still very active today as a community social center. Held outside under tents on the Expo grounds, the festival offers plenty of camaraderie, entertainment and wonderful Italian food. Hours are 5 PM to midnight on Friday, 10 AM to midnight Saturday and noon to 6 PM on Sunday.

Cats of Wisconsin
Exhibition Hall at Expo Center, 1919 Expo Way, Madison • (608) 231-1618

Always held the first full weekend in June, this show draws about 30 breeds of cats or about 250 felines altogether. Judging is continuous Saturday and Sunday, from 1 to 4 PM. All proceeds from the show either fund a scholarship annually awarded to a UW veterinary student or benefit feline medical research. The show always has many cat-related vendors and a booth staffed by the UW Veterinary School. Admission is around $4 for adults and teens and $1 for children younger than 12.

Tuesday Noon Concerts
King St. corner of Capitol Grounds, Madison • (608) 266-6033

Free one-hour, outdoor concerts begin at noon every Tuesday from June through September at the King Street corner of the Capitol grounds. Music varies from '40s swing to country and some ethnic, but no rock 'n' roll. The concerts are a mutual endeavor by the Music Performance Trust Fund and City of Madison. In case of rain, concerts are moved inside the Capitol, unless the group performing is too large.

Parade of Homes
Various sites in and around Madison • (608) 288-1133

Do you enjoy touring homes? Are you looking for ideas for remodeling your kitchen? More than 30 new homes go on display each year for the Madison Area Builders Association (MABA) Parade of Homes. Prices of models begin at about $200,000 and go up. The parade always takes place over a period of 16 days (over three weekends) in June and incorporates three or four sites in Madison and/ or adjacent burgs, including Middleton,

Fitchburg, Sun Prairie and Waunakee. Expect ticket prices to be around $8 on site ($7 in advance) for adults and teens and $3 ($2 in advance) for children 12 and younger. Senior citizens can view the homes on the first Wednesday of the show for $3. Don't worry how hot it gets outside; all homes are air-conditioned.

Hometown USA Festival
Hometown USA Park, Verona
• (608) 845-6626

The entire town and then some turn out for Verona's annual hometown celebration taking place the weekend that includes the first Sunday in June. You can always expect carnival rides, an arts and crafts fair, musical entertainment, tractor pull, classic car show and parade (1 PM on Sunday). Hours are 5 to 10 PM Thursday; 6 PM to midnight Friday; noon to midnight Saturday and noon to dusk on Sunday.

Cows on the Concourse
Capitol Square, Madison
• (608) 221-8698

Only in Madison could you wake up one summer morning, go Downtown to the Capitol Square to buy fresh produce from the Farmers' Market and pet a cow in the process. This event, which usually takes place the first Saturday in June, is a salute to the dairy industry and the Dairy State. After all, June is Dairy Month, and nowhere is it more appropriately celebrated than here. Music begins at 9 AM, and concessions selling everything dairy, including the legendary State Fair cream puffs, line the Square from 9 AM to 1 PM. Of course, we shouldn't have to remind you, but bring the kids.

Dane County Breakfast on the Farm
Various farms throughout Dane Co.
• (608) 256-8348

Typically the third Saturday in June, load the family into the sedan and head out to the country to take part in a big, old-fashioned farm breakfast held at a different farm in Dane County each year. The location is announced each spring. From 6:30 (for the early risers) to 10:30 AM, scrambled eggs, ham, cheese, rolls and even sundaes are ladled out in huge portions. The cost is very reasonable: about $3 for everyone 11 and older and $2 for children 3 to 10. Children younger than 3 eat for free.

June Jam
Exhibition Hall at Expo Center, 1919 Expo Way, Madison • (608) 276-6606

Think you're pretty good on the basketball court? Prove it. Organize a team and take part in June Jam, a three-on-three basketball tournament held the first full weekend in June as a fund-raiser for Madison YMCA. Games by teams of three are continuous. Prizes and trophies are awarded to the top teams in four divisions: Youth, Open (18 and older), Master (45 plus) and Elite (top division). The event is coed and attracts about 350 to 400 teams from throughout the Upper Midwest. The entry fee per team is about $70.

Rhapsody in Bloom
Olbrich Botanical Gardens, 3330 Atwood Ave., Madison • (608) 246-4550

Billed as "Madison's largest garden party," Rhapsody in Bloom is to summer what the Frostiball is to winter (see the January entry). They're equally elegant affairs and sell out weeks in advance. Always on a Saturday night in mid- to late June, patrons are invited to tour the gardens, a glass of wine in hand, then enjoy a sit-down dinner followed by dancing to live music. Everything takes place outdoors under white canopies, weather permitting, of course. (Only one year did a wind kick up so fast, a diner got smacked in the forehead by a flying roll. There were, however, no injuries.) Tickets for hors d'oeuvres, dinner (the bar is extra) and entertainment in '98 were $65. This is one garden party where you're urged to buy and take home the centerpieces, usually perennial plants that can be replanted in your own garden. Hours of the event are 6 to 11:30 PM. All proceeds benefit Olbrich. It's really a lovely affair.

Paddle & Portage
Downtown Madison • (608) 255-1008

Here's another event unique to Madison. It involves racing a 1.5-mile course in a canoe or kayak on one lake (Mendota) and then portage 1.5 miles across the Isthmus, past the Capitol, put your vessel into a second lake (Monona) and paddle another 1.5 miles,

The World Dairy Expo is the biggest show of its kind in the world, attracting almost 70,000 people.

ending at a lakeshore park (Olin-Turville) for awards. The event, a fund-raiser for Downtown Madison Inc., usually attracts about 600 participants and almost as many spectators. Entry fees are about $20 for one person and $35 for a two-person team. The race, usually held the third Saturday in June, begins at James Madison Park at 10 AM.

Badger State Summer Games
Various venues throughout Madison
- **(608) 251-3333**

The finals of this Olympic-style sports festival for Wisconsin residents take place in Madison over a three-day weekend at the end of June. (The winter event takes places in Wausau in February.) More than 15,000 male and female athletes of all ages compete in 26 sports including kayaking, cycling, golf, soccer, fastpitch and slow-pitch softball, swimming, volleyball and wrestling. There is no admission to any of the events. For information about qualifying, call the listed number.

Flags of Freedom
Sun Prairie High School, 220 Kroncke Dr., Sun Prairie • (608) 837-2547 Ext. 4104

Each year, usually on the last Saturday in June, a dozen high school marching bands from around the state come to Sun Prairie to participate in a parade and marching-band competition sponsored by the Sun Prairie Band Boosters. The parade down Main Street begins at 2 PM. Competition takes place later that night, usually beginning at 7 PM on Ashley Field at Sun Prairie High School. Tickets cost around $5 at the gate.

Attic Angel House and Garden Tour
Homes in and around Madison
- **(608) 238-0980**

Each year for more than 40 years, people have looked forward to this annual house and garden tour that showcases about a half-dozen beautiful homes in or around Madison. The event always is held on a Monday, usually in late June, from 10 AM to 8 PM. The cost is between $8 and $10. For an added fee, patrons can enjoy a luncheon served between 11 AM and 1 PM at a nearby country club. A free shuttle transports people between homes and the luncheon site.

Also part of this fund-raiser, sponsored by Attic Angel Association (money goes to support community projects), is an Attic Sale held at Edgewood High School, usually the Friday and Saturday before the house tour. For early admission, 8:30 to 10 AM that Friday, a ticket or entry fee (about $8) is required. From 10:30

AM to 3 PM on Saturday and 8:30 AM to 1 PM on Sunday, entrance to the sale is free.

Concerts on the Square
Capitol Square, Madison
• (608) 257-0638

Referred to as Madison's "biggest picnic of summer," Concerts on the Square is a series of six outdoor pops concerts performed on the Capitol grounds every Wednesday night for six consecutive weeks beginning the last Wednesday in June. (In case of rain, the concerts are postponed a night.) Instituted in 1984 as a means of getting people to remain or come Downtown after work, the concerts were an overnight success. They attract so many people that it's sometimes difficult to find a place to spread your blanket. For that reason, many people come early and visit with family and friends long before the concerts begin at 7 PM. Concessions open at 5:45 PM.

If you don't have time to pack a box supper, many area restaurants will gladly have one made up for you and delivered to the Square if you give them advance notice. Prior to the first concert, Madison newspapers publish a listing of participating restaurants and their menus, including several selections for kids. The Chamber also rents a number of upclose picnic tables, mostly to businesses, for the entire series. If you're invited to sit at one, remember: Your undivided attention is required. On the grass, in a sea of humanity, the mood is much more relaxed.

For these concerts, the Wisconsin Chamber Orchestra changes from its usual classical repertoire to a pops orientation, sometimes even with Beatles songs thrown in.

July

Back Porch Concerts
Dean House, 4718 Monona Dr., Monona
• (608) 222-5783

Every Thursday evening during July and often running into August, local musicians playing everything from ragtime to classical music perform outdoor concerts at the Dean House. The concerts, which begin at 7:15 PM, are sponsored by the Historic Blooming Grove Historical Society.

Monona Community Festival
Winnequah Park, Monona
• (608) 222-8565

A day (sometimes two, depending on which day of the week our nation's birthday falls) of entertainment, food (beer tent, too) and plenty of old-fashioned games is devoted to Monona's Fourth of July celebration in Winnequah Park along Lake Monona. Festivities, including water fights, a firecracker hunt, kiddie parade and softball tournament, are capped by an impressive fireworks show at dusk on July 4. Activities begin midmorning.

Rhythm & Booms
Warner Park, 1511 Northport Dr., Madison • (608) 833-6717

Occurring the first Saturday in July, this Independence Day fireworks celebration draws 100,000 people from all over the state. The pyrotechnics show culminates a day of fun-filled festivities made up of children's activities, live entertainment, bingo games and carnival rides. Traditional fireworks are teamed with laser lights in a computerized performance set to music. It's truly state-of-the-art. At about 9:30 PM, F-16s fly overhead to indicate the show is ready to begin. Donations are always appreciated, but there is no admission fee to enter Warner Park to watch the fireworks, which are also visible from across Lake Mendota at the Memorial Union Terrace or just to the north at Governor Nelson State Park.

Because so many people come to Warner, on the North Side of Madison, getting out of the park is a pain in the neck. Have a little patience, please. It's not unusual to leave the park at 10 PM and not get home until midnight. A free shuttle bus runs from the parking lot of Madison Area Technical College to the park, in order to eliminate some congestion. Is the show worth the hassles? Absolutely. People come back year after year.

Drums on Parade
Camp Randall Stadium, 1440 Monroe St., Madison • (608) 241-3171

Occurring on Thursday night in mid-July, Drums on Parade is a drum-and-bugle concert performed by seven top corps, mostly from the Midwest, who have been invited by the Madison Drum and Bugle Corps to participate. The beat and the moves are outstanding. Showtime is 7:30 PM. Tickets are $12 reserved and $7 general admission ($10 at the gate).

Art Fair on the Square
Capitol Square, Madison
• (608) 257-0158

Almost 500 juried artists from across the country and from overseas make this one of the largest outdoor art fairs in the state. Jewelry, wearable art, original paintings, pottery and furniture all are represented, with items priced from $5 into the thousands. Best get there at about 9 AM, an hour before the show is publicized to begin either Saturday or Sunday the second full weekend in July, or expect to walk slowly and en masse, counterclockwise, with most of South-Central Wisconsin. It's a very popular event. Proceeds from artists' application fees and booth rentals benefit the Madison Art Center.

Art Fair off the Square
Martin Luther King Jr. Blvd., Madison
• (608) 798-4811

Begun almost 20 years by a group of Wisconsin artists who didn't feel the Art Fair on the Square showcased enough home talent, this show — also juried, with about 130 artists and crafters — is completely separate. But few art lovers browse through one without also looking at the other. In between the two shows are food and drink booths and stages featuring live entertainment. Hours are the same as Art Fair on the Square (see the previous entry).

Olbrich Home Garden Tour
Homes in and around Madison
• (608) 246-4550

The spectacular gardens of eight private homes in or around Madison are opened to the public for two days (Saturday and Sunday) in mid-July for this garden tour benefiting Olbrich Gardens. Homes in a different neighborhood are featured each year. Tickets, about $10, are available from Olbrich, all Felly's Flowers locations and at the homes on the days of the tour.

Night at the Zoo Benefit Dance
Henry Vilas Zoo, 702 S. Randall Ave., Madison • (608) 278-5400

Although we'll never know what the zoo animals really think, even those that aren't nocturnal seem eager to join in the festivities for the annual Night at the Zoo Benefit Dance, sponsored by the Greater Madison Board of Realtors. The mid- to late-July event takes place 8 PM to midnight on a Saturday night. Tickets are $12 ($10 in advance), with food and drinks extra. Posters and T-shirts, sporting one animal or another, are always hot sellers. Money raised goes toward the construction of new zoo buildings.

Earlier in the day, from 10 AM to 2 PM, the Realtors sponsor a Kids Day, with plenty of activities and entertainment to keep them busy. The event is free.

Dane County Fair
Expo Center, 1919 Expo Way, Madison
• (608) 224-0500

Some people go to the Dane County Fair to eat, some to ride on the Ferris wheel and others to see the animals and exhibits. If you have a day, you can do it all. One of the largest county fairs in the state, this one occurs the third week in July, from early evening on Tuesday, when the carnival rides open, through Sunday. One popular attraction is the petting zoo, featuring at least a dozen baby animals — and if the pigs are racing, you should definitely be there to watch.

The barns are filled with bunnies, ducks, chickens, swine, llamas, mice (in cages), horses, cows, sheep and even snakes. The

---

INSIDERS' TIP

Attendance for the annual Wisconsin Deer & Turkey Expo has more than doubled in the past 10 years, from 11,000 people to more than 25,000. Once the show attracted primarily men. Today, women make up the biggest increase at the gate.

Exhibition Hall is filled with commercial vendors and 4-H educational projects by area youth. Entertainment takes place there and also on outdoor stages. Generally, hours are from 10 AM to whenever the midway clears out, although most of the special exhibits and booths close at 9 PM. The cost is $5 per person 12 and older; children ages 6 to 11 pay $2. Weekly passes are available. A separate parking fee is not charged for this event.

Maxwell Street Days
State St., Madison • (608) 266-6033

Always occurring the Friday and Saturday following the Art Fair on the Square (the weekend after July 4th), this festival-like sale is not only a bargain-hunter's paradise, but also a fun-filled happening with plenty of live music and food. A wide variety of clothing, books, CDs, videos, home decorative items and sporting goods can be had dirt-cheap from State Street merchants who sell from tables set up outdoors. Of course, some of the items are off-season, but who cares? Winter in Wisconsin is always just around the corner. Hours of Maxwell Street Days are 9 AM to 5 PM both days.

WaunaFest
Centennial Park, Waunakee • (608) 849-5977

An annual community festival, WaunaFest takes place the last weekend in July. Live entertainment, food, carnival rides, tug-of-war games and an arts and crafts fair are all part of the fun. Festivities begin at 5 PM on Friday and usually continue until midnight. Hours on Saturday are 9 AM until midnight; on Sunday, everything closes down at 5 PM. The parade down Main Street begins at noon on Sunday.

August

Kids Day
Capitol Square, Madison • (608) 266-6033

The first Tuesday of every August, mothers and child-care providers are invited to bring all the wee ones down to the Square between the hours of 11 AM and 1 PM to romp on the Capitol lawn and enjoy free entertainment. Many arrive by bus clutching brown-bag lunches. It's not unusual for day-care centers to ask the children to dress up for the day — in sunglasses and funny hats, for instance. With between 800 and 1,000 preschoolers parading around the Capitol, Kids Day turns out to be quite a show.

Sun Prairie Sweet Corn Festival
Angell Park, Sun Prairie • (608) 837-4547

Lots of activities are on tap during Sun Prairie's four-day festival, typically held the third weekend of August: carnival rides, a craft fair, petting zoo, beer tent and live entertainment. But the biggest attraction of all is sweet corn, served in the height of Wisconsin's corn season, but only on Saturday and Sunday (noon to 8 PM) of the fair. Bring some friends and be ready to chow down. Corn is sold by the "tote box" containing from a dozen to 15 ears. The cost in previous years has been $2.50 per person. To move the lines along, salt shakers are hung by string from clotheslines. Hours of the festival are 6 to 11 PM Thursday and Friday and noon to almost midnight Saturday and Sunday.

Sundae in the Gardens
Olbrich Gardens, 3330 Atwood Ave., Madison • (608) 246-4551

The American Horticultural Society, celebrating its 75th year in '97, selected this event as one of 75 "spectacular botanical celebrations" across the country to commemorate its diamond anniversary. Live music, games and plant information are all part of Sundae in the Gardens. But many families come just to enjoy a grilled brat or ice cream. Admission is free, although there is a charge for food and some games.

Triangle Ethnic Fest
Braxton Place, Park St. and W. Washington Ave., Madison • (608) 256-7808

Held the third Sunday in August, from 11 AM to 6 PM, the Triangle Ethnic Fest showcases a variety of ethnic dance and international foods and crafts in a family setting to celebrate the diverse ethnic heritage of the Bayview neighborhood, commonly referred to as the "Triangle." In the beginning of the 20th century, immigrants moved into the neighborhood just west of the Square because of the affordable housing available. Today, many of those homes are gone, torn down to make way for modern office buildings, medical centers and affordable rental housing. There is no admission to the festival.

Middleton Good Neighbor Festival
Fireman's Park, Middleton
• (608) 831-5696

This festival, always scheduled for the fourth weekend in August, is as friendly as its name. It begins at 5 PM on Friday with a fish fry and ends late afternoon Sunday with a slice of pie a la mode if you so desire. All activities take place at Fireman's Park, near Middleton High School, except for the parade, which always starts at 12:30 PM on Sunday and runs down University Avenue. Other traditional events include a mini-parade for kids on Friday, bingo, free live entertainment and a beer tent throughout the weekend, a pancake breakfast (Saturday morning) and a chicken barbecue (Sunday). There are also carnival rides and a nifty craft fair (Saturday and Sunday) noted for its large selection of handmade doll clothing and accessories.

Parade of Condominiums
Various sites in and around Madison
• (608) 288-1133

Started in 1996 by the Madison Area Builders Association, the Parade of Condominiums features about 10 sites, each of which may have three or four units open for viewing. If you're in the market for a condo, here's a great way to get an overview of what's available in Madison and surrounding communities. Models cost $100,000 and up. The event usually runs one full week, which includes two weekends. Hours are 3 to 8 PM Monday through Friday and noon to 6 PM Saturday and Sunday. Tickets are about $5.

September

Career Fair
Monona Terrace Convention Center,
1 John Nolen Dr., Madison
• (608) 252-6342

If you're seeking a job, this one-day employment fair in early September can help steer you in the right direction. (See the previous March entry for more information.)

Taste of Madison
Capitol Square, Madison
• (608) 831-1725

If you like to sample a little bit of a lot of things, this event on Saturday and Sunday over Labor Day weekend is made for you. Name your favorite cuisine — Oriental, Jamaican, Italian for starters — and it will be available at one or more of the 80 food booths operated by area restaurants. Samples average between $1 and $3 a piece. Beer, soft drinks and coffee are also available as well as plenty of live entertainment throughout the weekend. This means music, special programming for kids and a walking race for waiters balancing a tray of full wine glasses.

On Sunday beginning at 9 AM, a 5K "Race of the Taste" and a 2-mile family fun walk take place. Call (608) 276-6606 to register in advance.

Edgefest
Edgewood High School, 2219 Monroe St., Madison • (608) 257-1023

Held the weekend after Labor Day as a fund-raiser for Edgewood High School, this three-day festival is Madison's rite of passage into fall. It begins at noon on Friday with a "Lunchfest" and huge garage sale and continues throughout the weekend, ending at 5 PM on Sunday. In between is a variety of live entertainment, games, a bake sale, beer tent

---

INSIDERS' TIP

Sometimes you can judge the size and success of an event by the number of portable toilets requested. For Rhythm & Booms, the July fireworks display, the entire supply in the state of Wisconsin is depleted.

and craft fair. Six performances of the popular Edgefest Follies, a variety show featuring many enthusiastic parents, take place inside the school. Saturday morning, two fun runs — 5K and 2K — wind through the Arboretum nearby.

Madison Book Fair
Capitol Square, Madison
• (608) 251-6226

Held the first Saturday after Labor Day, from 9 AM to 4 PM, this event is a book lover's dream. Anything associated with books is happening here. Vendors on the square that day represent publishers, authors, mail-order catalogs and area bookstores. You can look at books or hear some of them being read.

Dane County Humane Society Dog Jog
2250 Pennsylvania Ave., Madison
• (608) 246-3342 Ext. 14

In Madison, people love their dogs so much, they turn out by the thousands — people and their four-legged friends — to participate in the Dane County Humane Society's annual Dog Jog fund-raiser, which takes place on a Sunday morning in mid-September. Most people walk their dogs instead of jogging the 2-mile course that begins and ends at the UW School of Veterinary Medicine, 2015 Linden Drive W. The entry fee includes both a T-shirt for the master and a bandana for the dog. Nary a problem has ever erupted during the event — at least, not among the dogs.

The Town and Country Antiques Show and Sale
Stock Pavilion, 1675 Linden Dr., Madison
• (608) 264-6440

Madison's most prestigious antiques show and sale is annually sponsored by the State Historical Society over a weekend in mid-September. The event usually features about 30 Wisconsin and out-of-state dealers who bring to the show a wide variety of antiques and collectibles. Hours are 10 AM to 7 PM on Saturday and 10 AM to 4 PM on Sunday. Tickets are $5. A benefit preview night with live music and a cash bar is usually planned for the Friday before the show opens. Call for information and ticket prices.

Everyone can get into the act at Madison's many festivals and events.

The Willy Street Fair
800 to 1000 blocks of Williamson St., Madison • (608) 256-3527

Over a span of 20 years, this neighborhood festival, sponsored by Common Development, Wil-Mar Neighborhood and the Crystal Corner Bar and held the third Sunday in September, has turned into a popular community-wide event. The fair, from 11 AM until 7 PM, features four stages with almost continuous live entertainment, plenty of food and arts and crafts. A short parade occurs at noon. In case of rain, the fair is postponed a week.

October

Chili Cook-off
Edgewood Motel, 101 W. Broadway, Monona • (608) 222-2385

This neighborly cooking event, sponsored by the Monona Grove Businessmen's Association to raise money for local charities, usually occurs in late September or early October, on a Saturday when the Wisconsin Badgers footballers are not playing at home. Between 24 to 50 cookers start chopping their ingredients for their favorite chili recipe at about 9 AM. Judging by a panel of local celebrities usually occurs at 1 PM, after which everyone is invited to buy samples of the various offerings for 50¢ per cup. Because the supply never lasts very long — less than an hour — the Businessmen's Association also cooks up huge pots of chili to sell along with beer and soft drinks. Be prepared: The contestants often turn out "hot" stuff, and beans are allowed! In addition to the "Best Chili Award," other cookers are singled out for best display, best costume, most unusual recipe and best of show for combining the best of everything. The day ends about 3:30 or 4 PM.

Isthmus Jazz Festival
Madison Civic Center, 211 State St., and other Madison locations
- **(608) 266-9055**

This weekend-long festival, sponsored by Friends of the Madison Civic Center, has helped create a healthy jazz scene in Madison. Major shows with such headline names as Ray Charles and Miles Davis take place in the Madison Civic Center. But there are also late-night jam sessions and other shows, some of which feature high school students, at other venues. Many of the events are free.

World Dairy Expo
Expo Center, 1919 Expo Way, Madison
- **(608) 224-6455**

The biggest dairy show of its kind in the world, World Dairy Expo draws representatives to Madison from all over the United States and up to 70 foreign countries for five days (Wednesday through Sunday) during the first week in October. Average attendance is between 65,000 and 70,000. In fact, one reason for adding on to the Expo Center was to be able to accommodate the needs of this show, which spotlights everything that is happening in the dairy industry today, from new milking machines and computer services to different kinds of cattle feed.

While this is primarily an industrial trade show, the seven breeds of dairy cows on exhibit and some of the educational dairy and food booths are interesting draws for the general public. Hours of the show are 10 AM to 5 PM. Admission is about $5 per person for anybody 12 and older. There is no parking fee for this show.

Fall Flower Show
Olbrich Gardens, 3330 Atwood Ave., Madison • (608) 246-4551

Olbrich celebrates the colors of autumn with this two-week Fall Flower Show beginning mid-October and featuring a different artistic theme every year. What remains constant, however, is the beautiful array of blooming chrysanthemums. Admission is free, and if you come the day after the show closes, you can buy pots of chrysanthemums used in the show.

Unbridaled Wedding Alternatives Party
Location changes annually
- **(608) 257-3214**

Interested in eloping on a Caribbean island and need something different but smashing to wear? Prefer an herbal wedding bouquet of flowering oregano, rosemary and lavender over roses? The Unbridaled Party, held on a Sunday in late October or early November, showcases local artisans who provide alternatives to traditional wedding products and services. Hours of the show are 10 AM to 5 PM. Tickets are about $5.

Halloween At the Zoo
Henry Vilas Zoo, 702 S. Randall Ave., Madison • (608) 288-1133

If you enjoy things that go bump in the night, you'll love the Tunnel Of Terror built and operated by the Madison Area Builders Association (MABA) and its Women's Council as a

---

INSIDERS' TIP

Despite the fact that it's only five miles in length, the Crazy Legs Run attracts participants from all over the world. Former UW students have such a good time, they find an excuse to come back no matter where they happen to be living.

fund-raiser for the zoo. It's open either the weekend before or of Halloween, beginning at 2 PM on Friday and lasting all day Saturday and Sunday. There is a nominal entrance fee.

If you have little kids that aren't quite ready for the scary stuff, take them trick-or-treating at the zoo Saturday afternoon. Area businesses donate candy and other items. In previous years, Rayovac Corp. has even given away small flashlights.

November

Winter Art Festival
Monona Terrace Convention Center, 1 John Nolen Dr., Madison
- **(608) 798-4811**

Sponsored by the Wisconsin Alliance of Artists and Craftspeople Inc., this show is typically held mid-November and showcases a variety of holiday-related gift items, jewelry, wearable art, pottery and fine art by 120 Wisconsin artisans. It's the winter version of the Art Fair off the Square. Hours are 10 AM to 6 PM Saturday and 10 AM to 4 PM on Sunday. Admission is $3 per person, although children younger than 12 are admitted free. Snacks and drinks are available at the show.

Madison Holiday Parade
Area around Capitol Square, Madison
- **(608) 831-1725**

Always held the second Sunday in November, beginning at 1 PM, this holiday parade features about 80 units made up of bands, dance troupes, floats, gigantic helium-filled balloons and Santa Claus, of course. Even Bucky Badger and Alice in Dairyland usually drive by. The parade route, around the Capitol Square and down E. Washington Avenue, is about a mile long. No matter how cold it can be, people line up along the curb, often with cups of hot chocolate in hand. (Hint: You might want to bring lawn chairs and blankets.) But if you won't be around to see it, don't worry. The parade is usually televised Thanksgiving and Christmas days.

International Holiday Festival
Madison Civic Center, 211 State St., Madison • (608) 266-6550

Annually sponsored by Friends of the Madison Civic Center, this festive event always takes place on a Sunday mid-November and points out just how ethnically diverse Madison is. Every space of the Civic Center, including both theaters, are utilized for 25 performances scheduled throughout the day, as well as for an international craft bazaar. Upstairs in the Starlight Room, a cafe is set up to serve dishes from around the world. There is no admission.

Holiday Art Fair
Madison Art Center, 211 State St., Madison • (608) 257-0158

A wonderful way to welcome the holidays, Holiday Art Fair usually is held the third weekend of November. The fair, sponsored by the Madison Art League, consists of three floors of finely crafted work by Midwest artists. Much of it is suitable for gift-giving (although it's next to impossible to leave without also buying something for yourself). Items range from ornaments and whimsical decorative pieces to beautiful hand-knit sweaters and silk ensembles. There is also a separate room showcasing homegrown Wisconsin food products. Hours are noon to 6 PM Friday, 10 AM to 5 PM on Saturday and 10 AM to 4 PM on Sunday. Admission is $3.

Kwanzaa Holiday Fair
330 W. Mifflin St., Madison
- **(608) 255-9600**

Held every year at the Madison Senior Citizen the Saturday after Thanksgiving, this Kwanzaa celebration of African-American life takes place from 10 AM until 4 PM and features for sale a variety of clothing, crafts and

---

INSIDERS' TIP

Over a two-day period during the Sun Prairie Sweet Corn Festival, held annually each August, more than 85 tons of sweet corn are cooked and served.

books, all of which have an African accent. Kwanzaa candle and libation ceremonies are held several times throughout the day. Food is also available. There is no entrance fee.

December

Jingle Bell Run
Begins at Vilas Park, 1339 Vilas Park Dr., Madison • (608) 221-9800

Sponsored by the Arthritis Foundation, this cold-weather run/walk takes place the second Saturday in December no matter how cold or snowy it might be. About 1,000 hearty souls turn out to either walk 5K or run a 5K or 10K course through the Arboretum. Festivities begin at 1 PM. The entrance fee is about $15. Call the listed number to register, and remember to avoid the icy patches.

Holiday Home Tour
Various sites throughout Waunakee • (608) 849-5977

Eight homes, fully decorated for the holidays, are opened to the public the first Saturday and Sunday in December. In between touring you'll have time to shop and take advantage of all the activities happening downtown, including horse-drawn carriage and sleigh rides. The cost of the tour, which includes a fashion show and lunch, is $25.

Holiday Fantasy In Lights
Olin-Turville Park, 1155 E. Lakeside St., Madison • (608) 222-7630

More than two dozen animated and illuminated displays, including Santa and his reindeer, come to life during the month of December at Olin-Turville Park, courtesy of the International Brotherhood of Electrical Workers, Local #159, and the local chapter of the National Electrical Contractors Association. Motorists make a giant loop around the park, accessible from John Nolen Drive on the South Side, and listen to holiday music and narration via a closed-frequency radio station while passing by the wired sculptures. There is no admission charge.

Holiday Flower and Train Show
Olbrich Gardens, 3330 Atwood Ave., Madison • (608) 246-4551

Large-scale model trains weave through a crimson forest of more than 600 blooming poinsettias during Olbrich's winter holiday show taking place most of the month of December. Each year, members of the Wisconsin Garden Railroad Society bring their trains to travel Olbrich's rails and staff the show, open from 10 AM to 4 PM Monday through Saturday and 10 AM to 5 PM on Sunday. Admission is free. Come at 2 PM Sundays, with the exception of Christmas, and enjoy holiday music, also free of charge.

Capitol Christmas Pageant
State Capitol, Madison • (608) 233-9165

Two late afternoon performances of this pageant, consisting of scenes enacting the events surrounding the birth of Jesus, are typically held the first Sunday of December unless it falls on Thanksgiving weekend. Then it occurs the following Sunday. Actors are high school volunteers. The pageant also features a main choir, echo choir and brass ensemble.

Firstar Eve
Various locations in Downtown Madison • (608) 252-4050

A variety of fun, family-related activities make up a citywide, nonalcoholic New Year's Eve party sponsored by Firstar Bank between 6 and 10 PM. Events include face-painting, storytelling, hayrides and dancing, all topped off by early fireworks at about 9:30 PM. Performance sites are Firstar Bank on the Square, State Historical Museum, the Capitol Rotunda and Madison Children's Museum. Advance tickets are about $3 for adults and $1 for children ages 5 to 15. Children younger than 5 are admitted free. Family passes for less than $10 also are available.

Madison offers children places they never get tired of — the zoo, for instance — and things to do on the spur of the moment all year round.

Kidstuff

We hope you'll keep this book in a handy spot so the next time your child moans, "Mom . . . what can I do?!" you can just flip to this chapter. With a little bit of exertion — for activities such as sledding in particular — and coaxing, we think you can make the most of whatever leisure time you and/or your children have available. But finding the time is the hardest part.

Have you ever heard of the "hurried child?" The phrase could have been coined in Madison. Many children residing here have more hectic schedules than their harried parents — fueled by school, sporting events and classes in any subject imaginable. But when you can find the time for spur-of-the-moment fun, look to our suggestions or ask other parents for tips and memorable experiences. Parent Teacher Organization (PTO) meetings are, especially, great times to exchange such chit-chat.

This chapter lists places that children never get tired of (the zoo, for instance), things to do on the spur of the moment and ideas for special outings. We also offer a list (see this chapter's Close-up) to help you plan birthday parties and information about summer programming and camps.

To cover all the bases, make sure you also read our Attractions, Arts, Festivals and Annual Events, Sports and Parks and Recreation chapters.

Education Made Fun

Madison has many places where children can have fun and learn at the same time. Although they might be too young to appreciate the significance of living in a city that is a state capital as well as home to a major university, they reap the benefits every day.

Isthmus

Madison Children's Museum
100 State St., Madison
• **(608) 256-6445**

The variety of participatory exhibits continually unfolding here teach as well as entertain children ages 1 through 12. Kids are invited to crawl through a giant fish to learn more about ecology, photograph their shadows, grow their own vegetables and then "serve" them at the juice bar and even travel around the world. Exhibits and special programming change frequently. Call ahead to find out what's new, but always know there is something going on that they will enjoy.

Museum and gift shop hours are 10 AM to 5 PM Tuesday through Sunday. If you have a very young child, you might be interested in Toddler Tuesday. From 9 to 10 AM each Tuesday, the museum opens exclusively for children 3 and younger and their adult caregivers. Admission is $3 for everyone 2 and older, except the first Sunday of every month when admission is free. Memberships also are available. There is no admission to enter the gift shop, which is filled with an assortment of games, toys and books in every price range.

Madison Public Library — Central Branch
201 W. Mifflin St., Madison
• **(608) 266-6300**

While the Madison Public Library's central branch (a.k.a. Central Library) offers the greatest selection of educational items and opportunities for children, all branches are wonderful places to visit (see our Literary Scene chapter). Something is almost always happening, except during the month of May when the children's library staff is kept busy making the rounds of area schools.

The Madison Kids Cafe series offers programs for school-age children, and the library has plenty of story-hour and video programming for preschoolers. There are books, CDs and computer software to borrow. Downtown, multimedia work stations allow children to experiment with a variety of computer programs on site. During the summer, the library sponsors reading incentive programs for young children and adolescents. Keep abreast of activities through the library's newsletter. Some programming requires registration. Call (608) 266-6345 for more information about youth services. All activities are free.

Hours are 8:30 AM to 9 PM Monday through Wednesday (until 6 PM Thursday and Friday) and 9 AM to 5 PM on Saturday.

Wisconsin Veterans Museum
30 W. Mifflin St., Madison
• (608) 264-6086

Maybe young children are unable to fully comprehend the travesties of war, but this museum, with its lifelike settings, offers hands-on information about Wisconsin's contribution to historical conflicts, from the Civil War to the Persian Gulf War. Visits are self-guided with the assistance of videotapes viewed through color monitors in the main galleries. For group tours, call (608) 266-1854.

Before leaving the museum, don't forget to take a turn at the submarine periscope that protrudes through the roof of the building and provides a panoramic view of Downtown. For more information about the museum, refer to the Attractions chapter.

Campus

Dairy Cattle Center
815 Linden Dr., Madison
• (608) 262-2271

Maybe it's not a skill most kids will ever use, but watching cows being milked can be exciting, unless, of course, you already live on a farm. No tours of the UW-Madison cattle barns are offered, but the public is invited to view the milking of the school's 90 dairy cows at 3:30 PM and 3:30 AM every day free of charge. Naturally, there are very few takers in the morning. To make the outing complete, walk over to the Babcock Hall Dairy, 1605 Linden Drive, and enjoy the fruits of the labor — ice cream!

Geology Museum
1215 W. Dayton St., Madison
• (608) 262-1412

What can kids expect to see at the Geology Museum? A blacklight mineral display and such intriguing vertebrates as a mesophippus (ancestral horse), saber-toothed cat, mastodon (Ice Age elephant) and an 18-foot mosasaur (marine lizard). The museum's extensive collection of fossilized invertebrates includes sponges, corals, snails, clams and cephalopods, including the squid.

A child growing up in Madison seldom makes it through school without several visits to this museum. But it's nice to go on your own, too.

Admission is free, although donations are appreciated. Hours of operation are 8:30 AM to 4:30 PM Monday through Friday and 9 AM to 1 PM Saturday. To arrange a group tour, call the number listed.

West Side

UW Space Place
1605 S. Park St., Madison
• (608) 262-4779

The fourth Saturday of each month at Space Place is saved for children ages 6 to 10. Beginning at 10 AM, a presentation is made on a space topic, after which children are invited to join in on a project. Kids always have something to bring home, whether it's a matching game on planet symbols or a homemade sundial. If you go, make sure you take enough time to view the exhibits and the display of satellites that have flown on space shuttles. Also, check out the computer games, including an astronomy version of Hangman.

The Kids in the Crossroads series features singing, storytelling, dancing and other amazements.

The UW Space Place is southwest of the Isthmus, a couple of miles from the UW campus.

Henry Vilas Zoo
702 S. Randall Ave., Madison
• **(608) 266-4732**

Head over to the new, $2.9-million "cat house" to see a Siberian tiger up close. For small children, feeding the goats at the Children's Zoo (open Memorial Day weekend through Labor Day weekend) is always a treat. You never know what you're going to find at the Children's Zoo, but often you'll see bear cubs, orphaned white-tailed fawns, miniature horses, spider monkeys, macaws and at least one badger, Wisconsin's state animal.

The weather doesn't have to be nice to enjoy the Discovery Center and Herpetarium building, the zoo's educational facility. Learning stations with microscopes and magnifiers are surrounded by displays of mammals, fish, birds, reptiles, amphibians and invertebrates. Many species are viewable underwater in simulated habitats.

The zoo is a favorite field-trip destination for area schools, but there are also summer zoo classes for children as young as 4. For older kids, a favorite is "Zoo Snooze," also affectionately referred to as "Bedtime with the Beasts." It's an overnighter in the Herpetarium. Can you imagine? Bedding down with snakes?

The best way to learn about classes, which fill up fast, and other special events taking place at the zoo is through the Vilas Zoological Society's *Zoo News*. But to receive a copy in the mail, you must become a zoological society member; call (608) 258-1460. For families, the cost is $25. A student membership is $15.

One more tip before we leave all the animals behind: The Vilas Zoo is one of the few places in the country where you can take a free camel ride, courtesy of Zor Shrine. The camels are there almost every Sunday during the summer months, from 10:30 AM to noon. Call ahead to make sure.

See our Attractions chapter for related information.

East Side

Olbrich Botanical Gardens
3330 Atwood Ave., Madison
• **(608) 246-4551**

Although the Bolz Conservatory isn't a real rain forest, it sure looks like one. The 50-foot-high glass pyramid is filled with more than 750 tropical plants. It's also thick with bamboo arbors, home to free-flying birds and one man-made waterfall for good measure.

Special games for children encourage exploration as they learn about a tropical environment. For instance, on a "Safari Hunt," the clue to find the Papyrus is "Growing in shallow waterways, this plant made paper in ancient days." Looking for plants that produce many common foods — lemon, cacao (the bean that makes chocolate), coconut, banana and cinnamon to name a few — also can be fun.

On weekends, children can monitor a science project by bringing home a plant cutting from the "Snipping Garden," part of the Bottle Biology Exhibit that showcases root systems and what decomposition looks like at the bottom of your compost pile.

Sometimes it's nice to visit the conservatory in the middle of winter just to remind very young children with few winters under their belts what summer is like.

It's open 10 AM to 4 PM Monday through Saturday and until 5 PM on Sundays. Admission is $1 (children 5 and younger are admitted free), except all day Wednesday and on Saturday mornings 10 AM to noon, when it's free for everyone.

On a Moment's Notice

When kids start whining and you, too, need a change of scenery fast, grab your hat and coat (or swimsuit, if the season allows) and take advantage of one of the following recommendations. Most suggestions here won't cost you a dime, although a cup of hot chocolate might taste good after sledding, and an ice cream cone is always a safe bet after an afternoon at the beach. (See our Parks and Recreation chapter for details about many of the following activities.)

When It's Too Hot To Move

Madison has 13 beaches staffed by lifeguards during the summer. There is also beach swimming near Oregon at **Goodland Park**, on the west shore of Lake Waubesa, and at **Mendota Park** in Middleton, off County Highway M.

Sometimes it's most convenient just to go to the beach nearest you (see our Parks and Recreation chapter). Yet, three of the larger and more popular ones are **Vilas**, on the north shore of Lake Wingra; **James Madison**, on the south shore of Lake Mendota and the closest beach to Downtown; and **Tenney**, farther east on Lake Mendota. The latter two are not handicapped-accessible. Vilas has an added attraction: Across the street is **Vilas Park** and the **Henry Vilas Zoo** (see this chapter's previous entry as well as the listing in our Attractions chapter).

INSIDERS' TIP

Free tickets go quickly for UW Professor Clint Sprott's magical Wonders of Physics shows, performed several times in February in Sterling Hall on campus. Call (608) 262-2927 for details or to have a member of the physics department demonstrate similar fests for a children's group or class.

Taking the Fuss Out Of Birthdays

If you're new to Madison, a neophyte when it comes to giving children's birthday parties or just plum out of ideas, read on. Help is a phone call away. Madison-area businesses are more than happy to pick up the slack. Some, in fact, not only provide food and entertainment, but also can supply invitations and party favors. All are in Madison except SwimWest Family Fitness Center (it's in nearby Middleton).

Some ideas include:

• **Playing laser tag** at Ultra Zone, 680 Grand Canyon Road, (608) 833-8880. This one is a big hit with older children, although it's also one of the more expensive ways to go. Party packages, with a six-person minimum, are about $12 per person, including one game, one large pizza, soda and either a membership to Ultra Zone for the birthday child or two free games.

• **Roller-skating** at Fast Forward, 4649 Verona Road, (608) 271-6222. The cost is about $60 for a party of eight, and that includes skating time, skate rental and the use of a party room. You bring the cake; Fast Forward supplies soft drinks and ice cream cups. Pizza can be ordered separately and delivered, or hot dogs can be purchased on site.

• **Allowing the kids to run wild** at Discovery Zone, 4617 Verona Road, (608) 274-5437, or Kid World Inc., 1701 Thierer Road, (608) 242-9636. A variety of parties are available at both facilities. Children work up an appetite playing indoors on colorful climbing and jumping equipment before settling into a party room for food, cake and soft drinks. Prices range between $10 and $14 per child, depending upon how many extras you choose.

• **Treating everyone to a sundae and carousel ride** at Ella's Deli, 2902 E. Washington Avenue, (608) 241-5291. A beautifully restored carousel outside this establishment makes stopping at this ice cream parlor, filled with old-fashioned treasures kids will adore, a real treat. One of Ella's most popular parties is "Humpty Dumpty" for $4.95 per person. It includes a choice of sundae, soft drinks, party paraphernalia and a free carousel ride for every child. Note: The carousel does close down for the winter, but the ice cream is good any time of year.

• **Swinging on an indoor play set** at Rainbow Play Systems, 6501 Seybold Road, (608) 273-2108. This manufacturer of outdoor redwood and cedar play structures hit upon a good idea when it decided to open its showroom for children's birthday parties. Not a bad way to advertise. Two-hour parties include more than an hour of play, with the remainder of time spent in the party room, where pizza, punch, banners, party hats, treat bags and cake are provided for $60 to $80 (maximum of 10 children, with an adult requested for every four kids).

In-line skating is a popular birthday party activity

Photo: Wisconsin State Journal/The Capital Times

— continued on next page

162 • KIDSTUFF

• **A movie and pizza** at Rocky Rococo's, 7952 Tree Lane, (608) 829-1444. For about $6 per child, Rocky's will do all of the work: plenty of pizza, breadsticks and pop, balloons, gift box for each child, decorations and invitations, too. Plus a movie, of course. This Rocky's is located one block east of the Mineral Point/Highway 12-18 intersection in space that once housed a restaurant/movie theater. That's why it's so ideal.

• **Playing indoor soccer or in-line hockey.** The three facilities that rent out courts and will either provide food and beverages or allow pizza and such to be brought in include the following: Capitol Sports Center, 4618 Verona Road, (608) 273-2633; Soccer World Inc. of Wisconsin, 4510 Helgesen Drive, (608) 222-8326; and Break Away Sports Center, 5964 Executive Drive, (608) 288-9600. Costs range from between $65 and $85 for a court and referee.

• **Tumbling** at Madtown Twisters, 7035 Old Sauk Road, (608) 829-2922, or Badger Gymnastics, 1922 S. Stoughton Road, (608) 221-8909, and 6901 Schroeder Road, (608) 271-1885. A variety of physical activities, including taking turns using the trampoline, make up these two-hour parties for about 10 children that range in price from $65 to $80, depending upon whether you bring the cake and beverages or the gym supplies them. Madtown also has a Sun Prairie gym at 601 S. Bird Street, 837-4555.

• **Swimming indoors** at SwimWest Family Fitness Center, 1001 Deming Way, (608) 831-6829; or at either one of the two YMCAs, 5515 Medical Circle, (608) 276-6600, and 711 Cottage Grove Road, (608) 221-1571. At SwimWest, eight children are included in the $75 cost (each additional child is $5), which includes a two-hour pool party with lifeguard and hostess to help serve lemonade provided by the facility. (Parents are asked to bring the cake.) At the YMCAs, parents must pay a small fee for each child ($4 for children younger than 12). Rooms can be rented separately.

• **Bowling and playing** at Alley Oops!, 13 Atlas Court, inside Dream Lanes, (608) 223-0700. This family-entertainment center offers pizza, a variety of skill games, a play area and bumper bowling. The cost per child is between $4 and $7, depending upon the activities chosen.

• **Letting them eat cake** at the Madison Children's Museum, 100 State Street, (608) 256-6445. Parties range in price from about $70 to $150, with a maximum of 15 children. They must also be scheduled six weeks in advance. One adult is required for every five children.

• **Climbing walls (literally)** at Boulders Rock Gym, 3964 Commercial Avenue, (608) 244-8100. Parties can be arranged for children 6 and older. There are two options available, but the one that doesn't limit the number of children is $75 minimum or $15 per child. That includes 1½ hours of gym time, harness and equipment rental, setup and cleanup, paper goods and instructor time.

• **Becoming creative** by painting pottery at Studio You, 2701 Monroe Street, (608) 231-2505. This is a fun, creative place to go, whether you're a kid or an adult and it's the only thing like it in Madison. Pieces of white bisque — everything from vases and plates to dog bowls — are available for painting. Once completed, they're glazed and fired on the premises and ready to be picked up in a couple of days. Parties range from $10 to $15 per person depending upon the ceramic pieces selected.

• **Turning the kids into nature detectives** at the new Aldo Leopold Nature Center, 300 Femrite Drive in Monona, (608) 221-0404. For a 90-minute party for 10 children that includes party favors, a one-hour program on a nature topic of your choice and party room, the price is about $70. You bring the cake and pop. The center supplies all utensils.

James Madison is open from noon to 6 PM. Hours of the other two are 10 AM to 8:30 PM. Beaches open Memorial Day weekend and close Labor Day. But if the bacterial count gets too high, which often happens come mid-July or August, the city will close certain beaches for as long as they remain affected.

Madison has no public pools. The city has seven private neighborhood facilities and three associated with country clubs that require membership fees and often have a waiting list to join.

Outlying Area

Walter R. Bauman Outdoor Aquatic Center
2400 Park Lawn Place, Middleton
• (608) 836-3450

After more than $2 million in renovations and two years in the works, Middleton's greatly enhanced outdoor aquatic center opened to the public in June of '98. Named after Walter Bauman, a former Middleton mayor, the pool, which can accommodate more than 600 swimmers at a time, offers two water slides and three water spouts. The refurbished diving well has a board and a 6-foot drop slide. There are also two sand volleyball courts on the premises.

Weekday hours are 1:30 to 8 PM, and weekends the pool is open from 11 AM to 8 PM. Daily admission for ages 3 to 17 is $2 for city residents, $2.50 for school-district residents and $3 for nonresidents. Adult rates are slightly higher. Summer family memberships are available to residents of the Middleton-Cross Plains School District.

Monona Pool
1011 Nichols Rd., Monona
• (608) 222-3098

Monona Pool is open from Memorial Day through Labor Day, and the public is welcome to cool off during open swims Monday through Friday 1 to 4:30 PM and 6:30 to 8:30 PM. On Saturday and Sunday, hours are 1 to 8:30 PM. The cost per visit is $1.50 for Monona residents and $3 for nonresidents (anyone younger than 5 is free). Seasonal passes are also available for residents and nonresidents.

The facility includes a concession stand, water slide, two diving boards and a separate wading pool for infants and small children. During the off-season, call (608) 222-4167 for information.

Sun Prairie Aquatic Center
920 Linnerud Dr., Sun Prairie
• (608) 837-7433

If you're willing to drive a little distance, your children will love the Sun Prairie Aquatic Center; it's the next best thing to the water parks in the Wisconsin Dells (see our Daytrips chapter). Sun Prairie residents receive a discount, but the daily fee for nonresidents is still quite reasonable, about $2.50 for children and $3.50 for adults. Infants younger than 6 months get in free. The pool is usually open 1 to 4 PM and 5:30 to 8:30 PM weekdays and generally noon to 4 PM and 5 to 8:30 PM Saturday and Sunday. During the off-season, call (608) 837-3449.

Jungle Gyms and All That Jazz

Because of its size and proximity to the zoo, **Vilas** is one of the most popular playgrounds in the city. It's earmarked by an "Old Woman in the Shoe" slide that young kids adore. There are two play areas with wonderful climbing structures, swing sets and monkey bars separated by enough wide-open spaces for young children to run around until they drop. Vilas is also a great spot to picnic.

M.Y. (Monona Youth) Dream Park along Healy Lane in Monona's Winnequah Park, com-

---

INSIDERS' TIP

Older children and teenagers enjoy playing disc golf on an 18-hole course in Elver Park, 1301 S. Gammon Road, on the far West Side. Remember to bring your Frisbee. The course is open spring and summer.

pleted in the fall of '97, is a 10,000-square-foot playground designed by kids specifically for kids and built by more than 3,000 volunteers. The wood structure includes all the necessities — slides, swings and parallel bars — positioned in various castle, spaceship and automobile shapes. There is a separate play area for younger children ages 2 to 5 called the "Tot Lot." The playground is open year round and is a short walk from the Monona Pool.

When school isn't in session, we'd also recommend taking children to playgrounds at **Dudgeon School**, 3200 Monroe Street, on the West Side, and **Lapham**, 1045 E. Dayton Street, on the East Side — although most any school or park in Madison will do.

Indoor playgrounds aren't as plentiful. There is **Discovery Zone**, described in the subsequent Fun For a Price section, and several small facilities connected with fast-food restaurants. One of the nicest is **McDonald's**, 6910 Odana Road, near West Towne.

Alley Oops!, part of Dream Lanes Bowling Center, 13 Atlas Court, on the East Side, is another good choice. The 400-square-foot play area is filled with tubes, slides, a sea of balls and a trampoline.

Take a Hike

UW Arboretum
1207 Seminole Hwy., Madison
• (608) 262-2746

Most children view hiking as "boring," unless it's directly related to friends, games or an adventure. But that's why the UW Arboretum is so appealing. Each trip out can easily become an adventure. Kids can follow numerous paths through open prairie grass or into deep woods. Five minutes from your car, you'll think you've left Madison far behind.

But what we think kids will enjoy the most is looking for small creatures along the Gardner Marsh Boardwalk, about a half-mile in length, that is easily accessible from the first parking lot in the Arboretum off Mills Street. Wheelchair-accessible, the boardwalk was completed in 1996.

The Arboretum is also a great place to ride bicycles. Traffic is usually light because no through traffic is allowed except from noon to 6 PM Sundays.

See our Attractions chapter for additional information about the UW Arboretum.

Freezing Cold, but Nice

Ice Skating

While lake skating is officially sanctioned by the city for a brief few weeks after the lakes freeze, we recommend you take your children to one of the many neighborhood park rinks maintained by the city or either of two lagoons: **Tenney Park**, 1440 E. Johnson Street, on the East Side; or **Vilas Park**, 1339 Vilas Park Drive, on the West Side. Both have large, groomed skating areas, warming shelters and separate, lighted hockey rinks. Hot chocolate is sold too.

Ice skating, in all its many forms, is a tradition in Madison. Next to soccer, ice hockey is one of the most popular and competitive sports on the high-school level. Remember the great Olympic speedskater Eric Heiden who won five gold medals in 1980? He's from Madison.

For recreational indoor skating, try any of the following:

Campus

Camp Randall Sports Center
1440 Monroe St., Madison
• (608) 263-6566

For skating indoors, no matter the season, Camp Randall Sports Center is a good place

---

INSIDERS' TIP

The Saturday of Memorial Day weekend is very festive at Henry Vilas Zoo. That's when the Children's Zoo opens for the season. Balloons are always given out and there is plenty of live entertainment to enjoy — in addition to what the animals provide, of course.

to go. Public skating is available noon to 1:10 PM and 5:30 to 7:20 PM Monday, Wednesday and Friday; 1:30 to 3:30 and 7:10 to 8:30 PM Saturday; and 1:30 to 3:30 PM Sunday. The cost is $2.50 for adults and $1.25 for students. Skate rental is an extra $1.25.

West Side

Madison Ice Arena
725 Forward Dr., Madison
• (608) 246-4512

Availability of indoor ice skating varies at this facility almost daily, depending on the season, level of skating and hockey schedule. Always call ahead for an updated message. Lessons are available as well as skate rentals ($2 per person). Sessions range from $3 to $5 for adults; children and seniors cost less.

East Side

Hartmeyer Arena
1834 Commercial Ave., Madison
• (608) 246-4512

Public skating and ice-skating lessons are available at Hartmeyer, although open-skate times vary widely. Costs are the same as at Madison Ice Arena (see the previous entry). As with Madison Ice Arena, always call ahead for an up-to-date schedule.

Outlying Area

Eagle's Nest Ice Arena
103 Lincoln St., Verona • (608) 845-7465

Open, public skating is available Saturdays and Sundays, but hours are likely to change, so we suggest you call ahead. The cost of skating is $2 per person per session, and skate rental is $1.50.

Mandt Ice Arena
400 Mandt Pkwy., Stoughton
• (608) 873-7528

The ice rink is usually open October through March, but the schedule for open skating varies depending on other events taking place there. Always call ahead. The cost of an open skating session is $5 per person. There is no skate rental.

Sun Prairie Ice Arena
1000 Bird St., Sun Prairie
• (608) 837-4434

Again, the schedule for open skating varies depending upon what other sporting activities are occurring at the rink, so please call ahead. The cost to skate is $3 per person and $2 for skate rental. The rink is open year round.

Sledding and Tobogganing

Because of the area's rolling topography, some children are lucky enough to be able to sled in their own backyards. If your lot is flat, don't despair. There are plenty of places to go. It just depends upon how much of a daredevil your child is.

The closest thing to an actual toboggan run is at **Elver Park**, 1301 S. Gammon Road, on Madison's far West Side. Be careful, however. The slope is pretty steep, and the trip down can be harrowing. Frankly, we much prefer the two-tiered hill at **Cherokee Middle School**, 4301 Cherokee Drive, on the near West Side. It's much gentler, although not always the easiest one to climb up, especially if you're pulling a child. On the East Side, on a par with Elver, is the hill on which the **Dane County Human Services Department** sits, at 1202 Northport Drive. It's quite a show for the employees inside on those wonderful days when school is called off because of too much snow.

As a safety reminder to parents and their children, please do not sled too close to trees, and once down the slope, quickly get out of the way of other sledders barreling down behind you. Walk back up in a single file at the far side of the hill, out of the way of the action.

Skiing

The city grooms almost 30 kilometers of cross-country ski trails at seven city parks and two golf courses, and many of those trails are flat enough for young beginners to maneuver. Maps are available from the Madison Parks Department, (608) 266-4711.

Rental equipment for adults and children is available from the **Village Peddler**, (608) 221-0311, 5511 Monona Avenue, Monona; **REI**, (608) 836-6680, 7483 West Towne Way, near West Towne Mall, Madison; or **Odana Golf Course**, (608) 266-4078, 4635 Odana Road, Madison.

The nearest downhill ski slope is **Tyrol Basin**, (608) 437-4135, in Mount Horeb, southwest of Madison. If you're planning on doing a lot of downhill skiing, look into a season pass there.

See our Parks and Recreation chapter for detailed entries and related information.

Swimming

Madison Area Technical College
Truax Campus, 3550 Anderson St., Madison • (608) 246-6093

Just because it's cold outside doesn't mean you can't go swimming. A perfect place to do it is the Truax campus of Madison Area Technical College, on the far East Side. Family swims usually are available 6:30 to 8:30 PM Tuesday, Thursday and Friday and noon to 2 PM Saturday. But the schedule often changes, so call ahead to verify times. The cost is about $2 per visit for adults and $1 per visit for children younger than 16. No one younger than 16 is allowed to swim without an adult present.

YMCA
5515 Medical Cir. (West Side), Madison • (608) 276-6600
711 Cottage Grove Rd. (East Side), Madison • (608) 221-1571

While most people who use the YMCA are members, it is possible to purchase a day pass to use the swimming pool or other facilities. The price ranges from $4 for children to $8 for adults or $16 for a family. Family swims are hosted every Friday night from 6:45 to 8 PM. Open swims are also available daily at various times. Call for a schedule.

Fun for a Price

Here are some places to go that cater to children . . . for a price, of course. Depending upon how the rest of your day has gone, it might be the best money you spend all week. Hours and rates are subject to change without notice so call ahead if price, especially is an issue. Many of the businesses mentioned here also do birthday parties. If you're in the market, refer to this chapter's related Close-up.

West Side

Discovery Zone
4617 Verona Rd., Madison
• (608) 274-5437

Especially when it's too cold to play outside, this glorified indoor jungle gym consisting of multicolored slides, mazes, laser tag and climbing structures is heaven to a young child, especially if he or she has a friend along. Hours of operation are 10 AM to 8 PM Monday through Thursday, until 9 PM Friday and Saturday and 11 AM until 7 PM on Sunday. The cost is $4.99 for children 38 inches or less in height and $7.99 for children taller than 38 inches up to age 16. Adults and kids younger than 1 get in free with a paying child. Don't expect to drop off your child so you can go do some shopping: A parent or guardian must remain on site at all times. Remember, socks are required to play.

Fast Forward
4649 Verona Rd., Madison
• (608) 271-6222

Many a parent has had to crawl off the rink on hands and knees after attempting a maneuver they hadn't tried since high school. Even so, roller skating remains a rite of passage for many families.

Public skating is available here in sessions that include 7 to 10 PM Friday, 10 AM to noon (for children 10 and younger and their parents) and 1 to 4 PM on Saturday. Teens are attracted to "Rap, Rhythm and Jam" night 9:30 PM to midnight every Saturday. There's also "Cheap Skate Night," 6:30 to 8:30 PM Wednesday night, when parents skate free with a child.

Depending upon the sessions, entrance fees range from $3 to $5, with family passes available at certain times. Skate rental is $1.50 for roller skates and $3 for in-line skates.

Schwoegler Park Towne Lanes
444 Grand Canyon Dr., Madison
• (608) 833-7272

Here's something that will particularly appeal to the teenager in your house. This and

There are many places in Madison where children can learn and have fun at the same time.

several other area bowling alleys (see subsequent entries) are offering blacklight (a.k.a. "lunar" or "cosmic") bowling, on Monday and Saturday nights after league play ends (9 PM or later). Bright lights are replaced by black lights that pick up glow-in-the-dark strips on the lanes and turn special bowling balls pink and orange. Laser beams, pop music and sometimes even fog rolling out from the pin pits adds to the fun. The cost ranges from $1.50 to $2.25 per person per game, depending on the night.

And remember, if you wear a white T-shirt, it will glow too.

Ultra Zone
680 Grand Canyon Dr., Madison
- **(608) 833-8880**

Laser-beam tag, especially appealing to older children and adolescents, is one of the newer fads to hit Madison. The trick is to avoid getting "hit" by a beam of light shot by your opponent(s). The facility is open 4 to 11 PM Tuesday through Thursday, 2 PM to midnight Friday, 10 AM to midnight Saturday and noon to 10 PM Sunday. The only thing that will slow kids down is the cost. For nonmembers, it's $6.50 for 15 minutes of actual play. Children who pay to become members ($12) receive a discount.

George Vitense Golfland
5501 W. Beltline Hwy., Madison
- **(608) 271-1411**

Remember the old-fashioned miniature golf courses with spinning windmills, Eiffel Towers and an assortment of other obstacles to go through, under or around? Vitense Golfland is it. The two 18-hole courses have been augmented over the years, but the flavor remains true to the original course.

During the peak summer months, the facility is open 7:30 AM to 11 PM Sunday through Thursday and until 11:30 PM Friday and Saturday. In Madison, one of the first signs of spring is the opening of the golf range here. (February 21 in 1998 — what a year!) If all goes well, the par 3 course opens sometime in March. Everything buttons down for the winter at the end of October.

Cost of miniature golf is $3.50 for children and $4.50 for adults. The par 3 course is $4.50 for children 12 and younger and seniors 55 and older and $5.50 for adults. Batting cages are also available (10 pitches for 50¢).

East Side

Dream Lanes
13 Atlas Ct., Madison • (608) 221-3596

This bowling alley offers blacklight bowling Friday and Saturday nights after league play ends (9 PM or later). Blacklight bowling costs about the same or slightly more than regular bowling. See the previous Schwoegler Lanes entry for details.

Boulders Rock Gym
3964 Commercial Ave., Madison • (608) 244-8100

Since Madisonians love everything about the outdoors, we knew it would only be a matter of time before a climbing gym opened here. While geared primarily to adults, Boulders will allow children to climb with a certified parent. Classes also are offered to children, and every Friday night is Kid's Night.

The gym has 8,000 square feet of climbing space, a bouldering cave, 42 top ropes and 28 lead lines. Hours of operation are 4 to 11 PM Monday through Thursday, 4 to midnight Friday, 10 AM to 6 PM Saturday and noon to 6 PM Sunday. The cost is about $11 per day although memberships are available as well as week-long day camps during the summer.

Kid World Inc.
East Point Plaza, 1701 Thierer Rd., Madison • (608) 242-9636

Thank goodness there are indoor playgrounds on both sides of town where kids can run off excess energy no matter how nasty it is outside. Kid World Inc., in East Point Plaza shopping center, has three separate play areas, one of which is designated for children 3 and younger, and another for children 40 inches and taller. Everyone is invited to tear around in the third area. There are ball pits, padded fun machines, roller runs and rope walks. There is no cutoff age, but a parent must remain on the premises.

Hours are Monday through Thursday, 11 AM until 8 PM; Friday and Saturday, 10 AM to 9 PM; and Sunday, 11 AM until 7 PM. Price of admission for children older than 2 is $4.95 (add $1 on Friday and Saturday); children ages 1 to 2 are $3.95; and kids younger than 1 are free.

Rollerdrome
1725 N. Stoughton Rd., Madison • (608) 244-7646

Rollerdrome is to the East Side what Fast Forward (see previous entry) is to the West Side. There are roller-skating sessions from 7 to 10 PM Wednesday, 7:30 to 10:30 PM Friday, 2 to 4:30 PM and 7:30 to 10:30 PM Saturday and 2 to 4:30 PM Sunday. The cost is $3 to $4.50. Skate rental is about $1 more. From noon to 1:30 PM Saturday the Rollerdrome has a Kiddie Matinee for children 11 and younger and their parents. The cost is only $2.

Outlying Area

Green Golf Center
3110 Laura Ln., Middleton • (608) 831-5559

Open from March until the end of October (weather permitting, of course), the Green Golf Center offers 36 holes of miniature golf ($3.25 for 18 holes, $5.75 for unlimited play), a par 3 course ($7 for adults, $5.50 for juniors younger than 16 and senior citizens) and driving range ($4.25 to $9.25 depending upon the size of the bucket of balls). A snack bar is inside; group and private golf lessons are also available. In the height of the summer season, the facility is usually open from 8 AM until 10 PM.

INSIDERS' TIP

In the Discovering Primates building at Henry Vilas Zoo, a "power grip" offers visitors the opportunity to test their upper-body strength against the apes. After hanging on the bar just 15 seconds, you'll have a real appreciation for the stamina of gibbons who can swing through the trees for up to five hours at a time.

Rude's Lanes
210 E. Holum St., DeForest
- **(608) 846-5959**

Rude's offers Glo 'N' Bowl Friday and Saturday nights after league play for $2 per person per game. See the previous Schwoegler Park Towne Lanes entry for details about blacklight bowling.

Free Entertainment

A lot of activities mentioned previously in this chapter are free and entertaining for children. So are the next two. But we feel that they deserve to be in a category all to themselves. To learn more about an International Children's Festival at the Madison Civic Center every March, refer to our Festivals and Annual Events chapter.

Now, it's SHOW TIME!

Kids in the Crossroads
Crossroads Lobby, Madison Civic Center, 211 State St., Madison
- **(608) 266-6550**

Almost every Saturday from September to May, two free shows (11 AM and 1 PM) are presented in the Civic Center's Crossroads lobby. The "Kids in the Crossroads" series, underwritten in part by brothers Irwin and Robert Goodman of Goodman's Jewelers, showcases a variety of entertainment including puppeteers, storytellers, folk singing, ethnic dancing and amazing science experiments. The second performance each Saturday is signed for the hearing-impaired.

Mad-City Ski Team
Lake Monona, Law Park, 355 John Nolen Dr., Madison • (608) 255-2537

We're big fans of the Mad-City Ski Team that performs a free water-skiing show every Sunday night during the summer months, June through August, on Lake Monona, along the shores of Law Park. The show begins promptly at 7 PM. Some parking is available at Law Park or, for a small fee, you can park at the Monona Terrace Convention Center nearby. In fact, you can see the show from the Rooftop Garden of the center, although most people take advantage of bleacher seating inside the park.

The Mad-City Ski Team is made up of about 100 adults and children. For more information, call the Madison Convention and Visitors Bureau at the number listed.

Especially for Teens

New Loft (teen center)
112 N. Fairchild St., Madison
- **(608) 251-7175, Ext. 102**

This Downtown hangout for teens ages 14 to 18 offers a variety of activities every day of the week except Sunday. Weekdays, the facility is open after school from 3:30 to 8:30 PM. Teens gather to play games, including pool, chess and checkers; seek help from available tutors; participate in a photo lab or theater group; or simply talk. A membership fee of $5 is good for the entire year.

There are also planned activities every day of the week. For instance, the latest movie rentals are shown on Thursdays, and different cultures are explored in an Arts Around the World program Wednesdays. Dances, with DJs, are held every Friday night from 7:30 to 11:30 PM with an admittance fee of $5 that includes pizza and soft drinks. On Saturday evening, with live bands scheduled from between 7:30 to 11:30 PM, the cost is $4.

Drugs and alcohol are not allowed on the premises. Anybody who tries to bring any in is banned from the premises for life. As an extra word of precaution, we suggest that young, newly licensed drivers not drive Downtown until they have had several months of driving experience. Madison, with all its one-way streets, can be confusing, especially after dark.

Camps

Day Camps and Classes

Day camps have become a way of life for many Madison-area children who have working parents. But, if you're a kid, it's far easier (and more enjoyable, we might add) to get up at the crack of dawn to go swimming, horseback riding and play tennis with friends than it is to roll out of bed for school.

Usually during the first week of March, Madison School-Community Recreation, a department of the Madison Metropolitan School District, sponsors annual summer preview **activity fairs** at Memorial High School (on the West Side) and La Follette High School (on the East) for parents to learn about what kinds of camps, organized sports activities, enrichment programs and classes are available either through the school district or other organizations serving area families. Dates for the fairs are usually announced in February school newsletters, but you can also find out by calling (608) 266-6070.

If you are looking for full-time day camps to keep your child occupied for most of the summer, two organizations that can offer monumental help are the **YMCA of Metropolitan Madison**, (608) 276-6606, and **After School Inc.**, (608) 233-9782. Prices for full-day camps five days a week for school-age children range from $80 to $100 per week, depending upon the activities involved and age of the child. The YMCA operates programs throughout Dane County. After School primarily serves the West Side of Madison and Middleton.

Both organizations are mindful that older children, ages 11 to 14, should be allowed greater freedom than younger children. Field trips and activities are planned with that in mind. Especially popular is After School's "Wandering Wisconsin." A dozen children, accompanied by two adults load into a van and drive to a state park where they camp for a week. The cost is $200.

Registration for summer programs usually begins mid-March. Don't tarry or you might be left out. (For more information about child-care options, see our Child Care chapter.)

Resident Camps

In Wisconsin alone, there are about 200 summer camps for children. Some are traditional, focusing on watersports, horseback riding and singing around a campfire. Others zero in on a particular interest such as soccer, basketball, music or computer programming.

If your child has enjoyed day camps in the past, is at least 7 or older and has expressed an interest in attending an overnight camp, this might be a good time to nudge him or her out of the nest, if only for a few days. Going with a friend often eases last-minute jitters.

Camp fees vary but generally range from $15 to $55 per day at those operated by nonprofit organizations such as the Girl Scouts, Boy Scouts or YMCA. Independent, privately run camps range from about $35 to $100 per day. In addition, some camps charge extra for some activities such as horseback riding.

While the summer preview fairs annually sponsored by the Madison School-Community Recreation Department primarily focus on day camps (see previous section), a few resident camps near Madison are represented. So are some sports camps directed by UW-Madison athletic coaches. (To track down information about a specific sports camp operated by a coach, call the UW Athletic Office, (608) 262-1866.)

For even more options, however, contact the **American Camping Association**'s Wisconsin office in Milwaukee, (414) 967-8185, and ask for a free directory listing of ACA-accredited camps in the region. For a national guide costing $10.95, call (800) 428-CAMP. Both can offer real peace of mind.

Camps approved by the American Camping Association are subject to on-site inspections and must meet certain standards ad-

> **INSIDERS' TIP**
>
> A family membership in the Madison Nordic Ski Club enables children to cross-country ski every Wednesday after school at Odana Hills Golf Course. Call (608) 222-1928 or the club's hotline, (608) 233-MADK, for information.

dressing everything from how food is prepared and stored to the qualifications of medical personnel and other staff members. If you're considering a camp for your child that isn't accredited by the American Camping Association, you need to do some serious homework. Visit the site, inquire about the ratio of campers to counselors and check the credentials of staff members. Ask for references and a full list of camp policies. In short, make sure the camp is a safe, inviting environment for your child.

The following is a list of accredited camps often attended by Madison-area youth. It represents just a sample of what is available.

Bethel Horizons
Wis. Hwy. 1, Dodgeville • (608) 257-3577

Bethel Horizons is a nonprofit, Lutheran-based church camp that has a diverse summer program but also provides environmental education for school groups and organizations throughout the year. It's noted for its nature center.

Camp Black Hawk
N2674 Black Hawk Rd., Elton
• (715) 882-2641

Although this is a Girl Scout camp, non-Scouts are welcome to attend. Activities include canoeing, backpacking, arts and crafts, sailing, swimming, etc. Camp Black Hawk offers one- and two-week sessions from June through August.

Camp Gray
E10213 Shady Lane Rd., Reedsburg
• (608) 356-8200

Close to Mirror Lake State Park, Camp Gray is a Christian camp operated by the Catholic Diocese of Madison. It offers a broad range of programs including a ropes course, sports, drama and horseback riding. One- and two-week sessions are offered.

Phantom Lake YMCA Camp
YMCA Camp Rd., Mukwonago
• (414) 363-4186

This is one of nine resident camps in Wisconsin operated by the YMCA. There are eight six-day sessions during summer, two of which are coed. Camping skills, gymnastics, kayaking and archery are offered along with swimming, sailing and tennis.

The Madison Children's Museum makes learning fun.

Camps Wawbeek and Pioneer
Wis. Hwy. 13 N., Wisconsin Dells
• (608) 277-8288

This residential camp is operated by Easter Seal Society of Wisconsin for children and adults with physical disabilities. The wide range of activities includes riflery, swimming, basketball and archery.

Hoofbeat Ridge Resident Camp
5304 Reeve Rd., Mazomanie
• (608) 767-2593

This family-operated coed camp specializes in horsemanship and horse care. One-, two- and three-week sessions are available. Hoofbeat also offers day camps with daily bus transportation from Madison.

Interlaken
7050 Old Wis. Hwy. 70, Eagle River
• (414) 967-8240

Operated by the Milwaukee Judaism Community Center, this camp is in the North Woods on Lake Finley. It is a Jewish camp with kosher food, but children don't have to be Jewish to attend. Traditional camp activities are offered as well as windsurfing, water skiing, soccer and video production. Sessions are two to eight weeks in length.

What makes Madison such a lively, affordable arts community is not the road shows or big headliners that roll through town on their way someplace else, but a rich and diverse base of home talent that often performs for free.

The Arts

People who complain about the high cost of entertainment in and around Madison sometimes get laughed off the street. (And if they don't, they really should.) Even a ticket to hear the Rolling Stones here was substantially cheaper than the very same concert in New York or Chicago.

Yet, what makes Madison such a lively, affordable arts community is not the road shows or big headliners that roll through town on their way someplace else, but a rich and diverse base of home talent that often performs for free. That's right. Between the UW-Madison dance, theater and music departments and other dedicated artists, there is something happening almost all the time, with the quality of entertainment far surpassing what you have to pay for it nearly all of the time. Madison has its own children's, professional, experimental and senior-citizen theater companies and a wide variety of dance troupes. During the summer months, a week doesn't go by without a community orchestra or chamber ensemble playing outdoors for free.

Besides actual performances, many other exciting things are happening in Madison related to the arts. In spring 1996, the Monroe Street Arts Center opened on the near West Side. Serving both children as young as 4 and adults, the nonprofit operation is offering classes in everything from t'ai chi exercise to photography, music and art. Private and group classes are available. Call (608) 232-1510 for information.

Some services are natural extensions of the arts. Theater Bus was founded in '76 to make the area's cultural events more accessible to adults 60 and older. For a fee, it provides transportation and tickets to many performances. Call (608) 257-0003 between 9 AM and noon Monday through Friday for information.

While we couldn't include everything in this chapter, we hope to give visitors and residents alike a feel for just how strong the arts pulse is in and around Madison. We've included some of the more active cultural organizations, venues and performance groups (for adults and children) plus art museums and other exhibition spaces including commercial galleries.

To learn even more about cultural and performance organizations throughout Dane County, ask for the 1997 edition of the very helpful *Dane County Cultural Resources Directory* (it's published every three years). Copies are free through the Dane County Cultural Affairs Commission, City-County Building, Room 421, 210 Martin Luther King Jr. Boulevard, Madison WI 53709. Also, for more information on the literary arts, see our Literary Scene chapter. For a guide to outdoor sculpture in Madison, refer to the "Attractions" chapter.

A Year of Special Events

September 1998 marks the beginning of the University of Wisconsin-Madison's year-long celebration of its 150th birthday, following closely on the heels of the State of Wisconsin's own sesquicentennial that concluded in spring of 1998. UW-Madison's celebration is highlighted by a series of community and statewide events, including lectures, concerts and special art projects.

While many details were still being worked out as this book went to press, some signature dates are established. They include the week of February 5, 1999, to commemorate the first day of classes. At that time, the School of Music will take center stage at the Kohl Center by showcasing the school's musical history with the help of the Marching Band, Jazz Ensemble, Concert Choir and Symphonic Orchestra.

A prominent national speaker is expected to cap off the sesquicentennial celebration in the fall of '99.

In anticipation of an influx of visitors, Transportation Services is releasing an updated map to include information about parking, bus routes and a walking tour of lower campus and the Bascom Hill historic district. There are even plans for Babcock Hall (dairy plant) to unveil a new flavor of ice cream during Alumni Week, May 2 through 7 of 1999.

A schedule of events will be available at various locations on campus including the Memorial Union. For information about UW-Madison's sesquicentennial celebration, call (608) 265-3044.

Minding the Cultural Store in Dane County

There are many organizations whose sole purpose is to promote and support the arts in and around Madison. The following four are especially instrumental in coordinating and sometimes producing cultural activities enjoyed by the public.

Arts Consortium
Humanities Building, Rm. 5542, 455 N. Park St., Madison • (608) 263-4086

Made up of more than 20 faculty members from the UW-Madison who are actively involved in creative writing, textile design, art history, theater and more, the Consortium was established in 1975 to coordinate arts activities on campus, provide a forum for academic and artistic issues and serve the general public by helping to develop cultural outreach and continuing education programs.

Dane County Cultural Affairs Commission
City-County Building, Rm. 421, 210 Martin Luther King Jr. Blvd., Madison • (608) 266-5915

This government agency was created in 1977 to support local arts and help promote the county's cultural resources. It has produced a variety of excellent artistic projects and informational publications and brochures for adults and children.

What people most look forward to, however, is the release of the commission's annual art poster, which always displays a work by a Wisconsin artist above a calendar for area art fairs. Thanks to funding from the private sector, 10,000 of these posters, suitable for framing, are distributed free each February through the City-County Building or the city or village halls of Fitchburg, Middleton, Monona, Stoughton, Sun Prairie, Verona and Mount Horeb.

To support the arts, commission grants totaling about $250,000 annually are awarded three times a year on a competitive basis to individuals, nonprofit organizations and public institutions seeking supplementary funds for cultural projects. Grant application deadlines are February 1, June 1 and September 1.

Madison CitiARTS
215 Martin Luther King Jr. Blvd., Madison • (608) 261-9134

This 12-member, appointed citizen commission advises the mayor and Common Council on civic arts-related projects and policies. It oversees the Art In Public Places Program, which provides funds for the placement of permanent works of art in Madison, and the CitiARTS Grants Program, which awards matching grants to individuals and organizations for visual, performing and literary arts. (Application deadline is April 1.) The staff also maintains gallery space in the Madison Municipal Building for local artists to exhibit their work, and, as part of S.O.S. Madison, funds are raised for the maintenance and landscaping of Madison's permanent outdoor works of art.

Mall-Concourse Office
215 Martin Luther King Jr. Blvd., Madison • (608) 266-6033

The Mall-Concourse office schedules free activities in five performance spaces on State Street and the Capitol Square and helps to

THE ARTS • 175

promote free cultural activities Downtown, including the Art Fair on the Square and Concerts on the Square.

Will the Curtain Please Rise

There are hundreds of devoted, talented performers in town who are just as happy entertaining in front of an audience gathered on a street corner as one seated in a legitimate theater. But to see Broadway touring shows, plays and big-name entertainers, the following venues — listed geographically so you'll know how much traveling time you'll need — are the most frequented places.

Isthmus

Dane County Memorial Coliseum
Rimrock at John Nolen Dr. (south of the Capitol Square), Madison
• **(608) 267-3999**

Elvis Presley, Liberace, Sonny and Cher in their heyday, Tina Turner, Fleetwood Mac, Billy Joel, Alice Cooper, Eric Clapton, Frank Sinatra and Red Skelton all have performed over the years in the Memorial Coliseum, part of the Dane County Expo Center. Because of its capacity to hold more than 10,000 spectators, it also hosts every circus and ice show that comes to town.

Hours for the box office are 9 AM until 5 PM Monday through Friday. It's closed Saturday and Sunday unless there is a show occurring or tickets go on sale for a big event, then hours vary. It isn't unusual for people to camp overnight (even in winter) to be first in line to buy tickets for some hot performers.

Esquire Theatre
11 E. Mifflin St., Madison
• **(608) 767-2550**

Actually, Esquire Theatre is the previous name of this venue, which had undergone a major face-lift and was awaiting its new name at the time this book went to press. More than $500,000 and a lot of elbow grease was used to transform the former movie house, built in 1971 a block off the Square, into a 265-seat auditorium for primarily live theater. Community theater groups began staging performances here in August 1998. Local groups using the facility include Reprise Theater, The Madison Theatre Guild, Strollers and Mercury Players. The box office had not opened by press time, but more information is available by calling the listed number.

Madison Civic Center
211 State St., Madison • (608) 266-9055 (Ticket Office), (608) 266-6550 (Administration)

Because the two theaters in the Madison Civic Center are filled all the time, it's difficult to imagine life here without them. Yet, this facility didn't even exist until 1980. (See the Attractions chapter for more background information on the building itself.)

The larger of the two auditoriums, the Oscar Mayer Theater, seats 2,200 people and annually showcases a wide variety of touring musicals, dance ensembles, orchestras and entertainers. Performers who have crossed the stage over the years include George Carlin, David Copperfield, Miles Davis, Ray Charles, Ella Fitzgerald, Mikhail Baryshnikov and Lily Tomlin. The Madison Symphony Orchestra and Madison Opera also perform here.

The smaller, 300-seat Isthmus Playhouse showcases plays and smaller ensembles. It's home to two local theater companies, Madison Repertory Theater and CTM Productions. The Civic Center also features several meeting rooms and reception areas including the versatile Starlight Room that some arts groups also use as a performance space.

To take advantage of the antique Barton pipe organ (it's still in excellent working condition) in the Oscar Mayer Theater, the Civic Center annually sponsors a silent film series with old classics starring Charlie Chaplin, Harold Lloyd, Buster Keaton and W.C. Fields. It really takes you back to the '20s, to the era when the forerunner of the Oscar Mayer, the old Capitol Theatre, was built to host vaudeville and movies.

Free family entertainment is often featured over the noon hour on Saturdays in the Crossroads area between the two the-

Memorial Carillon

A visit to Madison isn't complete without hearing "the bells" ring on campus.

The University of Wisconsin Memorial Carillon (see also our Attractions chapter) is played by carillonneur Lyle Anderson almost every Sunday afternoon during the school year. Throughout the spring semester a 30-minute concert begins at 3:15 PM Sunday, although the bell tower is open to the public from 3 to 4 PM. And at 1 PM Wednesday and Friday during the spring semester, a short, 15-minute recital is presented. During the fall semester and eight-week summer session, Anderson performs from 3 to 4 PM Sunday. In addition, on Thursdays in July, a 7:30 PM concert is followed by a tour.

The UW Memorial Carillon is at the top of Bascom Hill along Observatory Drive, between Ingraham Hall and the Social Science Building. Built in 1935, it is 85 feet tall and made of Madison sandstone. Fifty-six bells ranging from 15 to 6,800 pounds give the carillon a 4½-octave range. To make sure the bells will ring as announced here, call (608) 262-1197 for a recording of the current season's schedule.

The University of Wisconsin's Carillon Tower is a visual and aural icon on campus.

INSIDERS' TIP

UW's School of Music annually sponsors more than 300 performances by student ensembles, resident faculty ensembles and guest artists. For upcoming events, call the Concert Line at (608) 263-9485.

aters and the Madison Art Center. (See the Kidstuff chapter.)

Ticket Office hours are 11 AM to 5:30 PM Monday through Friday and 11 AM until 2 PM Saturday. The box office also remains open before and during shows in either theater. There is no service charge when buying tickets at the Ticket Office window, in the lower level of the Civic Center. However, a handling fee is added to phone and mail orders.

Campus

Fredric March Play Circle
800 Langdon St., Madison
• (608) 262-6333

The Fredric March Play Circle, upstairs from the Wisconsin Union Theater in the Memorial Union, is named for illustrious actor Fredric March, who graduated from the UW-Madison. The 168-seat auditorium is used regularly for films and lectures as well as for student productions. Call the listed number for upcoming events and prices.

Humanities Building
455 N. Park St., Madison
• (608) 263-1900

The Humanities Building houses most of the UW music classrooms and faculty studios as well as the Wisconsin Center for Music Technology, a sophisticated computer-music laboratory. The building has three performance spaces: the 770-seat Mills Concert Hall, the 220-seat Morphy Recital Hall and Eastman Recital Hall, which seats 175 people. For concert information, call (608) 263-9485.

Kohl Center
601 Dayton St., Madison
• (608) 262-1440

While the Kohl Center is home to UW hockey and basketball, the arena can also seat up to 17,000 people for big-name entertainers such as Shania Twain who performed here in July 1998. The phone number listed above is a branch of Ticketmaster. (For more information, see the Attractions and Sports chapters.)

Lathrop Hall
1050 University Ave., Madison
• (608) 262-1691

This Renaissance Revival-style building has housed UW dance programming since 1910 and was renovated to the tune of $4.6 million in 1997-98. Most noticeable is a greatly enhanced auditorium, the 240-seat Margaret H'Doubler Performance Space, named after the late dancer who developed the first college degree in dance in the entire country in 1926 at the UW-Madison. Featured throughout the school year are dance recitals/performances by faculty, students and guest artists. No box office is connected with the building. Tickets are sold through the Union Theater box office and at the door prior to a show. Although Lathrop Hall is in a congested area of campus, parking is usually available at Grainger Hall (across University Avenue) or at Lot 20, three blocks west of Lathrop.

Music Hall
925 Bascom Mall, Madison
• (608) 263-1900

Built in 1878 and renovated in 1985, Music Hall includes the 385-seat Carol Rennebohm Auditorium and is the home of University Opera. Many concerts and recitals by UW music students and faculty also are performed here. To find out what's happening each week, call (608) 263-9485.

Vilas Communications Hall
821 University Ave., Madison
• (608) 262-1500

Vilas Hall is the home of the Department of Theatre and Drama and its performance arm, University Theater. Plays are staged in either the Ronald E. Mitchell Theatre, a 321-seat auditorium with a thrust stage, or the Gilbert V. Hemsley multiform performance space seating 150. The box office is open 11:30 AM to 5:30 PM Monday through Friday and 30 minutes before a performance.

Wisconsin Union Theater
800 Langdon St., Madison
• (608) 262-2201

Considered the cultural hub of the UW-Madison, the Wisconsin Union Theater is in the Wisconsin Union along the campus lakefront. Almost 60 years old, the theater has a seating capacity of 1,300. As a multipurpose performance facility, the art deco-designed theater attracts a wide range of international artists in music, dance and theater — Gregory Peck is one example — to perform for and with students. Annual offerings include the Union Theater Concert Series, the Union Theater Performance Series and Travel Adventure Film Series. For armchair travelers, the latter is very popular. All events are open to the public.

The box office is open from 11:30 AM to 5:30 PM Monday through Friday and noon to 5 PM on Saturday. To be put on the Union Theater's mailing list, call the listed number.

West Side

Oakwood Theater
6209 Mineral Point Rd., Madison
• (608) 231-3451

This 230-seat auditorium, which is part of the residential retirement community of Oakwood Village (see our Retirement and Senior Services chapter), is often rented out by schools and nonprofit groups for plays, recitals and other performances. Many events are staged expressly for the residents and their families. These include a fund-raising variety show, *Encore*, held in even years, usually late winter or early spring. If you have talent to spare, you may want to volunteer.

East Side

Barrymore Theatre
2090 Atwood Ave., Madison
• (608) 241-8633 (Ticket Office),
(608) 241-8864 (Administration),
(608) 241-2345 (24-hour taped info line)

This 800-seat auditorium dates back to December 1929 when it first opened as a posh vaudeville movie palace with an opulent Spanish hacienda theme. It was the first theater in Madison built for talking pictures, and the original stars in the domed ceiling continue to twinkle today.

In '87, thanks to concerned residents who didn't want to see it razed, the theater was partially restored and is now owned by the Schenks Atwood Revitalization Association for the community it serves.

The Barrymore showcases a variety of mainstream and alternative entertainment. Appearing on stage in the past: Arlo Guthrie, Red Hot Chili Peppers, Lyle Lovett, The Second City National Touring Company, Green Day and the Lesbian Variety Show. Occasionally, special films also are shown. The administrative office is open noon to 5 PM Monday through Friday. Tickets can be ordered during those hours too.

Brave Hearts Theatre
1988 Atwood Ave., Madison
• (608) 249-9299

With seating for up to 90 people, this performance space opened about five years ago to give fledgling performance groups an economical space to stage their work. It's been home to dance, music, theater and video productions. It can also be rented out for private parties and workshops.

Mitby Theater
3550 Anderson St., Madison
• (608) 243-4000

Completed in 1986, the Mitby Theater, on the Truax campus of Madison Area Technical College, is one of the newest auditoriums in the city and the most practical at 985 seats. In addition to MATC performance groups, many citywide, nonprofit organizations utilize the space. Box office hours are 11 AM to 4:30 PM Monday through Friday and one hour before showtime.

Outlying Area

Stoughton City Hall Theater
381 E. Main St., Stoughton
• (608) 873-6677

Built in 1901, this 700-seat theater is on the second floor of Stoughton's City Hall. The first play ever performed in the auditorium was *The Doctor's Warm Reception*. Through the years, the theater has been the site of traveling road shows, lectures, political rallies, concerts and high school graduation ceremonies.

The Elvehjem Museum of Art on the UW-Madison campus is home to an impressive collection.

Performing Arts

Whatever your pleasure — dance, music or theater — there's plenty of it to go around in South-Central Wisconsin. We've listed some of the more active arts groups alphabetically under the three headings listed above — plus a fourth, multidisciplinary arts — since many perform at a variety of venues depending upon the season and availability of auditoriums. Besides, it's relatively easy to get anywhere in Madison if you're not fighting rush-hour traffic. Outlying community theater groups are listed separately as are organizations catering especially to children.

Some of the larger residency companies either have normal business hours or abbreviated ones. For the smaller ones, you'll simply have to leave voice mail. The following groups are not organized geographically because so many rehearse and perform at various area venues.

For more suggestions on how to spend a night out, see the Nightlife chapter.

Dance

Jazzworks
3009 University Ave., Madison
• (608) 845-2649

Established in 1980, Jazzworks is made up of two performing companies: a Senior Youth Ensemble for older children to learn and perform a broad repertoire in dance, and a semiprofessional Jazzworks Dance Company that presents the work of both local and national choreographers and collaborates with other performing artists. The Company stages shows throughout the year in major venues and smaller settings ranging from outdoor art fairs to public schools and senior centers. Classes are also available.

Kanopy Dance Theatre
Gateway Mall, 600 Williamson St., Madison • (608) 255-2211

One of the oldest and most active dance companies in Madison, Kanopy specializes in modern dance, with choreography heavily influenced by the work of Martha Graham. Creative-dance classes and workshops for children and adults are available in addition to about six annual company shows. Kanopy has its own performance space, which seats about 150 people and is used by other dance companies and schools teaching everything from yoga and karate to belly dancing. Due to the relatively small seating capacity, shows sell out quickly; plan accordingly.

Metro Dance
3009 University Ave., Madison • (608) 238-3009

This nonprofit production organization supports local dancers by providing affordable teaching and rehearsal space, encouraging choreographic exploration and promoting outreach activities such as school residencies, lecture demonstrations and concerts. It is directed by Charmaine Ristow, who has been active on the dance scene in Madison for nearly three decades. Schools and companies originating there are Ballet Madison, Jazzworks (see previous listing) and Performance Tech.

One of Metro Dance's newest projects is a staging of *The Nutcracker*, produced in late November and available to all young dancers who audition.

Madison Folk Dance
40 Fuller Ct., Madison • (608) 241-3655

The general public is invited to participate every Wednesday and Sunday evenings in Eastern European folk dancing, with an hour lesson preceding open dancing, from 8:30 to 11 PM. No fees are charged. Dancing usually takes place at 1127 University Avenue, but during the summer months, weather permitting, dancing takes place outdoors on the Library Mall. See the next entry for the performance arm of Madison Folk Dance.

Narodno International Dancers
40 Fuller Ct., Madison • (608) 241-3655

Narodno presents traditional, Eastern European folk dances, songs and music. The troupe of 20 dancers wears regional costumes and performs primarily at multicultural festivals held throughout the state of Wisconsin.

UW Dance Program
Lathrop Hall, 1050 University Ave., Madison • (608) 262-2353

A variety of dance, including ballroom, ballet, modern and African, is presented throughout the school year by dance students and faculty members in special concerts and master classes open to the public. Occasionally, guest artists also are featured. Performances take place in the newly renovated Lathrop Hall.

Music

Capitol City Band
(608) 835-9861

The best place to catch this 22-piece band, organized in 1969 and directed by UW-Madison School of Music Professor James Latimer, is on Thursday evenings during the summer at Oscar Rennebohm Park, 115 N. Eau Claire Avenue on the West Side. Concerts begin at 7 PM. The band also performs at neighborhood centers and parks throughout the county and occasionally at Olbrich Gardens (see our Attractions chapter). Outdoor concerts are free.

The Festival Choir
(608) 238-8030

A chamber ensemble of 40 voices, The Festival Choir was started in 1972 to perform a varied repertoire of chamber music from Renaissance to modern. The choir presents its own series of concerts at various venues in Madison as well as in cities and towns all over southern Wisconsin. It also presents spring madrigal dinners.

Madison Brass
908 Birch Haven Cir., Monona • (608) 221-8047

This brass quintet performs widely in the area for weddings, festivals, at special church services and even in parades. A jazz trio called Touch Of Brass is associated with the group.

Madison Jazz Society
(608) 877-4171

The Madison Jazz Society was organized in 1984 to foster and stimulate interest in jazz music. The organization sponsors six programs throughout the year and an annual jazz festival in May (see our Festivals and Annual Events chapter).

Madison Municipal Band
Madison Area Technical College, 3550 Anderson St., Madison • (608) 246-6055

Formed in 1955, this 60-member band is one of the oldest community bands in South-Central Wisconsin. An offshoot of MATC's music department, the band draws musicians from folks as young as 18 to seniors in their 70s and performs a wide variety of music on the lighter side. It performs for civic functions, at nursing homes and in parks. Rehearsals are 7:30 PM Thursdays at MATC's Downtown Campus.

Madison Opera Inc.
333 Glenway St., Madison
• (608) 238-8085

Founded in 1961, Madison Opera stages three to four standard operas a year featuring both professional guest artists and local talent. In 1993 the organization received international attention when it commissioned and premiered *Shining Brow*, an opera about the life of Frank Lloyd Wright. The company performs in the Oscar Mayer Theater of the Madison Civic Center and other venues.

Madison Symphony Chorus
211 N. Carroll St., Madison
• (608) 257-3734

Performing with the Madison Symphony Orchestra and by itself, this 150-member community chorus presents its main show every March at the First Congregational United Church of Christ, 1609 University Avenue. It rehearses every Tuesday evening at the Downtown Campus of Madison Area Technical College. Singers must audition to join.

Madison Symphony Orchestra
211 N. Carroll St., Madison
• (608) 257-3734

Getting ready to celebrate its 75th anniversary in the year 2000, this 90-piece Madison orchestra is conducted by John DeMain and performs traditional symphonic and pops music. For its subscription series — eight concerts with performances on Saturday and Sunday — internationally recognized musicians and conductors are often featured as guest artists. A resident company of the Madison Civic Center, the orchestra also annually performs an educational concert for school children and another, in April, geared to the entire family. For auditions and information, call the listed number. For tickets, call the Madison Civic Center box office, (608) 266-9055.

MATC Jazz Ensemble
Madison Area Technical College, 3550 Anderson St., Madison • (608) 246-6055

This 20-member student ensemble directed by Jeff Peronto performs about six concerts during the school year at MATC. It's noted primarily for a Big Band sound.

UW-Madison Arts Outreach Program
Humanities Building, Rm. 5542, 455 N. Park St., Madison • (608) 263-4086

Through permanent residency programs, Madison-area residents and visitors receive a tremendous musical bonus by being able to attend concerts, the majority of which are free, by such nationally recognized classical groups as the Wisconsin Brass Quintet, the Wingra Woodwind Quintet and the Pro Arte String Quartet (see this chapter's Close-up). In addition, student ensembles from the band, orchestra and choral areas of the School of Music perform a number of statewide concerts.

INSIDERS' TIP

Ticketmaster outlets are available in Madison at the Boston Stores (East and West Towne Malls); University Bookstore, 711 State Street; and NRM Music (Westgate Mall). You can also charge tickets by phone, (608) 255-4646. Ticketmaster charges a convenience fee per ticket on all orders. And remember, Ticketmaster outlets accept cash only.

UW's Internationally Acclaimed Pro Arte

On a cool May afternoon in 1940, concert-goers hastened into the Union Theater to hear the third of six concerts being performed by the Belgian Pro Arte Quartet, a guest of the UW-Madison.

Yet, before the musicians had an opportunity to pick up their bows, Clarence Dykstra, then president of the university, made an important, shocking announcement. The Nazis had invaded Belgium, home of three of the musicians. (The other was from Britain.) Doing everything in his power to keep the musicians safe, Dykstra secured an extended residency for the four, signaling the beginning of UW-Madison's Pro Arte Quartet, the oldest artist-in-residence ensemble at an American public university.

Today, often praised by musical publications and acclaimed as a "first-rate quartet" by *The New York Times*, the Pro Arte has been besieged over the years with invitations to perform in Asia and Europe as well as at the White House.

In 1965, as the UW School of Music continued to expand, a faculty woodwind quintet ensemble, the Wingra Quintet, was formed, followed two years later by the Wisconsin Brass Quintet. Few universities can boast of the same musical accomplishments. Like the Pro Arte, members of these two ensembles are allotted generous performance time and act as musical ambassadors for the school. Chamber music devotees from around the world would openly gasp if they knew Madisonians can regularly hear the Pro Arte for free during some Sunday afternoon concerts at the Elvehjem Museum of Art.

Not until 1974 did the quartet hire its first woman. Martha Blum stepped in as second violinist and joined her husband, violist Richard Blum. She retired in '88, and after an unprecedented 34 years, he stepped down in 1991. The two continue to reside in Madison.

The Pro Arte Quartet

Today the Pro Arte is made up of violinists David Perry and Suzanne Beia, both of whom joined the group in '95; cellist Parry Karp; and violist Sally Chisholm. Karp has been part of the group (save for one year) since 1976.

Throughout the years, the Pro Arte has maintained a dedication to classical and contemporary string chamber music with a repertoire including works by Mozart, Schubert, Beethoven, Bartok and Samuel Adler. Its music can be heard on the Laurel, Gunmar, Centaur and CRI record labels. For more information about the Pro Arte and other UW in-residence musical ensembles, call the Arts Outreach Program, (608) 263-4086.

UW-Madison School of Music
Humanities Building, Rm. 3561, 455 N. Park St., Madison • (608) 263-1900

When classes are in session, a day seldom goes by when there isn't a concert or recital occurring on campus. Student groups include the University of Wisconsin Chamber and Symphony orchestras, Concert Band and a variety of ensembles: Wind, Black Music, Jazz, Early Music, Percussion and Javanese Gamelan, made up of percussion, brass and wood instruments. A sold-out event every spring is a performance by the Varsity Band led by Michael Leckrone. Also well attended are the Faculty, Concert and Guest Artist Series. Tickets are often free or minimally priced. Call the School of Music or Arts Outreach Program for a calendar of events.

Wisconsin Chamber Orchestra
22 N. Carroll St., Ste. 104, Madison
• (608) 257-0638

Incorporated in 1962, the Wisconsin Chamber Orchestra is best known for its outdoor series of summer Concerts on the Square performed before 100,000 picnickers. Its mainstay programming, however, is a subscription series of four concerts with a repertoire ranging from Baroque to contemporary. Indoor concerts are performed at a variety of venues. Educational programming and concerts are also provided for elementary school-age children. The orchestra is made up of a core group of about 35 musicians, although as many as 50 take part in the summer concerts.

Wisconsin Singers
Humanities Building, Rm. 5530, 455 N. Park St., Madison • (608) 263-9499

Considered musical ambassadors for the UW-Madison under the sponsorship of the UW School of Music and Wisconsin Alumni Association, this group of about 16 entertainers performs a choreographed medley of old-time favorite show tunes throughout the state at various banquets, conventions and other events.

Multidisciplinary Arts

The following groups combine several art forms.

TAP-IT New Works
1957 Winnebago St., Madison
• (608) 244-2938

Under the guidance of co-artistic directors, Danielle Dresden and Donna Peckett, TAP-IT creates and produces original theater works that promote the art of tap dancing. Concerts, workshops, classes and demonstrations are held at TAP-IT's studio on the East Side and in other venues. Activities are geared for all ages.

Synergy! Jazz
535 S. Shore Dr., Madison
• (608) 255-3786

Dancers and musicians fuse jazz, modern and classical elements of dance and music in high-energy performances and lecture demonstrations. Call director Corinne Heath for information.

Theater

Broom Street Theater
1119 Williamson St., Madison
• (608) 244-8338

Founded in 1968, Broom Street Theater is one of the oldest, year-round experimental theaters in the United States. Most of the time Broom Street stages original works by Madison playwrights under the tutelage of theater founder and Madison icon Joel Gersmann, who

---

INSIDERS' TIP

In 1979, former Beatle Paul McCartney purchased the rights to the march song, "On Wisconsin," an immediate hit in Wisconsin even though the song was originally written in 1908 by W.T. Purdy and Carl Beck for a University of Minnesota contest. In 1959, it became the Wisconsin state song.

writes and directs many of the productions himself. You can label Broom Street's work bizarre, creative and/or provocative, but never dull. Broom Street operates out of its own small theater, a converted garage on the East Side.

CTM Productions
228 State St., Madison • (608) 255-2080

From *Peter Pan* and *Little Women* to an annual rendition of *A Christmas Carol*, CTM Productions presents five or six family shows annually. Most feature a large cast of adult and child actors. A resident company of the Madison Civic Center, CTM has been in operation for more than 30 years under the directorship of Nancy Thurow, who has watched several generations of actors grow up on stage. Many of them hone their acting techniques at CTM's Summer Drama School, open to children ages 5 to 19.

Madison Repertory Theater
211 State St., Madison • (608) 256-0029

Commonly referred to as The Rep, Madison Repertory Theater is the city's only professional theater company. Performing seven shows per year, it offers a rewarding playbill of 20th-century classics and contemporary works. Begun in a school basement in 1969, the group moved to the Civic Center in '80 and realized its dream of going professional in '88. Most plays are staged in the Isthmus Playhouse. An annual recipient of grant money from the National Endowment for the Arts for "excellence, vitality and diversity," The Rep has a wide base of support — about 2,800 annual subscribers.

Madison Savoyards
(608) 231-9005

This organization of devoted Gilbert and Sullivan fans has been staging one musical production every summer in late July or August in the Union Theater since the early '60s. In 1997, a second production (in December) annually was added. A large cast of about 60 volunteer actors are backed by a full orchestra.

Madison Theater Guild
2410 Monroe St., Madison
• (608) 238-9322

Dane County's oldest community theater group — founded in 1946 — performs a wide variety of drama and comedy. The company also provides another service, especially popular around Halloween: It rents out vintage clothing, shoes and accessories from its huge costume shop above the theater office, a converted firehouse. Call (608) 238-0009 for information. Office hours for the Guild are 2 to 6 PM Monday, Wednesday and Friday.

Mercury Players Theater Company
1344 Spaight St., Madison
• (608) 251-1886

Mercury Players was organized in 1994 to present original pieces of theater — often black comedy and one-acts — that otherwise might not receive a voice on stage. The group's intent is to challenge both actors and the audience to sample something they haven't tried before and to react in ways they might not expect.

Reprise Theatre Inc.
4558 Wis. Hwy. 78, Black Earth
• (608) 767-2550

This acting company for senior citizens — the only one in the state as far as we know — rehearses at Edgewood College and performs throughout the area, often at senior centers (see our Retirement and Senior Services chapter). All actors are 55 and older, and stage experience is not a requirement for joining the group. The company usually produces one or two plays or musicals each year for a general audience in addition to shorter works for touring. In keeping with its emphasis, Reprise stages work of interest to senior citizens who often are allowed in to the performances for free.

Strollers Theater
649 Sheldon St., Madison
• (608) 238-8183

This small, all-volunteer company performs five plays every year at various locations. Since organizing in 1958, Strollers has gained a solid reputation for staging intimate, thoughtful theater. Its seasons are interesting ones, encompassing both classics and contemporary, alternative works. Both experienced and inexperienced actors are welcome.

Thriving arts programs offer entertainment for performers and spectators.

University Theater
Vilas Communications Hall, 821 University Ave., Madison
• **(608) 262-1500**

The performance arm of UW-Madison's Department of Drama, University Theater provides a wide range of entertaining and often very reflective work. During the school year its casts are made up of students and faculty. But the public is welcome to audition for summer productions. University Theater works alongside other UW performance groups including the Theatre for Children and Young People, Asian/Experimental Theatre and University Opera, the latter of which is a combined effort of the Department of Theatre and Drama and the School of Music.

Outlying Area

Middleton Players Theater
7009 Friendship Ln., Middleton
• **(608) 831-2521**

This community theater group performs two to three shows annually — primarily Broadway musicals and comedies. Started in '91, the group usually performs in the auditorium of Middleton High School.

Stoughton Village Players
2709 Rolling View Rd., Stoughton
• **(608) 873-7455**

The Village Players was formed in 1973 to stage live theater for Stoughton audiences. The group produces two to four plays and musicals every year at the City Hall Auditorium, upstairs in City Hall on Main Street. Norwegian ethnic comedy always is produced around Syttende Mai (see the "May" section of our Festivals and Annual Events chapter).

Sun Prairie Civic Theatre
(608) 837-8217

In existence since the early '70s, this community group presents a variety of theater every year including two musicals, one comedy and a children's show. Most performances take place in the auditorium of Sun Prairie High School. The organization encourages people of all ages to participate.

Especially For Children

The following organizations provide artistic and performance outlets for children. They are not alone. Many area theater, dance and music schools, including some of those mentioned previously, offer performance opportunities in addition to classes.

Other suggestions include the Monroe Street Fine Arts Center, described in this chapter's introduction; the Family Music Learning Center, which is part of Ward-Brodt Music Mall just off the Beltline; Forbes-Meagher on the West Side; the Kehl School of Dance, with schools in Madison, Verona and Waunakee; the Stoughton Dance Studio; Virginia Davis School of Dance on the East Side; and Studio One Dance School and West Side Performing Arts Inc. on the West Side. For a complete listing, look under appropriate headings in the Yellow Pages.

Dance

Performing Arts For Children
549 Zor Shrine Pl., Madison
• (608) 833-9772

This new performing arts company for children was established in 1998 to provide a noncompetitive vehicle in which young people could explore creative expression. The ballet, *The Sleeping Beauty*, the organization's first show, was staged in the spring of '98 and will be repeated every other year. On the off year, a different show, encompassing other forms of dance and music, will be featured.

Wisconsin Dance Ensemble
6320 Monona Dr., Monona
• (608) 222-5552

Associated with Monona Academy School of Dance, the Wisconsin Dance Ensemble performs *The Nutcracker* every December in the Madison Civic Center, featuring more than 200 local dancers. Another ballet is produced in the spring.

Music

Madison Boychoir
1021 University Ave., Madison
• (608) 233-5736

Founded in 1971, the Madison Boychoir teaches boys ages 8 to 14 self-discipline and an appreciation for music within a choral setting. The choir has performed with the Harvard Glee Club and a variety of Madison-area orchestras. State, national or international tours are conducted annually. The 11-month program includes rehearsals twice a week, public concerts and two music camps. Auditions are required.

Madison Children's Choir
(608) 238-SING

Girls and boys from 4th grade through high school are invited to take part in one of the five choruses that make up the Madison Children's Choir. Between 200 and 250 children participate annually. Auditions are required for placement. The main goal of the organization is for children to have fun singing and learn to enjoy various styles of music, although children who excel at singing also have an opportunity to maximize their talent. Each of the five choruses performs a formal concert at least twice a year. Rehearsals are once a week.

Madison Drum and Bugle Corps Association
(608) 241-3171

The association directs two performance-oriented music organizations: Madison Scouts is for young men ages 17 to 21; the Capital Sound is for both sexes ages 14 to 21. Operating since 1938, the association sponsors a drum and bugle competition for each group every summer. (See the Festivals and Annual Events chapter for details.)

Opera for the Young
(608) 277-9560

Opera for the Young was established in 1970 to bring live opera productions to school audiences. Each year, the company mounts a touring production of abridged operas sung in English and performed by regional artists for young people who, in turn, perform some of the cameo roles. Schools who sponsor a performance are given detailed preparatory materials in advance. Recent productions include *Hansel and Gretel*, *The Pirates Of Penzance* and Sousa's *El Capitan*. Today, the company tours not only throughout the state but also in northern Illinois.

Wisconsin Youth Symphony Orchestras
Humanities Building, Rm. 1625, 455 N. Park St., Madison • (608) 263-3320

Four separate orchestras encompassing 360 students from about 80 schools make up the Wisconsin Youth Symphony Orchestras, established in 1966 to meet the symphonic educational needs of aspiring young musicians living in South-Central Wisconsin. Children in grades 5 through 12 are accommodated. Local concerts are performed in Mills Concert Hall on the UW-Madison campus, although national and even international tours are occasionally organized for the students.

Theater

Playtime Productions
6003 Winnequah Rd., Monona • (608) 222-1033

Drawing young actors and theater lovers in grades 3 through 12 from all over the area, Playtime Productions annually stages two original fairy tales "with a twist" written and directed by Teddy Studt. The cast of children, usually about 25 strong, performs all over Sauk and Dane counties but rehearses at the Monona Library. The price of admission to each these shows is nominal if not free. These family shows are almost always musicals, lasting just more than an hour.

Stagecoach Players
112 N. Fairchild St., Madison • (608) 266-6420

Stagecoach was organized in 1948 to provide summer theater experiences for Madison high school students. The troupe travels in a large truck and trailer and performs for adults and children outdoors at Madison parks, beaches and the Farmers' Market. Sponsored by the Madison School-Community Recreation Department, the program is seven weeks long.

Visual Arts

From nationally recognized art museums to a wide range of galleries, the Madison area is rich in exhibition space (although some hardworking, under-appreciated regional artists might not think so). Large, community-wide art fairs are held each July and around the winter holidays (see our Festivals and Annual Events chapter). Also, in addition to spaces described here, hospitals, restaurants, government office buildings, shopping centers and libraries regularly host shows. Even artwork in the Governor's Executive Offices is rotated three times a year.

So, wherever you are, take the time to look around. For a roundup of outdoor, permanent sculpture, see the Attractions chapter.

Art Museums and Exhibition Spaces

Isthmus

Madison Art Center
211 State St., Madison • (608) 257-0158

Specializing in contemporary art, the Madison Art Center, a nonprofit independent museum, has an impressive permanent collection of 4,500 works, mostly by American artists. Photography, sculpture, paintings, a large number of works on paper and even video works are contained within the collection.

Renting space from the Madison Civic Center, the Madison Art Center averages between 10 and 12 exhibits annually, with permanent works rotated regularly for viewing on the third floor. Major shows are sometimes organized with other out-of-state art museums. Every other year, the Art Center works with the Madison Metropolitan School District to showcase the fine work being done by students in a roundup called "Young At Art."

Art Partners, one of two volunteer arms of the Madison Art Center, semiannually sponsors Gallery Night (a tour of local galleries), field trips to area studios and other social events. The Gallery Shop connected with the Art Center offers a wide selection of art books, posters and note cards in addition to handcrafted decorative art items, including glasswork and jewelry. The Madison Art Center sponsors the Art Fair On the Square each summer. (See our Attractions chapter as well as Festivals and Annual Events for more information.)

The Madison Art Center is open 11 AM to 5 PM Tuesday through Thursday, 11 AM to 9 PM Friday, 10 AM to 9 PM Saturday and 1 to 5 PM Sunday. It's closed Mondays and some holidays. Admission is free; so are the majority of special exhibitions.

Campus

Elvehjem Museum of Art
800 University Ave., Madison
• (608) 263-2246

More than 14,000 works, ranging in date from 2300 B.C. to the present, make up the art collection of the University of Wisconsin housed in the Elvehjem (pronounced EL-ve-hem). The collection includes significant holdings in European and American paintings, sculptures, prints and drawings from the 15th through 20th centuries. Of special note are ancient Greek vases and coins. Several hundred works of art are added every year through gifts, bequests and/or purchases.

The Elvehjem produces about 16 exhibitions throughout the year. It also sponsors lectures, films, gallery talks and a Sunday chamber music series. Catalogs and brochures are regularly published to accompany major exhibitions.

The museum is open 9 AM to 5 PM Tuesday through Friday and 11 AM to 5 PM Saturday and Sunday. It's closed on Mondays and some holidays. Admission is free. Access to an elevator is available from the Murray Street entrance. (See the Attractions chapter for more information.)

Gallery of Design
1300 Linden Dr., Madison
• (608) 262-8815

Associated with the UW-Madison's School of Human Ecology, the Gallery of Design is one of the university's newest artistic centers, having opened in 1991. It offers lectures and other educational activities in addition to exhibitions centering around the design of living spaces and textiles.

Although rarely on display for the general public, the Helen Louise Allen Textile Collection, considered one of the largest and most comprehensive university textile collections in the country at 12,000 pieces strong, is housed here. Strengths of the collection include American quilts and coverlets, American and European domestic needlework and ethnographic textiles from Latin America and Southeast Asia. There are early Christian ritual cloths, a 10-foot-long silk cummerbund woven in 1648 for the Shah of Baghdad and dowry hats from Bethlehem.

Hours during planned exhibitions are 11 AM to 4 PM Tuesday through Friday and 1 to 4 PM Sunday. The collection office is open 9 AM to 5 PM Monday and Tuesday and 9 AM to 1 PM Wednesday. Researchers must call (608) 262-1162 to make an appointment to see the Allen Collection.

Wisconsin Union Art Collection and Theater Galleries
Memorial Union, 800 Langdon St.
• (608) 265-3000

An art committee within the governing body of the Memorial Union maintains the Union Collection, which is composed of more than 800 two- and three-dimensional works of art collected since the '20s. The collection is rotated through the halls, galleries and offices of the Memorial Union and Union South (see Attractions). Occasionally, special exhibits by students and faculty are featured. Galleries normally are open 10 AM to 8 PM when school is in session.

West Side

DeRicci Gallery
Edgewood College, 855 Woodrow St.
• (608) 257-4861 Ext. 2881

This active gallery is on the second floor of DeRicci Hall on the Edgewood College campus just off Monroe Street. About a dozen shows are hung throughout the year and change almost monthly, although the gallery is usually closed over winter break; otherwise, it's open 8 AM to 9 PM daily. Regional artists vie to have their work individually showcased between student and faculty shows.

Commercial Galleries

In addition to the galleries listed here, many of which are within a couple of blocks of one another on Monroe Street, some antique, home and specialty shops listed in the Shopping chapter also carry one-of-a-kind, decorative items. The majority of galleries are open normal business hours, unless otherwise stated. Call ahead to find out about evening hours.

Isthmus

Fanny Garver Gallery
230 State St., Madison • (608) 256-6755

For more than 25 years, the Fanny Garver Gallery has been providing two- and three-dimensional exhibits by established and upcoming American artists. Always available are original paintings, graphics, jewelry and works in wood and clay. The gallery also has hosted annually the traveling exhibit of exquisite jewelry boxes and small chests curated by Tony Lydgate, a nationally known woodworker.

Red Deer Gallery
125 State St., Madison • (608) 251-8011

Popular items at this gallery, which opened in 1995, specializes in handcrafted Native American art, are dream-catchers by the Ho-Chunk and Ojibwa tribes and sand paintings like those used by the Navajo in sacred healing ceremonies. Red Deer also offers a wide selection of Pueblo pottery and jewelry made by the Navajo, Hopi, Zuni and Santo Domingo tribes. Native American books, music, handmade drums, cedar flutes and craft kits are available too.

West Side

Antique Gallery
6608 Mineral Point Rd., Madison • (608) 833-4321

This small gallery specializes in old maps, prints and some paintings from around the world, mostly from the 19th century. It's open by appointment only.

Calabash Gifts
2608 Monroe St., Madison • (608) 233-2640

After going to South Africa on a five-month sabbatical with her professor husband, Leah Kessel came back with so many ethnic, handcrafted items, she decided to open a small gallery. That was in '96. Although the majority of jewelry, paintings, sculpture and wall hangings are one-of-a-kind, some manufactured goods are also available. Especially noteworthy are the wooden animal sculptures, some of which are 5 feet tall. The gallery is closed Sundays and Mondays except by appointment.

Grace Chosy Gallery
1825 Monroe St., Madison • (608) 255-1211

Another longtime gallery in Madison, Grace Chosy features a wide variety of decorative American arts and crafts, including paintings, drawings, sculpture, glass, jewelry and ceramics. Primary focus, however, is on Midwestern art and two-dimensional wall art as opposed to crafts. The gallery opened Downtown in 1979 and moved to the near West Side in the mid-'90s. It's closed Sundays and Mondays.

The Last Square
5944 Odana Rd., Madison • (608) 278-4401

The Last Square, in Odana Plaza, specializes in limited-edition prints and posters of military art, much of which is historic in nature. The gallery represents as many as 250 artists. The store also carries books, miniature soldiers and related military-theme items.

McMillan Gallery
1719 Monroe St., Madison • (608) 238-6501

Specializing in original fine American crafts, McMillan offers a wide range of decorative items, from original paintings and metalwork to ceramics and jewelry. But it's the collection of hand-blown glass that grabs the most attention here. The gallery is in Knickerbocker Place.

Nature's Gallery
6712 Odana Rd., Madison • (608) 827-5841

The name of the gallery says it all. Original pieces of environmental art, including seascapes and wooded scenes, are featured along with renowned Wyland marine-life sculptures. Nature's Gallery is in the White House Shoppe strip mall near West Towne. It's closed Mondays.

Valperine Gallery
2701 Monroe St., Madison
• (608) 256-4040

Valperine Gallery, in a new but stately building not far from campus on the upper end of Monroe Street, encompasses a wide range of media but is especially noted for its selection of original watercolors by local and regional artists. Its opening-night gallery receptions are always well-attended and fun.

Wild At Heart Studios and Gallery
4082 University Ave., Madison
• (608) 238-5180

This interesting gallery specializes in two distinct areas: wildlife art and aviation art. Some limited-edition lithographs of noteworthy, historical aircraft are signed by the artists as well as by those who flew them on important missions. Owner Donald Patrick Pate is a corporate pilot whose hours vary, therefore, so do the store's. But you can usually catch him there evenings or weekends. To make sure, call ahead. Wild At Heart is in the corner of the Walnut Grove Shopping Center near Hilldale Shopping Center.

East Side

Spaightwood Galleries
1150 Spaight St., Madison
• (608) 255-3043

In a landmark Victorian home on the near East Side, Spaightwood is in a class by itself, offering more than 7,000 works (prints, drawings, paintings and sculpture) from the 15th century to the present. The collection is quite remarkable, with more than 1,000 old master prints and drawings, about that many 19th-century works, including examples from Blake and his school in England; the Romantics, Pre-Impressionists, Impressionists and Post-Impressionists. Renowned artists whose work can be viewed in depth at Spaightwood include Alechinsky, Chagall, Durer, Garache, Goya, Matisse, Miro, Picasso, Motherwell, Joan Mitchell, Tapies and Titus-Carmel. Spaightwood is open Saturday and Sunday and by appointment other days of the week.

Tandem Press
201 S. Dickinson St., Madison
• (608) 263-3437

Tandem Press is a nonprofit print-making workshop and fine arts press operated under the direction of the UW Department of Art. Nationally recognized print makers are invited to Madison to make special-edition contemporary prints and work with graduate students in art. These prints are then nationally marketed and sold. The workshop is open Monday through Friday or by appointment on weekends.

Wisconsin Center For Paper Arts
811 Williamson St., Madison
• (608) 284-8394

Twenty-one artists specializing in making handmade paper by a variety of methods, from beating old cotton rags to cooking corn and hemp, work out of this center that also offers classes in creating handmade paper and other arts utilizing paper. Some paper bowls, boxes and other pieces are for sale at the working studio, which doesn't have specific business hours. Interested parties should call ahead.

Outlying Area

Artisan Gallery
6858 Paoli Rd., Paoli • (608) 845-6600

A little off the beaten path but certainly worth the extra drive, the Artisan Gallery is in old Paoli Creamery in the small village of Paoli. (Take Exit 92 off U.S. Highway 18/151 southeast of Verona.) Inside, the original work of

---

INSIDERS' TIP

You don't have to be an artist to turn out "works of art" at Studio You, 2701 Monroe Street. A wide variety of plain bisque pieces, including vases, platters and even dog dishes, are provided as well as all the brushes and paints needed to turn out a one-of-a-kind keepsake. As part of the fee, the studio glazes and fires the pieces for you. Call (608) 231-2505.

200 American artists (75 percent are from Wisconsin) is showcased. You can easily spend the greater part of a morning or afternoon here viewing the array of pottery, woodwork, blown-glass and stained-glass decorative items, handmade paper, metalwork, jewelry and fiber art in addition to paintings, drawings and prints.

If you get hungry, stop for a bite in the adjacent, 20-seat Paoli Creamery Cafe overlooking the Sugar River; it's only open for brunch and lunch. Both the restaurant and gallery are closed Mondays.

Gary's Art & Frame Shop
2029 Parmenter St., Middleton
• **(608) 831-2231**

Gary's, owned by Gary Milward, who also operates the McMillan Gallery on Monroe Street (see previous listing), carries a wide selection of limited-edition prints and posters. Also available is a smattering of hand-blown glass, jewelry and other art pieces, although Gary's specializes in prints and framing.

Lazzaro Signature Gallery of Fine Art
184 W. Main St., Stoughton
• **(608) 873-2000**

If you've never been to Lazzaro Signature Gallery, you'll be astonished at the breadth of contemporary fine art available in this small South-Central Wisconsin town's establishment. It's no wonder Signature Gallery attracts patrons from Chicago and both coasts. Chronicling the ideas and processes that go into contemporary art, the gallery has recently expanded to display the work of international as well as American artists. The main gallery makes up the entire first floor. A more intimate gallery with smaller pieces is on the lower level.

CTM Productions has thrilled families for years.

Shows change about every seven weeks. The gallery is closed Sunday and Monday to the general public but is open those days by appointment.

Newell Gallery & Fine Wine
315 E. Main St., Waunakee
• **(608) 849-8422**

Housed on the first floor of a beautiful Victorian-style farmhouse dating back to 1925, this gallery carries a variety of two- and three-dimensional American art including a nice selection of oil and pastel paintings. The kind of work for sale continually changes. Imported and domestic wines also are sold, and wine tastings are frequent in the gallery. Newell's is closed Mondays (Sundays, too, during the summer). Appointments, however, can always be made.

It isn't just the variety of attractions that Madison's visitors and residents like. It's also the fact that so many of them are free — even the zoo.

Attractions

In this chapter we get down to the heart of Madison — all the things that make it tick and underscore its wide appeal. Individually, these attractions are noteworthy. Together they are incredible, encompassing a wide variety of interests and fun. There aren't many places where you can take a tour of the hallowed halls of the state Capitol in the very center of the city and then enjoy a secluded hike through tall prairie grass in the University of Wisconsin's Arboretum. Within 5 miles of one another, they showcase two very different sides of Madison.

But it isn't just the variety of attractions that visitors and residents like. It's also the fact that so many of them are free — even the zoo.

To help you find just what you're looking for while planning your day, week or new start in our city, we've broken down this extensive listing into five categories. Under "What Makes Madison Unique," we include those spots, such as the Governor's Residence, that are synonymous with the city. They'd be difficult to duplicate elsewhere.

There are also separate headings for "Museums," "Outdoor Public Art" (you're likely to bump into a piece or two if you do any walking at all), "Hot Spots on the UW-Madison Campus" and "Historical and Architectural Highlights" to steer history buffs and Frank Lloyd Wright fans in the right direction. All attractions are wheelchair-accessible unless otherwise noted.

Prices and hours are as up-to-date as we can make them. Please call ahead, however, if you need precise information. Also, while we include such favorite outdoor spots as the UW Arboretum and Picnic Point in this chapter, you'll have to turn to Parks and Recreation for a roundup of city parks and beaches.

For expanded coverage of some points of interest described here, refer to chapters on Kidstuff and the Arts. And if you intend to spend any time at all on Madison's college campuses — UW-Madison, Edgewood College or Madison Area Technical College — you should peruse our Higher Education chapter.

That's a lot of reading, we know. But it's the only way to appreciate and enjoy all that Madison — indoors and outdoors — has to offer.

What Makes Madison Unique

In trying to organize this chapter as best we could, we came up with a handful of attractions that defy normal categorizing but are most certainly major attributes of the city. Madison wouldn't be Madison without them.

Isthmus

State Capitol
Capitol Square, Madison
• **(608) 266-0382**

The first glimpse of Wisconsin's State Capitol many people see is a bird's-eye view as they pass overhead, flying into Madison. Wings of the regal-looking, white-domed granite building face the four main diagonal streets of the city. With lakes on two sides, there's no mistaking which city is below. Look closely and you'll see the dome is topped by a gilded bronze lady, *Wisconsin*, by Daniel C. French. Does his name sound familiar? French is also responsible for the Lincoln Memorial in Washington, D.C.

You wouldn't know it to look at it, but *Wisconsin* weighs 3 tons and stands 15 feet 5 inches tall. In her left hand she holds an eagle perched on a globe, and her outstretched right hand points ahead to symbolize the state motto, "Forward." In 1990, she underwent a face-lift to the tune of $100,000 — almost five times more than her original cost. The tedious cleanup required 12,800 tissue-thin, 3-inch-square sheets of gold leaf. But she's worth every ounce.

Modeled after the nation's Capitol — at precisely 284.4 feet it's only 3.5 feet shorter — the present Wisconsin Capitol is the third to be built on the same site. (After 25 years, the first was replaced by a larger building that subsequently was destroyed by fire.) Completed in 1917, this latest edition was designed by architect George Post and took 11 years to build at a cost of $7.25 million — a huge chunk of change in those days. Walk in and you'll see why it took so long and why preservationists fiercely oversee any remodeling projects. The interior of the Capitol features 43 varieties of stone from around the world, decorative murals, glass mosaics and hand-carved furniture. Go into the rotunda, look 200 feet up into the dome — the only granite dome in the nation and the largest by volume — and you'll see Edwin Blashfield's mural, *Resources of Wisconsin*.

Another visual highlight is the Governor's Conference Room, styled after the small council chambers of the Doge's Palace in Venice. Everything in the room, including 26 allegorical paintings by Hugo Ballin in gilded frames looks palatial, even the French walnut furniture. But the wood floor is good ol' Wisconsin hardwood. Other impressive rooms filled with priceless murals and imported marble are the State Supreme Court, the Senate Chamber and the Assembly.

Especially on a sunny, warm spring or summer day, take time out to enjoy the Capitol grounds — 6.5 acres of lawn and the site of political rallies and protests, band concerts and family picnics. The gardens are especially beautiful in late April and early May, when more than 50,000 tulips bloom. Later in the season, you can buy these bulbs at a greatly reduced price — they sell fast! — to plant at home.

Free tours depart from the information desk on the ground floor three times each in the morning (9, 10 and 11 AM) and afternoon (1, 2 and 3 PM) Monday through Saturday and at 1, 2 and 3 PM Sundays. Groups of 10 or more are advised to make a reservation through the listed number.

Dane County Farmers' Market
Capitol Square, Madison
• (920) 563-5037

It's the place to be seen, take a leisurely stroll around the Capitol, welcome spring and bid adieu to autumn. One of the oldest and largest open-air farmers' markets in the country, this Dane County institution turns the Capitol Square into a bountiful banquet of bakery goods, fresh vegetables, herbs, honey, homemade jams and fruit, offset by a wonderful array of flowers, both freshly cut and ready to plant. From late April to November, it happens each Saturday morning from 6 AM to 2 PM. (A smaller version takes place on Wednesdays during the summer months, June through August.) Among the area markets, this one offers the greatest selection of produce and uniquely Madison ambiance. For more on the Dane County Farmers' Market, see the Close-up in our Festivals and Annual Events chapter.

Another independently managed Saturday morning market at Hilldale Shopping Center saves people living on the West Side a drive Downtown.

Madison Civic Center
211 State St., Madison • (608) 266-6550, (608) 266-9055 box office

A performing arts center for Madison was discussed for nearly a century and originally proposed as part of a failed attempt to build a Frank Lloyd Wright-designed civic building at Law Park, now the site of the Monona Terrace Convention Center. In 1974, the city purchased the old Capitol Theatre — once a thriving spot for vaudeville — and several adjoining stores. Following years of extensive renovation, the Madison Civic Center opened its doors in the winter of 1980.

Much effort has been made to retain the ornate splendor of the old Capitol Theatre stage and 2,200-seat auditorium (renamed the Oscar Mayer Theater in tribute to the Madison food company that made a major donation to the refurbishing effort). The carpeting is identical in design to the original, and the gold-fringed maroon draperies are also perfect reproductions. Two large chandeliers to the sides of the stage were made by piecing together five smaller fixtures saved from the original foyer. The theater is a regal monument to the past with one drawback: Space between seating rows is tight (people weren't as tall back then). If you happen to have extra-long legs, you might want to request an aisle seat.

The pride and joy of the auditorium is a 69-year-old pipe organ, believed to be the oldest Barton (from Bartola Musical Instrument Company in Oshkosh) in Wisconsin and the only one in the state that hasn't been moved from its original site. The organ is still used often to accompany the center's silent film series and other special events. The center also includes the Isthmus Playhouse, an intimate, 350-seat theater built around a thrust stage with no seat more than seven rows out. Its design is as modern and sleek as the Oscar Mayer is showy. Connecting the theaters with the Madison Art Center is a multilevel Crossroads lobby that doubles as a casual performing site for a variety of festivals and free children's performances.

Note the center's whimsical stained-glass signs guiding visitors to their seats, exits and restrooms. They were designed by area artist Dennis Pearson, who has built an artistic reputation on life-size, fiberglass, animal-shaped "Beasties" (they look much kinder than they sound). He incorporates the same colorful imagery of farm animals and birds, on a much smaller scale of course, into his signs. And don't leave the premises without checking out the bright-red graphic visible from the Henry Street entrance. Added in 1993, *Faces* was created by Reed Sendecke Design and consists of a foam base 40 feet wide and almost 33 feet high covered with stucco. (For more information on programming at the Madison Civic Center, see our Kidstuff and Arts chapters.)

You can arrange a tour of the Madison Civic Center, including the backstage area, by calling the number listed. The center's administrative hours are 8 AM to 4:30 PM Monday through Friday. On weekends, the building is open from 10 AM to 5 PM for activities and programming and often much later into the evening if a performance is scheduled.

Madison Public Library — Central Branch
201 W. Mifflin St., Madison
• **(608) 266-6300**

Have an hour or two to kill? It's a short walk from the Capitol Square to the "Central Library," where magazines are available online. You don't have to turn a single page. Together, the Central Library and its seven Madison branches hosted more than 1.7 million visitors in 1997 who checked out everything from books and books-on-tape to videos, CDs and educational toys. (See our Literary Scene and Kidstuff chapters for more information.)

Hours for the Central Library are 8:30 AM to 9 PM Monday through Wednesday, 8:30 AM until 6 PM Thursday and Friday and 9 AM to 5 PM on Saturday. Sad to say — to keep operating costs down, all libraries in Madison are closed on Sunday.

Monona Terrace Community and Convention Center
1 John Nolen Dr., Madison
• **(608) 261-4000**

"Wake up, go places, do something with the beautiful site Nature gave you," Frank Lloyd Wright challenged Madison constituents in 1939.

Fifty-six years later, long after the celebrated architect's death in 1959, Wright's concept is a reality. (For a history and architectural description of Monona Terrace, see the related Close-up in the Politics and Perspective chapter.) Visitors are welcome to wander through the building from 9 AM to 5 PM daily to admire Wright's vision and the view of Lake Monona from the Grand Terrace inside or from the outdoor rooftop garden (closed during inclement weather or for special events).

Guided tours are available at 11 AM and 1 PM for a cost of $2 per person Wednesday through Sunday. On Monday and Tuesday, they're free. Groups of 10 people or more are urged to call ahead. A gift shop filled with Wright stuff is located inside the center and is open 10 AM until 3 PM Monday through Sat-

The Henry Vilas Zoo is one of the few free accredited zoos in the country.

urday and 11 AM until 3 on Sunday. During the day, 350 stalls in the adjoining parking ramp are open to the public, but if there is an event taking place, it's sometimes difficult to find a spot. Cost is 75¢ per hour. Enter off W. Wilson Street or the eastbound lane of John Nolen Drive.

West Side

Henry Vilas Zoo
702 S. Randall Ave., Madison
• **(608) 266-4732**

One of the few free accredited zoos remaining in the nation, this popular county attraction was built on land deeded to the city in 1904 by prominent Madison attorney and businessman William S. Vilas and his wife, Anna, in memory of their son, Henry. A multifaceted renovation project started several years ago and continuing today has made the facility much more comfortable for animals and visitors alike.

The Herpetarium and Discovery Center offers a multitude of hands-on exhibits and classes for children. It's especially appreciated during the fall and winter when the Children's Zoo closes for the season (see our Kidstuff chapter). A new $3-million primate house gives the apes much more space for cavorting and entertaining human gawkers. A cat complex, just completed in 1997, includes two large natural habitats for the lions and tigers, both equipped with pools for humid summer days and heated rocks for frosty evenings.

Future plans call for the bird house, built in 1913, to be converted into a visitors center, making room for a new aviary that is expected to cost another $3 million. Yet, even the zoo isn't immune to Madison politics. Monkeygate erupted in 1997-98 when the UW-Madison announced it was sending two primate colonies it had maintained at the zoo for behavioral research studies to new locations in Texas and Louisiana. The university had lost national funding that covered the costs of maintaining the animals. The Monkey Protection Fund was launched, and even the Governor's wife got involved, but to no avail. In spring of 1998, the monkeys left.

While many zoos are larger, few are better maintained or offer more fun. Special zoo events include trick-or-treat stops and a haunted house each Halloween and an outdoor benefit dance every summer. An active zoological society, (608) 258-1460, helps make this zoo one of the most viable in the country.

Henry Vilas Zoo is a short drive from the Capitol Square, adjacent to Vilas Park and across the street from Vilas Lake and Beach. There are two concession stands in the zoo and another at the beach. Zoo grounds are open 9:30 AM to 8 PM June through Labor Day, but only until 5 PM September through May. Hours are 9:30 AM to 4:45 PM year round for all buildings except the Discovery Center, Children's Zoo and Primate Center, which don't open until 10 AM.

UW Arboretum
1207 Seminole Hwy., Madison
- **(608) 263-7888**

Decades of carefully planned restoration, led by such illustrious naturalists as Aldo Leopold and John Curtis, have turned this 1,280-acre tract on the near West Side of Madison into a rare ecological microcosm of pre-settlement Wisconsin. Only in the Arboretum do prairies, conifer forests and wetlands exist side-by-side. Flowering trees in the landscaped Longnecker Garden, containing the largest collection of woody plants in the state, are a favorite draw in May when hundreds of varieties of lilacs and crab-apple trees are in full bloom. In early fall, the 10-foot-tall bluestem grass of Curtis Prairie, the oldest restored prairie in the world, equally beckons.

With increased interest in native plants and landscaping, the Arboretum, with its vast collection of wild flowers hardy to a northern climate, is a natural garden for everyone to enjoy and study. But mostly the Arboretum, with more than 20 miles of marked trails, is a favorite and natural hideaway for walking, biking, cross-country skiing or simply sitting a spell. Several convenient lots are available where you can park your automobile and hike, but the Arboretum is only open to cars for through traffic from noon to 6 PM on Sunday. All other times, you must turn around and exit the way you entered.

Seeds of the UW Arboretum's development date back to the 1920s when several astute Madison citizens, intent on maintaining public access around Lake Wingra, convinced university officials to purchase and revitalize the land. It was a tall order back then, especially since the land — mostly old farm fields and broken-down pastures — looked nothing like it does today. Thankfully, people such as botanist Norman Fassett, landscape designer G. William Longnecker and Leopold took on the challenge. Today, dedication to and enthusiasm for maintaining and improving this ecological treasure remains unabated. The UW Arboretum is served by a wide consortium of conservationists and volunteers alike.

The grounds are open year round from 7 AM to 10 PM daily. There is no admission fee. The McKay Visitor Center includes a visitor information desk, small bookstore, library and space for exhibits. It's open weekdays from 9:30 AM to 4 PM and weekends from 12:30 to 4 PM (11 AM to 3 PM from June to August), excluding holidays. Public tours and other programs take place on most weekends. Call ahead for a list of activities.

UW Space Place
1605 S. Park St., Madison
- **(608) 262-4779**

If you'd like to learn more about space science or operating a telescope, check out Space Place, a perfect example of how a community can benefit by having a world-class university at its doorstep.

Space Place opened in 1990 as an outreach program by UW-Madison's Astronomy Department and Astronomy Lab to share pertinent research and knowledge about space with the general public. Programming is free and geared to both families and adults. Mark your calendar. The second Tuesday of each month beginning at 7 PM, Space Place presents a speaker, usually from the university, to address a variety of related topics pertaining to astronomy. Often, the lectures are geared to the latest space discovery. To hear what to watch for in the coming month, attend the "Eyes on the Sky" program, held at 7 PM the fourth Tuesday of every month. If it's a clear night, patrons are invited after dark to go outside to the Space Place's parking lot and peer into the night sky through telescopes. If you have your own, bring it along. Experts in attendance will be glad to help you.

The second and fourth Saturday of each month is saved for children ages 6 to 10 (see our Kidstuff chapter for more information). Visitors should note that Space Place is not on campus, rather it's to the south (our West Side of Madison), a short drive away.

East Side

Executive Residence
99 Cambridge Rd., Madison
• (608) 266-3554

This Southern Classical Revival home in the influential East Side village of Maple Bluff has been the home of Wisconsin governors and their families since 1949. Built on the shores of Lake Mendota in 1927, the house was sold by a Madison banker to the state for $47,500. That was a bargain, because even in '49 it was already assessed at a value of $200,000. Current Gov. Tommy Thompson is the 11th governor to live there.

The house has 34 rooms, including seven bedrooms, 12 bathrooms (the four teenage daughters of former Gov. Tony Earl were delighted to learn they no longer had to share a single bathroom) and seven fireplaces. This adds up to 16,000 square feet of living space, excluding the lower level. The wrought-iron fence along Cambridge Road originally encircled the first state capitol in Madison.

In 1965, the home was extensively remodeled at a cost of $249,000. Since then, other less extensive restoration and remodeling projects have been made possible through the nonprofit Residence Foundation set up by former Gov. Warren Knowles' wife Dorothy.

In the expansive front entry, the 500-pound bronze chandelier, attached for safety reasons to a steel beam in the attic, is a copy of an original 1900 candle lantern. Its twin hangs in the White House foyer. Free public tours of the first floor and gardens take place beginning at 3 PM on Thursdays from April through August. When all decked out for the winter holidays, the Executive Residence is also open briefly to the public.

Olbrich Botanical Gardens
3330 Atwood Ave., Madison
• (608) 246-4550

"A Garden For All Seasons" is the catch phrase for the city-owned Olbrich Botanical Gardens. Truer words were never spoken. In the dead of winter, when snow blankets the gardens outside, there's still an opportunity to enjoy Madison's version of a rain forest: a 50-foot-high, pyramid-shaped, glass-enclosed tropical conservatory thick with bamboo arbors, exotic flowers and lacy ferns. Along about January, the tropical setting is a sight for sore eyes, and the singing of canaries and waxbills are music to frostbitten ears.

The completion of the Bolz Conservatory in 1991 was a landmark occasion for the gardens, established in the early '50s and named for Michael Olbrich, a founder of the Madison parks system. But much attention also has been paid to the large building complex and 14 acres of specialty gardens that together host a variety of classes, shows, art exhibits, indoor and outdoor band concerts and fund-raisers. The biggest event of all is the posh annual garden party, "Rhapsody In Bloom." Tickets for that July event always sell out quickly (see our Festivals and Annual Events chapter).

Many people visit Olbrich to get ideas for their home gardens. They enjoy meandering through the Courtyard Garden, a formal area modeled after the traditional herb gardens of England; the Lavender Garden, where all plants have lavender-colored blooms or leaves; the old-fashioned Rose Garden; and the celebrated Butterfly Garden, showcasing plants that attract different species of butterflies. Other garden varieties are Rock, Touch and Smell, Thyme and Sage and Everlasting Wreath. The latter is filled with foliage that can be dried and made into decorative arrangements.

Any of the gardens is a great place to host a small wedding ceremony, and many couples do choose to tie the knot there. Call Olbrich for rental and catering information. Events not to be missed include the Spring Flower Show

Photo: JMAR Foto Werks

The Allen Center Gardens are on the UW-Madison campus.

in mid-March, the spring plant sale in early May and the Holiday Show each December (see our Festivals and Annual Events chapter; for information on children's activities, see our Kidstuff chapter).

One of Madison's crown jewels, Olbrich Gardens sits across from Lake Monona, 2.5 miles east of Downtown. The outdoor gardens are open 8 AM to 4 PM November through March, 8 AM to 5 PM September, October, April and May and 8 AM to 8 PM during June, July and August. The conservatory is open year round from 10 AM to 4 PM Monday through Saturday and 10 AM to 5 PM Sunday. The gift shop is open the same hours as the conservatory. Admission to the center and outdoor gardens is free. The cost to visit the conservatory is $1 for adults and children 6 and older. Between 10 AM and noon on Wednesday and Saturday, admission is free.

Museums

The Downtown area encompassing the Square and upper end of State Street is often referred to as "Museum Mile." Practically brushing shoulders are the Madison Art Center, Children's Museum, Veteran's Museum and State Historical Society Museum. Others listed here are only a short hike or drive away, except the four historical museums in the "Outlying Area" subsection.

Isthmus

Elvehjem Museum Of Art
800 University Ave., Madison
- **(608) 263-2246**

Named for Conrad A. Elvehjem, the 13th president of UW-Madison (1958 to 1962), the museum was established in 1970 to store, exhibit and study the university's extensive art collection. Some decorative objects date back to 2300 B.C. In addition to exhibiting a wide range of art (see our Arts chapter), the museum acts as a regional educational and cultural center, providing lectures, films, a Sunday afternoon chamber music series and other performances.

The building was designed by Chicago architect Harry Weese and financed with privately donated funds. In addition to 26,000 square feet of exhibition space, there are four auditoriums, office space for the Department of Art History, seminar rooms, a museum shop and the prestigious Kohler Art Library, which houses more than 300 periodicals. If you're visiting the Elvehjem for the first time, don't miss *Generations* (see the subsequent entry in this chapter's "Outdoor Public Art" section), an outdoor sculpture on the plaza in front of the museum on University Avenue.

The museum is open 9 AM to 5 PM Tuesday through Friday and 11 AM to 5 PM Saturday and Sunday. Admission is free. Access to an elevator is available from the Murray Street entrance.

Madison Art Center
211 State St., Madison • (608) 257-0158

The Art Center, a nonprofit museum of contemporary art, attracts a wide audience not only for its exhibits (see our Arts chapter), but also for its wonderful gift shop, a gallery all to itself and the special events it sponsors throughout the year. Two favorites are the outdoor Art Fair held each July around the Capitol Square and the Holiday Art Fair held each November in the galleries.

The Madison Art Center and Madison Civic Center share a common entrance off State Street. For information about joining the Madison Art Center's volunteer organization, the Madison Art League, call Barbara Banks at the listed number.

Gallery hours are 11 AM to 5 PM Tuesday through Thursday, 11 AM to 9 PM Friday, 10 AM to 9 PM Saturday and 1 to 5 PM on Sunday. The Art Center is closed on Mondays. There is no admission fee.

Madison Children's Museum
100 State St., Madison • (608) 256-6445

With nearly 9,000 square feet of exhibit space, the Madison Children's Museum, the first children's museum established in the state, is filled with imaginative, hands-on activities geared for children ages 2 to 10 and often centered around the arts, the environment and/or science (see our Kidstuff chapter for details).

Incorporated in 1981, the private, nonprofit museum serves schools in a 14-county area and is supported by donations from foundations, corporations and individuals. Its biggest fund-raiser is the annual summer sale of Pleasant Company (maker of the American Girl series of dolls) seconds and returns, attracting mothers and their eager daughters from across the country. Although tickets are now sold in advance, people have been known to wait hours to get through the warehouse doors.

Museum and gift shop hours are 10 AM to 5 PM Tuesday through Sunday. It's closed on Monday. Admission is $3 for all visitors 2 and older, except on the first Sunday of every month when admission is free. Memberships are also available.

State Historical Museum
30 N. Carroll St., Madison
• (608) 264-6555

Utilizing artifacts, dioramas, audiovisual programs and illustrations, the State Historical Museum is doing an admirable job tracing and interpreting Wisconsin's past and present. The museum just passed an important milestone itself, having celebrated its 150th birthday in 1996. Permanent and temporary exhibits on the second, third and fourth floors are dedicated to examining the history of the state. A gift shop on the first floor carries a wide selection of books, native arts, cards and other souvenirs in keeping with Wisconsin heritage. An exhibit tracing the settlement of Wisconsin explores the early Woodland People, the state's geographical landscape and its wealth of natural resources instrumental in industrial and agricultural development. Visitors can enter a lead mine, a re-creation of the St. John mine in Potosi, Wisconsin; they can also calculate how far a person could expect to travel in one day by stagecoach, rail, steamboat or on foot. Other exhibits showcase just how important a role 19th- and 20th-century im-

---

INSIDERS' TIP

The Kohl Center is the first arena in the United States to use a variable rise system for its 1,500 end seats. This means it takes only six minutes to change the seating configuration from basketball to hockey and vice versa. The complete changeover from one sport to the other takes only three hours.

migrants played in the ethnic and cultural history of Wisconsin.

A division of the State Historical Society of Wisconsin, the museum presents a family-oriented program every Saturday beginning at 10:30 AM. Subjects are not restricted to Wisconsin history. From 12:15 to 1 PM on the first and third Tuesdays of each month (except December and January), adults are invited to bite off a little history over the noon hour by bringing a brown-bag lunch to the museum's "History Sandwiched-In" lecture series. Hours of operation are 10 AM to 5 PM Tuesday through Saturday and noon to 5 PM Sunday. The museum is closed Mondays and most holidays. Entrance to the museum and all programming is free.

UW Geology Museum
1215 W. Dayton St., Madison
• **(608) 262-2399, (608) 262-1412 tourist information**

Have you ever seen a 1,300-pound copper nugget? It's a popular stop on a tour of the UW Geology Museum. On exhibit are many other minerals and rocks, including an amethyst geode, pyrite crystals and angel-wing calcite. Visitors are invited to walk through a model of a limestone cave with all the trimmings — stalactites, stalagmites, drips and even echoes — and learn what Wisconsin looked like during the Great Ice Age. A large part of the museum houses an extensive collection of marine fossils — Wisconsin was once covered by an inland sea — and dinosaurs. A 33-foot-long Edmontosaurus excavated in South Dakota was the first dinosaur to be restored in Wisconsin. (See the Kidstuff chapter for more information about the museum, a hot spot for field trips.)

Admission to the museum is free, although a donation of $1 per person (with a minimum of $15 for guided tours) is appreciated. Hours of operation are Monday through Friday, 8:30 AM to 4:30 PM and Saturday, 9 AM to 1 PM. Parking is tough to find around Weeks Hall (on the corner of Charter and Dayton streets), the building that houses the museum. On-the-street parking is easiest to find on Saturdays, unless a sports event at UW is scheduled. In that case, you won't find a spot nearby.

Wisconsin Veterans Museum
30 W. Mifflin St., Madison
• **(608) 264-6086**

On the Capitol Square, the Wisconsin Veterans Museum is anything but a staid assortment of military mementos — quite the contrary. A series of lifelike dioramas set up in the two main galleries take visitors everywhere from the jungles of Vietnam to snow-covered forests in Europe in relating the roles Wisconsin men and women played in major national and world conflicts, from the Civil War to the Persian Gulf War.

To highlight the role of military aviation during the 20th century, three aircraft are suspended from the gallery ceiling, including a World War I Sopwith "Camel" biplane. Sixteen scale models of 19th- and 20th-century ships — including, of course, the USS *Wisconsin* — are also on display. Children especially enjoy using the submarine periscope that protrudes through the gallery roof and offers a panoramic view of Downtown Madison. Visits are usually self-guided with the assistance of videotapes that can be seen and heard on color monitors throughout the museum. But groups can arrange for a personal tour by calling (608) 266-1854. The adjoining gift shop contains a wealth of valuable resources for school history projects.

Entrance to the museum is free. Hours are Tuesday through Saturday 9:30 AM to 4:30 PM and Sunday noon to 4 PM (April through September). The museum is closed on Mondays and holidays.

Outlying Area

Middleton Area Historical Museum
7410 Hubbard Ave., Middleton
• **(608) 836-7614**

To learn about Middleton's history, visit the city's historical museum in the Rowley House, built in 1867 and the home of three generations of doctors. While Middleton was settled in the mid-1800s, a terrible fire in June 1900 destroyed 19 buildings, wiping out almost the entire business district. Photos of that fire are included in the museum, along with a piece of carpeting one resident watered down and kept on the roof of his house to keep it from burning.

Hours of operation are 1 to 4 PM Tuesday and Saturday from mid-April to mid-October, or by appointment for group tours. There is no admission charge, but donations are appreciated.

Historic Blooming Grove Historical Society Museum
4718 Monona Dr., Monona
• (608) 222-5783

Artifacts from 1850 to 1900 are on display in this pre-Civil War (1856) restored building, the former home of the Nathaniel W. Dean family. Dean, a gentleman farmer who also operated a dry goods and grocery store in downtown Madison and was an original stockholder in the Inn on the Park Hotel, moved into the hotel in 1872 because his wife got tired of living "clear out in the country." The house served as the clubhouse for the Monona Golf Course for 50 years, until 1972, when the historical society saved it from the wrecking ball and turned it into a museum.

No public hours are available, but Robert Bean (who's often mistakenly called Dean) will be glad to set up a tour for you; call the listed number. The Dean House is the site of ice cream socials and community band concerts during the summer and sleigh rides in the winter (see our Festivals and Annual Events chapter). Donations are gratefully accepted.

Stoughton Historical Museum
324 S. Page St., Stoughton
• (608) 873-4797

The first building in Stoughton to be placed on the National Register of Historic Places, the Historical Museum, a couple of blocks off Main Street, was built in 1858 as a church. Today, it records a bustling village of yesteryear with a display of antique farm implements and everyday artifacts, some of which Norwegian settlers brought with them from the Old Country.

It's sometimes hard to catch this museum open, although it certainly comes alive during the city's annual three-day May Syttende Mai Celebration (see our Festivals and Annual Events chapter). The museum is open Saturdays and Sundays May through September. There is no admission fee, but donations are appreciated. The museum is not wheelchair-accessible.

Sun Prairie Historical Library and Museum
115 E. Main St., Sun Prairie
• (608) 837-2915

Historical artifacts relating to the Sun Prairie area are housed in this museum, open from 2 to 4 PM Wednesday, Friday and Saturday from May through Labor Day and the same hours Saturday and Sunday from Labor Day through November. Inquire about the lectures and audiovisual presentations about Sun Prairie conducted by museum staff members. There is no admission fee, but donations are accepted.

Hot Spots on the UW-Madison Campus

One of the biggest attractions in Madison is the university, and no visit to the Capital City is complete without a walk or drive on campus, which hugs the southern shores of Lake Mendota. More information about UW-Madison can be found in the Higher Education chapter. But for a thumbnail sketch on how best to enjoy the sights on campus, read on.

Kohl Center
601 W. Dayton St., Madison
• (608) 263-KOHL

This new $76 million sports arena, named after U.S. Sen. Herb Kohl, who donated almost one-third of the total cost of the impressive building, is the 17,142-seat home for UW-Madison's men's and women's basketball teams and hockey team. Opened in January of 1998, the Kohl Center occupies the southwest corner of Dayton and Frances streets, just a 10-minute walk from the lower end of State Street and the heart of the UW-Madison campus. Walking may be your only option for sporting and other events if you don't have a pre-arranged parking pass. For parking information, call (608) 262-3126.

Inside the complex is The Badger Store, operated by University Book Store from 10 AM to 5 PM Monday through Saturday and during all Kohl Center events, sporting and entertainment-related. Tours can be arranged by calling (608) 265-4138. Otherwise, you'll have to be content to visit either the store or ticket office.

Art lovers will want to make arrangements for a tour just to view Dale Chihuly's *Mendota Wall*, described later in this chapter under the "Public Art" heading. For more information about the Kohl Center, see our Sports and Arts chapters.

Memorial Union
800 Langdon St., Madison
• **(608) 265-3000**

Often referred to as the "heartbeat," "soul" or "living room" of the university, the Memorial Union, which opened in 1928, has become the center of recreational, social and cultural programming on campus. Built with private money raised through a successful fund-raising drive after World War I, the building was designated a war memorial for those who fought in World War I. (Later, when Union South opened in 1971 soon after the height of the anti-war movement on campus, it was considered a "peace" memorial.) Appearances by controversial political speakers, bookings of innovative art exhibits, dance, theater and film performances and scheduling of special mini-classes on such diverse subjects as windsurfing and art appreciation draw thousands of people here daily.

But nothing attracts more people than the view from Union Terrace, nestled against the southwestern shore of Lake Mendota. No other spot in Madison is more popular, especially on a warm Friday evening when live music is featured. Through the years, the Terrace's signature metal sunburst chairs — 600 strong — have generated such fond memories for people that the Union is now selling them, with one slight difference: The Terrace chairs melt into the sunset in warm shades of yellow, orange and green; the chairs for sale are bright Badger red and white.

The Memorial Union is also home to the famous Rathskeller, patterned after the old German beer halls and stylized by high arched ceilings, heavy oak tables and German mottos and murals of student life drawn on the walls; the Union's Great Hall, originally envisioned as a retreat for women who weren't given free reign of the building until the early '40s; and Lakefront Cafeteria, which has been upgraded and improved a number of times over the years. (For information about performance venues in the Memorial Union, see the Arts chapter.)

The Union is open to everyone, although you must be a member (students are automatically members) to buy beer or to join the university's outdoor club, the Hoofers, which maintains about 100 sailboats behind the Union and offers instructions and a chance to compete in a variety of participatory sports including mountain climbing, scuba diving and skiing. For membership information, call 262-2263.

Hours of operation of the Memorial Union vary somewhat according to the school calendar, but generally it's open 7 AM to 11 PM Monday through Friday, 8 to 12:30 AM Saturday and 8 AM to 11 PM Sunday. The Memorial Union is closed during winter break.

Union South
227 N. Randall Ave., Madison
• **(608) 263-2600**

Union South opened on the southwest side of campus in 1971 to serve a growing student and faculty population. Although not as large or historically significant as the Memorial Union, Union South offers a wide range of programming including free DJ dances, blood drives and live music. Also available are bowling, billiards and table tennis. It has a full-service cafeteria, Einstein's; a deli; and the Red Oak Grill restaurant. Union south, which sits near Camp Randall Stadium, where home football games are played, offers pregame entertainment and postgame music and dancing. Hours are the same as the Memorial Union (see previous entry).

UW Babcock Dairy Plant
1605 Linden Dr., Madison
• **(608) 262-3047**

Don't leave campus before sampling the university's own Babcock brand of ice cream, made fresh daily at the UW Babcock Dairy Plant on Linden Drive (take Charter Street south off Observatory Drive to Linden Drive). More than 100 flavors are interchanged annually, with at least a dozen different ones available every day. (Chocolate-chip cookie dough continues to be a hot seller in addition to old standbys vanilla and chocolate, of course.) Visitors are invited to watch ice cream being made mid- to late mornings, Monday through Saturday, from an observation deck overlooking the plant. About 350 gallons are distributed daily to dorms and cafeterias around campus.

Store hours are 9:30 AM to 5:30 PM Monday through Friday and 10 AM to 1:30 PM Saturdays. Don't fret. If you can't make it to Babcock, ice cream is sold at both unions, too (see previous entries).

The Scenic Side

Lake Shore Path
From Memorial Union to Picnic Point

The winding, wooded Lake Shore Path runs along Lake Mendota's shoreline for about 2.5 miles, beginning from behind the Memorial Union to Picnic Point. It's these hidden paths and expansive lakeside frontage that make this campus one of the most beautiful in the Midwest.

Picnic Point
At the mouth of University Bay of Lake Mendota

Whether you take the Lake Shore Path or drive, make sure you visit Picnic Point, a half-mile-long finger peninsula at the western edge of campus. Parking is available near University Bay Marsh, at the entrance to Picnic Point. The tip of the peninsula is only accessible by foot or bicycle. Because it's a well-known spot, don't expect much privacy in spring or summer. But the view across the lake of Madison and the university is spectacular.

Washburn Observatory
1401 Observatory Dr., Madison
- **(608) 262-9274**

On top of the hill and to the left on Observatory Drive is the Washburn Observatory. Built in 1881, its refractor telescope, 15 inches in diameter, was considered one of the largest at that time. The public is invited to look through this telescope on the first and third Wednesdays of each month (if the sky is at least 75 percent free of clouds). From April to October, the observatory opens at 9 PM; from November to March, it

Bascom Hall on the UW campus graces the top of Bascom Hill.

opens at 7:30 PM. Reservations are not required, so be prepared at times to wait in line outdoors. There is no admission fee.

You can catch a breathtaking view of the lake through a car window while driving along Observatory Drive (ascending the hill from Park Street near the lake).

UW Memorial Carillon
Observatory Dr., Madison
- **(608) 262-1197**

Sometimes people in a hurry pass the UW Memorial Carillon, to the right on Observatory Drive, without even noticing it. But they don't soon forget once they've heard the bells ring — on Sundays, 3 PM during the fall semester and 3:15 PM during the spring semester (usually through the first week in May). During colder months, the tower is open, and you're welcome to step inside to listen. A cumulative gift of graduating classes from 1917 to 1926, the 85-foot-tall sandstone tower contains more than 50 bells, sent over from England, that range individually in weight from 15 to 6,800 pounds. For more information, refer to the Arts chapter.

Allen Centennial Gardens
Babcock and Observatory Drs., Madison
• (608) 265-8502

West of Washburn Observatory, the beautiful Allen Centennial Gardens collectively serve as an outdoor classroom for UW-Madison's Department of Horticulture. Funded entirely by private gifts, the gardens are named for Oscar and Ethel Allen. After Allen, a UW professor of bacteriology, died in 1976, his wife, a botanist and former member of UW-Madison's horticulture faculty, gave money in her husband's name to help establish the gardens. Ethel Allen still resides in Madison.

The 2.5-acre plot is divided into a variety of shrub, herb and ornamental gardens containing hundreds of exotic plants as well as those native to Wisconsin. As they've matured, the gardens have become a popular spot for weddings and receptions. Next door is a beautifully restored Victorian Gothic house in which the first four College of Agriculture deans lived with their families. Today it houses the Experimental Farms offices, but nobody will care if you take a peek inside. During the growing season, the gardens are open from dawn to dusk, although parking is easiest in the evenings and on weekends.

Outdoor Public Art

In Madison, public art receives the same kind of relentless interrogation and second-guessing as does erecting the majority of government buildings. Everybody has an opinion, and each varies widely. Helping to spur interest was the establishment in 1979 of Madison's "1 percent for art" program in which the city set aside 1 percent of the cost of new or renovated building projects for public art. That program has since been replaced by an Art In Public Places grant process. In 1980, the Wisconsin legislature established its own "percent for art program" to help pay for visual art in or around buildings constructed by the state. The program is administered by the Wisconsin Arts Board.

The following roundup of public art in Madison is not meant to be an all-inclusive list. It does not contain outdoor art erected by private businesses, nor even all those funded by tax dollars. It does include the most celebrated and likely to be seen pieces and, quite honestly, the ones we like the best. To learn more about Madison's outdoor public art, buy a copy of *Common Joy II*, written by Frances Hurst with accompanying verse by Fran Rall, available at area bookstores and some specialty stores. Hurst pulled together much of the information presented here.

Isthmus

Entrance Arch to Madison Area Technical College
211 N. Carroll St., Madison

In the name of progress and practicality, some noteworthy buildings must come down. But to keep their memories alive, occasional compromises, thankfully, can be made. Such is the case with a classical Beaux Arts-style stone arch now standing alone as a gateway to the modern downtown campus of Madison Area Technical College, one block north of the Capitol Square. It was once the entrance to Madison Central High School, dedicated in 1907. Cass Gilbert was the New York architect who designed the building and arch.

Amphitheater in the Plaza
State St. and the Capitol Square, Madison

This pavilion-like structure, supported by six stone columns and topped with a dome of stainless-steel mesh, was installed in 1993 at the head of State Street. Amphitheater in the Plaza is the name of the site; the actual sculpture by L. Brower Hatcher is called *Forum of Origin*. You might call it a working piece because it was designed to offer not only visual interest on the corner, but also performance space, often used for downtown festivals.

Stand in the center and look above. Netted in the steel mesh are small bits of cast bronze, aluminum and iron in the shapes of things near and dear to the hearts of Wisconsinites. They include the state bird (robin), state animal (badger), oh-so plentiful deer, corn and, of course, cheese. The Amphitheater is truly a public art piece because the public actually had a chance to vote among three designs selected by a Madison committee. Of more than 700 people who chose to participate, almost half chose this one.

Living The Dream
210 Martin Luther King Jr. Blvd., Madison

This limestone bust of Martin Luther King Jr., by Frank Brown, was erected in front of the Municipal Building in 1993. It's surrounded by six small plaques of historical scenes that include the civil rights march from Selma to Montgomery, Alabama, and King's family mourning his death.

Col. Hans Christian Heg
Capitol Square at King St., Madison

This bronze sculpture on the Capitol grounds at the junction of King Street immortalizes Col. Hans Christian Heg (1829-1863), a Norwegian native who was state prison commissioner before organizing an all-Norwegian brigade to fight in the Civil War. Heg never lived to see his 34th birthday: He died in the battle of Chickamauga. The Norwegian Society of America commissioned Paul Fjelde to make this 12-foot sculpture and two identical bronze castings to be erected in Lier, Norway (Heg's birthplace), and Waterford, Wisconsin (his burial place).

Forward
Capitol Square at State St., Madison

Erected in 1996, this bronze sculpture is a copy of the original beloved copper lady that was named for the state's motto, "Forward," and originally created for the Wisconsin building at the World's Columbian Exposition in Chicago in 1893. Standing sentry for 100 years at the juncture of N. Hamilton, Pinckney and Mifflin streets, the sculpture was removed in '96 because inclement weather over the years gradually was destroying it. Artist Jean P. Miner Coburn — raised in Madison and only 28 years old when she made *Forward* using a technique called repousse (also used on the Statue of Liberty) — never envisioned the statue being outside in the first place. When the state announced its plans to remove *Forward* and dedicate the space to a new memorial to honor police officers, a committee headed by Sue Ann Thompson, wife of the governor, was formed to raise enough money — $67,000 — to pay for a reproduction. The donations also funded a pedestal for *Forward* to enable her to be exhibited once again, this time indoors at the State Historical Society building on the UW-Madison campus, 816 State Street, where she stands today.

Hieroglyph
201 W. Mifflin St., Madison

This 12-foot bronze sculpture, funded by a gift from the Oscar Mayer Foundation, was installed in 1965 when the library was new. Created by O.V. Shaffer, a former Beloit College art professor, the semi-abstract piece is, as Hurst describes, "curiously inscribed with figures half-emerging from canyons or caves on the sides [that] suggest the voices of silence which come down to us from past civilizations and still speak."

Otis Redding Memorial
Rooftop Garden, Monona Terrace Convention Center, 1 John Nolen Dr., Madison

After singer Otis Redding died en route to Madison to perform, when his private plane crashed into Lake Monona on December 10, 1967, fans raised money for three curved, pink Portuguese marble benches that graced Law Park (a few miles from the spot where Redding died) until the Monona Terrace Convention Center was built. Now they've been moved to the Rooftop Garden, where they are expected to garner even more attention. (Just three days before he died, Redding had recorded one of his most memorable hits, "Dock of the Bay.")

Spare Time
111 Main St., Madison

For almost 20 years, John Martinson's whimsical "stick man" of painted steel has been dangling his legs over the roof of the M&I building on the Capitol Square, watching everyone passing by and everything happening on the Square from outdoor concerts to arts fairs and political rallies. Eleven-feet-tall, with only his head and feet showing, "Spare Time" has seen it all.

Timekeeper
Law Park, West Side of Lake Monona, Madison

Little did artist Robert Curtis know just how significant his work would become with the construction of the nearby Monona Terrace

ATTRACTIONS • 207

Photo: Wisconsin State Journal/The Capital Times

The Henry Vilas Zoo has an active zoological society.

Convention Center. *Timekeeper* consists of a granite boulder (ancient), fragments of columns and arches (classical period) and two steel slabs (modern) to denote how time marches on in the architectural design of buildings. It was installed in 1983.

Wisconsiana
101 S. Webster St., Madison

Approaching the General Executive Facility (GEF) III State office building at the north end of E. Doty Street, Hurst describes the scene this way:

One sees an archway formed of three blocks of red granite, one supported on the other two. They are squared and highly polished except for appearing to be broken off at the top. Six similar columns ranging in height from three to eight feet study the courtyard between the archway and the building.

Lloyd Hamrol, a California sculptor, won a 1988 competition sponsored by the Wisconsin Arts Board to create *Wisconsiana*, the name given to the eldest daughter of the Pecks, the first family to settle in what is now Madison. Their home is said to have stood where this state office building now stands. Hamrol is quoted in *Common Joy II* as describing his piece as "a kind of pushing forward of the front door of the State. It's a symbolic act of welcome."

Untitled Light Sculpture
120 N. Henry St., Madison

More than 700 feet of neon tubing shaped into a broad arc and chandelier-shaped light sculpture dominate the entrance to the modern red and blue Federal Courthouse built in 1986. The red-orange neon light, designed by New York City artist Christopher Sproat, softens the stark entrance and is especially appealing after dark.

Untitled Mural
At the foot of Olin Terrace, Madison

Now only partially visible by passing through the Monona Terrace Convention Center tunnel, Richard Haas' *trompe l'oeil* (French for "fool the eye") mural has never received the public recognition this major piece by a celebrated artist deserves. Perhaps because the site was really only visible by boat from Lake Mendota or through the window of an automobile, its imaginative details and ties to Madison were never fully appreciated. The future of this piece now depends upon how the convention center is eventually finished off. The mural incorporates figures of prominent men associated with Madison history including Native American Chief Blackhawk and Frank Lloyd Wright, whose original design for a civic center became the basis for Monona Terrace.

Wisconsin Law Enforcement Memorial
N. Hamilton St., side of the Capitol, Madison

Since 1844, four years before it became a state, Wisconsin has lost 195 law enforcement officers in the line of duty. All of their names are inscribed on a monument installed during the summer of 1998 on the Capitol grounds.

INSIDERS' TIP

One museum that may not be quite as well known as others in the Capital City is the Madison Museum of Bathroom Tissue which houses, according to its curators, the "world's largest collection of toilet paper." Started in 1992, the museum today exhibits more than 1,000 two-ply rolls "borrowed" from various famous sites including Graceland, Lambeau Field, Ellis Island and the Alamo. Ordinarily, the museum is open for viewing several evenings a week or by appointment. But as this book went to press, curators were seeking a new location for the museum. Call Carol Kolb at (608) 251-8098 for information. And, yes, donations are kindly accepted, appropriately labeled, of course.

Campus

Generations
800 University Ave., Madison

This sculpture is in front of the main entrance to the Elvehjem Museum of Art (see the previous "Museums" section in this chapter for details). Commissioned from New York artist Richard Artschwager, it consists of three white plastic domes, two of which stand on stainless-steel posts.

Lincoln
500 Lincoln Dr. (in front of Bascom Hall), Madison

Though not as memorable as the Lincoln Memorial, Madison residents and university students would think Bascom Hill empty without this seated sculpture of Abraham Lincoln created by Adolph A. Weinman. A gift of Thomas E. Brittingham, a UW-Madison alumnus and regent, the statue was dedicated in 1909 but was moved to its present site and raised on a platform in 1919. During spring finals week, students often gather to study under his benevolent gaze.

Maquina
1415 Johnson Dr., Madison

One of the newest and most fascinating public pieces in Madison, *Maquina* (meaning "machine" in Spanish) is the centerpiece of the Engineering Mall. It's an 18-foot-high sculpture fabricated in stainless steel that interacts with water as a liquid, vapor and solid, along with compressed air, sound and light. It's an engineering marvel, with special effects controlled by engineering students from a laboratory underneath the mall and also by visitors who can pass a hand over infrared "eyes" to change the pattern of water spouting from the adjoining fountain. The sculpture was donated by William Conrad Severson, a 1947 art graduate, as a thank-you to the university. Said Severson: "Attending the UW was an important step in my life and in my father's life." (His father was one of 15 children and the only one to come off the farm to graduate from the UW.)

A life-size sculpture of an engineering student, *Between Classes*, is on the steps of Engineering Hall. It was created by artist J. Seward Johnson Jr. Students have been known to "dress up" the statue depending upon the season. He's been seen sporting everything from a red Wisconsin cowboy hat during football season to a grass skirt in anticipation of spring break.

The Mendota Wall
Inside the Kohl Center, 601 W. Dayton St., Madison

This 140-foot sculpture made up of bright orange, green, blue and yellow tendrils of glass was designed by renowned glass artist Dale Chihuly of Seattle, who was a graduate art student at the UW-Madison during the mid-'60s. It is a stunning, massive piece that some feel is a fish out of water in a "rah-rah" sports arena, no matter how well-designed the building is. Location aside, it's still a sight to behold. Chihuly has said the piece evokes the images of Lake Mendota he remembers while studying and living in Madison. And, yes, in case you're wondering, the piece is occasionally dusted — by UW art students specializing in glass. The sculpture is somewhat visible from the arena's Gate A, although it's better to arrange a tour, (608) 265-4138, if you want a good look.

East Side

Act
Olbrich Park, 3330 Atwood Ave., Madison

This 26-foot work consisting of four flat aluminum figures never got the attention it deserved until it was moved in 1988 to a park setting with Lake Monona in the background. Created by New York sculptor William King, *Act* was commissioned for a small concrete plot behind the Madison Civic Center as a tribute to that venue's opening. Alas, the space was too congested to show off the piece to its full advantage. The move was a good one. Money for the work was collected through a fund-raising campaign spearheaded by the Madison Art Center and a matching grant from the National Endowment for the Arts.

Fiddleheads
Olbrich Botanical Gardens, 3330 Atwood Ave., Madison

This hand-carved, 12-foot limestone sculpture by Middleton artist Sylvia Beckman captures nature at one of its finest moments: the curled emergence of ferns every spring. The sight is an especially welcome one following a bitterly cold Wisconsin winter. "*Fiddleheads* is an enlarged shape that hopefully evolves thoughts of spring and the prospect of new beginnings," Beckman states in *Common Joy II*. The simple concept is appropriate to its site and is an easy one to embrace.

Historical and Architectural Highlights

Madison has more than its share of historic buildings, many of which were built of sandstone shortly after Madison became a city in 1856. The stone was quarried near Hoyt Park, the hills of Shorewood, where Meriter Hospital-Park now stands, and Maple Bluff.

A series of Madison Heritage pamphlets outlining detailed, historical walking tours of various Madison neighborhoods unfortunately is out-of-print for the most part. But they and other materials about historical Madison can be perused at the Greater Madison Convention & Visitors Bureau, 615 E. Washington Avenue; the State Historical Museum, 30 N. Carroll Street (see this chapter's "Museums" section); and the Central Library, 201 W. Mifflin Street.

Some of the largest, oldest and most ornate homes, with backgrounds as colorful as the people who lived in them, are in the Mansion Hill District, bordered by James Madison Park to the north and the Capitol Square and State Street to the south. Because of its rising ridge and the successful developers, statesmen, university professors and merchants who settled there, the area sometimes was also referred to as "Yankee Hill," "Aristocracy Hill" and "Big Bug Hill."

A short walk off the Square toward Lake Mendota along N. Pinckney to Gilman and Gorham streets puts you in the heart of the Mansion Hill District. Many of the early homes there reflect the Romanesque Revival flair of German-born architect August Kutzbock and his partner, Samuel Hunter Donnel. Please keep in mind that the sampling of homes described subsequently, unless otherwise noted, are privately owned and not open to the public. Please enjoy them from the sidewalk only.

Isthmus

Bashford House
423 N. Pinckney St., Madison

This Italian villa-style house is named after Sarah and Robert Bashford, who lived in the house from about 1889 to 1911. Over his career, Robert held several political offices, including mayor in 1890. Sarah was the daughter of the home's previous owners, Anna and Morris Fuller, who operated a successful agricultural-implement dealership, with sales throughout the Midwest. Jottings from August Kutzbock's journal indicate he might have had a hand in the early design of this house, built in 1855. Old photographs show the home once featured elaborate gingerbread detailing on balconies and porches and a formal flower garden to the south, which long ago was covered over by an apartment building. In the 1930s, this house, like so many others in the neighborhood, was divided into apartments and rooms.

Gates of Heaven Synagogue
300 E. Gorham St., Madison

The first synagogue in Madison and one of the oldest surviving synagogues in the country, this early German Romanesque Revival sandstone and brick structure is considered one of August Kutzbock's finest works. Over the years, since being built in 1863, it's also housed a kindergarten, funeral home and churches of varying denomination. Originally at 214 W. Washington Avenue, it was successfully moved to its current site on E. Gorham Street in 1971, thanks to a group of Madison citizens who couldn't bear to see it demolished. Today it's owned by the city and rented out for private functions including meetings and weddings. Call the Parks Division, (608) 266-4711, for information.

Grace Episcopal Church
6 N. Carroll St., Madison

Completed in 1858, Grace Episcopal Church is the oldest building on the Capitol Square and the only remaining church of four that fronted the Square during the 19th century. It is constructed of sandstone, and its Gothic revival style was designed by James Douglas of Milwaukee. Additions have been

The UW Memorial Union Terrace is a popular gathering spot.

constructed throughout the years. Today, the congregation includes 450 families. Especially noteworthy is the stained-glass baptistry window designed and made by Louis Tiffany's firm in New York in 1899.

Keenan House
28 E. Gilman St., Madison

This was the last of four houses constructed on the Pinckney-Gilman corner. It is thought to have been designed in 1857 by August Kutzbock for Napoleon Bonaparte Van Slyke, although the Yankee banker and his wife, Laura, never lived here. Rather, the unusual German Romanesque Revival building is named after Madison physician Dr. George Keenan and his wife, Mary, who resided here from 1900 to 1916.

Kendall House
104 E. Gilman St., Madison

On Gilman, across Pinckney from the Keenan House, is a sandstone home built for John Kendall of New York in 1855. It was the first of the four houses at the corner of Pinckney and Gilman. Also designed by August Kutzbock, it was built with a low, hipped roof and cupola. Although modernized over the years, the house remains an important, historical building in the district.

Keyes House
102 E. Gorham St., Madison

Built in 1853, this large, brick Italianate-style house was named for Elizabeth and Elisha Keyes, the latter of whom was a powerful state political figure appointed postmaster by Abraham Lincoln in 1861. While serving 20 years in that position, Keyes also was elected twice as Madison's mayor. Later, in 1886, he was elected for a third time. The Keyes made extensive alterations to the house, which was built for another Madison couple. Take note that the original front yard of this house has been preserved as Period Garden Park, founded when individual citizens bought the land and then convinced the city to maintain it as a park, rather than allow construction of a proposed 24-apartment building. With cast-iron lamps, decorative walks and park benches, it's a nice place to go to visualize the mood and ambiance of Mansion Hill during its heyday.

The McDonnell-Pierce House
424 N. Pinckney St., Madison
• (608) 255-3999

Considered one of the finest remaining examples left in the United States of German Romanesque Revival architecture, characterized by tall, arched windows and ornate cornices, the house was built in 1857-58 for Alexander and Francie McDonnell. The ornate stonework resembles that of the second capitol in Madison (which burned), for which Alexander McDonnell was the contractor. The two buildings also shared an architect — August Kutzbock. Today this home, resurrected in 1987 as the Mansion Hill Inn, Madison's celebrated European-style, 11-room luxury inn, looks as elegant as it did more than 100 years ago, thanks to extensive renovation (see our Hotels and Motels chapter).

Inside the 9,000-square-foot mansion is a four-story, oval-shaped mahogany spiral staircase leading to a belvedere. Light passes into the marble foyer through etched Venetian windows. Twin parlors showcasing leaf friezes on the ceilings are replicas of those in the Capitol's Assembly and Senate chambers. Although the interior once was divided into apartments, the ornate exterior, set off by buttresses and arched windows, was never altered. Care to pamper yourself in Madison Victorian splendor? This is the place to do it.

Old Governor's Residence
130 E. Gilman St., Madison

Built in 1856, this structure, now the Knapp Memorial Graduate Center, was the executive residence for 17 Wisconsin governors beginning in the year 1885. The Italianate-style home made of locally quarried sandstone was built by Julius T. and Catherine White and sold in 1857 to one of Madison's first settlers, real-estate developer George P. Delaplaine and his wife, Emily. The site of lavish parties, it was purchased for $15,000 in 1883 by Jeremiah Rusk when he was elected governor, then sold to the State after extensive remodeling "for a sum not to exceed $20,000." A sweeping wraparound veranda with Ionic columns was cut way back in the 1960s, after being purchased in 1950 by the university with Knapp funds.

The Mark of Frank Lloyd Wright

Frank Lloyd Wright designed 32 buildings for Dane County. Only 11 were built, and eight still stand today. Of those described subsequently, one, the Lamp House, is Downtown; the others are within an easy drive west of the Capitol Square. (For more information about the flamboyant architect, see the related Close-up in our History chapter and the Spring Green entry in our Daytrips chapter.)

Isthmus

Robert M. Lamp Residence
22 N. Butler St., Madison

This simple, cube-like brick home was designed by Wright in 1903 for his longtime friend, Robert Lamp. A block off the Capitol Square, the original two-story home was designed with a garden on the roof. Subsequent owners added a third floor.

West Side

Unitarian Meeting House
900 University Bay Dr., Madison
- **(608) 233-9571**

Wright was 78 years old in January 1946 when he was commissioned to design the Unitarian Meeting House. It was completed in 1951. Now overshadowed by development, the Meeting House, considered one of the world's most innovative examples of church architecture, was designed on a knoll overlooking farmland and Lake Mendota. Two additions, designed by Wright-schooled Taliesin Associated Architects, were added in 1964 and 1990. Constructed primarily of native limestone, copper and glass, the original triangular building demonstrates the architect's ability to "connect the indoors with the outdoors." A glass prow in the auditorium affords the

---

INSIDERS' TIP

The scented geraniums in Olbrich's "touch and smell" garden are ancient herbs native to the African Cape. The leaves, when rubbed, release fragrant oils smelling like rose, citrus, even chocolate!

building impressive height without a steeple. Guided tours are offered May through September from 1 to 4 PM Monday through Friday and 9 AM to noon on Saturday. A donation of $2 per person is requested. For group tours, call the listed number.

E.A. Gilmore Residence
120 Ely Pl., in University Heights, Madison

Often referred to as the "Airplane House" because of its projecting "wings" that evoke a biplane, this 1908 home in University Heights on the near West Side of Madison constitutes the only local example of Wright's mature Prairie style. It once offered a view of four Madison lakes.

Herbert Jacobs I Residence
441 Toepfer Ave., Westmorland neighborhood, Madison

This L-shaped house with a carport and flat roof (not exactly practical for Wisconsin winters) is on a corner lot in the modest Westmorland neighborhood on the near West Side. This was the first truly Usonian house (1937) designed by Wright to be affordable for the average American. It was constructed on a concrete slab floor and used radiant heating. In the 1980s, new owners rehabilitated and made some cosmetic modifications to the house.

John C. Pew Residence
3650 Lake Mendota Dr., near 3100 block of University Ave., Village of Shorewood

Perched on a ravine overlooking Lake Mendota on the West Side of Madison, this Wright-designed home is difficult to see from the street through all the foliage. The house, constructed of limestone and cypress, has only 1,200 square feet of space but seems larger because of such details as a lapped wood ceiling. The Pews, who became friends of Wright and William Wesley Peters, who supervised the general contracting, lived in the house from the time it was built in 1940 until the early '80s, when they decided to retire and sell it. Since that time, some carefully executed renovations have been made. For instance, the original wood-slat kitchen floor has been replaced by flagstone.

Quiet Getaway

West Side

Forest Hill Cemetery
1 Speedway Rd., Madison
• **(608) 266-4720**

History buffs who want to get a feel for early Madison shouldn't leave town without taking a walking tour of Forest Hill Cemetery on Madison's West Side. Owned by the City of Madison, the cemetery contains the graves of many persons who played significant roles in the history of not only the city and state, but also the nation.

A self-guided, 1.4-mile walking tour points out many highlights of the cemetery where Native Americans built effigy burial mounds thousands of years ago. Buried here several Madison luminaries: Ebenezer Brigham (1789-1861), the first permanent white settler in Dane County; William F. Vilas (1840-1908), postmaster general and Secretary of the Interior under Grover Cleveland, who bequeathed $30 million to the UW and Vilas Park to the city; and Robert "Fighting Bob" La Follette (1855-1925) and other members of his prominent Wisconsin family. La Follette, a member of Congress, led the Progressive Movement, and his wife, Belle Case La Follette (1859-1931) was the first woman to graduate from the UW Law School. John Bardeen, winner of two Nobel prizes in physics, is also buried here. So are eight former Wisconsin governors.

A wonderful brochure outlining the walking tour of Forest Hill prepared by the Forest Hill Cemetery Committee of Historic Madison Inc. is available through the cemetery office at the site.

Wisconsin has long been an effective incubator for writers. Carl Sandburg, Thornton Wilder and Laura Ingalls Wilder spent parts of their lives in Wisconsin.

The Literary Scene

If you love books and enjoy talking about them nearly as much, you'll find plenty of kindred spirits in Madison. There are at least 165 registered book clubs here with more than 2,000 members. The bigger bookstores sponsor many of them, but you'll also find them through churches and civic groups such as the Madison Junior Woman's Club, and neighborhoods. The Madison Public Library has a "Book Talk" group led by a UW-Madison English professor. Many of the groups get considerably more specific than "fiction or nonfiction."

Borders Book Shop (West) has a longstanding group, open to the public, that spotlights literature for young adults. Borders (East) has groups for fans of science fiction, general fiction, gay literature, women's literature and history. Booked for Murder has clubs for mystery lovers; A Room of One's Own has groups for those who prefer travel, contemporary women's fiction and lesbian literature. The dozen groups based at Canterbury Bookseller are for those who want to zero in on contemporary literature, current events, classics, women's spirituality or Pulitzer Prize winners.

Some of the Madison clubs have also been able to meet Wisconsin-based authors such as Jackie Mitchard (*The Deep End of the Ocean*, *The Most Wanted*), Jane Hamilton (*A Map of the World*, *The Short History of a Prince*) and Agate Nesaule (*A Woman in Amber*). Frank McCourt, author of *Angela's Ashes*, also held court at a Madison bookstore recently.

Local book lovers also have the Book Fair on the Square, which is usually held each September (see our Festivals and Annual Events chapter). The event is hosted by local booksellers, and in addition to row upon row of bargain books, there are poetry readings, entertainment stages and a silent auction of autographed books.

A Brief History

Wisconsin has long been an effective incubator for writers. Carl Sandburg, Thornton Wilder and Laura Ingalls Wilder spent parts of their lives in Wisconsin.

The father of the modern ecology movement, Aldo Leopold, did most of his writing in Madison. In 1998 events marked the 50th anniversary of the publication of his classic *A Sand County Almanac*. Leopold worked at the U.S. Forest Products Laboratory in Madison before going on to chair the UW-Madison department of game management.

Wisconsin's most prolific writer, author of more than 150 books as well as articles, short stories and poetry, was August Derleth. Derleth lived in the Wisconsin River town of Sauk City, a short drive from Madison.

The natural beauty of Wisconsin's landscape has inspired many other writers as well. *The Glacier Stopped Here* is a moving anthology of poems published by the Dane County Cultural Affairs Commission. In it is "The Makings of Happiness" by renowned poet Ron Wallace, a UW-Madison professor.

Another writer, Sterling North, who spun yarns about the raccoon Rascal, grew up on a farm not far from Madison. His older sister, Jessica Nelson North, was a poet and author in her own right. Her second novel, *Morning in the Land*, is set in Wisconsin during the pre-Civil War era.

Edna Ferber, John Muir and Zona Gale are other writers with Wisconsin roots. Visit your nearest library for a complete listing of Wisconsin authors and prepare to embark on your own adventure through their works. (See our Close-up in this chapter on current literary stars from Wisconsin.)

Bookstores

As the home of one of the nation's top public universities, the Wisconsin Supreme

THE LITERARY SCENE

Court, the state legislature and numerous other noteworthy entities, Madison literally has millions of volumes of books. More than 50 bookstores do a brisk business here, and in recent years, Madison has attracted some wonderful new superstores to the city's already substantial repertoire.

State Street, which runs from the Capitol to Bascom Hill on the UW-Madison campus, is a favorite haunt for people who love to rummage through used-book stores filled with offbeat and often esoteric volumes. Other stores are hidden away on side streets in the area as well.

Isthmus

A Room of One's Own
307 W. Johnson St., Madison
• (608) 257-7888

Open since 1975, this unique bookstore is a fixture on Madison's literary scene. The store specializes in books by and about women, with a huge selection of self-help titles, volumes dealing with lesbian and gay issues, spirituality and books written for and by women of color. You'll also find a diverse selection of cassettes, CDs, jewelry, T-shirts, cards and posters plus an on-site coffeehouse.

Avol's Bookstore
240 W. Gilman St., Madison
• (608) 255-4730

Patrons will discover an extensive collection with thousands of used and out-of-print books in a variety of subject areas including history, philosophy and art. The shop has what is probably the city's best selection of classic cookbooks.

Bookworks
109 State St., Madison
• (608) 255-4848

This is a place to take treasured books for restoration and finding rare books. Bookworks buys secondhand books.

By the Light of the Moon
212 Henry St., Madison
• (608) 250-9810

By the Light of the Moon, just off State Street, shines its light on women's authors. In addition to books, you also will find music by female artists, handcrafted gifts, jewelry, cards, candles, lotions and bath salts — everything you'll need to feel pampered. (Also see our Shopping chapter for related information.)

Canterbury Booksellers Coffeehouse
315 W. Gorham St., Madison
• (608) 258-9911

This bookstore in a beautifully restored 1924 building that was originally a car dealership may have more charm per square inch than any bookstore in Wisconsin. You'll find thousands of authors and titles carefully displayed, and comfortable places to sit and look at them. Canterbury has a unique children's section — with a castle for kids to play in. The castle is filled with interesting books, including many on the arts and ballet, plus children's stories written in foreign languages. Children are invited into the castle for story hours every Tuesday at 11 AM.

It's a great place to stop for afternoon tea and finger sandwiches. There is also a full vegetarian menu for lunch and dinner, with wine and beer available. This is also the home of the delightful Canterbury Inn, a bed and breakfast that occupies the second floor of the building (see our Bed and Breakfast Inns chapter).

McDermott Books
449-D State St., Madison
• (608) 284-0744

Two levels connected by a spiral staircase with 3,000 secondhand books make this store a mandatory stop for any book lover. McDermott also has a special section of books on Wisconsin and the region, but the store's greatest emphasis is on academic titles and literature. McDermott's buys per-

---

www.insiders.com
See this and many other Insiders' Guide® destinations online — in their entirety.
Visit us today!

sonal libraries, review copies and out-of-print books.

Mimosa Community Bookstore
210 N. Henry St., Madison
• (608) 256-5432

Mimosa offers self-help books and titles on spiritual growth, empowerment and healing. The soothing atmosphere is perfect for browsing. There is also a fine selection of New Age music and the best Celtic harp selection around. A resident cat has the run of the place, demonstrating the various cat condos that are also for sale here.

More Books! On State Street
310 State St., Madison
• (608) 258-8084

The motto of this store is, "No T shirts! No cappuccino! Just more books!" You'll find primarily secondhand books and some new titles — all of it recreational reading. The store specializes in mystery, fantasy, science fiction, horror, thrillers and related novels. The shop gets more arrivals daily. Don't forget to visit the second-story book nook.

Paul's Book Store
670 State St., Madison
• (608) 257-2968

If you're looking for rare or out-of-print volumes, check out the inventory at Paul's. In business since 1954, this smaller bookstore has a substantial collection of used books in many academic disciplines. The staff also will consider buying your books or, for that matter, your entire library.

Pic-A-Book
506 State St., Madison
• (608) 256-1125

Magazines, both foreign and domestic, line the displays at Pic-A-Book. Read about your favorite topic or purchase a rare magazine. Pic-A-Book also has a wide variety of books and comics to suit just about any sense of humor.

Rainbow Bookstore Cooperative
426 W. Gilman St., Madison
• (608) 257-6050

This eclectic bookstore, a couple blocks from the UW campus, specializes in the newest, cutting-edge titles in culture and media studies, politics, economics, social theory and the history of radical movements. Rainbow has been cooperatively owned and managed since 1989, and it's a favorite of many an academic.

Shakespeare's Books
18 N. Carroll St., Madison
• (608) 255-5521

Since it was established in 1933, Shakespeare's Books has grown to house an inventory of 250,000 tomes. This is Madison's largest used- and rare-books store. In fact, it's one of the largest in the Midwest. Shakespeare's Books is just across from the State Capitol, so just drive toward the dome.

Shakti Book Shop
320 State St., Madison
• (608) 255-5007

This store is one of Wisconsin's most comprehensive sources of metaphysical books.

INSIDERS' TIP

Work on the *Dictionary of Regional American English* has been under way in Madison since 1965. The comprehensive series of dictionaries looks at regional speech, the origins of slang words that became part of mainstream English. Field work to track down the origins of everyday words was done throughout the United States in the 1960s. So far, three volumes (3,005 pages) carrying the project through the letter O have been published. Two more volumes are expected to carry it through Z.

Current Literary Stars

People in Madison have known Jackie Mitchard since the 1970s when she was columnist for Madison's afternoon daily newspaper, *The Capital Times*. Her first novel, *The Deep End of the Ocean*, made the rest of the literary world aware of her work in 1996. Her tale about the kidnapping of a child and its effect on his family jumped to No. 1 on *The New York Times* bestsellers list after Oprah Winfrey made it the first selection of her Book Club. A movie based on the book, starring Michelle Pfeiffer, is in the works, and a Madison event tied to the movie's opening is expected to be held in the autumn of 1998.

Mitchard's second book, *The Most Wanted*, was released in May 1998. It's a very different kind of book than *Deep End*. It revolves around the relationship between a female attorney and a teenage girl who marries a Texas prison inmate. Mitchard describes it as being about "the continuous war between reckless passion and common sense." Meanwhile, Madisonians can still enjoy her column, "The Rest of Us," in *The Capital Times*. The column is now widely syndicated.

Children's book author Kevin Henkes is another Madison resident who has earned national acclaim. *The New York Times* recently had this to say about his work: "Every once in a while — and in children's books, it's only once in a very great while — there is a book so delightful, so exuberant, honest and evocative of the passionate life that children live as we look on, that one considers nailing a proclamation to the door of a local bookseller or wearing a copy around one's neck to advertise it." The review, which took up an entire page of the Sunday "Book Review" section, was about *Lilly's Purple Plastic Purse*.

"In all of children's literature there is just a handful of characters we think of as family — Madeline, Winnie the Pooh and Charlotte come to mind. When this young generation is old enough to reflect on the ones it loved, Lilly will probably lead the pack," the review continued.

Henkes has published 23 books since, at age 19, he left UW-Madison to try to make a living as an artist in New York. His first book, *All Alone*, was published in 1982. Henkes' writes prose, but with a simplicity and emotional power that give his books a poetic quality. His book, *Owen*, was a 1994 Caldecott Honor Book. Drawing on his childhood in nearby Racine where he grew up in a family of five children, Henkes' books take a humorous yet compassionate look at growing up, life changes and sibling rivalry. Henkes' books are treasured for their brightly colored pen and ink drawings.

Madison resident Jacquelyn Mitchard is author of *The New York Times* No. 1 bestseller *Deep End of the Ocean*.

Two UW-Madison English professors have also earned national reputations. Poet and novelist Kelly Cherry wrote *In the Wink of an Eye* and *My Life and Dr. Joyce Brothers*. Lorrie Moore's short story collections include *Anagrams*, *Like Life* and *Self-Help*.

Describing her works as psycho-biographies, historical novelist Margaret George came out with *The Memoirs of Cleopatra* in 1997. Past epics include *The Autobiography of Henry VIII* and *Mary Queen of Scotland and the Isles*.

— continued on next page

Author Agate Nesaule now lives in Madison, but she was born in Latvia just before the outbreak of World War II. Her searing account of her exile from her homeland, *A Woman in Amber*, was published in hardcover in 1995 and in paperback in 1997. It has been translated into German, Danish, Swedish and Latvian, and is now part of courses on memoir writing, women's studies and immigrant history. Nesaule was previously a professor of English and women's studies at UW-Whitewater, and she's now working on a novel.

Jerry Apps has become the chief chronicler of a rural Wisconsin that is quickly disappearing. Apps, a retired education professor from UW-Madison-Extension now lives in Madison, but he grew up on a farm in Wild Rose. In 1977 he published a book about Wisconsin's barns, which is still selling briskly. "In the Midwest, we're almost all just a few generations off the farm," Apps said, explaining the public's fascination with barns. Since then he has written books about Wisconsin's one-room schoolhouses like the one he attended, its mills and its breweries. He also wrote a volume about rural wisdom. His latest project is a book about Wisconsin's creameries.

Madison children's author Sheri Cooper Sinykin found her niche in books for adolescents that deal with real-life topics such as bulimia, death and family conflicts.

Joan Zeier, another Madison writer who tackles the problems of adolescence, is author of *Stick Boy* and *The Elderberry Thicket*.

Raymond Blum takes a very different approach to writing for young people. Blum's *Mathemagic* is a collection of number magic tricks for children 9 and older. Blum, a middle-school math teacher, captivates his readers with calculator capers and mental maneuvers using playing cards, dice, coins and calendars.

Madison's many other writers of note include author Marshall Cook, a writing guru of national stature; playwright Ed Amor; and many talented, award-winning poets such as Ron Wallace, Janet Shaw, Max Garland, Andrea Musher and Russell King.

It also carries jewelry, minerals, meditation and aromatherapy supplies, music, incense and tabletop fountains.

State Historical Museum Gift Shop
30 N. Carroll St., Madison
- **(608) 264-6555**

This is one of the city's finest sources for books on Wisconsin history, genealogy, Native Americans and ethnic specialties. The shop carries more than 3,000 titles, and many of them are entertaining and educational books for children.

Campus

University Book Store
711 State St., Madison
- **(608) 257-3784**

No doubt, this is the mother of all Madison bookstores. Generations of UW-Madison students have wandered these stacks in search of required texts for their courses. The quintessential college bookstore, University Bookstore offers aisle after aisle of academic books, art supplies, study aids, plenty of collegiate wear and just about anything you need to augment your life as a student. But it doesn't end in this mammoth store. Madison's largest bookstore now has four locations in all — two on State Street and two at Hilldale Shopping Center, University Bookstore and UBS for Kids (see subsequent entries).

University Book Store's Digital Outpost
673 State St., Madison • (608) 257-3784

If you love computers and electronics, this University Bookstore subsidiary is worth a stop. Patrons will discover personal computers, high-performance calculators and audio equipment plus a huge selection of computer

West Side

Barnes & Noble Booksellers
7433 Mineral Point Rd., Madison
• (608) 827-0809

If you're looking for the latest bestseller, a hard-to-find book or anything in between, you are likely to find it at this huge, newer West Side bookstore, the second-largest Barnes and Noble in the country. Barnes and Noble of Madison lives up to its national reputation, delighting readers of all ages and interests. Barnes and Noble has an extensive computer section. The store hosts book signings, children's programs and many other events; call the listed number for details. Barnes and Noble's second level is filled with used and discontinued books; it's a paradise for any book lover on a budget.

The Book Rack
Market Square, 6648 Odana Rd., Madison • (608) 829-3191

This one-room store is filled to the brim with used paperbacks targeted to youth readers on up, all nicely organized and lovingly cared for by a friendly staff. Buy books at half their cover price or trade two for one the same price and type.

Booked for Murder Ltd.
Lakepoint Commons, 2701 University Ave., Madison • (608) 238-2701

If you love mysteries and whodunits, visit Booked for Murder. The shelves are loaded with about 20,000 mystery, detective, suspense and espionage books. This store also caters to puzzle lovers of all types with a wide selection of crosswords, mystery puzzles, games and more. The shop also carries children's mysteries and books on audiotape.

Borders Book Shop
3416 University Ave., Madison
• (608) 232-2600

Borders Books Music & Cafe
2173 Zeier Rd., Madison
• (608) 240-0080

Another national chain and newer Madison superstore, Borders quickly has gained a reputation for having a topnotch inventory. Book lovers may browse unimpeded for hours among the store's 120,000 volumes or seek out the store's knowledgeable staff for quick assistance in finding titles. The 15,600-square-foot bookstore on University Avenue has a bright, casual atmosphere, an espresso bar, wide aisles and chairs for shoppers who like to scan before they buy. Most hardcover books sell at 10 percent off list price, and 30 percent discounts are applied to *New York Times* hardcover bestsellers. The newer store on Zeier Road is about three times bigger, and it has music, videos, and a larger periodical selection.

Frugal Muse Books, Music & Video
High Point Centre, 7475 Mineral Point Rd., Madison
• (608) 833-8668

No shopping trip to Madison's West Side is complete without a stop at the Frugal Muse. The selection of new and used books — both hardcover and paperback — is outstanding. If you want to sell your books, this is where you'll probably get the best price for them. And that's why you'll find so many barely touched current bestsellers here. The store also has terrific cookbooks. You can discover hard-to-find vinyl (remember record albums?), audio books, CDs, music cassettes and videos. You can also get a discount on new Pleasant Company books here.

INSIDERS' TIP

Alfred Hitchcock's 1960 movie *Psycho* was written by Wisconsin writer Robert Bloch and based on the killing spree of Wisconsin man Ed Gein. Gein spent his last years at Mendota Mental Health Institute in Madison.

THE LITERARY SCENE • 221

This Madison bookstore is a treasure trove for avid readers. The city has a strong literary tradition so bookstores are plentiful.

Madison Church Supply
820 S. Park St., Madison
• **(608) 256-1214**

At this South Side store, you will discover a collection of books on spirituality, feminist theology, Catholicism and liberation theology. Madison Church Supply also offers children's books with religious themes and a large selection of Bibles, spiritual music and gifts.

20th Century Books
1115 S. Park St., Madison
• **(608) 251-6226**

This is a great place to find books on popular culture, science fiction, comics, mysteries and film/TV.

University Book Store
Hilldale Shopping Center, 702 N. Midvale Blvd., Madison
• **(608) 238-8455**

If you want to look like a UW Badger or read like one, visit the University Book Store at Hilldale. This smaller version of the State Street store (see the previous entry) offers fiction and nonfiction, gifts, greeting cards, art supplies and clothing with UW insignias.

UBS for Kids
Hilldale Shopping Center, 702 N. Midvale Blvd., Madison • **(608) 238-3332**

UBS for Kids often invites children to come down in their pajamas for an evening of stories. The shop carries a large variety of children's books, including the latest award-winning titles. You'll also find gifts for kids and educational games.

East Side

Aardvark's Bookstore
2750 E. Johnson St., Madison
• **(608) 249-6778**

Book lovers have been trading books at this store since it opened in 1976. Aardvark's

---

INSIDERS' TIP

Madison native Thornton Wilder won three Pulitzer Prizes for *The Bridge of San Luis Rey, Our Town* and *The Skin of Our Teeth.*

sells paperbacks, specializing in fiction, historical and contemporary novels and romances, mysteries, suspense science fiction, fantasy, horror — you name it. Aardvark's also has some nice secondhand children's books and some nonfiction.

Half-Price Books, Records and Magazines
4250 East Towne Blvd., Madison
• **(608) 244-1189**
Nakoma Plaza, 4543 W. Beltline Hwy., Madison (West) • **(608) 273-1140**

Local outlets of this national chain sell used and new books of national and regional interest, sheet-music classics, videos and books-on-cassette. Whether you are looking for books on travel, religion, cooking, the arts, self-help or just about any topic, this is a great store to begin your hunt. New books arrive daily, and you can sell your secondhand books and pick up a few dollars toward some new purchases.

Pooh Corner
East Pointe Plaza, 1617 Thierer Rd., Madison • **(608) 242-1880**
Homestead Shoppes, 6116 Mineral Point Rd., Madison (West)
• **(608) 231-0211**

This bright, friendly store offers a tremendous selection of children's books including award-winning titles. The stores also has educational videos, toys and some fun Winnie the Pooh collectibles. Pooh Corner is one of Madison's very first children's bookstores and has earned a reputation for excellence and exceptional staffing. (See the Young At Heart section of our Shopping chapter for related Pooh Corner information.)

The stores merged with the Highsmith Education Station in 1995, which strives to connect customers with many ways of learning besides books. You will find educationally stimulating toys and other products in areas such as science (budding meteorologists will love it here), math, language arts, chemistry, art, music (you'll find everything from simple shakers to kits for building your own piano keyboards), tapes and CDs. Products are suitable for children from infancy through teens.

Reading for Free

Madison has numerous public and specialty libraries free for the browsing and borrowing. Anyone who lives in South-Central Wisconsin (including Dane and six other counties) can obtain a free library card good at any of approximately 60 public libraries.

Isthmus

Madison Public Central Library
201 W. Mifflin St., Madison
• **(608) 266-6300**

Central Library is the hub of the Madison Public Library System. Library patrons can borrow not only volumes and volumes of literary works of art, but also audiocassettes, videos, compact discs, toys and even framed art reproductions. The library hosts frequent book talks supported in part by the Wisconsin Humanities Council, with funds from the National Endowment for the Humanities; call the listed number for schedules.

Central Library has dictionaries and books for learning 68 languages. For more than 25 of those languages, the library maintains a sampling of fiction and nonfiction books in the language. The Central Library also has magazines in Spanish, French and German. Also through Madison Public Library, readers can access an extensive large-print collection. Among large-print editions are numerous bestsellers and other popular fiction and nonfiction titles. Many special services are available to patrons with disabilities; call for details.

INSIDERS' TIP

The Vesterheim Genealogical Center in Madison is the nation's largest repository of information on Norwegian immigration to the United States.

You can call various Central Library departments for specialized information (all area codes are 608): Reference, 266-6350; Administration, 266-6363; Audiovisual Services, 266-6318; Circulation, 266-6308; and Youth Services, 266-6345.

Historical Society Archives Division
816 State St., Madison • (608) 264-6460

The Archives Division is the official archival repository for Wisconsin state and local government records and holds nongovernmental data collected from individuals, organizations, churches, businesses and other record creators. Within the collection are Wisconsin state and local government records; unpublished primary research source materials; approximately 2 million photographs; more than 25,000 maps and atlases; and the holdings of the Wisconsin Center for Film and Theater Research.

The visual materials archives are on the same floor but is a separate division; call (608) 264-6470. More published government records are available in the Historical Society Library on the second floor of the building (see the next listing).

Historical Society Library
816 State St., Madison • (608) 264-6534

The Historical Society's comprehensive library collection features Wisconsin history; genealogy and local history; political, economic and religious history; anthropology and archaeology; social reform and radical groups; left- and right-wing political and social movements; women and women's groups; immigrant groups and ethnic minorities; and Wisconsin state and local publications.

Dane County Law Library
210 Martin Luther King Jr. Blvd., Madison • (608) 266-6316

The Dane County Law Library has a small collection of family-related legal materials, with an emphasis on Wisconsin law. These resources may be used in the library by Dane County attorneys and the general public. The Dane County Law Library distributes the following family law-form packets free of charge:

• Motion to Change Court Ordered Child Support/Maintenance
• Order to Show Cause for Remedial Contempt of a Divorce or Paternity Judgment
• Motion to Change Custody of Physical Placement
• Affidavit and Order to Waive Required Mediation
• Motion for Contempt for Failure to Cooperate with Family Court Counseling

Campus

You probably will need a Wisconsin driver's license to check out books from UW-Madison libraries. But anyone, regardless of residency, can stake out a seat and read within the library to their heart's content. Of course, even librarians and library patrons can't read all the time; sometimes they must sleep. Remember, if you pick out a really long book or are researching a project, you may have to come back the next day and finish.

College Library
Helen C. White Hall, 600 N. Park St., Madison • (608) 262-3245

In this multilevel library, you can find students studying industriously, even on Friday and Saturday nights! Helen C. White Hall has books on just about any subject — fiction and nonfiction. The collection emphasizes introductory material useful to UW-Madison undergraduate studies, along with significant selections on personal and career development.

Cooperative Children's Book Center (CCBC)
4290 Helen C. White Hall, 600 N. Park St., Madison • (608) 263-3720

The library collection contains review copies of newly published juvenile trade books, recommended children's and young adult trade books, historical children's books, contemporary and historical reference materials related to children's and young adult literature, children's and young adult books by Wisconsin authors and illustrators and alternative press books for children. Books do not circulate, but you may read on site.

Criminal Justice Reference and Information Center
L140 Law Library, 975 Bascom Mall, Madison • (608) 262-1499

The Criminal Justice Center provides a research base for anyone interested in the criminal justice system. Users include faculty and students from the entire UW system as well as private educational institutions, law enforcement and correctional personnel, district attorneys, judges, inmates, task forces and commissions.

Institute for Environmental Studies (IES) Library
15 Science Hall, 550 N. Park St., Madison • (608) 263-3064

This collection focuses on current environmental issues, specifically subjects dealing with energy and land use. You also will find information here about air pollution, water issues and the Great Lakes.

Middleton Health Sciences Library
1305 Linden Dr., Madison
• (608) 262-2371

This library, centrally located on campus behind the Medical Sciences Center, houses more than 140,000 books and 9,700 periodical titles. The collection focuses on basic and clinical biomedical sciences, health-services administration, history of health sciences, clinical and experimental psychology, nursing and allied health.

Social Work Library
1350 University Ave., Madison
• (608) 263-3840

The Social Work Library contains information on social-work education and research as well as resources pertaining to divorce, addiction, child abuse, mental retardation, aging, human sexuality, AIDS and other topics.

Steenbock Memorial Library
550 Babcock Dr., Madison
• (608) 262-9635

Materials in this library are related to agriculture; animal, plant, food or life science; genetics; landscape architecture; veterinary medicine; natural resources; family studies; and consumer sciences.

Library Branches

Each of the Madison-area library branches is linked to collections throughout South-Central Wisconsin. Using computers within the library, you can request books and have them sent to the branch nearest you. Check with the reference desk for assistance in learning to use the operator-friendly computer system. You may also renew books from home using a touch-tone telephone.

Many Madison libraries have children's programs, summer reading incentives for school children, reading groups and other activities. Check with librarians for a list of current events.

Branches of the Madison Public Library include the following:

•West Side — South Madison Branch, 2222 S. Park Street, (608) 266-6395; Meadowridge Branch, 5740 Raymond Road, (608) 288-6160; Monroe Street Branch, 1705 Monroe Street, (608) 266-6390; and Sequoya Branch, 513 S. Midvale Boulevard, (608) 266-6385.

•East Side — Hawthorne Branch, 2817 E. Washington Avenue, (608) 246-4548; Lakeview Branch, 2845 N. Sherman Avenue, (608) 246-4547; and Pinney Branch, 204 Cottage Grove Road, (608) 224-7100.

Literary Organizations

Cheap At Any Price Poets' Collective
317 N. Brearly St., Madison • No phone

This collective of Madison area poets was formed to provide local poets with opportunities to have their work heard. The group hosts regular open poetry readings twice a month and sometimes travels to Chicago and other cities. CAAP publishes a free monthly newsletter and participates in annual poetry competitions.

Council for Wisconsin Writers
(608) 233-2484

The council is dedicated to honoring and nurturing Wisconsin writers. CWW publishes a newsletter and sponsors statewide projects, a speaker's bureau and an awards program. Membership is open to anyone interested in supporting Wisconsin Writers. Contact Russell King at

P.O. Box 55322, Madison WI 53711 for details about membership and events.

Madison Storytellers' Guild
3126 Buena Vista St., Madison
- **(608) 249-5030**

The Madison Storyteller's Guild is an informal affiliation of storytelling enthusiasts who gather monthly for the sharing of stories. Meetings are held September through May on the third Saturday of each month, usually in the evening. Locations vary. Storytellers and story listeners are welcome. In addition, the guild sponsors storytelling concerts and events to explore and promote the art of storytelling. For details, call Susan Gilchrist evenings and weekends at the listed telephone number.

Wisconsin Screenwriters Forum Inc.
UW-Madison Liberal Studies and the Arts, 610 Langdon St., Madison
- **(608) 262-3447**

WSF is organized for writers interested in television and motion pictures, including independent production. Call for a copy of the newsletter or a list of workshops. WSF also holds writing competitions, sponsors workshops and is involved in one-on-one tutoring. Contact Christine DeSmet at the listed address and phone number.

The Writers' Place
7 N. Pinckney St., Ste. J, Madison
- **(608) 255-4030**

This nonprofit literary center offers educational and inspirational support for Wisconsin's writing community. The Writer's Place offers creative-writing workshops and classes, a newsletter, peer critique groups, readings and an annual literary contest.

Silver Buckle Press
236 Memorial Library, UW Campus, 728 State St., Madison
- **(608) 263-4929**

The Silver Buckle Press offers educational opportunities for interested individuals and groups with its working museum of letterpress printing equipment. Silver Buckle has a publishing program and sponsors workshops and conferences related to printing and the book arts.

Abraxas Press
(608) 238-0175

This nonprofit literary organization publishes an independent small-press poetry magazine, *Abraxas*, with an international readership. Write to editor Ingrid Swanberg, P.O. Box 260113, Madison WI 53711 for writer's guidelines and information about submissions.

You'll find plenty of places to spend your money in Madison, from big national businesses in home decor, electronics and apparel to the independent, specialty stores that make shopping here a unique experience.

Shopping

It should come as no surprise that a white-collar city like Madison would have more than its share of shopping opportunities, from large regional malls serving all of South-Central Wisconsin to small, one-of-a-kind stores often grouped together in neighborhood clusters.

The bottom line is, you'll have plenty of ways to spend your money in Madison. And while Madisonians have, especially within the past five years, been discovered by big national names in home decor, electronics and apparel, it's the independent, specialty stores on which we focus the most attention in this chapter because they are what make Madison shopping unique. We begin with a roundup of the three largest malls in Madison, East and West Towne and Hilldale, followed by a description of three popular shopping clusters — State Street between the UW-Madison campus and Downtown; Monroe Street on the near West Side; and Williamson Street on the East. Following that is a listing of the kind of small shops that are fun to poke around in whether you're a visitor or a resident.

Major Malls

Because shopping in Madison could be the subject of a book all to itself, we've only listed the two large regional malls, East and West Towne, and Hilldale, a popular and thriving specialty mall with a focus on upscale clothing and products for the home. Somewhat smaller but still significant are South Towne, anchored by Kohl's Department Store, and Westgate on the near West Side, home to Famous Footwear (with corporate offices in Madison) and T.J. Maxx.

In addition to the three malls described in this chapter, there are several other smaller yet significant malls, including a new one that opened in 1997 — Prairie Towne Center — off Mineral Point Road about a mile west of West Towne. It's notable as Madison's introduction to Target, Old Navy and CompUSA. A sizeable Land's End Inlet (like an outlet, only better) is also located there. For avid boaters, the opening of a West Marine in '98, near South Towne Mall, was big news.

West Side

Hilldale Shopping Center
702 N. Midvale Blvd., Madison
• **(608) 238-6640**

Though older, Hilldale is not as large as West and East Towne malls, but what it lacks in size, it makes up for in style. A straight, 3-mile shot from the Capitol, on the corner of Midvale Boulevard and University Avenue on the near West Side, Hilldale was built in 1962. Today, after periodic expansions and renovations — a major $4.5 face-lift occurred in 1997 — the shopping center features about 50 stores and services.

If the regional malls bring the rest of the world to Madison, then Hilldale shows off the best of Madison. Shops are, for the most part, upscale, one-of-a-kind and locally owned. One exception to the latter is Marshall Field's department store, the central hub of Hilldale. It may be corporate, but it fits.

Hilldale, more classic than faddish, is the first large mall in Madison to offer a masseuse on the premises; it also sponsors its own farmers' market in the front parking lot from May through October. Imagine, buying carrots and Anne Klein all in the same morning. That's Madison.

Home to some of the better locally owned women's apparel stores, Hilldale offers Jan Byce's, Square One, Woldenberg's For Women and Rupert Cornelius. (See subsequent separate entries in this chapter.) For classic, upscale men's clothing, there's Woldenberg's For Men. A wide selection of dress shoes is available at Field's, Woldenberg's or the Shoe Gallery across

University Avenue in Walnut Grove Shopping Center, where another longtime women's apparel store — Yost's — is also located. Falling under the category of "upscale casual," a phrase that underscores Madison living, is the Boot Barn, Cornblooms and Morgan Shoes.

Like the shops, restaurants are a bit more upscale. The closest thing to a food court is the Upstairs/Downstairs Restaurant & Deli and Chocolate Shoppe.

Given everything we've just said, it might seem incongruous to add that Hilldale also has a Walgreen's and Wolff Kubly housewares/hardware store (with one of the best watch departments in town). Yet, anyone who shops Hilldale regularly wouldn't have it any other way. And seniors like the fact they can shop at Field's and then pick up groceries at the end of the mall. Sentry Foods is open 24 hours a day. Some people wish all of Hilldale was.

Mall hours are Monday through Friday, 10 AM to 9 PM; Saturday, 10 AM to 5:30 PM; and Sunday, noon to 5 PM.

West Towne Mall
66 West Towne Mall, Madison
• **(608) 833-6330**

When West Towne Mall opened up on the far West Side of Madison in October of 1970, Odana Road was little more than a frontage road for the Beltline Highway. Today, as a result of traffic attracted by West Towne, Odana is a main business artery for the West Side, home to a multitude of strip malls, automobile dealerships (some of which wisely got there first) and professional buildings.

Following several expansions over the years, the latest completed in '97, West Towne is home to 105 retail businesses. It's owned by the Richard E. Jacobs Group, based in Cleveland, Ohio. Anchoring the mall are four large department stores: the Boston Store, Sears, JCPenney and Younkers (all noted for numerous, wonderfully discounted sales). In between are a variety of specialty shops and food vendors selling everything from coffee and hot pretzels to leather goods, fine jewelry and athletic wear.

Across the city from one another, West Towne and East Towne malls draw from all of South-Central Wisconsin. As the two largest shopping centers in the Greater Madison area, they feature many big-name national retailers, especially in men's and women's apparel. (See our subsequent write-up for East Towne Mall.)

So who are the big players at West Towne? That, of course, depends upon your tastes, but those who are into name-dropping might like this impressive roundup: Abercrombie & Fitch, Gap and Gap Kids, Gymboree, Limited, Casual Corner, Victoria's Secret, The Disney Store, Bath & Body Works, American Eagle, Williams Sonoma, Ann Taylor and Eddie Bauer.

Madison is a very athletic-conscious town, and stores like Athlete's Foot and Champs provide enough Nike, Reebok and Adidas wear to keep anyone active and fit.

The mall also has a bookstore (Waldenbooks), toy store (Kay-Bee Toy & Hobby Shop), large candy store (Mr. Bulky), coffee emporium (Gloria Jean's), several card and gift shops and a sizeable food court.

This shopping story doesn't end with the mall itself. Almost a dozen warehouse-size stores and restaurants have sprung up behind West Towne within the past decade. Within walking distance are Best Buy and Circuit City, both of which carry a wide range of electronics; a Cost Plus World Market and Pier 1 Imports that overflow with home decorative items; Kohl's Department Store, a great place to find reasonably priced sportswear and lingerie; Recreation Equipment Inc. (REI) that has its own climbing wall; one of the largest Barnes & Noble bookstores in the country; and numerous specialty and furniture stores.

Chain restaurants represented include Olive Garden, Red Lobster, Mountain Jack's and Chili's. McDonald's, of course, and Taco Bell are right inside the mall.

Normal mall hours are 10 AM to 9 PM Monday through Saturday and 11 AM until 6 PM on Sunday.

STATE STREET

Experience Madison's Most Famous Street

THE SOAP OPERA

319 STATE STREET • (608) 251-4051

A State Street Landmark for Over 25 Years

The most extensive selection of cruelty-free body care, perfume & gift products found anywhere

Full service gift wrapping & shipping service available

OPEN 7 DAYS/EVENING HOURS
800-251-7627
www.thesoapopera.com

CANTERBURY Booksellers Cafe Inn

A cozy setting for serious browsers, focusing on fiction, poetry, and children's literature--with a full service cafe and a fanciful B&B above the bookstore.

315 W. Gorham 258-9911
www.madisoncanterbury.com

Celebrating the non-necessities of life - beautiful gifts, jewelry and accessories.

LITTLE LUXURIES
214 STATE STREET • 255•7372

OPEN EVERY DAY AND EVENINGS

Puzzlebox
A CURIOSITY EMPORIUM

230 STATE STREET, MADISON, WI
608-251-0701
MONDAY - SATURDAY 10-8
SUNDAY 12-5

State Street is a great place to shop, dine and people watch.

East Side

East Towne Mall
89 East Towne Mall, Madison
• **(608) 244-1501**

The easiest way to describe East Towne is just to add "ditto" for everything written about West Towne (see previous entry). Also owned by the Richard E. Jacobs Group, East Towne opened across town in '71, a year after West Towne, and, in one sense, has been steadily catching up ever since.

That's doesn't mean East Towne has trouble attracting tenants — not in the least. But some national retailers like The Disney Store and Gap often test the waters at West Towne before committing to both sides of town. Demographics for the West Side profile a consumer with a bit more spending money in his or her pocket, although that distinction is starting to blur with so much residential development now occurring on the East Side and beyond, namely in Sun Prairie and Cottage Grove.

Like West Towne, East Towne is anchored by the Boston Store, JCPenney, Sears and Younkers. As mentioned, it has Gap and Disney, but no Gap Kids. But it also offers a Victoria's Secret, Limited, Casual Corner, Waldenbooks, Eddie Bauer, Champs and several of the same jewelry stores. In place of Abercrombie & Fitch, it has the less expensive Lerner New York, although both are owned by the same parent company. One day, who knows!

Commercial development around East Towne, easily accessible from E. Washington Avenue and the U.S. Highway 151 Exit off I-90/94, exploded in the early '90s. Nearby, you can shop at a large Burlington Coat Factory, Highsmith Education Station, Best Buy and a large Home Goods Store (which makes up for the Bed, Bath & Beyond now on the West Side). Even the same restaurants, Mountain Jack's, Red Lobster, Chili's and Olive Garden, back up East Towne as they do West Towne.

Most people who live in Madison shop the mall closest to them, although it's easy to get from one to the other in 20 to 30 minutes by using the Beltline. It's human nature to think that something always looks better on the other side of the fence. Some people swear that even the department stores carry different merchandise. We think it's all a matter of luck and timing, but if it's simply a matter of not finding your size, clerks are more than happy to call across town for you.

One big advantage of East Towne is its proximity to Interstate 90/94 and a number of hotels that have sprung up for that very same reason. Store hours are the same as West

Towne — 10 AM until 9 PM Monday through Saturday and 11 AM to 6 PM on Sunday.

Neighborhood Shopping

Madison is the sum of its many neighborhoods, noted for their historical significance, beauty and, sometimes, shopping. The following three especially fall into the latter category. Take the time to enjoy them individually for they vastly vary in personality.

Isthmus

State Street

Running from the State Capitol to the eastern edge of the UW-Madison campus, State Street is a bustling pedestrian mall filled with interesting, offbeat art galleries, eateries and small boutiques selling everything from Bucky Badger memorabilia to high fashion, unique jewelry, decorative home items, T-shirts, and yes, even "cheeseheads" (see this chapter's "Homegrown Products" Close-up).

Altogether, there are almost 200 shops and services along this street as well as 50 coffeehouses and restaurants serving everything from Eastern Mediterranean to Greek, Mexican and Italian. (Do you like cappuccino? It's available on almost every street corner.) You'll be hard-pressed to find a more eclectic, devil-may-care shopping and restaurant district anywhere else in the state.

Because State Street attracts all kinds, including occasionally the homeless, State Street has come under particular scrutiny of late, and plans are under way to aesthetically improve the popular shopping district and eliminate any panhandling. While there is always room for improvement, we believe State Street and the Capitol Square are great places to meander, and on those few summer and spring weekends when a festival isn't occurring Downtown, street musicians and outdoor cafes keep the place pretty lively. Even in winter, the street takes on a glow when about 25,000 miniature white lights are strung on the trees lining the street.

There are many places to check out on State Street. Teenagers and young adults naturally gravitate to the **Exclusive Co.**, 122 State Street, a music store with some of the lowest CD prices in town; and **Urban Outfitters**, 604 State Street, near campus, that offers trendy clothing and dorm/apartment decor.

Other shops of note include **Little Luxuries**, 214 State, a gift shop just like its name; **Tropic Jewel**, 449 State, a jewelry and bead store; **Soap Opera**, 319 State, an institution here that preceded the bath and body craze; **The Puzzlebox**, 230 State, a fun toy and game store for young and old alike; and **Fontana Sports Specialities**, 251 State, an upscale sporting goods store. (Look under separate headings for more information.)

Remember, lower addresses are near the Square; higher ones are closer to campus. With that said, it's a Madison tradition to refer to upper State Street as being near the Capitol and lower State Street as close to campus. Totally confused? You'll catch on. All of State Street is within walking distance of Downtown museums and the Madison Civic Center.

Parking ramps most convenient to the Capitol Square and "upper" State Street are the Civic Center Ramp, with entrances off Mifflin and Dayton streets; and the State Street/Capitol Ramp, accessible from Frances and Lake streets. Closer to campus and "lower" State Street is the State Street/Campus ramp, also accessible from Frances and Lake streets.

State Street stores and restaurants are open every day of the week, beginning at 10 AM, with extended evening hours during the summer. Don't forget to mark Maxwell Street Days on your calendar. (See the "July" section of the Festivals and Annual Events chapter.)

West Side

Monroe Street

On the near West Side of Madison, near the edge of the UW-Madison campus and not far from the Henry Vilas Zoo and Lake Wingra, Monroe Street offers 1.5 miles of locally owned specialty shops, small eateries and galleries. Businesses are primarily lumped in a five-block area from 1500 to 1900 Monroe and then again from 2400 to 2800. In between is Edgewood High School and College.

The one word that sums up the shopping here is "arty." This is where you'll find a wide selection of fine arts and crafts (refer to the gallery entries in the Arts chapter), unusual home decorative items, natural-fiber clothing and imported specialty foods.

For instance, **Atlas Delicatessen**, 1923 Monroe, offers homemade pastas and dozens of oils and vinegars in addition to fresh-made dishes and sauces (see our Restaurants chapter). Immediately next door is **Breadsmith**, one of the better bread bakeries in town.

Stores to which people naturally gravitate are **Orange Tree Imports**, 1721 Monroe Street, a wonderland of decorative items, kitchenware and gifts; **Katy's American Indian Arts**, 1817 Monroe, showcasing handmade American Indian jewelry at better prices than you'll find in Santa Fe; and **Wild Child**, 1813 Monroe, a children's clothing store specializing in natural fabrics that the store itself dyes in bright colors. (See separate listings for some of these stores and others in the latter part of this chapter.) New in 1988 is **Bill Paul LTD Studio**, an upscale menswear store (see separate listing).

Away from campus, on the upper end of the street, more small shops and galleries are clustered in **Knickerbocker Place**, taking up the 2600 and 2700 blocks. One of the more visually appealing strip malls in Madison, it's predominately built of brick to blend architecturally with the neighborhood buildings. Located there is **Studio You**, a workshop in which visitors are welcome to come in and paint pottery. All supplies are available on the premises. Both children and adults are welcome. (For more information, see "Taking the Fuss out of Birthdays" Close-up in the Kidstuff chapter.)

You'll find some of Madison's favorite restaurants on this street, including **Bluephies**, in Knickerbocker Place, and **Pasqual's Southwestern Deli**, 2534 Monroe. (See our Restaurants chapter for details.)

In case you get all the way up Monroe Street to **Mallatt Pharmacy**, 3506, and **Parman's Service Station** next door, say "hi" for us. Mallatt's is a small pharmacy doing business the old-fashioned, know-every-customer way as well as the modern way (it does a brisk business in costume rental and accessories). The Parman brothers, Junior and Keith, continued to pump gas and clean windshields, just as their father did before them, until state law required them to pull their tanks in the fall of 1998. But they still do automobile repairs for everyone in the neighborhood. The business is more than 50 years old and still looks the same. Monroe Street indeed has stood the test of time. That's what makes it so neat.

East Side

Williamson Street

If any shopping district best fits the fiercely independent mood of Madison from the 1960s and early '70s, it has to be Williamson Street, commonly called "Willy Street." Nowhere is the entrepreneurial spirit greater or the mix of merchandise more unpredictable. If State Street is the heart of Madison, Willy Street is its soul.

This is a place where storefronts are still affordable and odd sorts of things greatly appreciated. With the nearby Monona Terrace Convention Center now up and running, Willy Street will be getting more than a second look by many people. The trick will be to promote the neighborhood without damaging its core existence as a home for those kinds of unusual and avant garde stores that wouldn't be able to exist anywhere else. Willy Street has stuck around so long, it's back in style again.

When you enter a store on Williamson Street, nine times out of 10 the owner will be the one waiting on you. Because of that, hours of operation are sometimes sporadic. Few stores are open on Monday — or even before 11 AM other days of the week. Evening hours vary.

Epitomizing Willy Street as an interesting assortment of old and new is **Pick More Daisies**, 1216 Williamson. A cross between a gift and antique shop, it's one of the newer additions on the street. (See the separate listing in the subsequent "Little Luxuries" section.)

Almost directly across the street is **Reality Check**, "an alternative place to buy stuff" like new and recycled clothing, hemp products, candles, used CDs, beads and modestly priced gift items by neighborhood artisans.

Where To Go for Cheddarheads and Other Wisconsin Treats

There are a couple of things you need to know about shopping in the Greater Madison area that ring true, really, for the entire state.

Predominate colors, no matter the season, are red and white and green and gold.

Cheddar wedges are not only good to eat; they're often worn on the head. But you probably already knew that from television coverage of the '97 Super Bowl.

For the widest selection of Wisconsin-inspired merchandise, especially logo apparel for the UW-Madison Badgers and Green Bay Packers, head to State Street where many stores carry T-shirts, mugs, posters and other popular memorabilia. Some shops, however, are in the business of selling nothing but team sports clothing. That's how fanatical the fans are here.

One of the biggest operations is **Name of the Game**, with two locations on State Street, both of which carry Badger wear exclusively. The folks who own Name of the Game also own five **Bormann's Apparel** stores that also specialize in Badger and Packer mania. They carry a wide selection of clothing and accessories including everything from warm-up suits, leather jackets and football jerseys to cheerleader outfits for children. Bormann's Apparel stores are in the Westgate Mall on the near West Side; 2526 Allen Boulevard, Middleton; 4120 Monona Drive, Monona; 1191 N. Sherman Avenue on the northeast side; and 225 Junction Road in Prairie Towne Shopping Center on the far West Side.

— continued on next page

Cheddarheads were sported by members of the world-champion Green Bay Packers on *The Tonight Show*.

The nonprofit **W Club**, which raises money for UW Athletics, has three stores in Madison. Only UW-Madison merchandise is carried, and if you care to pay the price, you can come home with some limited-edition, Badger-inspired artwork not sold anywhere else. Named **Bucky's Locker Rooms**, the larger of the three stores is in the Kohl Center. Another is at Hilldale Shopping Center, corner of University Avenue and Midvale Boulevard. The original Bucky's remains tucked away in the corner of the UW Fieldhouse.

For classic UW-logo apparel, we also highly recommend **The University Book Store**, an independent business (despite the name) with the largest of its three stores at 711 State Street adjacent to Library Mall. A variety of university memorabilia, including inexpensive notebooks and pens, is also available at a second location in Hilldale Shopping Center and through its children's book store, **UBS For Kids**, also in Hilldale.

If you're looking for the classic, foam cheese-wedge hat that's made Wisconsin famous, the best place to head is State Street. Many stores carry them.

But if you truly are hungry (no, the foam cheese wedge won't help), call or drop by the following Madison establishments for some good eats:

For a wonderful selection of fine foods and one-of-a-kind gifts made in Wisconsin, try **Moze's Gourmet Specialities**, 1925 Monroe Street. This is a great place to find smoked fish, specialty cheeses, wild rice, special chutneys, gourmet popcorn and even dessert sauces. Gift boxes and baskets can be made up. Non-edible items include T-shirts, tote bags, artist carvings and cookbooks written in Wisconsin.

If time is of the essence, but you'd still like to have or send a memento of Wisconsin, call **PRESENTing WISCONSIN** at (888) FROM WIS. Gift packages are available for $18 to almost $100. They're filled with products for which the state is famous, including cheeses, maple syrup, specialty jellies and dried cherries and cranberries just for starters.

Rick's Olde Gold, 1314 Williamson Street, is an institution. It carries used furniture and stereo equipment in addition to a full line of ethnic-inspired imports and secondhand gold jewelry. Just walking through the door is an experience.

One very interesting shop that is often difficult to find open is the **Linen Closet Gallery and Gift Shop**, owned and operated by a Jamaican native who is studying at the UW-Madison. The Linen Closet carries paintings by local artists, some ethnic jewelry and clothing but specializes in fine Nigerian bed and table linens by a process called adire, similar to batik but much more subtle. The gallery has limited hours: 1 to 5:30 PM Tuesday through Friday and 10 AM to 5:30 Saturday and Sunday. Often, you just have to pass by. The store has no phone.

Two very interesting shops on the west end of Williamson, closer to the Downtown area, include **Wooden Voices** and the **Linen Closet Gallery and Gift Shop**, owned and operated by a Jamaican native who is studying at the UW-Madison to become an art teacher. Both stores are filled with multicultural riches.

Wooden Voices sells a variety of handmade instruments such as African drums and Egyptian shakers. The store is also a treasure chest for ethnic clothing, baskets and decorations.

The **Linen Closet** carries paintings by local artists, some ethnic jewelry and clothing but specializes in fine Nigerian bed and table linens by a process called adire, similar to batik but much more subtle. The gallery has limited hours: 1 to 5:30 PM Tuesday through Friday and 10 AM to 5:30 Saturday and Sunday.

Street parking is usually easy to find on Williamson Street.

… SHOPPING

Store-by-Store

While it's impossible to write up every shop in and around Madison, we've included those independent businesses that have wide appeal to visitors and/or help to better define the area. We've organized them in alphabetical order under "Antiques and Collectibles," "Athleticwear," "Children's Clothing," "Home Decor and Accessories," "Jewelry," "Men's Apparel," "Resale Shops," "Simple Pleasures," "Women's Apparel" and "Young At Heart." Stores that defy categorization but make Madison unique are lumped at the end under "In A Class By Themselves."

Shops maintain normal business hours unless otherwise stated. Evening hours vary, so call ahead. Stores that typically are closed on Sundays often remain open that day during the holiday season.

Antiques and Collectibles

Though the Greater Madison area has always been noted more for its cutting-edge innovations than antiquity, there is a thriving business here in antiques and collectibles.

West Side

Atomic Interiors
961 S. Park St., Madison
• **(608) 251-5255**

People may think of this shop as carrying antiques, but it really specializes in quality, mid-century, modern furniture, specifically classic designer pieces primarily from the '30s through the '60s. Three names prominently represented in the store include Herman Miller, Heywood-Wakefield and Knoll Furniture. All are vintage pieces except some new ones by Miller. Owners of Atomic Interiors live in Madison but also operate a store in Wrigleyville Antique Mall, 3336 N. Clark Street in Chicago. Hours in Madison are limited: noon to 3 PM Wednesday through Friday and 11 AM until 5 PM on Saturday.

Chris Kerwin Antiques & Interiors
1839 Monroe St., Madison
• **(608) 256-7363**

Direct importer of English and Oriental antiques, Chris Kerwin has been in business for nearly 30 years. She has made her mark on not only many homes in the area, but also many of the country clubs, including the prestigious Madison Club. She's as much involved in interior design as selling high-end decorative antiques and jewelry. The shop has an extensive collection of botanical prints, some of which date back to the late 1600s. The store is closed on Sundays.

Janet's Antiques
815 Fern Dr., Madison • (608) 238-4474

This business, in operation since '73, is in an old building built in 1935 for a German immigrant couple who operated a sausage factory in it and served beer and brats on the side. Later it was turned into apartments. Today it houses a wide selection of restored antique furniture from the 18th and 19th centuries as well as china, glassware and jewelry. Janet produces a newsletter four times a year that's filled with interesting tidbits and new finds. Call to be put on the mailing list.

Stony Hill Antiques
2140 Regent St., Madison
• **(608) 231-1247**

This is a small shop crammed with unusual, wonderfully aged pieces, including Oriental carpets, tribal masks, fine art, ethnic weavings and Americana books. But it's textiles for which this shop is most noted. In many ways, Stony Hill, in operation for 20 years on the same corner

---

INSIDERS' TIP

The Lower Level of Yost's, 201 State Street, a locally owned clothing store for women, always carries half-price apparel and discontinued bridal dresses. In the latter category, some items valued up to $1,000 sometimes sell for as little as $99. Of course, you have to be the right size.

Monroe Street

Experience Madison's Most Charming Street

Voted Madison's Best Specialty Shop

Cookware
Glassware
Gadgets
Toys
Jewelry
Soaps
Cards
Candies

ORANGE TREE IMPORTS
1721 Monroe Street • 255-8211
Open 7 days a week

The Flower Shop

CUSTOM FLORAL SERVICES

Weddings • Special Events
Corporate Events • Gift Baskets
Interior Floral Design • and more

**1725 Monroe Street
(608) 255-4414**

KATY'S AMERICAN INDIAN ARTS

Where the tradition continues...

- Zuni hand carved fetishes
- Hopi band rings
- Navajo contemporary & traditional jewelry
- Pendleton Blankets

1817 MONROE STREET • 251-5451

Imagine comfortable clothes, creative jewelry...

Think Indigo Moon

indigo moon

257-9477
1809 MONROE ST.
OPEN DAILY

Monroe Street

PAINT YOUR OWN POTTERY

America's hottest new activity is now in Madison. STUDIO YOU provides an easy, comfortable, and fun activity for people of all ages!

- Adult/Children's classes
- Birthday Parties
- Spouse activities during conventions

WALK-INS WELCOME!
2701 Monroe St., Madison, WI
608-231-2505 • 608-231-2594 fax
studioyou@sprynet.com

Capture the essence of an American tradition with a unique selection of hand-forced wrought iron lamps and funiture. Rowe Pottery Works has a selection of plant stands, planters, candles, salt glaze stoneware, ironware and home accessories that bridge the centuries.

ROWE POTTERY WORKS.
1843 MONROE STREET
608-256-7693
M-SAT 10-5 • SUN 11-5

---

near the edge of the university, is more an art gallery than an antique store. The shop is closed Sunday and Monday.

East Side

Antiques Mall of Madison
4748 Cottage Grove Rd., Madison
• (608) 222-2049

Housing one of the biggest collections of antiques in the area, this mall represents between 60 and 70 dealers from all over Wisconsin and beyond who rent individual spaces or stalls within the 18,000-square-foot building. It takes a while to peruse everything under this roof. And merchandise changes daily. What's your pleasure: furniture, jewelry, toys, books, pictures, guns, automobile memorabilia, china, glassware, Depression glass, clothing and even old fishing lures. It's all under one roof. Do-it-yourselfers won't want to miss the room with "Furniture in the Rough."

Buy and Sell Shop Inc.
701 E. Washington Ave., Madison
• (608) 257-3956

When your son or daughter starts band, this might be the place to look for a perfectly good but used instrument. Or you might find a vintage camera, stereo or gold watch here. This is a shop of a million items — all different. And it might look like junk until you begin scavenging.

INSIDERS' TIP

Madisonians like to shop, and often they don't even leave home to do it. National Decision Systems of San Diego, a market research firm, ranked Madison in '97 as one of the top 10 metropolitan areas in the country for catalog shopping.

A cross between an antique and salvage shop (some items are new), the Buy and Sell Shop fixes things when they can, or they mark them way down and let you try. Walking through these doors is always an interesting venture. The store, in operation since 1958, is closed on Sunday.

Florilegium
823 E. Johnson St., Madison
• (608) 256-7310

It might be a mouthful to pronounce, but Florilegium in Latin means "gathering of flowers," and in keeping with the name, many of the antique treasures sold here showcase a floral design. This is the place to go for antique flapper and wedding dresses, cake toppers and vintage beaded items, from lamp shades to evening bags. Antiques and needle art go hand-in-hand here. The store is closed Sunday and Monday.

Hopkins and Crocker Inc. Art and Antique Gallery
807 E. Johnson St., Madison
• (608) 255-6222

This shop specializes in traditional 18th-, 19th- and early 20th-century traditional furniture and accessories including Oriental rugs, oil paintings, prints and plenty of old English brass and silver. The store is open Tuesday through Saturday, noon to 5 PM.

Kappel's Clock Shop
2250 Sherman Ave., Madison
• (608) 244-6165

Open since 1972, this shop specializes in new and antique traditional decorative clocks, from miniature brass ones to gigantic grandfathers, and ships to customers all over the country. Though small in size, the shop carries one of the biggest selections of antique clocks in the United States. If you do stop by, you won't easily forget the 12-foot-high, handmade Pennsylvania grandfather clock on display that is more than 200 years old. The shop is closed Sunday and only open until 2 PM on Saturday.

Mapletree Antique Mall
1293 N. Sherman Ave., Madison
• (608) 241-2599

Open seven days a week, Mapletree represents about 60 dealers that rent space and cases to showcase antiques and collectibles from the 1860s through the 1960s. This is a good place to find military memorabilia and vintage dolls.

Vintage Interiors
2615 E. Johnson St., Madison
• (608) 244-3000

If you want a quick visual lesson in the history of modern interior design, you'll find it at Vintage Interiors. This shop specializes in items for the home — dinnerware, appliances, furniture, fabrics and lighting — that showcase the cutting-edge and design shifts of the modern movement from the late 1800s through the early 1900s. The shop is only open noon to 6 PM Tuesday through Saturday.

Outlying Area

The Angelic Rabbit
1827 Parmenter St., Middleton
• (608) 827-9490

One of the newer antique/gift shops to open in the area, The Angelic Rabbit specializes in antique furniture, pewter and kitchen collectibles as well as unusual handcrafted works, including a line of dresses for little girls, ages 2 to 5, made out of antique lace, chenille bedspreads, hankies, etc. The store is closed on Sunday.

Broadway Antiques Mall
115 E. Broadway Ave., Monona
• (608) 222-2241

About 70 dealers, mostly from Wisconsin, are represented in this 14,500-square-foot mall filled with antique furniture and collectibles. New items are delivered daily.

Coffee Mill Antique Mall
3472 Hoepker Rd., Sun Prairie
• (608) 837-7099

In operation for almost 20 years, Coffee Mill Antique Mall is jam-packed with furniture, dishes, clocks, utensils, jewelry, toys, lamps and other home accessories. Items are brought in "as is" and priced accordingly. If you're looking for reproductions of antique hardware to mend or refinish a piece of furniture, Coffee Mill is a good place to find them.

Icehouse Antiques
195 E. Main St., Stoughton
- **(608) 873-1778**

Stoughton is well suited for antique stores because the entire Victorian downtown has been designated a National Register Main Street Historic District. This building, a former restaurant and ice house, dates back to the 1880s. Today it's filled with a variety of antiques and collectibles, furniture and glassware ranging from the Victorian era to the 1950s. Remember the old glass bubble lights once used to decorate Christmas trees? We found some here.

The Middleton Antiques Mall
1819 Parmenter St., Middleton
- **(608) 831-5515**

The Middleton Antiques Mall opened in May 1998 in the city's first building, a restored general store that in the past has housed a number of furniture stores. Everything in the 13,700-square-foot store is pre-1950. The building itself dates back to 1850. A wide variety of furniture, glassware, jewelry and quilts is represented by more than 75 dealers.

Stoughton Antique Mall
524 E. Main St., Stoughton
- **(608) 877-1330**

This is another Stoughton shop brimming with antiques. The building housing Stoughton Antique Mall dates back to 1890. It was originally a tobacco warehouse. The two-story mall represents as many as 75 dealers displaying a wide range of kitsch. If you're downtown in Stoughton, take the time to peruse the selection. You'll never know what treasure you'll unearth.

Athleticwear

Madison is moving every minute, and that's why even department stores carry many lines of sports and exercisewear, and large chain stores, including Active Sports, Athlete's Foot, The Finish Line and Champs, all have at least one store in Madison. But the following independent stores also specialize in clothing and equipment for one or more sports.

Isthmus

Active Endeavors of Madison
119 King St., Madison • (608) 255-7482

Carrying an assortment of outerwear for traveling or hiking and a wide assortment of camping equipment, Active Endeavors is loosely associated with two similar stores in the Chicago area. This shop caters to its active customers by keeping a watercooler outside.

Fontana Sports Specialties
251 State St., Madison • (608) 257-5043

From scuba diving to in-line skating, fly fishing and just plain hiking, Fontana carries a wide variety of both equipment and clothing with such big names as Columbia, The North Face and Gramicci setting the scene. This is a great store to check out during State Street's Maxwell Street Days (see our Festivals and Annual Events chapter).

Gazelle
132 State St., Madison • (608) 255-4967

This little shop specializes in the latest dancewear and women's fitness clothing for aerobics and running. Capezio dance shoes also are carried, and if you can't find the exact style or size you're looking for, Gazelle will be glad to do a special order. The store is usually closed on Sunday, although hours are sometimes extended during the summer months. Monday through Friday, it opens 11 AM.

Movin' Shoes
604 S. Park St., Madison • (608) 251-0125

About 2 miles from the Capitol Square, Movin' Shoes is more than a running specialty shop; it's the "running center" of Madison where information about area-wide running events is available. Shoes here are not simply sold, they're explained in great detail. A full line of running apparel is also available. The store's longevity — in existence for well more than 20 years — indicates just how long running has been popular in Madison. It's closed on Sunday.

Sports Savers
510 State St., Madison • (608) 255-3343

While this store carries athleticwear and accessories for a variety of participatory sports, including skiing and tennis, it specializes in in-line skating, which is very popular in Madison. In fact, Sports Savers is one of the few places in town that rents in-line skates.

West Side

Sepp Sport Inc.
1805 Monroe St., Madison
• **(608) 257-7956**

This small sporting-goods store specializes in only two sports — cross-country skiing and tennis. Both are extremely popular in Madison, underscoring why Sepp Sport has been around for more than 20 years. For personalized service, this is a great place to come. The store is closed on Sunday.

Walters Swim & Sun
1639 Monroe St., Madison
• **(608) 256-7946**

You won't find a better selection of Lycra suits, especially Speedo and Tyr, than at this Madison institution that has been outfitting city swim teams for many years. In addition to swimsuits for children, men and women, Walters carries brand-name T-shirts and some exercisewear in addition to other swimming accessories, including goggles, sunscreen and clogs. The store is closed on Sunday.

East Side

Carl's Paddlin' Canoe and Kayak Center
617 Williamson St., Madison
• **(608) 284-0300**

Carl's carries athleticwear appropriate for paddling, including Gore-Tex jackets, hats, footwear, etc. The shop sells and rents canoes and kayaks. If you're looking to get into the sport, classes are available here as well as tours on area lakes and the Wisconsin River.

Outlying Areas

Middleton Cycle and Fitness
6649 University Ave., Middleton
• **(608) 836-3931**

For hockey, swimming, biking or soccer, Middleton Cycle and Fitness is a good place to come for clothing and equipment at prices that won't break the bank.

Rutabaga
220 W. Broadway, Monona
• **(608) 223-9300**

If you're a canoe enthusiast, this is the place to come. Rutabaga's staff is very knowledgeable and offers the latest equipment and clothing for any paddling sport. This shop annually sponsors Canoecopia every March (see the listing in the Festivals and Annual Events chapter). Rental paddling equipment is also available.

Children's Clothing

In addition to the following independent stores, there are many children's apparel stores in Madison's major malls (see the previous "Major Malls" section toward the beginning of this chapter). Department stores, including JCPenney, Marshall Field's, Boston Store and Younker's, also carry a wide selection of children's clothing.

West Side

Alphabet Soup
Hilldale Shopping Center, 702 N. Midvale Ave., Madison • (608) 238-1329

This is a place where a doting grandmother can do a lot of damage to her bank account. In addition to fancier dresses you won't find elsewhere, Alphabet Soup carries a complete line of play and dress-up clothing for infants and children. It also sells fairy-tale-like shoes, stationery including birth announcements, fun gifts for mothers and babies and one-of-a-kind items such as hand-painted furniture. Madison used to have several stores specializing in upscale children's clothing; this is the only one left. Sizes range from newborn to 16.

Wild Child
1813 Monroe St., Madison
• **(608) 251-6445**

This unique store is known for its brightly colored long johns and T-shirts hand-dyed by the staff. All clothing sold here is 100 percent cotton and is primarily casual — meaning it

Not just another cookie-cutter mall.

There is shopping. And then, there is Hilldale. A relaxing atmosphere with a one-of-a-kind mix of casually cosmopolitan shops, everyday essentials and exquisite luxuries. From fine art to designer fashions, premium housewares to best-selling books, stylish footwear to educational toys, and so much more await for you to explore. Come. Enjoy. And indulge in the unique taste that has helped shape Hilldale since 1962.

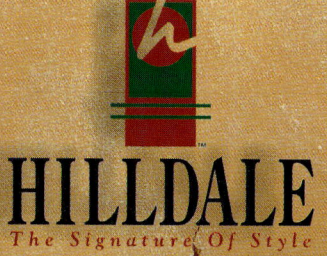

HILLDALE
The Signature Of Style

University Avenue at Midvale Boulevard • Customer Service Center (608) 238-6640
Monday — Friday 10 a.m. — 9 p.m.; Saturday 10 a.m. — 5:30 p.m.; Sunday noon — 5 p.m.
Some stores and restaurants may have additional hours.

Madison's only quality Irish & Celtic shop,
featuring music, jewelry, clothing, foods, tea & gifts from Ireland, England, Scotland and Wales.

patrick's LOOK of the ISLES

(608) 231-1707

This classic mohair Teddy Bear is one of the many Steiff pieces that can be found at Playthings. These and other collectible items, including, Madame Alexander, Götz and Corolle dolls, along with Little Gem Bears and Muffy and Hoppy Vanderbear are just a few of the many lines we offer. Stop by and see for yourself why our products truly "Entertain, Educate and Fascinate children of all ages!"

PLAYTHINGS

(608) 233-2124

Come visit...
Come browse...
Find your style at Jan Byce's

Jan Byce's

Designer fashions and accessories

(608) 233-1606

WEHRMANN'S OF MADISON

Since 1886

Offering an extensive selection of luggage, business cases, daily planners, wallets, leather goods, all travel necessities and unique gifts imported from all over the wotld.

Discover the quality and personal attention that you expect and deserve.

Wehrmann's Travel Shop

(608) 238-7156

HILLDALE
The Signature Of Style

UNIVERSITY AVENUE AT MIDVALE BOULEVARD
MONDAY - FRIDAY 10A.M. - 9P.M.; SATURDAY 10A.M. - 5:30P.M. SUNDAY NOON - 5P.M.
CUSTOMER SERVICE CENTER: **(608) 238-6640**

SHOPPING • 241

The Hilldale Shopping Center enjoyed an expansion and renovation in 1997.

can go anywhere in Madison. You'll find separate sizes for girls and boys, from newborn to size 14, although much of the clothing is unisex. The store is closed on Sundays.

Home Decor and Accessories

Madison is home to more than a dozen large furniture stores including Steinhafels, 2164 W. Beltline Highway, and Ethan Allen, 5302 Verona Road. Stores specializing in solid oak, maple and cherry furniture include Woodworks, 6641 Watts Road, and Shelf & Dining Furniture Ltd., 2217 S. Stoughton Road and 4657 Verona Road.

The following specialty stores are locally owned and emphasize home accessories and gift items as much as furniture.

Isthmus

Rubin's Furniture
317 E. Wilson St., Madison
• (608) 255-8998
670 S. Whitney Way, Madison (West Side)
• (608) 274-5575
4207 Monona Dr., Madison (East Side)
• (608) 222-0069

Rubin's "mother" store, Downtown on Wilson Street, contains more than four floors — 60,000 square feet of space — of fine contemporary furnishings. This is where ideas get started. In business in Madison for more than 60 years and now managed by the third generation of the same family, Rubin's has its own art gallery, Gallery 323, focusing on the work of national and international artists in all media. The West Side store specializes in Scandinavian and more modestly priced furniture, and the store on Monona Drive acts primarily as a warehouse and furniture outlet for the other two stores. There are some great bargains here.

West Side

Capital Columns
6710 Odana Rd., Madison
• (608) 829-3458

A home, garden and museum shop all rolled into one, Capital Columns offers everything from hand-blown glass to bookends, planters, fountains, statues and Tiffany lamps. One corner of the store is dedicated to items with a nautical motif. What's really unique about this store, however, is the fact that most of the decorative items for sale have historical or architectural significance.

Century House Inc.
3029 University Ave., Madison
• (608) 233-4948

Another longtime business in Madison, Century House is 50 years old, and the beautiful old building in which it is housed is 150 years old. It was a former tavern built to last. The original Century House store carries many imported gifts and home accessories including picture frames, tabletop and kitchen housewares and works of art in glass, wood and metal. The furniture annex mostly features teak and cherry pieces from Denmark and a wide selection of Scandinavian rugs to match. This business has stayed in one family the entire time.

Dimaggio's Euro Design
High Point Center, 7475 Mineral Point Rd., Madison • (608) 833-4790

Behind West Towne Mall, Dimaggio's is a trend-setting contemporary home-furnishings store offering everything from unique candles and photo frames to sculpted lighting fixtures and unusual glass end tables. Prices are moderate. If you're looking for decorating ideas or something new to spice up a room, this is a wonderful place to start.

Douglass China and Gifts & Dimension 2
Hilldale Shopping Center, 702 N. Midvale Blvd., Madison • (608) 233-0330

Together, these two stores specialize in contemporary housewares, fine gifts and tabletop accessories to beautify the home. This is a great place to splurge. In addition to china and cut-crystal glassware, Douglass China sells many one-of-a-kind, signed art-quality pieces in ceramic and glass. Downstairs, Dimension 2 offers modestly priced kitchen and household items, from salad bowls and timesaving utensils to gourmet pasta and whimsical salt and pepper shakers. Many a bride registers on both floors.

Rowe's Pottery Works
1843 Monroe St., Madison
- **(608) 256-7693**

A smaller version of the Rowe Pottery shop in Cambridge (see our Daytrips chapter), this one also carries signature stoneware in addition to a wide range of home decorative items including linens, wall hangings, candles, iron work and even some furniture. However, if you want to check out pottery "seconds," you'll have to travel to Cambridge.

Vintage Door
2503 Monroe St., Madison
- **(608) 231-0040**

New in 1998, this small furniture store is an offshoot of Zander's Interiors, a commercial and residential design firm next door. Featured are fine furniture and accessories.

Jewelry

Madison has a wonderful array of fine jewelry stores, many of which specialize in custom-design work. We've singled out the following three, either because of the contribution they've made to Madison or the fact they are bit more unusual. Please take note: We're not recommending them over others. For a complete listing, refer to the Yellow Pages.

Isthmus

Goodman's Jewelers
220 State St., Madison • (608) 257-3644

While there are many interesting little jewelry shops springing up in and around Madison, this one deserves mention just for its longevity and the fact that its owners, Goodman brothers Irv and Robert, are longtime Madison philanthropists. The store prides itself on quality and service — everything from changing a battery in a watch to custom-designing a ring. Many State Street stores have come and gone, but Goodman's has been going strong for nearly 65 years.

West Side

BR Diamond Suite
6409 Odana Rd., Madison
- **(608) 274-4848**

BR Diamond doesn't advertise, is tucked away in a small business suite rather than higher-priced retail space and keeps its inventory at a minimum in order to pass on savings to customers. In business for more than 10 years, the small jewelry boutique is operated by two Madison natives who specialize in fine craftsmanship and custom work.

Outlying Area

University Coin Stamp & Jewelry
6801 University Ave., Middleton
- **(608) 831-1277**

Unique to the area, this shop features fine jewelry as well as rare coins and stamps. While most jewelry is new, about a quarter of it is purchased from estate sales. Prices for these pieces usually are relatively less. The shop, which is closed on Sunday, carries a wide selection of gemstones, although no custom work is done on the premises.

Men's Specialty Clothing

Many of these stores have become Madison traditions, perhaps because men's fashion trends aren't as fickle as women's.

The Jazzman Isthmus
340 State St., Madison • (608) 256-2062

When this store first opened on State Street, it was considered real hip. It still has a funky twist, but a funny thing happened on the way to success. Early customers — many of them were college-age — grew up, and

---

INSIDERS' TIP

A variety of antique, flower and art shows take place in Madison's indoor malls on weekends throughout the year. They're usually publicized in calendars of events in Madison newspapers.

Jazzman has grown right along with them. Today the store offers contemporary sportswear and dressy menswear for men ages 18 to 60. The store offers a greater selection of color than most traditional menswear shops and everything from briefs to wallets, jewelry and sunglasses. Jazzman also has a nice selection of men's hosiery, both novelty and everyday wear.

West Side Bill Paul LTD Studio
1904 Monroe St., Madison
• **(608) 280-0653**

One of the newer upscale men's stores in Madison, this one is within walking distance of the UW-Madison campus. The shop features a wide selection of business and sportswear attire and accessories including Robert Talbott ties, Ike Behar shirts and Oliver, Hilton and Tallia suits. Though the store is fairly new, staff members are well known in Madison men's retail. Bill Paul is closed Sunday and Monday.

D.W. Zemke Traditional Clothiers
Heritage Square Shopping Center, 708 S. Whitney Way, Madison • **(608) 274-6447**

If you believe you're judged by what you wear, Zemke's is a good place to shop for high-quality menswear in a very traditional vein. Zemke sells lasting style and, for hard-to-fit gentlemen, will measure to order. Shoes and other accessories as well as corporate casual and formal business attire are available. Heritage Square Shopping Center is at the corner of Odana Road and Whitney Way.

Rundell's Menswear
7475 Mineral Point Rd., Madison
• **(608) 829-2532**

This is not only the oldest menswear store in Madison, but also one of the oldest retail stores in the entire city. It started on the Square in 1888 and didn't move out to the West Side until November 1995. Today, the third generation of the Rundell family manages this shop, which features a wide selection of moderately priced casual and professional clothing. (In Madison, the lines increasingly blur together. Sports jackets and slacks are much preferred over three-piece suits.) The shop specializes in clothing for big and tall men but carries all sizes. It's closed on Sundays.

Suiter's Limited
High Point Center Shopping Center, 7475 Mineral Point Rd., Madison
• **(608) 827-0777**

New to Madison in the fall of '97, Suiter's carries a nice selection of upper-end business and casual menswear offset by such brands as Hart Schaffner & Marx, Austin Reed, Axis, Robert Talbott. Also carried are Johnston & Murphy shoes. The store is closed on Mondays.

Woldenberg's Men's Apparel
Hilldale Shopping Center, 702 N. Midvale Blvd., Madison • **(608) 233-4300**

Woldenberg's Men's and Women's (see subsequent section) share space at Hilldale and pride themselves as much on service as the high-quality fashions. Both cater to designer wear. Woldenberg's Men's carries such brands as Burberry of London and Jack Victor of Montreal. The store specializes in classic, lasting designs, although some sportswear items, like colorful, hand-knit Coogi sweaters from Australia, speak volumes for themselves.

Resale Shops

Vintage clothing is "in," so much, in fact, that some of the trendier stores are now selling "recycled" clothing along with new items. But the following stores are, with a couple exceptions, exclusively resale, specializing in "nearly new" items. For imagination and originality, just the names of some of these stores deserve recognition.

Isthmus

Juju & Moxie
458 W. Gilman St., Madison
• **(608) 255-4002**

If you're into vintage clothing, especially from the 1940s through the '60s, this is one place to look for hidden treasures. The shop carries clothing for men and women and such accessories as hats, shoes, jewelry and

Something for everyone

- Packer sweatshirts and Badger books
- Frank Lloyd Wright books and posters
- Fishing stories and hunting books
- Baseball caps and T-shirts
- Golf books and golf videos
- Calendars and coffee mugs
- Dilbert and Far Side merchandise
- Postcards and puzzles
- Dane County and Wisconsin atlases
- Books and merchandise written by your favorite reporters and columnists ... George Hesselberg, Ron Seely, Catherine Murray, Julianne White, Marv Balousek, Pearl Swiggum and more!
- Gift Certificates

Pick up your daily **Wisconsin State Journal** or **Capital Times**, start a subscription, pay for a subscription, or place an Online classified ad.

the news store
EAST & WEST TOWNE MALLS

purses. It opens at 11 AM Monday through Saturday and noon on Sundays.

Ragstock
329 State St., Madison
- (608) 251-3419

Before there were resale shops in Madison, there was Ragstock. It carries trendy recycled clothing with an emphasis on military surplus. Many university students have clothed themselves here. Some new apparel also is sold.

West Side

Community Thrift Store
1814 S. Park St., Madison
- (608) 250-1986

Patterned off San Francisco's Community Thrift Store, this store, which opened in May of '98, relies on almost all volunteers for staff. Money raised from the sale of donated items — clothing, furniture, household goods and toys — is split among nearly 60 partner nonprofit organizations whose members help keep the store full. Anyone who drops off recycled goods can designate which of the charities should benefit from the merchandise being sold. The Community Thrift Store is located on the southwest side of Madison, south of the Square.

Elite Repeat Of Madison
6652 Odana Rd., Madison
- (608) 833-8881

Specializing in high-quality women's clothing, Elite Repeat, in the Market Square Shopping Center, carries many brand names in all sizes. It can clothe you for any occasion, even your wedding day. Accessories are also available. The shop is closed on Sunday.

Music Go Round
694 S. Whitney Way, Madison
- (608) 271-3939

This franchise specializes in recycled musical instruments; owners are as interested in buying as selling. Everything but the really big items — pianos and organs — is available. It's a great place to shop for middle-school students taking band for the first time.

Once Upon A Child
706 S. Gammon Rd., Madison
- (608) 276-8076
1625 Thierer Rd., Madison (East Side)
- (608) 243-1284

This shop carries new and used children's clothing up to size 12 plus strollers and other baby equipment including swings, car seats and playpens.

Play It Again Sports
720 S. Gammon Rd., Madison
- (608) 277-1988
4100 E. Washington Ave., Madison (East Side) • (608) 249-5201

Name the sport — baseball, in-line skating, cross-country skiing, even karate — and Play It Again Sports can outfit your children in either reduced-price new or used sports equipment and accessories. After all, when their feet are growing two sizes a year, just buying shoes becomes an expensive venture.

Susan's Closet Resale Boutique
6650 Mineral Point Rd., Madison
- (608) 833-1033

Susan's specializes in higher-end, recycled clothing for women — jeans, outerwear, formal and wedding gowns and everything in between — with accessories to match. Emphasis is on current rather than vintage styles. All sizes — junior (good for prom time), mater-

---

INSIDERS' TIP

One of the oldest retail stores in Madison is *Rundell's Menswear*, now at 7475 Mineral Point Road on the West Side. More than 100 years old, it was started by Sydney P. Rundell, a traveling shirt salesman who came to Madison, liked what he saw and decided to stay.

Department, specialty and discount stores are in abundance in Madison.

nity, petite, women's and plus — are available. The shop is closed Mondays.

Women and Kidstore Resale
6798 Watts Rd., Madison
• **(608) 274-4477**

One of the largest and oldest resale shops in the area, this store carries, on consignment, a wide selection of maternity wear and children's clothing, books, toys, bedding and other related items (but no used sports equipment). The shop is beginning to carry more professional clothing for women and furniture. It's closed Sundays.

East Side

Flashback Denim 'n' More
817 E. Johnson St., Madison
• **(608) 256-4501**

This small shop is a favorite haunt of teenagers. While it carries a wide variety of used clothing for men and women, Flashback specializes in vintage jeans, both denim and corduroy. It's also a good place to find an inexpensive Hawaiian shirt, army surplus clothing and used leather jackets. The store doesn't open until 11:30 AM most weekdays and 2:15 PM on Monday. On Saturday it's open 10 AM to 7 PM.

Kid E-Corner
306 N. Lawn Ave., Madison
• **(608) 249-9436**

This store carries a full line of kids clothing through size 14, furniture, toys and accessories such as car seats for newborns.

Wear It Again
1645 Thierer Rd., Madison
• **(608) 249-6901**
315 E. Main St., Sun Prairie
• **(608) 825-2035**

In 1998, Wear It Again opened a second store near East Towne Mall featuring women's, men's and maternity clothing. It's original store in Sun Prairie specializes in brand-name casual and business wear for women, sizes 3 to 32. Clothing accessories for women also are sold. The stores are closed on Monday.

Outlying Area

Puttin' On The Ritz
2407 Allen Blvd., Middleton
• (608) 831-7480

A resale institution in the area, Puttin' On The Ritz carries casual and designer clothing for men, women and children, a wide assortment of accessories including jewelry and purses and some housewares. The store is closed on Sunday.

Smarty Pants Resale Shop
208 E. Main St., Sun Prairie
• (608) 825-6686

Smarty Pants specializes in children's clothing up to size 12 but also carries some specialty items including toys, books and small baby equipment. The store is closed Sunday and Monday.

Simple Pleasures

These are the kind of gift shops that sometimes double as galleries, filled with beautiful glassware, jewelry, candles, bath and body lotions, etc., that make great gifts for everyone, yourself included. This is not an all-inclusive list, but rather some of our favorites. Please note: Other shops with "simple pleasures" can be found under "Young At Heart" and "Home Decor and Accessories." And don't forget to consider museum shops listed in our Arts chapter. We've only listed independently owned stores, although as we've already mentioned, Madison also has its share of stores like Cost Plus World Market, Williams-Sonoma and Pier 1 Imports.

Isthmus

By the Light of the Moon
212 N. Henry St., Madison
• (608) 250-9810

As you can guess, the moon and stars show up a lot in gift items available through this store that is meant to be a positive influence for women. Books, music, handcrafted gifts, jewelry, candles and aromatherapy products are available.

Little Luxuries
214 State St., Madison • (608) 255-7372

Obviously, this shop is tailor-made for this category. There are small things of beauty, including a wide selection of aromatic candles and jewelry to attention-grabbing whimsical folk art such as wood long-tailed cats and fishing frogs. The shop carries hand-blown glasses and a limited number of special clothing accessories. It's all under one roof.

Soap Opera
319 State St., Madison • (608) 251-4051

In operation for more than 25 years, this store is visually appealing inside and out. The majority of its bath and body products are unique because owners Chuck Beckwith and Chuck Bauer offer their own line of biodegradable, cruelty-free items and custom-blend fragrances in addition to brand names. Today, mail orders make up about 20 percent of its business because visitors and former residents who try their products aren't about to switch.

West Side

Angels For All Reasons
7475 Mineral Point Rd., Madison
• (608) 833-7072

After the death of their daughter, Larry and Bonnie Anderson would put up a Christmas tree every year filled with angels in her memory. It made them feel closer to her. So caught up did they become in collecting and noticing angels, they opened a retail store in the fall of '97 specializing in everything "angelic." Items for sale include collectibles, music boxes, jewelry and books.

The Flower Shop
1725 Monroe St., Madison
• (608) 255-4414
6110 Mineral Point Rd., Madison
• (608) 233-5304

The Flower shop is a full-service, custom florist and more. Both locations also contain primitive antiques, regional handicrafts, small gifts and decorative home items including many encompassing, as you might expect, the love of gardening. The Mineral Point location can be found in a 130-year-old farmhouse that was saved when the Homestead Shoppes (a strip mall) was built around it. It is one of the most appealing strip malls in the city.

Katy's American Indian Arts
1817 Monroe St., Madison
• (608) 251-5451

Think Southwest and you'll naturally gravitate toward this 25-year-old business that specializes in Native American art including Pueblo pottery, Zuni fetishes and beautiful handcrafted beaded and silver jewelry. It's Madison's answer to Santa Fe. Other home accessories, including Pendleton wool blankets, are also available.

Orange Tree Imports
1721 Monroe St., Madison
• (608) 255-8211

Readers of *Wisconsin Trails* voted Orange Tree Imports one of Wisconsin's favorite specialty shops. It's filled with small toys, imported foods and candies, kitchenware, glassware, jewelry, greeting cards and a host of other interesting gift items. If you can't find something appealing here, you just aren't looking closely enough.

Oriental Specialties
Hilldale Shopping Center, 702 N. Midvale Blvd., Madison • (608) 233-8899

Oriental Specialties has one of the largest and best collections of sterling silver jewelry in Madison. It also carries many home decorative items from the Far East and women's natural-fiber clothing.

Patrick's Look of the Isles
702 N. Midvale Ave., Madison
• (608) 231-1707

Whether you've got Irish blood in you or not, you'll enjoy Patrick's, the only Irish and Celtic store in Madison. The small shop, located in the Hilldale Shopping Center, carries a wide variety of imported foods, jewelry, music, collectibles and clothing from England, Scotland, Ireland and Wales. This is the place to find such treasures as Royal Tara china, Gallway crystal and the Crabtree & Evelyn line of soaps and body lotions. Looking for a walking stick? You'll find some unusual ones here.

The Perfume Shop
Walnut Grove Shopping Center, 4140 University Ave., Madison
• (608) 233-7100

Though the location has changed in recent years, this shop has been going strong since 1934, selling basically the same product: fine, imported perfumes and colognes for men and women. Good perfumes, according to owner Knud Tinglev-Hansen, never go out of style ("... the only trail they ever leave behind is a hint of elegance"). Even stores like Neiman-Marcus in Chicago refer customers to Tinglev-Hansen.

East Side

Lighten Up
2086 Atwood Ave., Madison
• (608) 244-3848

From Starry Nights electric and candle lights to holographic lamps, this store contains a little bit of everything unique and a little different. It takes its name from the number of "Lighten Up" items in stock including light strands in the form of chili peppers, cows, pink flamingos, moose, pigs, even log cabins. You can decorate your yard every week and never run out of choices.

Pick More Daisies
1216 Williamson St., Madison
• (608) 255-7090

Contemporary picture frames, vases, an alternative card line, handmade jewelry, bath items and an assortment of small toys and puzzles share space with antiques and other collectibles in this interesting little neighborhood shop on Williamson Street. The store is closed on Sunday and doesn't open until 11 AM weekdays.

Outlying Area

Artisan Gift Shop
Lake Edge Shopping Center, 4116 Monona Ave., Monona • (608) 221-3200

If you're looking for those delightful mice and rabbits called Charming Tales, here's a good place to find them. The Artisan Gift Shop carries a wide selection of figurines, dolls, plates and other collectibles in addition to personal-care products, unusual candles and other home accessories and jewelry. It's in Lake Edge Shopping Center at the corner of Monona Avenue and Buckeye Road.

Clock Tower Crafts
120 E. Main St., Stoughton
• (608) 873-6699

Country crafts by Wisconsin artists, collectibles, stamps, jewelry and a variety of other small gift items are sold here in a shop that looks old-fashioned because of its original wood floor. Because of Stoughton's Norwegian heritage, the store also carries small rosemaling pieces. Upstairs, it's Christmas every day except during the winter holidays when it's all moved downstairs. All holidays are celebrated with gift items. The shop is closed on Sunday.

Cottage Grove Company Store
219 S. Main St., Cottage Grove
• (608) 839-3034

An interesting little shop to happen upon, the Company Store carries everything from cigars to original art. Prominently displayed is the owner's own State Line jewelry. She cuts sterling silver pins in the shapes of states and then appropriately places a gem stone for the customer's home city. The store is open by appointment only on Sunday.

Crescent Bear & Bath Boutique
212 W. Main St., Waunakee
• (608) 849-8550

This small shop specializes in collectible teddy bears in all price ranges — from $4 to more than $700. It also carries other gift items including fragrant soaps, lotions and candles. In this neck of the woods, Crescent Bear is also a big supplier of Beanie Babies and greeting cards.

Happy Pastime Hummels & Collectibles
1800 Parmenter St., Middleton
• (608) 831-4200

For a wide selection of collectibles, you'll be hard-pressed to find a better selection in the state. The store specializes in Hummels and Lladro figurines from Spain. There are also hundreds of dolls, plates and Old World Christmas ornaments as well as those designed by Radko. Careful, you might begin a new collection. The shop is closed on Sunday.

Lighthouse Nautical Gifts
6309 Monona Ave., Monona
• (608) 221-1630

Opened in the spring of 1998, this store is filled with collectible lighthouses, wooden ships, brass lanterns, porthole mirrors, nautical figurines, netting and anything else you might think of that falls under the nautical category.

The Pepperberry
1920 Parmenter St., Middleton
• (608) 831-0101

It will take you a while to browse through this shop filled with one-of-a-kind gift and home items including customized arrangements made of dried and silk flowers, Victorian bears, tapestry place mats and table runners, gardening treasures and a variety of hand-painted lampshades. But the shop isn't geared only to a woman's taste. There are gifts for men, too, many of which center around favorite sporting activities, including hunting and golf. For children, a special corner is filled with an assortment of games, toys and cute accessories.

Women's Apparel Stores

From JCPenney to the Gap and Ann Taylor, there are plenty of places for women to buy clothing. The shops listed here, however, are Madison born and bred.

Isthmus

Camille's
133 W. Johnson St., Madison
• (608) 258-1426

This small boutique just off State Street offers high-quality contemporary classics and designer wear for women. It provides many extra services including free alterations and wardrobe consultation. Accessories such as scarves and jewelry are available. The store is closed

Cambridge's arts, crafts, furnishings and antique shops have followed the lead of pioneer Rowe Pottery Works, which helped establish Cambridge as a community of artisans.

Sunday and most evenings, but private appointments are accepted during those times.

Karen & Co.
418 State St., Madison • (608) 258-5500

Karen & Co., a short walk off the Square, offers quality contemporary women's apparel and accessories, both casual and professional. Many brand names are represented. Much of the clothing featured here is bought with ease of traveling in mind. It's a sister store to Sassafras Ltd. (see subsequent entry), a block away. The store is closed on Sunday.

The Peacock
512 State St., Madison • (608) 257-7730

The Peacock features clothing, much of it in natural fabrics, that is a bit more offbeat and flowing than most ready-to-wear. Styles here are relaxed, comfortable and primarily casual in keeping with Madison's laid-back lifestyle. This store offers more than just apparel and clothing accessories, however; it also sells small gift items and home accessories.

Razzmatazz
126 State St., Madison • (608) 257-0002
328 State St., Madison • (608) 256-1222

This women's apparel boutique has two locations on State Street and offers imported fashions, both casual and dressy.

Sassafras Ltd.
307 State St., Madison • (608) 258-5510

Carrying sizes 4 to 14, Sassafras dresses the professional woman more than the college student. In retail lingo, it's lines are "bridge," or higher-end, sportswear. The shop carries mostly natural fabrics — lots of rayon and cotton — along with clothing accessories and some lingerie. The store is closed on Sunday.

Scoshi
410 State St., Madison • (608) 256-7630

This is a women's contemporary, specialty-clothing store featuring moderate to better career, dress and sportswear. Sizes from 4 through 12 are available.

Sedona
330 State St., Madison
• (608) 256-1222

Carrying everything from satin gowns to casual knits and Doc Marten shoes, Sedona is one of the funkier women's apparel stores on State Street.

Yost's
201 State St., Madison • (608) 257-2545
Yost's New Traditions
Walnut Grove Shopping Center, 4010 University Ave., Madison
• (608) 238-7189
Yost's Bridal and Formal
Walnut Grove Shopping Center, 4010 University Ave., Madison
• (608) 231-2221

Yost's is the closest thing to a local women's department store. It carries contemporary, traditional-style women's apparel including bathing suits, sportswear and a full line of outerwear with many name brands represented. The store's bridal and formal shop is situated alongside a smaller, more upscale version of the downtown store, New Traditions, in the Walnut Grove Shopping Center. Check out Yost's Lower Level on State Street, where there are bargains to be had.

West Side

Atelier — Art To Wear
2616 Monroe St., Madison
• (608) 233-7575

Here's a wonderful little women's apparel shop filled with wearable art by artisan Gerri Ager, who prefers working with natural fabrics including cotton, rayon and silk. Featured are many silkscreen pieces and one-of-a-kind, hand-knit sweaters. Custom orders are welcome. Ager designs her fashions for women who want to be noticed but not conspicuous. The shop is open from 11 AM to 5 PM Monday through Saturday or by appointment.

Galway Bay
2536 Monroe St., Madison
• (608) 238-3335

Galway is a small shop specializing in natural-fiber fabrics that look casual and are comfortable to wear and easy to maintain. Much of the clothing is made out of cotton, rayon or Tencel, a natural fiber made from recycled wood pulp. A lot of ethnic-inspired beaded and costume jewelry dresses up many of the outfits. The store is closed on Sunday.

The Glorious Woman
Lakepoint Commons, 2701 University Ave., Madison • (608) 231-0025

Owner Gloria Martony thought it was a shame not to have a women's specialty shop that carried clothing and accessories for all sizes, petitie and plus. So she opened one. If you're looking for something unique, this is a good place to come. The shop carries such brands as Flax, Fenini and Liz & Jane. Martony makes beaded jewelry that is also for sale in the store.

Indigo Moon
1809 Monroe St., Madison
• (608) 257-9477

This is a fun shop featuring comfortable, colorful and creative ready-to-wear items with an ethnic and contemporary feel. Accessories and some small gift items are also available. Indigo Moon is closed on Sunday.

Jan Byce's
Hilldale Shopping Center, 702 N. Midvale Blvd., Madison
• (608) 233-1606

With an emphasis on comfort but with lots of style, Jan Byce's carries classic and contemporary designer wear. Everything from sportswear to suits (including many pants suits) and outerwear is available. Clothing purchased here makes a statement: We know a woman who saw Joan Lunden on *Good Morning America* wearing the same suit she purchased there. Need we say more?

Rupert Cornelius — The Women's Store
Hilldale Shopping Center, 702 N. Midvale Blvd., Madison
- **(608) 231-2621**

Rupert Cornelius features lots of specialty, comfortable dress lines such as Eileen Fisher, Flax and Carol Turner. Apparel, for the most part, is casually elegant, flowing and made of natural fabrics; emphasis is on the fabric rather than the cut. And most everything sold here is washable. The store has been in operation since 1970 and carries a nice selection of handbags, belts and jewelry.

Square One Outfitters
Hilldale Shopping Center, 702 N. Midvale Blvd., Madison • (608) 233-8363

Newly remodeled, Square One Outfitters features contemporary, artistically inspired clothing in fabrics that are easy to pack and wear well while traveling. With that in mind, the store also sells soft-side luggage, tote bags, satchels, backpacks and all kinds of little travel accessories to put into them.

Suzen Sez
2421 University Ave., Madison
- **(608) 238-1331**

The shop promotes its fashions as clothes "with an attitude" for women who don't like to take themselves too seriously. The upper-end selection of women's clothing and accessories at Suzen Sez in Madison (there is a larger store in Cambridge) is tastefully playful and comfortable to wear.

Woldenberg's Women's Apparel
Hilldale Shopping Center, 702 N. Midvale Blvd., Madison • (608) 233-4300

In business since 1910, first on the Square and now at Hilldale Shopping Center, Woldenberg's continues to offer its specialty: designer women's clothing and accessories. If you have a big occasion looming and want to look like a million bucks, this is a good place to visit. In addition to on-site alterations, Woldenberg's also provides a personal shopping service. Woldenberg's mix includes apparel by St. John Knits and Louis Ferard and shoes by Stuart Weitzman. Everything from sportswear and outwear to evening wear is sold in sizes 4 through 18.

Young At Heart

You don't have to be a kid to enjoy shopping at the following stores, which are filled with a wide variety of creative games, toys, gadgets and decorations that range from educational to outlandish, outrageous to cute and cuddly, but always fun and interesting. For birthday presents and all the trappings, these are good places to check out.

Isthmus

The Puzzlebox
230 State St., Madison • (608) 251-0701

In the toy specialty market, The Puzzlebox has set the pace in Madison. Offering everything from imported building sets to yo-yos guaranteed to spin, this shop is ideal for anyone with a fanciful whim. Plan on staying awhile once you enter. In addition to the main State Street store, The Puzzlebox also operates the gift shop in the Concourse Hotel and Governor's Club, 1 W. Dayton Street, just off the Square.

West Side

JT Puffin's
Heritage Square Shopping Center, 5505 Odana Rd., Madison • (608) 274-5613

Stop in here for five minutes and you're likely to stay an hour. Though small in size, it's loaded with a wide selection of stickers, stuffed animals, magnets, imported games, magic tricks, puzzles, jewelry, soaps and a full line of greeting cards and balloons.

The Learning Shop
714 S. Gammon Rd., Madison
- **(608) 277-8747**
5225 High Crossing Blvd. (East Side)
- **(608) 241-0261**

The store is just like it sounds. It offers educational and creative toys and software and one of the best designer pencil collections in town. It's also great for birthday treats. Into Legos? The store carries many sets of that popular brand along with Playmobil, Thomas and Brio.

Playthings
Hilldale Shopping Center, 702 Midvale Blvd., Madison • (608) 233-2124

When shopping at Hilldale Shopping Center, don't overlook this store that specializes in the unusual and unique. It carries many imported toys and other items including whimsical lunch boxes. Looking to begin a doll collection? Here's one place to start.

Pooh Corner Bookstore
6116 Mineral Point Rd., Madison
- **(608) 231-0211**
1617 Thierer Rd. (East Side)
- **(608) 242-1880**

This was the first children's bookstore in Madison, and it remains one of the best. Pooh Corner carries wonderfully illustrated storybooks, chapter books and all the classics for readers of all levels. Also available are puzzles, art supplies, travel games for the car and stuffed animals that relate to popular book characters — Babar, Clifford and Paddington Bear. And, of course, Pooh. (See the Literary Scene chapter for more information.)

Whoops! & Co.
7416 Mineral Point Rd., Madison
- **(608) 833-2280**

Often referred to as Beanie Baby Central, this whimsical shop in the Cambridge Court Shopping Center carries an interesting array of toys, games and stuffed animals — both educational and purely for fun. Close your eyes as you approach the counter or you might be tempted by all the cute little gadgets and critters stacked nearby.

East Side

Highsmith Education Station
1601 Thierer Rd., Madison
- **(608) 249-9787**
6122 Mineral Point Rd., Madison (West Side) • (608) 233-1539

The larger of the two Highsmith stores is the Thierer Road shop, but both offer the same mix of computer software, quality games and a variety of learning products and art supplies to stimulate the imagination. This shop is now associated with Pooh Corner Bookstore (see previous entry as well as our Literary Scene chapter); they're adjacent to one another in both locations.

In a Class By Themselves

The following shops don't necessarily fit into any of the categories listed in this chapter. Nevertheless, they are so entrenched in Madison, it's hard to leave them out. So here goes.

West Side

American TV Appliance & Furniture
2404 W. Beltline Hwy., Madison
- **(608) 271-1000**
5201 High Crossing Blvd., Madison
- **(608) 271-1002**

Madison has its share of electronic, appliance and furniture stores — some large national chains and some small, family-owned businesses (unfortunately in dwindling numbers). But American TV, as it's called by anybody who has been around awhile, is truly a success story. Erupting from a television repair business in the 1950s, American TV now competes with the big players like Sears, Circuit City and Best Buy. The original store on the West Side is now the size of three football fields, and the East Side location on High Crossing Boulevard, added later, is the same size. Owner Lenny Mattioli doesn't appear in his own ads anymore, but that's because he now has eight stores to manage, including three in Milwaukee, one in Rockford, Illinois, and one in Appleton, Wisconsin.

East Side

Burnie's Rock Shop
901 E. Johnson St., Madison
- **(608) 251-2601**

The more things change, the more they stay the same. Retailing is very competitive in Madison, and some say the market is oversaturated — unless you have a one-of-a-kind specialty store like Burnie's that supplies local collectors and lapidarists with rocks, mineral specimens, gem stones and jewelry-making equipment. Raw materials and finished products are sold, from polished rocks for 10¢ to large amethyst geodes. Even if you're not into lapidary, you'll find this store fascinating. It's open every day of the week except Sunday and looks much the same as it did years ago. That's comforting, don't you think?

Outlying Area

Monona Bait & Ice Cream
4516 Winnequah Rd., Monona
- **(608) 222-1929**

If you stop by this small shop across from Lake Monona, you not only can buy live bait but also order a cone made with Babcock ice cream or even a hamburger. Kids in the neighborhood love riding their bikes here. During the winter, Monona Bait & Ice Cream is closed on Wednesday. During the summer, hours are extended from 8 AM until 10 PM.

Orchids by the Ackers
4823 County Hwy. Q, Waunakee
- **(608) 831-4700**

If you like orchids, you'll love Orchids by The Ackers, which is more than a family-owned greenhouse — it's an attraction. Hundreds of varieties are raised and sold here, including some very rare and novel ones. It's the largest orchid grower in the state and the second-largest in the Midwest. The greenhouse is open every day of the week from the end of April through mid-June and is closed on Sunday the rest of the year.

Wintersilks
2700 Laura Ln., Middleton
- **(608) 836-1857**

This mail-order catalog company specializing in high-quality silk clothing — everything from long johns to sweaters and dresses — operates an outlet store adjacent to its warehouse and offices on Laura Lane in Middleton. Both first-quality and imperfect merchandise are available. The store is open every day.

A professional women's volleyball team pounded its first spike at the Field House in February 1998, and a new pro indoor football team hit the artificial turf inside the Dane County Coliseum a few days later.

Sports

Madison sports lovers had plenty of excitement in 1998.

A professional women's volleyball team pounded its first spike at the Field House in February, and a new pro indoor football team hit the artificial turf inside the Dane County Coliseum a few days later. That brings to four number of minor league teams in the city.

Observers say the proliferation of pro sports here is because the UW-Madison's teams have such loyal followings that organizers of professional leagues figure they can tap into local sports mania.

Another major happening for local sports fans in 1998 was the opening of the magnificent $76 million Kohl Center arena on campus. The men's and women's basketball teams immediately moved into the state-of-the-art facility after many years at the Field House. The Badger hockey team is scheduled to move into the Kohl Center in October 1998, leaving the Dane County Coliseum (and possibly sparking some legal wrangling). Another change is the ticket center's moved from the Field House to the Kohl Center.

And, at long last, women's hockey was added to the list of varsity sports at UW-Madison.

The main attraction of 1998, though, was the Green Bay Packers' march to the Super Bowl, where they lost to the Denver Broncos. When last seen on national television, Packer fans were the ones with the cheese wedges on their heads, pulling up their shirts to show green- and gold-painted bellies.

The previous year, the Packers, led by quarterback Bret Favre, won the Super Bowl, and brought home the Lombardi trophy that goes with it. People in Wisconsin believe it belongs here, since it is named for the legendary Green Bay Packer coach of the 1960s, Vince Lombardi.

The other team many Madisonians root for is the University of Wisconsin Badgers. They, too, had a respectable season. They were invited to the Outback Bowl, in Tampa, Florida, but couldn't pull off a win. In 1994 the Badgers won the Rose Bowl.

Fashion-wise, Badger fans also wear cheese wedges on their heads, but the customary clothing is red and white. If your Bucky Badger wardrobe isn't up to snuff, you can buy the perfect thing from street vendors outside Camp Randall Stadium.

For years Badgers fans had much in common with Green Bay Packers fans — a good thing, because many support both teams. Their teams worked hard, but they were losers. The revival of both football teams has bolstered the spirits of fans dramatically.

When there are no Packer or Badger games, Madisonians also keep watch over some other fine teams: Milwaukee's Brewers and Bucks and Madison's Monsters, to name a few. The Chicago Bulls also have a strong following in Madison, but you'd be hard-pressed to find anyone here who roots for "da Bears." And if you've got a Dallas Cowboy fan in the family, well, let's just say it's usually best to keep that information to yourself.

Here is some of what Madison sports fans can watch.

Baseball

Madison Black Wolf
2920 N. Sherman Ave., Madison
• (608) 244-5666

In 1996 Madison welcomed a new pro baseball team, the Madison Black Wolf, of the Northern League. They finished their 1997 with a 34-50 record.

The team is locally owned and had a slate full of lively promotions. A kid's club offers children general admission tickets to every Sunday home game for $5.

The Black Wolf's 86-game season kicks off in late May and extends until September. Box tickets for Black Wolf games are $6; general admission and kids and seniors box seats are $5, and general admission for kids and seniors is $4.

The Black Wolves are the third baseball team to try their luck in Madison. The Madison Muskies pulled up anchor in 1993 after 12 fairly successful years. The Mad Hatters left Madison after one profitless season.

Milwaukee Brewers
Milwaukee County Stadium, 201 S. 46th St., Milwaukee • (414) 933-1818, (800) 933-7890

With County Stadium just about 90 minutes away, Madisonians find it easy to keep an eye on Brewers action. In 1998 the Brewers left the American League and joined the National League. That means teams like the Chicago Cubs and the St. Louis Cardinals, which have big followings throughout the Midwest, will be coming to Milwaukee.

Watching Brewers baseball is hardly a passive spectator sport. Fans not only have to endure rigorous tailgating parties in the hours just prior to the game — and often for hours after the event, win or lose — but many also leave Milwaukee County Stadium hoarse from their sideline coaching duties. The cheap seats are also famous for all the foot-stomping that goes on in an effort to distract opponents. On opening day of the 1997 season, excited Brewers fans caused such a ruckus by throwing souvenir baseballs onto the field that officials almost forced Milwaukee to forfeit the game.

The former Seattle Pilots — now the Brewers — came home to Milwaukee in 1970. The current stadium has a natural grass surface and holds 53,192 fans.

The Brewers' 162-game regular season runs from April through September. Tickets are usually easy to get. Prices range from $5 to $18, and season tickets are available. To reach County Stadium from Madison, take I-94 east to Milwaukee, then look for the Stadium exit.

The Brewers are expected to move to their new home, Miller Park, in time for the season opener in the year 2000. The Miller Park project has caused much consternation in southern Wisconsin due to the imposition of a sales tax to fund construction. The new park will seat fewer fans, just 42,500, but the facility will be much larger and luxurious than County Stadium. The most spectacular feature of the $250 million Miller Stadium design is its retractable roof. The roof will remain open most of the time, but in case of foul weather, it can be closed, and the game will go on. When the roof is closed, the stadium will be able to be heated to 15 degrees above the outside temperature or cooled by 10 degrees, depending on the weather. Fans formerly chilled to the bone on occasion by Lake Michigan's "breezes" likely will be grateful for the added barrier.

Basketball

Milwaukee Bucks
Bradley Center, 1001 N. Fourth St., Milwaukee • (414) 227-0500

Founded in 1968-69, the Milwaukee Bucks have enjoyed good times and bad times in the National Basketball Association. The team has the distinction of being the newest team to win a championship in the history of professional sports. The Bucks won the league title in their third season, bolstered by center Kareem Abdul-Jabbar.

Longtime Bucks fans miss the success of the 1970s and 1980s and hope that, like the Packers, their team will rally and bring home another championship. The Bucks begin their 82-game schedule in late October and continue through April.

Since 1988, the Bucks have played at the Bradley Center. To reach it, take I-94 east to I-43 to the Kilbourn/Civic Center Exit. The second traffic light is N. Fourth Street. Turn left and go two blocks, and you'll see the Bradley Center on the left.

Ticket prices range from $6 to $50. Multi-ticket packs and season tickets are available.

Wisconsin Badgers — Men
UW Athletic Ticket Office, Kohl Center,
601 W. Dayton St., Madison
• (608) 262-1440

Coach Dick Bennett, who came to UW-Madison in 1995, is known as a defensive strategist. The team had a disappointing season in 1998, but that did nothing to deter attendance. There is a waiting list for season tickets. The season begins in early November and ends in early March.

The team's new home in the Kohl Center has two balconies stacked atop each other so that the rows farthest from the court will be closer and have better views than in most other new arenas (see our Close-up on the Kohl Center).

Single-game tickets cost about $14 and $16.

Wisconsin Badgers — Women
UW Athletic Ticket Office, Kohl Center,
601 W. Dayton St., Madison
• (608) 262-1440

University of Wisconsin women's basketball has come into its own since the arrival of coach Jane Albright-Dieterle. She has an impressive record for four seasons at UW-Madison, earning an invitation to the 1998 NCAA Tournament after the team's 21-9 season.

Her team also has the third-highest attendance among women's collegiate teams in the nation. Attendance skyrocketed since the coach's arrival to an average of 10,400 in its 1998 season. That's up nearly 9,000 from the pre-Albright-Dieterle days. That growth is due not only to the Badger women's improved play, but also to the burgeoning interest across the nation in women's basketball. It's also a popular family event because tickets are cheap and easy to get. The active involvement of the coach and her players in the community — and their willingness to stand for hours signing autographs and talking with fans — has also enhanced interest in the Badger Women. If you want to be a little more cynical, you'd also note that since tickets for men's basketball, football and hockey are usually sold out, the Athletic Department's marketing pros had extra time to pump women's basketball.

The Badger women begin their season in early November and conclude in March.

Season tickets for women's basketball cost $60. Single-game tickets are $7 for adults, $3 for UW students and $2 for youth and seniors.

Football

Green Bay Packers
Lambeau Field, 1265 Lombardi Ave.,
Green Bay • (920) 496-5719

Even before the Pack scored a resounding 1997 Super Bowl victory over the New England Patriots, it was a challenge to get tickets. At Lambeau Field, or the "Frozen Tundra" as it's known, ticket agents estimate that if you put your newborn's name on the waiting list for season tickets, they'd get them by the time they were 30 or 40. There are more than 30,000 names on that list, and about 20 or so get the prize. Once a family gets Packer season tickets, they never seem to let go. Spouses wrangle over them in divorce courts, and siblings dispute parental wills. This is not surprising when you consider that Packer fans paid good money for clomps of sod from the playing field that was being resurfaced, and many have home shrines to their idols.

When Packer stock was sold to the public in 1998, some of it wound up in green-and-gold frames on living room walls.

The Packers played their inaugural game at fabled Lambeau Field, then known as City Stadium, on September 29, 1957 — a win over the Chicago Bears. (A bitter Packers-Bears rivalry continues to this day.) Nine years later, after the death of coach Curly Lambeau, the stadium was renamed. Lambeau Field now seats in excess of 60,000 fans.

Preseason play begins in August; the 16-game regular season begins Labor Day weekend. If by chance any tickets are available, prices range from $32 to $90. It's more likely, however, to find single-game tickets advertised in a newspaper or by word of mouth.

To obtain tickets and travel packages for away games, call (920) 490-0220. If you go to a game at Lambeau, go early and have a tailgate party amid the Frozen Tundra. You'll never forget it.

To get to the field from Madison, take U.S. Highway 151 to U.S. 41 (just before Fond du

Kohl Center

Madison christened the Kohl Center, a $76.4 million state-of-the-art sports and entertainment arena, in 1998.

As exciting as that was, it was bittersweet for many longtime UW-Madison basketball fans, who were feeling nostalgic about the team's leaving the rickety old Field House, known as "The Barn." The musty 67-year-old building with its cramped wood bleachers was notorious for having acoustics so bad that Badger fans could make enough noise to scare opponents.

Close-up

The goal of the Kohl Center architects was to create a place that was intimate for fans but noisy enough to intimidate visiting teams, and still be suitable for concerts and other entertainment. The gently curved building on West Dayton Street, just west of the Capitol Square, has precast concrete panels made with ground mica to give it a granite-like look. Other elegant touches are its terrazzo floors and Portugese limestone tile walls. The 30,000-square-foot arena is filled with light from north- and south-facing windows that stretch around it.

The key art element in the Kohl Center is *The Mendota Wall*, a 140-foot span of colorful glass tendrils that greets patrons. The sculpture was designed by glass artist Dale

— continued on next page

The UW men's basketball team inaugurated the Kohl Center in January 1998.
By the way, Wisconsin won. Go Red!

Chihuly, who says the piece evokes his memories of Madison when he was learning to blow glass as a graduate art student here in the mid-1960s. He now lives in Seattle.

It's a basketball-first facility, but it will be the only Big Ten arena to house both basketball and hockey. With a seating capacity of 16,500, it ranks second in size among Big Ten schools. State basketball tournaments and the individual state wrestling championships will be held here.

Like the beloved Barn, it's noisy. But its designers describe it as "controlled noise." Sound hits all seats in the house at the same moment. The new facility has plastic seats with arm rests and treatments on the walls and ceilings that reflect mid-range sounds like yelling, but absorb the highs and lows.

The state-of-the art sound system makes the Kohl Center desirable for concerts, speeches and other events. Aerosmith tested its acoustics at its first major concert in February 1998. Dance troupes, ice shows and concerts are on the docket. *Lord of the Dance* was an attraction four months after the Kohl Center opened.

Among its other assets: Big 18-wheel trucks can drive right up to the floor and unload equipment for concerts or other events; it has 333 wheelchair and wheelchair-companion seats, tactile and audible phone directories and assisted-listening devices; 18 concession stands; a 2,400-square-foot retail store; a 2,300-square-foot sports medicine facility; an 1,800-square-foot interview room; a 1,600-square-foot strength and conditioning room; 14 ticket windows; eight locker rooms; and six memorabilia display areas.

One of the most welcome changes will be the number of bathrooms: 26 sparkling and spacious restrooms at the Kohl Center compared to two at the 67-year old Field House. That includes seven small "family restrooms" where parents can bring a small child of the opposite sex. The bountiful bathrooms jibe nicely with the university's plans to aggressively hawk concessions like extra large sodas.

Athletes will have access to study areas and a 22,000-square-foot practice gym with three courts (basketball or volleyball), and there is a 2,000-capacity room for functions. Each team has its own locker, and near the training rooms are areas with hydrotherapy and medical personnel, a huge equipment room with laundry facilities and full-service kitchen for team meals and catered events. The kitchen will also serve the 36 luxury suites that go for $35,000 a year.

The arena is named for Herb Kohl, a Democratic U.S. senator and owner of the Milwaukee Bucks basketball team, who contributed $25 million for arena. His substantial gift was part of the $49.4 million in private funding raised for the project. No state money was used.

It's predicted that the center will attract 800,000 to a million people annually to 113 events, support 750 jobs and create more than $56 million in economic activity in Dane County each year. It is technologically equipped to handle national media, which will make it competitive with Milwaukee, Chicago and Minneapolis for major events that previously bypassed Madison. Because of the popularity of men's and women's basketball at UW-Madison, the Kohl Center is expected to be profitable in its first year because of ticket and concession revenue. About 2,000 seats are reserved for students.

The Kohl Center is within walking distance of a number of bars and restaurants. The closest are Babes at the Depot, 640 W. Washington Avenue, and the Nitty Gritty Restaurant and Bar, 223 N. Frances Street. Slightly farther away are Josie's Spaghetti House, 906 Regent Street, and the Greenbush Bar, 914 Regent Street. To the north in the University Square shopping center are Paisan's, Beijing Restaurant and Mango Grill. State Street, the main drag on campus which has many other bars and restaurants, is three blocks away.

Lac). Proceed north on U.S. 41 to Green Bay; watch for Lambeau Field signs.

School buses provide transportation to the games from most Green Bay motels for a nominal charge. Parking at Lambeau Field costs $10.

Wisconsin Badgers
Kohl Center, 601 W. Dayton St., Madison • (608) 262-1440 (UW Athletic Ticket Office)

Badger football games for many years were more successful as social events than gridiron displays. The band got most of the attention. But since the arrival of coach Barry Alvarez in 1990, the quality of play has improved and the fans have had more reason to cheer. Wisconsin's appearance in the 1998 Outback Bowl was its fourth bowl game in the last five years. The others were the Rose Bowl in 1994, the Hall of Fame Bowl in 1995 and the Copper Bowl in 1996.

A 261-pound sophomore tailback named Ron Dayne has given the Badgers' fans something to talk about: a possible Heisman Trophy. Dayne, who also competes in the weight events for Wisconsin's defending Big Ten-champion track team, caught fire in the second half of his rookie year and broke a slew of records in the process. College football's second-largest tailback, Dayne broke nearly every NCAA freshman rushing mark. In 1996 Dayne joined only 10 other players in college history to rush for more than 2,000 yards and eclipsed the all-time Big Ten rushing record in the process.

People who attended Badger football games at Camp Randall Stadium in previous decades — and lived to tell about it — have war stories about student-section traditions like body-passing. It was often more interesting to watch what was going on in the stands than on the field. The mischief escalated to the point where it was no longer clear whether police could control the crowd for its own safety. University officials cracked down on fans, enforcing rules against drinking and rowdy behavior after the 1986 Wisconsin-Indiana game when 13 fans were arrested and 177 more ejected from the game. Another incident occurred in November 1993 when jubilant fans crashed the field during the Wisconsin-Michigan game and several people were trampled. Fortunately, all the victims recovered.

Badger games are safe now. Fans now confine themselves to cheering and save their boisterous energy for the Fifth Quarter. That's when director Mike Leckrone strikes up the UW band, and the fans flood out on the field to dance to the music. Win or lose, it's always great fun to be a Badger.

Season tickets for football go on sale in April. Single-game ticket sales begin in July. Tickets are $24. Obstructed-view and end zone seats cost $12. The regular season includes 11 games.

Hockey

Madison Monsters
Dane County Coliseum, 1881 Expo Mall E., Madison • (608) 251-2884

The Madison Monster's hockey team, of the United Hockey League (they were previously in the Colonial Hockey League), got off to a slow start in a city that sometimes seems obsessed with Badger hockey. But the team has worked hard to gain attention and seems to gain momentum each year. Its 37-game season runs from October to March.

The Monsters always have entertaining, if gimmicky, promotions going on, and a goofy green mascot, Maddy. A highlight is when peewee skaters come out and try their sticks on the ice during intermissions. The Monsters made it to the CHL playoffs in 1997, challenging the Thunder Bay Thunder Cats, winner of three of the five previous Colonial Cups. In the end, Thunder Bay also won the

---

INSIDERS' TIP

U.S. Sen. Herb Kohl is the only member of the Senate to own a pro basketball team, the Milwaukee Bucks. He was the largest donor for the Kohl Center.

1997 playoff series, taking home three wins to the Monsters' two.

Monsters tickets range in price from $9 to $12 for adults and $7 to $12 for youth. You can purchase single-game tickets at the Dane County Coliseum box office or at any Ticketmaster outlet. Season tickets and ticket packages are available.

Wisconsin Badgers
Kohl Center, 601 W. Dayton St., Madison • (608) 262-1440 (UW Athletic Ticket Office)

The University of Wisconsin Badgers are without a doubt Madison's premier hockey attraction. Diehard followers schedule surgery, weddings and maybe even funerals around the Western Collegiate Hockey Association's timetable. Badger hockey fans often spend more time on their feet than in their seats. This is definitely another sport with a lot of audience participation.

The Hockey Badgers are five-time title winners in the WCHA, the third-highest title total in collegiate hockey. When the Badgers are working together on the ice, it's grace in motion.

The Hockey Badgers have had a fair share of successful alumni. Former Badger iceman Mark Johnson scored the goal that allowed the United States to beat the Soviet Union in the 1980 Winter Olympic Games in Lake Placid, New York. He is now an assistant coach at the UW. As of this writing, 28 Badgers have made it into the professional leagues.

The team is scheduled to move to the Kohl Center in October 1998. Tickets are $14. Call the listed number to have your name placed on the season-ticket waiting list.

The UW added ice hockey as the 12th sport for women in 1998. The team will begin a full schedule of varsity competition in 1999-2000. Recruitment of players will be underway until then. One unresolved question is who will be the competition. There are many women's collegiate hockey teams on the East Coast, but few in the Midwest.

You can thank the gold medal won by the U.S. women's hockey team in Nagano for moving that proposal along. Until recently only colleges on the East Coast had women's hockey teams. Programs have already started in Minnesota and are expected to be formed in Michigan and Ohio.

Volleyball

Wisconsin Fury
UW Field House, 1440 Monroe St., Madison • (608) 222-4922

The Field House got new life in 1998 with the debut of the Wisconsin Fury women's volleyball team. The team is part of the five-year-old National Volleyball Association, which includes the Kansas City Lightning, St. Louis Spirits, Nebraska Tornados, Colorado Thunder and the Iowa Blizzard.

The roster includes many UW-Madison alumni under the direction of Coach and General Manager Sonny Calvetti.

The 1998 regular schedule ran February through April with all home games at the Field House. Tickets are $3, $5 and $8. Tickets are available at the door.

Indoor Football

Madison Mad Dogs
Dane County Coliseum, 1881 Expo Mall E., Madison • (888) 316-DOGS

Madison got a third football team to root for in 1998 when the Madison Mad Dogs played their first game at the Dane County Coliseum. Indoor football abides by the same rules as the outdoor game, but its faster paced.

The regular season begins in April and ends in August. The other teams in the Professional Indoor Football League are the Green Bay Bombers, Tacoma Thunder, Minnesota Monsters, Louisiana Bayou Beast, Great Britain Spartans, Texas Bullets, Utah Catzz and the Honolulu Hurricanes. The Mad Dogs have a 22-man roster, many of them leading area athletes.

Ticket prices start at $6 and can go as high as $35 for VIP seats. All kids seats are $3 off except VIP seats. One potential perk is that balls that go into the stands are fair game, and you get to keep them. In the outdoor sport, courtesy demands that you send the ball back into the game.

Whether you want to pack a picnic lunch, fish, boat, hike or just sit and listen to the call of wild birds and the rustle of the wind through prairie grasses and trees, the parks offer respite from ordinary life.

Parks and Recreation

Madison's notorious climate doesn't mean people here don't enjoy outdoor recreation. Being surrounded by lakes means that at virtually any time of day in the spring, summer and fall, the city offers scenes of colorful sails of windsurfers and sailboats billowing across the horizon.

The lakes are put to good use in winter, too, with ice-boating a popular sport in Madison since the 1890s, ice skating and cross-country skiing.

Although Madison parks are rarely empty, when spring arrives it's hard to find even a path, sidewalk or street empty of pleasure or power walkers, in-line skaters, joggers or bikers. As for parks, they just seem to come alive, not only with flowers and squirrels, but also with Frisbee games and softball.

Parks

Madison is famous for its thousands of acres of parkland. Beautiful parcels have been acquired bit by bit, thanks to early city fathers who started the Park and Pleasure Drive Association around the turn of the century. Their vision has paid off magnificently. Our parks provide interesting destinations for those interested in geology, wildlife, Wisconsin history and nature. Whether you want to pack a picnic lunch, fish, boat, hike or just sit and listen to the call of wild birds and the rustle of the wind through prairie grasses and trees, the parks offer respite from ordinary life.

Madison's passion for parks may have inspired its neighbor, Monona, as well. In 1997 the Monona Youth Dream Park opened in Winnequah Park. The 10,270-square-foot community-built playground has what some say is the biggest play structure in Dane County. The park was designed by children and built by volunteers — including inmates from local minimum security prisons. (For more information about this playground and others in Madison, refer to the Kidstuff chapter.)

There is no admission fee at Madison parks. Hours are 4:30 AM to 10 PM daily. Shelters, which close at 9:30 PM, are available for group activities for a fee of $40 for weekdays or $55 on holidays and weekends; the fee is $35 for half-days. You can drink alcohol without a permit in Madison parks, but you need a permit if you intend to sell alcohol. The fee for pitching a tent for an event is $103.50. There is a $45 "amplified sound" fee if you want to have a band or DJ in a park. Dog permits are $10 a year or $1 a day. Ski and boat launch permits are good in both city and county parks (see the section on county parks). The Parks Division, which maintains administrative offices at 215 Martin Luther King Boulevard, has additional information on Madison parks; call them at (608) 266-4711 regarding golf passes and shelter reservations.

To learn more about some area parks, see our Kidstuff chapter. For information about the UW Arboretum, see our Attractions chapter.

A Picnic in the City

The city of Madison has more than 200 parks. Many of these are neighborhood parks just within skipping distance for children who want to zip down a slide, indulge in a quick game of basketball or play catch. Many are flooded in winter for skating. Hockey is one of the local passions, and children often practice in the neighborhood rink. Many parks are much grander, with lake frontage.

Pedestrian paths wind their way through acres of lush vegetation, and lovely foot bridges arch over waterways, inviting you to pose someone you love for a romantic "candid" photo.

Even with more than 360,000 county residents vying for time at the parks, remarkably we've discovered you can almost always find a bench or picnic table when you get the urge to sit and rest. It's not uncommon for residents here to carry a blanket in the car in case an opportunity for picnicking arises. Why worry about packing a lunch? If you've got your blanket, there are plenty of restaurants ready to provide you with a box lunch or carry-out.

Here's a sampling of our biggest and best.

West Side

Elver Park
1240 McKenna Blvd., Madison

On a typical day at Elver Park, you're likely to come across someone who has dropped a line into a pond in search of panfish. Within the length of a Frisbee toss, you'll also see people picnicking, jogging, strolling babies or biking. Elver Park has one of the most popular sledding hills on Madison's West Side; you might even see a few skiers.

There's a lot to do even when the snow disappears. The park has three tennis courts, baseball and soccer fields and a large children's play structure. Wide, paved trails — frequented by walkers, joggers, bicyclists and in-line skaters — wind through the park past two fishing ponds filled with bluegill. The perimeters of the park are heavily wooded, and there's lots of open green space for Frisbee, sunbathing and other activities. The park has a large pavilion as well as tables for picnicking.

To reach this beautiful Madison park, take the Gammon Road exit from the Beltline and travel south.

Vilas Park and Beach
1339 Vilas Park Dr., Madison

Right next door to the Henry Vilas Zoo (see our Attractions chapter), Vilas Park is popular for picnics and other recreation. The park's large pond entices anglers, both pint-size and adult. Vilas has a large amount of play equipment including the famous "Old Woman Who Lived in a Shoe" slide and other perennial favorites with Madison's youngest residents and visitors. There's a separate toddler playground for young children who are just learning the ins and outs of playground play and aren't yet ready to hang with the big kids.

Vilas Beach, on Lake Wingra, draws huge summer crowds of swimmers and sandcastle designers on hot summer days. The park also hosts spectacular events such as regatta for collegiate rowing teams.

To visit Vilas Park, take the Fish Hatchery North Exit from the Beltline, travel north to Wingra Drive and take a left. You'll see Lake Wingra and the park in about two blocks on the left.

East Side

Olbrich Park
3300 Atwood Ave., Madison

Although Olbrich is best known for its splendid botanical gardens (see our Attractions chapter), the wonders of Olbrich Park extend far beyond where the lilies bloom. The western border of Olbrich Park is the northeastern shore of Lake Monona. This park has a busy boat landing and popular swimming beach. Families with young children are particularly fond of the lakeside with toddler-size play equipment at the north end of the park.

If you choose to picnic here, you'll have great views of boaters and water skiers. The park also has two soccer fields, a softball diamond, walk/jog path, four sand volleyball courts, two tennis courts and two basketball courts. Bring your kite — lake breezes and large open spaces make this a great place to launch trick and traditional kites.

Olbrich Park is along Atwood Avenue. Take the Beltline to the Monona Drive Exit and fol-

Madison's lakes provide anglers with plenty of opportunities to test their skills.

low it north. Monona Drive becomes Atwood Avenue just before you reach the park.

Tenney Park
1300 Sherman Ave., Madison

There's water, water everywhere at this popular and sublimely beautiful historic park with beachfront on Lake Mendota and lots of ponds and channels for anglers. The East Side park has a picturesque bridge that is a favorite spot for photographers, and it has a small sandy beach and a shoreside beach house. Numerous trees dot the landscape, providing picnickers with shade and anglers with privacy and solitude. Children's play equipment, including swings, can be found near the beach on the southeastern shore of Lake Mendota.

In the nucleus of the park, you'll find a building that serves as a summer picnic shelter and winter warming hut for ice skaters. Tenney Park has a walk/jog path, a sand volleyball court, basketball court and three tennis courts. You can also learn a little physics while hanging out at this park: A lock and dam complex allows small boats to travel from Lake Mendota to other lakes in the Madison chain via the Yahara River.

From I-90/94, take the U.S. Highway 151 (E. Washington Avenue) Exit, travel southwest toward the Capitol to First Street. Take a right on First Street, traveling down First until it ends and intersects with E. Johnson Street. Turn left on Johnson. Tenney Park will be on your right just after you cross Fordem Avenue and the bridge.

Warner Park
1101 Woodward Dr., Madison

As the home of the Black Wolf baseball team (see our Sports chapter), there's seldom a dull moment at this huge Madison park. Warner Park boasts just about any facility you desire in a sports-and-recreation area, with several baseball diamonds, a skating rink and ponds, a Vita fitness course and extensive paths for biking, walking, in-line skating or jogging.

The paths offer plenty of opportunities for communing with nature — lots of beautiful wild birds, wetlands, green space and shoreline.

Your biggest decision of the day may be what to do first. During a recent visit we heard a toddler exclaim: "Daddy, Daddy, we can fish or throw rocks!"

For younger children, there's a small, relatively new play structure on the northeast corner of the park, along Northport Drive, near the intersection with Troy Drive.

From I-90/94, take U.S. Highway 151 (E. Washington Avenue) Exit and then travel southwest toward the State Capitol to Aberg Avenue (Wis. Highway 30). You'll go right on Aberg; there's no other choice. At the intersection of Aberg and Packers (Wis. Highway 113), following the airport exit signs, travel north on Packers to Northport Drive (still Wis. 113). Warner Park is on the left just past Shereman Avenue.

Taking on the County

Dane County has about 25 parks, ranging from the undeveloped to full-blown green spaces with vast recreational facilities.

If you have a couple hours to relax, jump in the car and check out one of Dane County's many multiple-use, four-season parks. In no time at all, you'll be tramping up and down trails, gazing at scenic natural vistas and wondering why it took you so long to get out and explore. Most of the trails in Dane County parks are used for hiking during non-snow months and for cross-country skiing when nature allows. Pets are allowed in parks if they are kept on a short leash. (If you own a dog, please read the "Exercising Fido" section later in this chapter.)

All Dane County parks are open for regular use from 5 AM to 10 PM year round, and there are no admission fees. There are other fees however: Trail passes for mountain bikes, cross-country skiing and horseback riding cost $15 a year or $2 a day; dog permits, $10 a year or $1 a day; alcoholic beverage permits, $10 per day; and shelter fees, from $40 to $50. You can rent picnic tables in increments of six for $42; volleyball and horseshoe equipment can be rented for $2. Boat launch fees are $16 for county residents, $25 for nonresidents, $5 for Dane County residents older than 65 and $5 for disabled individuals.

You can find campsites at the following parks: Babcock, Brigham, Mendota and Token Creek. Reservations are available on a first-come, first-served basis. Campsite passes range from $1 per person to $15 per site. Camping is limited to seven consecutive nights. For campsite reservations and information on all permits call (608) 246-3896.

The following is a list of major Dane County parks, dividing the county geographically.

Northwest

Festge Park/Salmo Pond
U.S. Hwy. 14, 1.5 miles west of Cross Plains

A visit to this park area is a two-for-one deal. On one side of U.S. Highway 14 you'll find Salmo Pond, a large fishpond perfect for young anglers. The state Department of Natural Resources keeps the pond stocked with trout, and you'll also likely find some bass, perch and panfish. Black Earth Creek runs alongside Salmo Pond and is subject to DNR catch-and-release regulations, so review these before you drop in a line. You can pick up a regulations booklet when you purchase your fishing license, or call the DNR at (608) 266-2621.

On the opposite side of U.S. 14, Festge Park offers a softball field, three shelters, plenty of picnic tables, some play equipment and three hiking/cross-country trails ranging in length from .2 to .6 mile. The park has a 100-foot-high overlook to provide you with a memorable view of the countryside.

Fish Lake Park
Fish Lake Rd., near West Point

As its name suggests, this small park provides anglers access to Fish Lake, a 250-acre body of water with a depth of 62 feet. The park has a boat landing, picnic tables, play equipment and a picnic shelter. Fish Lake contains bluegill, northern pike and largemouth bass.

You can reach Fish Lake Park via U.S. Highway 12, turning north onto County Highway KP, right on County Highway Y, left on Mack Road and right on Fish Lake Road.

Indian Lake Park
Wis. Hwy. 19, Berry

Probably the most memorable part of our latest visit to this park was meeting a small garter snake that was relaxing in some long grass next to the walk path. After we startled it (and vice versa), the garter snake checked us out, smelling the air with its tongue. Then, apparently deciding we were harmless enough, it continued on its way.

Indian Lake, one of Dane County's largest parks, drew its name because it was the site of a Native American community. A trail has now been developed along the entire lake and includes 900 feet of elevated boardwalk at the shallow end. This is a good place to take neophyte anglers to fish for bluegill and bass. You can launch canoes and other nonmotorized boats from the park's boat landing.

Indian Lake has another interesting bit of history. A settler named John Endres constructed a small stone chapel at the pinnacle of a hill (in what is now Indian Lake Park) to fulfill a religious vow he'd made, asking that his family be spared in a diphtheria epidemic. Visitors to the tiny chapel frequently leave fresh flowers for the Virgin Mary. A guest book chronicles visitors' names and dates.

The hike up the hill to the chapel is moderately difficult with numerous wood steps and platforms. However, you'll find some places to rest along the way and enjoy myriad wildflowers and birds.

Indian Lake does not allow individual camping but has group campgrounds for use by youth organizations.

Take U.S. Highway 12 north out of Madison to U.S. Highway 19 and turn left; you'll soon see the park on the left.

Walking Iron Park
636 Hudson Rd., Mazomanie
• (608) 246-3896

You can hike or ride horseback on the trail at this 200-acre park, which has prairie restoration and forested areas. There are a few picnic tables, but this is mostly a conservation area. The park is a 45-minute drive west of Madison on Highway 14; it's entrance is through Mazomanie Village Park. If you are unloading a horse trailer, you can enter the park through the second trail head on Beckman Road, where there is a parking lot.

Central

Babcock Park
U.S. Hwy. 51, near McFarland

You can camp, fish, boat or just play at Babcock Park, situated on 2,000-acre Lake Waubesa. The park has 25 campsites with electricity, showers, a fish-cleaning facility and a protected boat launch designed to make launching headache-free, even on windy days. You're most likely to hook panfish or a largemouth bass, but the lake also offers up an occasional walleye, northern pike, muskie or smallmouth bass.

Take U.S. Highway 51 south from the Beltline. You can find the park off U.S. 51, near the village of McFarland.

Goodland Park
Goodland Park Rd., Dunn

On the western shore of Lake Waubesa, Goodland Park is favored for swimming and boating. This smaller park has two shelters, volleyball, tennis and basketball courts and softball. The lake is nice for canoeing and fishing. Panfish and largemouth bass are the most prevalent species, but you can also reel in northern pike, muskies and smallmouth bass.

Travel U.S. Highway 14 south from Madison toward Oregon (the Park Street S. Exit) and exit at McCoy Road. Turn left on McCoy Road, turn right after one block on County Highway MM, go another block and turn left onto E. Clayton Road (turns into Larsen Road), then follow it to Goodland Park Road and turn left.

Lake Farm Park
Off U.S. Hwy. 51, near McFarland

Picnicking, hiking, fishing, softball and soccer are just a few of the ways you can wile away an afternoon at Lake Farm Park. Another option is to hike the Native American

Archeological Trail to learn more about the area's history from 10,000 B.C. to 300 A.D.

Lake Farm Park has a fish-cleaning facility where you can fillet the "big ones" — bass, pike or panfish — you pull from Lake Waubesa. The park is open for group camping (i.e., Girl Scouts), but single-family camping is not available.

This county park is off U.S. Highway 51, south of the intersection with U.S. Highway 12/18.

Mendota Park
County Hwy. M, near Middleton

This busy park on the northwest shores of our largest lake, Mendota, is one of the most popular camping areas in the county parks system as it provides sites with electricity and lake access and is close to shopping in Middleton. The park has soccer, volleyball, tennis, play equipment and a nice beach. You can also fish for your dinner. Panfish are abundant, and other common species in Lake Mendota include northern pike, walleye and bass. Some muskies also are present, according to county park department reports.

Mendota Park is on County Highway M near the intersections of County highways Q and M.

Token Creek Park
Off U.S. Hwy. 51, Burke

There are lots of places to play at Token Creek. You'll find two softball fields, two modern play structures, five sand volleyball courts, four horseshoe pits and many other facilities. Campers using one of the park's 38 campsites have access to electricity and showers. An elevated boardwalk takes you across a unique sedge meadow marsh for a closeup of wildlife and vegetation. In winter, you can cross-country ski here and access Dane County's 260-mile snowmobile trail system, and horseback riding is permitted.

You can reach the park by traveling north on U.S. Highway 51 from the Madison city limits.

Southwest

Brigham Park
County Hwy. F, Blue Mounds

If you've wanted to visit the Cave of the Mounds (see our Daytrips chapter), consider combining your trip with a stop at Brigham Park. Just 1.5 miles past the cave entrance, Brigham Park has camping for tents, campers and motorhomes, a group campsite, some older play equipment and a nice scenic overview. You'll find picnic tables and a shelter at this shaded park named after Ebenezar Brigham, one of Dane County's first white settlers. Brigham Park also has a self-guided nature tour.

The park entrance is on County Highway F, north from U.S. Highway 18/151.

Stewart Park
County Hwy. ID, near Mount Horeb

Just outside the city of Mount Horeb, Stewart Park is a large park centered by Stewart Lake and Dam. You can fish for bluegill and bass in the lake now, but in a couple years you'll probably have better luck since the county is about to begin a large-scale rehabilitation project at the lake. Stewart Lake Park has four hiking trails, three shelters, a variety of play equipment and lots of green space for romping. It's a nice place to walk about and visit after a trip down Mount Horeb's "Trollway" (main street shopping area). See Daytrips for additional information.

From Madison, drive west on U.S. Highway 18, then turn north on County Highway ID.

INSIDERS' TIP

There are big plans for Ahuska Park in Monona, Madison's immediate neighbor. Organizers hope to build a $3.3 million indoor ice arena in the park, which stretches along Broadway on the city's south side, for hockey and figure skating. Before that happens there will be soccer fields by the end of 1999, then baseball fields and tennis courts.

East

Cam-Rock Park
County Hwy. B, Cambridge

This 300-acre park was created through the efforts of local citizens and the Cambridge Foundation. You can picnic along the meandering river, watch for herons and other unusual birds, or take advantage of the many recreational facilities. The park has a large wood play structure with three bridges and a tower, horseshoe pits (bring your own horseshoes), fire rings and room to hike, ski and mountain bike.

Take U.S. Highway 12/18 west toward Cambridge, turn right on County Highway B and watch for the park entrance on your right.

State Park Wanderlust

Dane County is fortunate to have three state parks within its boundaries. Each offers diverse opportunities for recreation, hiking, picnicking and other pursuits. Admission rates are as follows: daily passes, $5 for Wisconsin residents and $7 for nonresidents; and annual passes, $18 for Wisconsin residents and $25 for nonresidents. Wisconsin residents who are 65 and older pay only $3 for a daily pass and $9 for a yearly sticker. If you own two cars and will be using both at the parks, you may purchase a second annual vehicle sticker at half-price.

Blue Mound State Park
Off County Hwy. K, Blue Mounds
- (608) 437-5711

This park — which extends over the Dane County line into Iowa County — is the best-kept secret in the Wisconsin State Park System. Don't tell anybody, but it has a huge, heated swimming pool! If that's not enough to get you packing, consider the 78 campsites, nature center, modern play equipment, amphitheater, three hiking trails (up to 2 miles long) and access to the Military Ridge Bike Trail. Two 40-foot-high observation towers offer panoramic views of the countryside.

Camping fees are $7 for Wisconsin residents on weekdays and $9 on weekends. (Nonresidents pay $2 more each night for camping.) To use the pool, it's $1 for adults and 50˘¢ for kids younger than 12.

Take U.S. Highway 18/151 west from Madison to Blue Mounds, then watch for signs.

Governor Nelson State Park
5140 County Hwy. M, Middleton
- (608) 831-3005

Situated on the northwest shore of Lake Mendota, Governor Nelson Park is the perfect setting for a Sunday picnic or fishing excursion. Facilities include a boat launch, large fish-cleaning station, modern play structure and numerous picnic tables. You can hike nature paths in search of the panther-shaped Indian mound, see plenty of varieties of wildflowers or just relax on the beach. Lake Mendota anglers commonly catch northern pike, walleye and both largemouth and smallmouth bass. Panfish are plentiful, and you might be lucky enough to bag an occasional muskie. This is a day-use park; no camping is available.

Take the Beltline west to County Highway K, then turn right. At the intersection with County Highway M, turn right; the state park will be on your left.

Lake Kegonsa State Park
2405 Door Creek Rd., Stoughton
- (608) 873-9695

Lake Kegonsa literally means "lake of the many fishes" in the Winnebago language, and anglers who have spent numerous hours casting into its depths no doubt agree. Walleye, northern pike and largemouth bass are common in Lake Kegonsa and, of course, there's an abundant supply of panfish. If you're lucky you'll catch a smallmouth bass or even a muskie to take home for supper.

Lake Kegonsa is a favorite spot for family camping ventures. The park has 80 campsites, many of which are fairly heavily wooded; only one site, which is handicapped-accessible, has electricity. Other handicapped-accessible sites are available as well. Swimming, hiking, boating and water skiing are popular pastimes, and children have lots of room to just run and play. You'll find a small playground, volleyball court and two horseshoe pits near the campground. You can get a volleyball or set of horseshoes free from the park office with a $5 deposit.

The 1.2-mile White Oak Nature Trail takes you past Native American burial mounds and a pine plantation.

Lake Kegonsa State Park is near Stoughton. Take the Beltline east (toward Cambridge) and turn right on County Highway MN. The park is on the right side of the road.

Exercising Fido...

Taking your pup to the park can be good exercise for both you and your pet. The City of Madison and Dane County have set up some guidelines to allow dog lovers and others to maintain peaceful co-existence.

In the City Parks

In Madison, marked portions of Brittingham, Sycamore and Warner parks are now open to unleashed dogs, as is part of Quann Park. The city also has zones for leashed dogs in Brittingham, Sycamore and Warner parks, as do Elver, Hoyt, Marlborough, Spring Harbor, Yahara Parkway and Burr Jones Field. Dogs are permitted on leashes in all Dane County parks, and the county also offers five off-leash areas. They are in Indian Lake Park, Token Creek Park, Prairie Moraine (off Highway PB, south of Verona), Viking Park and Yahara Heights Park (Highway 113).

Taking a dog in either city or county parks requires a permit, which costs $10 each year. The county also offers daily permits for $1. City permits are acceptable for use in county parks and vice versa. The permits are available at the city Parks Division office at 215 Martin Luther King Jr. Boulevard, Suite 120, or at the Dane County Parks Department office at 4318 Robertson Road.

In the State Parks

Once again, pets are required to be on a short (less than 8 feet long) leash when inside a Wisconsin state park. Pets can't be left alone in any section of the park, including the campground. Pets are not allowed in picnic areas, on beaches or in any park buildings, but you can have them at your campsite and on designated hiking trails. As in other parks, you are required to clean up after your animal or face a $116.90 fine. Plastic bags usually are available at state parks.

Greenspace at the University of Wisconsin

Allen Centennial Gardens
620 Babcock Dr., Madison

One of the most gorgeous spots in Madison on a summer day is this 90,000-square-foot garden surrounding a National Historic Landmark Gothic Victorian house that was one of the campus' first dean's residences. The gardens are used for teaching and research, but they're open every day of the year from dawn to dusk, with the best floral displays from June through September. Look for the Victorian garden, iris garden, exotic-shrub garden, arbor and vine display, small fruit garden, and herb and medicinal garden. Other gardens have such intriguing names as sinister garden and edible garden, while still others are categorized by their locations, such as the terrace garden, water garden, bog garden and rock-alpine garden. Finally, if you have a touch of wanderlust, visit the English, Italian and French gardens or, closer to home, the new American garden and Wisconsin wildflower garden. (Additional information about the Allen Centennial Gardens is listed in the Attractions chapter.)

Recreation

Archery

Archery Center
2421 Stoughton Rd., Madison
• (608) 244-8686

Whether your childhood hero was Robin Hood or Maid Marian, you might get a kick out of honing your skills with a bow and arrow. The Archery Center, which is on Madison's East Side, has eight lanes open from noon to 9 PM weekdays and 10 AM to 4 PM on weekends. The cost is $5 an hour per person, including equipment. Adult supervision is required for children.

Madison's more than 200 parks can satisfy the urges of hikers, swimmers, skaters and picnickers to budding tennis pros.

Ballooning

Up, up and away! Experience the freedom and wonder of flight without having to battle with baggage and ground transportation or worry about getting a window seat. Madison has several reputable hot-air balloon companies ready to help you get a new perspective. When you fly, interestingly enough, the temperature in the balloon's basket is usually about the same as on the ground. Nevertheless, leave your shorts and sandals at home even if it's a scorcher; for safety reasons, balloon passengers are encouraged to wear long pants and athletic shoes on their trip through the clouds.

Isthmus

Sky Aces Inc.
202 N. Henry St., Madison
- **(608) 255-2935**

With Sky Aces, your balloon launches from Madison's West Side, and you travel over the lakes and Downtown before landing in the countryside. Sky Aces offers morning and afternoon flights from late April or early May until October. Flights last from one to 1½ hours. At the landing, you are treated to champagne (if you're 21 or older) and a free T-shirt. The fee is about $165 per person. Gift certificates and dinner packages are available.

Outlying Area

Cattails to Clouds Hot Air Balloon Rides
2535 County Hwy. AB, McFarland
- **(608) 224-1100**

This is the only Madison ballooning company that flies year round. Cattails to Clouds has daily flights April through October and flies on weekends from November through March. You can choose from one of 60 starting points in Dane County or join a prearranged flight. Flights last about an hour and include a preflight briefing, flight certificate and souvenir photos. The cost is about $135 per person, depending on flight type. Champagne and T-shirts may be purchased if you desire. Bring a camera and binoculars.

Token Creek Hot Air Balloons Inc.
3807-B Wis. Hwy. 19, Token Creek
- **(608) 241-4000**

Token Creek balloons have been flying over Dane County since 1981. The Token Creek season extends from May through October. Flight prices vary according to time, beginning with weekday sunrise flights at $135 per person and ranging to weekend evening flights at $179 each. Flights originate in Token Creek, north of Madison, and travel paths differ; you should allow about three hours for your ballooning adventure. Champagne and snacks are served at flight's end. Bring your camera, staff advise, and more film than you think you'll ever need.

Bicycling

Even in the dead of winter, bicyclists are part of Madison's street scene. Many businesses promote bicycle commuting as a way to keep employees physically fit. But in truth, bicyclists around here don't need much encouragement. Bicycling for pleasure is one of the favorite pastimes in Madison. There are many favorite spots to bicycle in the city, especially on trails that line the lakes. A bike path was even included in the design of Monona Terrace Convention Center. Safety is emphasized among local bicyclists, and you rarely see them without helmets.

Bike Trails

Glacial Drumlin Trail
Off County Hwy. C, Delafield
• (608) 646-3025

Just east of Madison, in the village of Cottage Grove, lies one of the state's most popular bike trails. From its starting point across from the Cottage Grove Post Office, Glacial Drumlin Trail traverses 47 miles to Waukesha along an abandoned railroad bed. The trail has a smooth, packed limestone surface. Several towns — Deerfield, Lake Mills, Sullivan, Dousman and Wales — are along the way if you need to stop for refreshment or have trouble with your bicycle.

Anyone 16 or older using the trail between April 1 and October 31 must have a state trail pass. Annual trail cards cost $10, daily cards are $3, and you can use them on any state trail. You can purchase trail cards from local vendors and park rangers along the trails or at Lake Kegonsa State Park (see our previous "Parks" section for details).

Military Ridge State Park Trail
4175 State Rd., Dodgeville
• (608) 935-5119

Take U.S. Highway 151 south out of Madison toward Fitchburg and Verona to begin your trek on the scenic Military Ridge State Park Trail. You may park your car in the designated trail parking area near the intersection of County Highway PB and U.S. 151. The 39.6-mile state trail connects the communities of Dodgeville and Fitchburg. The trail is 8 to 10 feet wide with a packed limestone surface. The trail has a 2 to 5 percent grade and 48 bridges, all with planked decks, curbs and railings. Along the way, you will see farmland, forest, wetlands, prairies and several small communities.

Although no camping is allowed on the trail, you may choose to exit into Blue Mound State Park (see subsequent "Camping" and previous "Parks" sections), near Blue Mounds, for overnight R&R. Call Blue Mound State Park, (608) 437-5711, for details. If you're older than 15, you need a state trail card ($3 daily, $10 annually) to use the trail.

Mountain Biking

If mountain biking makes your heart flip-flop, you'll find many Madisonians share your passion. Two county parks — **Badger Prairie Park** and **Cam-Rock Park** (see previous "Parks" section) — have mountain bike trails. Call (608) 246-3896 or (608) 242-4576 for information. **Quarry Park** (see "Parks"), a city park on the West Side, also welcomes mountain bikers; call (608) 266-4711.

To gain a copy of the *Wisconsin Biking Guide* with trail maps and information about facilities across the state, call (800) 432-TRIP.

Rentals

If you don't have a bike, don't let that stop you from touring or at least taking a spin around a lake. Three bike shops in town rent bicycles by the day, week or month:

Budget Bicycle Center
1202 Regent St., Madison
• (608) 251-8413

Mountain and hybrid bicycles rent for $15 daily, $45 per week or $125 per month. Trailer bikes for kids rent for $15 daily and Burley trailers for $5 per day. One-, three-, five- and 10-speed bicycles rent for $7 a day, $21 a week or $60 a month. Car racks rent for $10 a day. Helmets and locks come with the rentals.

Williamson Bicycle Works
601 Williamson St., Madison
* **(608) 255-5292**

Mountain and hybrid bicycles (a cross between 10-speed and mountain bikes) and trailers for kids are rented for $10 a day or $50 for a week. Tandem and recumbent bicycles are rented for $30 a day. Helmets are included and locks are $2.

Yellow Jersey
419 State St., Madison • (608) 257-4737

Bike rentals begin at $7 daily for touring bikes and $9.50 for mountain bikes. Some rental packages include bike locks and helmets. If you'd like to try a bicycle built for two, ask about tandem bike rentals.

Resources

Wisconsin Off-Road
Bicycling Association
P.O. Box 1681, Madison, WI 53701

This group meets monthly at a Madison restaurant to plan excursions. Dues are $20 for a single or family membership. To learn about current happenings, write the association at the listed address or pick up a copy of the "Break Away" section of the *Wisconsin State Journal*, (608) 252-6100.

Bicycle Federation of Wisconsin
* **(608) 251-4456**

The federation publishes an annual, full-color event booklet with information on Wisconsin bicycle rides, races and tours. The cost is $2. To receive one, write to the federation at P.O. Box 1224, Madison, WI 53701.

"400" Trail Depot
* **(800) 844-3507**

The 22-mile Wisconsin "400" Bike Trail between Reedsburg and Elroy — with its wetlands, sandstone bluffs, rolling croplands and abundant wildlife — is known as Wisconsin's most beautiful bike trail. You can write to Trail Headquarters, P.O. Box 142, Reedsburg, WI 53959, for more information.

Billiards

You can find a pool table at just about any tavern in town. But if you're looking to play billiards, you might want to chalk up your cue at one of the following:

Isthmus

Cue-Nique Billiards
317 W. Gorham St., Madison
* **(608) 251-1134**

Who wants to break? Cue-Nique has more than 20 tables, including 16 of the 9-foot-long variety. The cost of play for two people varies from $6.25 an hour on a weekday afternoon to $7.50 on a weekend night. Each extra player pays 50¢ an hour. The game room is open from 11 AM until bar time. Regular leagues play on Monday and Tuesday nights, and there are 9-ball tournaments on Thursdays. Smoking is allowed, and you can purchase beer and grill food on site.

West Side

The Green Room
5618 Odana Rd., Madison
* **(608) 277-8588**

Rack 'em up on one of 25 tables at the Green Room where two or more players can shoot for $7 an hour on weekday afternoons or $10 an hour on weekends. Monday through Friday, the Green Room offers a special deal: A player can shoot from 11 AM until 7 PM for just $9. The Green Room serves food and drink. The surroundings are spacious and well-ventilated. Call to find out when the next leagues will start.

Bowling

Madison has an abundance of bowling centers including established and newer facilities. League bowling is very popular, so it can be difficult to find open bowling in the early- to mid-evening hours. If you think you might like to participate in a league, call one

West Side

Schwoegler Park Towne Lanes
444 Grand Canyon Dr., Madison
• **(608) 833-7272**

The Schwoegler family got into the bowling business in 1912 in Downtown Madison. The business has since moved to the West Side and has grown to 36 lanes, about 35 leagues, a bar and grill, an arcade and a pro shop. Twelve lanes can accommodate bumpers, which makes it a perfect place for birthday parties. After bowling, kids can retreat to the party room for pizza and cake. Day care is available during the day for league bowlers. Costs usually range from $1.50 to $2.25 per person per game, but sometimes there are special reduced rates (see our Kidstuff chapter).

East Side

All Star Lanes
3587 E. Washington Ave., Madison
• **(608) 241-5000**

Open since August 1996 at the corner of E. Washington Avenue and Stoughton Road, All Star Lanes offers 16 lanes, a sports lounge for adults and game room for kids. The center has open bowling daily (call for open-bowling times and league information) and offers birthday parties and bumper bowling for kids. The cost per game is $1.75 for juniors and $2.25 for adults. You can rent shoes for $1.25.

Bowl-A-Vard
2121 E. Springs Dr., Madison
• **(608) 244-7246**

This is a favorite recreation hub with 40 lanes, a top-notch bar and grill, nightclub and dance bar, pro shop, daily open bowling, sand volleyball and horseshoes and more leagues than you could shake a pin at! Bowl-A-Vard does kids' birthday parties and has pop-up bumpers. The cost per game is $2.40 for adults and kids. Shoe rental is $1.50.

Dream Lanes
13 Atlas Ct., Madison • **(608) 221-3596**

With 38 lanes of automatic scoring and an extensive game area for the kids, Dream Lanes is a popular family entertainment site. Try out the "ultra bowling" on Friday and Saturday nights. Bowlers take to the lanes in the dark, with black lights making pins and lanes glow. Fog, lasers and music contribute to make this a fun, out-of-this-world experience. Dream Lanes also has several leagues, a frequent-bowlers club and an on-site Pizza Pit. Game prices are $1.75 weekdays for all ages and $2.25 on weekends. You can rent bowling shoes for $1.50 a pair.

South Side

Badger Bowl
506 E. Badger Rd., Madison
• **(608) 274-6662**

Even non-bowlers relish trips to Badger Bowl (just off the Beltline at Rimrock Road) where delicious and hearty homemade soups draw a daily lunch crowd. Senior, adult and youth bowling leagues are available, and morning and afternoon babysitting is offered to league bowlers. Badger Bowl's party room is a popular spot for private gatherings, and there's live entertainment in the lounge on Friday and Saturday nights. Call ahead for daily open-bowling times, which vary. Badger Bowl has 30 lanes. Day games cost $2 each, while games rolled after 9 PM cost $2.30 each. Shoe rental is $1.25.

Outlying Area

Bowling Green Recreation Center
7625 Lisa Ln., Middleton
• **(608) 831-2030**

If you're into bowling, virtual golf, softball, sand volleyball or just lounging around, Bowling Green Recreation Center is ready for you. In business for 20 years, the center keeps expanding its offerings. Bowling Green has 20 lanes of bowling and a game room

First you skate as fast as you can and jump into a pile of snow. Pure joy.

with big-screen TVs. Birthday and group packages are available. The center is just off the West Beltline in Middleton, behind Fitzgeralds. It'll run you $2.25 per game to bowl; rental shoes cost $1.

Prairie Lanes
430 Clarmar Dr., Sun Prairie
• (608) 837-2586

League bowling is big at Prairie Lanes, but more recreational bowlers will also find open daily bowling before 4 PM and after 9 PM. The center has 32 lanes, a pro shop and grill. Prairie Lanes also has pop-up bumper bowling and a few games for the kids and the young at heart. At Prairie Lanes, everyone bowls for 75¢ per game on Mondays. Other days, youth 17 and younger bowl for $1.60 per game and pay $1 for shoe rentals, while adults pay $2 per game and $2 for shoe rentals.

Viking Lanes
1410 U.S. Hwy. 51, Stoughton
• (608) 873-5959

Whether you're looking for a family pizza-and-games experience or a traditional Friday night out with fish fry and bowling, Village Lanes offers plenty of entertainment opportunities. There are 16 bowling lanes, a big-screen TV in the lounge and a separate banquet hall for parties, class reunions and receptions. Bumper bowling and birthday parties add to the fun. It costs $2 per game to bowl most nights, although on Mondays and Wednesdays bowlers pay $1 per game. Shoe rental costs 75¢ per pair.

Camping

The following is a brief overview of camping opportunities. Please review the previous "Parks" section for additional information.

Public Facilities

Outlying Area

Blue Mound State Park
Off County Hwy. K, Blue Mounds
• (608) 437-5711

This park — which extends over the Dane County line into Iowa County (see the previous "Parks" section) — includes 78 campsites, four with electric hookups. Camp fees are $7 for Wisconsin residents on weekdays and $9 on weekends. (Nonresidents pay $2 more each night for camping.) This state park also features a nature center, modern play equipment, an amphitheater, hiking trails and access to the

Military Ridge Bike Trail (see the previous "Bicycling" section). Two observation towers offer views of the surrounding countryside. Blue Mound's pièce de résistance is a huge, heated swimming pool ($1 for adults and 50¢ for kids younger than 12).

Lake Kegonsa State Park
2405 Door Creek Rd., Stoughton
- **(608) 873-9695**

Lake Kegonsa State Park gives Dane County residents and visitors a fun, wilderness-style camping experience right in their own backyard. The campground is about 20 minutes from Downtown Madison. The park has 80 family campsites, most of which are heavily wooded. A few double campsites and handicapped-accessible campsites are also available. With fishing, swimming, bicycling and some short nature trails, this park provides a terrific setting for introducing young children to camping. You must have a state sticker on your vehicle to enter the park (see the previous "Parks" section). You can reserve a spot via telephone from June to August, Monday through Friday, 9 AM to 4 PM. Camping fees vary from $7 and $9 Sunday through Thursday nights for residents and nonresidents respectively to $9 and $11 Friday and Saturday nights.

Dane County Parks and Campgrounds
4318 Robertson Rd., Madison
- **(608) 246-3896**

The Dane County Park System provides a variety of camping opportunities for families and individuals. Registrations are on a first-come, first-served basis. Camping is limited to seven days, and reservations are accepted for some parks. You can also reserve shelters for family reunions and other gatherings. Here's a peek at Dane County parks.

Babcock Park is on the second lake in Madison's chain, Lake Waubesa. All 25 campsites are wired with electric hookups. Campers have access to a protected boat launch, fish-cleaning facility and showers.

Brigham Park, in northwestern Dane County, offers a rustic campground with 25 sites ($10 per night; no electricity) and self-guided nature and history tours.

Mendota Park is another popular county park and campground due to its proximity to Middleton and Madison. (It's even on a bus line.) The park has a boat launch and 30 shaded campsites ($15 a night) with electricity. The park is within walking distance of several Middleton apartment complexes, so the park is usually busy.

Private Campgrounds

With the large number of public campgrounds available, private campgrounds in the Madison area are few and far between. Here are a couple to try.

Outlying Area

Madison KOA Campground
4859 County Hwy. V, DeForest
- **(608) 846-4528**

This KOA campground has more than 80 pull-through sites with full hookups including sewer. The campground also has 11 tent sites with electric and water. Young guests can swing or teeter-totter on the playground while older guests play pool and video games inside the main building. The cost is $22 for a site with full hookups for two guests or $18.50 for two people at a tent site. An additional $2 per person is charged for any number over two.

Viking Village
1648 County Hwy. N, Stoughton
- **(608) 873-6601**

Campers can play mini-golf and soccer or swim in the outdoor pool at Viking Village near Stoughton. The private campground offers 71 campsites, including a tent-camping area. All

---

> **INSIDERS' TIP**
>
> **Wisconsin offers outstanding freshwater snorkeling at places such as Devil's Lake, about a hour's drive from Madison.**

campsites have electricity and water. There's a good-size playground and sand area for children next to the swimming pool. Fees are $23 per night for a site with electricity and water, $27 with sewer and $20 for a tent site.

Canoeing, Kayaking and Rowing

With the many lakes and other waterways in Wisconsin, canoeing opportunities are only a short stone's skip away. In fact, Madison was named one of the top 10 cities in the country for paddling by *Canoe and Kayak* magazine in October 1995.

All Madison-area lakes are connected by the Yahara River. You can expect calm paddling unless it's windy — then the lakes get choppy. Paddling gives you an opportunity to experience "the wilds" of Dane County firsthand — to see things you would never see zooming down a highway. You might get to say hello to a glossy muskrat, paddle close enough to eyeball a crane or watch a beaver busily creating his empire. It would be a rare day, indeed, if you came home with no nature tale to tell.

Rentals

If you don't own a water vessel, it's easy enough to rent one. You might try one of the following:

Carl's Paddlin' Canoe and Kayak Center
617 Williamson St., Madison
• (608) 284-0300

At Carl's, the staff can offer advice on where to paddle and set you up with a canoe or kayak. Aluminum canoe rentals start at $25 a day. Or, you might want to try a composite tandem or solo canoe. A (two-person) tandem is $40 a day, while the solo canoe is available for a $30 rental fee. Kayaks rent for $30 for the first day. The rental canoe center drops the rate per day for those desiring prepaid, longer rentals, and they will supply foam block systems for transporting the canoes on your vehicle. Life jackets and paddles are included.

Rutabaga
220 W. Broadway, Madison
• (608) 223-9300

Rutabaga gives you the option of renting canoes right off the dock (on the Yahara River) or for transportation elsewhere. The Yahara River will take you into the Madison chain of lakes. Off-dock canoe rentals vary depending on size, ranging from $10 to $20 a day. Off-dock kayak rentals are $10 and $20 a day, depending on the kayak. If you rent a canoe or kayak for transportation to another site, fees vary from $25 to $40 a day. A rental includes paddles, life jackets and a foam block-and-strap system for transporting the canoe atop your car.

Nau-Ti-Gal
5360 Westport Rd., Madison
• (608) 244-4464

If you want to combine an afternoon or early evening lake outing with good food, drive out to the Nau-Ti-Gal restaurant where you can rent a canoe for $6 an hour and paddle away from its pier. For a little extra exercise, rent a pedal-powered aquacycle for $8 per hour. The season runs from Memorial Day to Labor Day. (See our Restaurants chapter for food-related information about Nau-Ti-Gal.)

Mendota Rowing Club
622 E. Gorham St., Madison
• (608) 238-2637

Join competitive or recreational rowers for a unique workout. New members must complete an instructional class. Four-week sessions begin at $65. All necessary equipment is provided.

Climbing

Boulders Rock Gym
3964 Commercial Ave., Madison
• (608) 244-8100

Conquer the indoor challenges at Boulders, on Madison's East Side, where you can find 8,000 square feet of climbing space, a bouldering cave, 42 top-ropes and 28 lead lines. The cost is $10 per day. See the entry in our Kidstuff chapter for hours and related information.

Fishing

Game and pan fish are plentiful in Lake Mendota, encouraging year-round fishing. But before you cast, make sure you've got a license. Out-of-state residents are asked to pay $34 for an annual license, $13 for a four-day license or $20 for a 15-day license. A Wisconsin resident fishing license is $14 a year. You can purchase the licenses just about any place fishing gear is sold.

Once you have your license in hand, grab your pole and some bait and get ready to angle. A commonly viewed bumper sticker here relates that "a bad day fishing is better than a good day working." If you think that theory rings true, then you might want to head out to one of our gorgeous parks. Many anglers choose to drop lines in the Yahara River or one of Madison's beautiful lakes (see the previous "Parks" section for details about fish populations).

Dane County Parks
4318 Robertson Rd., Madison
• **(608) 246-3896**

Babcock Park offers shore and boat fishing and a fish-cleaning facility at scenic Lake Waubesa. You can also camp at the park, which is near McFarland on U.S. Highway 51.

Friends swear by the fishing at Festge Park/Salmo Pond, where anglers will find a pond and pier surrounded by nearly 70 acres of wooded parkland. The Dane County park is 1.5 miles west of Cross Plains on the south side of U.S. Highway 14, off Scherbel Road.

At sunset on most summer nights, you can see fish jump and flip their way all across Lake Kegonsa.

Fish Camp Launch, a 10-acre park at the inlet of the Yahara River to Lake Kegonsa, is off County Highway AB, about a mile northeast of the intersection of U.S. 51 and County Highway AB.

Fish Lake Park, on the west end of Fish Lake, offers anglers a chance to try their luck with northern pike, largemouth bass and pan fish. Directions to this northwestern Dane County park are a little complicated; you'll need a map.

For more information on Dane County parks, see the previous "Parks" section or call the listed number.

Fitness Training

No matter how you like to work up a sweat, Madison likely has a health and fitness club that can accommodate you. Before you sign on the dotted line, however, spend a day working out at the club and getting to know the staff. Most clubs offer one-day passes for a nominal fee or will give you a free one-day pass to try out the facility. In selecting a club, it's a good idea to check out the traffic at the times you'd like to work out. Is there room for you on a stepper, on the track or in an aerobics class? What about parking? Some clubs are so busy right after work that you may have difficulty finding a spot. If you have children, does the facility provide child care? Is it free, or is there an additional charge? Are there some different types of youth activities so the kids don't have to do the same thing day after day when you work out?

Check the Yellow Pages for a complete listing of health and fitness clubs. Here are a few recommendations to get you started. Daily rates at the following places usually are less than $10.

Isthmus

Madison Athletic Club
44 E. Mifflin St., Madison
• **(608) 256-5656**

If you're looking for individually designed and supervised exercise programs, state-of-the-art fitness equipment and free weights, then the Madison Athletic Club may be the place for you. Services include fitness and body-composition evaluations, tanning and personal trainers.

The club has a $200 initiation fee and costs $40 a month for a one-year membership. Short-term passes are available. The club opens 6 AM weekdays and 8 AM weekends.

East Side

Gold's Gym Health Fitness
& Beyond
361 Blettner Blvd., Madison
• **(608) 244-4653**

Madison's newest fitness center is the 21,000-square-foot Gold's Gym. It has an entire floor devoted to cardio-exercise, the only computerized circuit training in the city, weight training, private saunas, nutrition programs, massage and free day care. Specialty courses such as cardio-karate and t'ai chi are added regularly. The first Gold's Gym, in Venice, California, was a haven for muscle men, but there are now 550 gyms for regular mortals in the United States, all with full reciprocity. The rates are $29 to $47 per month for unlimited access to the facilities.

West Side

Princeton Club
6680 Odana Rd., Madison
* **(608) 833-8746**
1726 Eagan Rd., Madison (East)
* **(608) 241-2639**

If you like to do step aerobics at 5:45 AM, then step over to the Princeton Club to check out its extensive list of classes. The Princeton Club recently purchased the Odana Road club and is remodeling it as part of a major expansion. Amenities at both clubs, which are open 24 hours, include aerobics classes for all levels, more fitness equipment — treadmills, bikes, rowing machines, skiers and Stairmasters — than you can shake a towel at. The club also has a 25-yard lap pool and a walking/running track. After a tough day at the office, you can come back to the club to relax in the hydrotherapy whirlpool, steam room or sauna.

Princeton Club members pay no initiation fee. Membership rates are $40 a month for a 12-month contract and $35 a month for a 24-month contract. The rate for additional family members is half-price, and the cost for children is $10 a month.

Outlying Area

Harbor Athletic Club
2529 Allen Blvd., Middleton
* **(608) 831-6500**

Choose from two membership plans at this health club, depending on your fitness goals. The club opens at 5 AM Monday through Saturday and 7 AM Sunday. Services include weight loss and management, aerobics, fitness machines, personal trainers, swimming lessons, child care, racquetball, an indoor track and youth fitness area.

Membership fees are assessed by the number of family members and type of plan, ranging from $35 per month for an individual to $85 a month for a family of four on a two-year plan. The initiation fee for one year is $75.

Prairie Athletic Club
1010 N. Bird St., Sun Prairie
* **(608) 837-4646**

If you're new to Madison's East Side or live in one of the eastern outlying communities, you should probably walk through this fitness club before you sign on at any other. Prairie Athletic Club (PAC) is huge, with more than 110,000 square feet devoted to nearly every type of exercise possible. The club recently opened a new indoor aquatic facility, which includes warm-water therapy and a warm-water family pool, bringing the total number of PAC pools to eight. Members have reciprocal rights with Harbor Athletic Club in Middleton (see previous entry).

PAC has child care and a strong youth program. Kids' activities include organized gym sports, swimming lessons, aerobics, weight training and racquetball.

Membership fees are based on four levels, depending on what services you would like to use. Rates range from $29 a month for an individual and $42 a month for a couple to $49 a month for an individual and $71 a month for a couple, depending on the length of term and membership level. The initiation fee varies from $200 to nothing, depending on the length of contract.

Golf

The snow's barely off the links around here when golfers are already duffing shag balls across brown grass. Course superintendents usually allow golfers on the fairways around April 1. The season continues until mid-October and occasionally runs into November.

Madison has a wide variety of golf courses to challenge beginners, intermediates and experts. The city has also been home to some golf giants: The most famous are Andy North, winner of two U.S. Opens, and Steve Stricker, winner of two major PGA tournaments in 1996.

After you polish up your clubs and before you call for a tee time, you'll likely want to know a little bit more about golfing in Madison. Here's a overview of the city's public-access, 18- and nine-hole courses. Please note that all course yardages listed are from the middle (men's) tees.

Regulation Courses

West Side

University Ridge Golf Course
7120 County Hwy. PD, Madison
• (608) 845-7700

University Ridge is considered Madison's premier public course and has earned accolades from *Golf Digest*. The par 72 layout measures 6825 yards. The front nine meanders over lush greenlands, while the back nine is carved out of dense Wisconsin woodland. The Robert Trent Jones II course has 80 sand traps and two water hazards. No. 10 is considered the most challenging. The 456-yard, par 4 hole is tree-lined and requires two solid shots to get on the green guarded by bunkers on the right.

Greens fees for playing the Ridge are $28 for nine holes and $49 for 18. Cart rental is $15 for 18 holes. Club rentals, lessons and golf supplies are available on site. To reserve a tee time, call six days in advance.

University Ridge is near Verona.

East Side

Yahara Hills Municipal Golf Course
Off U.S. Hwy. 12/18, east of I-90, Madison • (608) 838-3126

Yahara Hills Muni is our city's largest course, boasting two 18-hole courses. The west course (par 72, 6841 yards) is wide open and designed for beginner to intermediate players. The east course (par 72, 6968 yards) has narrow fairways suitable for championship-style play. The course is often busy, but you can reserve a tee time up to a week in advance.

It costs $11 to play nine holes or $20 for 18 holes. Cart rentals are $11 for nine holes and $22 for 18.

Lake Windsor Country Club
4628 Golf Rd., Madison
• (608) 846-4713

This non-municipal public course offers 27 holes nestled along the shoreline of Lake Windsor. You can play nine holes (par 36, 2890 yards) for $13 to $15 or 18 holes (par 72, 6228 yards) for $18 to $25. Cart rental is $7 per rider for nine holes or $12 per rider for 18 holes. To reach the course, take Interstate 90/94 westbound to the Windsor Exit and follow signs to Golf Road. Reservations are accepted no more than one week in advance.

Odana Hills Municipal Golf Course
4635 Odana Rd., Madison
• (608) 266-4724

Odana Hills traditionally is one of the busiest golf courses in the state, in part due to its location along Madison's West Beltline. The par 72 layout measures 6486 yards. The wide-open course has something to challenge all levels of golfers.

You can golf 18 holes for $20 or nine holes for $11. Cart rental is $11 for nine holes or $22 for 18 holes. To reserve a time, call up to a week in advance. Reservations are also accepted just one day in advance.

Outlying Area

Door Creek Country Club
4321 Vilas Rd., near Cottage Grove
• (608) 839-5656

Golfers must successfully maneuver 87 traps and 16 water hazards at Door Creek, a par 71, 6408-yard layout. This open course was farmland just a few years ago; now it has lots of small trees. Door Creek has an executive (shorter) nine-hole course and regulation 18-hole course.

You can play nine holes for about $13 and 18 holes for about $23. Cart rental is $5 and $10 per person for nine and 18 holes respectively. To reach Door Creek, follow County Highway BB (Cottage Grove Road) to Vilas Road, turn right and follow the signs.

Foxboro Golf Club
1020 County Hwy. MM, south of Oregon
- **(608) 835-7789**

Oregon's Foxboro Golf Club is another relatively new, shorter course (par 71, 6013 yards). This is a good course for beginners and others who want to improve certain skills because the layout is wide open with few hazards.

You can play nine holes for $13 or 18 holes for $23. Cart rental is $12 or $20 respectively. Reservations are requested one week in advance, but even if you haven't reserved a time, call to see if you can walk on. To reach Foxboro, take Park Street south from the Beltline to the second Oregon exit (about 8 miles).

The Meadows of Sixmile Creek
Wis. Hwy. 113, north of downtown Waunakee • (608) 849-9000

The Meadows of Sixmile Creek opened in 1997 in the Madison area. Designed by Ken Killian, the 18-hole links course features bentgrass tees, greens and fairways. While the layout will remain fairly open until young trees mature, it's designed with a lot of mounds, very undulating, large greens and plenty of hazards. Nine ponds come into play on 11 holes including the par 3 No. 14, which is surrounded on three sides by water. This par 72 course measures 6469 yards.

Tee times are required and can be made by the general public up to a week in advance. Cost for 18 holes is $26 weekdays and $34 on weekends. A cart is $12 per person for 18 holes. A special twilight rate ($26 including cart for all the holes you can play) is offered after 4 PM on Friday, Saturday, Sunday and holidays.

Pleasant View Golf Course
4279 Pleasant View Rd., Middleton
- **(608) 831-6266**

Pleasant View has both an executive nine-hole course and a regulation 18-hole course. On the executive course, the longest hole is 180 yards. The 18-hole course is a rolling, par 72, 6436-yard challenge for seasoned golfers.

It costs $13 to $15 to play nine holes or $23 to $26 to play 18 holes. Cart rental is $12 a person for 18 holes. For reservations, call up to a week in advance. To reach the course, take the West Beltline to the Old Sauk Road Exit West, turn left and travel about a mile to Pleasant View Road, turn right and go about another mile to the golf course.

Sun Prairie Country Club
Happy Valley Rd., Sun Prairie
- **(608) 837-6211**

Sun Prairie Country Club features a wide-open, par 72 course that measures 6809 yards. It's one of the longest courses in the area and has some of the area's largest greens, giving golfers the benefit of larger targets and greater opportunities for breathtaking, beautiful long putts.

Greens fees are $13 for nine holes or $20 for 18. Cart rental is $12 or $20 respectively. For tee times, call up to one week in advance. Take U.S. Highway 151 north to the American Parkway Exit, take a right on Hoepker Road to County Highway C, take a left on C and go 4 miles to Happy Valley Road; follow the signs.

Tumbledown Trails Golf Course
7701 W. Mineral Point Rd., Middleton
- **(608) 833-2301**

Tumbledown Trails is the Madison area's newest public, 18-hole course. The par 72 layout measures 6501 yards. Tumbledown's front nine has lots of sand. The back nine, on the other hand, features numerous water hazards.

Greens fees are $12 to $13 for nine holes and $20 to $24 for 18 holes. You can rent a cart for $10 for nine holes or $20 for 18. Walk-ons are permitted but sometimes get turned away depending on scheduled reservations; your best bet is to call in advance for a tee time.

Nine-Hole Courses

West Side

George Vitense Golfland
5501W. Beltline Hwy., Madison
- **(608) 271-1411**

George Vitense Golfland offers a nine-hole, par 3 course that is ideal for beginners. Lessons for children are available. Fairways range

Madison's many beaches are favorite places to cool off.

from 67 to 137 yards. All holes are lighted for nighttime play. Hazards include seven bunkers.

It will cost you only $5 to play nine holes or $7.50 to play 18. Pull cart rental is $1.50, and rental clubs are available for $2.75. George Vitense also has a driving range and miniature golf. No need to call ahead — you can golf on a first-come, first-served basis. To find the course, turn south at the Whitney Way Exit.

Glenway Municipal Golf Course
3747 Speedway Rd., Madison
• (608) 266-4737

If you're looking for a short, par 32 course, try Glenway Municipal Golf Course on Madison's near West Side.

You can golf nine holes here for just $10.50. Cart rentals are $8 on weekdays and $11 on weekends. The evenings are always busy, but you may be able to pick up a tee time if you're willing to golf before 5 PM. To reach Glenway from the Beltline, take Midvale Boulevard to Mineral Point Road, then turn right. Mineral Point becomes Speedway Road at the course.

East Side

Monona Municipal Golf Course
111 E. Dean Ave., Madison
• (608) 266-4736

Monona Municipal is just off Monona Drive on Madison's East Side. It's a challenging course because the final three holes are played around duck-filled ponds.

The fee for nine holes is $11. Carts can be rented for $9. You may call up to a week in advance for a tee time.

Outlying Area

Nine Springs Golf Course
2201 Traceway Dr., Fitchburg
• (608) 271-5877

Nine Springs has six par 3 holes and three par 4 holes. This is a good course for those who wish to hone their iron skills.

The cost to play is $6.50, except for youth and senior citizens, who can play for only $3.50 before 4 PM on weekdays. Pull carts are available for $1.50, and you can rent a set of clubs for $3. From the Beltline, take the Fish Hatchery Road Exit south for about 1.5 miles to Traceway Drive, then turn right.

Hiking

Governor Nelson State Park
5140 County Hwy. M, Westport
• (608) 831-3005

More than 4 miles of wildflower-framed hiking trails wind through this state park, with the Indianola Trail (the park's longest) covering 2.4 miles. The hiking trails provide a wilderness "yellow brick road," leading travelers through hardwood forest, oak savannah, restored prairie land and marsh. The unpaved trails vary in difficulty. Hikers will find a scenic overlook of Lake Mendota and a 358-foot panther effigy mound, among other wonders.

Swimming, picnicking, fishing and boating are other popular pastimes at Governor Nelson State Park. Nature programs for children are held every Wednesday in June, July and August, and you can pick up explorer activity books at the park office for children through 6th grade.

A state park admission sticker is required to use the park. For Wisconsin residents, daily passes cost $5; annual stickers, $18. Cars with out-of-state plates pay $7 for a daily pass or $25 for a yearly pass.

Dane County Parks
4318 Robertson Rd., Madison
• (608) 246-3896

Park your car or lock your bike and explore one of Dane County's beautiful parks for a closer look at history, nature and ecology. Here's a sampling of what awaits:

Badger Prairie Park, east of Verona, offers campers access to Military Ridge State Park Trail (see the previous "Bicycling" section) and the National Ice Age Hiking Trail.

Cam-Rock Park, near the intersection of U.S. highways 12 and 18 at County Highway B, is a 300-acre park that serves as a refuge for ducks and geese in the spring and fall. Hikers can travel along the banks of scenic Koshkonong Creek.

Indian Lake Park, one of Dane County's largest, has miles of nature trails, including a trail with an elevated boardwalk that circles the entire lake. Another trail winds its way to a hilltop with a scenic overlook of the valley and an historic chapel.

Lake Farm Park is the site of the Native American Archaeological Trail, a fascinating .5-mile-long, self-guided tour with markers describing history from 10,000 B.C. to 300 A.D.

Horseback Riding

Wisconsin Hoofers
Pleasant View Stables, 1422 Pleasant View Rd., Middleton • (608) 262-1630

Trail rides ($11 for a one-hour trip) and horseback-riding lessons ($15 per lesson with an eight-lesson minimum) are offered through the Wisconsin Hoofers sports club at Pleasant View Stables. Membership is $30 per semester; Hoofers is open to the public.

Ice Skating

You can skate at many of Madison's outdoor parks and lagoons. Vilas, Tenney and Warner parks have large lagoons that are cleared for skating when conditions permit. The lagoon at Vilas is where former local Olympic speed skaters Eric and Beth Heiden often practiced. Even tiny neighborhood parks are flooded and cleared for skating in this ice-crazy city. Call (608) 266-4711 to ask which rinks are open.

Rental skates are available at some facilities (Tenney Park, for example), or you can purchase a pair of secondhand skates for $10 to $20 at a used-equipment shop.

Outdoors

East Side

Tenney Park
Off E. Gorham St. near Fordem Ave., Madison

One of the most popular spots with skaters, Tenney Park in winter includes large ponds on which to cut a figure-8. Rental skates cost about $3 per hour ($1 each additional hour) at the warming hut, which is open until 9 PM.

Warner Park
1511 Northport Dr. (Wis. Hwy. 113), Madison

Warner Park is another cold-weather hotspot for skaters. Beside plenty of skating space on the frozen lagoon, the park includes a warming hut that's open until 9 PM. No skate rentals are available at Warner Park, so bring 'em if you've got 'em.

Indoors

Figure skaters, hockey players and recreational skaters constantly vie for time on Madison's indoor ice. That means open-skate times fluctuate greatly. It's a good idea to call before you leave home to make sure the ice hasn't been rescheduled.

Madison's two indoor rinks are: **Hartmeyer Ice Arena**, 1834 Commercial Avenue, (608) 246-4512; and **Madison Ice Arena**, 725 Forward Drive, (608) 271-1304. For more information about these and other area rinks, check the Kidstuff chapter.

In-Line and Roller Skating

Certain streets, most stores and, for some reason, even the majority of school grounds are off-limits to in-line skaters in metropolitan Madison.

Even with these prohibitions, there is no shortage of frontier for 'bladers to explore. Streets and bike paths around the lakes Mendota, Monona and Wingra continue to draw recreational and hard-core skaters. Then again, if you're truly determined to in-line skate, you can find a path just about anywhere. (Some of our favorite routes are through new developments with those spanking new, smooth streets.)

Rinks

Rink roller skating continues to be popular in Madison, and a relatively new phenomenon in our community — roller hockey — is generating enthusiastic support. (For additional information, also refer to the Kidstuff Chapter.)

West Side

Break Away Sports Center
5964 Executive Dr., Madison
- (608) 288-9600

This sports center is geared up for in-line hockey with two air-conditioned rinks. The center caters to soccer players in the winter and in-line skaters in the summer. Leagues and instruction are available. Individual fees for league play are $65 for an eight-game schedule. No rentals are available on site. On Wednesdays, open skating (no sticks or pucks) is available from 2:30 to 4 PM for $3 per person.

Fast Forward
4649 Verona Rd., Madison
- (608) 271-6222

Fast Forward offers open skating, birthday parties and roller hockey with skaters using traditional skates and in-line models. With its smooth floors, mood lights and happenin' music, this skate center is a hit with old and young alike. Strap on some skates yourself for a trip back in time or watch your children experience some good old skating fun. Roller-hockey teams organize in April and early July. Costs for individuals are $50 for an instructional league (11 and younger) or $65 for recreational (all ages) or competitive leagues (12 and older). Team entries are $550.

East Side

Rollerdrome
1725 Stoughton Rd., Madison
- (608) 244-7646

Admission and skate rental is $4.50 combined on Friday and Saturday nights, 7:30 to 10:30 PM, at this popular East Side skating center. The Rollerdrome is closed Monday, Tuesday and Thursday but rocks weekend afternoons (2:30 to 4:30 PM) and Wednesday nights. In-line skates and traditional skates can be rented on site.

Soccer World Inc.
4510 Helgesen Dr., Madison
- (608) 222-8326

Soccer World turns into "roller-hockey world" in the summer when soccer players tend to move outdoors for their recreation and indoor soccer fields are converted to roller rinks. In-line leagues get going in early April. The cost to participate is about $55 a person. Soccer World also hosts a springtime clinic for in-line skaters.

Skate Rentals

If you've not skated before and think it might be fun, consider renting a pair. Rentals are available from the following outfitters:

Isthmus

Sports Savers
510 State St., Madison • (608) 255-3343

Sports Savers rents in-line skates for $5 an hour, $15 a day or $12 after 5 PM until noon the next day. A $150 deposit is required.

East and West Sides

Play It Again Sports
4526 Monona Dr., Madison (East)
- (608) 222-3210
720 S. Gammon Rd., Madison (West)
- (608) 277-1988

You can rent in-line skates at both Play It Again Sports locations. The cost is $5 an hour, $15 a day or $35 for a weekend. Be prepared to provide a $200 deposit.

Line Dancing

Dry Bean Saloon and Smokehouse
5264 Verona Rd., Madison
- (608) 274-2326

If you want to learn some new steps, check out the line-dancing lessons at the Dry Bean,

---

INSIDERS' TIP

Interested in hang-gliding and para-gliding? Join the UW Hoofer Gliding Club, (608) 262-1630.

on Madison's West Side. Dance instructors take to the floor Tuesday, Wednesday and Thursday nights, beginning at 6:30 PM. Lessons cost just $2 each, and after you learn the moves, you can strut your stuff at the Dry Bean any night of the week. (See our Restaurants and Nightlife chapters for more information about the Dry Bean.)

League Sports

Madison School-Community Recreation
1045 E. Dayton St., Madison
• **(608) 266-6070**

Men's and women's basketball, baseball, softball and volleyball leagues play weeknights during each of the respective seasons. Registration and participation fees cover the cost of officials, facilities, trophies, timekeepers and league administration. Usually teams play in six-team leagues with a 10-game schedule played at facilities throughout Madison. You must be 18 or older to participate in all sports except baseball and softball (16 and older). Special leagues are open to players 35 and older.

Martial Arts

If you want to learn to defend yourself or just want the discipline and fitness of a martial art, you'll find that Madison has a variety of schools available. Here's a short list to get you started.

Isthmus

Aikido of Madison
2219 Atwood Ave., Madison
• **(608) 231-3935**

Instruction in this Japanese art of self-defense is open to men, women and children. Aikido is a defensive rather than offensive martial art, so participants learn to use their opponent's force to take control of a situation. Proficiency is measured with a belt system leading up to Black Belt. If you want to check it out, call to find out when you can observe a class. Family and student rates are available.

West Side

Karate America
330 Westgate Mall, Madison
• **(608) 273-4111**

Karate America has six schools in the Madison area offering instruction to adults and children. Karate America teaches a tae-kwon-do-based system of ancient blocks, strikes and stances. Students learn skills associated with improving balance, coordination, body control and mental discipline. Call for information about current introductory offers. Karate-instruction costs vary depending on the frequency of lessons.

Outlying Area

Ring's All-American Karate
116 Owen Rd., Monona • (608) 221-9704
536 Southing Grange, Cottage Grove
• **(608) 839-3605**

With schools in Monona and Cottage Grove, Ring's Karate currently has an enrollment of 200 students from preschool age through adult. Ring's teachers help students develop martial-arts skills, self-discipline and self-esteem. The school has a reputation for providing students with positive, fun and interesting learning experiences. Introductory programs begin at $14.95 and include a free uniform. Ring's has after-school child-care programs (they provide transportation from schools), and the martial arts school offers full-day karate camps during school breaks. Evening aerobics classes are available for adults.

Miniature Golf

Vitense Golfland
5501 W. Beltline Hwy., Madison
• **(608) 271-1411**

Test your mettle with mini-golf on one of Vitense's two 18-hole courses. Greens fees are $4.50 for adults and teens and $3.50 for kids 12 and younger. Afterward, you might want to check out the driving range or batting cages. The course is just north of the Whitney Way Exit off the Beltline, on Madison's West Side. It's open 7:30 AM to

11 PM seven days a week during warm weather.

Paintball

Apocalypse Paintball Inc.
W9496 County Hwy. CS, Poynette
• **(608) 635-7324, reservations**
(800) 303-8222

If you want to feel the excitement of battle without the agony of bullets, get ready to go on maneuvers at Apocalypse Paintball in Poynette, about 30 minutes north of Madison. The recreational facility has nine playing fields equipped with such niceties as vehicles, land bridges, forts, ponds, trenches, bunkers and swamps to make them interesting. They also include a three-story tower and a village. Plan your survival strategy, then don protective gear, a semiautomatic, CO_2-powered gun and rounds of paintballs to take on your co-workers, classmates, family or friends.

Field rental is $11 per person per day, and you can rent a semiautomatic paint gun and safety mask for $11 as well. One hundred rounds of paintballs cost $7. Apocalypse Paintball is open March through late November. Reservations are necessary except for Sundays and Wednesdays when walk-ons are invited.

Racquetball

YMCA
711 Cottage Grove Rd., Madison (East)
• **(608) 221-1571**
5515 Medical Cir., Madison (West)
• **(608) 276-6600**

The YMCA offers league play, group and individual lessons and an open-challenge court. To participate in a league, players must declare an experience level and be Y members. The annual fee for an adult is $360; the annual family membership is $516. League fees are $7 to $10.

If it's been a while since you picked up a racquet or if you want to improve your skills, you might want to take a lesson. One-hour lessons are available to the public ($20) and Y members ($10). Group lessons meet for four-week sessions. The cost is $8 for Y members and $16 for the general public. To play in the open-challenge court, you need to be a Y member or purchase a day pass ($8 for an adult, $14 for a family).

Running/Walking

If you like to walk and run for exercise, the only boundaries are your endurance, schedule and "No Trespassing" signs. Madison has numerous walking paths, and you can find joggers and walkers in any park and on just about any sidewalk in the city. If you want to view some new scenery while you walk — maybe even see some wildlife — check out a state park or the UW Arboretum (see the next entry as well as our Attractions and Kidstuff chapters).

University of Wisconsin Arboretum
McKay Visitor Center, 1207 Seminole Hwy., Madison • **(608) 263-7888**

The UW Arboretum is open from 7 AM to 10 PM daily and is considered a haven for joggers, walkers, bicyclists and cross-country skiers. Stop in at the McKay Center to pick up a map and more information about the Arboretum. Special tours are held throughout the year. Try the "Searching for Spring" tour, a night walk to listen for owls, or one of the numerous early morning walks. The Arboretum has more than 20 miles of trails and fire lanes for walkers to use. Bikes must stay on paved drives; in-line skates are not permitted.

Movin' Shoes
604 S. Park St., Madison
• **(608) 251-0125**

This club organizes both fun runs and track events. Coaching is available. Call for information about membership and/or planned events.

Sailing and Sailboarding

If you want to learn how to make the wind work its power for you, consider taking lessons in sailing, sailboarding and a number of other watersports through **UW Memorial Union**, 800 Langdon Street, (608) 262-3156, or **UW Hoofers**, same as previous address,

(608) 265-4663. Anyone is welcome to join UW Hoofers, the most extensive outfitter in Madison. Equipment rental is available at the Union, (608) 262-7351, for members of the sailing club — an annual membership costs about $160 a year.

Sailing and sailboarding are popular activities on lakes Mendota, Monona and Wingra.

Skiing

Cross-Country Skiing

Cross-country skiing enthusiasts love Madison's more than 30 kilometers of ski trails. Hiking trails in Madison-area parks are transformed into cross-country trails in winter.

You can find trails for all levels at the following places:

Cherokee
5002 School Rd., Madison

Cherokee has two Nordic trails measuring 3.6 kilometers. The trails are set in the picturesque Cherokee Marsh, which mean there is plenty of wildlife to see as you ski through the area.

Elver Park
1301 S. Gammon Rd., Madison

Three trails representing three ability levels cover 8 kilometer. This is one of Madison's most well-used parks throughout the year. In winter, you can send the children down the sledding hill while you take on one of the beautiful trails.

Monona Golf Course
111 E. Dean St., Madison

Beginning skiers will find an easy 3.6-kilometer trail at Monona Golf Course. This course is surrounded by beautiful woods, and a historic landmark house is a special feature.

Odana Golf Course
4635 Odana Rd., Madison

Odana features nice beginner trails. It's hard to believe that this pretty golf course, with its ponds and wildlife, shares a name with Odana Road, which is known for its traffic congestion. If so inclined, you could ski to several West Side shopping malls within a few minutes.

Olin-Turville Park
1155 E. Lakeside St., Madison

Two courses — one easy, one moderate — cover a total of 2.1 kilometers. This park is one of Madison's oldest and most beautiful, with its setting on Lake Monona and a splendid view of Lake Monona, the Monona Terrace Convention Center and the Capitol. The park itself is lit up with holiday lights throughout much of the winter.

Owen Conservatory
6021 Old Sauk Rd., Madison

Skiers will find one intermediate, 2.6-kilometer trail at the conservatory. The densely wooded area makes it possible to block out any thoughts of city life during most of the time you spend on this trail.

Warner Park
1511 Northport Dr. (Wis. Hwy. 113), Madison

Warner Park offers cross-country skiers an easy, 4-kilometer trail. This park is one of the city's biggest and most geographically interesting, with woods, lagoons and hills. Its a favorite spot for skiers who like to birdwatch.

University of Wisconsin Arboretum
McKay Visitor Center, 1207 Seminole Hwy., Madison • (608) 263-7888

When the snow flies, avid cross-country skiers head to the UW Arboretum. Open from 7 AM to 10 PM daily, the Arboretum allows skiing on certain footpaths and service roads during the winter. You can pick up a map at the McKay Center, open weekdays from 9:30 AM to 4 PM and weekends from 12:30 to 4 PM.

Downhill Skiing

For downhill skiing, head north to Devil's Head (40 minutes north in Merrimac) or Cascade Mountain (30 minutes north of interstates 90 and 94), or cruise over to Mount Horeb's Tyrol Basin. It's safe to say that, in Wisconsin, the farther north you travel, the better the skiing.

Cascade Mountain
Off I-90/94 Exit 106, Portage
• **(608) 742-5588, (800) 992-2SKI**

Cascade features 21 runs, the longest of which is a mile. This ski hill is a particularly popular destination for student ski trips. Cascade Mountain is about a 45-minute drive from Madison. This ski hill is a particularly popular destination for student ski trips and is known for its big moguls and narrow runs. It has a powerful snowmaking system that creates a blizzard nearly every night. There are lifts but no overnight accommodations. Food is available in a casual restaurant. Cascade Mountain is about a 45-minute interstate drive from Madison.

Devil's Head Resort
Off I-90/94, Merrimac
• **(608) 493-2251, (800) 472-6670**

Devil's Head offers 22 runs and a vertical drop of 500 feet. Of the ski hills close to Madison, it has the most and the longest runs with lifts. You can stay overnight in its attractive resort and convention center. The resort is a straight shot north from Madison (about a 35-minute drive on westbound I-90/94).

Tyrol Basin
Bohn Rd., Mount Horeb
• **(608) 437-4135**

This is the Madison area's best snowboard hill with a half-pipe. Tyrol is nestled in scenic hills and has a lovely chalet with a cafeteria-style restaurant, but no overnight lodging is available. You'll find 11 runs, chairlifts and a rope tow on a very gentle bunny hill.

To reach the hill from Madison, take U.S. Highway 18/151 north to County Highway E and turn right, then proceed to County Highway JG (near Mount Horeb); turn left onto Bohn Road.

Skydiving

Seven Hills Skydivers
7530 Wis. Hwy. 73, Marshall
• **(608) 244-5252**

If you've always wondered how it would feel to jump out of an airplane, Seven Hills Skydivers can train you to jump in less than a day. You must be at least 18 years old and weigh less than 230 pounds to jump. First-jump packages and tandem jumps cost $150.

Soccer

Soccer World Inc.
4510 Helgesen Dr., Madison
• **(608) 222-8326**

This indoor facility on the East Side offers adult and youth soccer leagues in the spring, fall and winter. Twelve-member teams pay fees between $325 and $585, depending on skill level and type of play. Soccer instruction for adults and children costs from $30 to $45, depending on session length. If you just want to join a pickup game, drop by Friday afternoons and play from 3 to 5 PM for $5.

YMCA
711 Cottage Grove Rd., Madison (East)
• **(608) 221-1571**
5515 Medical Cir., Madison (West)
• **(608) 276-6600**

Come to the YMCA for youth soccer leagues and micro soccer (three-on-three games with no goalie). Recreational and traveling leagues cost $20 for Y members and $30 for the general public. Regular leagues for players ages 4 to 9 focus on skill building and teamwork; fees are $18 for members and $40 for nonmembers.

Swimming

Here is a roundup of places where you can make a splash, indoors or out. We also include information on swim clubs and private pools that have modest membership fees. Swimming is also available at area health clubs, some of which are described in this chapter's "Fitness Training" section. (For spots that are especially suitable for children, see our Kidstuff chapter.)

Public Beaches

Madison has 13 free public beaches staffed by lifeguards during warm weather: Warner, east shore of Lake Mendota; Tenney, southeast shore of Lake Mendota; Vilas, north shore of Lake Wingra; Olin-Turville, southwest shore of lake Monona; Ester, Waunona Bay; B.B. Clarke and Hudson, north shore of Lake Monona; Olbrich, northeast shore of Lake Monona; James Madison, south shore of Lake Mendota; Bernie's, south shore of Monona bay; Brittingham, north shore of Monona Bay; Marshall, far west shore of Lake Mendota; and Spring Harbor, southwest shore of Lake Mendota. B.B. Clarke, Olbrich, Tenney, and Vilas are open 10 AM to 8:30 PM; all other beaches are open noon to 6 PM. Certain beaches occasionally may close because of bacterial levels. For information call (608) 266-4711. Occasionally, beaches close due to high bacterial levels; watch for signs.

You'll also find beach swimming near Oregon at Goodland Park on the west shore of Lake Waubesa; at Mendota Park in Middleton off Highway M; and at Fireman's Park in Verona at 195 Paoli Street (Wis. Highway 69).

Outdoor Pools

Madison currently has no public outdoor swimming pools. There are, however, a number of private pools. Check the Yellow Pages for information. For a nice daytrip to a pool, consider visiting one of the following.

Monona Pool
1011 Nichols Rd., Monona
- **(608) 222-3098**

Open to Monona residents and nonresidents, this outdoor pool offers afternoon and evening swim sessions. Residents pay $1.50 per day or $30 for an annual pass. Nonresidents 5 and older pay $3 per visit or $60 for a summer pass. Water aerobics, swimming lessons and swim teams also are offered; contact the Monona City Hall, (608) 222-2525, for details.

Sun Prairie Aquatic Center
920 Linnerud Dr., Sun Prairie
- **(608) 837-7433**

Brave the water slide, try out a new dive or splash off the summer heat in the Sun Prairie pool, one of the Madison area's finest summer recreation centers. The pool offers daily afternoon and evening sessions and may be rented for special events. The pool starts at zero-depth and gets progressively deeper, so even toddlers can enjoy water exploration. An adjoining sand area with plenty of toys makes an afternoon at the pool even more enjoyable. Daily fees are $3.50 for nonresident adults and $2.50 for nonresidents 17 and younger. Get there early if you want a lounge chair.

Indoor Pools

Madison School-Community Recreation
1045 E. Dayton St., Madison
- **(608) 266-6077**

Working through the Madison school district, this program offers inexpensive swimming lessons ($17 per session) at points across the city. Discount passes also may be purchased for open swims.

West Side

SwimWest Family Fitness Center
1001 Deming Way, Madison
- **(608) 831-6829**

Swimwest offers a new facility with a pool and fitness room for a family or individuals who love the water. You can purchase a family membership for $300 without water aerobics classes or $375 with water aerobics classes. Or, you can try out the facility with a fitness pass at a single-person rate of $45 for 12 visits or $60 for a 12-visit family pass. The passes do not have expiration dates. Swimwest has earned an excellent reputation for swimming instruction. Classes are small, usually with only four students per instructor, and cost $8.50 per lesson. During warm weather, you can choose between indoor or outdoor lessons.

East Side

Madison Area Technical College
3550 Anderson St., Madison
- **(608) 246-6093**

Warm water and super-clean facilities make this a great place to bring the kids to swim or enjoy some good clean adult fun. The pool has open-swim hours on Tuesday, Thursday and Friday evenings and from noon to 2 PM

Saturdays. You must be 16 years old to swim without an accompanying adult. The fee is $4 for adults and $1 each for children.

YMCA
711 Cottage Grove Rd., Madison (East)
- **(608) 221-1571**

5515 Medical Cir., Madison (West)
- **(608) 276-6600**

To swim you will need to join the Y or purchase a day pass for a nominal fee. Both Madison YMCAs offer a variety of swimming lessons and "aquacise" programs and have family swim times.

Swim Clubs

Youth competitive swimming is a big sport in Madison. The following clubs draw kids from all over the Madison area. If you think you might be interested in joining a swim club, call a private or public pool or one of these swim clubs:

Badger Dolphins Swim Club
- **(608) 276-SWIM**

This club focuses on swimmers from 7 years old through high school age. Swimmers practice on weeknights at local high schools. Fees vary and are paid by semester.

Mad-Town Aquatics Swim Team
- **(608) 828-1695**

Mad-Town Aquatics is a competitive swim team for aquaphiles ages 6 to 18, with year-round training and competition. Fees are tied to age.

Madison Aquatic Club
- **(608) 257-4823**

This team offers competitive swimming for kids ages 6 to 18. Practices are held year round at Edgewood High School and supplemented in the summer with practice at the Shorewood pool. Fees vary depending on age, ability level and the swimmer's goals. The club also offers a stroke clinic for young swimmers.

UW Clinic Research Park Aquatic Center
621 Science Dr., Madison
- **(608) 263-7936**

The center offers adult swim lessons (private, semiprivate or group), lap swimming (you must sign up for one of five specific time slots), deep water running and aqua aerobics classes. Also available are arthritis, fibromyalgia and ai chi (water t'ai chi) programs in its warm water pool. Fees vary.

Other Pools

Madison, which has three country clubs with access to pools, also has a number of private pools that offer membership to anyone for fees in the $400-per-summer range, which make them attractive to many middle-income families:

High Point Swim Club
901 N. High Point Rd., Madison
- **(608) 831-8486**

There are lap, diving and children's pools at this club. Lessons in water ballet, swimming and diving are available. The club has swimming and diving teams. The complex also has two tennis courts, a basketball area and a sand volleyball court.

Parkcrest Swim and Tennis Club
1 N. Yellowstone Dr., Madison
- **(608) 233-3573**

There are lap, diving and children's pools here. Lessons in water ballet, swimming and diving are available. The club has swimming and diving teams. Other recreation is available, too, with two tennis courts, a basketball area and a sand volleyball court.

INSIDERS' TIP

The Bally Total Fitness U.S. Triathlon Series came to Madison in July 1997, and its sponsors hope to make it a regular event. The triathlon included a swim in Lake Wingra, a bike race through the UW Arboretum and a run through Vilas Park and the Arboretum.

Ridgewood Pool
6022 Hammersley Rd., Madison
- membership (608) 271-4614,
pool (608) 271-9283

This is one of the city's older private pools, established in 1958. It's now a well-maintained complex on landscaped grounds in the Orchard Ridge neighborhood. The complex has four pools including a diving well and a baby pool. Swimming, diving and water ballet lessons are available. Evening swim lessons are being offered for the first time since the pool opened, to help working families. There are active swim and dive teams, a water ballet show and water aerobics. Special events include ice cream socials and carnivals.

West Side Swim Club
702 S. Whitney Way, Madison
- (608) 273-1955

There are two pools here: an L-shaped pool with a diving well at the bottom and a children's pool. There is a snack shack where members can buy such things as hot dogs and chips. A grill is provided, so members can bring their own meat to cook. The club has swimming and diving teams and offers lessons in swimming, diving and water ballet.

Tennis

Campus

Neilsen Tennis Stadium
1000 Highland Ave., Madison
- (608) 262-0410

Players can choose from 12 indoor and six outdoor courts at this facility — considered one of the Midwest's best. Fees are based on a tiered system, giving preference to UW students and faculty, but the public may also use courts. Indoor rates for UW students are $2.50 for singles and $1.25 per person for doubles per tennis "hour" (75 minutes). High school students, non-UW college students and UW faculty, staff and their spouses pay a rate of $6 per hour for singles and $3 per person for doubles. For the general public, the indoor rate is $14 an hour for singles and $7 per person for doubles. Outdoor court rates range from less than a $1 per hour to $5, depending on your status.

West Side

John Powless Tennis Center
6122 Schroeder Rd., Madison
- (608) 274-6262

Whether you are looking for indoor, outdoor, hard or clay courts, you can find them here. If your skills aren't quite what you'd like them to be, the tennis center offers a variety of lessons. Eight-week group sessions for adults and juniors are offered in the fall, winter and spring.

Indoor court rentals start at $27 a tennis hour (75 minutes). You may use the ball machine for $4 an hour. If you join the club, membership dues are paid monthly. Rates are $92 per month for individuals, $162 for couples, $216 for families with children younger than 21 and $65 for juniors and senior citizens. The club has a initiation fee of $100 for singles and $150 for couples and families.

Ultimate Frisbee

Madison Ultimate Frisbee Association
- (800) GET-UPAH

In 1993, the Madison Ultimate Frisbee Association brought the World Championships to town, drawing teams from 100 countries. Ultimate continues to draw disc fanatics to the Mad City, which serves as the site of about six tournaments a year. The Madison Ultimate Frisbee summer league has grown to approximately 400 players, with 14 to 20 participants on each team. Most teams play twice a week during the summer season.

Ultimate Frisbee stresses sportsmanship and fair play. Players are responsible for their own foul and line calls and resolving their own disputes.

Cost per league member is $15, including a T-shirt and disc.

Volleyball

Several area taverns host sand-volleyball league play. Teams are made up of employees from area businesses, but singles usually have no trouble finding a team on which to play. Team fees for a 13-week session run about $135.

To get started, contact the following: **Pooley's**, 5441 High Crossing Boulevard, Madison, (608) 242-1888; **Alt'n Bach's Town Tap**, 2602 Whalen Lane, Madison, (608) 271-9955; **The Whitehouse Tavern**, County Highway I, Waunakee, (608) 249-1659; **Club Tavern**, 1915 Branch Street, Middleton, (608) 836-3773; **Curveball Sports Bar & Grill**, 2611 Branch Street, Middleton, (608) 831-0436; and **Black Bear Inn**, 320 Cottage Grove Road, Cottage Grove, (608) 839-5222.

Additional options include the following:

Madison School-Community Recreation
1045 E. Dayton St., Madison
- (608) 266-6077

Co-ed, men's and women's volleyball at three skill levels is played weeknights at school gymnasiums around the city. Teams are chosen each night from the pool of players in attendance. There is a $35 fee for a 14-week session.

East and West Sides

YMCA
711 Cottage Grove Rd., Madison (East)
- (608) 221-1571
5515 Medical Cir., Madison (West)
- (608) 276-6600

Adult-league sand-volleyball teams play for seven weeks each spring and summer. Levels include beginner and intermediate. Team registration fees range from $75 to $90, depending on the number of Y members on your team.

Water Aerobics

All area health clubs with pools offer water aerobics to members. If you're not a club member, don't despair; there are other options.

YMCA
711 Cottage Grove Rd., Madison (East)
- (608) 221-1571
5515 Medical Cir., Madison (West)
- (608) 276-6600

Water-aerobics classes are free to Y members, but the public can splash, too, for a fee. Classes are held in the mornings and evenings for all levels. Fees range from $25 to $58. Water aerobics are a particularly nice way for people who haven't exercised for a while to start getting more active. Before you take any exercise class, check with your doctor.

Wheelchair Basketball

Madison School-Community Recreation
1045 E. Dayton St., Madison
- (608) 266-6077

Who says you have to run to be good at basketball? Not these Madison kids. Youth ages 8 to 17 meet once a week for wheelchair-basketball instruction and competition. MSCR works with Madison Wheelchair Athletics Inc. (MWAI) on this volunteer-run program.

ALWAYS
in tune

Let **Rhythm** entertain you every Thursday in The Capital Times and Wisconsin State Journal. It's Madison's most complete entertainment guide.

Daytrips

Madison's appeal is only enhanced by the small, outlying villages and towns that imbue an overpowering sense of historic tradition, ethnic heritage and rural pride into South-Central Wisconsin. From the towering rocky cliffs of Devil's Lake to the emerald-green Wisconsin River valleys, the countryside is awash in scenic beauty and down-home hospitality.

Whether you're a new resident or here simply for a short visit, take some time out to relax and go "daytripping" from Madison. We've selected four options with destinations that are easy to get to and within a 50-mile radius of the Capital City. But, of course, there are many others, including Wisconsin Dells and surrounding communities. They are covered in a separate chapter.

Note that for listed telephone numbers with a 608 area code, you'll first have to dial 1 or 0 plus the area code when calling from Madison. (Two exceptions are Cambridge and Mount Horeb.)

Trip 1: Cambridge, Fort Atkinson and Janesville

If You Like Quaint, Visit Cambridge

A 20-mile drive east of Madison on U.S. Highway 12/18 will take you into the center of Cambridge, a thriving little shopping/artisan community noted for its many quaint storefronts in restored turn-of-the-century brick buildings.

Main Street, especially, is a Victorian treasure. Many old buildings, including the grist mill and wagon factory, languished for a number of years until the late '70s, when a large bequest from the late A.R. Amundson and his wife, Irene, enabled the Cambridge Foundation to embark on a village-wide revitalization program. Today, these same buildings are prime retail space for stores selling antiques, gourmet food items, specialty clothing, art and, especially, pottery.

Jim Rowe helped to turn Cambridge into the salt-glazed stoneware capital of the world when he opened up shop in 1975 as a one-man operation. Today, Rowe Pottery employes about 130 people, and its two-story showroom, **Rowe Pottery Works**, has become a showpiece for home decorative items as well as stoneware. (Check the back room for greatly reduced seconds.) Rowe Pottery also has a retail store on Monroe Street in Madison. For more artisan-quality, handcrafted pottery and ceramic pieces, check out **Wells Clay Works**, **Cambridge Woodfired Pottery** and **Montage**.

Cambridge is the only place we know of in South-Central Wisconsin that annually hosts a pottery festival. Held during a Saturday and Sunday in mid-June at West Side Park, the festival includes a pottery show and sale as well as a competition that draws potters from across the country.

The Country Inn & Pub, 206 W. Main Street, with its old-fashioned, home-cooked meals, is a destination unto itself in this village of 1,000 people (see the listing under "American" dining in the Restaurants chapter). For a piece of pie or cup of soup, we also heartily endorse **Sherry J's Curve Cafe**, a small-town eatery on U.S. Highway 18, just before you cross the Koshkonong Creek into Cambridge.

Before or after eating, make sure you have enough time to explore the many interesting shops along or just off Main Street. Some of our favorites include **The Pantry**, filled with many Wisconsin food products; **Sienna River Gallery**, showcasing rustic carvings, weavings and other woodsy decorations;

Sugar Bakers, a shop of interesting, Victorian-inspired gifts and clothing in the Wagonfactory Mercantile, built in 1892 as a manufacturer of farm wagons and buggies; Music and Memories, a wonderful place filled with hundreds of music boxes, some of which are truly priceless; **Glorious Woman** and **Suzen Sez**, two upscale women's clothing stores that also have retail outlets in Madison (see the Shopping chapter).

Nearby on Lake Ripley is the **Eva Ruxton's Shop**, a gift shop filled with handcrafted items. In a big white frame house surrounded by a picket fence, the store was established in the mid-60s by Eva and now is operated by her daughter-in-law, Sally Dale. It's open April through December. The **Cambridge Antique Mall**, representing about 25 dealers and within an easy walk of Main Street, is in a restored, 100-year-old former Lutheran church.

Celebrating its 150th anniversary as a village in 1997, Cambridge has long been a popular summer retreat for Chicagoans because of its proximity to spring-fed **Lake Ripley**. Ole Evinrude, inventor of the outboard motor, was fond of vacationing here, as was Arthur Davidson. (Guess which motorcycle he helped launch with his brother William, sister Elizabeth and Mr. Harley?) Children's author Edward Edson Lee, better known by his pen name of Leo Edward, based many characters and plots for several series of children's books he wrote in the '20s and '30s on his experiences and friendships in Cambridge.

Canoeing is popular on **Koshkonong Creek**, running directly through Cambridge, and just a few miles north is access to the **Glacial Drumlin Bike Trail** (see the "Bicycling" section of our Parks and Recreation chapter), which runs 47.2 miles from Waukesha to Cottage Grove following the old railroad bed of the Chicago & Northwestern.

For more information about the Cambridge area, call the **Cambridge Chamber of Commerce** at (608) 423-3780. In addition to the Pottery Festival, mark the first weekend of December on your calendar. That's Cambridge's **Country Christmas** — a scene that could come right out of Charles Dickens' *A Christmas Carol* — complete with strolling carolers, roasted chestnuts and a madrigal dinner served at the Cambridge Inn & Pub.

A Variety of Pleasures in Fort Atkinson

Traveling about 10 miles southeast on U.S. Highway 12/18 will bring you into Fort Atkinson, home of the **Hoard Museum and Dairy Shrine** (named after former Wisconsin governor, W.D. Hoard) and **Fireside Restaurant & Playhouse**.

On U.S. 12, the Hoard offers a wide variety of exhibits including an overview of the Black Hawk War, early decorative arts, an ornithology display of 400 specimens, 19th-century tools and Native American artifacts. A new exhibit room has items relating to Abraham Lincoln and the Civil War. The museum is housed in the 1841 **Dwight Foster House**, the restored pioneer home of Fort Atkinson's founder and the oldest dwelling in town.

The adjacent Dairy Shrine will tell you everything you ever wanted to know about dairy farming in America, serving as an appropriate salute to the Dairy State.

The museum's summer hours (June through August) are 9:30 AM to 4:30 PM Tuesday through Saturday and 1 to 5 PM Sunday. The rest of the time, the complex is open 9:30 AM to 3:30 PM Tuesday through Saturday and 1 to 5 PM the first Sunday of each month. There is no admission charge. For information, call (920) 563-7769

The Fireside is more than a dinner theater. It's a Wisconsin tradition dating back more than 30 years. Theater, encompassing mostly well-known Broadway shows, is performed in-the-round, preceded by dinner in a very glamorous setting highlighted by a rushing stream and fountains. The 1-acre complex also includes five shops. Prices for dinner/theater range from about $45 to $60 per person, depending upon the day of the week. Call (800) 433-9505 for reservations and in-

SPRING GREEN AREA
It's All Happening Here

Free comprehensive guide:
800-588-2042
Box 142, Spring Green, WI 53588
www.execpc.com/~spring/

- the remarkable House on the Rock
- Frank Lloyd Wright's Home: Taliesin
- classics at American Players Theatre
- quiet beauty on the Wisconsin River
- recreation: Golf, Bike & Canoe
- full range of Lodging & Dining
- distinctive Shops & Galleries
- June Art Fair Weekend
- and, within an hour's drive to many other Major Attractions

---

formation. The theater is on the south side of Fort Atkinson on Wis. Highway 26.

For more information about Fort Atkinson, contact the **Chamber of Commerce**, (920) 563-3210.

History and Autos: Top Draws in Janesville

From Fort Atkinson, drive 25 minutes south on Wis. Highway 26 to Janesville, site of many historic buildings, including the 26-room, Italianate-style William Tallman House in which Abraham Lincoln stayed for two nights in 1859. It's the only private residence in Wisconsin still standing that can boast of that honor.

Constructed between 1855 and 1857, the **Lincoln-Tallman House**, 440 N. Jackson Street, off Wis. Highway 26, had many amenities for its day, including large walk-in closets, central heating and an indoor privy. It was built by William Morrison Tallman, an attorney who moved to Southern Wisconsin from New York with his wife, Emeline, a woman who knew exactly what kind of home she wanted.

Offering a regal glimpse of upper-class life during the mid-1880s, the Lincoln-Tallman House — all 26 rooms on five levels, from basement to cupola — is open for tours on weekends year round and every day June through September from 9 AM to 4 PM. The home is especially appealing when dressed up in old-fashioned Victorian splendor for the winter holidays, from mid-November through December. More than 75 percent of the home's furnishings are original. Admission is $5 for adults, $4.50 for seniors and $2.50 for students, kindergarten through 12th grade. Call (608) 756-4509 for information.

Visitors can also tour the **General Motors** assembly plant in Janesville, the largest GM plant under one roof in the country. It's been operating since 1920. Free tours ordinarily take place Monday through Thursday at 9:30 AM and 1 PM, although it's wise to call ahead, (608) 756-7681. Reservations are needed for groups of 10 or more.

No matter the season, a beautiful place to stroll is **Rotary Gardens**, featuring nine gardens, a wildlife sanctuary and visitor center. Open every day of the week during daylight hours, the 15-acre site is at 1455 Palmer Drive off Wis. Highway 11. Call (608) 752-3885 for information. Admission is free, although donations are encouraged.

In recent years, Janesville has become known throughout the world as the home of **Miracle, the white buffalo**, born August 24, 1994, on the 45-acre farm owned by Dave, Val and Corey Heider. The first white buffalo calf known to be born since 1933, Miracle represents a sacred symbol of unity and prosperity to Native Americans. While now more cinnamon-colored than white, and a mother herself (having had her first calf in the spring of '98), Miracle continues to attract many visitors who are welcome to view the animal most days from 10 AM to 5 PM at the farm. But it's wise to call ahead, (608) 752-2224, for directions and any changes in the visitation schedule.

For more information about the Janesville area, call the **Janesville Convention & Visitors Bureau**, (800) 48 PARKS.

Bus Tours

If you're here for a visit but don't have access to a car, you can still enjoy many outlying attractions by hopping a Gray Line Madison bus. Day tours are available from Madison to the House on the Rock, Wisconsin Dells and Baraboo and Taliesin in Spring Green. Buses will pick up passengers from the Gray Line office, 3 S. Pinckney Street, or from any major hotel in Madison. Visitors can also sign up for a three-hour sightseeing tour showcasing the best of what Madison has to offer — sweeping vistas of both lakes, the UW-Madison campus, historic Mansion Hill and the Governor's Mansion. With the recent opening of the Frank Lloyd Wright-inspired Monona Terrace Convention Center, the bus company has recently added a drive-by tour of homes and buildings in Madison designed by the celebrated architect. This trip can be combined with one to Taliesin, Wright's estate. Coming to town with a group? Gray Line will tailor a sightseeing package to suit special interests and needs. Also, inquire about sightseeing/hotel packages. Call **(608) 257-8983** in Madison or **(800) 256-6820**.

Trip 2: Spring Green and Dodgeville

Area Overview

The opening of the Frank Lloyd Wright-influenced Monona Terrace Convention Center in Madison is focusing even more attention on **Taliesin**, Wright's 600-acre, hilly estate in Spring Green where he lived and worked for much of his life — and which remains the summer home of Taliesin Architects and the Frank Lloyd Wright School of Architecture. Tours of the individual buildings are fascinating, even if you're not particularly a fan of Wright.

But the Spring Green/Dodgeville area offers a lot more to the daytripper, both in unique tourist attractions, like the **House on the Rock**, and natural beauty, such as **Tower Hill State Park**, on the edge of the Wisconsin River. The fact that Spring Green is now home to a first-class resort, **The Springs**, with its 18-hole championship golf course, is making this area even more desirable.

Spring Green

The Arty Side of Spring Green

About a 45-minute drive from Madison via U.S. Highway 14 through Cross Plains, Black Earth (home of the **Shoe Box**, with one of the largest selection of shoes in the entire Midwest) and Mazomanie (site of the **Old Feed Mill**; see the entry in our Restaurants chapter), Spring Green is a small village of about 1,400 people. Still, you can see the influence of Wright in many of the homes and commercial buildings, most notably the round **M&I Bank** building on Jefferson Street, the main street through town.

The **Old Post House** pays homage to Wright with an outdoor garden and Flying Dutchman Bar designed by W. Wesley Peters, Wright's stepson-in-law and protege, who is also responsible for the aforementioned bank building. One of the oldest restaurants in the state, dating back to the Civil War days, the Old Post House serves hearty food for lunch and dinner.

Spring Green has developed a creative aura, partly because of Wright, partly because of the existence of **American Players Theatre** nearby (see the subsequent discussion), but also because of two galleries showcasing the work of Wisconsin artists.

The larger and more established of the two is **Jura Silverman Gallery**, 143 S. Washington. Housed in a former Wisconsin cheese

Frank Lloyd Wright's Taliesin home is a popular stop for visitors to Spring Green.

warehouse, the Jura Silverman Gallery showcases an extensive collection of prints, paintings, photography, sculpture, pottery, jewelry, mixed media, art furniture, jewelry, wood carvings and basketry.

Excluding Madison's Art Fair on the Square, the **Spring Green Arts and Crafts Fair** is probably the most anticipated arts and crafts fair in South-Central Wisconsin. Featuring as many as 240 artists, it's traditionally held in the center of town the last weekend of June. This fair attracts many of the same artists as the Madison fair does. Only the crowds are smaller — and sometimes the prices are, too.

More to See and Do

One of the newest attractions in Spring Green is the **American Calliope Center**, on U.S. Highway 14. Owner Bill Griffith now has 10 antique, fully restored calliopes, that were used to play music at tented circuses throughout the first half of the century. The rarest is one with 43 whistles Griffith found in Williamsburg, Virginia, made in 1914. There is no admission to the museum, which is open seven days a week from 10 AM to 8 PM from April through December. The center has a large gift shop to tempt your wallet.

Spring Green proper is within a couple of miles of the **Lower Wisconsin River**, which offers plenty of opportunities for swimming and canoeing. But please be cautious. Always swim with a buddy and know that sandbars can drop off suddenly any time. A summer season doesn't pass without at least one tragic drowning. The river can be treacherous, even for the best swimmers.

For scenic walks and canoeing, a good place to start is **Tower Hill State Park**, one of the state's smallest but most unique parks, with access off County Highway C. A short (but nearly vertical!) hike will take you to the reconstructed shot tower used in the manufacturing of lead shot during the mid-1800s. It's only one of six like it in the United States. Inside the park is a canoe landing into Mill Creek with access to the Wisconsin River. A daily or seasonal state park pass is needed for entry. For more information, call (608) 588-2116. Remember the bug repellant when you visit this park or golf nearby at The Springs. Certain times of year, the mosquitoes can be fierce.

Making the Most of Taliesin

Although raised in Madison, Frank Lloyd Wright spent many a childhood summer living and working for his Uncle James in the Wisconsin River valley near Spring Green. His mother came from a large Welsh family, the Lloyd Joneses, many of whom settled there. So Wright was very much at home in the Wisconsin countryside, where he first contemplated integrating nature with mortar and bricks. He built **Taliesin**, his home, on the side of a hill he could see from his uncle's house and where he loved to romp as a child.

You'll see something here to commemorate every decade of Wright's career: the **Visitor Center** (across Wis. Highway 23 from Taliesin), designed by Wright designed in '53 and used for a number of years as a restaurant; the five buildings on the estate; and the nearby **Unity Chapel** (in which young Wright had a hand), a gathering spot for all the Lloyd Joneses. No other place in the world can make that claim.

Wright spent nearly 50 years working on Taliesin. He never stopped adding to it or changing it until the day he died. Twice the house was seriously damaged by fire. Each time, he started over, determined to make it better than before. Only in recent years have public tours of Wright's private living quarters become available. The furnishings, many of which were designed by Wright, and his impressive collection of Asian art are as intriguing as the house, a vanguard of Prairie-style modern architecture.

Yet, it was at the **Hillside Home School** — designed in 1902 for his two aunts, school teachers both, who opened one of the nation's first co-educational boarding schools — where Wright first broke "the box" of prevailing architecture, making space flow instead of trapping it. It's been said that parents arriving for the first time at the school were hesitant about allowing their children to enter for fear the walls wouldn't hold.

Other buildings Wright designed on the property are the **Romeo and Juliet Windmill Tower** (1896); **Tan-y-deri** (Welsh for "under the oaks") **House** (1907), built for his sister Jane; and **Midway Farm**, one of the most handsome barns in existence (1938).

Ironically, after he died in 1959, Wright was buried in the yard of the Unity Chapel, his grave marked by a natural, rough stone (it's still there) as he likely would have wanted. However, in the mid-'80s, upon the death of his widow, Wright's body was exhumed and cremated with hers by her prior request. (For more background about Wright, see the History chapter.)

All tours of Taliesin begin at the **Frank Lloyd Wright Visitor Center**, at the intersection of Wis. Highway 23 and County Highway C and operated by the Taliesin Preservation Commission. It features a bookstore and gift shop, exhibits and an informal cafe. The visitor center is open from 8:30 AM to 5:30 PM during the Taliesin touring season, May 1 through October 31. Table service at the cafe is offered daily 11 AM to 3 PM and also on weekends for breakfast beginning at 8:30 AM. Carry-outs are available from 9 AM to 5 PM. Tickets for seven different tours can be purchased from the center, although advance reservations are required for the two-hour House Tour, four-hour Estate Tour, Photography Tour and Tea Circle Tour (only June through September). During the latter, visitors can converse with folks working at Taliesin just as Wright would often do at the end of a productive day. For prices and times, call the Visitor Center at (608) 588-7900.

Enjoying the Classics on Balmy Evenings

In the late '70s, four dedicated, talented actors/administrators moved here from the East Coast to fulfill a dream: produce classical theater in an outdoor setting. They bought 110 rolling, wooded acres and, scraping together every last dime they could raise, built a Elizabethan-style wood stage in a natural amphitheater on property 4 miles south of Spring Green near what is now the Wright Visitor Center. Their dream was to produce the works of Shakespeare in a manner and setting true to the playwright's original vision.

Physical amenities have greatly added to theater comfort, although right from the start, **American Players Theatre (APT)** established a sterling reputation for staging renowned works of Shakespeare — in a manner the Bard himself would have approved of, we believe — as well as other classics by such notable playwrights as Moliere, Sheridan and Wilder.

The season runs from mid-June through the beginning of October and usually includes five plays performed in repertory

Norwegian culture thrives in Little Norway.

Tuesday through Sunday, with both matinee and evening shows on Saturday. There is plenty of room to picnic before the show, and gourmet boxed suppers can be ordered in advance through the box office. There is a relatively steep, 10-minute walk up to the theater, but shuttle service is available from the parking lot for those who need it. Tickets range from about $18 to $33. To receive a schedule or purchase tickets, call the box office at (608) 588-2361.

The House on the Rock

Heading south on Wis. Highway 23 through the lush Wyoming Valley, the distance between Spring Green and Dodgeville is about 18 miles — a beautiful drive in any season. Halfway there, you'll happen upon Wisconsin's No. 1 tourist attraction: **The House on the Rock**.

Built as a retreat atop a sandstone, 60-foot-high chimney of rock by Alex Jordan in the early '40s, the 13-room, multilevel house remains the focal point, although the complex has expanded greatly over the years into a museum featuring an odd assortment of things. Among the treasures contained inside is the world's largest carousel, with 269 animals (none of which are horses) and more than 20,000 lights. It's just a shame you can't ride it.

You'll walk your feet off at this attraction, although the best is still at the beginning: The house's glass-enclosed Infinity Room projects out over the valley more than 200 feet, making you feel like you're suspended in air; "The Streets of Yesterday" with its gas-lit Main Street; and "The Music of Yesterday" exhibit with the world's largest collection of automated music machines and instruments. More recent additions include the Transportation Building, which encompasses (among other things) a Burma Shave sign collection.

A reclusive man who lived almost all of his life in a small apartment in Madison, Jordan died in 1989. A year later, new owner Arthur Donaldson added **The Alex Jordan Creative Center** as a tribute to the man who built The House on the Rock. It includes a one-hour informational program that takes you behind the scenes of the huge complex.

Shopping and dining (at a pizza parlor and a small, buffet-style cafe) are available at the facility. The regular season begins March 15 and ends with the last weekend in October. Hours are 9 AM to 8 PM, with the last tickets sold at 7 PM. Prices range from $3.50 for children ages 4 to 6 to almost $15 for anyone 13 and older. Call (608) 935-3639 for other details.

From mid-November until early January, there is a special Holiday Tour showcasing one of the largest assortments of Santas you'll ever see in one place.

Make sure you give yourself at least four hours to do justice to this eclectic museum. And at that, you'll probably be cutting it short. Be aware that strollers are not allowed in the building, and both the entry Gate House and House on the Rock do not accommodate wheelchairs.

Plenty to Do in Dodgeville

Continuing south 8 miles on Wis. Highway 23 from The House on the Rock will bring you into Dodgeville (46 miles from Madison), a community of about 4,000 people and county seat of Iowa County. The courthouse, which you can't miss as you come into the downtown area, is the oldest in Wisconsin. It was erected in 1859.

Dodgeville is an eclectic mix of old and new. It's entire downtown business district was listed on the National Register of Historic Places in 1996. But the city is also progressive and modern. It's home to the **Lands' End** clothing and home furnishings mail-order company, which employs up to 7,000 people during the peak holiday season. The company offers free tours and welcomes people to their own visitor center from May through October; call (608) 935-9341.

If you like woodworking and crafts, be aware that **The Walnut Hollow Woodcraft Outlet** has a warehouse-full of overstocks and irregulars at greatly reduced prices. Walnut Hollow is to your right on Wis. 23 as you enter Dodgeville from the north. But before you get there, you'll pass a Dodgeville institution, the **Don Q Inn**, one of the first hotels or motels in Wisconsin to offer fantasy suites, some of which can be toured every Saturday and Sunday at 2:15 PM. You can't miss the place; there's a Boeing C-97 transport airplane parked out front.

Within the past several years, a number of interesting shops and galleries have opened in Dodgeville. Along Iowa Street, the main street in town, don't miss **Thistle Hill Tabletop Company**, a shop filled with interesting and artful items for simple living and entertaining; **Carousel Collectibles & Antiques**, specializing in carousel art and restoration; and **Metropolitan Art**, which is both a modern-art gallery and school. And, of course, there is a **Lands' End** outlet, too. If you get hungry, stop in at **The Short Story Cafe** — in the back of the Short Story bookstore — where lunch is served 11 AM to 2 PM daily.

Dodgeville operates an **Information Center** on Wis. Highway 23 and U.S. Highway 18/151 — between the only two stoplights in Iowa County — from Memorial Day through Labor Day. This is a good place to pick up a "Historic Walking Tour" brochure, which provides many interesting tidbits about the area. The center is open 9 AM to 5 PM seven days a week. Housed here is the **Iowa County Historical Museum**, displaying a wide variety of artifacts contributed by local citizens. For information about Dodgeville, call (608) 935-5993.

Just outside Dodgeville is the entrance to **Governor Dodge State Park**, the second-largest state park in Wisconsin and a popular camping site for locals as well as visitors.

If You Have Time . . .

While we've tried to limit side trips to within 50 miles of Madison, we'd be derelict if we didn't at least mention **Mineral Point**, which is just another 8 miles farther south on Wis. Highway 23 from Dodgeville. It's a destination unto itself and can be most conveniently reached by taking U.S. Highway 18/151 out of Madison.

Founded in 1827, Mineral Point was once a booming lead-mining town, but after the California Gold Rush hit in 1849, Mineral Point was never quite the same again. In one day alone, supposedly 60 wagons left for California.

After languishing for a number of decades, Mineral Point began rebounding during the mid-20th century. Today it's a thriving artisan community and architectural treasure, the latter of which was heavily influenced in the 1800s by an influx of miners from Cornwall, England, who were excellent stone masons. They constructed many buildings of locally quarried limestone. If you visit Mineral Point, you can't leave without sampling a Cornish pasty or visiting **Pendarvis**, a group of restored Cornish miner homes on Shake Rag Street — so named because women used to wave a cloth from their doorways to summon their husbands home from the mines when it was time for dinner.

A couple of events you should know about: the annual **Fall Art Tour**, held one weekend in October, when artists open their studios, many of which are tucked away in the rolling hills surrounding Mineral Point; and the semiannual **Antiques Show**. The antique shops alone will keep you busy no matter when you visit.

For more information about Mineral Point, contact the **Mineral Point Visitors Bureau**, (608) 987-3201, or visit the city's Visitor Center, a small stone building in the shadow of the Mineral Point water tower.

Returning to Madison via U.S. Highway 151, look for the County Highway K Exit, just south of Barneveld, to visit one of the newer vineyards in the area. **Botham Vineyards and Winery** was opened in '94 by Peter Botham in partnership with his father, Dr. Richard Botham, a retired Madison surgeon. Our favorite Botham wine is the Upland Reserve, a medium-bodied red. Botham Winery offers free wine tastings 10 AM to 5 PM Wednesday through Sunday, mid-April through December 24. Wine tastings are also offered on the weekends mid-March through mid-April. For information, call (608) 924-1412.

Trip 3: Mount Horeb and Blue Mounds

From shopping the Trollway to investigating the deep contours of the Cave of the Mounds, the Mount Horeb/Blue Mounds area offers plenty of sightseeing and recreational opportunities.

If you get hungry en route, veer off U.S. Highway 18/151 at the Verona Exit, immediately turn left on County Highway PB and you'll be at one of the most scrumptious chocolate candy stores around. **Candinas Chocolatier** makes more than a dozen kinds of chocolate truffles daily on the premises. Pace yourself; they're addictive.

To request more information about the area, call the **Mount Horeb Area Chamber of Commerce**, (608) 437-5914.

Mount Horeb: Troll Capital of the World

Within a 25-minute drive south of Madison is the Norwegian-inspired village of Mount Horeb, "Home of the Trolls." This is a fun place to visit for myriad reasons, including antique hunting, troll sighting and downhill skiing at nearby Tyrol Basin.

The Main Street of Mount Horeb is called the **Trollway**, and upon seeing this Scandinavian community for the first time, you'll know why. More than a half-dozen trolls carved out of tree trunks stand sentry along the curb in front of various specialty shops and other local businesses. Many were carved by master carver Mike Feeney, including one of the most photographed, "The Peddler," in front of **Open House Imports**, a treasure chest of Norwegian finery.

Take your time poking around the four antique shops on the main drag, but save time to visit a truly unique site, the **Mount Horeb Mustard Museum**, 109 E. Main Street, which has the largest collection of prepared mustards in the world. The museum was started and is operated by a former Wisconsin assistant attorney general, Barry Levenson, who started collecting mustards like many people

---

INSIDERS' TIP

The distinctive shiny surface of salt-glazed pottery is produced by throwing rock salt into a kiln while pottery is being fired. You've no doubt seen examples of Rowe Pottery. You might even own some. It's gray stoneware with blue cobalt designs.

do baseball cards. His collection got so big, he quit the practice of law and opened a store in 1986.

What do you do in a mustard museum? You learn how mustard is made; you discover new ways of using it; and you sample kinds you never thought existed before buying a jar yourself. You won't be able to resist. The museum is usually open 10 AM to 5 PM seven days a week.

Blue Mounds: Enjoying the Countryside

You can spend a day in Mount Horeb, or you can spend a day exploring sites in the nearby rolling Blue Mounds countryside just west of Mount Horeb. Here are some suggestions.

The temperature is a constant 50 degrees in **Cave of the Mounds**, one of the most significant caves open to the public in the Upper Midwest. Discovered in 1939, after a quarry blast revealed its entrance, Cave of the Mounds is filled with interesting stalactites, stalagmites and other formations. Don't get too nervous when guides turn out the lights to show just how dark it can get down there. The cave is open every day mid-March through mid-November, 9 AM to 7 PM Memorial Day weekend through Labor Day and until 5 PM spring and fall. In winter, it's open 9 AM to 5 PM weekends. Admission costs $9 for adults and teens and $4.50 for children ages 5 to 12. Children younger than 5 get in free. Cave of the Mounds is 3 miles west of Mount Horeb, just off U.S. Highway 18/151. Call (608) 437-3038 for more information.

You'll think you've landed in Norway when you visit **Little Norway**, 3 miles west of Mount Horeb on County Highway JG in a lush, secluded valley named Nissedahle, which is Norwegian for "Valley of the Elves." The museum complex is made up of historic buildings, many of which were built by a family of Norwegian immigrants during the 1860s. They include a home, barn, tool shed and grainery. One of the most impressive is the restored, multi-gabled Norwegian Pavilion from the 1893 World's Columbian Exposition in Chicago. Inside the buildings you'll find one of the largest privately owned collections of Norwegian antiques in the country. Little Norway is open May 1 through the last Sunday in October. Hours during July and August are 9 AM to 7 PM; the rest of the time, the facility closes at 5 PM. Tickets are $7 for adults, $6 for senior citizens and $2.50 for children ages 6 to 12. For information about guided tours, call (608) 437-8211.

Recreational activity is available year round. Both **Governor Dodge** and **Blue Mound** state parks are nearby (see the "Parks" section of our Parks and Recreation chapter), and the 39-mile **Military Ridge Trail** (see the "Bicycling" section of our Parks and Recreation chapter), open to hikers and bikers in the warmer months and cross-country skiers in winter, passes through Mount Horeb. **Tyrol Basin**, the closest ski hill to Madison, is especially noted for its snowboarding facilities. The 6-mile drive from Mount Horeb to the ski hill showcases the rolling Wisconsin countryside at its best. Watch out, however, for wandering deer.

Trip 4: New Glarus and Monroe

New Glarus and the Green County seat of Monroe have two things in common: a vibrant Swiss heritage and lots of cheese. In fact, Swiss cheese is considered "gold" in the heart of Wisconsin cheese-making country. We've listed highlights of the two communities subsequently, but for more information, contact the **Green County Tourism Bureau** at (800) 527-6838.

To get to New Glarus and Monroe, head southwest from Madison on U.S. Highway 18/151 to Verona and turn right onto Wis. Highway 69. A nice diversion on the way there or back is the **Artisan Gallery** in Paoli that showcases the works of more than 200 artists (see our Arts chapter). Inside and to one side of the gallery is a small cafe, the **Paoli Creamery**, overlooking the Sugar River. It's a great, out-of-the-way spot for lunch but you do need reservations, especially on weekends. Also across the street from the gallery, the **Schoolhouse Shops**, inside an old, renovated one-room schoolhouse, are fun to explore.

New Glarus: America's "Little Switzerland"

Twenty-five miles south of Madison on Wis. Highway 69/39, in the heart of picturesque Green County farmland, is the small village of **New Glarus**, commonly referred to as America's "Little Switzerland" because the Swiss influence is visible everywhere you turn — in the architecture, the shops and pageantry still avidly practiced today.

The village was established in 1845 by immigrants from Glarus, Switzerland, eager to make a fresh start in America following an economic crisis in their homeland. Quickly, they established a cheese-making industry that remains an important economic boost to the area. You can sample home-produced cheeses from many of the shops in town or, if you prefer, kalberwurst or Landjaegger sausage. We, on the other hand, go straight for the Swiss chocolate and pastries. One good place to light for the latter is the **New Glarus Bakery & Tea Room**, 534 First Street, in the middle of the downtown district. The second-floor restaurant serves salads, sandwiches and soups — that is, if you make it past the bakery on the main floor.

For a relaxing evening, we're partial to dining on the expansive balcony of the **New Glarus Hotel**, Sixth Avenue and First Street, offering authentic Swiss cuisine, polka music and a sweeping view of everything below. From the street, the chalet-like hotel is an equally colorful sight, set off by rows of traditional, flower-filled window boxes. Reservations are recommended. Call (800) 727-9477.

Not everything in this small village is old. It's also home to the **New Glarus Brewery**, a microbrewery that opened in 1993 and quickly made a name for itself. At the intersection of County Road W and Wis. Highway 69, the New Glarus Brewery offers free tours from noon to 4:30 PM Saturdays from May through November. Call (608) 527-5850 for details.

Exploring the History of New Glarus

Everywhere you look, Swiss heritage is alive and thriving in New Glarus, but the following two spots best capture and explain the Old World traditions on which this village was founded.

The **Swiss Historical Village Museum**, overlooking the village from a hillside on the west edge of town at 612 Seventh Avenue, includes 14 either original or replica buildings, each of which depict a facet of Midwestern pioneer life. Buildings include a print shop, log church, blacksmith shop, cheese factory, schoolhouse and general store. The complex is open May 1 through October 31. Admission costs $5 for folks 14 and older and $1 for kids ages 6 through 13. For more information, phone (608) 527-2317.

Three floors of painted furniture and priceless Swiss antiques are housed in the **Chalet of the Golden Fleece Museum**, 618 Second Street, built in 1937 as a private residence by Edwin Barlow, who eventually donated the chalet and his impressive collection to the village of New Glarus. Items of special interest include a jeweled watch once owned by King Louis XVI, a 300-year-old Swiss slate-and-wood-inlaid table and a Swiss porcelain-tile stove dating back to 1760. The museum is open from May through October. Admission is $3 for adults and $1 for students ages 6 to 17. Phone (608) 527-2614.

A Great Place to Shop

If you like to poke around in shops, you'll enjoy **Roughing It in Style**, specializing in rustic furniture, clothing, jewelry and home accessories; **Peter's Briar Patch**, eight rooms of gifts and collectibles in an old Victorian house; **Simple Gifts Gallery**, specializing in folkart and Shaker-designed products; and **Roberts Drug Store**, where you'll find everything Swiss. All the stores are within easy walking distance of one another in the heart of downtown New Glarus.

Celebrating with the Swiss

Wisconsin is famous for its wide variety of ethnic festivals, three of which occur annually in New Glarus and center around staged entertainment. These include the **Heidi Festival**, usually the last full weekend in June; the **Volksfest** (Swiss Independence Day), the first Sunday in August; and the **Wilhelm Tell Festival**, on Labor Day weekend, which dates back to 1938.

The Mustard Museum in Mount Horeb is home to the world's largest collection of mustards — more than 2,800!

The **New Glarus Maennerchor**, a men's choir group, is the official sponsor of Volksfest and always performs a concert following an official ceremony marking Swiss Independence Day. A play retelling the story of Heidi — the fair-haired, pigtailed little girl featured in the classic children's book of the same name — is the highlight of the Heidi Festival. And the story of Swiss independence is the basis of the Wilhelm Tell drama performed three times over the Labor Day weekend, including one performance in German. For ticket and other festival information, contact the **Green County Tourist Bureau** at (800) 527-6838.

Need we add that each of these special events affords plenty of opportunity to eat, shop and listen to some of the best yodeling this side of Switzerland.

Sugar River State Trail

One of the most popular and scenic trails in Southern Wisconsin for recreational biking and hiking is the **Sugar River State Trail**, which follows an abandoned railroad bed in Green County for 23 miles, passing over streams and through wildlife refuges and rolling farmland. In the winter, this trail is used for snowmobiling and cross-country skiing.

Headquarters for the trail is in the old railroad depot in New Glarus where you can rent single and tandem bikes and make arrangements to have someone drop you and your bike (using your car) at any one of the other three entry points — Monticello, Albany and Brodhead — and then return and park your car in New Glarus so it is waiting for you when you finish your ride. These arrangements should be made in advance by calling (608) 527-2334. All bikers 16 and older need to purchase either a daily or seasonal trail-use permit before using the trail.

Monroe: Cheese, Cheese and More Cheese

With a population of more than 10,000, Monroe is Green County's largest city as well as its seat of government. It's also known as the "Swiss Cheese Capital of the USA."

If you like Gruyere, Swiss or Limburger cheese, Monroe is a great place to savor the best. Several cheese factories offer tours, including **Alp and Dell**, (608) 328-DELL, the only cheese factory in the United States that processes Gruyere cheese the old-fashioned way, in a copper vat. Check in at the **Monroe Wel-**

come Center-Historic Cheesemaking Center housed in a renovated railroad depot on Wis. Highway 69 as you arrive from New Glarus, 16 miles to the north (see previous section).

Beside cheese, Monroe, which dates back to the 1930s, is noted for its many historic buildings including the **Green County Courthouse**, an impressive Romanesque-style building that's the focal point of the downtown square. A "Historic Monroe Walking Tour" booklet is available for a nominal fee at the Monroe Area Chamber of Commerce office, 1505 Ninth Street.

Also, just off the square is the **Green County Historical Museum**, 1617 Ninth Street, in a former Universalist church built in 1861 that was used to store wheat and wool for the Union Army during the Civil War. Tools and other artifacts dating back to the mid-1800s are on display. A fully furnished schoolhouse built in the late 1800s is adjacent to the museum.

Cheese Country Recreational Trail

Following the former bed of the Milwaukee Road railroad, the **Cheese Country Recreational Trail** is one of the newer trails, and unlike other state-owned ones, it's all-terrain, meaning ATVs and horseback riders are as welcome as hikers and bikers. (Rental bikes are available nearby at the Gasthaus Motel.) In winter, that means snowmobilers also have access, so don't say you haven't been warned.

Entrance to the 40-mile trail is at the **Monroe Welcome Center**. It parallels the Pecatonica River and ends at Mineral Point (see previous "If You Have Time . . ." section). Permits are necessary for anyone using the trail, which is closed during deer-hunting season in mid-November. (That's probably a very wise move.)

With Noah's Ark billed as the largest water park in America, and another whopper, Family Land, attracting more water demons, it's little wonder that 3 million people flock annually to the Wisconsin Dells/ Lake Delton area.

Wisconsin Dells

When the Wisconsin Department of Tourism asked 4th-graders across the state to rate their favorite Wisconsin vacation destination, the Wisconsin Dells came out on top, hands down. (Madison took third place.)

Said one enthusiastic student: "I like the water parks. I like going down the slides because they make me scream!"

With Noah's Ark billed as the largest water park in America, and another whopper, Family Land, attracting more water demons, it's little wonder that 3 million people flock annually to the Wisconsin Dells/Lake Delton area. People either love all the hype and cheap thrills associated with this man-made, teeming wonderland or think they're stuck in a nightmare.

Yet, within minutes of one of the most commercialized, fun-seeking strips in the country is a beautiful stretch of unspoiled land and water. The Wisconsin Dells is truly a study in contrasts: crowded and serene; tacky and majestic; flashy and utterly captivating. The fact this popular tourist destination represents both nature at its best and, as Wisconsin writer Tracy Will aptly describes, "kitsch run amok," makes it an unusual, eclectic getaway. During separate visits, we've enjoyed many aspects of the Dells, from following our own "screaming" children down Black Thunder at Noah's Ark to playing a leisurely round of late autumn golf at the challenging Trapper's Turn golf course.

With advance planning and the proper attitude, trips to the Wisconsin Dells can be great sport. Let this chapter help guide you. (For phone numbers listed in this chapter, first dial 1 or 0 and then the area code, 608.)

A Historical Primer

On the very eastern edge of the Driftless Area, the portion in Wisconsin and neighboring states that was never covered by glacial ice sheets, the Dells received its celebrated deep gorges seemingly overnight about 14,000 years ago. A swift flood caused by a nearby glacial melt tore through the area. The rushing water quickly eroded the soft sandstone cliffs that had been formed layer by layer for millions of years, leaving behind the state's foremost waterway, the Wisconsin River. The sudden exposure of the beautiful cream and pinkish hues of the towering cliffs, coupled with interesting deep cracks and narrow crannies, has turned this portion of the river into one of nature's stunning works of art.

In 1909, the Kilbourn Dam was built, separating the Wisconsin Dells into lower and upper regions, the latter of which offers the most secluded and majestic scenery. More than 2,800 acres of shoreline there are preserved by the Wisconsin Department of Natural Resources.

According to historical data gathered by the Wisconsin Dells Visitor & Convention Bureau, Native Americans (especially the Winnebagos whose descendants continue to reside in the area) named the river Mekousing for "where the waters gather." Early French explorers pronounced it "Ouisconsin" and described the topography as "dalles," meaning "a slab or tile-like rock." Yet when first settled on a bluff above the river, the town of Wisconsin Dells was named Kilbourn City, after an early railroad magnate who recognized the potential of the area as a tourist destination even back in the 1880s. It was renamed Wisconsin Dells in 1931.

Today, it is impossible to tell where the village of Lake Delton, established in 1848, ends and the Wisconsin Dells begins, although the latter is used as a catchall for all that goes on in the area.

Tourism is the primary industry, bringing in more than $348 million each year, in large part from the 71 attractions, 65 restaurants, 6,385 lodging rooms and more than 3,000 campsites, the majority of which are on or just

312 • WISCONSIN DELLS

off the two main strips — Wisconsin Dells Parkway (U.S. Highway 12) and Broadway Avenue.

Getting There

The Wisconsin Dells is 192 miles northwest of Chicago and 50 miles north of Madison at the junction of U.S. Highway 12, Wis. Highway 16 and Interstate 90/94.

During inclement weather, we always recommend taking the Interstate north from Madison to Wisconsin's largest playground. Otherwise, we like U.S. Highway 12, which is a far more scenic drive and winds by many of the outlying attractions we discuss later in this chapter. But please, keep your eyes on the road. This highway is heavily traveled at times and is the source of much heated political debate as to whether or not it needs to be widened. No matter the route you decide to drive, the trip is a little more than an hour in length.

A Place for All Seasons

While the Dells attracts the most tourists during the summer months when the water parks are open and a wide variety of activities — from bungee jumping to boating to go-cart racing — are in full swing, it has, within the past decade, become a popular destination for all seasons.

The area offers more than 600 miles of groomed snowmobile trails, and cross-country skiing is at its best in nearby state parks. Within miles of the Dells downtown area are three downhill ski areas: Christmas Mountain Village Resort, Cascade Mountain and Devil's Head Resort and Convention Center.

Horseback riding doesn't stop when the leaves fall. Canyon Creek Riding Stable provides winter riding and sleigh riding as does Christmas Mountain. In fact, the Fake Out Festival, occurring in mid-January and highlighted by snow- and ice-sculpting competitions, is rapidly gaining more converts, although it has a long way to go to beat the Great Wisconsin Dells Balloon Rally held the weekend after Memorial Day.

It's hard to think of the Dells as a quiet getaway, but that's what it can be when the crowds thin out in early September. The phenomenal (albeit seasonal) success of the water parks has prompted many hotels to build elaborate indoor water playgrounds of their own (see the subsequent "Where to Stay" section) that are especially appealing when a blanket of snow is covering all of Wisconsin.

Some attractions, including the **Ho-Chunk Casino & Bingo Parlor**, on U.S. Highway 12 between Baraboo and the Dells (Exit 92 off the interstate), are big draws, no matter the season or, for that matter, the time of day. While we're not high rollers, we hear the all-you-can-eat buffet, served from about 11 AM until 3 PM and again from 5 to 10 PM, is very good. The casino, owned and operated by the Ho-Chunk Nation, never closes. Truly. Call (800) 746-2486 for information. While all the places mentioned here use the 608 area code, from Madison it is necessary to always dial 1 and the area code first, before the number.

Popular Attractions

There is enough to see and do in the Wisconsin Dells to keep families happily occupied for days. It all depends upon what your interests are. But the following suggestions are primary attractions that show off both the scenic and fun-loving sides of the area. Pace yourself. It's impossible to do everything in a day — or even a long weekend. Your children won't mind returning, believe us.

Water Parks

There are three water parks, all of which are within a couple of blocks of one another along Wisconsin Dells Parkway. All three water parks offer concessions and picnic pavilions (you can save a lot of money by bringing your own food and drinks). All-day passes range from about $15 to $23; be sure to ask about special rates for children and evening admission. Discount coupons often are avail-

---

www.insiders.com

See this and many other Insiders' Guide® destinations online — in their entirety.

Visit us today!

able through area publications and, beginning the week after school lets out for the summer, through the Madison School-Community Recreation Department, 1045 E. Dayton Street, Madison, (608) 266-6070, from 8 AM to 2:30 PM on Fridays during June, July and August.

To avoid long lines, be ready to hit the slides as soon as they open, or stick around during the dinner hour when the majority of families head home.

Noah's Ark
Wisconsin Dells Pkwy., Wisconsin Dells
• (608) 254-6351

The 65 acres at Noah's Ark supposedly qualify it as the largest water park in the world — and it's still growing. It includes two Lazy Rivers, two wave pools and a multitude of water slides including the Dark Voyage, in which parties of up to five speed through dark tunnels in large inner tubes. Go-carts, kiddie bumper boats, miniature golf and several play areas for children also are available. Noah's Ark opens at 9 AM daily from Memorial Day through Labor Day, and water activities continue until 8 PM — although at the beginning and end of the season, hours might vary slightly. Admission is $22.99 for adults and kids 3 and older; kids younger than 3 get in free.

Family Land
Wisconsin Dells Pkwy., Wisconsin Dells
• (608) 254-7766

Family Land provides water slides, miniature golf, the large interactive Huck's Landing water-activity center for young children and the 85-foot Demon's Drop that's not for the faint of heart. With nine kiddie slides alone, we think Family Land is ideal for families with wee ones. A snack bar and picnic and play areas also are available. The park opens at 9 AM every day from Memorial Day through Labor Day; water activities continue until 8 PM. Admission is $17.95 per person 3 and older; kids younger than 3 get in free.

Riverview Park & Waterworld
Wisconsin Dells Pkwy., Wisconsin Dells
• (608) 254-2608

Riverview doesn't offer as many water slides activities (about 30 altogether) as Noah's Ark or Family Land (see previous entries), but rather combines the "wet and wild" scene with a bevy of amusement rides — a roller coaster, sky ride and seven go-cart tracks — many of which are geared to young children. Food and picnic facilities also are available. During peak season, Riverview is open 9 AM to 11 PM with the water rides closing at 8 PM. An all-day, unlimited pass costs $15.99 for everyone 6 and older; $8.99 for kids 5 and younger. Riverview is open daily from 9 AM to 8 PM.

Boat Rides

The noisy DUK (pronounced "duck") amphibious vehicles — historically significant for having transported U.S. soldiers from ship to land during the D-Day invasion at Normandy during World War II — are so much apart of the Dell's mystique, nobody should pass up riding in one . . . at least once. Children adore the idea of traveling by land and water as college-age drivers run on with personable, endless chatter. Seating up to 21 passengers, each Duck weighs 7 tons and measures 8 feet wide, 9 feet high and 32 feet long.

Two companies operate Duck tours of the Lower Dells, with boats leaving about every 10 to 15 minutes in peak season. Tours last one hour, from mid-May through mid-October.

To really enjoy the geological wonders of the area, tours of both the Lower and Upper Dells are in order. But if you only have time to take one boat ride, take it to the Upper Dells where narrow, lush, fern-filled canyons showcase the very best of what the Wisconsin Dells has to offer.

An evening cruise will take you to Stand Rock (also available by automobile) where Native American songs and dances are performed by members of the Winnebago tribe. For information about Stand Rock, call (800) 223-3557 extension 60.

Dells Duck Tours
1550 Wisconsin Dells Pkwy., Wisconsin Dells • (608) 254-6080

The hourlong Lower Dells Duck tour takes passengers on roads, but mostly on water along the Lower Wisconsin River, Lake Delton and Dell Creek. Tickets cost $13.50 for persons 12 and older, $8.50 for children ages 6 through 11 and nothing for children 5 and younger. A tour of the Upper Dells (one hour and 15 minutes) is also available on the boat company's *Mark Twain*. Passengers view 16 scenic sites, but no stops are made. The cost is $13.50 for persons 12 and older; children's tickets are $8.50. A combination ticket for both trips is available for $20 (adults) and $12 (children).

Original Wisconsin Ducks
1890 Wisconsin Dells Pkwy., Wisconsin Dells • (608) 254-8751

Tours of the Lower Dells area take passengers through cool, secluded wilderness trails as well as sections of the Wisconsin River. A variety of unusual ferns are pointed out along the route. Ticket prices are $13.75 for anyone 12 and older and $8.75 for children ages 6 through 11. Children 5 and younger can ride for free.

Dells Boat Tours
11 Broadway, Wisconsin Dells • (608) 254-8555

This company offers tours of both the Upper and Lower Dells. The Upper Dells tour is about two hours long and includes two stops where passengers can debark and explore walkways through such beautiful canyons as Witches Gulch. The Lower Dells tour is one hour long with no stops.

Boats leave daily from 9 AM until 6 PM during the height of the tourist season but operate on a limited schedule from mid-April throughout the spring and after Labor Day through the end of October, weather permitting. The cost of the Upper Dells boat ride is $14.75 for individuals 12 and older and $7.50 for children ages 6 through 11. Children 5 and younger ride free. The tour of the Lower Dells is about $9.95 and $5 respectively. Or you can buy a combination ticket for rides of both the Upper and Lower Dells for about $18 (12 and older) and $9.50 (ages 6 through 11).

Tommy Bartlett's Amusements

Spend any time in the Dells and you'll soon learn that the master showman of the area is Tommy Bartlett. Forty-five years ago, he started a water-skiing show on Lake Delton that today has become the "Ski, Sky and Stage" entertainment extravaganza (see next entry).

Ski, Sky and Stage
560 Wisconsin Dells Pkwy., Wisconsin Dells • (608) 254-2525

What Tommy Bartlett began 45 years ago as a water-skiing show on Lake Delton has become a entertainment spectacle filled with everything from amazing juggling and trapeze acts to superb water-skiing feats. (When he turned 70 in '84, Bartlett himself got up on skis.) Shows happen rain or shine at 1, 4:30 and 8:30 PM. We recommend the last of the day because it ends with fireworks. Ticket prices range from $10.50 to $16.50 plus tax. (Children 5 and younger get in free if seated on an adult's lap.) Entrance to the thrill show is off Wisconsin Dells Parkway, next to the Copa Cabana Resort Hotel & Suites.

Bartlett's Robot World & Exploratory
560 Wisconsin Dells Pkwy., Wisconsin Dells • (608) 254-2525

Open since 1982, Bartlett's Robot World & Exploratory, adjacent to Ski, Sky and Stage (see previous entry), features more than 100 hands-on scientific and educational exhibits. The newest attraction here is a MIR Russian Space Station, one of only three in existence. Visitors can walk through the module, which was designed to serve as living quarters and

---

INSIDERS' TIP

The Upper and Lower Dells Boat Tours and several other attractions offer a 20 percent discount card to people 55 and older who apply by mail. In advance of your visit, write Dells Associated Boat Lines, P.O. Box 208-C, Wisconsin Dells, WI 53965.

Waterparks are a popular attraction at the Wisconsin Dells.

scientific research center for astronauts during extended stays in space. Hours are 8 AM to 10 PM from Memorial Day weekend through Labor Day. Hours vary the rest of the year; please call ahead. Admission is about $8.75 plus tax for adults and school-age kids; children 5 and younger get in free.

Golf

In recent years, the Wisconsin Dells has made great strides in demonstrating it has more to offer than water parks and fudge shops. Nowhere does this show up more than with golf. New courses have opened, and others have been greatly improved. Tee times are available from April through October, weather permitting. But if you're planning to play on a summer weekend, best make your tee time weeks in advance. The courses fill up fast. [Ed. note: The following yardages are from the men's (middle) tees. Prices offered are for peak season.]

Christmas Mountain Village
S-944 Christmas Mountain Rd., Wisconsin Dells • (608) 254-3971

A four-season family resort, with downhill and cross-country skiing available in the winter, Christmas Mountain offers an 18-hole, par 71 golf course as part of its complex, which is away from the madding crowd but within 5 miles of downtown. Many improvements have been made to the course in recent years. The front nine features narrow, tree-lined fairways and plenty of water hazards; the back nine is more rolling. The par 71 course measures 6300 yards.

Christmas Mountain Resort includes lodging, full-service restaurants, a bar, pro shop and both an indoor and outdoor swimming pool. Tennis and horseback riding also are available. Golf packages are available to guests. The public can golf for $48 (including cart) on weekends and $40 on weekdays.

Coldwater Canyon Golf Club
4065 River Rd., just north of Wisconsin Dells • (800) 254-8489

Hills, narrow fairways and small greens make this nine-hole, par 33 course — one of the oldest in the state — much more difficult than its 2444-yard total length might indicate. Built in 1923 along Coldwater Canyon of the Upper Dells, it's adjacent to one of the loveliest resorts in the area, Chula Vista. The clubhouse serves food and drinks. Greens fees are $14 for weekend play, $13 during the week. Riding carts are an additional $13.

Devil's Head Lodge And Convention Center
S6330 Bluff Rd., Merrimac
• (608) 493-2251

Set amid the Baraboo Hills in Merrimac, a short drive from the Dells, the mature, wooded par 73, 6336-yard course offers as many challenging holes as it does beautiful views. An old stone wall even cuts across two of the fairways. In winter, the resort turns into a ski area, offering some of the best skiing in the immediate area. During the summer, green fees are $56 with cart, on weekdays, they're $46. Golf packages, including accommodations, are available.

Trapper's Turn
1.5 miles off U.S. Hwy. 12, Wisconsin Dells • (608) 253-7000

One of the most beautiful courses in the Dells, Trapper's Turn opened in 1991 and makes wonderful use of its hilly topography. (Expect a lot of sidehill lies here.) No two holes are alike, and there is plenty of trouble to get into if you stray too far from the fairways. The 18-hole course includes a clubhouse with a bar and grill and pro shop. Greens fees are $55 from noon Sunday until 3 PM Thursday and $65 Friday, Saturday and until noon Sunday (including cart, which is required during those times). After 3 PM Thursday, the cost is $41 with a cart and $31 without, although most people find Trapper's Turn a very difficult course to walk; the par 72 layout measures 6203 yards.

Wilderness Hotel and Golf Resort
511 E. Adams St., Wisconsin Dells
• (608) 253-GOLF

One of the oldest golf resorts in the Dells, dating back to the '20s, this complex and course were renamed when totally revamped in the mid-'90s. The par 72 layout measures 6000 yards. Nine holes were redesigned to take advantage of the hills, woods, cliffs and canyons in the area. The hotel has one of the area's most extensive indoor and outdoor water playgrounds (see the subsequent "Where to Stay" section), and the course is the home of the Galvano Golf Academy, which offers two- to seven-day golf clinics for women, men and juniors. Special golfing packages are available. Summer greens fees are $52 with a cart (required), $48 weekdays with a cart and $35 without one. Twilight rate, after 4 PM, is $30 with a cart and $20 walking.

Entertaining Extras

Go-carting, miniature golf, horseback riding, fishing, canoeing, personal-watercraft riding and even helicopter rides are readily available at the Dells. For information about a specific activity, call either the Wisconsin Dells Visitor & Convention Bureau, (800) 223-3557 Extension 60, or the Wisconsin Dells/Lake Delton Chamber of Commerce, (800) 94 DELLS. Here are some other suggestions.

Crazy King Ludwig's Adventure Park
1851 Wisconsin Dells Pkwy., Wisconsin Dells • (608) 254-5464

One of Wisconsin Dells's newer attractions, Crazy King Ludwig's Adventure Park is housed in what looks like a medieval castle. The go-cart attraction includes the six-story-high Home Run Racers and a half-mile-long track that winds through the interior of the castle. Hours are 9 AM to midnight during summer. Cost is $4.50 per ride, six rides for $20 or an all-day pass for $27.

Big Chief Go-Kart World
Wisconsin Dells Pkwy., Wisconsin Dells
• (608) 254-2490
County Hwy. A, Wisconsin Dells
• (608) 254-2490

Big Chief bills itself as the largest go-cart facility in the area, with 13 tracks in all between its two locations. Three roller coasters also are available at the Wisconsin Dells Parkway site. Both locations are open 9 AM to midnight during the summer season. All rides require one token ($5). Day and night passes are available for about $30.

The Crystal Grand Music Theatre
Wis. Hwy. 23, Wisconsin Dells
• (608) 254-4545, (800) 696-7999

Maybe it's not Branson, Missouri — not yet, anyhow — but the Wisconsin Dells does have its own 1,400-seat country music theater, the Crystal Grand, which opened in '94.

Notable headliners include Willie Nelson, Johnny Cash and Barbara Mandrell. Shows are scheduled twice a month year round. Ticket prices begin at about $16 and go up, depending upon an entertainer's popularity. The Crystal Grand Music Theatre is just off U.S. Highway 12, or take Exit 89 from Interstate 90/94.

Storybook Gardens
Wisconsin Dells Pkwy., Wisconsin Dells • (608) 253-2391

Very young children will enjoy a trip to Storybook Gardens, a parklike setting in which storybook characters come to life. Visitors can sit down to dinner with the Three Bears, take a carousel or train ride, watch live entertainment and grab a snack at the Ginger Bread House (without worrying about being eaten by the mean, old witch.) Open only during summer months — 10 AM to 5 PM weekdays and Sunday and until 6 PM Saturday, Storybook Gardens costs $8.99 for anyone 12 and older and $7.99 for children ages 2 through 11. Kids younger than 2 get in free.

Lost Canyon Carriage Rides
Canyon Rd., off U.S. Hwy. 12 at County Rd. A, Lake Delton • (608) 254-8757

Temperatures can drop by 10 to 15 degrees (bring along an extra jacket or sweater) when you take a horse and carriage ride into Lost Canyon on the south shore of Lake Delton. Carriages leave approximately every 10 to 15 minutes. Some of the sandstone gorges are so narrow, it's difficult for the wagons — each seats up to 15 passengers — to get through.

This attraction is open from 8:30 AM to 8 PM daily May through September and on weekends in October. Hours shorten after Labor Day, so please call ahead. The cost is about $5.50 for folks 12 and older and $3.25 for children ages 4 through 11. Children younger than 4 ride free.

H.H. Bennett Museum
215 Broadway, Wisconsin Dells • (608) 253-2261

Thanks to photographer H.H. Bennett, inventor of the stop-action camera shutter, beautiful landscapes of the Dells area are well documented as far back as 1865, when he and his brother, George, opened a photography studio that, for a number of years has been operated as a museum by the H.H. Bennett Foundation (Bennett family) in downtown Wisconsin Dells. Recently bought by the State of Wisconsin, the museum will be closed, beginning in the fall of 1998 for restoration purposes, and then reopened in the year 2000 as the ninth historic site in the state.

Where to Stay

Because Wisconsin Dells is just a little more than 50 miles from Madison, there's no reason to stay overnight, but many families and couples do, just to get away for a night or two. The city is home to a number of historically significant bed and breakfasts including the Bennett House Bed and Breakfast, named after H.H. Bennett (see the previous section's H.H. Bennett Museum entry) who originally resided in the home. On the flip side, in keeping with the cheap-thrills-and-frills image along the main drags, many hotels try to transport guests to mythical lands or lush, artificial settings.

Yet, most noteworthy about the Dells is the number of resort-like hotels that have large outdoor and indoor pool complexes to attract families in summer and winter. When cabin fever strikes at the end of January, it's time to pack up the kids and head for the Dells, even if you never leave the hotel. Off-season, there are bargains to be had; room rates are often half as much as they are in summer. Here are only a few suggestions.

Carousel Inn & Suites
1031 Wisconsin Dells Pkwy., Wisconsin Dells • (608) 254-6554, (800) 648-4765

Guests can visit the outdoor Lollipop Lagoon featuring Gum Drop Falls, a water slide on top of a mountain of "cotton candy." If that looks too steep, cool your heels on Banana Split Island. All rooms (about 100 altogether) feature refrigerators. Some units have whirlpools. Prices range from $130 to $295 in the high season. The complex also has an indoor pool.

Black Wolf Lodge
U.S. Hwy. 12, immediately off I-90/94, Wisconsin Dells • (608) 253-2222, (800) 559-WOLF

The new Black Wolf Lodge, built in 1997, acts as a North Woods paradise. Built by the same family who gave the Dells Noah's Ark, it features a 20,000-square-foot indoor water park with slides, waterfalls and winding rivers. It has, in fact, the largest indoor water facility of any hotel in the country. When the kids get tired of swimming, take them across the hall to enjoy a large game room. The atrium lobby is meant to resemble a gigantic log cabin, and it's filled with Indian artifacts and hand-carved, rustic furniture. Completed in time for the summer of '98 season is an outdoor pool area featuring a four-story-tall waterslide.

The 206 units all have microwaves and refrigerators and, depending upon size, sleep from four to eight people. Room rates range from $159 to $299 plus per night during peak summer season. If you intend to visit Black Wolf during the summer or any weekend, you should book months ahead. That's how popular this place already is.

Ramada Inn RainTree Resort
1435 Wisconsin Dells Pkwy., Wisconsin Dells • (608) 253-4386, (888) 253-4FUN

Opened in 1997, this 122-unit features a jungle theme for its indoor and outdoor water-recreation areas that together offer more than 70 different activities including water basketball and a lily-pad walk. All rooms are equipped with a microwave and refrigerator. Units range from a room with two queen beds and a sofa sleeper to a two-bedroom suite sleeping up to eight. Rates range from about $150 to $235 per night.

The Polynesian Resort Hotel & Suites
857 N. Frontage Rd. • (608) 254-2883, (800) 272-5642

One of the first hotels in the Dells to offer indoor and outdoor mini-water parks and family-oriented suites, The Polynesian features Captain Kids Lagoon outside and The Water Factory inside, adjacent to a poolside bar for the grownups. The outdoor play area includes a 40-foot pirate ship equipped with slides and water cannons. The hotel has 58 standard rooms and 172 suites including several two-bedroom units (with three TVs) sleeping up to eight comfortably. Rates range from $110 to $285 a night during the summer. Take Exit 87 off I-90/94.

Wilderness Hotel and Golf Resort
511 E. Adams St., Wisconsin Dells • (608) 253-4653, (800) 867-WILD

The Wilderness Hotel is home to the three-story-high Wilderness Fort Exploratory, a water-activity center with more than 30 hands-on activities for children including several slides. The outdoor water facility includes four pools, waterfalls and a tube ride. Each unit has a microwave and refrigerator. The top-of-the-line accommodations option is an 800-square-foot whirlpool suite with two queen-size beds, a sleeper sofa and small kitchenette. Rates range from $110 to $275 per night from Memorial Day through Labor Day. (Also, see the previous listing for the Wilderness Golf Course in this chapter's "Golf" section.)

Holiday Inn
703 Frontage Rd., Wisconsin Dells • (608) 254-8306, (800) 543-3557

Though there aren't as many recreational gimmicks built in, size-wise, we think the Holiday Inn offers one of the best indoor/outdoor pool values in town. It doesn't seem as crowded either. The Mystic Waters Aqua Dome is a 36,000-square-foot complex housing five pools, three whirlpools and two water slides, one of which (outdoors) is 100 feet long. During the summer months, the hotel caters to families by providing supervised play activities including movies and puppet shows for children. There are 228 standard rooms, some of which have microwaves and refrigerators. Rates range from $130 to $144 per night in peak season.

Chula Vista Resort
4031 River Rd., Wisconsin Dells • (608) 254-8366, (800) 388-4782

Built on a bluff overlooking the Wisconsin River, the Chula Vista Resort showcases the scenic beauty of the Wisconsin Dells at its best and transports visitors away from the hustle and bustle on the strip. To remain competitive, the Chula Vista has enhanced both its outdoor and indoor pool areas and offers "Suite Dreams" fantasy whirlpool suites. Couples can enter "The Final Frontier" or pretend they're out of the country on an "African Safari." Save "The Wild Wild West," however, for when the kids come along. They'll love sleeping in covered wagons; you can take the tepee. Also inquire about the new suites added in '97 — each equipped with Super Nintendo and computer modem jacks. The price of a standard room begins at $109 per night during peak season. The complex includes an outdoor grill, restaurant and pizzeria. In winter, ice skating and snowmobiling are available.

Historic Bennett House B&B
825 Oak St., Wisconsin Dells
- (608) 254-2500

Looking for a romantic getaway . . . without the kids? It is possible at the Dells if you stay at a bed and breakfast like the Historic Bennett House, the restored elegant home of the area's famous photographer, H.H. Bennett. While the inn offers a number of fine antiques to look at, bedrooms have been designed with comfort in mind. There is one suite, with a small living room and private bath downstairs and two bedrooms upstairs, with a bath that can be either shared or rented as a private one. Room rates are generally $70 to $95 a night.

Seth Peterson Cottage
Mirror Lake State Park, Lake Delton
- (608) 254-6551

The only Frank Lloyd Wright-designed rental cottage in existence, a one-bedroom hideaway above Mirror Lake in Mirror Lake State Park, can be rented overnight with a two-night minimum ($225 nightly). Construction of the Seth Peterson Cottage began in 1959, the year Wright died. It eventually was purchased by the State of Wisconsin but then restored and turned into a rental cottage by a nonprofit organization, the Seth Peterson Cottage Conservancy, in the early '90s. Although the cottage is never advertised, word has traveled fast (we were told that it's booked nearly three years in advance; cancellations may provide your only chance to stay here). It is rented out years in advance by Wright fans from all over the world. For information, call the conservancy at the listed number. Public tours are available the second Sunday of each month from 2 to 4 PM for $2. Just show up; no reservations are needed.

Where to Eat

Recognizing that the Wisconsin Dells is a kids' paradise tells you a lot about the kind of food available: pizza, hamburgers and more pizza topped off by a box of fudge. Just kidding.

While you'll find many places to grab a snack or light meal, there are several others we like to go to for more leisurely dinners catered to grownups (although there isn't a restaurant in the area that doesn't also accommodate children).

Cheese Factory The Restaurant
521 Wisconsin Dells Parkway S., Lake Delton • (608) 253-6065

Operating out of a renovated cheese factory, this vegetarian restaurant is noted for its fine international cuisine, old-fashioned soda fountain and cappuccino bar and homemade desserts such as Key lime pie. The food is delicious, but be forewarned: No smoking is allowed, nor is alcohol served. Reservations are accepted only for parties of six or larger. During the summer, on Friday and Saturday nights, live entertainment is featured. Cheese Factory is open for breakfast, lunch and dinner.

The Del-Bar
800 Wisconsin Dells Pkwy., Lake Delton
- (608) 253-1861

One very popular spot that's always crowded in the height of the summer — it's on the main drag and within walking distance of many hotels — is The Del-Bar. This Wisconsin Dells institution has been serving steak and seafood since the late 30s. Some preferred seating is available, although the cocktail lounge is always a lively place to hang out. The Del-Bar is open for dinner year round.

Dells Boat Tours let visitors enjoy unusual sandstone formations.

Field's Steak 'n Stein
Wis. Hwy. 13, Wisconsin Dells
- **(608) 254-4841**

You can dine in Victorian splendor under gleaming chandeliers at Field's, which is especially noted for its prime rib. Field's is another Dells restaurant legend, having been in operation for more than 40 years. Reservations are accepted. Field's, open year round for dinner only, is 2 miles north of the junction of Wis. Highway 13 and Wisconsin Dells Parkway. The restaurant sometimes is closed on Sunday and Monday during the off-season.

The Ishnala Supper Club
Ishnala Rd., Lake Delton
- **(608) 253-1771**

Best known of all the restaurants in the area for its beautiful setting — perched on a bluff overlooking Mirror Lake and surrounded by 117 acres of secluded woodland — is The Ishnala Supper Club. The menu includes prime rib, steak and seafood. The restaurant doesn't take reservations so expect to cool your heels some on a busy summer weekend unless you arrive early. Also, please note that there is no smoking in the dining room. Ishnala is open for dinner from Memorial Day weekend through mid-September only. There is a full-service bar.

From the Dells, take U.S. Highway 12 south to Gasser Road, which deadends on Ishnala.

Monk's Bar & Grill
220 Broadway, Wisconsin Dells
- **(608) 254-2955**

This downtown Wisconsin Dells eatery — famous for its hamburgers — celebrated its 50th anniversary in 1997. It's open for lunch and dinner all year, with food served until midnight during the summer months. (When you see how many people linger and shop on Broadway during a warm, Friday night, you'll know why.) A full bar is available. This place is a popular hangout, so don't expect too much privacy. In fact, you might as well bring the kids!

On the Way to the Dells

If you have the time or inclination, you can find lots to do and see on the way to Wisconsin Dells via U.S. Highway 12. Some places, like Baraboo, are destinations unto themselves. Attractions are free unless otherwise noted.

Sauk-Prairie

Along the Wisconsin River, about halfway between Madison and Wisconsin Dells on U.S. Highway 12/Wis. Highway 78, are the combined villages of Sauk City and Prairie Du Sac, now known as Sauk-Prairie. In late fall and winter, bald eagles can be seen soaring over the tops of the bluffs nearby.

Merrimac Ferry
Wis. Hwy. 113, Merrimac

Traveling 10 miles on Wis. Highway 78 northeast from Sauk-Prairie to Wis. Highway 113 brings you to Merrimac, site of the Merrimac Ferry, a free car-ferry service maintained by the Wisconsin Department of Transportation that crosses the Wisconsin River. It's open 24 hours daily, weather permitting, usually from mid-April to December. The trip across the river takes only five minutes, but the ferry is small and extremely popular, so expect to wait on a busy summer weekend. Unless you intend to ride it both ways, it makes more sense to hit this attraction on the way back to Madison from the Wisconsin Dells. Take Wis. Highway 113 out of Baraboo into Merrimac. After crossing the river, take Wis. Highway 188 to Wis. Highway 60 and proceed through Lodi,

---

INSIDERS' TIP

To learn more about the geological makeup of the Wisconsin Dells, read *Glacial Lake Wisconsin* by Lee Clayton and John W. Attig (Geological Society of America Inc., Boulder, Colorado, 1989). Sign up for a geological tour of the Dells through Time Travel Geological Tours, (608) 253-2123.

which is 4 miles west of an I-90/94 entrance ramp.

Wollersheim Winery
Wis. Hwy. 188 • (608) 643-6515, (800) VIP-WINE

Across the river, tucked into the southern slope of Sugarloaf Bluff, Wollersheim Winery is a small regional vineyard and winery with a charming European atmosphere. More than 140 years old, Wollersheim has established quite a name for itself, its vintners having learned how to grow grapes that are able to withstand the rigors of harsh Wisconsin winters. Guided daily tours during the summer take visitors to the underground limestone caves where wines continue to age in wood casks.

Wollersheim Winery is open year round, with free wine tastings available from 10 AM to 5 PM. The Wine Garden, where cheese and a glass of wine can be enjoyed, is only open from mid-May through October. Festive times to visit are October for the Grape Stomp Festival and November during the annual release of Wollersheim's Ruby Nouveau. One of the signature wines is a crisp, slightly sweet white wine, Prairie Fume.

To get to the winery, turn right onto Wis. Highway 188 just before you get to Sauk-Prairie. Wollersheim is 2 miles from U.S. Highway 12.

Baraboo

Just 15 minutes south of the Wisconsin Dells, Baraboo is home to the Circus World Museum, International Crane Foundation and Devil's Lake State Park, where 500-foot bluffs, reachable by hiking trails, tower over a crystal-clear lake. A combined, discounted ticket for the circus, cranes and trains plus tram rides at Devil's Lake State Park is available through the Baraboo Area Chamber of Commerce and area motels; call (800) BARABOO.

Circus World Museum
426 Water St. (Wis. Hwy. 113), Baraboo • (608) 356-0800

The biggest attraction in Baraboo, the Circus World Museum was built at what is considered to be the birthplace of the Ringling Bros. Circus, which wintered along the banks of the Baraboo River from 1884 to 1918. The museum, open daily year round (10 AM to 4 PM Monday through Saturday and 11 AM to 4 PM on Sunday), houses a variety of circus memorabilia including 150 antique circus wagons. Admission is $3.25 for adults and $1.75 for children.

From May through the first week of September, live circus performances are presented daily under a 2,000-seat big top on the property. Admission to the grounds during the summer season is $11.95 for adults and teens, $5.95 for children ages 3 through 12. Children younger than 3 are admitted free. There are also special evening and senior-citizen rates.

But you don't have to leave Madison to relive the excitement of what it was like when the circus came to town. At the beginning of each July, many of the vintage wagons are loaded onto a train for a two-day trip that winds through downtown Madison on its way to Milwaukee, where circus activities ensue for the next three days. Kids and local politicians clamor to get on board.

Devil's Lake State Park
Wis. Hwy. 123, 3 miles south of Baraboo • (608) 356-6618

Devil's Lake State Park is open year round, although it's most peaceful during the spring and fall — or even in winter, when cross-country skiing is a popular activity. On a hot summer weekend, the place resembles a water park at the Dells. The park has 408 campsites for which reservations are accepted from May through October. If you have small children, keep an eye on them. Climbing rocks looks like a lot of fun (and it can be), but it's wiser and safer to remain on manicured trails. These trails lead to heights affording spectacular views of the deep lake and surrounding countryside. For information about park fees and rules, call the listed number.

International Crane Foundation
Shady Lane Rd., off U.S. Hwy. 12, between Baraboo and Wisconsin Dells • (608) 356-9462

The only facility of its kind in the world, the International Crane Foundation raises all 15 species of cranes — found on five of seven continents — for breeding and release into the wild. Many of these unique birds can be viewed during guided and self-guided tours from May through October. Admission is $6 for adults and kids 12 and older, $5 for seniors and $2.50 for children ages 5 through 11. Children younger than 5 get in free. Joining the foundation allows unlimited admission. Hours are 9 AM to 5 PM daily. Facilities include a museum, gift shop and free picnic area.

Mid-Continent Railway Museum
Wis. Hwy. 136, North Freedom
- **(608) 522-4261**

OK, this place is actually west of Baraboo on Wis. Highway 136 in North Freedom, but it's worth the side trip. You can experience turn-of-the-century railroading, embarking on a vintage steam train for a short trip into the countryside at the Mid-Continent Railway Museum. The depot at North Freedom was built in 1894, and the museum displays an impressive collection of old and rare engines and cars. For the railroad buff, this place is heaven. The museum is open mid-May through the end of August with daily rides at 10:30 AM and 12:30, 2 and 3:30 PM. It's also open Saturday and Sunday through mid-October.

Especially popular are the autumn-color tours, the Santa Express during the last weekend in November and snow train always scheduled for the President's Day weekend (Friday, Saturday and Sunday) in February. (The latter two offer first-class dining options and always sell out quickly.) The cost of riding the rails is ordinarily $9 for adults and teens, $5.50 for children ages 3 to 12; kids younger than 3 get in free. A family ticket, good for two adults and two or more children, is $25.

Reedsburg

From North Freedom, continuing northwest on Wis. Highway 136 to Wis. Highway 23/33 will bring you to Reedsburg, a small town (population 6,500) at the southern end of the 22-mile-long 400 State Trail, (800) 844-3507.

Pioneer Log Village and Museum
Wis. Hwy. 33, Reedsburg
- **(608) 524-3419,**

Heading east from Reedsburg on Wis. Highway 33, you can't miss this 11-building historical site operated by the Reedsburg Historical Society. It includes a school, a church, a blacksmith shop and a country store dating back to 1850. Hours of operation are 1 to 4 PM Saturday and Sunday from Memorial Day weekend through September. It's also open Memorial Day, Fourth of July and Labor Day no matter the days of the week they fall on. There is no admission fee, but donations are appreciated.

Yep! A move with the Stark Company is as easy as going around the block!

We'll take care of all the details because..... we know when it comes to relocating employees and their families even the smallest details are of the utmost importance.

STARK
COMPANY REALTORS®
A family tradition since 1908

Relocation Division
717 John Nolen Dr., Madison, WI 53713
800/779-4037 x353 ☎ 608/256-9018 x353
jjaeger@starkhomes.com
http://starkhomes.com

RELO
EMPLOYEE
RELOCATION
COUNCIL

RDC
RELOCATION
DIRECTORS
COUNCIL, INC.

Real Estate

If you're looking for a Madison home in the over-$250,000 price range, this is a good time to buy. The local luxury home market has an abundance of offerings, and you can find relative bargains these days. The healthy supply is due, in part, to the local Parade of Homes, an extremely popular event that every year results in 35 or so new executive residences, many of them built before a buyer has been lined up (see our Festivals and Annual Events chapter). In addition, new developments on recently annexed land have also added many upscale homes to the market.

In the lower price range, the pendulum has swung toward the sellers. The more modest houses tend to be snapped up quickly in what today is a healthy, if not bullish, real estate market. There were about 4,200 home sales in Dane County in 1997, with an average time of 73 days on the market.

A trend local experts have observed in Dane County is that more single young people are buying homes, rather than renting apartments. This age group often looks toward condos in the Downtown area or near Lake Monona as a means of building an investment and increasing daily convenience. It's also become more common in the last 10 years for single people to get together and pool resources for a home purchase.

What's the Bottom Line?

The average home in Madison in 1997 was assessed at $132,800, compared to $121,306 in 1993. But prices in Madison cover the spectrum. Just a quick look at low-end price listings for three-bedroom homes reveals a wide range: $89,000 for a vintage Cape Cod with a single-car garage and large fenced yard on the city's east side; $200,000 for a classic Colonial in the well-established Nakoma area; $154,900 for a West Side ranch with separate master bedroom suite and two-car garage; and from $300,000 to more than $1 million for most of the homes on Madison's two major lakes, Monona and Mendota. Lakefront property prices have been skyrocketing for at least a decade, and there's no sign of that changing.

One of the newer upscale neighborhoods is the Bishop's Bay development in Middleton (see our Neighborhoods chapter). It's centered around a private golf course and on a lake, and you are unlikely to find a house less than $500,000.

Prices in the Madison area compare quite favorably to those in many other parts of the country. People moving in from either coast or even nearby Chicago find their home-purchasing dollars go a lot farther here. If you're moving in from a less populated area or a southern state, however, you will probably find home prices in Madison to be higher than what you are used to.

Vicki Martin, of Century 21 City Wide, says many home buyers are shocked when they discover what property taxes will be on their new homes, and some of these people then opt to purchase a less-expensive residence. Property taxes for some can mean the difference between purchasing a $130,000 home or a $150,000 home, she says.

According to the Madison City Treasurer's Office, the average tax bill in 1997 was $3,537 (based on a $132,771 house). Property taxes within Dane County can vary by as much as $600, depending on location. Taxes in adjoining counties are somewhat less; however, if you choose to live outside Dane County and work in Madison, expect much higher transportation costs.

On the up side, according to Martin, people from metropolitan areas are used to paying to send their children to private schools, something most Wisconsinites don't do because the high taxes we pay provide for an excellent public school system (see our Education chapter).

Buyers are often so busy with work and other responsibilities that they will only consider homes that are in top condition; they don't want to have to deal with replacing anything, not even the carpets. Experts say that buyers who are willing to consider doing a little work on a home may be able to find a bargain. If you are looking for a referral of certified remodelers, contact the Madison chapter of the **National Association for the Remodeling Industry** (NARI) at (608) 222-0670. The metropolitan area also has an active builders' association that puts together a variety of annual shows including the Parade of Homes. Call the **Madison Area Builders Association**, (608) 288-1133, for a free directory of the association's 750 members.

Help For First-Time Buyers

If you are a first-time buyer, you will find several programs available to help you purchase your first home. **Home Buy** is a program funded by the State of Wisconsin Department of Administration Division of Housing and the city of Madison. This program provides a secured no-interest loan to eligible home buyers to cover partial down payment and closing costs. Eligibility is determined by family size and income. For details, call (608) 266-4223.

Affords is a lease-purchase ownership program developed in part by the Madison Community Development Authority. Through the program, designed to help new home buyers overcome the barriers associated with down payments and closing costs, the home you wish to buy is purchased by the Community Development Authority, then leased to you on a lease-purchase agreement. For information on Affords, call (608) 267-8734.

WHEDA is a state program designed to provide affordable financing for development of rental housing, to empower people to buy homes, to expand small business and to help farmers be successful. The program operates with income limits; in Dane County the household-income limit is currently $46,500. For details, contact WHEDA at (800) 33-HOUSE or (800) 334-6873 Extension 613.

Home buyers may also qualify for **Federal Housing Administration** (FHA) loans, which also are subject to household-income limits. Ask your banker for more information.

Relocation Experts

The thought of packing up and moving — whether it's cross-country or just a few hundred miles — can intimidate even the most organized person. Add to the equation a couple of children, some pets and concerns about starting a new job, and you've more than doubled the consternation. Before you start hyperventilating, pause and take a deep breath. Remember, you don't have to go it alone. Statistics show that about a third of those purchasing homes in Madison annually are from outside the area. That means many services are available to help you relocate. Although you might only move a handful of times in your lifetime, relocation experts deal with moving questions and problems every single day. Take advantage of their experience. They can help you take the pain out of moving and avoid common pitfalls by arming you with information.

"At Home in Madison" is a new multimedia opportunity to investigate Madison schools and neighborhoods before you decide where to buy a home. It marks the first time the private sector, the city and its school district have collaborated on an effort to inform prospective home buyers. For information on the program call Home Savings at (608) 282-6000 or visit the offices at 2 South Carroll Street, Madison.

Here's a list of some experienced relocation specialists.

Visitors to the Parade of Homes can see the latest in building and decorating.

First Weber Group Inc.
429 Gammon Pl., Madison
• (608) 833-3711, (800) 236-8133
relocation line

First Weber has helped new and transferred employees find their niche in Madison since 1967. The company provides an area-orientation tour and video, Internet access and information on elder care and day care. It also will make arrangements for school appointments.

RE/MAX Preferred
4868 High Crossing Blvd., Madison
• (608) 241-5500, (800) 236-8262
relocation office

RE/MAX offers a wide range of services to help you sell your old home and purchase a new one, including a guaranteed sales program and corporate home buy-out plan. RE/MAX has prepared an extensive relocation informational packet for prospective clients.

Restaino Bunbury & Associates
7701 Mineral Point Rd., Madison
• (608) 833-7777, (800) 637-1178
relocation line

Ron Restaino and Tom Bunbury, the principals in this real estate, development and relocation firm, are experienced hands in the Madison real estate market. The firm has three offices with more than 75 Realtors and did $210 million in sales in Dane County in 1997. Restaino Bunbury offers orientation tours, relocation counseling, school and child-care assistance, spouse career counseling and interim rental information.

Stark Company Relocation Division
717 John Nolen Dr., Madison
• (608) 256-9018, (800) 779-4037 Ext. 353
relocation line

If you are thinking about relocating to Madison or south-central Wisconsin, Stark invites you to imagine the possibilities by viewing an 11-minute video, which provides an in-depth introduction to the city and a discussion of Madison's finer points. The Stark team also can help you arrange short-term housing if you need it. The company provides information on employment-assistance networking for spouses, area tours and pre-counseling sessions and can help ease the move for children with a special video and packet.

Apartment Living

In a town with more than 40,000 university students, there is ample rental housing available. If you are looking for an apartment, therefore, you might want to consider letting someone else help you with some of the legwork. The best way to start is usually by deciding in which part of the city you will be spending most of your time (either for work, school or entertainment), how much time you want to spend commuting and what mode of transportation you will use. Then, take a look at your budget and determine how much you can afford to pay for rent.

Don't forget to add in utility bills when formulating your financial plan. In winter months heat bills can be upwards of $100 per month, and depending on how much ventilation your apartment has, you might want to run an air conditioner at least part of the summer. **Madison Gas and Electric** (MG&E) will give you last year's high and low utility bills for a specific apartment; call (608) 252-7222.

Many leases in the Madison area expire on August 15, just before the start of the school year. Some landlords list fall vacancies as early as January. The best selection of fall-available apartments is found between March and May. Students often advertise on bulletin boards at the student unions if they have apartments to sublet or are looking for roommates.

If you are a student at UW-Madison or the downtown Madison Area Technical College (MATC) complex, remember that parking is almost always a problem (or premium priced) on campus. Therefore, it's wise to choose an apartment within easy walking or biking distance. If you prefer to be farther out, look for a place with quick access to a bus route. Check the bus schedules before you sign a lease to make sure they will work out for you. Find out what weekend bus services will be available.

Many apartment styles are available near campus — from old-fashioned flats with spacious living rooms and hardwood floors to modern units with the latest in kitchen gadgets.

In general, prices go down and amenities increase as you move away from the UW campus. In most cases, renters are asked to provide landlords with a security deposit equal to a month's rent at the lease signing. Under local ordinance, your landlord must pay you the interest on that deposit accrued over the length of your rental term, provided you pay your rent on time. Most landlords require a one-year lease, but sometimes you can negotiate for a shorter period.

The **Tenant Resource Center**, (608) 257-0006, can offer you valuable assistance if you have questions or concerns about renting. The center also publishes a handbook on tenant's rights in Wisconsin. Be prepared to ask your potential landlord several important questions: Do the property owners make needed repairs quickly? Are security deposits usually returned promptly to tenants? What complaints have been leveled against the property owners?

Your landlord is required by law to observe several minimum housing codes governing necessities such as hot water, garbage disposal, security and fire protection. The leasing agent must provide you with a list of any outstanding building code violations when you are looking at the apartment. If you have concerns, visit the City Building Inspection Unit, 215 Martin Luther King Jr. Boulevard, and fill out a brief information request form. Fair housing laws prohibit anyone from intimidating, harassing or threatening you in an effort to prevent you from leasing a specific rental property. In addition to the usual protections for race, religion and sex, you cannot be discriminated against in Madison for age, sexual orientation, handicap, political beliefs, physical appearance, student status or your source of income. For more information, call the **Madison Equal Opportunity Commission** at (608) 266-4910.

You can access helpful information on available rentals through the following channels.

Campus Assistance Center
420 N. Lake St., Madison
• (608) 263-2400 off-campus housing services

UW-Madison students can find the answers to oft-asked questions about off-campus housing at this office. The Campus Assistance Center also maintains a housing listing service.

Rent-Search
2329 Atwood Ave., Madison
• (608) 243-1430

For 20 years, Rent-Search has been helping match renters to available rental housing in Dane County. For a $35 fee, Rent-Search

Looking to buy a home?

Checked your computer lately?

www.wisconsinhomes.com

FIND OVER 4,000 PROPERTY LISTINGS
in the South Central Wisconsin Multiple Listing Service (MLS).
Complete with photographs and descriptions.
You'll also find a directory of agents, firms, related services and
mortgage information.

www.madison.com

ON THE MOVE is a newcomer's guide
to Madison and its many parts. Complete with
information about many
area neighborhoods.

SOUTH CENTRAL WISCONSIN
MULTIPLE LISTING SERVICE
now on-line!

Searching for a new home just got a little easier!

Produced by

REALTOR® | EQUAL HOUSING OPPORTUNITY

MLS™

WISCONSIN STATE JOURNAL
The Capital Times

provides you with listings and access to a 24-hour update service during a three-month period. You provide the service with a rent payment range, any specific lease requirements, dwelling-styles preferences and information about your pets, if any. Landlords list with the service for free. You can register by phone with a credit card, or stop in; no appointment is needed.

Property-Management Firms

Alexander Company
660 W. Washington Ave., Madison
- (608) 258-5580

Don't want another cookie-cutter apartment? The Alexander Company can help you find a unique apartment among the 500 units it owns in renovated historic buildings; many one- and two-bedroom apartments are near UW-Madison or the Isthmus. The average monthly rent for a two-bedroom apartment is about $900.

Gorman and Company Inc.
131 W. Wilson St., Madison
- (608) 257-8778

Since 1984, Gorman and Company Inc. has been managing properties across southern Wisconsin. The company has numerous residential, multifamily properties in Madison, suitable for many lifestyles and ranging in size from one-bedroom through three-bedroom units. In addition to apartment rentals, Gorman and Company handles some condominium sales.

Haen Real Estate
650 N. High Point Rd., Madison
- (608) 829-1155

Choose from six styles of rental homes in this innovative, new apartment-home community on the far West Side. Seventy single-family ranch and two-story homes, beginning at 1,300 square feet, are available for rent, ranging from $1,095 to $1,285 per month. Each home has a landscaped yard, patio and attached garage. Most have first-floor laundry rooms with washers and dryers. Renters must sign a minimum one-year lease. Waiting lists are common.

Munz Corporation
133 S. Butler St., Madison
- (608) 255-9433

Contact Munz to learn about openings in some of Madison's most popular apartment communities, including several East Side properties. Munz Corporation was founded in 1970. Richard Munz was an early developer of multifamily housing in South-Central Wisconsin, and the firm continues to be a frontrunner. It also specializes in corporate apartments and short-term housing for executives. Munz-managed apartments offer all the comforts you need to feel pampered and secure.

Oakbrook Corporation
440 Science Dr., Madison
- (608) 238-2600

Oakbrook Corporation manages property throughout the Midwest, including approximately 1,500 apartments in Dane County. The company specializes in market-rate apartments and rental housing for senior citizens. Oakbrook Corporation also manages property for commercial developers.

Ridgewood Country Club Apartments
2001 Traceway Dr., Madison
- (608) 271-5955

One of Madison's largest property-management firms, Ridgewood oversees more than 850 apartments and townhomes. One-, two- and three-bedroom units are available. Rents range from $530 to $880 a month. Tenants have access to two outdoor pools, tennis courts and golf, and pets are allowed. Short-term leases are available.

Rental-Information Publications

Apartment Guide & Renters Handbook
21 N. Henry St., Edgerton, Wis.
- (608) 884-3367, (608) 258-9292

This comprehensive apartment guide walks you through rental properties, neighborhood by neighborhood. This resource can help you narrow your focus, providing you with information on size and number of units, beginning rents, types of leases available, pet policies, amenities and parking, among other details. The publication also includes a glossary of legal terms often included in lease agreements.

Greater Madison Apartment Showcase
6402 Odana Rd., Madison
• (608) 278-8188

This full-color, pocket-size guide takes you through historic properties to the city's most modern, fully appointed rental offerings. Maps direct you to an index of rental properties so you can explore possible neighborhoods.

Start Renting Inc.
102 N. Franklin St., Madison
• (608) 257-4990

This biweekly publication is available for free at hundreds of Madison area locations. Apartments are listed by location, size and price.

Wisconsin State Journal/ The Capital Times
1901 Fish Hatchery Rd., Madison
• (608) 252-6100, (608) 252-6200

Classified advertisements in the morning and afternoon daily newspapers can provide you with the most up-to-date real estate and rental listings around. The Internet address is http://www.madison.com.

Real Estate Firms

Madison is home to nearly 400 real estate firms. But how can you ensure that the firm you pick will be right for you?

• Check on experience, education and productivity. Experienced agents know the market and the process, thus they have the best chance of quickly and smoothly helping you buy a home.

• Does your Realtor hold a professional designation (such as GRI, CRS or CRP)? These designations suggest a commitment that goes beyond earning a real estate license.

• As you drive around, do you see the agent's yard signs? A proliferation of these signs suggests familiarity with the area market.

• Does the agent seem interested in sharing expertise and market knowledge, or do you get the feeling that he or she is just telling you what you want to hear?

Most real estate firms now offer buyer brokerage. Buyer brokers can help you look after your interests. When you retain a buyer broker to help you locate a new home, the broker is paid a percentage fee similar to that paid a real estate agent — often 3 percent of the home price. Sellers usually end up paying the costs of a buyer broker, so it can be very much to your advantage to engage a buyer broker to help you navigate the market and negotiate a deal. For a referral, contact the **National Association of Buyer Representatives**, (608) 223-1860, 2800 Royal Avenue.

Beginning in summer 1997, "Most on Madison," the Web page for the *Wisconsin State Journal* and *The Capital Times*, began providing consumers with a full MLS listing of available residential offerings. The homepage address is http://www.madison.com.

We've compiled a list of some of the area's largest real estate firms to get you started.

Century 21 Advantage Gold
5402 Mineral Point Rd., Madison
• (608) 231-5858

Century 21 Advantage Gold specializes in residential and development sales throughout Dane County. The real estate firm is part of the Century 21 nationwide network, but like other Century 21 offices, Advantage Gold is independently owned and operated. Advantage Gold has 22 full- and part-time agents working from six offices. Services include free market analysis, computerized listings, national relocation and buyer brokerage.

Century 21 Affiliated
2800 Royal Ave., Madison
• (608) 221-2121

One of Madison's largest real estate firms, Century 21 Affiliated has 156 agents. The firm maintains five offices in Madison, including one at East Towne Mall. Century 21 Affiliated specializes in residential properties and can direct you to available homes all over Dane County.

Century 21 City Wide
1334 Applegate Rd., Madison
• (608) 273-2800

Century 21 City Wide's 38 real estate experts are knowledgeable about residential and income property opportunities across the city, in Dane County or throughout South-Central Wisconsin. The Century 21 office offers corporate relocation services, nationwide relocation assistance and buyer brokerage.

Coldwell Banker Sveum Realtors
2927 S. Fish Hatchery Rd., Madison
• (608) 276-3161

Coldwell Banker Sveum Realtors provides residential-sales services and sales and leasing of commercial, industrial and investment properties. Thirty-six real estate agents work at this busy firm. Coldwell Banker Sveum also has a home-mortgage network that helps you determine if you are getting the best possible deal on home financing.

ERA Krause Real Estate and Builders
1001 W. Main St., Sun Prairie
• (608) 837-4644

This 26-year-old firm recently opened a second office (in Cross Plains) so staff can better serve western Dane County. ERA Krause has 13 full-time agents. The company is involved in existing home sales, new residential and commercial properties and development. ERA Krause offers the option of steel-frame homes, which look and cost about the same as wood-built houses. Construction videos are available.

First Weber Group Inc.
429 Gammon Pl., Madison
• (608) 833-3355, (800) 236-8133

One of Dane County's largest realty agencies, First Weber offers eight offices in the greater Madison area with 230 real estate agents. In 1995, First Weber boasted more than $320 million in sales, with an average home price of $144,200. First Weber is locally owned and has been in business since 1967. The company specializes in single-family homes throughout Dane County.

Mardi O'Brien Real Estate
225 W. Beltline Hwy., Madison
• (608) 274-4646

Mardi O'Brien Real Estate specializes in waterfront and higher-end properties, including single-family dwellings and condominiums. The firm handles properties all over Dane County and also is involved in sales of residential income properties. Mardi O'Brien Real Estate was founded in 1974. New owners acquired the company in 1996.

McGettigan Company
5430 Century Ave., Middleton
• (608) 836-3626

Although this company is just 4 years old, founder Brian McGettigan has been in Dane County real estate for 25 years. The firm has three agents and specializes in home and condominium sales in Dane County. Currently McGettigan Company is helping to develop a new condominium community in Waunakee.

RE/MAX Preferred
6442 Normandy Ln., Madison
• (608) 276-8110

RE/MAX Preferred offers East Side (see "Relocation") with two Dane County offices (and three in outlying areas). RE/MAX logged more than $187 million in sales in 1,559 transactions in Dane County in 1997. The firm has about 62 agents who pride themselves on having some of the best sales production records in Dane County. RE/MAX offers all types of residential and commercial real estate services including buyer brokerage.

Restaino Bunbury and Associates
7701 Mineral Point Rd., Madison
• (608) 833-7777

Associates at Restaino Bunbury have on average 10 years of experience in Dane County's

---

INSIDERS' TIP

The current renaissance in Downtown Madison has meant many high quality new condominiums and apartments are available.

The Madison area has many friendly and reliable real estate companies to help you with your real estate needs.

real estate market. The firm has three offices and 72 agents ready to help you with your real estate needs. Restaino Bunbury handles sales of existing homes in neighborhoods throughout the Greater Madison area and is involved in new construction and development. The company specializes in condominium sales.

Simon and Voss
1818 Parmenter St., Middleton
• **(608) 831-3234**

Founded in 1988, Simon and Voss has 12 sales associates and two partners. The firm is committed to community involvement, and two Simon and Voss Realtors currently serve on the 10-person Madison Board of Realtors. Simon and Voss handles commercial and residential real estate. The firm tends to focus on home sales in Middleton and on Madison's West Side.

Stark Company
717 John Nolen Dr., Madison
• **(608) 256-9011**

With more than 175 employees in six offices throughout South Central Wisconsin, the Stark Company maintains an aggressive lead share in the Madison market. Stark offers a full menu of real estate services including residential sales, mortgage financing, insurance coverage and relocation assistance. Stark has been a leader in residential sales since 1908.

Builders

Whether you've made a firm decision to build or you're just kicking around the idea, you'll want to talk with the people who make homes happen. For a complete listing of Madison builders, contact **Madison Area**

Builders Association, 5936 Seminole Centre Court, (608) 288-1133.

Here's a sampling of Madison builders.

Design Shelters
2020 Eastwood Dr., Madison
• (608) 249-3251

Design Shelters has built some of Dane County's most spectacular, architect-designed homes since it was established in 1976. The firm builds about a dozen homes per year with annual sales of $4 million. Design Shelter homes range from 2,000 to 10,000 square feet and are priced between $250,000 and $1 million.

Don Simon Homes
2800 Royal Ave., Madison
• (608) 223-2626

This builder offers custom-built residences on homesites throughout Dane County. Depending on location, size and style, Don Simon homes are priced from $110,000 to more than $200,000. The builder has a reputation for easing the way for first-time home buyers. The company was founded in 1956 and has been featured in the Madison Area Parade of Homes.

Ehlers Construction Inc.
680 Grand Canyon Dr., Madison
• (608) 833-8005

Ehlers Construction has been designing, constructing and remodeling homes in the Madison area for 20 years. Terry Ehlers says the key to his company's success is listening to clients and maintaining communication throughout the process.

Impala Custom Homes
6617 Seybold Rd., Madison
• (608) 271-8500

Large, upscale homes ranging in price from $200,000 to $300,000 are Impala Home's trademark. The builder has constructed more than 2,000 homes since the company started in 1966. Impala constructs homes on sites in some of Madison's most desirable locations. A three- to four-bedroom home typically ranges in size from 2,000 to 3,000 square feet. Impala offers basic floor plans that home buyers can modify and expand.

Loren Imhoff, Homebuilder
7919 Airport Rd., Middleton
• (608) 831-1900

If you visit the Parade of Homes, you will no doubt see a breathtaking and unique Imhoff home. The builder constructs about six custom homes each year. Imhoff homes range in price from $250,000 to $1.2 million; some are as large as 10,000 square feet. Imhoff, who constructs custom cabinets in each of his homes, builds on sites across southern Wisconsin.

Michael F. Simon Builders
817 S. Division St., Waunakee
• (608) 849-5916

The Simon family has been building homes in the Madison area since 1893, and is a frequent participant in the Parade of Homes. Simon homes stress energy efficiency by incorporating greater use of insulation and using passive solar energy and airtight construction techniques. Large, arched windows contribute to the beauty of many Simon homes. In addition to residential construction, the Simons have also built churches and commercial buildings in the area. Most floor plans range from 3,000 to 5,000 square feet; costs vary widely. Bring in your ideas or plans for a free estimate.

Midland Builders
6709 Raymond Rd., Madison
• (608) 271-4444

Midland Builders has been constructing homes in Madison for 45 years. Visit open houses in Midland neighborhoods to discover how you can customize one of the company's 100 floor plans to suit your needs. Many homes are priced

INSIDERS' TIP

If you've got a million or so to spend on a house, some of the best places to look in the Madison area are Bishop's Bay, the Highlands and on Lake Mendota in Shorewood Hills or the Town of Westport.

in the $130,000 range and include 1,100 square feet of living space plus a full basement.

Monson Construction Co. Inc.
414 D'Onofrio Dr., Ste. 100, Madison
• (608) 274-1127

Current Monson Construction projects include upscale apartment complexes, single-family-home subdivisions, custom family homes and several commercial buildings. Since 1954, president Terry Monson has built more than 1,000 custom family homes and earned a reputation for excellence. He has been honored with numerous industry awards and has been in the Madison Parade of Homes continuously since 1967.

Nichols Design and Construction LLC
5874 Tree Line Dr., Madison
• (608) 273-4807

The owner of Nichols Design and Construction is a professional architect and licensed engineer as well as experienced homebuilder. In business for 23 years and a longtime Parade of Homes participant, Nichols Design has built homes as costly as $2.5 million in the past three years. The builder, however, likes diversity and enjoys building custom single-family homes of all styles. If you want a starter home, a large house with plenty of room for a growing family, an "empty nest" paradise or an executive showplace, they will work with your plans or start from scratch. Home prices start at $130,000, and Nichols builds on scattered sites across Dane County.

Princeton Custom Homes Inc.
1009 S. Whitney Way, Madison
• (608) 274-7747

Whether you're looking for a moderately priced ($110,000 to $120,000), newly constructed home in a nice development or are planning to build a fantasy house with all the amenities in the half-million dollar range, Princeton Custom Homes can provide you with a wide range of options. The builder offers on-site design using your plans or adapting existing plans to suit your needs. Princeton has a solid reputation and has participated in the Madison Parade of Homes for more than 20 years. The builder works on sites all over Dane County. Princeton also constructs multifamily homes and does remodeling.

Wick Homes
400 Walter Rd., Mazomanie
• (608) 795-2261, (800) 442-9425

Wick Homes, a division of Wick Building Systems Inc., has built more than 25,000 homes in Wisconsin and neighboring states in the past 30 years. Home prices range from $60,000 to more than $300,000 in more than 75 floor plans and hundreds of options. Wick Homes constructs 220 homes per year, and buyers can be living in their new homes within 40 days of the contract agreement. Components are built in the Wick factory and then quickly erected on site, which Wick says helps them meet tight deadlines, adhere to budget and improve quality control.

Yahara Builders Inc.
2927 S. Fish Hatchery Rd., Madison
• (608) 276-3166

Yahara offers custom-built homes — your site or theirs — throughout the Madison area. Homes begin at 2,500 square feet and $250,000, then are limited only by your budget. In previous years, Yahara created several outstanding residences for the Parade of Homes.

Check over the brochure...

Check With the Experts

MGE's do-it-yourself checklist of energy-saving standards for your home.

mgoe.

We have a brochure full of ways to save energy and money.

Call for your free copy of *Check With the Experts* today:

252-7117.

Save over time.

mgoe.®
life enhancing energy™

GS0412 R-6/98

©1998, Madison Gas and Electric

Neighborhoods

Madison is in the midst of a growth spurt that is pushing out its eastern and western borders.

The population in Dane County is 398,233, making it the second-fastest growing county in Wisconsin with an 8.3 percent increase in the number of residents between 1990 and 1997. That is due, in part, to Madison's so-called recession-proof economy that is the result of it being a university town and the state capital.

Growth has been swallowing farmland surrounding Madison. As a result, land-use planning is a subject that anyone running for public office is expected to have strong opinions about. But you can be sure that runaway urban sprawl is not likely to happen here. There are too many active environmentalists in Madison to let that happen.

The past year has also seen an unprecedented boom in Downtown construction, triggered by the Monona Terrace Convention Center and the Kohl Center arena. Apartments, condominiums and hotels are being built on the isthmus, or are in the planning stages. Restaurants and upscale bars are opening downtown at a dizzying rate.

What all this means is that if you're looking for a place to live in Madison, you'll have a lot of choices. The city has a number of charming historic neighborhoods. New lots are being sold in outlying areas. There are many new housing developments to choose from. And the many neighborhoods that sprang up after World War II, many of them with big yards, are being remodeled.

What almost every Madison neighborhood has in common is green space nearby. Madison has a long history of aggressively purchasing land for parks. You're never far from community parks, beaches and boat landings, churches and shopping. Neighborhood schools often serve a dual purpose as community centers, hosting adult basketball games, youth soccer and T-ball, continuing-education classes, aerobics and Scout meetings.

The average assessed home value in Madison in 1997 was $132,800. The typical house is usually described as a well-maintained three-bedroom ranch with about 1,100 square feet and an attached garage in a nice neighborhood.

To help you zero in on the neighborhoods you might be interested in, we have clarified and expanded our usual geographic locations. For further detail and neighborhood maps, obtain a copy of *A Guide to Madison's Neighborhood Associations* from the City Department of Planning and Development, 215 Martin Luther King Jr. Boulevard, (608) 266-4635.

Where it is possible, we mention which public schools children in the neighborhoods attend. But school boundaries are often changed, so make sure to ask a real estate professional about schools if it is your intention to buy a home in Madison.

Isthmus

The Isthmus area is the heart of downtown Madison, our center of local, county and state government and home to numerous professional offices and associations. Due to its proximity to the Madison campus, the area offers a wide selection of rental properties. Home prices range from $60,000 to $250,000 in the six neighborhoods that make up the Isthmus area.

Bassett

The Victorian homes here were built by 19th-century Irish and German immigrants. Famous Wisconsin Progressive "Fighting Bob" La Follette and his wife, Belle, also lived here for a while. These days, the Bassett area — bordered by University Avenue to the north,

Broom Street to the east, N. Shore Drive to the south and N. Frances Street to the west — primarily houses university students. About 2,500 apartments and 100 single-family homes can be found within the neighborhood, which is served by Franklin-Randall Elementary School, Hamilton Middle School and West High School. Neighborhood residents can walk to shopping on State Street or picnic and play Frisbee at nearby Brittingham and Law parks. Four major bus routes give residents easy access to many other parts of the city. The average assessed value in 1997 was $110,000.

Capitol

This small conglomeration of several neighborhoods encompasses about 270 acres. It is one of Madison's oldest sections, centered around the Capitol Square. Here you will find the Mansion Hill historic district with its distinctly elegant 19th-century homes. Some of Madison's most spectacular specimens of historic architecture are here, much of it built of local sandstone. Residents of the Capitol area have the luxury of being bordered by Madison's largest lakes, Lake Mendota to the north and vistas of Lake Monona to the south. Residents of the Capitol area have the luxury of being bordered by Madison's largest lakes, Lake Mendota to the north and a stretch of Lake Monona to the south. Butler and Blair streets mark the eastern borders; Broom and Carroll streets are to the west.

This lively area offers plenty of entertainment and cultural opportunities, with quick access to parks and beaches, bike paths, shopping, churches, the civic center, museums and other attractions. Like the Bassett area, most of the residential properties in this neighborhood are rental units. However, the area has some remarkable single-family homes. Students (kindergarten through 12th grade) from this neighborhood may attend Lapham-Marquette or Franklin-Randall elementary schools, O'Keeffe or Hamilton middle schools and East or West high schools. The average 1997 assessed value just east of the Capitol Square was $104,700, and $109,100 west of the Square. However, those figures do not reflect the old mansions that sell for hundreds of thousands of dollars.

Langdon Street

Another landmark historic neighborhood set on the shores of Lake Mendota, Langdon Street is a student area known now for its stately period Revival-style fraternity and sorority houses. There's something going on here day and night.

In early days this splendid old neighborhood was home to university faculty members and Madison's "upper crust." Residents can walk to State Street, the Memorial Union, all of the university's major libraries and Madison's Central Library (see our Attractions chapter). This area is served by all of the city's major bus routes. The assessed value of the average home in 1997 was $139,900.

Marquette (a.k.a. Wil-Mar)

This historic neighborhood, sliced by the Yahara River, is currently a red-hot real estate market. It is bordered on the south by Lake Monona. Its most famous street, Williamson — or Willy Street — had its heyday in the 1960s as an anti-establishment refuge. That heritage is celebrated today through events such as the Willy Street Fair (see our Festivals and Annual Events chapter) and a waterfront festival. Residents are proud of their area's colorful past and its continuing spirit of cooperation.

The neighborhood is a mix of older, multistory single-family homes and apartments, with about 100 condominiums and some highly sought-after lakefront properties. The area includes two historic districts. The 19th-century homes were built largely by blue-collar workers, although you will find many huge, beautiful Queen Anne houses in the area. Many single people and childless couples have moved into the neighborhood and are undertaking major renovations of the historic properties. The 1997 average assessed value in Wil-Mar was $94,800, although housing prices along the lake can run more than $300,000.

Madison's first cemetery was in this neighborhood, about a block from Lake Monona. It was moved long ago, and in its place there is now the lovely Orton public park, with a Victorian gazebo and trees as old as the city. It's a popular place for weddings and picnics.

To get a concentrated taste of this neighborhood, go to the Williamson Street Coop, which was organized in the Vietnam era and has evolved into a well-run center for organic foods. There's also a charming little people's park on Willy Street. Residents are within easy walking distance of downtown, shopping areas, beaches and major bus lines. Primary- and secondary-school students attend Lapham-Marquette or Lowell elementary schools, O'Keeffe Middle School and East High School.

Old Market Place

The Old Market Place neighborhood is one of Madison's most historically significant sections. Its East Dayton Street marks the site of Madison's first African-American community. Visitors to the area will discover architectural diversity, including the venerable Gothic Revival-style Leitch House, on the Lake Mendota shoreline, which is now open as the Livingston Bed and Breakfast Inn (see our Bed and Breakfast Inns chapter).

Seven major bus routes pass through this area, connecting residents with East and West Towne malls (see our Shopping chapter), University of Wisconsin-Madison and Madison Area Technical College (see Higher Education). The neighborhood has about 90 single-family homes, a smattering of condominiums and more than 1,000 apartment units. Residents and visitors alike enjoy relaxing in James Madison Park on Lake Mendota. Primary- and secondary-school students attend Lapham-Marquette Elementary School, O'Keeffe Middle School and East High School. The 1997 average assessed home value was $102,400.

Schenk's-Atwood (a.k.a. Atwood-Winnebago)

Two Indian mounds, small hills shaped like a bear and a lynx, can still be found in this historic neighborhood's Lakefront Park. During the Civil War the area was known as Union Corners, a way station on the road from Milwaukee to Madison. For a while it was known as a resort area, as it's on the eastern shore of Lake Monona. But factories on the East Side of Madison changed that, and blue-collar residential development grew.

Between 1900 and World War II this area was known as a German and Norwegian enclave. The neighborhood's once-lively shopping began to falter after the war, when malls in outlying areas began to take over. Today, the neighborhood has many young residents, as well as some elderly who've been living in the area since they were young. Since 1982 renovation has put a fresh face on many of the area's buildings, including a theater and a dairy barn that now houses business offices. Olbrich Gardens, which is one of Madison's most treasured assets, is on Atwood Avenue. Lowell School was built in 1916 on circus grounds in the neighborhood, and one of Madison's most beautiful Catholic churches is on Atwood Avenue.

Rayovac (formerly French Battery and Carbon Co.) began here, and the theater now known as the Barrymore was built in the Spanish hacienda style in 1929. The Yahara River Parkway is here, too. The meandering little Yahara River that connected lakes Monona and Mendota was broadened and turned into a beautiful parkway in the early 20th century. Today, the neighborhood is on the upswing, with considerable renovation under way. The average assessed value in 1997 was $88,400.

Tenney-Lapham

The huge appeal of the Tenney-Lapham neighborhood comes from the sprawling beauty of Tenney Park, a picturesque mecca for ice skaters and nature lovers since the early 1900s. You can walk down the park to the architecturally distinctive Sherman Avenue Historic District. Local social events include a summer ice-cream social, fall spaghetti dinner, winter caroling party and annual garden tour.

Housing consists of more than 500 early 20th-century single-family homes, about 1,200 apartments and a few condominiums. The average assessed values in the Lapham School-Breese Stevens area is $96,800. Tenney Park's average price is $133,600.

Area residents are never far from water. The Tenney-Lapham neighborhood is bordered by Lake Mendota to the north, the Yahara River to the east, E. Washington Avenue to the south and N. Livingston Street to the west. Primary- and secondary-school students attend Lapham-Marquette Elementary School, O'Keeffe Middle School and East High School.

Near West

The near West Side neighborhoods offer comfortable living within easy walking or short driving distance to the zoo, public golf courses, parks and many other attractions. Homes here can be found between $96,500 and $225,000, according to 1997 assessed values. Neighborhoods have established vegetation, well-kept homes and diverse populations. Most homes in this area are older and vary in style from ranches to English Tudors.

Bayview and Brittingham-Vilas

The Bayview and Brittingham-Vilas neighborhoods are composed mostly of apartments and duplexes with about 500 older, single-family homes. These are primarily rental neighborhoods targeted at UW students. Residents here can relax at Brittingham Park and Beach, on Monona Bay, or take the kids to community playgrounds. The neighborhood is bordered by Regent Street to the north, W. Washington Avenue to the east and south and S. Park Street to the west. Children from this area can attend Randall-Franklin Elementary, Hamilton Middle School and West High School.

The Brittingham-Vilas area offers diverse worship opportunities including Beth Israel Center, Islamic Center and five Christian churches. Residents are close to numerous healthcare facilities and specialty shops. Here you can find some of the city's least expensive housing with an average assessed value of $84,300.

Dudgeon-Monroe

The Dudgeon-Monroe neighborhood is home to two of Madison's oldest surviving buildings, former stagecoach stops named the Plough Inn (a.k.a. "Plow in and Stumble Out"), which is now a beautiful bed and breakfast inn, and the Spring Tavern, which is now a private residence. The neighborhood is filled with beautiful wetlands, and you'll find spots here for hikes, wildlife watching and renting a canoe.

The area is primarily made up of neatly kept older, single-family homes (about 1,200). Points of interest in this area include three private schools — Edgewood Elementary School, Edgewood High School and Edgewood College — Dudgeon Center for Community Programs, Glenwood Children's Park, Edgewood Park and the UW Arboretum. The neighborhood association hosts an annual summer solstice celebration at Wingra Park. Monroe Street also has some of the most interesting shops in all of Madison, such as Orange Tree Imports and Chris Kerwin Antiques and Interiors, some ethnic restaurants and coffee bars. The 1997 average assessed home value was $131,900.

Nakoma

Nakoma is one of Madison's most desirable neighborhoods. It was first platted in 1915 as a country suburb, with winding roads, a golf course, parks and tennis courts. As the city grew up, Nakoma grew with it. Most of the homes were built by the 1950s. In Nakoma you will find a wide range of architectural styles, especially its stone versions of English revival styles, and many Colonials. The lots tend to be tiny, but landscaping and mature foliage make many of them lovely.

Nakoma is one of the more exclusive neighborhoods on the near West Side with 1997 assessed values averaging $217,700. Parks include Nakoma Park, Tillitson Greenway and Hiawatha Circle.

Primary- and secondary-school students living in Nakoma attend Thoreau Elementary School, Cherokee Middle School and West High School. Neighbors get together for a fall celebration, Twelfth Night Dinner and Play, a Tulip Time Progressive Dinner, July 4th festivities and a Halloween party.

Westmorland

Westmorland residents have many recreational opportunities in close range. Glenway and Odana public golf courses are nearby

The Olbrich Park neighborhood enjoys botanical gardens and one of the city's best sledding hills.

along with an arboretum, a zoo and neighborhood parks. Nearly 900 single-family homes and about 60 apartments are in Westmorland. Annual events include a Fourth of July festival, children's Halloween party, skating party and an adult winter dance. Average assessments in 1997 were $133,500.

Radio Park and Sunset Hills

Radio Park and Sunset Hills sit on the edge of Hoyt Park, which is one of Madison's oldest and most beautiful parks. The densely forested park has walls, park shelters, tables and barbecues made of stone during the Depression by WPA workers. An observatory drive through the park offers a panoramic view of Madison's West Side. These small neighborhoods consist primarily of single-family homes, including some dramatic International-style residences.

Residents are close to shopping at University Hill Plaza, The Highland, Shorewood Shopping Center, University Place, Hilldale Shopping Center and Walnut Grove. Nearby Glenway Golf Course further enhances the area. Students attend Midvale or Lincoln elementary schools, Hamilton Middle School and West High School. The 1997 assessments in Sunset Hills averaged $225,500.

Sunset Village

The Sunset Village neighborhood is made up of small two- and three-bedroom homes. The area is bordered by University Avenue, Mineral Point and N. Midvale Boulevard. Residents are primarily "empty nesters," young families and single professionals. The average assessed value is $134,700.

Regent

Within the Regent neighborhood, you can find historic homes designed by Frank Lloyd Wright, Louis Sullivan and George Maher. There are about 1,200 single-family homes and the same number of apartments here, most dating to before World War II. Homes here tend to be higher priced than in other near West neighborhoods. The neighborhood also has a few condominiums and duplexes. Streets in this area tend to follow a traditional grid pattern.

A focal point of the Regent neighborhood is West High School, near the intersection of Speedway and Regent Street. Nearby Forest Hill Cemetery is the final resting place of many prominent Madison citizens, and there are Union and Confederate sections for Civil War dead. Homes around the high school sell for about $160,000, but you'll find a few in the $300,000 plus range as well.

Vilas-Edgewood Avenue

Here's where to live if you don't mind being awakened by an occasional hippopotamus bellow. Surrounded by Henry Vilas Zoo, Regent Street, Randall and Edgewood avenues and Monroe Street, Vilas neighborhood has about 400 single-family homes, including numerous rentals, 175 duplexes and 160 apartments. Many of the city's most charming older homes can be found here, but they are usually on miniscule lots. Neighborhood children attend Franklin-Randall Elementary, Hamilton Middle School and West High School.

In addition to having a free zoo and huge city park in their midst, residents have a close-up look at Madison's earliest history with the Curtis Effigy Mounds (for more information about Native American mound builders, see the History chapter). Average assessments were $189,900 in 1997.

University Heights

This neighborhood was platted at the turn of the century. A hilly topography and curving streets attracted many university faculty members, who built large and attractive homes. University Heights is now a popular spot for walking tours, with outstanding buildings by the greatest of the Prairie School architects Frank Lloyd Wright and Louis Sullivan, its Craftsman and bungalow-style homes, and a number of fine Queen Anne-, Georgian- and shingle-style dwellings. Olin House, the English-style brick mansion occupied by the president of UW-Madison, is here too. A number of them simply can't be put into categories.

The neighborhood is home to one of the oldest congregations in Madison, The First Congregational Church, a lovely red-brick Georgian-style building, and the landmark 1906 Randall School. The average assessed value in 1997 was $253,600.

Eagle Heights

Eagle Heights is more commonly known as "married-student housing" for the University of Wisconsin. The wooded, students-only neighborhood sits on Second Point, along the Lake Mendota shoreline. In recent years, UW has upgraded its housing so apartments now offer such niceties as dishwashers. There's a strong sense of cooperation and community within Eagle Heights as well as a diverse international population. Elementary students from this area attend Shorewood Elementary School in the prestigious nearby Village of Shorewood Hills. Property here is owned by the UW and rented to students.

West

West neighborhoods offer a wide variety of styles and prices that can meet virtually any need. Residents are within an easy walk or a short drive of shopping, parks and many other attractions. The median home price here is about $148,000, but homes can be found between $85,000 and $365,000. Neighborhoods have established vegetation, numerous parks and diverse populations. Most homes in this area were built since 1945 and vary in style from ranches with single-car attached garages, to classic Colonials and contemporary designs.

Appalachian Ridge

Appalachian Ridge is a small development of 21 homes that traces its roots back to the 1950s and '60s. Although the neighborhood has no parks of its own, residents are in close walking distance to Woodland Hills Park and Owen Park. The quiet, tree-lined neighborhood attracts quite a few varieties of birds. Homes sell for about $200,000. Schools include Crestwood, John Muir, Jefferson and Memorial.

Faircrest

Anchored on Mineral Point Road, one of Madison's main thoroughfares, Faircrest is another well-established neighborhood with many mature, large trees. The neighborhood is a nice mix of condos, single-family homes, duplexes and apartments. Residents work to gain a sense of community by publishing a neighborhood directory and sponsoring numerous events including guided nature walks, a spring bash, food drive, progressive dinner and a cookie exchange.

Faircrest dwellers are served by three Madison Metro bus routes. Recreational centers include the Owen Conservation Park, Nautilus Point Park, Parkcrest Swim and Tennis Club and Mineral Point Park. Students attend Glenn

Stephens or John Muir elementary schools, Jefferson Middle School and Memorial High School. The 1997 average assessed value in the Faircrest-University Heights neighborhood was $177,100.

Glen Oak Hills

Glen Oak Hills contains about 375 single-family homes and a few dozen duplexes and apartments amid lots of park land. The neighborhood is framed by Old Middleton Road, N. Whitney Way, Regent Street and Rosa Road. Residents with shopping on their minds can easily head to nearby Odana Road, Westgate Mall, Hilldale, Shorewood and a variety of other shopping centers. Three bus routes extend to Glen Oak Hills. The average assessed value in 1997 was $113,800.

The Highlands

The Highlands is a quiet, prestigious neighborhood that began to take shape in 1911. It is on a series of hills that form the western slope of the basin of Madison's lakes. The principle road through the Highlands is a horseshoe shape, which has contributed to its rustic, wooded character. This 131-acre neighborhood, with its winding roads, has about 95 single-family homes having assessed values of $431,100. However, some top $1 million, making The Highlands one of the most expensive neighborhoods in the city, home to many executives and UW doctors. The Highlands is within walking distance of University Hospital.

Architecture here covers a wide range, but the most unusual Highlands mansion would have to be the Edenfred, which is 180 feet wide but just one room (26 feet) deep. The odd shape was to make the most of hilltop breezes and give every room a view from the crest of a hill that overlooks Lake Mendota. The Highland's best known mansion, though, is Brittingham House, owned by the university.

The neighborhood has two greenways and Skyview Park. A few homes date back to World War II, but most are newer. Residents enjoy an annual Wisconsin River canoe trip.

Nearby, the tiny Skyview Terrace neighborhood has about 35 single-family homes on 28 acres.

Hill Farms

Students and young people just starting out often find homes in Hill Farms. The area has more than 1,600 apartments, offers steady bus traffic and is within walking distance of several shopping areas, seven churches and numerous restaurants.

Hill Farms has about 700 single-family homes with a 1997 average assessed value of $159,000. The area is best-known as the site of the Hill Farms State Office Building (you can renew driver's licenses and purchase car tags here), and the headquarters for the American Red Cross are here.

Mendota Beach Heights

Mendota Beach's 260 acres, as you might guess, are snuggled against the shores of Lake Mendota. Homes consist of about 350 single-family dwellings, a dozen condos, some duplexes and more than 100 apartments. Area schools include Crestwood, Glenn Stephens, Jefferson and Memorial. Lakeshore properties are at least double the price of homes without lake views: from $300,000 to $500,000. The average 1997 assessed value for the neighborhood, however, was $146,800.

Midvale Heights-Tokay

Midvale Heights-Tokay is another cohesive neighborhood with a diverse population spanning all age groups. About 3,500 people live in the area bordered by Mineral Point Road, Midvale Boulevard, Odana Hills Golf Course and S. Whitney Way. The area primarily consists of single-family homes, with a

---

INSIDERS' TIP

The Mansion Hill Historic District can be found north of the Capitol Square around Gilman and Pinckney Streets. You will find a sandstone Victorian mansion at each of the four corners and several other memorable buildings along the streets.

few condos and duplexes and about 160 apartments. Midvale Heights has well-established foliage, including lots of tall hardwoods and plenty of hedges and flower gardens. The average assessed value was $125,000 in 1997.

Parkwood Hills

The 318 acres that make up Parkwood Hills are divided by streets named after some of America's most prized natural wonders, such as Mount Rainier, Bryce Canyon and Carlsbad Caverns. The newer neighborhood has about 500 single-family homes, with an average assessed value of $216,000. There are about 160 condominiums and apartments.

This neighborhood includes James Madison Memorial High School and borders on Owen Park Conservancy. Shopping is close-at-hand at West Towne Mall, Market Square, Odana Plaza and the Odana Shoppes.

Spring Harbor-Indian Hills

Just west of Blackhawk Country Club is the Spring Harbor neighborhood, named for an inlet on Lake Mendota. Residents have a huge selection of parks and greenways, including eight parks within the 380-acre neighborhood itself. The area consists of about 700 single-family homes, several condos and duplexes and 500 apartments. The average assessed value was $146,800 in 1997. The average of Spring Harbor lakeshore property was $324,000.

Saukborough-Woodland Hills

Woodland Hills is a neighborhood where energy conservation is for many a way of life. Many of the more than 100 single-family contemporary homes have incorporated passive solar and other energy-saving technology into their designs. Woodland Hills Park is a focal point for the neighborhood. The average assessed value is $230,000.

Stonefield Woods-Ridge

Stonefield Woods-Ridge shares many amenities with Woodland Hills. Children from both neighborhoods attend Crestwood Elementary, Jefferson Middle School and Memorial High School. Prices for homes in this area average about $200,000.

Far West

The far West Side neighborhoods contain some of Madison's newest developments. The prices run from $109,200 to a half-million dollars. Neighborhoods include Millstone, Oakbridge, Sauk Creek, Walnut Grove, Wexford Ridge and Wexford Village.

Access to points east of these far West Side developments can easily be gained by hopping on the W. Beltline Highway. Traveling by car to the UW-Madison campus and downtown Madison will typically take 20 to 30 minutes during rush hour and about 5 to 10 minutes less during other times.

These developments are typically less than 25 years old, and as you go farther west, the developments are newer. From Gammon Road to the W. Beltline, single-family homes and condominiums dominate the landscape with a smattering of upscale apartments. In the 1990s, developments west of the W. Beltline began springing up, with homes typically smaller than those to the east. There also are more apartments and condominiums west of the W. Beltline.

Millstone

The Millstone neighborhood, west of Gammon Road off Colony Drive, consists of 16 smaller single-family homes with an average price of about $130,000. The Oakbridge community and the Sauk Creek neighborhood are small developments bordered to the west by the W. Beltline, to the east by S. High Point Road, to the south by Mineral Point Road and to the north by Old Sauk Road.

INSIDERS' TIP

Many people who like to hike choose to live in the UW-Arboretum area, where you can walk on city streets for hours without getting near a car.

Home Lending

HOME SAVINGS

Education Funding

Retirement Planning

Children's Savings

Helping you achieve your life events

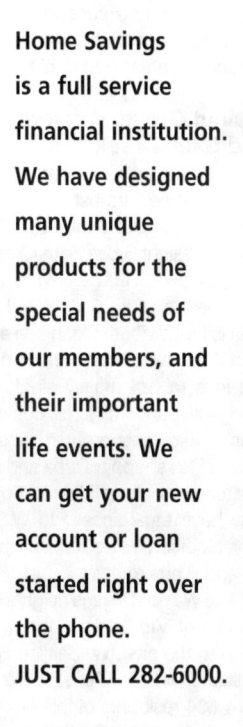

Home Savings is a full service financial institution. We have designed many unique products for the special needs of our members, and their important life events. We can get your new account or loan started right over the phone.
JUST CALL 282-6000.

Our commitment to the community is a commitment to you.

Downtown, West, East, Northport, Stoughton

Five locations | One number | 282-6000

www.home-savings.com

FDIC INSURED

EQUAL HOUSING LENDER

The area is best described as a small neighborhood that combines the flavor of contemporary designs with the feeling of Old Country charm.

The area's 1,300 residents live in a mix of single-family homes, duplexes, condominiums and apartments. Single-family homes range from about $125,000 near Mineral Point Road to more than $300,000 in the Sauk Creek Estates area. Madison Metro bus routes service the neighborhood residents with primary and secondary service. Shopping, churches and day-care providers also service the area's residents.

Walnut Grove, Wexford Ridge and Sauk Creek

The Walnut Grove and Wexford Ridge neighborhoods are just west of Gammon Road and south of Old Sauk Road. The assessed value in Walnut Grove/Sauk Creek is $205,800; in Wexford Village (with Sawmill and Longmeadow), it's $183,800. Housing in this area is typical for the Madison area. The more than 3,500 residents of these neighborhoods live in a mix of mainly single-family homes along with condominiums, duplexes and apartments. Residents are very close to the West Towne Mall shopping area and myriad restaurant choices along Mineral Point Road, and they have easy access to W. Beltline Highway. Madison Metro services the area with its J, I and P bus routes.

The Wexford Village neighborhood borders the city of Middleton to the north, Gammon Road to the east, W. Beltline Highway to the west and Old Sauk Road to the south. Most of the 1,634 residents of this neighborhood live in single-family homes that are best described as two-story contemporaries with two- or three-car attached garages. Since the development is relatively new, the area is not heavily wooded, but residents have planted many trees and other vegetation that, in a few years, will become mature landscaping and add to the area's beauty.

Madison's far West Side is home to numerous restaurants and shops and Madison's newest retail mecca, Prairie Towne Shopping Center, which is anchored by the area's first Target store and is also home to the region's only CompUSA store.

Students attend Crestwood, John Muir and Glenn Stephens elementary schools, Jefferson Middle School and Memorial High School.

Northeast

Much of the development in the Madison's Northeast dates back to the 1950s. Many of the early residents of this area worked for companies east of the capitol, such as Oscar Mayer. The median home price is $90,000, with most in the $79,000 to $182,000 range. Styles range from small cottages to contemporary homes. There are also numerous apartments and condos in Northeast Madison.

From Brentwood Village, you can easily walk to nearby Warner Park for minor-league baseball games and the city's blockbuster Fourth of July celebration. The Mendota-Hill Farms bus provides area residents with a link to the city's other major bus routes.

Brentwood Village-Bruns

Slightly more than 200 single-family homes and 350 apartment units line the streets in Brentwood Village. Residents have fast access to the Northgate, Lakewood and Sherman Plaza shopping areas as well as to Warner Beach on Lake Mendota. Primary- and secondary-school students attend Lakeview or Emerson elementary schools, Sherman Middle School or East High School. The average assessed value is $117,000.

Burke Heights

The focal point of Burke Heights is Sycamore Park. You'll find fewer than 100 single-family homes and 150 apartments in this neighborhood, which is bordered by Sycamore Avenue to the north, Sycamore Park to the east, Commercial Avenue to the south and Stoughton Road (U.S. Highway 51) and a railroad to the west and northwest. The setting offers quick access to major roads including Wis. Highway 30.

Residents enjoy such annual rituals as a summer neighborhood picnic, neighborhood garage sale, spring cleanup and a Christmas cookie exchange. The 1997 average assessed value in this Stoughton Road-Commercial Avenue neighborhood is $92,100.

East Bluff

East Bluff has the distinction of having Madison's oldest condominium association. Area residents express pride in their diverse ethnic backgrounds, ages and lifestyles. The condominium community includes about 175 two- and three-bedroom homes.

Residents are close to Warner Park and Beach, Northgate Shopping Center and Sherman Plaza. Two buses have regular stops in the area, and it's a quick drive to the Dane County Regional Airport. East Bluff is bordered by Troy Drive, N. Sherman Avenue and Northport Drive. School children attend Lakeview Elementary, Black Hawk Middle School and East High School. The 1997 average assessed home value was $101,100.

Hawthorne

Hawthorne residents enjoy easy access to major thoroughfares and shopping at East Towne Mall, Madison East Shopping Center, Princeton Place and Essex Square. The neighborhood is bordered by Stoughton Road (U.S. Highway 51) and includes a portion of Wis. Highway 30. Housing includes about 570 single-family homes, 170 two-unit apartments and 400 multiple-unit apartment buildings.

Students attend Lowell or Hawthorne elementary schools, Sherman Middle School and East High School. Residents have a community center and community gardens. Home values averaged $92,700 in 1997.

Kennedy Heights

The Kennedy Heights neighborhood consists of 104 two- and three-bedroom apartments centered around a community center and playground. The area is served by Lindbergh Elementary School, Black Hawk Middle School and East High School. Nearby shopping areas include Sherman Plaza and Northgate. Area attractions include Cherokee Lake and Marsh, Warner Park and Beach, the Lakeview Hill Conservancy and the Dane County Regional Airport. Residents can hop on a Mendota-Hill Farms bus to travel to other points of interest in the city.

Lakeview Hills

Lakeview Hills frames three sides of the scenic Lakeview Woods County Conservancy Park. School children attend Gompers, Lakeview or Lindbergh elementary schools, Black Hawk Middle School and East High School. Three bus routes provide citywide transport, and residents have nearby shopping at Lakewood Plaza, Northgate Shopping Center and Sherman Plaza.

Lakeview Hills has about 1,000 single-family homes, 175 condominiums and 190 apartments. You'll find four churches in this neighborhood, which had average assessed home values of $101,100 in 1997.

Norman Acres

Next to East Towne Mall and Reindahl Park, Norman Acres is home to about 200 residents. Housing includes about 40 single-family homes and 25 apartments. The area is bordered by Duke Street, Crescent Road, Independence Lane, E. Washington Avenue and Portage Road.

Children living in Norman Acres can attend Sandburg Elementary, O'Keeffe Middle School and East High School. There are three neighborhood churches. Shopping is varied and plentiful. Residents have easy access to a major road (E. Washington Avenue) leading either Downtown or out to interstates 90 and 94. Norman Acres average assessed home values in 1997 were $121,900.

North Lake Mendota

As its name suggests, North Lake Mendota rests on the shores of Madison's biggest lake. Just 140 single-family homes make up this neighborhood, which also is bordered by Cherokee Marsh, Northport Drive and Troy Drive. Nearby, you'll find Central Wisconsin Center and Mendota Mental Health Center.

Area schools include Mendota Elementary, Black Hawk Middle School and East High School. Bus service is available, and it's a short ride to Northgate Shopping Center, Lakewood Plaza or Sherman Plaza. While the average assessed value here in 1997 was $128,700, lake shore residents have average assessed values of $346,300.

Reindahl Park

Residents of Reindahl Park can frolic at Holiday Bluff Park, Village Green East Park, Sun Gardens Park or (of course) Reindahl

Park. The neighborhood features about 200 single-family homes, 10 duplexes and 165 apartments. There is a neighborhood garden at Reindahl Park. Local events include an annual block party, Halloween party, Christmas caroling and a home-improvement contest.

Those who live in Reindahl Park can take advantage of the many educational and cultural opportunities offered at the nearby Madison Area Technical College. School children attend Sandburg Elementary, O'Keeffe Middle School and East High School.

The 1997 average assessed value in this neighborhood in the East Washington Avenue and Stoughton Road area is $85,100.

Sherman

The heart of the Sherman neighborhood has many beautiful homes on Lake Mendota, and many distinguished historic homes throughout. The community takes its name from its major north-south thoroughfare, which was once the favorite route from Downtown to the once rural areas that now make up Madison's East Side. Housing consists of about 900 single-family homes, 140 condos, 100 duplexes and 85 apartments.

Neighborhood amenities include four churches, three bus routes, Hartmeyer Ice Arena, Sheridan Triangle Park, Windom Way Park and Warner Park and Beach. Maple Bluff Country Club is nearby. Area schools include Emerson or Mendota Elementary, Sherman Middle School and East High School. Housing in the area ranges from cottages to large lakeshore homes.

Sherman Village

Take the Lakeview/Burr Oaks or the Sherman Ltd. bus to visit Sherman Village. Points of interest include Cherokee Country Club, Cherokee Conservancy and Marsh and a handful of neighborhood parks. More than 1,000 single-family homes and 439 condominiums make up this neighborhood that borders Cherokee Country Club's golf course. Youth attend Gompers, Lindbergh or Lakeview elementary schools, Black Hawk Middle School and East High School.

The 1997 average assessed value in Northport-Sherman Avenue is $99,000.

Cherokee Park

This neighborhood takes its name from the nearby Cherokee Marsh. The development includes a large number of condominiums and townhouses, and single family homes. Some residences face the golf course and country club of the same name. The average assessed value in 1997 was $179,900.

Truax

The Dane County Regional Airport was formerly known as Truax Field. The Truax neighborhood consists of 120 apartment units on 18 acres. Residents gather together for an annual community picnic and pre-election party. Nearby attractions include East Madison Community Center and Community Gardens, Madison Area Technical College and, of course, the airport. Area schools include Hawthorne Elementary School, Sherman Middle School and East High School.

The homes in the Truax neighborhood had an averaged assessed value in 1997 of $92,700.

East

It's almost impossible not to find a tree-lined street in Madison, particularly on the established East Side, where hardwoods have had 20 to 30 years of growth. The East Side is considered a good place for young families just starting out. However, you will also find a significant number of long-term residents who swear by the area's convenience and comforts.

Within the East Side, you'll find diverse housing options, ranging from post-World War II construction to new growth. In blocks with modest, 1950s-era ranches, you will find homes with single-car garages and full basements. Residents are proud of their nice, green lawns, but you'll find little in the way of formal landscaping. Hedges often mark side property boundaries.

As you proceed toward the central East Side, you begin to see larger ranch homes of 1,500 to 1,800 square feet with attached garages. These homes were constructed mostly in the 1960s and 1970s, but you'll find an occasional contemporary or Colonial. Streets here tend to wind through the rolling topography; many are boulevards.

Bordering the UW Arboretum, Nakoma is one of Madison's oldest and most beautiful neighborhoods.

East Buckeye-Droster

Bordered by E. Buckeye Road, I-90 and the Chicago Northwestern Railroad, East Buckeye is a surprisingly quiet and peaceful community. The assessed value here is $125,400. About 1,500 Madisonians make their homes in this neighborhood of about 650 single-family homes, 40 duplexes and about two dozen apartments. Five churches are nearby, and neighbors can reach four major shopping areas within a matter of minutes.

East Buckeye children attend Allis and Elvehjem elementary schools, Sennett Middle School and La Follette High School. Mira Loma Park provides a beach and other outdoor recreation.

Olbrich Park-Cottage Grove Road

Olbrich Park, with its botanical gardens, green space and lengthy beach, is the jewel of Eastmorland. You can launch your sailboat here or just sit on the beach and enjoy the sun setting over the Capitol dome. Housing includes about 1,400 single-family homes, 80 duplexes and 50 apartments. The average assessed value is $87,700.

The neighborhood — bordered by Milwaukee Street, Stoughton Road, Cottage Grove Road and Lake Monona — has several other smaller parks. Five churches can be found nearby. Public schools include Schenk Elementary, Whitehorse Middle School and La Follette High School.

Elvehjem

At the center of the Elvehjem neighborhood is Elvehjem Elementary School, a 100-percent barrier-free public school. The neighborhood's 4,500 residents live in approximately 1,300 single-family homes, 126 duplexes and 116 apartments. Highlights of the neighborhood include Elvehjem Park, two smaller parks and several acres of Nature Conservancy forest. The area is bordered by Cottage Grove Road, I-90, E. Buckeye Road and Chicago Northwestern Railroad.

This neighborhood had 1997 average assessed home values of $133,300.

East Emerson

Bordered by Commercial and Packers avenues to the north, North Street to the east, E. Washington to the south and First, Fifth and Sixth streets to the west, East Emerson is served by four bus routes. Residents have plenty of close-by recreational opportunities at Demetral Field, Emerson Elementary's playground and East High's athletic fields and courts. Shopping is available at Camelot Square, Fiore Shopping Center, Princeton Place and several other nearby centers.

The neighborhood has about 600 single-family homes, 286 two-unit apartments (some duplexes, mostly upper/lower units) and 160 multi-unit apartments. Students attend Emerson Elementary, Sherman Middle and East High schools. The average assessed value in 1997 was $86,700.

Glendale

In Glendale you're close to schools, shopping, golf courses and beautiful Taylor Conservation Park. Border streets include Stoughton Road (U.S. Highway 51), Glenview Drive, Admiral Drive and Bjelde Lane. School children living here can attend Glendale Elementary, Sennett Middle School and La Follette High School. The area has several shopping centers, and the public can use Glendale Elementary's playground and La Follette High School's athletic fields when the school district is not using the facilities. Glendale homes had a 1997 average assessed value of $110,600.

Heritage Heights

Heritage Heights offers one- and two-story single-family homes along tree-lined, wide, winding streets. Residents can choose from several parks including Heritage Heights Greenway, Kennedy Park and Heritage Prairie Conservation Park. Designated schools for the area are Kennedy Elementary, Whitehorse Middle School and La Follette High School. This neighborhood has about 800 single-family homes and a handful of duplexes. The average assessed value is $132,000.

Hiestand

About 3,600 residents live in the Hiestand neighborhood. Children attend Schenk and Kennedy elementary schools, Whitehorse Middle School and La Follette High School. The neighborhood consists of about 300 single-family homes, 200 duplexes and 650 apartments. Recreational opportunities can be found at Hiestand Park, Hiestand Conservation Park, Swanton Greenway and Honeysuckle Park. Neighborhood boundaries are Commercial Avenue, Wis. Highway 30, Milwaukee Street and S. Stoughton Road. The average 1997 assessed home value was $117,700.

Lake Edge

The Lake Edge neighborhood frames the grounds of Monona Grove High School, although the area is now part of Madison, not Monona. Nearby shopping areas include Lake Edge Shopping Center and South Towne Mall. Four large churches are in or near this neighborhood, which is served by two bus routes.

About 1,000 single-family homes, 42 duplexes and 40 apartments make up the Lake Edge neighborhood. Children attend Frank Allis Elementary School, Sennett Middle School and La Follette High School. Parks include Lake Edge Park, Quaker Circle and the Frank Ellis Elementary playground. You'll find houses with a 1997 average assessed value of $100,600.

South of the Beltline Highway

From peaceful and affluent Arbor Hills, tucked up against the University of Wisconsin Arboretum (see our Attractions chapter) to Broadway-Simpson, the frequent target of urban renewal efforts, the South Madison neighborhoods run the gamut in terms of the lifestyles they afford.

NEIGHBORHOODS • 351

The UW Arboretum, Monona Bay shoreline and Turville Woods are natural attractions that draw many residents to South-Central Madison. Few can resist lingering to enjoy the quiet, natural beauty. Fishing, jogging, in-line skating and cycling are just a few of the ways residents commune with the outdoors. Residents can quickly access stores along the S. Beltline Highway or at South Towne.

Homes in this area range in price between $63,000 and $265,000. Higher-priced homes can be found in Arbor Hills and Waunona Way, while the least expensive housing is found in the Bram's Addition, Burr Oaks and Capitol View Heights neighborhoods.

Arbor Hills

Arbor Hills is primarily composed of high-quality, newer single-family homes with an average assessed value of $176,000. Many have spectacular, wooded yards. School children attend Leopold, Cherokee and West High schools. The neighborhood association sponsors an annual meeting, garage sale, Fourth of July children's parade and Santa visits.

Bay Creek

Bay Creek, a neighborhood of 1930- and 1940-era single-family homes with about 600 apartments and 160 duplexes, is nestled along the shores of Monona Bay. Residents enjoy Bernie's Beach on the Bay, Olin-Turville Park and the Franklin Playfield. Bay Creek area children attend Franklin-Randall Elementary, Hamilton Middle School and West High School. St. Mark's Lutheran Church serves as the site of political and educational forums as well as Bay Creek neighborhood meetings and picnics.

It is one of the few places in city where you can find modestly priced waterfront property. The average assessed home value in 1997 was $127,100.

Bram's Addition

Just up Wingra Creek is Bram's Addition, a small neighborhood of about 140 modest single-family homes and 160 apartments. Bram's Addition has two parks and a playground. Students in this neighborhood attend nine different Madison-area schools. Nearby shopping areas are South Park Street, South Towne Mall, Nakoma Plaza, the Madison Shopping Plaza and the Villager Shopping Center. The average assessed home value in 1997 was $90,900.

Broadway-Simpson

The Madison Police Department's "blue blanket" has helped to revitalize the Broadway-Simpson area. Those efforts, coupled with initiatives by concerned local parents, have improved the area.

Although south Madison has had its share of knocks, passersby would never know it. Nearly all of the 60-some single-family homes and apartment buildings in the area are well-maintained, with nice lawns and trees. Broadway-Simpson has about 860 apartments, many of which are older, four-unit building. The average 1997 assessed home value was $111,700.

Burr Oaks

Burr Oaks is bordered by Sequoya Trail, Cypress Way, Magnolia Lane and Fish Hatchery Road. The neighborhood has about 80 one- and two-story single-family homes and 250 apartments. Youth residing in this area may attend Lincoln Elementary, Cherokee Middle School and West High School.

The 1997 average assessed value in the Burr Oaks-Lincoln School area was $90,300.

Moorland-Rimrock Road

The Moorland-Rimrock Road area consists of some newer multilevel single-family homes, some older ranches and two-stories, about 60 duplexes, 600 apartments and 360 mobile homes; the total area is about 450 acres. The neighborhood hosts a spring garage sale, holiday potluck and spring cleanup. This community is close to shopping at South Towne Mall and nearby strip centers, the Coliseum and Expo Center, and has quick access to the Beltline. Children attend Allis Elementary, Sennett Middle and La Follette High schools. Homes in the Rimrock Heights-Moorland Road neighborhood had an average 1997 assessment of $114,700.

Waunona Way

The Waunona Way neighborhood follows the southern shoreline of Lake Monona.

Three parks enhance the area, giving residents and visitors plenty of recreational and exploring opportunities. This neighborhood consists of some expensive lakefront properties, many one- and two-story homes on heavily wooded lots, about 60 condominiums, 10 duplexes and 860 apartments. Youth attend Glendale Elementary, Sennett Middle School and La Follette High School. The average 1997 assessed home value was $108,800.

Southwest

The southwest neighborhoods include Allied-Dunn's Marsh, Greentree, Maple Prairie, Meadowood, Orchard Ridge, Prairie Hills, Skyview Meadows and Westhaven. The median home price for this area is $130,000, with homes costing from $69,000 to $300,000. Single-family homes in this area are typically ranch-style, bi-level and tri-level homes, and Colonials with attached garages. Much of the development in southwest Madison occurred between 1950 and 1980.

High Point Estates

This new development near Elver Park south of Gammon Road has huge custom homes with an average assessed value of $285,400. The area is full of former Parade of Homes residences, and construction continues. The lots are not large compared to the houses, and the vegetation is just now starting to mature to the point where the area no longer has the raw look of a new development. The architecture is mixed, but you'll find a lot of Georgian-style homes and many that can best be described as transitional— a mix between contemporary and traditional.

Allied-Dunn's Marsh

Allied-Dunn's Marsh is a melting pot of cultures with a mix of home styles. The community has about 450 single-family homes (many with detached garages), 72 duplexes and more than 1,000 apartments. Neighborhood events include an All-Cultural Fest and spring cleanup. The neighborhood is tucked between the UW Arboretum and Dunn's Marsh, between the cities of Madison and Fitchburg.

Greentree

The Greentree Neighborhood Association sponsors a July 4th parade and picnic, the Greentree Gallop (a run/walk), Halloween bonfires, family skating, a variety of holiday events and a spring dinner-dance for adults. In this 320-acre neighborhood, set between Schroeder and Hammersley roads, you will find four neighborhood parks. Three bus routes serve the area.

Greentree has about 600 single-family homes and 115 duplexes. Schools include Falk Elementary, Akira Toki Middle School and Memorial High School. Whitney Square and Westgate offer a variety of shopping experiences. The average assessed value is $159,900.

Meadowood

Meadowood is a staircase-shaped neighborhood with more than 1,000 single-family homes, 16 condominiums, 80 duplexes and 275 apartments. Youth attend three elementary schools, Akira Toki Middle School and Memorial High School. Much of the development in this area occurred in the late 1960s and 1970s. Area residents can choose from six neighborhood parks. Meadowood and Orchard Ridge are served by a major bus route. Residents have easy access to Meadowood Shopping Center, Midvale Plaza, Nakoma Plaza, Westgate Shopping Center and Whitney Square. The average assessed value is $123,000.

Orchard Ridge

Orchard Ridge is known as a good place for families who want big yards. It's relatively easy to find lots with mature shade trees and privacy. The neighborhood sprang up in the 1960s, so you'll find lots of sprawling homes, many of which are undergoing extensive renovation because people want to stay in the area. The neighborhood is a mix of single-family homes (about 700), condos, duplexes and apartments (about 200). The average assessed value is $146,000, although some recent sales prices have been much higher.

One of the big draws here is the Ridgewood Pool. It is a big, beautiful private swimming club that offers excellent instruction programs and has one of the best-known swim teams in the area. The pool offers adults-only times too, as well as events such as ice-cream socials, a carnival and a water-ballet extravaganza. Orchard Ridge hosts its own Fourth of July celebration with a parade and a neighborhood-wide garage sale.

Most of the kids in the neighborhood walk to Orchard Ridge Elementary, Toki Middle School or Saint Maria Goretti (K-8); some students attend Spring Harbor Middle School. Secondary students attend Memorial High School. The three churches within walking distance are Good Shepherd Lutheran, Orchard Ridge United Church of Christ and Saint Maria Goretti.

The neighborhood also has the Meadowridge Branch of the public library and a public tennis court, Flad Park, which has play structures and a winter skating rink. Within five minutes you can drive to any of seven malls, including Westgate, Hilldale and the mammoth West Towne. Two major supermarkets are included in the malls.

Crestwood-Glen Oak Hills-Merrill Crest

Crestwood is an enclave of many International-style homes that, with their flat roofs, corner windows and spare lines, were considered avant garde when they began appearing in the 1940s. Homes in the area have a 1997 average assessed value of $113,800.

Prairie Hills

About 4,600 Madisonians make their home in Prairie Hills among three parks: Pilgrim, Waltham and Homestead. Nearby shops are found at Gammon Place, Grand Canyon Place, Market Square and Odana Plaza. Prairie Hills youth can attend Orchard Ridge, Huegel or Falk elementary schools, Akira Toki Middle School and Memorial High School. Look for homes valued at $126,700, according to the 1997 assessment rolls.

Skyview Meadows

Skyview Meadows is a small, family-oriented community with residents from diverse backgrounds. The neighborhood association has worked to improve Raymond Ridge Park, planting more than 100 trees and purchasing playground equipment. The neighborhood has a mix of single-family homes and apartments. Skyview Meadows neighbors gather together for a summer picnic, Halloween party, holiday caroling, July 4th parade and Easter egg hunt. Many of the homes in the well-maintained area sell for about $140,000.

Westhaven

Bordered by the city limits to the west, Westhaven is a neighborhood of more than 1,000. Housing consists of a mix of single-family homes, condos, duplexes and apartments, centered on Westhaven Trails Park. Children attend Orchard Ridge, Huegel or Falk elementary schools, Toki Middle School and Memorial High School. The 1997 average assessed home value was $126,700.

Villages

Within the area commonly known as Madison are some independent communities. Two of the largest are the villages of Shorewood Hills and Maple Bluff.

Shorewood Hills is very popular with University of Wisconsin faculty members. The village tends to have large custom homes on private, wooded homesites. Shorewood Hills has its own elementary school and a community pool. The average 1997 assessed value is $255,634.

Maple Bluff, on Madison's East Side, is the location of the Wisconsin Governor's Mansion and Maple Bluff Country Club. Maple Bluff offers executive homes, with an average assessed value of $295,009, flanking very wide streets and boulevards in an estate setting.

Outlying Area

Madison's outlying communities offer the benefits of small-town living — very little crime and traffic — combined with easy access to metropolitan resources. Most of these communities have independent school districts (see our Schools chapter). All have grocery stores, banks, convenience stores, gas stations and established park systems. Recently, these outlying communities have seen an increase in local healthcare services, as it has become common for major Madison health networks to build rural community clinics.

Choosing to live in one of Dane County's small towns is a matter of personal taste and priorities. And while life in Madison's 'burbs is very similar to life in some parts of the city, there are subtle differences. You lose some of the diversity that makes Madison so intriguing and special, and you have to drive several miles each time you want to go into town. On the other hand, in small towns you don't have to wait in long lines to vote or to check out at the grocery store. And you don't have to pull out your driver's license every time you write a check.

Here are some of Dane County's smaller communities. We include rental rates in case you prefer to get a feel for living in a community before buying property there.

Cross Plains

Cross Plains (population 2,350) has boomed in the last five years with a tremendous amount of new construction. The city has a mix of old and new businesses and has begun adding a fair number of nationally and regionally known names to its business community, including Lands End. Homes in this western suburb vary in style and size. Most of the houses in the downtown area are typical of 1920s to 1950s construction standards: detached garages, two-story designs and narrow, deep lots. In the recent past, developments on the Madison-side of Cross Plains include large, modern homes on large lots as well as upscale condominiums.

Some rental housing is also available. A two-bedroom condo rents for about $625 a month. The average assessed value is $88,791.

DeForest

DeForest (population 5,200) is snuggled between bustling Interstate 90 and U.S. Highway 51 yet maintains a quiet, small-town flavor. With its own school system, several churches and a variety of shopping, dining and healthcare services, the community is quite self-sufficient. There's been a great deal of new construction in DeForest in the last five years. The average assessed home value is $97,930. You can often rent a small duplex for about $650 per month.

Fitchburg

Within the boundaries of Fitchburg (population 17,000), you can find some of Dane County's grandest — and most expensive — homes. If you're looking for an executive residence, you might focus your hunt on **Seminole Hills**, **Seminole Forest**, **Seminole Village**, or the new **Highlands of Seminole** (which has bicycle paths, plans for a neighborhood market center and a location adjoining the UW Arboretum). Many homes have 4,000 or more square feet, circular drives, pools and three-car garages. Home designs feature distinctive brick and stone exteriors. The large, professionally landscaped lots with mature trees and vegetation add to the area's restful ambiance.

Fitchburg has plenty of other housing options, including budget apartments, spacious duplexes, condos and single-family homes on wooded acreage. Fitchburg has quite a bit of rental housing — both apartments and duplexes. The average assessed home value is $142,096, although the community has a large number of far more expensive executive homes. More affordable options are available, such as two-bedroom apartments renting for about $550 per month.

Fitchburg does not have its own school district. Youths are bused to neighboring districts, including Madison schools.

McFarland

McFarland (population 5,500) has had steady growth over the last decade and has added services accordingly. A recent grassroots effort resulted in the village's first public library. McFarland has a substantial selection of newer, midsize family homes on good-size lots, bordered by wide, tree-lined streets. In the older sections of town, you will find smaller, heavily wooded lots; many homes are on waterways. McFarland has its own school district. The average assessed home value is $129,039. A two-bedroom apartment rents for $450 to $500 a month.

Middleton

Middleton (population 13,500) developed strong school and community-service systems early on, partly due to the influences of the large number of UW-Madison faculty who lived

NEIGHBORHOODS • 355

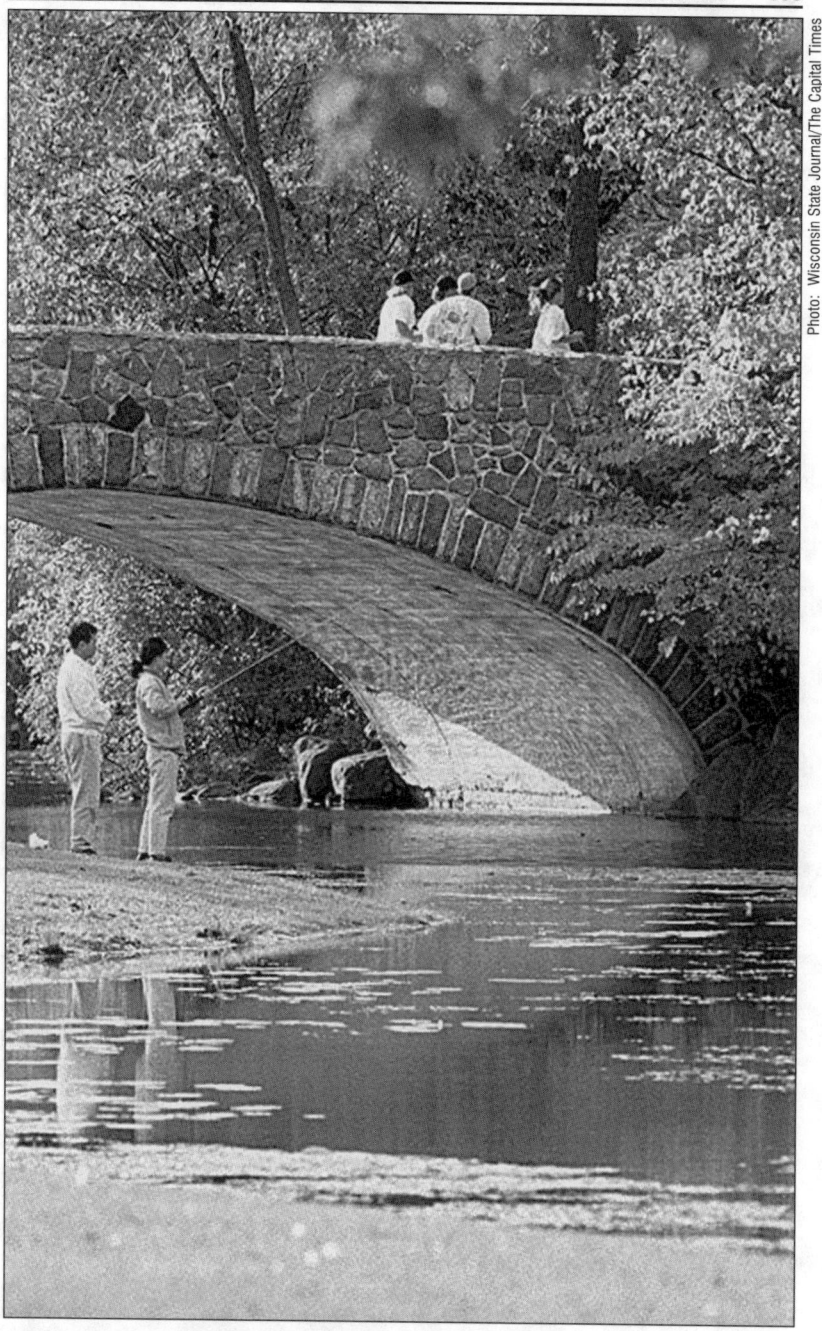

Boasting more than 200 parks, many of the city's neighborhood parks are within skipping distance.

there over the years. As Madison has grown westward, the two communities' borders have come together. City residents have access to a number of parks and Madison Metro bus service. Suburban living with city bus service is a combination that draws many area residents to Middleton.

This friendly community offers a reputable public school district, plentiful shopping, fine and casual dining and lots of upscale rental property. The city is beautifully landscaped, and newcomers will find a variety of apartments, condos and single-family homes.

Middleton's most prominent new development is **Bishop's Bay**, centered around a championship golf course. Lakefront property, as usual, is a valued commodity.

In addition to recent commercial growth along University Avenue and W. Beltline Highway, Middleton has seen a rebirth in its historic downtown. Homes in Middleton vary from small, older ranches and two-story dwellings near downtown to ultramodern, multilevel homes near Bishop's Bay that sell in the $1 million range. The average Middleton-Cross Plains home, though, was assessed in 1997 for $128,438. The city also has a large number of rental units. Two-bedroom apartments rent for between $495 and $600 a month.

Middleton Hills is a new 150-acre development designed by the late Marshall Erdman, a prominent Madison architect, to reflect traditional neighborhood experiences and offer an appealing old-time atmosphere. Residential and commercial properties are mixed, so you can walk to buy most everything you need. Many of the homes have friendly-looking front porches, so people will mingle with their neighbors, and houses are set close to the street. This is a development for families who want to avoid "garage homes," those developments where you drive up and down the streets and see nothing but huge garages.

Monona and Cottage Grove

Monona (population 8,700) and Cottage Grove (population 2,300) are about as different as two communities can be, yet the pair shares an excellent school system.

The average home sale price in Monona — an established, urban community surrounded by Madison and perched on the shores of Lake Monona — is $135,957. Monona is home to a fair number of "empty nesters." The city has several nice parks, a popular aquatic center and its own library.

Cottage Grove, on the other hand, is a mecca for young families. The community has two beautiful elementary schools (Taylor Prairie was built in 1995). Cottage Grove has seen a huge construction boom in the past five or six years. The average home sale price is about $104,561. Duplex and quad rentals are available, with rents between $750 and $895. A major employer for those living in the community is American Family Insurance.

Oregon

Oregon (population 4,800) has experienced some fairly rapid growth in the last 10 years but is still considered one of Madison's more rural bedroom communities, probably due to surrounding farmland. Residents have a good selection of local shopping and dining establishments. The village has its own golf course, public school system (the high school has been lavishly renovated) and a nice recreational facility with a pool.

The average assessed home value is $119,231. Most of the new construction in Oregon since the mid- to late-1980s includes construction of ranch, bi-level, tri-level and two-story homes in all regions around the village's older downtown area.

Stoughton

Stoughton (population 10,000) is one of Dane County's most colorful small towns. The city strives to keep its Norwegian heritage intact through annual celebrations such as

---

INSIDERS' TIP

The Dudgeon-Monroe neighborhood is a good choice for those who want a hint of wilderness close to their front door.

Syttende Mai (see Festivals and Annual Events), a May celebration that includes canoe racing, a distance run, parade and appearances by the Norwegian Dancers, a multi-talented high school group. Stoughton residents can find lots of athletic and cultural experiences right in their own backyard.

Since about 1990, the city's north side and the perimeter of Lake Kegonsa have experienced quite a bit of new construction. Stoughton has one of the largest collections of 19th-century homes in Wisconsin, in a wide range of architectural styles. One of the old dwellings has Nordic dragons on the roof to ward off evil spirits. You'll find a lot of major renovations underway in Stoughton these days.

The average home sale price is $104,069. Some rentals are available. You can usually find a two-bedroom apartment for less than $500 a month.

Stoughton is the only rural community in Dane County with its own hospital, which is a full-service facility. The town has its own school district, numerous clinics and plentiful shopping, including a lovely historic main street district. The town's major employers are Nelson Industries and Stoughton Trailers (see our Overview chapter).

Sun Prairie

Sun Prairie (population 15,500) has an aquatic center that is envied by many metro Madison residents. This community has a historic downtown and has expanded its commercial offerings significantly since the early 1990s. Sun Prairie has its own school system, several nice parks and a variety of restaurants. It's also very close to one of Madison's largest cinemas and shopping areas.

The city has many nice older and contemporary homes and a good selection of rental units. The average assessed value is $112,786. Two-bedroom apartments start at about $530 per month.

Verona

Verona (population 5,400) has gone from being a sleepy rural community to a bustling small town that serves as the hub for surrounding subdivisions. The community has several health clinics, banks and a fair number of dining establishments. The average home sale price in Verona is about $115,550, although many of the newer homes cost two or three times that much.

Most of the homes in the downtown area are 40 to 60 years old but are very well preserved. New construction in Verona since the late 1980s includes large development plots of ranch, bi-level, tri-level and two-story homes.

Wanuakee

Residents say this is the "only Wanuakee in the world." This popular Madison bedroom community (population 5,900) has its own school system, shopping options and some excellent German dining. The average 1997 assessed home value was $125,768. A two-bedroom apartment can be found for about $560 per month.

In Closing . . .

The Madison area and its close neighbors offer everything from cosmopolitan urban life to, literally, isolated farm life complete with livestock, all within a short drive. This may very well be the perfect place for a person who wants it all.

It's common knowledge that some of the best child care in the nation is available in Madison.

Child Care

Because Madison is so often singled out for being one of the top places to live, it's easy to take certain quality-of-life benefits for granted. Right on the top of that list belongs reliable, high-quality day care for working parents.

County registration or state licensing is mandatory for child-care centers and family child-care providers serving more than three children younger than 7. And while that in itself doesn't always ensure the best care, it does mean that regulated child-care providers do receive periodic home visits. County-registered and state-licensed providers are required to attend classes to be trained before becoming fully regulated, but a new category, provisional child-care provider, does not require training.

Above and beyond normal procedures, local day-care centers and home-care providers are urged to voluntarily meet additional, more stringent standards set by the City of Madison and/or the National Association for the Education of Young Children (NAEYC). Both establish certification or accreditation by rating such criteria as health and safety, staffing numbers, staff qualifications and physical environment. Primary consideration, however, is given to the child's fundamental experience. Is he or she happy and relaxed while playing and learning? That's the bottom line.

Statewide grants being issued within the past several of years has spurred many centers to improve the quality of their programming and seek accreditation. About 25 in the greater Madison area are now accredited by the National Academy of Early Childhood Programs, the program arm of NAEYC, and 100 family day-care homes and centers have earned city certification.

This kind of commitment speaks well for the entire community. It's common knowledge that some of the best child care in the nation is available in Madison.

Begin Your Search Early

The fact that good day care exists doesn't necessarily mean it is easy to find or always affordable. Openings for infants whose care is labor intensive are especially scarce. Yet, for the most part, shortages have not occurred, as was originally feared, with the implementation of welfare reform (commonly referred to in Wisconsin as W-2). Experts in the field are concerned that some of the 3,000 children younger than 6 who were expected to be enrolled in day care when their welfare-enrolled parents returned to work are home alone or are being watched by older siblings being taken out of school to babysit. But that's a subject for another day.

According to most recent statistics available from Community Coordinated Child Care (4-C), a nonprofit, child-care referral agency (see listing in the subsequent Referral Services section), enrollment in regulated child care in Dane County was 17,785 between March 1996 and March 1997. That number is slightly more than the previous year but still down a bit from what it had been in the early '90s. The increased availability of full-day kindergarten in Madison area schools is believed to be one factor for the slight decline in tuition-paying parents. The number of county-funded instances of child care increased in all categories of care.

Welfare reform is also affecting some of the ground rules for the regulation of day care in Wisconsin. Temporary "provisional" status given those providers seeking training has been made a permanent category, thus eliminating the child-care training requirement in some instances. Parents need to be aware that provisional providers do not have as much training as other regulated providers.

To find a day-care center or home that best meets your family's needs, begin your search early — before your baby is even born — and do your homework. Know what's available. The child-care market is driven by the accredited and certified centers at the top who fill up the fastest and are likely to be the most expensive. But don't rely on price or accreditation alone. Parents need to be sophisticated as to the wealth of available options and organized in their search in finding the best match for their children.

Contact providers with specific information about what your needs will be. Visit at least two homes or centers for comparison and spend time observing children at play. Meet the instructors who will be taking care of your child. Discuss your expectations regarding discipline, sleep habits and meals. Ask for and check references. Most of all, talk to other parents.

What You Can Expect to Pay

There is no way around it.

Paying for child care is very much like paying college tuition. It takes a big bite out of the family budget. Just how expensive you view it depends upon income and previous experience. Value for the money, child care in Madison is considered a bargain by many white-collar, two-income families. Others are discovering that the cost of full-time day care, especially for infants, is too much of a cross to bear. Day-care costs in the Madison area have been rising between 4 and 5 percent annually over the past couple of years. And part-time day care is becoming increasingly harder to find as more facilities only offer full-day slots to better coordinate staffing and programming needs.

Here is a breakdown in costs compiled annually by 4-C from regulated providers in Madison. Statistics cited are for one child per week for full-day care. Outside city limits, the cost of child care is slightly less — between $5 and $8 an hour. Also, some centers and homes do offer reduced rates for a second child.

• Average cost for an infant 1 or younger in a day-care center is $160, with a range from $115 to $180. For an infant in a day-care home, it's $140, with a range from $70 to $180.

• For toddlers (ages 1 to 2) the average cost in day-care centers is $154, with a range between $115 to $178. Family day-care providers charge, on the average, $136, with a range between $70 and $210.

• Centers offer a special rate for 2-year-olds. The average cost is $138, with a range between $95 and $173.

• For preschoolers (ages 2 to 5 in home settings and ages 3 to 5 in centers) the average cost is $132 (center), with a range from $95 to $179. In family day-care homes it's $131, with a range from $60 to $210.

The majority of rates hover near the average or are slightly higher. The highest rates might include care for children with special needs. Some fees for infants and young toddlers also include the cost of diapers.

Referral Services

The following agencies can help make your search for quality day care go a little smoother. All are in Madison except one, which is in Washington, D.C.

Community Coordinated Childcare Inc. (4-C)
50 Odana Ct., Madison
• **(608) 271-9181**

4-C is a nonprofit child-care resource and referral agency serving Dane, Dodge, Sauk, Jefferson and Columbia counties. Its computer database of available openings is a great resource for parents seeking child care. This agency can also provide brochures and other information for helping parents conduct a more effective in-home or out-of-home child-care search and better understand tax credits and regulations. An excellent guide available through 4-C is Selecting Quality Child Care.

The agency registers family child-care providers for Dane County and certifies day-care centers for the City of Madison. There is

---

www.insiders.com

See this and many other **Insiders' Guide®** destinations online — in their entirety.

Visit us today!

a nominal service fee for parents whose combined income is more than $25,000.

Extended Day Care Project
1502 Greenway Cross, Madison
- (608) 273-3318

Extended Day Care Project helps parents in Dane County who have children with developmental disabilities find appropriate child care. Children from birth to age 12 are served. County funded, the agency works closely with local child-care centers to provide both training and other kinds of assistance, whatever is needed to care for a particular child. Parents should be advised, however, that there is a waiting list for Extended Day Care's services.

Satellite Family Child Care Inc.
3200 Monroe St., Madison
- (608) 233-4752

Satellite is a nonprofit agency that provides city certification to family child-care providers and acts as a referral network for parents hoping to find and optimize quality day care in a home setting. Satellite loans large equipment such as toys, high chairs, double strollers and gates to professional providers. It also offers additional consulting services to establish and maintain good communication between providers and parents and to ensure a safe, caring environment for children. While Satellite mostly places children in Madison homes, the agency also works with a few providers in Verona, Middleton and Fitchburg. There is no fee for referrals, but parents pay a one-time, $20 enrollment fee if a child is placed and a quarterly fee based on the number of hours the child is cared for weekly.

National Academy of Early Childhood Programs
- (800) 424-2460

Contact the academy to receive a free list of accredited programs in the Madison area. Day-care facilities that are accredited by this national organization have met a stringent set of guidelines to promote a child's well-being. Assessment is voluntary. The mailing address is 1509 16th Street N.W., Washington, D.C. 20036.

Madison has many quality child-care facilities.

Assistance for Low-Income Families

Low-income families can seek monetary assistance for day care through the City of Madison's Office of Community Services, (608) 267-4996, and/or the Dane County Department of Human Services, (608) 242-6200.

While there is often a waiting list for subsidized day care, low-income parents are urged to inquire about benefits as soon as a need arises. City day-care funding goes to parents who are working, looking for work or are in an approved job-training course for two years or less. Criteria for low-income county funding is changing rapidly as it's coordinated closely with welfare reform. Call for information.

In-Home Care

Parents have many ways to locate an in-home provider, including advertising the position on job boards at local grocery stores or in local newspapers and shoppers. (See our Media chapter for ideas.) Child-care providers also often post advertisements, so it's wise to scrutinize the classified ads. Sometimes the best avenue for finding a cherished nanny is simply by word-of-mouth. Let your friends, pastor, neighbors and co-workers know you are looking for in-home care.

Parents should be advised that in-home care is not regulated by the state or city. Proceed cautiously. For a list of important questions to ask potential care-givers, contact 4-C (see the previous entry in the Referral Services section).

To find college students interested in child-care work, call or mail your request to the following Madison addresses: Edgewood Placement Office, 855 Woodrow Street, Madison, Wisconsin 53711, (608) 257-4861; MATC Job Placement Office, 3550 Anderson Street, Madison, Wisconsin 53704, (608) 246-6401; or UW Student Job Center, 432 N. Murray Street, Room 333, Madison, Wisconsin 53706, (608) 262-5627.

Nanny Services

Two agencies in the Madison area, **Select Day Care Personnel Services Inc.**, 301 S. Bedford Street, Madison, (608) 255-3839, and **Be My Nanny**, 1822 Helene Parkway, Suite 4, Madison, (608) 277-8282, provide placement for live-in, live-out, part-time or full-time nannies. Representatives of both services say they carefully screen candidates in learning everything they can about an individual, from information about prior employment to child-care philosophy and skills. Background checks are routinely run to eliminate those with criminal or serious driving violations. Families then interview potential candidates and make the final decision.

Finder fees can be substantial, based in part upon how many hours per week a nanny is employed. In Madison, salaries for full-time nannies range from $250 to $350 per week. The hourly wage for part-time care ranges from $6 to $10.

Minding The Kids After School Lets Out

Children who have graduated from after-school day-care programs in Madison have fond memories of that block of time sandwiched between school letting out for the day and 5:30 in the evening when parents arrived to retrieve them, usually as they were finishing art projects in the school cafeteria.

One parent talks about the time a school nurse called to say her child wasn't feeling well and wanted to come home.

"Yes, I do feel sick now," said the 6-year-old. "But if I come home, will you take me back for 'after-school?'"

There are two primary agencies operating after-school programs in the majority of public schools and some private ones in and surrounding Madison (see subsequent listings). They also provide all-day programming on weekdays when school is not in session as well as summer camps (see our Kidstuff chapter). Students often are divided into two age categories: kindergarten through 2nd grade and 3rd through 5th grades. While after-school day care cuts off at the end of 5th grade, summer day camps are open to middle schoolers.

A word to the wise. Don't delay in signing up for after-school care. Slots at some schools fill up quickly. Find out which agency offers programming in your child's school and be sure to register as early as you can, usually in the spring for the following fall.

After School Inc.
601 N. Whitney Way, Madison
• **(608) 233-9782**

After- and before-school programs operated by After School primarily take place in Madison public schools on the West Side of Madison. The agency also coordinates after-school care at two Madison private schools,

---

INSIDERS' TIP

Community Coordinated Childcare Inc. (4-C) in Madison helps more than 4,000 parents a year locate regulated child-care options and provides training and technical assistance to 2,000 child-care providers annually.

Wingra and Eagle, and in some elementary schools in Middleton, Stoughton and Mount Horeb. Before-school programs including breakfast operate at Wingra and Eagle and in Mount Horeb. Parents can sign up their children for as few as two days a week and as many as five. Dismissal time is 5:45 PM (until 6 PM in Mount Horeb and Stoughton). The monthly cost for a five-day after-school program is $188. Summer and full-day care on non-school days are billed separately.

East Side YMCA
711 Cottage Grove Rd., Madison
• (608) 221-1571

The YMCA, through its East Side location, operates 23 school-age programs throughout Dane County. Although half of them are in Madison schools, the majority are on the East Side. Outlying communities served include Sun Prairie, Middleton, Verona, Cross Plains, Waunakee, Stoughton and Windsor. Children must be picked up from the schools by 5:45 PM. Summer and full-day care on non-school days are also available. The monthly cost for a five-day, after-school program is $180.

Support Groups

Numerous support groups and agencies serve families in Dane County, especially those with hardships or special needs. Here are several that can provide camaraderie or just calm the waters in times of stress. Addresses, when given, are for Madison.

La Leche League of Madison
• (608) 232-MILK

The league offers information and support to women interested in breast-feeding. Resources include a bimonthly newsletter, loan library and phone counseling. The group meets once a month.

Mothers of Multiples (Moms)
W9242 Old Hwy. 60, Lodi
• (608) 592-7236

Monthly support meetings are usually attended by mothers, but fathers are welcome too. Activities sponsored by the organization include resales, picnics, an annual holiday party and the publication of a newsletter.

Parental Stress Center
2120 Fordem Ave., Madison
• (608) 241-4888, (608) 241-2221
(24-hour stress line)

If you're feeling angry or stressed out and don't know where to turn, call the listed stress line or attend a support group for parents called Parents Anonymous. The Parental Stress Center is dedicated to the prevention of physical and sexual abuse and neglect of children.

Ronald McDonald House
2716 Marshall Ct., Madison
• (608) 232-4660

This facility, like all Ronald McDonald Houses throughout the country, offers low-cost overnight accommodations for families with ill children in area hospitals. Families or guardians must be referred to the house by hospital personnel.

Wisconsin First Step
Lutheran Hospital-La Crosse 1910 South Ave., La Crosse, Wis. • (800) 642-STEP

Sponsored by the Wisconsin Council on Developmental Disabilities, First Step is a statewide computerized information and referral service dedicated to helping families and professionals find services for children younger than 6 who have special needs. The service is free.

Public Schools Are WORKING In Wisconsin!

Wisconsin students are consistently among the best in the nation. Our students outscore students nationally on assessment tests. Our high school completion rate is among the highest in the country. By building on what we know works, all children will leave school prepared for life and the jobs of the future.

www.weac.org

Let's Build on the BEST!

WISCONSIN EDUCATION ASSOCIATION COUNCIL
WEAC

Schools

Harping on the pluses and minuses of public education is quickly becoming an American pastime. Everyone wants to fix something about their school system. Wisconsinites are certainly no different, except change isn't as great an issue here in South-Central Wisconsin as protecting the high caliber of education already in place without increasing taxes.

Over the past 10 years, Wisconsin students taking the American College Test (ACT) for entrance into college scored as high or higher than other students in the United States. (Students from Upper Midwestern states consistently outperform their peers in other states on this test.) The state always ranks high on the National Assessment of Education Progress 3rd- and 8th-grade reading tests, and for those students not interested in a post-secondary education, Wisconsin is leading the way in designing youth-apprenticeship job programs such as School To Work.

School districts in this neck of the woods have equally as high or higher standards than the state itself. District scores on assessment tests overall meet and often exceed state averages. Hotly contested school board elections in Madison and neighboring towns attract more voters and ignite more controversy than presidential campaigns. But that's because people care.

This chapter highlights the Madison Metropolitan School District, those serving Madison's surrounding communities and private schools. Boundaries are not neat and tidy. Children living in villages and towns of the same name might go to schools in different districts. Even some children with Madison addresses attend schools in other districts. If you are moving, make sure you know which schools your children will be attending.

In the past, if you sent your child to an out-of-district school, you paid the price, literally. But under a new state Open Enrollment law enacted in 1998, children from one district can request to attend school in another district without any financial penalties as long as there is room in the school, no school loses more than 3 percent of its total student body and racial imbalances aren't created as a result. The law also allows districts to refuse transfer requests from students who have been expelled. Transfer requests must be made early, in February for the following September, and be approved by both the resident and nonresident district. Families are notified in April.

The start of school varies a little depending upon how many snow days each district builds in. Most public schools, however, including those in Madison, start the week before Labor Day and end the first week in June.

In Wisconsin, children must turn 5 by September 1 to enroll in kindergarten that same year. Registration and testing begins the previous spring. The Wisconsin Department of Health and Family Services requires students enrolling in public schools to be current with vaccinations for diphtheria, tetanus, pertussis, polio, measles, mumps, hepatitis B and rubella.

Public Schools

Madison Metropolitan School District
545 W. Dayton St., Madison
• **(608) 266-6270**

The second-largest school district in the State of Wisconsin, Madison Metropolitan School District (MMSD) covers about 65 square miles, including all or part of the cities of Madison, Fitchburg and Monona, the villages of Maple Bluff and Shorewood Hills and the towns of Blooming Grove, Burke,

Madison, Middleton and Westport. Total enrollment is more than 25,000 students.

The district has 30 elementary schools, 10 middle schools and five high schools including an alternative, citywide school for students who learn better in a nontraditional environment. In addition, Madison offers a wide selection of academic and arts-related summer enrichment classes, early childhood programs for children with disabilities and a 4-year-old kindergarten for children at risk. Administratively, the district is organized around the four high school attendance areas: East and La Follette on the East Side of Madison; Memorial and West on the West Side.

Every year each school submits a School Improvement Plan with goals related to student achievement, attendance, participation in school programs and climate (safety) of the school. These annual plans are developed by a team of teachers, administrators, students and parents to give more autonomy to individual schools in addressing the needs of their students.

While MMSD is beset with challenges in the immediate years ahead, its reputation for delivering superb educational programs, from early childhood through high school, remains rock-solid. In choosing Madison as the best place to live in America in '96, *Money* magazine cited the quality of education as a big factor. Madison also received a perfect 100 percent ranking from *Ladies Home Journal* at the end of '97 for "quality of education" in naming Madison the "Best City For Women." And a national business magazine, *Expansion Management*, has consistently ranked Madison, in terms of quality of education, as one of the top-10 school systems in the country. Especially impressive was Madison's score by *Expansion Management* for graduate outcomes — 146 out of a possible 150. This category looks at graduation rate and scores on the ACT and SAT college entrance exams.

Despite sometimes heated debates over building referendums and teacher contracts, public confidence, overall, remains high. It's a reason why the percentage of Madison residents sending their children to private schools is far less than in many other urban areas and several percentage points below the state average.

In preparing for the future, every school in the district is now electronically linked. Libraries are online, and computers have been integrated into the curriculum beginning in kindergarten.

Even more important, Madison is preparing students for an increasingly complex world by implementing in stages its Madison Schools 2000 strategic plan to which hundreds of educators and parents have given input since 1991. In raising expectations for all students, the cornerstone of the plan calls for assigning learning standards at different intervals in all the core subjects. For example, by the end of 8th grade, students must show they have mastered certain mathematical skills, from basic computation and measurement to algebraic reasoning. Its objectives to be met by the year 2000 are simply stated: "100 percent student success, 100 percent graduation and 100 percent post-secondary success."

With an overall 30 percent minority population in the elementary grades, Madison is becoming more sensitized to issues of multiculturalism. Within the curriculum itself, an appreciation and knowledge of ethnic differences is emerging. It's a challenge in the making — one that sets Madison schools apart from outlying districts with predominately white student populations. Preparing children to work and live in a diverse, rapidly changing world is an important by-product of a MMSD education.

There is no documentation to prove white flight, although it is continually being studied. Families who do move out of Madison usually cite housing needs as a reason. But one looming problem the district knows it must meet head on is serving more effectively the growing percentage of low-income, educationally disadvantaged students without draining resources from its other educational programs.

Another problem is aging buildings. Unlike outlying communities with burgeoning school populations, Madison is experiencing

---

www.insiders.com

See this and many other **Insiders' Guide®** destinations online — in their entirety.

Visit us today!

Edgewood High School

FOR COLLEGE. FOR LIFE.

EDGEWOOD HIGH SCHOOL
2219 MONROE STREET
MADISON, WI 53711
608/257-1023

At Edgewood High School, we prepare students for college and for life. An Edgewood education focuses on the spiritual, academic, physical and social development of each student rooted in the Sinsinawa Dominican values of truth, justice, compassion, community and partnership. For admissions information, call 257-1023.

---

stable or only modest enrollment growth. Building new schools is not a priority, even though a new technology-focused charter middle school opened in the fall of '97 on the South Side. But keeping its aging schools healthy is a problem, especially in the face of state-imposed spending limits. Seventy percent of school facilities are more than 30 years old, and the district is wrestling with ways to pay for new roofs, furnaces, etc.

Says one Madison administrator about the challenges ahead: "The world is much more complex; we understand that even with a high level of student achievement, the economic world and society are changing so fast, it's like shooting at a moving target."

Outlying Districts

A rapidly rising school population is one of the biggest challenges facing communities surrounding Madison. When push comes to shove, new schools are being built, although savvy, bottom-line voters are demanding fiscal responsibility in the planning and construction of new facilities.

DeForest Area School District
520 E. Holum St., DeForest
• (608) 846-6500

DeForest Schools are within a 90-square-mile area bordered by U.S. Highway 51, Wis. Highway 19 and Interstate 90/94, which links the area with Madison, 6 miles south. The district serves the communities of DeForest, Hampden, Leeds, Bristol, Burke, Vienna, Windsor and portions of Sun Prairie and Madison. Approximately 3,600 students attend eight facilities made up of five elementary schools, one middle school and one high school.

A separate building, the O.S. Holum Education Center, houses kindergarten and an early childhood program to address the special learning needs of children 3 to 6 years old.

The middle school was built in 1988 to provide the appropriate setting for the district's Interdisciplinary Team Organization in which a group of students are assigned to a team of teachers. The resulting "family-like" environment has been very well received. To enforce positive behavior on the high school level, the district has implemented a "Catch Kids Being Good" program in which students are rewarded for doing good deeds and practicing good citizenship.

DeForest, like other bedroom communities around Madison, has vacant land that continues to attract new residential development. School population is on the rise. The district is hoping to pass a referendum in 1998 that would ease overcrowding in the middle and high schools by funding a new high school and turning the existing one into a middle school for 7th- and 8th-graders.

McFarland School District
5101 Farwell St., McFarland
* **(608) 838-3169**

McFarland is a relatively small school district serving just fewer than 2,000 students in kindergarten through 12th grade. The district is sandwiched between Stoughton, Oregon and Madison. It contains two elementary schools (kindergarten through 4th grade), one middle school (grades 5 through 8) and a high school with about 600 students. A new elementary school will open in the fall of '99, and money is also being spent to remodel the high school.

Learning experiences for kindergarten through 2nd-grade students are extended beyond the walls of the classroom. Students correspond with their journal pals at Indian Mound Middle School and McFarland High School. At least one performing arts program or activity is planned each month during the school year in the elementary level.

McFarland High School was one of the first schools (there are only a few) in the area to incorporate a four-period school day in which classes are 90- instead of 45-minutes long. Administrators believe it improves the school climate and focus of learning. Classes once completed in one semester are now done in nine weeks.

McFarland's record mirrors many districts in the area. More than 90 percent of the 3rd-grade students who take the Wisconsin Third Grade Reading Test perform above the state average.

Middleton-Cross Plains Area School District
7106 S. Ave., Middleton • (608) 828-1600

The Middleton-Cross Plains Area School District serves more than 4,800 students in grades kindergarten through 12. To reach 4-year-olds with specific needs, it also offers early childhood programs including the nationally recognized "Camper Classroom" in which a teacher pulls up to a student's house or apartment literally in a camper filled with books for individual tutoring. The district encompasses eight municipalities covering 70 square miles, from the western shore of Lake Mendota to the Village of Cross Plains.

One of the fastest growing districts in the area, Middleton-Cross Plains has, since the early 1990s, built two new schools, renovated three others and constructed an indoor pool adjacent to the high school. Today, it operates seven elementary schools, two middle schools and one high school on a budget of approximately $27 million.

As part of the charter school initiative, the district set up an alternative high school program that has attracted about 60 students. More than 70 percent of the graduates of Middleton High School pursue education beyond high school, with nearly 65 percent selecting a four-year college or university.

Monona Grove School District
5301 Monona Dr., Monona
* **(608) 221-7660**

With four elementary schools, one middle school and one high school, Monona Grove serves students residing in the City of Monona and the Village and Town of Cottage Grove. Total enrollment is about 2,600 students.

After failing the first time, a $23 million referendum passed in 1997, enabling the district to build new a new high school on the site of the existing one, which was built in 1955 as a "temporary" structure. If all goes well, the new school will open in the fall of '99. With more families moving into Cottage Grove, there might soon be the need for a third elementary school there.

INSIDERS' TIP

Not many people know that Milt McPike, principal of East High School in Madison, is a former reserve defensive back for the San Franciso '49ers. But everybody knows how well respected he is within the school community. In '97, he was named Principal of the Year in the State of Wisconsin by the Association of Wisconsin School Administrators.

Every school in Madison's district is linked electronically.

In addition to grades kindergarten through 12, Monona Grove offers early childhood and pre-kindergarten programs for younger children who have been determined through screening to have special needs.

Oregon School District
200 N. Main St., Oregon • (608) 835-3161

The Oregon School District includes pre-kindergarten through grade 12 and encompasses an area of approximately 85 square miles, taking in parts of Dane, Rock and Green counties. About 3,200 students are served through three elementary schools, one middle school and one high school. In May 1996, district residents approved an almost $21 million referendum to authorize remodeling and additions for two of the grade schools and the high school. Improvements included a new 750-seat multipurpose auditorium for Oregon High School.

According to Wisconsin Manufacturers and Commerce, Oregon ranks as one of 46 Wisconsin "Best of Class" districts by attaining above-average achievement while spending less than the state average per pupil. In Oregon, that's $7,113.

Stoughton Area School District
211 N. Forrest St., Stoughton
• (608) 877-5000

In 1996, the passage of a $26 million referendum to remodel existing schools and build two new schools brought the number of elementary and middle schools to five and changed the grade configuration in the district. Now kindergarten through 4th grade, 5th and 6th grades and 7th and 8th grades are all in separate schools. High school remained the same (9th through 12th grades), although the building was extensively remodeled and expanded. Even district offices moved.

Stoughton serves approximately 3,350 students in a 100-square-mile area that encompasses all of the city and parts of about a dozen townships including Pleasant Springs, Dunn, Dunkirk, Deerfield, Rutland and Albion.

The school district provides a comprehensive curriculum including agriculture and business courses in high school. As a result of adding more support staff and implementing alternative programs for students in need, the percentage of students dropping out has decreased over a span of 15 years, from 3.9 percent to .1 percent. About 74 percent of Stoughton graduates go on to college or seek additional vocational training.

Sun Prairie Area School District
509 Commercial Ave., Sun Prairie
- **(608) 837-2541**

With an average growth rate of 2.5 percent per year, Sun Prairie currently serves about 4,500 children living within a radius of 85 square miles that includes the City of Sun Prairie; parts of the townships of Sun Prairie, Bristol, Burk, Cottage Grove, Blooming Grove and Hampden; and a small corner of Madison.

In the fall of '97, two new, identical middle schools opened (the existing one was torn down), bringing the number of schools in the district to eight.

The Sun Prairie schools are noted for the business partnerships they've cemented since the early 1990s within the community. Today, more than 30 local businesses have adopted classrooms, the majority of which are elementary level. Teachers are urged to take advantage of summer internships with area businesses, and an exchange program in which teachers work for a day at a local business and business people are invited to come into the classroom and teach, has been very successful.

Verona Area School District
400 N. Main St., Verona • (608) 845-6451

At one point in time, Verona was the fastest growing district in the state, increasing by a whopping 28 percent in a four-year time span. Since 1988, that large influx of students necessitated building two new elementary schools and a new middle school, adding a major addition to the high school and even building new district offices. Enrollment today is nearly 4,000 students. If a referendum passes in 1998, two more schools — one elementary and one middle school — will be built.

Verona is also one of the districts to consistently make Wisconsin Manufacturers and Commerce's "Best of Class" list, which measures achievement as it relates to expenditures per pupil.

However, what sets Verona apart right now is its willingness to adopt charter schools. These publicly funded schools aren't as rigidly state regulated as traditional public schools, thus allowing greater parental input and innovation. In 1995, Verona was the first district in the state to open a parent-initiated charter school, New Century, an elementary school featuring multi-age classrooms and integrated learning. A second school, Verona Core Knowledge, stresses direct, teacher-led instruction and a more traditional core-subject curriculum. Enrollment in either school is open to all children in the district. However, Verona Core Knowledge has a waiting list. In 1998, the school also came under public attack for not being as racially diversified as the district itself.

Students from the City of Verona make up only about a third of the district that also includes the western section of Fitchburg, the Maple Hills/Prairie Grove neighborhoods of Madison and small sections of several different townships.

Waunakee Community School District
101 School Dr., Waunakee
- **(608) 849-2000**

The Waunakee School District's student population has been steadily growing, requiring the construction of a couple of new schools in recent years. Today, it has two elementary schools, an intermediate school (grades 5 and 6), a middle school and high school.

Ten miles north of Madison, the 56-square-mile district is bordered by Lake Mendota to the south, DeForest School District to the east, Middleton to the west and Lodi to the north. Enrollment is 2,563.

Of the nearly 200 teachers who work for the district, a number have been singled out for awards within the past several years. Two

Preparing children to live in a diverse, rapidly changing world is an important goal of educators.

have been named Teachers of the Year for the state of Wisconsin. Another was selected as a National Science Teacher.

Also recognized by Wisconsin Manufacturers and Commerce for using tax dollars wisely, Waunakee, in meeting the needs of all students, has developed work experience and apprenticeship programs. More than 94 percent of students at Waunakee High School graduate, and 85 percent of those graduates go on to post-secondary education.

Private Schools

The majority of non-public schools in south-central Wisconsin are church schools. In Dane County alone, approximately 3,500 children attend Catholic schools, some of which are more than 100 years old.

Other schools cater to academically gifted children and those with special needs. The following list incorporates a wide variety, big and small, of what is available in the area.

West Side

Blessed Sacrament School
2112 Hollister Ave., Madison
• **(608) 233-6155**

Blessed Sacrament is a Catholic elementary school providing a quality Christian and academic education for 330 students in kindergarten through grade 8. The school features multi-age classrooms, an experienced staff and a prime location on the near West Side that is easily accessible from Downtown. After-school care is available for students in grades 1 through 6.

Eagle School
1201 McKenna Blvd., Madison
• **(608) 273-0309**

Founded in 1982, Eagle School offers an enriched, accelerated education for about 150 gifted children in kindergarten through grade 8. The admission process for this school on the far West Side of Madison includes testing

---

INSIDERS' TIP

In Madison, 45 percent of high school students take advanced math courses, compared to only 7 percent statewide.

and visits by potential students and their parents. Both before- and after-school care are available. Children entering kindergarten must be 4½ or older.

Edgewood Campus Grade School
2324 Edgewood Dr., Madison
• (608) 257-7726

Encompassing a beautifully wooded campus near Vilas Park, Edgewood is a Catholic private school emphasizing academic excellence, cultural arts and Christian values. The school has about 270 students in kindergarten through grade 8. Four-year-olds are accepted into a half-day (afternoon) pre-kindergarten program. After-school care is available for students in kindergarten through grade 4.

Edgewood High School
2219 Monroe St., Madison
• (608) 257-1023

When Edgewood High School opened in 1881, there was little else around it on the near the West Side of Madison. Now it's sandwiched between stately neighborhoods and quaint shops, although its large rolling, wooded campus continues to set this school apart. The only Catholic high school in Dane County, Edgewood offers a college-preparatory curriculum for 600 students, who often drive 50 miles or more one way to attend. More than 95 percent of graduating seniors go on to college. Religious courses and community service are required, and students are expected to follow a written code of behavior.

High Point Christian School
7702 Old Sauk Rd., Madison
• (608) 836-7170

High Point is a nondenominational school seeking to provide a program of academic excellence within the context of a Christian viewpoint. The school stresses traditional family values, and art, music and literature are evaluated from a moral as well as artistic perspective. Also, the curriculum emphasizes a phonetic approach in teaching reading skills. The school has 175 students in kindergarten through grade 8.

Madison Central Montessori School
4337 W. Beltline Hwy., Madison
• (608) 274-9549

Montessori accommodates about 100 students from preschool through grade 6. The school specializes in nongraded classes of mixed-age children who gain practical and intellectual knowledge from individual exploration of language, math, geography, art and music. All materials are designed for independent learning.

Our Lady Queen of Peace
418 Holly Ave., Madison
• (608) 231-4580

In the quiet neighborhood of Westmorland on Madison's near West Side, Queen of Peace emphasizes a strong academic program within a Catholic educational framework. Many families move into the neighborhood just to be closer to this school that teaches kindergarten through grade 8. It's the largest Catholic school in the area, with almost 500 students. The school was enlarged in '96 to accommodate more kindergartners and add more space for physical education, science and foreign language classes. After-school care is available.

Our Redeemer Lutheran School
1701 McKenna Blvd., Madison
• (608) 274-2830

Operated by Our Redeemer Lutheran Church, the school educates children from kindergarten through grade 8. A staff of eight instructors teaches 112 students. The curriculum consists of basic courses of instruction as required by the State of Wisconsin. In addition, daily religion classes are conducted

---

INSIDERS' TIP

Each year, Madison has nearly 50 National Merit Scholar Finalists, whereas across the nation a district of Madison's size typically has no more than two.

to provide students with a thorough knowledge and understanding of Scripture. Extracurricular programs include music and athletics. Preschool is available Tuesday and Thursday afternoons.

St. Maria Goretti School
5405 Flad Ave., Madison
- (608) 271-7551

While parishioners of St. Maria Goretti receive preference, the Catholic school is open to everyone in the community. About 205 students in kindergarten through grade 8 attend. The traditional curriculum is augmented by a strong school philosophy that "each child is first and foremost a unique creation of God and as such deserves love and an opportunity to develop to his or her potential."

Walbridge Academy
7035 Old Sauk Rd., Madison
- (608) 833-1338

Walbridge specializes in a very low student-teacher ratio to accommodate children with learning disabilities, attention deficit disorder or those simply in need of a structured, individualized setting. Instructors match teaching styles to learning styles for children in grades 1 to 8. Tutoring on all grade levels is also available. No after-school care is available, although two day-care centers are right across the street if parents choose to utilize them.

Wingra School
3200 Monroe St., Madison
- (608) 238-2525

Wingra is a small, independent elementary school serving about 150 children of diverse family backgrounds, abilities and needs in kindergarten through grade 8. It was founded in 1972 by parents and teachers influenced by a version of progressive school then often referred to as informal, or British, primary education. It features a theme-based integrated curriculum and mixed-age classrooms equipped with materials to meet children's varied interests. Kids love the campus because it has one of the best sliding hills of all the schools in Madison. Before- and after-school day care is available.

East Side

Abundant Life Christian School
4901 E. Buckeye Rd., Madison
- (608) 221-1520

The student body of Abundant Life represents 60 different churches. There are 421 children taught in kindergarten through grade 12. A Bible-centered education within traditionally structured classrooms is emphasized.

Calvary Christian Academy
5301 Commercial Ave., Madison
- (608) 249-6445

At Calvary, children in grades 1 to 12 work individually at their own pace assisted one-on-one by teachers using a Bible-based curriculum. The school of only about 50 students is set up like a one-room schoolhouse, with multiple grades working together.

Eastside Evangelical Lutheran School
2310 Independence Ln., Madison
- (608) 244-3045

Eastside has nine teachers instructing kindergarten through grade 8 for a student body of 163. The academic curriculum is based on Christian principles and influenced by Bible teachings. Eastside Lutheran incorporates a public-school curriculum into its religion-based program. With one teacher per grade, the student/teacher ratio is about 18-to-1.

Holy Cross Lutheran School
2670 Milwaukee St., Madison
- (608) 249-3101

Holy Cross provides a Christ-centered educational experience for 156 children in preschool through grade 8. The school sets high academic standards, and all subjects are taught within a Scriptures framework. Average student assessment on the annual Iowa Test of Basic Skills ranks in the upper 20 percent.

Omega School
949 E. Washington Ave., Madison
- (608) 255-6879

Omega is a nonprofit school for adults seeking their high school equivalency diplomas. Tuition is free, but there is a $25 testing fee.

Operation Fresh Start
1925 Winnebago St., Madison
• **(608) 244-4721**

This private, nonprofit alternative school accommodates students between the ages of 16 and 24 who wish to earn a high school equivalency diploma. Tuition is free, but a referral by the public school system or other governing body is needed to be eligible to attend.

Seventh Day Adventist School
900 Femrite Dr., Madison
• **(608) 222-5775**

More than 50 years old, this church school serves about 40 students in grades 1 to 8. There is cross-age tutoring, multi-grade classrooms and a student-teacher ratio of 11-to-1. After grade 8, students either attend public high school in Madison or a Seventh Day Adventist boarding high school in Columbus.

Madison's public schools are recognized for providing superb educational programs, from early childhood through high school.

Outlying Area

Churches in small cities and villages surrounding Madison have their own schools. This is not a definitive roundup but lists some that are better known and/or have been around for many years. Some, in fact, have been in existence for more than a century.

Country Day School
5606 River Rd., Waunakee
• **(608) 278-4039**

Dane County's newest private school opened its doors in the fall of 1997 as a college-preparatory school for about 50 students, pre-kindergarten through 4th grade. Country Day School plans to add grades every year and eventually be a high school, too. But first it has to find a permanent home. Although land was donated to the school in the Town of Westport, on the north side of Lake Mendota, some residents in the area who didn't want a school nearby managed to prevent Country Day School from building. The school has gone back to the drawing board and is hoping to answer all concerns.

Tuition is between $4,000 and $7,000 a year, with the lesser amount covering half-day pre-kindergarten. Financial aid is available.

Immaculate Heart of Mary School
4913 Schofield St., Monona
• **(608) 222-8831**

As a Catholic school, Immaculate Heart of Mary seeks to provide opportunities for learning as well as growth in Christian values. It serves about 250 students in kindergarten through grade 8. A traditional curriculum is featured, with a maximum of 25 students per class. Multiple parishes from Madison and surrounding communities attend.

INSIDERS' TIP

Class size and individual attention is a big issue for area school districts. Madison enjoys a licensed instructional staff member for every 11.6 students, compared to the state average of one for every 13.8 students.

Kinderhaus
5700 Pheasant Hill Dr., Monona
- (608) 224-1234

Kinderhaus opened in the fall of 1996 as the first school patterned after the German Waldorf model of education, which is based on the development of the child and emphasizing parental involvement. Three- and five-day preschool and mixed-age kindergarten for ages 3 through 6 is now being offered. In the immediate future, the school intends to add grades 1 through 8, a year at a time.

Peace Lutheran School
232 Windsor St., Sun Prairie
- (608) 837-5346

In the heart of Sun Prairie, Peace Lutheran School is growing by a grade a year. As in a one-room schoolhouse, the school has about 31 students in four grades, 1st through 4th. Fifth grade will be added in the fall of 1998; grade 6 in the fall of '99. Half-day kindergarten is also offered. The traditional academic curriculum is centered around God's word.

Sacred Heart Catholic School
219 Columbus St., Sun Prairie
- (608) 837-8508

Sacred Heart began teaching pupils long before the first subdivision opened in Sun Prairie — even before the streets were paved. The school celebrated its 100th anniversary in 1992. This Catholic school emphasizes a vigorous academic curriculum for 412 students in kindergarten through grade 8.

St. John The Baptist School
114 E. Third St., Waunakee
- (608) 849-5325

Including preschool, St. John has about 260 students, with one class per grade through grade 6. The mission of St. John is "to develop each student's potential to become well-rounded members of the community by stressing Catholic liturgy, traditional Christian values and the basic skills necessary to meet the challenges of an ever-changing society."

St. Peter Catholic School
7129 County Trunk A, Middleton
- (608) 831-4846

St. Peter School is a small, rural Catholic elementary school serving fewer than 60 students in grades 1 through 6. The environment offers a student/teacher ratio of about 15-to-1 amid a curriculum steeped in strong Christian ethics and values.

Western Koshkonong Lutheran School
2632 Church St., Cottage Grove
- (608) 873-6011

This country church school with 65 students was established more than 70 years ago to provide a traditional education with a Christian viewpoint to members and nonmembers of the Koshkonong Lutheran Church. Commercial or residential development has yet to catch up with Koshkonong. The school is between Cottage Grove and Stoughton with bus service provided by the Stoughton School District. Children in preschool through grade 8 go here.

Whether it's taking a few cooking classes through a local Indian food shop or going through a rigorous doctorate program at UW-Madison, opportunities to learn are everywhere.

Higher Education

Madison's personality as a city is defined, to a large extent, by the University of Wisconsin campus that rolls along the shore of Lake Mendota, just west of the Capitol. The colorful parade of students, as well as the nightlife, businesses and restaurants that spring up to cater to them, has an impact on everyone who lives here.

Madison is a place where debate is endless, and learning is woven into every aspect of community life. Whether it's taking a few cooking classes through a local Indian food shop or going through a rigorous doctorate program at the university, opportunities to learn are everywhere.

The cultural events, museums and sports events at the university and other local campuses add a myriad of possibilities to the quality of life here.

University of Wisconsin-Madison

The UW-Madison's sprawling 900-acre campus is famously picturesque, with rolling lawns, scenic pathways, fountains and gardens. Its fine collection of historic stone and brick buildings have, most of the time, been gracefully interwoven with new architecture.

Since it was created in 1848, the flagship of the Wisconsin public university system has become one of the nation's finest institutions of higher learning. *U.S. News and World Report* has listed UW-Madison as tied for third overall among top public universities in the country.

UW-Madison students and faculty have gone on to distinguish themselves and the university. UW-Madison's legacy includes 13 Nobel Prize recipients, 21 Pulitzer Prize winners, four Rhodes Scholars and 10 recipients of the esteemed National Medal of Science.

One UW-Madison professor whom Congress has been paying close attention to lately is Joanne Cantor of the communication arts department. She has spent 15 years studying how children are damaged by images, especially violent ones, on television and in movies. Among her many surprising findings are that sometimes even Disney movies and wholesome TV shows like *Little House on the Prairie* can terrify children for many years after the viewing. Her book, *Mommy, I'm Scared*, will be published by Harcourt Brace in late 1998.

Late in 1996, UW-Madison biologist Neal First won the world's most prestigious agricultural award, the Wolf Prize in Agriculture, for his work on the development of systems of bovine embryo cloning, gene transfer and in-vitro production of livestock embryos. Techniques pioneered in First's lab are now common procedures in human in-vitro fertilization clinics.

Alumni records for UW-Madison reveal two astronauts, Jim Lovell and Brewster Shaw; Magnetic Resonance Imager (MRI) inventor Raymond Damadian; Emmy Award-winning actor Daniel J. Travanti; rock singer Steve Miller; two professional athletic team owners, Kenneth Behring of the Seattle Seahawks and Allan "Bud" Selig of the Milwaukee Brewers; and many others who have left their mark, large or small.

About 40,000 students are enrolled at UW-Madison, which has the third-largest number of international students of any university in the nation. Minority enrollment is about 8 percent.

As budgets tighten, the university's commitment to educating the people of the state has become more important. UW Board of Regents' policy states that no more than 25 percent of the university's undergraduate enrollment may come from outside Wisconsin's borders.

The fall semester usually kicks off the last week of August. The student district is clustered within about a 3-mile radius of campus. Student housing has improved dramatically during the last decade. Before then, students were generally crammed into old houses as rickety as they were overpriced. A recent wave of building in the student neighborhoods has meant that students can find better housing at more reasonable prices.

Some 27,800 undergraduates are now enrolled in bachelor's degree programs chosen from majors from within eight colleges and schools: Agricultural and Life Sciences, Business, Education, Engineering, Family Resources and Consumer Sciences, Letters and Science, Nursing, and Pharmacy. UW-Madison's undergraduate business school is ranked seventh overall in the nation, while the university's undergraduate chemical engineering program is second overall in the United States, according to *U.S. News & World Report*.

According to *Wisconsin Week* (the university's paper of record for UW-Madison faculty and staff), 91 percent of undergraduates at UW-Madison say they are satisfied with the university, and 90 percent of students say they would enroll here again if they had a chance to do it over. In terms of overall quality of instruction, 63 percent of undergrads describe it as "excellent" or "very good" — up from 53 percent in 1995. Also of interest in the survey, one-seventh of students reported involvement in faculty research, and 27 percent of students reported involvement in some type of volunteer service during the academic year.

The university is third nationally in the number of graduate degrees it awards. The 1998 national rankings by *U.S. News and World Report* puts the following UW-Madison graduate programs in the top 10: education, audiology, rehabilitation counseling, social work, speech pathology, veterinary medicine, chemistry, computer science, economics and sociology. Within the top 20 are engineering, medicine (primary care), nursing, pharmacy, biological sciences, English, geology, history, mathematics, physics, political science and psychology.

The university's three professional schools — law, medicine and veterinary medicine — have a current enrollment of 1,910 students.

UW Medical School has a strong reputation for innovative medical education, especially in primary care. With its links to UW Hospitals and Clinics, students have the opportunity to work with nationally recognized specialists in such areas as oncology, pediatric lung diseases, ophthalmology, radiology and surgery. (For more information, see our Wellness and Healthcare chapter.)

Building dreams . . .

As students work to build academic records and career foundations, the university continues to grow and build in virtually every discipline — from biochemistry and engineering to dance.

To mark the 70th anniversary of the UW-Madison dance major program, a renovation costing more than $4 million completed in 1998 transformed the second-floor gymnasium of Lathrop Hall, a 1910 structure that has long housed UW-Madison's dance program, into a state-of-the-art performance space. The Lathrop Hall renovation won a historic preservation award in 1998 from the Madison Trust for Historic Preservation.

One of the most glamorous new buildings on campus is the $40 million Grainger Hall, completed in 1993. The five-story building contains 30 modern classrooms, two large lecture halls, a superb auditorium and a two-story library. Leading-edge instructional technology is incorporated throughout the building. To meet the demands of executive management education, the Fluno Center is being added. Also, the business school has a new evening MBA program.

---

www.insiders.com

See this and many other **Insiders' Guide®** destinations online — in their entirety.

Visit us today!

The big architectural event on campus in 1998 was the opening of the $76.4 million Kohl Center arena, where the men's and women's basketball teams and the hockey team will play (see the Close-up in the Sports chapter).

Other recent or ongoing campus construction projects are under way, including:

• a $16 million upgrade of the UW law school;

• the renovation of the Red Gym, an 1894 Norman-style red-brick building on the lake that resembles a medieval fortress, which for many years was the center for sports, social, political and cultural events and the home court for UW basketball teams from 1911 to 1930 (it now holds a visitors center and admissions offices);

• a major addition and research greenhouse for the Department of Biochemistry;

• new outdoor basketball and volleyball courts adjacent to the Southeast Recreation Facility (SERF) and a student-funded expansion of SERF resources.

Campus landmarks . . .

The first Biotron in the world, where environmental conditions such as temperature, humidity, barometric pressure, air flow, light intensity and length of day can be controlled for experimental purposes, opened on the UW-Madison campus in 1966.

The Nielsen Tennis Stadium, built in 1968, is said to be the largest building of its kind in the world. The stadium contains 12 tennis courts, six squash courts, galleries for 1,500 people and a large players' lounge.

The Memorial Union, often described as "the living room of the campus," has several dining rooms, theaters, lounges, meeting rooms and game rooms, in addition to the German-style Rathskeller and the lakeshore Terrace. The first section of the Union was built in 1928, and there have been three subsequent additions.

Science Hall, built in 1888, is one of the buildings designated as a National Historic Landmark on campus. It is said to be the second building in the nation built with steel-beam construction, and the oldest still standing. The architecture is Richardsonian Romanesque, and the young Frank Lloyd Wright helped su-

EDGEWOOD COLLEGE
MADISON, WISCONSIN

Weekends, Days, or Nights

- More than 40 undergraduate majors in the humanities, sciences, arts, business, education, and nursing

- Graduate programs in business administration, education, educational administration, religious studies, nursing and marriage and family therapy

- Classes offered on variety of schedules for traditional and working adult students

- Personal attention in small classes from faculty who know your name

- Access to UW-Madison libraries and classes for specialized study

- Learning resource center, career and counseling services

- Internship opportunities

- Continuing education classes for a wide variety of interests

- Financial aid packages and flexible payment schedules negotiable

257-4861
Admissions Office
855 Woodrow Street
Madison, Wisconsin 53711
www.edgewood.edu

The Time's Right In Your Life!

pervise its construction. See our Attractions chapter for more about this building.

The heart of the campus is Bascom Hall, which was built in stages beginning in 1859. It is the center of the Bascom Hill Historic District and a national landmark. The Renaissance Revival-style building now holds administration offices. In front of Bascom Hall is the most famous symbol of the campus, the statue of a seated Abraham Lincoln, which was unveiled in 1909.

The 85-foot tall sandstone Carillon Tower was the cumulative gift of graduating classes from 1917 to 1926. Its more than 56 bells, each weighing between 15 and 6,800 pounds, give the Carillon a 4½-octave range. A carillonneur from the School of Music gives Sunday afternoon concerts, and you'll hear them on some summer evenings as well. Our Arts chapter provides more information about this structure.

Across the Observatory Drive from the Carillon Tower is the Washburn Observatory, which at the time it was built in 1879 had the largest refractory telescope in the nation. The first telephone line in Wisconsin ran from Washburn to Music Hall for setting of the clocks. The Pine Bluff Observatory farther west is now used for most academic purposes, but Washburn is still used for teaching and is open to the public on the first and third Wednesdays of each month. It is on the National Register of Historic Places.

Camp Randall was originally a Civil War training ground, a hospital and a stockade for Confederate prisoners. Currently it is the home of intercollegiate athletic and recreational facilities, a small park and the Memorial Arch, completed in 1912. Nearby is the Field House, which, until the Kohl Center was completed, was the home of UW basketball.

The Elvehjem Museum of Art, built in 1970, houses the university's collection of paintings, prints, drawings, sculpture and decorative arts dating from 2300 B.C. to present. It maintains an active schedule of temporary exhibitions, and regularly hosts a classical musical quartet. Again, see our Arts chapter for more information.

Regarding research . . .

UW-Madison continues to pave the way in diverse areas of research. Highlights include the following:

• The Arboretum, developed due to the efforts of naturalist Aldo Leopold. This outdoor-research lab is internationally recognized for ecological restoration of forests, wetlands and other habitats.

• McArdle Laboratory for Cancer Research, the first university-based cancer research center in the United States (1940). McArdle Labs focus on cancer treatment and research, including the use of tamoxifen for breast cancer.

• The Center for X-ray Lithography, the Physical Science Laboratory and the Synchrotron Radiation Center — three major UW science research facilities off campus, near Stoughton.

• Space Science and Engineering Center, which specializes in atmospheric studies of the earth and other planets, helping scientists interpret long-term effects.

• University Research Park, west of campus, where UW researchers work hand-in-hand with more than 60 businesses helping them apply and benefit from scientific advances.

Students, faculty and Wisconsin residents wishing to research just about any topic can use the UW library system, the 14th-largest library collection in the United States. The campus has more than 40 libraries. The largest are Memorial Library and Helen C. White Library, both on the east end of campus.

The University of Wisconsin-Extension also has a wide range of course offerings. And for educational pick-me-ups, the Memorial Union on campus offers mini-courses on such varied topics as massage, photography and clog

---

INSIDERS' TIP

The National Organization for Women, launched by Kathryn Clarenbach and Betty Friedan in 1966, was first housed in Clarenbach's faculty office on the UW-Madison campus

HIGHER EDUCATION • 381

This Badger backer must be a swimmer — Bucky doesn't have webbed feet as a rule.

dancing. Extension courses have been around 25 years, are amazingly popular and offer a variety that continues to surprise.

The campus map included in this chapter details some of these features and a few more. Pick up an inclusive map at the Campus Assistance Center, 420 N. Lake Street, (608) 263-2400.

Other Institutions

Cardinal Stritch University
8017 Excelsior Dr., Madison
• (608) 831-2722

Students applying to Cardinal Stritch University are required to have previous work experience to qualify for enrollment, and that work experience may qualify for college-level credit. The college offers three undergraduate business degrees and three graduate degrees — business administration, management and health-services administration — as well as some certificate programs in sales and sales management.

Headquartered in Milwaukee, the Madison branch serves about 600 students. Applications are accepted year round, and new classes begin every month.

Concordia University Madison Center
2909 Landmark Pl., Madison
• (608) 53713, (608) 277-7900

The Madison center of Concordia University offers three undergraduate majors: management and communication, liberal arts, and healthcare administration. Associates or bachelor's degrees are awarded.

The school recommends that students be at least 25 years old with seven years of work or "life" experience. Academic credit is given for real-life experience, such as skills and information they've learned on the job. The adult accelerated program allows students to concentrate on one subject area for four weeks, with 20 hours of homework per week. Then it's on to another subject area.

For undergraduate programs, students attend class one night a week and can earn three credits in four to six weeks, going on to receive a degree in as few as 18 months.

No graduate programs are based in Madison. Those are available at Concordia's headquarters in Mequon, a suburb of Milwaukee. However, people in Madison who want to take Concordia's graduate courses without commuting to Mequon can do so through the modern equivalent of correspondence courses. Students communicate with the campus and faculty via electronic mail. Papers, assignments and forms are sent back and forth by e-mail, and students participate in interactive conferences with faculty and fellow students by computer, fax, telephone or express mail.

Concordia University was founded in 1881 by the Lutheran Church-Missouri Synod.

Edgewood College
855 Woodrow St., Madison
• (608) 257-4861, (800) 444-4861

Edgewood College, on Madison's Lake Wingra, was founded by the Sinsinsawa Dominican Sisters and was established as a junior college for women in 1927. The private college now has about 1,450 undergraduates and 500 graduate students. Edgewood offers weekday classes for traditional resident and commuter students, weekend and evening undergraduate and master's degree programs and continuing-education classes. Admission requirements include a high school minimum GPA of 2.7 and appropriate ACT or SAT scores.

The school offers intercollegiate men's and women's basketball, soccer and tennis; women's softball and volleyball; men's baseball; men's and women's golf; cheerleading and intramurals. A major construction boom is under way on the Edgewood campus. A new science facility will open in spring 1999. When finished it will be the only science facility in the country that is shared by students from kindergarten through college level. (A private elementary and high school shares the campus.) The facility will make it possible for college students to student teach without leaving campus.

The next phase of construction will be a four-story humanities center, with a new student union and auditorium, to be completed in the spring of 2000. A new parking ramp for 300 cars, plus an increase in surface parking, should eliminate the college's previous parking problems.

High-Tech Careers
START HERE

ELECTRONICS CAREER TRAINING
- Digital, AC/DC
- Networking
- Windows NT
- Visual Basic
- C++
- Internet
- MCSE & MCSD
- 4 Year Degree in 3 Years
- Financial Aid, If qualified
- Employment Assistance

We're Committed To Your Success

HERZING COLLEGE OF TECHNOLOGY

CALL **1-800-582-1227**

Edgewood is accredited by the North Central Association of Colleges and Secondary Schools, National Council for Accreditation of Teacher Education and National League of Nursing. Students may choose to live off campus or in on-campus apartments or residence halls.

Herzing College of Technology
1227 N. Sherman Ave., Madison
• (608) 249-6611

Small classes, short-term career training, state-of-the-art equipment and personal attention are some reasons why students choose to attend Herzing College of Technology.

Formerly known as Wisconsin School of Electronics, Herzing College offers accredited training in electronics and computer technology. Curriculum choices include associate degree programs in electronics engineering technology, electronics and mechanical CAD drafting, and computer information systems. The school offers three bachelor's degree programs: electronics and computer technology, CAD drafting and computer technology, and computer information systems.

New students must have a high school diploma or equivalency and must pass entrance exams. Associate degree programs cover six semesters over a two-year period. An additional three to five semesters are needed to complete bachelor's degree programs. Part-time students are accepted.

Founded in 1948, the college merged in 1970 with Herzing Institutes to become part of an international vocational training program. In 1995, the college granted its first bachelor's degree as part of a minor program expansion. Herzing College also offers a number of certificate programs and is has Microsoft-authorized academic program (AATP) offering preparation courses for Microsoft certified systems engineer (MCSE) and Microsoft certified solutions developer (MCSD).

Herzing College graduates are in high demand by such companies as IBM, Rockwell, Allen Bradley and Motorola. Half-day and evening classes allow students time for class-related employment while attending school.

Madison Area Technical College
3550 Anderson St., Madison
• (608) 246-6100, (800) 322-6282 (toll-free in Wisconsin)

Madison Area Technical College, the technical and community college for the greater Madison area, offers more than 100 educational programs and serves approximately 50,000 students annually. Primarily a commuter college, MATC's main campus is off Stoughton Road (U.S. Highway 51), near the Dane County Regional Airport.

MATC has been branching out lately and now does a lot of training for businesses. Instructors from MATC might, for example, teach a group of employees at a business about a particular computer system. Such programs are customized to meet the needs of the business.

You will also find offbeat classes such as Beverage Mixology, or "Bartender U." The classroom contains a full-size bar, and the more advanced curriculum includes mixing such drinks as Pink Cadillacs, B52s and Grasshoppers. You'll also learn bar lingo and a thing or two about how to gracefully cut people off and about Wisconsin's tough liquor laws. For a few, the class counts toward an associate degree in hospitality and tourism management.

Among MATC's campus amenities are a Fitness Center and a wide range of cultural events, open to students and the general public. It is well known for its food service training, and the public can sometimes come in for special dinners in its Gourmet Dining Room. The dinners are held Tuesdays and Thursdays during the school year. For reservations call (608) 246-6369.

Students attending MATC can earn associate degrees in applied sciences (such as computer technology, public safety, industrial production, agriculture and health) and applied arts (commercial art, photography, interior design and occupational therapy). MATC also offers a variety of short-term (two years, one year or less) technical degree and diploma programs, emphasizing hands-on skills.

MATC is an alternative for college studies, providing many of the basic courses generally required by four-year universities. If students choose to pursue this course of study, however, they should communicate closely with officials at the university they intend to transfer to at the end of their MATC studies to ensure credit transfers. The school grants associate degrees in arts and liberal studies. High school students wishing to get a jump on their college or technical education may be eligible to take some MATC courses.

If you are interested in pursuing a career in the construction trades — bricklaying, carpentry and ironworking — the MATC apprenticeship department coordinates and oversees training for skilled trades through a combination of work-related schooling and on-the-job training (varying between two to six years). For information on the apprenticeship program, call (608) 246-5202.

Of great benefit to Dane County residents is MATC's adult- and continuing-education programs. Courses can be found as close as your local public school, covering a range of topics including computers, child care and financial planning. Adults also can earn high-school equivalency diplomas through MATC programs, and special classes are available for those learning English as a second language or preparing to become U.S. citizens.

MATC has nine South-Central Wisconsin education centers in addition to its main Truax Campus. Distance-learning opportunities are also available. In 1996 more than 1,000 students took 18 telecourses. MATC is now working to develop two-way audiovisual communication between all MATC campuses and as many as 40 area public school districts.

Admission requirements vary. The closing date for applications is July 1 for the fall semester and November 15 for the spring semester.

Madison College
31 S. Henry St., Madison
• (608) 251-6522

Formerly Madison Business College, this institution was renamed Madison College in June of 1998. The two-year junior college has plans to become a four-year institution within approximately two years. Plans are in place for a varsity sports program with football, basketball, men's baseball and women's volleyball. All the courses are business oriented,

---

INSIDERS' TIP

If you're looking for a gorgeous place to hold a wedding, the gardens of 1897 Agriculture Dean's residence, which was built in 1897, can be rented.

The many educational opportunities in Madison help make the city a popular place to live.

and Associate of Applied Science degrees are currently awarded. This is now a commuter college, but eventually a dorm will be built.

Madison Media Institute
One Point Pl., Ste. 1, Madison
• (608) 829-2728

Students at Madison Media Institute receive instruction to help them enter careers in radio and television broadcasting or recording and music technology. The student-teacher ratio is 12-to-1, and the school stresses a hands-on approach. Madison Media Institute, which traces its roots to 1969, has state-of-the-art equipment. The school has 4,300 square feet of classroom and studio space including six radio studios, a multiple-track radio production studio, a music-synthesis and computer lab and a 24-track digital recording studio.

Each semester is 15 weeks long (certificate programs require two semesters). Students may choose from five starting points during the calendar year. Applicants must have a high school diploma or equivalent.

Upper Iowa University Madison Center
4601 Hammersley Rd., Madison
• (608) 278-0350

This commuter campus caters to working adults who want to complete bachelor of science degrees in accounting, business, human resources management, marketing, management and public administration, human services and psychology. The Madison Center also offers a master's degree in business leadership.

Upper Iowa University traces its roots back to 1857. The Madison Center has been operating since 1981.

Most classes at the Madison Center are held weeknights and on Saturday mornings to accommodate busy adults. Six two-month terms are scheduled per year.

Hope your tour of Madison doesn't include us

(but should the need arise, we're here day and night)

New in town or just passing through? Meriter Hospital's Emergency Services provides medical care that may leave you thinking you never left home. Our board-certified emergency physicians, a pediatric physician, skilled nurses and other support staff work 24 hours a day, every day, to provide caring, quality emergency care.

Not sure whether you need to come in?
Call us at 267-6206. One of our registered nurses will find out more about your situation before recommending what you do next.

MERITER®
EMERGENCY SERVICES
202 S. Park St. • 267-6206
www.meriter.com

Healthcare

To be selected as the No. 1 Place To Live in '96 by *Money* magazine, Madison scored high on four major "quality-of-life" criteria. But it received the greatest number of points, 99 out of 100, for the excellence of its healthcare.

It's not surprising, then, that less than a year later, *American Health* magazine labeled the capital city "the healthiest city in the country for women" based on seven categories: women's health, career potential, crime index, environment, family life, fitness and urban stress.

Of course, it's small consolation to know you're living in a healthy spot when you're 15 pounds overweight and haven't exercised in a month. Even so, it's nice to know a healthy environment and excellent healthcare coexist here.

At Madison's doorstep are five general hospitals, more than 20 major medical clinics, 100 research and testing labs and UW-Madison's schools of medicine, nursing and pharmacy.

Having a teaching hospital within city limits benefits everyone in a number of ways by making Madison an ideal place for physicians to practice and stay current with medical advancements. Partnerships forged between the UW and community health facilities enable residents to enjoy innovative health services and take part in medical studies that otherwise wouldn't be available in a midsize city like Madison.

Affordable access to healthcare is as important as the quality of medical services. Credited with helping to improve the efficiency and reduce the cost of healthcare in Dane County is a wide network of managed-care companies. Health-maintenance organizations (HMOs) began operating in Wisconsin during the mid-1970s, although they didn't come into their own until the mid-1980s. Of the HMOs operating in Dane County, four of the largest are the following: Group Health, a consumer-sponsored cooperative with a primary affiliation with University of Wisconsin Hospital; Dean Health Plan Inc., owned by Sisters of St. Marys Health Care System of St. Louis and Dean Health System, and primarily affiliated with St. Marys Hospital; Physicians Plus Insurance Corp., owned by Physicians Plus Physicians, Meriter Hospital and Wausau Insurance; and Unity Health Plans based in Sauk City and owned by United Wisconsin Services, which is part of Blue Cross of Wisconsin. Area Unity subscribers primarily use UW Hospital, and Physicians Plus Physicians subscribers are sent to Meriter.

While the verdict is still out on the long-term effect of HMOs and whether they provide adequate and enough long-term coverage for chronic and life-threatening illnesses, newcomers should note that the health-maintenance organizations operating in South-Central Wisconsin are considered to be some of the better managed ones in the country. Yet, before signing on the dotted line of any healthcare plan, it's wise to read the fine print, talk to other consumers and ask enough questions to eliminate any surprises down the road.

The best way to find a dentist or physician is by word-of-mouth, although many established healthcare providers are not taking new patients. The Wisconsin Dental Association, based in Milwaukee, only provides referrals to patients on medical assistance. However, the organization will review complaints and provide some general information about individual members. Call (414) 276-4520.

The State Medical Society of Wisconsin, based in Madison, will share names of physicians who are members and provide some background information including age, medical school from which the person graduated

HEALTHCARE

and whether or not he or she is board-certified, but the organization does not give referrals. For more information, call 257-6781.

Under Meriter Hospital's "Doctor For You" program, referrals are available for more than 300 physicians practicing in Madison and the surrounding area. Call (608) 258-DR4U between 8:30 AM and 5 PM weekdays.

We start off this chapter with an introduction to the five hospitals in the area, followed by sections listing emergency and health-related support services. Finally, if you have a pet that needs to see a doctor, refer to the end of this chapter.

Good Numbers To Keep Handy

For an emergency or health-related question, look to these resources for help. Crisis lines are answered 24 hours a day. (The area code for numbers not otherwise designated is 608.)

Life-threatening, police and fire emergencies in Dane County, 911
UW-Madison Police & Security, 262-2957
Poison Control Center, (800) 815-8855
Crisis line for parents and teens, (800) 798-1126
Rape Crisis Center, 251-5126, 251-7273
Suicide Prevention, 251-2345
Overeaters Anonymous, 250-3980
Free Hearing Screening, 252-5252
Alcoholics Anonymous, 222-8989
Al-Anon, 241-6644
Narcotics Anonymous, 258-1747
Gamblers Anonymous, 255-1116
Anonymous AIDS Testing, 262-7330
Well-water Testing (for rural Dane County), 242-6515

Hospitals

All Madison hospitals are near one another, just west of the Capitol Square.

Low-cost overnight accommodations for families with ill children in area hospitals is available through the Ronald McDonald House, 2716 Marshall Court, near the UW Children's Hospital. Families or guardians must be referred to the house by hospital personnel. The Howard Johnson Plaza-Hotel, 525 W. Johnson Street, also offers reduced rates for the families of persons undergoing treatment at Madison hospitals or some clinics. Call the hotel, (608) 251-5511, for details. (See our Hotels and Motels chapter for related details.)

Isthmus

Meriter Hospital
202 S. Park St., Madison
• **(608) 267-6000 general information,**
(608) 267-6206 emergency,
(608) 267-6036 patient information

Celebrating its centennial year in '98, Meriter Hospital is a locally managed community hospital with 517 beds and a medical staff of 340 primary physicians and medical specialists.

The hospital offers a wide range of outpatient and inpatient surgical procedures and other medical services including 24-hour emergency and urgent care to patients of all ages. Its Birth and Family Services Department provides comprehensive, family-centered healthcare services to pregnant women, newborns and their families. Meriter's Birthing Center was the first hospital in the area to offer single-room maternity care. Working in partnership with the UW-Madison, the hospital is also singled out for the availability and quality of its high-risk obstetrical and neonatal care.

At Meriter's Heart Center, cardiac treatment and rehabilitation go hand-in-hand with programming aimed at reducing the incidence of heart disease. Preventive medicine is the cornerstone of an extensive community-outreach program highlighted by a multitude of classes and workshops geared to educating people about how to stay healthy.

Other strong areas at Meriter are orthopedics, neuroscience, physical rehabilitation, dialysis, sports medicine, evaluation of sleep disorders, psychiatry and drug-abuse programming.

There's no substitute for Experience

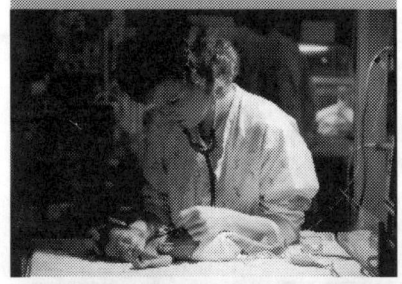

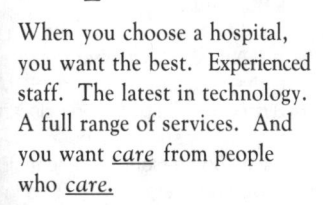

When you choose a hospital, you want the best. Experienced staff. The latest in technology. A full range of services. And you want _care_ from people who _care_.

At St. Marys Hospital Medical Center, we have 85 years in the business of caring for people in south central Wisconsin.

From our 24-hour emergency services to our birthing and pediatrics units, we care for the health of families. From our Cardiovascular Center to our Neuroscience Center, we bring the latest in technology to care for those with more serious illnesses.

St. Marys is a good neighbor, too. Classes and health information programs help keep you well, and support groups are available for your special health concerns.

Whatever you need, St. Marys can help.

When you choose a hospital, take a good look at St. Marys. When you choose a health plan, make sure St. Marys is a choice if you need hospitalization.

For more information, or a free brochure on St. Marys, call the Community Relations Department, (608)258-5065.

St♥Marys

St. Marys Hospital Medical Center • Madison, Wisconsin • (608) 251-6100

A MEMBER OF THE SSM HEALTH CARE SYSTEM

The hospital opened its new Emergency Services department in January 1998. It is accessible from Park and Brook streets.

St. Marys Hospital
707 S. Mills St., Madison
• (608) 251-6100 general and patient information, (608) 258-6800 emergency

Part of the St. Louis-based SSM Healthcare System owned by the Franciscan Sisters of Mary, this hospital has been serving residents of South-Central Wisconsin since 1912. Over the years, the 440-bed facility has been extensively renovated, and in 1993 a five-story patient-care wing was opened. The St. Marys campus includes an outpatient surgery center and an employee child-care center. Nearby is St. Marys Care Center (nursing home). St. Marys also operates an off-site adult day center and is part owner of a home healthcare organization.

The hospital and its affiliated physician group, Dean Medical Center, together own and manage more than 22 primary-care clinics. They also jointly own and operate the Surgery and Care Center, Davis Duehr (eye) Surgery Center and the Pediatric Specialty Clinics in Madison. Also, since 1972, St. Marys has been affiliated with the UW School of Medicine's three-year family-practice residency program.

A full range of inpatient and outpatient treatment and diagnostic services in primary care and nearly all specialties are offered through the hospital. But areas of special focus are cardiac services, perinatology, pediatrics, the neurosciences, geriatrics and emergency services. St. Marys offers health screenings, promotes support groups and sponsors a variety of health and fitness classes through its wellness entity, Health Works.

Campus

University of Wisconsin Hospital and Clinics
600 Highland Ave., Madison
• (608) 263-6400 general information, (608) 262-2398 emergency, (608) 263-8590 patient information

Established by the Wisconsin Legislature in 1924, University Hospital, as it is commonly known, moved to its current location on the far west end of campus in 1979. It was reorganized as a public authority in June '96.

Affiliated with almost 20 clinics in South-Central Wisconsin in addition to the 80 outpatient clinics that are part of its operation, University Hospital also shares its facilities with the UW Schools of Nursing and Pharmacy, UW Medical School and UW Comprehensive Cancer Center, the latter of which is one of only about 30 federally designated centers for cancer treatment and research in the country.

The hospital contains 479 beds, 59 of which are in five intensive-care units. One of those ICUs is for burn victims.

University Hospital is nationally recognized in a wide range of medical specialties including cancer care, pediatric lung diseases, ophthalmology, radiology and surgery. Its transplant program is ranked among the nation's best for procuring donor organs and achieving successful outcomes. Survival rates of UW transplant patients exceed expectations in all categories, according to a 1994 federal study.

A critical-care, helicopter transport service, Med Flight, lands on the roof of the hospital. It

---

INSIDERS' TIP

After Madison native Chris Farley died, his family and friends established The Chris Farley Foundation to combat drug and alcohol abuse. The Madison-born comedian was laid to rest in Madison's Resurrection Catholic Cemetery in 1998.

The UW Hospital and Clinics is recognized for excellence in a wide range of specialties.

was established in '85 to serve the western half of the state and is the largest service of its kind within Wisconsin.

UW Children's Hospital
600 Highland Ave., Madison
• (608) 263-7337

Housed within University Hospital (see previous entry), the UW's pediatric hospital contains 60 beds and is nationally known for medical treatment in many specialized areas including children's lung diseases and cancer.

West Side

William S. Middleton Memorial Veterans Hospital
2500 Overlook Ter., Madison
• (608) 256-1901 general and patient information, (608) 262-7012 emergency

The 170-bed medical center provides surgical, neurological and psychiatric care as well as a range of primary outpatient services to 235,000 veterans spread throughout South-Central Wisconsin and northwestern Illinois.

Dedicated in September 1951, the hospital operated as a tuberculosis treatment center until 1960 when the advent of new drugs for the disease greatly reduced the need for hospitalization. Today, the medical center lists as its strengths the cardiac surgery program, neurosurgery unit, epilepsy treatment center and center for geriatric research and treatment. The hospital also supports a veterans outreach center.

To forge an affiliation with the University of Wisconsin Medical School, a wing was added in 1979 to connect the hospital with UW's Clinical Science Center. In '95, as a means to streamline services, the Department of Veterans Affairs enacted a new system to group all of the country's VA hospitals into 22 Veterans Integrated Service Networks, or VISNs. Madison is now one of seven units of the VA Great Lakes Healthcare System (VISN 12) serving Wisconsin, Upper Michigan and northwest Illinois, including the Chicago region.

Outlying Area

Stoughton Community Hospital
900 Ridge St., Stoughton
• (608) 873-6611

Established in 1902, Stoughton Hospital is the fifth-largest employer in Stoughton, with a staff of about 260. The present 69-bed facility includes four additions since 1948. The most recent one in '94 made room for an ambulatory-care center and medical office building. A new day-surgery center opened in fall '95.

Stoughton is a full-service, community hospital serving people in Brooklyn, Cambridge, Cottage Grove, Evansville, Deerfield, McFarland, Oregon and Stoughton. It offers a wide range of diagnostic services and patient care and provides such community services as classes in babysitting and cardiopulmonary resuscitation (CPR) and recovery programs for chemical dependency. In addition to an emergency room, Stoughton Hospital has its own urgent-care center on site.

Immediate-Care Facilities

For treatment of non-life-threatening injuries or illnesses, a visit to an immediate-care facility is less expensive and usually less time-consuming than going to a hospital emergency room. Centers associated with a specific hospital and/or health-maintenance organization will treat anyone who walks in off the street. But it's wise to check with your health-insurance carrier first to guarantee coverage. If your insurance company can't be billed, you'll be expected to pay in cash when services are rendered. All facilities treat adults and children unless otherwise noted. Hours may have changed from those listed below so it's always a good idea to call ahead.

If you as a visitor to Madison become ill while staying in a name-recognizable hotel and do not want to go to an urgent-care center, you may request a "house call" through **Hotel Docs Inc.** at (800) 468-3537. Based in San Diego, California, the medical service has doctors on call 24 hours a day in more than 200 cities including Madison. The cost is $150 between the hours of 8 AM and 10 PM and $195 from 10 PM until 8 AM and on holidays. Be advised, however, that this service is for nonemergency medical problems only.

Campus

UW Doctors/Physicians Plus Urgent Care
University Hospital and Clinics, 600 Highland Ave., Madison
• (608) 263-7500

This clinic provides adult care only. Hours are Monday through Thursday 5 to 9 PM and Saturday and Sunday, 8 AM to noon.

General Pediatric Urgent Care
600 Highland Avenue, Madison
• (608) 263-6421

Care here is limited to children only. Hours are Monday through Friday 5 to 9 PM and Saturday and Sunday, 8 AM to noon.

West Side

Dean Urgent Care Center
202 S. Gammon Rd., Madison
• (608) 250-1525

Hours are 7 AM to 10 PM daily.

East Side

Dean Urgent Care Center
3434 E. Washington Ave., Madison
• (608) 246-2260

Hours are 7 AM to 10 PM daily.

Concentra Occupational Medical Center
1619 N. Stoughton Rd., Madison
• (608) 244-1213

Hours are 8 AM to 5:30 PM daily.

Outlying Area

Stoughton Hospital Urgent Care
900 Ridge St., Stoughton
• (608) 873-2564

Hours are 5 to 9 PM Monday through Friday and 9 AM to 11 PM weekends and holidays.

INSIDERS' TIP

In July 1997 *U.S. News & World Report* ranked University Hospital among the best hospitals in the nation in 11 different medical specialties.

Whether you're passing through town or moving to Madison, isn't it nice to know one of the nation's top-rated hospitals is just down the street?

At UW Hospital and Clinics, we provide expert care from tendonitis to transplants. And with more than 50 area clinics, there is sure to be one close by.

For unsurpassed medical care, choose UW Health. Call **263-8580** for the clinic nearest you.

Strong Medicine Tender Care

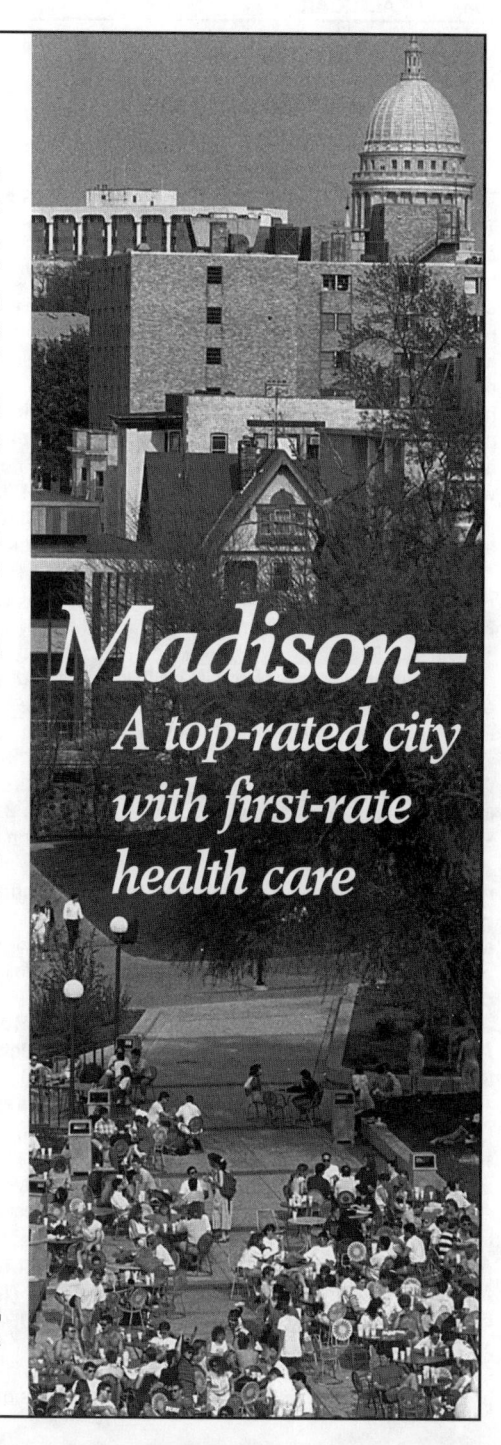

Madison–
A top-rated city with first-rate health care

UW Health
University of Wisconsin
Hospital and Clinics

Special Services and Support Groups

The following alphabetized list of organizations only represent a fraction of support services available in and around Madison. These do, however, disseminate information about a wide variety of health and living problems. Following this first general list are specific categories with services for mental health, drug abuse, coping with cancer and aiding the homebound/terminally ill. For a more complete listing of social, legal and health-related organizations, refer to the *Wisconsin State Journal's* annual "Answer Book" and/or *Isthmus'* "Annual Manual," both of which are published in late summer as free newspaper inserts. All addresses are in Madison unless otherwise noted.

Access to Independence
2345 Atwood Ave., Madison
• (608) 242-8484

This organization puts physically disabled people who want to live independently in touch with services that can help them do so.

AIDS Network
680 Williamson St., Madison
• (608) 252-6540

AIDS Network, formerly known as Madison AIDS Support Network, provides outreach, education and direct-care services for people who are HIV-positive or have AIDS as well as for their partners, families and friends in 13 counties, including Dane, in South-Central Wisconsin.

Alzheimer Association
517 N. Segoe Rd., Madison
• (608) 232-3400

This group provides information, support and community referrals to help reduce stress on families and caregivers dealing with Alzheimer's.

American Diabetes Association, Madison Chapter
6320 Monona Dr., Ste. 211, Monona
• (608) 222-3181

This chapter acts primarily as a referral service, linking area residents with the diabetic-support services and information they need.

American Heart Association of Wisconsin
4703 Monona Dr., Monona
• (608) 221-8866

Serving a seven-county area including Dane, the American Heart Association of Wisconsin disseminates information through literature and videos to help reduce premature death and disability from heart disease and strokes.

American Red Cross, Badger Chapter
4860 Sheboygan Ave., Madison
• (608) 233-9300
East Side blood-donor site, 3939 Lien Rd., Madison • (608) 233-9300

This Red Cross chapter, serving all of South-Central Wisconsin, offers disaster relief and blood services, instructions in first aid and water safety, and military counseling and referral. For young adolescents, it offers a babysitting certification program.

Arthritis Foundation, Wisconsin Chapter
802 W. Broadway Ave., Ste. 206, Madison • (608) 221-9800

The foundation acts as a clearinghouse for information to help improve the lives of those suffering from arthritis and supports research to prevent the disease from occurring at all.

Blue Bus Clinic
1552 University Ave., Madison
• (608) 262-7330

This specialty clinic diagnoses and treats sexually transmitted diseases. Anonymous HIV testing is provided. Blue Bus is operated by University Health Service but serves all area residents.

Briarpatch
512 E. Washington Ave., Madison
• (608) 251-1126, (800) 798-1126
24-hour crisis line

Counseling and temporary foster placement is offered through this organization for

HEALTHCARE • 395

teens and parents in conflict. Briarpatch also operates Teens Like Us, a support group for gay teens.

Easter Seal Society
101 Nob Hill Rd., Ste. 301, Madison
• **(608) 277-8288**

For people with physical disabilities, the Easter Seal Society provides a wide variety of referral, advocacy and educational help. It also operates the Wisconsin Craftsmen craft shop, 14 N. Carroll Street, which sells items made by artisans with disabilities. Also, the organization oversees summer camps near the Wisconsin Dells for adults and children. (See the Kidstuff chapter for related information.)

Epilepsy Center South Central
7818 Big Sky Dr., Ste. 117, Madison
• **(608) 833-8888**

This organization provides direct and indirect services for people with epilepsy in Richland, Juneau, Columbia, Sauk, Dodge and Dane counties.

First Call For Help
(608) 246-4357, 246-4360 TDD

This referral service links Dane County residents to services and programs that can help them in resolving an overwhelming concern or need.

Madison Area Chapter of the National Spinal Cord Injury Association
(608) 222-8302

Dedicated to serving people with spinal cord injuries or nerve system damage and their families, the association provides networking and referral services, recreational activities and publishes a newsletter.

Madison Department of Public Health
210 Martin Luther King Jr. Blvd., Rm. 507, Madison • **(608) 266-4821**
2713 E. Washington Ave., Madison
• **(608) 246-4516, (608) 246-4858 AIDS information line**

This arm of city government encompasses environmental health services, including investigations of complaints about animals, air quality and water quality. Public-health nursing also falls under this department. If you have a question about immunizations or free health clinics, call one of the listed numbers.

March of Dimes Birth Defects Foundation
320 Holtzman Rd., Madison
• **(608) 274-2590**

The March of Dimes is dedicated to preventing birth defects and reducing infant mortality. The agency provides helpful information about planning for the healthy births of babies and sponsors the WalkAmerica in Madison every spring (see our Annual Events chapter).

Meriter Hospital Women's Center
309 W. Washington Ave., Madison
• **(608) 258-3750**

This center offers a wide range of health-related classes and support groups of interest to women.

Public Health Nursing Services
Dane County Division of Public Health, 1202 Northport Dr., Madison
• **(608) 242-6520**

As a part of nursing services, childhood and adult tetanus immunizations are provided at no charge on a regular basis at various Dane County locations. Flu and pneumonia immunizations also are available for a small fee for persons 65 and older or who have a chronic illness. For more information about public health clinics that also provide blood pressure, vision and hearing screenings, call the listed number.

Survivors Of Suicide (SOS)
625 E. Washington Ave., Madison
• **(608) 251-2345**

This support group sponsored by the Mental Health Center's Emergency Services unit is open to people grieving over the death of a loved one by suicide.

Outreach
14 W. Mifflin St., Ste. 103, Madison
• **(608) 255-8582**

In seeking to provide a safe environment for lesbians, gays and bisexuals and their friends and families, Outreach offers counseling, crisis intervention, referrals and advocacy information. It also provides speakers for schools, churches and social agencies.

United Cerebral Palsy
1502 Greenway Cross, Madison
• (608) 273-4434

This agency offers support and services to children who have cerebral palsy as well as to their families.

Wheelchair Recycling Program
3531 International Ln., Madison
• (608) 243-1785

This statewide, nonprofit agency associated with the Madison Area Chapter of the National Spinal Cord Injury Association (see previous entry) collects and redistributes used wheelchairs, walkers, crutches, canes and other mobility devices. It repairs and recycles them for people in need — here and overseas.

Cancer Information and Support Groups

There is a wide network of support for Dane County residents diagnosed with cancer. Many support groups are organized by hospital personnel and focus on a particular kind of cancer. Health professionals can steer you in the right direction. So can the following organizations.

American Cancer Society, Dane County Unit
1 Point Pl., Ste. 100, Madison
• (608) 833-4555

If you've just been diagnosed with cancer and don't know where to turn, this agency will put you in touch with support groups and services. It also offers public educational programs.

CHAT
202 S. Park St., Madison
• (608) 267-6027

CHAT stands for Cancer Has Affected Tots to Teens. It's a cancer support group for children directed by Meriter Patient and Family Services.

I Can Cope
707 S. Mills St., Madison
• (608) 258-5065

This is an eight-session program taught by healthcare professionals for anyone touched in some way by cancer. It's supported by the American Cancer Society and administered through St. Marys Hospital (see this chapter's "Hospitals" section).

Home Healthcare

Home Health United
4801 Hayes Rd., Madison
• (608) 242-1516

One of Dane County's largest home-care agencies, Home Health United provides comprehensive services including nursing, personal care, home-health aides, therapists and medical and social services.

HospiceCare Inc.
2802 Coho St., Ste. 100, Madison
• (608) 276-4660

Through HospiceCare, terminally ill patients of all ages and their families receive a variety of at-home services to enhance their quality of life and assist with the kinds of physical, spiritual and emotional needs that arise when a person is dying. Bereavement care extends 12 months beyond the death of the patient. HospiceCare is community based and funded partly through Medicare and individual health-insurance programs.

INSIDERS' TIP

As part of a comprehensive stroke-prevention program begun at University Hospital, patients can be evaluated on a nonemergency basis for their stroke risk. Call (608) 265-8899.

FREE Madison Visitors Guide

Call **1-800-373-6376**

*The official guide of the
Greater Madison Convention & Visitors Bureau*

MADISON
convention & visitors bureau

http://www.visitmadison.com

Meriter Home Health
202 S. Park St., Madison
- (608) 284-3300

This service provides comprehensive home healthcare including nursing, therapy and needed medical equipment.

Mobile Meals
128 E. Olin Ave., Ste. 200, Madison
- (608) 257-6716, (800) 69-MEALS

A program of the Visiting Nurse Service (see next entry), Mobile Meals provides hot, nutritious noon meals to homebound residents of all ages in Madison, Middleton and northwest Dane County.

Visiting Nurse Service Inc.
128 E. Olin Ave., Ste. 200, Madison
- (608) 257-6710

This agency provides such home-care services as nursing, physical, occupational and speech therapies and hot noon meals (see previous Mobile Meals entry). In addition to providing home healthcare services, the organization also conducts foot-care and blood-pressure clinics at various sites in and around Madison.

Wisconsin Homecare Organization
5610 Medical Cir., Madison
- (608) 278-1115

This statewide umbrella organization can provide a listing of licensed home healthcare agencies.

Mental Health Services

Alliance for the Mentally Ill
2059 Atwood Ave., Madison
- (608) 255-1695

This group acts as support and provides mental health information to families and friends of people who suffer from a mental problem or illness.

Mental Health Center of Dane County
625 W. Washington Ave., Madison
- (608) 251-2341

For Dane County residents, the Mental Health Center offers comprehensive outpatient mental health services. It's also home to Emergency Services — available 24 hours a day at (608) 251-2345 — which provides immediate attention to a variety of serious emotional problems. Highest priority is given to the prevention of suicides.

Substance-Abuse Treatment Centers

Adolescent Alcohol/Drug Abuse Intervention Program
UW Hospital and Clinics, 122 E. Olin Ave., Madison • (608) 263-8173

This is a place for adolescents younger than 18 and struggling with a drug problem to turn for help. Services are confidential and free of charge.

NewStart
1015 Gammon Ln., Madison
- (608) 271-4144

A program of Meriter Hospital, NewStart offers hope and treatment to adults and adolescents suffering from chemical dependency. Both outpatient and inpatient services are available.

PICADA
2000 Fordem Ave., Madison
- (608) 246-7606, (608) 246-7600
information and referral

PICADA stands for Prevention and Intervention Center for Alcohol and other Drug Abuse. It works with individuals, families and entire communities to prevent and treat drug abuse.

INSIDERS' TIP

The Red Cross has free information on how to prepare for disasters, including winter storms. To receive materials, call (608) 233-9300 Extension 292.

Tellurian UCAN
300 Femrite Dr., Madison
- **(608) 222-7311**

Tellurian is home of the Teresa McGovern Center, named in memory of the daughter of former U.S. Senator and presidential candidate George McGovern, who donated money for the building. Teresa lived in Madison and died from alcoholism after valiantly trying to fight it for most of her life. Tellurian provides a wide range of social services for those who are mentally ill, addicted to drugs or homeless.

Alternative Medicine

A growing interest in holistic and preventive medicine — including aromatherapy, acupuncture, massage therapy and herbal supplements — has not gone unnoticed in Madison. Some health-insurance plans in the Madison area cover a portion of health-club memberships and chiropractic visits. A number of holistic clinics have sprouted up in the last several years. Check the Yellow Pages for complete listings, and talk to satisfied patients before making an appointment.

To clear up any confusion we might have on dietary supplements, we check in regularly with pharmacist Mike Flint, owner of Mallatt Pharmacy, an old-fashioned, service-oriented drug store at 3506 Monroe Street. We've also heard good things about Green Earth, 6771 University Avenue in Middleton and 2501 University Avenue on the West Side and 2094 Atwood Avenue on the East Side. A wide selection of organic foods and herbs is available at Whole Foods Market, 3313 University Avenue. It's a special oasis for luscious fruit in the middle of winter. But, of course, strawberries to die for don't come cheap in January in Madison.

When Fido Gets Sick

Madisonians do love their animals, and the variety of pet-sitting and grooming services, lodges, dog-training classes and pet stores available in and around Madison proves it. Some veterinarians even make house calls for routine checkups and inoculations. For a complete list of services, check Pet Grooming, Pet Shops, Pet Sitting Services, etc. in the Yellow Pages.

For emergency services there are several choices. Contact the Emergency Clinic For Animals, 229 W. Beltline Highway (Rimrock Road Exit), (608) 274-7772; Dr. Jens Luebow at the Madison Veterinary Clinic, 2125 N. Stoughton Road, on the East Side, (608) 249-8525; or the Veterinary Medical Teaching Hospital, associated with the UW-Madison's School of Veterinary Medicine, (608) 263-7600 or (800) DVM-VMTH.

Routine care for animals and birds of all types and sizes, from canaries and rodents to cows and horses, is also available through the teaching hospital on the UW campus, 2015 Linden Drive.

A handy book to have if you're a pet and/or dog lover is *Pet First Aid*, a combined effort by the American Red Cross and the Humane Society of the United States. Retailing for about $10, the book is available through the local Red Cross chapter (see the previous entry).

Madison is a great area for seniors because there are so many activities here for all ages that are free or low cost.

Retirement and Senior Services

If you are a senior looking to make Madison your home base, welcome to town. This chapter is full of helpful hints that will enable you or someone you love to make the very most of those retirement years — with an eye on keeping things affordable as well as enjoyable.

Madison is a great area for seniors because there are so many activities here for all ages that are free or low cost (see our Attractions and Arts chapters). If you have the time, you can explore interesting museums, continue your education, augment your income, pursue a new hobby or make a difference in your life and the lives of others by volunteering.

If you're at a point in your life where you want to make some changes in your lifestyle and give up routine maintenance tasks such as lawn mowing and grocery shopping, you can find services here that will take up those burdens. If you or someone you care for needs a little extra help around the house or on-site medical care, you can find a wide range of options here.

Madison has an active senior community, and these people serve to enhance the quality of life for everyone. It's not uncommon to find seniors manning the desks at local libraries, packing groceries at food pantries, working on city or school district committees, organizing sporting or cultural events or volunteering with literacy programs, information desks or rocking babies at hospitals.

The interests of seniors in South-Central Wisconsin are as varied and far-reaching as the people themselves. Whatever your hobbies, skills and goals, you are likely to find your niche here in Four Lakes country.

Where to Start

Madison's senior service organizations are divided geographically into four coalitions for the elderly. Each coalition has workers who provide the link between seniors, their families and the community. It is a coordinated effort to see that seniors get the help they need to stay independent. The coalitions include the following: East Madison/Monona Coalition, 4644 Cottage Grove Road, (608) 233-3100; North/Eastside Senior Coalition, 1400 E. Washington Avenue, Suite 144, (608) 255-8875; South Madison Coalition of the Elderly, 540 W. Olin Avenue, Room 137, (608) 251-8405; and Westside Coalition of Older Adults, 517 N. Segoe Road, Room 309 (608) 238-7368.

Another excellent resource for seniors is the *Over 60* directory published by Dean Medical Center and St. Marys Hospital Medical Center. This comprehensive booklet contains more than 100 pages of resources and lists activities and services for Dane County's senior citizens. You can find the booklet at local libraries and at the four coalition offices mentioned previously.

The coalitions are excellent places to get help and referrals, but there are other valuable outlets. Below, we describe some additional places to contact, including two aging advocacy groups in Madison.

Independent Living
437 S. Yellowstone Dr., Ste. 208, Madison • (608) 274-7900

This nonprofit, multi-service agency is dedicated to helping older adults maintain independence. Services include help with home chores — workers assist older adults and people with disabilities in their homes — and home sharing, in which older people with extra room in their homes are matched with individuals who exchange household help for free or reduced rent. Other important assistance programs include Meals on Wheels, in which workers deliver nutritious hot evening meals to older adults; home modification, in which an occupational therapist and staff evaluate a home for safety and accessibility; and volunteer services such as a daily safety check by telephone and performing minor home repairs. Another program, home care/respite services, provides qualified caregivers who offer temporary in-home care for people recovering from illness and respite for family members who are caring for an older adult at home. In addition, seniors can take advantage of financial counseling, such as assistance with checking and bank accounts, bills and insurance claims. Independent Living also offers transportation services.

Coalition of Wisconsin Aging Groups (CWAG)
5900 Monona Dr., Monona
• **(608) 224-0606**

CWAG is a nonprofit, nonpartisan statewide organization that focuses on matters of concern to the elderly. It represents Wisconsin's senior citizens on civic and political issues. The organization also helps through the Partner Care program and the Home Equity Conversion Reverse Mortgage program.

Wisconsin Elder Law Center (WELC)
5900 Monona Dr., Monona
• **(608) 224-0606**

WELC houses the Dane County benefit specialist program. It provides legal assistance to seniors in Dane County with problems related to government benefits and other elder law matters. The group also operates guardianship training projects and works on issues such as consumer protection and elder abuse prevention.

Food, Fun and Friends

During the years when you were in school, working a full-time job and/or raising your children, you probably had lots of contact with other people, making it easy to meet new people and forge friendships. As people retire and their children leave the home, however, they may find that their circle of friends begins shrinking. Senior centers, church groups and volunteer opportunities are all great avenues you can use to make sure you continue to meet new people and enrich your life.

Madison-area senior centers are more than just gathering places for retired citizens; the centers are involved with community action, the arts, health initiatives, continuing education and a whole spectrum of life-enhancement opportunities. Operating under National Council on Aging guidelines, senior centers strive to provide opportunities for older adults to use their capabilities and be productive in their communities. Check out the senior center near you. You may be surprised at what you'll find.

Isthmus

Madison Senior Center
330 W. Mifflin St., Madison
• **(608) 266-6581**

The Madison Senior Center sponsors health screenings, volunteer initiatives, special events, exercise programs and a variety of educational programs and discussion groups. The senior center serves nutritious lunches Monday through Friday and dinner too on Thursdays. Call (608) 266-6416 one day in advance to make your reservation; leave your name and the day of the meal you will be attending after the taped message. Seniors are asked to give a free-will offering; $1.50 per meal is suggested.

*Meriter Commons...
a downtown wellness and
retirement community.*

Meriter Retirement Center... *apartments with services*
110 S. Henry Street

Meriter Terraces... *C.B.R.F./Alzheimer's care*
345 W. Main Street

Meriter Health Center... *skilled nursing care*
334 W. Doty Street
Madison, WI

MERITERRETIREMENT   608-283-2000

West Side

Westside Senior Center
602 Sawyer Ter., Madison
• (608) 238-0196

Seniors on Madison's West Side can avail themselves of a wide range of social, volunteer and educational opportunities at the Westside Senior Center. The center serves noon lunch Tuesdays and Thursdays and 5:30 PM dinner Mondays and Wednesdays. Meals cost $4.73 per senior. In addition, the Westside Senior Center serves dinner and provides musical entertainment on the second and fourth Saturdays of each month, beginning at 5:30 PM.

Outlying Area

It would not be possible to list all of the diverse services provided by all Madison-area senior centers in this chapter. Please stop by or call the senior center near nest you for information about programs of interest. As these senior centers are miles apart, community residents tend to use the center in their own community for ease of access. All centers provide a wealth of activities to suit virtually any interest, so call the one nearest you for more information. Some Madison-area centers include the following: Belleville Senior Citizen Center, 130 S. Vine Street, Belleville, (608) 424-6007; Colonial Club Senior Center, 301 Blankenheim Lane, Sun Prairie, (608) 837-4611; DeForest Area Senior Center, 505 N. Main Street, DeForest, (608) 846-9469; Fitchburg Senior Center, 5510 E. Lacy Road, Fitchburg, (608) 275-7155; Middleton Senior Center, 1811 Parmenter Street, Middleton, (608) 831-2373; Monona Senior Center, 1011 Nichols Road, Monona, (608) 222-3415; Oregon Senior Center, 219 Park Street, Oregon, (608) 835-5801; Stoughton Senior Center, 248 W. Main Street, Stoughton, (608) 873-8585; Verona Area Senior Center, 304 Church Avenue, Verona, (608) 845-7471; and Waunakee Senior Center, 607 Reeve Drive, Waunakee, (608) 849-8384.

Just for Seniors

Many organizations exist with the mission of working to increase understanding between generations and help seniors meet the challenges of growing older. Some local resources include are described below.

American Association of Retired Persons (AARP)
8750 W. Brynmawr Ave., Chicago, Ill.
• (312) 714-9800
Madison Chapter • (608) 251-2277
Middleton Chapter • (608) 831-8935
Sun Prairie Chapter • (608) 837-5024

The AARP is a nonprofit, nonpartisan organization dedicated to helping older Americans achieve lives of independence, dignity and purpose. The national association is the largest organization of senior citizens in the United States with more than 33 million members. Anyone 50 or older, whether working or retired, may join. AARP members are involved in community, state and national affairs. The Madison chapter provides a refresher course for older drivers.

Dane County Commission on Aging
210 Martin Luther King Jr. Blvd., Madison • (608) 266-9063

The Commission on Aging, housed in the City-County Building, is responsible for policy planning and development on behalf of Dane County's elderly population. The commission sponsors communication forums for seniors, their elected representatives and senior service providers.

Dane County SOS Senior Council
122 State St., Rm. 401, Madison • (608) 256-7626

The purpose of this organization, also known as Save Our Security, is to organize and educate advocates for issues important to the elderly. SOS also maintains a reduced-cost healthcare program for members who are enrolled in Medicare Part A and Part B and have annual incomes below specified limits.

Elder Care of Dane County
2909 Landmark Pl., Ste. 101, Madison • (608) 278-2470

Elder Care provides support to older adults and their families. This community-based, not-for-profit organization offers many programs such as adult day centers (including a center specifically for adults with Alzheimer's) and a home-care program providing in-home personal-care services for the elderly and persons with disabilities. Other programs include supported-living retirement services and Elder Care Options, a program integrating healthcare and long-term care services for frail and disabled elderly persons.

The goal of Elder Care programs is to match services to the needs and desires of each individual in the least restrictive setting.

Golden Care
St. Marys Hospital Medical Center, 707 S. Mills St., Madison • (608) 258-5995

This free program is open to anyone 65 and older. As a Golden Care member, you can receive discounts on the following services and items: meals in the St. Marys dining room; prescriptions purchased from Dean and St. Marys pharmacies; eyewear purchased at Dean Optical centers; Health Works classes; Lifeline Personal Emergency response system; and help with Medicare problems including in-home assistance for homebound members.

Golden Care members receive a regular newsletter and are invited to attend free social and educational events.

Stretching Your Food Dollars

Senior Nutrition Sites

Numerous senior nutrition sites are scattered throughout the county. Participants are asked to donate what they can afford for their meals. Call for current meal schedules and reservation policies. Or stop by one of the following senior nutrition sites to obtain information and survey the facilities for yourself. On the Isthmus, you'll find Brittingham Apartments, 755 Braxton Place, (608) 251-4525; on the West Side are Bethany United Methodist Nutrition Site, 3910 Mineral Point Road, (608) 238-6381, and Lechayim Lunchtime Plus, 1406 Mound Street, (608) 278-1808. On the East Side is St. Paul's Lutheran Church, 2126 N. Sherman Avenue, (608) 244-3133.

Groceries and Home-Delivered Meals

If you would like to have groceries delivered to your home, many area stores are happy to cooperate. Grocery delivery service is available through Capitol Centre Foods, (608) 255-2616; Olde Time Grocery Delivery, (608) 224-0049; Shoppers Express, (608) 238-2917; Ken Kopp's, (608) 257-3594; and the

Williamson Street Co-op, (608) 251-0884. Miller & Sons Super Market in Verona, (608) 845-6478, and Stoughton's Mainstreet Market, Stoughton, (608) 873-8944, also deliver.

Home-delivered meals may be arranged by calling one of the following: Independent Living Inc., (608) 274-7900; Mobile Meals, (608) 257-6716; or your local senior center.

Free food commodities are distributed at sites throughout the Madison area. Call the Community Action Coalition at (608) 246-4730 or TDD 246-4768 for information. CAC can also give you referrals to local food pantries.

Innovative Ways to Reduce Food Bills

The Food Fair, Community Action Coalition
1717 N. Stoughton Rd., Madison
• (608) 246-4730

This cooperative buying program enables low-income individuals to receive groceries at reduced costs. Participants pay $13 a month in food stamps or cash, complete two hours of volunteer service per month and receive groceries in return.

Garden Program, Community Action Coalition
1717 N. Stoughton Rd., Madison
• (608) 246-4730

If you've got a green thumb and no place to put it to work, call the CAC to enroll in the Garden Program. Individuals receive seeds and garden space at various Madison locations for a small rental fee.

Free-Meal Sites

Madison has more than a dozen free-meal sites. Remember to always call first to ask about times and reservations. Among them are Broadway/Simpson Community Center, (608) 222-0291; East Madison Community Center, (608) 249-0861; Luke House, (608) 256-6325; Off the Square Club, (608) 251-6901; Plymouth Congregational UCC Church, (608) 249-1537; and Port St. Vincent, (608) 257-2036.

Low-Cost School Lunches

Public schools in Madison serve reduced-price hot lunches to senior citizens during times when school is in session. Call your local school for details.

Modifying Your Home

Project Home Inc.
104 N. First St., Madison
• (608) 246-3733

This program assists Dane County seniors and those with disabilities in repairing single-family, owner-occupied homes with handicapped-accessible construction. Project Home also provides help with energy conservation measures for homes of lower-income citizens who meet income guidelines for energy assistance.

Choosing a Retirement Community

If you've decided it's time to hang up your hedge trimmers and look for a retirement community where someone else can take over the yard work, here are some tips for selecting the community that's right for you.

When choosing a retirement community, one of the first things to think about is location. How far will you be from friends, family, shopping, churches and other important destinations?

You may be blessed with good health and think that there will never be a day when

INSIDERS' TIP

Some local lawyers participate in the AARP Network, providing legal services to AARP members at reduced rates and possibly making house calls if you are unable to travel.

you have to give up the car keys. But what happens when your vehicle is in for service or you have an illness or other physical condition that permanently or temporarily prevents you from driving? When looking at retirement communities, ask about public transportation, including transportation to and from the airport in case you want to take a trip or fly off to see a child or grandchild. The greater your independence in terms of getting around, the happier you are likely to be with your choice of a retirement community.

Once you've pinpointed some locations you would like to explore, figure out your budget: How much can you afford to spend on housing? Then set up a tour of some retirement communities to get a feel for what life would be like if you moved in.

It's usually a good idea to plan your visit during meal time or a community get-together so you can meet some of your potential neighbors and get an idea of how they like to spend their time. Ask them how satisfied they are with the community and what group activities, excursions or resources they like best. Also ask them what things they would like to see changed about the community.

Although you shouldn't spend all of your time talking with staff, do consider them a good resource for discovering the hidden benefits and costs of retirement life. Ask them to give you a calendar of monthly events or activities. Find out if these services are free or if they will cost you additional money. Is there a library, beauty shop or exercise room on site? Are housekeeping services available? What control will you have over the physical climate of your apartment to ensure that it is not too hot or too cold? Are utilities included in the cost of your rent? Is cable access available for your TV, and if so, who pays for it?

Ask questions that will give you insight into community management. Are most of the apartments rented? What's the usual rate of resident turnover? How does the management screen potential tenants?

As you walk through the community, watch how the staff and residents interact. Are they friendly, and do they call each other by name and chat for a few minutes about shared interests?

Safety and boundaries can help you feel like you are in a comfortable place. What type of security system is in place to ensure your personal protection and the safety of your valuables? Do individual apartments have good locks and security chains so neighbors can't burst in uninvited? Is there an emergency call system you can access if you suddenly have a problem? Is that system monitored 24 hours a day?

Look at the grounds. Are lawns and gardens well cared for? Are there benches and tables for residents who want to spend time outdoors? Does the community offer garden space for residents who want to plant a few vegetables, herbs or flowers?

As you walk through the facilities, take a look at the activities that are going on. Check the walls and bulletin boards for information about group trips or other events. Look at the physical upkeep of buildings. Are walls, carpets and furniture clean and in good condition?

Look at apartments with a critical eye to see if the accommodations will meet your needs. Try to think in terms of whether you will have room for the items you don't want to give up. If you have a hutch filled with treasured china, will there be a place for it? Is the bedroom large enough to accommodate your bedroom set or will you need to invest in something new? Find out the policies regarding pets and overnight guests. Is there a guest suite available for visiting relatives? Is there a nearby park for restless grandchildren?

How much money will you be required to pay up front? How can you get out of the housing arrangement if you find you are not happy or need to move elsewhere?

We have given you a lot of ideas for questions, but you probably have more of your own. Don't be afraid to take a list of questions along with you on your tours and jot down the answers so you can compare apples to apples when making your decisions. Moving can be expensive, and you want to find the best place for you — a home that will suit your needs for the years to come.

Here's a sampling of some Madison-area retirement communities to get you started. More options are included in the *Over 60* directory and in the Yellow Pages. Call the Fair Housing Council of Dane County, (608)

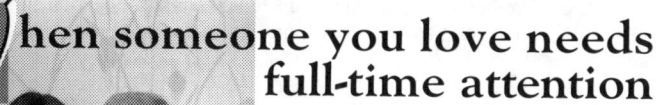

When someone you love needs full-time attention

When your mom or dad needs short- or long-term care, check us out. You'll be pleased to find top quality medical care, rehabilitative services and recreation programs in a comfortable home-like setting. Plus, you'll find attractive, updated rooms in a facility conveniently located in central Madison close to major medical clinics.

For a tour or free brochure, call St. Marys Care Center, 257-0781.

St. Marys Care Center

Madison's Catholic Rehabilitation and Nursing Home
1347 Fish Hatchery Road • Madison, WI (608)257-0781

A MEMBER OF THE SSM HEALTH CARE SYSTEM

251-5599, before you sign on the dotted line or write any checks.

Horizon Management Properties Senior Division
37 Kessel Ct., Madison
• (608) 274-2233

Whether you are looking for city living or country vistas, Horizon Management has several properties that may interest you. The management company specializes in providing affordable senior housing for independent seniors 55 and older. One- and two-bedroom units, ranging in size from 650 square feet to 1,100 square feet, are available at these modern, newer facilities throughout Dane County. Horizon properties include Country View in Waunakee, Meadow Grove in Madison, Taylor Ridge in Cottage Grove, Dempsey Manor in Madison, Pheasant Branch in Middleton, Greentree Glen in Madison and Sugar Creek in Verona.

Rents begin at about $320 and, depending on size, range to more than $600 per month. Underground heated parking is available at some locations for an additional fee (usually $35 a month). There's a $100 refundable deposit, but no entrance fee.

Isthmus

Meriter Retirement Services Inc. Retirement Center
110 S. Henry St., Madison
• (608) 283-2000

Choose from one- or two-bedroom apartments in this strikingly attractive Downtown retirement community. Services include daily meals, 24-hour emergency response, housekeeping, social activities, van services and laundry. From this location, residents have fast access to museums, the Capitol Square and farmers' market, State Street and the Civic Center.

Monthly rents start at $834. Entrance fees are $13,500 for a one-bedroom apartment, $21,500 for a two-bedroom apartment and $27,000 for a deluxe two-bedroom apartment.

The Village Cohousing Community
Corner of Mound and Mills Sts., Madison
- **(608) 246-8846**

After seven years of planning, Madison recently got its first cohousing community. Cohousing combines private housing with community aspects. It's a living concept developed in Scandinavia about 25 years ago in which residents have their own units but also share a common kitchen, recreation and other space and resources. It is how neighborhoods used to be, with seniors sharing their lives with neighbors of all ages. The concept is considered by its founders to be an ideal, protective situation for the elderly, as well as for single parents and women.

For information on local cohousing opportunities contact Design Coalition Architects, 2088 Atwood Avenue, at the number listed above.

West Side

Attic Angel Retirement Tower
602 N. Segoe Rd., Madison
- **(608) 231-5902**

Attic Angel residents have fast access to most of Madison at this centrally located, near-West Side community. The independent-living facility has 68 apartments and is within walking distance of Hilldale Shopping Center. It's also on a bus line. Residents pay a monthly fee that includes a 24-hour emergency call system, utilities, building maintenance, five nursing home days per year (at an adjacent nursing home), evening meals and biweekly housekeeping.

Studios and one-bedroom apartments are available starting at $983 per month with a $16,000 entrance fee for a studio; $1,074 and $23,700, respectively, for a one-bedroom, single occupancy; and $1,410 and $27,700 for one bedroom, double occupancy.

Oakwood Village Retirement and Health Care Community
6209 Mineral Point Rd., Madison
- **(608) 231-3451**

Rated in the top-20 retirement communities in the nation by *Choices* magazine, this pleasant community offers 211 apartments in a wooded West Side setting, close to shopping, restaurants and other amenities. Residents can supplement independent living with nursing and rehabilitation services as needed. The Oakwood Village Retirement Community has van service, an on-site pharmacy, coffee shop, theater (see our Arts chapter) and beauty shop. Daily meal service is optional.

Monthly rents begin at $602. It costs $1,000 to add your name to the waiting list. The waiting period is about two years.

Outlying Area

Colonial Acres Apartments
605 Chase Blvd., Sun Prairie
- **(608) 837-2124**

Just east of Madison is the growing community of Sun Prairie. Colonial Acres is an independent-living facility for seniors who want to live in their own place and have someone else handle day-to-day maintenance tasks, including shoveling Wisconsin's white gold. Studio and one- and two-bedroom apartments are available. Monthly rents start at $732, including utilities and monthly housekeeping service.

INSIDERS' TIP

Mature Lifestyles **is a free monthly publication filled with useful information of interest to local seniors. You'll find everything from investment advice to looking-for-love personal ads. P.O. Box 44327, Madison, 53744. (608) 274-5200.**

Colonial View Apartments
601 Thomas Dr., Sun Prairie
• **(608) 837-3174**

Senior citizens and disabled individuals seeking subsidized housing may want to check out the services at Colonial View Apartments. The apartments are next to the Colonial Club Senior Center, giving residents easy access to meal services and social events. Colonial View residents can access a variety of services on site including a coffee shop, beauty salon, exercise room and chapel. Rent for the one-bedroom apartments is based on income. There's currently about a two-year waiting list for apartments.

Middleton Glen
6720 Frank Lloyd Wright Ave., Middleton
• **(608) 836-8900**

A lot of seniors probably remember living in a town where everybody knew everybody, where you could walk to the store, where you could sit on your front porch and talk to the neighbors as they passed by. Towns like that pretty much got swept away in the 1950s and '60s as the big lawns and tract houses of suburbia drained the lifeblood out of Main Streets all over the country. Middleton Hills, the idea of the late architect Marshall Erdman, seeks to recreate that kind of lifestyle. Middleton Glen, a premier senior living community for middle-income people 55 and older, will be part of that.

The 55-residence, three-story structure is scheduled for occupancy in late summer of 1999. Floor plans range from 700 to 1,542 square feet and feature eat-in kitchens, walk-in closets, washer/dryer hookups and full-size appliances. Some of the units have unique balconies designed for privacy. The units are not rented, and they are not really purchased in the traditional sense, either. They will instead be available through a new financing concept in which the units are owned by a nonprofit corporation. Each unit will be purchased at "an equitable interest" to be negotiated. There are no deeds, no titles and no real estate taxes. When a resident decides to move or dies, 100 percent of the entrance fee plus appreciation will go to them or their heirs. The units are currently available for between $31,500 and $68,000.

The complex also includes a community room, country store, guest room, health and wellness area with a whirlpool, a hobby shop, library, craft room, walking paths and park and optional dining, along other common areas. Van transportation will also be available. Middleton Glen is sponsored by Meriter Retirement Services Inc. (see a previous listing). There will household chore assistance available and medical services can be arranged.

Transportation Services

55 Alive Driver Training Program
AARP, 18 Ellie Cir., Madison
• **(608) 222-9518**

An eight-hour refresher course costs just $8 and is offered to drivers 50 and older. Classes are held throughout Dane County. Call the instructor at the listed number for a schedule.

Driver Escort Program, RSVP
517 N. Segoe Rd., Ste. 210, Madison
• **(608) 238-7787**

This program provides escorted transportation for seniors and disabled individuals of any age. Volunteers use their own vehicles. Passengers must be ambulatory and have no other means of transportation. Donations are greatly appreciated.

There are 27 coordination centers serving Dane County, each with its own volunteer coordinator. The program operates 8 AM to 5 PM weekdays.

MetroRide of Wisconsin
4605 Pflaum Rd., Madison
• **(608) 223-0610**

MetroRide provides lift van service for elderly and disabled individuals to medical appointments and nutrition sites and for group grocery shopping excursions. Metro Ride accepts Medical Assistance payments. If you are not eligible for Medical Assistance, transportation to medical appointments begins at $15 and varies according to trip length. If you participate in a group ride — the van transports seniors from all over Madison — to a grocery store or nutrition site, the cost is $2 round trip.

The Art Fair on the Square offers delights for consumers of all ages.

Wisconsin Dept. of Transportation
4802 Sheboygan Ave., Madison
• (608) 266-2325

Renew your driver's license or purchase vehicle license plates here. The DOT also issues handicapped-parking identification and license plates — call (608) 266-3041 — and provides free driver-awareness training for adults 55 and older — call (608) 266-0614. Wisconsin has many styles of license plates, including one honoring the state's sesquicentennial.

Job Opportunities

It used to be when you reached age 65, you were given a gold watch and "put out to pasture." Adults of today, however, are often eager to stay involved in the business world, not only for the money, but also for the challenge and fun of it. Here are a few resources to help you nail down a job that's right for you.

Dane County Job Service
1819 Aberg Ave., Madison
• (608) 242-4900

Job specialists at Dane County Job Service assist people of all ages in finding work. The Madison office maintains listings of current jobs, provides information on retraining programs and helps you update your job-hunting skills.

Employment Options Inc.
2095 Winnebago St., Madison
• (608) 244-5181

Employment Options Inc. provides employment-related services for individuals who are unemployed, underemployed, in transition or having difficulty with current employment. Attend a free orientation to learn if any of these services would be helpful to you. Clients are charged for one-on-one employment counseling.

Goodwill Industries
1302 Mendota St., Madison
• (608) 246-3140

Goodwill Industries is well known for its low-cost retail stores, but it also provides vocational services for adults with disabilities and other barriers to employment. Call to learn about which Goodwill services might benefit you.

Over 55 Employment Service Inc.
1245 E. Washington Ave., Ste. 276, Madison • (608) 255-5585

Over 55 provides free job counseling and placement for Dane County residents 50 and older. The organization also maintains a job-listing service for employers who are interested in hiring older adults. Some job training is available.

United Refugee Services of Wisconsin
1245 E. Washington Ave., Ste. 84, Madison • (608) 256-6400

This nonprofit organization works to help refugees of all ages achieve self-sufficiency. Services include translation/interpretation, job placement, tutoring, outreach and advocacy. Refugees pay no fees for services.

Volunteer Opportunities

Retired Senior Volunteer Program (RSVP)
517 Segoe Rd. Ste. 110, Madison
• (608) 238-7787

The Retired Senior Volunteer Program (RSVP) of Dane County matches volunteers 55 and older with more than 200 agencies. RSVP sponsors the Driver Escort Program, the Friendly Listener Intergenerational Program, a grandparent program and self-skills program.

United Way of Dane County Volunteer Center
2059 Atwood Ave., Madison
• (608) 246-4380

Can you spare a kind word and a helping hand? The Volunteer Center is the clearinghouse for individuals interested in volunteering service to Dane County's nonprofit organizations. More than 1,000 volunteer opportunities are available. Call to find out what you can do. Volunteers are interviewed about their interests, then matched with local agencies.

Educational Opportunities

UW-Madison Division of Continuing Studies
Program Information and Publications Office, 610 Langdon St., Madison
• (608) 262-1156

Choose from more than 300 classes for adults of all ages. Topics include writing, foreign language, art, literature, fitness, history, music, astronomy, public speaking, dance, acting and others. Courses vary in length from one session to a full semester. For a catalog, call the listed number.

Dane County Cooperative Extension Office
1 Fen Oak Ct., off U.S. Hwy. 51, near Pflaum • (608) 224-3700

If you'd like to learn more about topics such as estate planning, financial counseling, nutrition and gardening, contact your local extension office for publications and videotapes. The office recently moved to its East Side location.

UW Madison Office of University Special and Guest Students
905 University Ave., Madison
• (608) 262-2115

Seniors can enroll in regular UW-Madison courses year round as special nondegree or guest students. If you take the course for credit, you pay the regular undergraduate tuition rate. If you enroll as a guest student for no credit, you may take courses at reduced rates.

Madison Area Technical College
211 N. Carroll St., Madison
• (608) 258-2443

Citizens older than 62 get a discount at MATC when enrolling in noncredit classes through the Adult and Continuing Education

Division; discounts depend on the class. In most cases, seniors pay only for materials. Course topics include retirement planning, crafts, creative writing and genealogy.

Participatory Learning and Teaching Organization (PLATO)
905 University Ave., Madison
• (608) 262-3309

PLATO features peer discussion groups, lectures and social events for older adults.

Health and Fitness Programs

Dane County Senior Olympic Games
(608) 242-1664

No matter what your skill level or type, you can enjoy participating in the Senior Olympic Games, usually held in late May. Events include golf, tennis, cribbage, bowling, horseshoes, swimming, pool basketball, dartball, table tennis, skeet, race walking and track events. Special events in 1997 included an afternoon dance, music festival and ice cream social. Registration for the first game event is $8; additional events are $3 each. The top three participants in competitive events receive medals.

Evora Pool and Health Club
605 Chase Blvd., Sun Prairie
• (608) 837-2124

Seniors can work out the kinks and develop cardiovascular conditioning at this special facility designed for people 50 and older. The warm-water pool is used for open swimming, aquatic exercise and strength and conditioning classes as well as an Arthritis Foundation aquatic program.

Goodman-Rotary Senior Fitness
1045 E. Dayton St., Rm. 120, Madison
• (608) 266-6071

This organization holds year-round classes in martial arts, swimming, water aerobics, yoga and healthy cooking. In summer, seniors can participate in par 3 and nine-hole golf or join a walk-about club. Mall-walking helps keep seniors fit when winter winds whirl.

St. Marys Health Works
5918 Odana Rd., Madison
• (608) 271-6400

Each winter, spring and summer, St. Marys Hospital offers courses on developing and maintaining healthy habits, emotional health, fitness, nutrition, CPR and first aid. Call for details.

Taking Time for Fun

Forbes-Meager Music Center
6301 Odana Rd., Madison
• (608) 271-1064

Music classes target beginners 50 years of age and older who want "immediate gratification." After the first lesson you will be able to go home and play a song. The cost is $20 for 10 lessons, and you can learn to play anything with keys: piano, organ, keyboard or accordion. The lessons are different than those offered to children. Children learn to sight-read music, whereas these classes take the simpler approach of learning to play by numbers. Many of the students here claim that since

INSIDERS' TIP

Older adults in the Madison area use a number of senior-friendly travel and tour companies. Look for their advertisements in *Mature Lifestyles* and the local newspapers. Among them are Jones Travel and Tour, (800) 236-3160 (for a catalog), Conventions Plus Tours and Burkhalter Cruise. Membership in the Mature Lifestyles Travel Club will get you discounts with all of them. Contact Lifestyles Travel Club, P.O. Box 44327, Madison, WI 53744.

they started playing an instrument they sleep better, use less medication, are more active and have lower blood pressure.

Madison Civics Club
2650 Penwall Cir., Fitchburg, WI 53711

This 85-year-old group, which now holds its events in the Monona Terrace Convention Center, is a 700-member organization that has brought an impressive array of speakers to Madison, including Amelia Earhart, Eleanor Roosevelt and, recently, actor Ed Asner, who came to talk about the entertainment industry's ethical responsibilities. Biologists, journalists, genetic engineers and politicians have also come to speak about cutting-edge social issues. For more information, write to Judy Winkel at the listed address.

Madison School-Community Recreation
112 N. Fairchild St., Madison
- **(608) 266-6423**

Classes in lapidary, painting, photography and ballroom dancing are among the many exciting opportunities offered through MSCR. In addition, seniors can find a wide range of hobby clubs. Pick up a free listing of recreation offerings at the local library or call the listed number.

St. Marys Health Works
(608) 271-6400

Fun classes offered through St. Marys change constantly, but there is always something of interest for active seniors. If you like cooking, you can choose from classes in ethnic cuisine as well as heart-healthy cooking. Dance classes are popular: A ballroom dance course teaches the basics of the fox trot, waltz, swing and jitterbug, and a Latin dance class for couples covers the rhumba, tango and cha cha. A creative memories class teaches participants how to crop and label photographs and create decorative photo album pages. Other classes focus on massage and American Heart Association CPR. The classes are open to the public, and the costs are minimal.

Theater Bus Inc.
302 N. Baldwin St., Madison
- **(608) 257-0003**

If you're a theater buff, join in the fun of the Theater Bus, specifically designed for folks older than 60. The bus picks up seniors at points all around Madison and transports them to theater productions and other special events such as a cruise of Milwaukee's harbor on Lake Michigan. A senior selection committee picks destinations. Trips usually range in price from $20 to $46 each.

Special Services

Books on Audio

Do you know someone who is visually impaired? Thousands of books and magazines on record or cassettes are available free of charge through the Milwaukee office of the Library Service for the Blind and Visually Handicapped; call (800)-242-8822. Local contacts in Dane County can be reached at (608) 266-6314 (Madison Public Library) or (608) 266-4419 (Dane County Library Service).

Tutoring

Madison Literacy Council
2007 Atwood Ave., Madison
- **(608) 244-3911**

The Literacy Council provides help for those who are learning English as a second language and English-speaking persons with less than a 5th-grade reading proficiency. Prospective tutors participate in a five-day workshop spread over two weeks. There is a fee to cover teaching materials. Tutors are then matched with adult learners. The Council is always looking for qualified seniors to serve as tutors.

Wisconsin
— *we've got you covered!*

Afternoons Monday thru Friday.
Weekender on Saturday morning.

Every morning — seven days a week.

Moving, planning a trip, or just want to know what's going on in Wisconsin?

It's easy.

Call 1-800-362-8333 to subscribe

Media

In terms of quality and quantity of news, it doesn't get much better than Madison. As the state capital and home to a major university, the city has always been a great place for news hounds, no matter the subject.

Political argument in these parts is elevated to an art form, and this means even the most lowly government budget meeting can quickly turn into a three-ring circus. Just the liveliness of the city and diverse goings-on in the surrounding countryside provide many things to do and cover.

Between two daily newspapers (four, counting the two covering UW-Madison news), monthly lifestyle and business magazines, four commercial television stations, more than a dozen radio stations and a number of thriving weeklies, there is no excuse for not knowing what is going on here.

Madison-based publications match the city's diverse personality and beliefs. It's home to the agnostic *Freethought Today*; the weekly African-American newspaper, *The Madison Times*; a humorous newspaper parody, *The Onion*, that is rapidly gaining fans across the country; and the liberal magazine, *The Progressive*. If you visit a library or shop at a major food center, look as you walk in and you'll find many free publications with timely and interesting tidbits about South-Central Wisconsin.

Newspapers

While you might not always agree with what's being written in Madison newspapers, you'll find no lack of publications to read. The city is in a class by itself. No other campus in the country currently has two independent competing student dailies. And while few cities even have two major dailies anymore, Madison may be the smallest market in the country to do so.

Because the *Wisconsin State Journal* and *The Capital Times* share advertising and the same building through a joint business venture, Madison Newspapers Inc., many people think they are one and the same. That's not true. Editorially, they are very different, and each has different ownership.

In addition to daily newspapers, Madison has a number of weeklies. The largest is *Isthmus*, whose stories always make for good dinner conversation. The *Isthmus* is free and readily available from libraries, coffeehouses and many retail stores throughout the city.

Almost all of the outlying communities are represented by small weeklies. We've listed those in a separate Community Newspapers section.

Dailies

Badger Herald
550 State St., Madison • (608) 257-4712

Published Monday through Friday during the school year and weekly during summer sessions, *Badger Herald*, is independently operated by UW-Madison students and specializes in campus news. It was started in September 1969, at the height of Madison's Vietnam protest era, to counteract the radical voice of *The Daily Cardinal*. Today neither newspaper is as far right or left, although the *Badger*, a broadsheet, is still considered the more conservative and business-oriented of the two. The press run during the school year is 17,000. *Badger Herald* is free and readily available on campus and at stores and restaurants on State Street.

The Capital Times
1901 Fish Hatchery Rd., Madison • (608) 252-6400

In Madison, politics is a way of life. People are driven by their convictions. So it is not surprising that when the *Wisconsin State Journal* began running editorials against then-U.S. Sen. Robert M. La Follette and the Progressive movement prior to World War I, an angry William T. Evjue, business manager of the

Wisconsin State Journal, decided he had only one recourse: to start another daily newspaper. That was The Capital Times, first published on December 13, 1917.

Both newspapers were published seven days a week in the afternoon until 1949, when increasing operational costs prompted the two to enter into a business agreement to form Madison Newspapers Inc. (jointly owned by The Capital Times Co. and Lee Enterprises). Although the two Madison dailies are run off the same presses and share advertising revenues, The Capital Times remains true to its "progressive" cause, with an editorial bent more liberal and daring than its across-the-hall neighbor.

Remaining in the afternoon slot (except Saturday), The Capital Times is delivered to homes in the city by 5:30 PM Monday through Friday and by 9 AM Saturday. Paid circulation is about 23,000.

While talk has circulated for years about combining them editorially, the two newspapers remain fiercely competitive, except for an occasional special section published in both newspapers and one common entertainment endeavor, "Rhythm," published on Thursdays. Also, because the State Journal serves many Capital Times readers on Sunday, the latter is given editorial space on Page 2 in the Journal's Sunday "Forum" opinion section.

The Capital Times continues to view itself as a crusader for the common people and, in that regard, loves to remind its readers of the important role it played in recognizing and exposing early on the dark side of anticommunist U.S. Sen. Joseph McCarthy.

The Daily Cardinal
Vilas Hall, Rm. 2142, 821 University Ave., Madison • (608) 262-5857

The Daily Cardinal has a long, rich history as a campus newspaper dating back to 1892. It's published Monday through Friday during the school year and, like the Badger Herald, is readily available throughout campus and Downtown. The Cardinal, while not nearly as liberal and outspoken as it was during the protest years of the late 1960s and early '70s, is still not afraid to speak its mind.

The Cardinal has a circulation of 10,000 and, although located in Vilas Hall, is completely independent of the university. Accumulated debt prompted the newspaper to cease publishing for nine months in the early 1990s. Although it was a hard lesson to learn, the Cardinal weathered the financial storm and is now on solid footing.

Wisconsin State Journal
1901 Fish Hatchery Rd., Madison • (608) 252-6100

The Wisconsin State Journal is the largest daily newspaper in Madison, with a weekday morning circulation of about 86,000 (164,000 on Sunday). Considered the more conservative of the two major dailies (see the previous Capital Times write-up), it's delivered to doorsteps by 6:30 AM.

Though tracing its roots to 1839, two years after Rosaline and Eben Peck arrived to become the first permanent white settlers in Madison (see our History chapter) and a year after the first school was established here, it wasn't until 1852 that the Wisconsin State Journal became Madison's first daily newspaper. Under the guiding ownership of David Atwood, the newspaper flourished in the last half of the 19th century, growing as fast as the city did. According to The Lee Papers: A Saga of Midwestern Journalism, Atwood frequently sent a correspondent to Civil War battles to supplement telegraph reports. Atwood himself visited camps of Wisconsin troops.

An equally guiding force at the turn of the century was Amos P. Wilder, who arrived in Madison in 1894 to become editor of the newspaper. Armed with a doctorate degree from Yale University and a pledge to seek out and cover the local news — a challenge his staff of reporters royally took to heart — Wilder remained editor until he was appointed U.S. Consul to Hong Kong by President Theodore Roosevelt in 1906.

Early in the 20th century, the newspaper was a staunch supporter of Robert "Fighting Bob" La Follette and his Progressive movement. That all changed under the tutelage of Dick Jones, who chastised the senator for his opposition to allowing the United States to enter World War I. The newspaper soon lost the support of most Progressives and quickly earned a pro-business, conservative stance, although its current staff of reporters are quite diverse in their political leanings.

In 1919, Lee Syndicate, the forerunner of today's publicly owned media corporation, Lee Enterprises, based in Davenport, Iowa, bought the *State Journal* for $200,000. Of all its media holdings, the Madison paper, distributed in 17 Wisconsin counties, remains the company's largest operation.

In the 1949 agreement with *The Capital Times*, the *State Journal* was switched to what was then the less lucrative morning market. In exchange it also was granted the right to publish the Sunday edition. What a deal! The Sunday *State Journal* contains a weekly television guide, with major cable and all local network stations listed; *Parade* magazine; and separate business, lifestyle, home, arts and editorial sections.

Weeklies

Agri-View
2001 Fish Hatchery Rd., Madison
• **(608) 250-4175**

Agri-View, a weekly newspaper with a circulation of about 46,000, is mailed to dairy and other farmers, mostly within the state of Wisconsin. Published Thursdays in South-Central Wisconsin by Madison Newspapers Inc., *Agri-View* is filled with news affecting farmers' livelihoods, including pending agricultural legislation.

Catholic Herald
702 N. Blackhawk Ave., Madison
• **(608) 233-8060**

Catholic Herald contains news of the Catholic diocese as well as other national and foreign religious news. As the official newspaper of the Catholic Diocese of Madison, it's distributed to 11 counties within Wisconsin and has a circulation of 31,000.

Cover Story
2013 Fish Hatchery Rd., Madison
• **(608) 250-4150**

This free shopper is delivered Sundays to the doors of more than 83,000 residents in Dane County. Featuring copy about the entertainment world, *Cover Story* is produced by Madison Newspapers Inc.

Isthmus
101 King St., Madison • **(608) 251-5627**

Though a relative newcomer to Madison — the first edition of *Isthmus* was published April 9, 1976 — the free weekly tabloid newspaper distributed on Thursdays has become a notable fixture on the Madison scene with a flair for provocative, investigative reporting and a liberal bent more in keeping with *The Capital Times* than the *Wisconsin State Journal*.

Distributed throughout Madison at stores, restaurants and other locations that receive heavy pedestrian traffic, *Isthmus* has a circulation of 63,000. And although it was created with an urban, Downtown feel, it has evolved through the years into a more mainstream publication.

One thing that hasn't changed is the paper's devotion to coverage of the arts scene. Look to a weekly roundup of reviews in addition to "Critic's Choice" in *Isthmus'* "Arts and Entertainment Guide" for a variety of solid suggestions.

Madison Business First
2001 Fish Hatchery Rd., Madison
• **(608) 250-4331**

With the economy booming in Dane and surrounding counties, businesses are finding they need more information. *Madison Business First* provides the business community of south-central Wisconsin with the news it needs to continue to flourish.

Because it has a business-to-business focus, this publication can concentrate on the nuts-and-bolts information that helps business people make informed decisions. Special reports probe behind the headlines to examine the trends and background on issues, and columnists provide advice on business-related topics.

The Madison Times
931 E. Main St., Ste. 7, Madison
• (608) 256-2122

Billed as "the paper that's more than black and white," *The Madison Times* is a free, weekly newspaper distributed throughout Madison and parts of Dane County each Friday. With a circulation of about 6,500, the newspaper was started in 1991 by editor and publisher Betty Franklin-Hammonds to ferret out more neighborhood news and items of special interest to African-Americans. Among its special sections is one for Black History Month and another saluting graduating high school seniors. *The Madison Times* is readily available in libraries and most Kohl's Food Stores in Dane County.

The Onion
33 University Sq., Ste. 270
• (608) 256-1372

If you don't know what *The Onion* is all about, expect to be shocked, then amused when picking it up for the first time. It looks and feels like a traditional newspaper. Only it's not. It's a parody with very cleverly executed satire. The free, weekly tabloid is published every Wednesday in Madison, Chicago, Milwaukee and Denver and Boulder, Colorado. The press run is more than 150,000 and growing. Chicago circulation was added the beginning of 1998.

Through its web site, *The Onion* is gaining many new fans — so many, in fact, that Disney's Hyperion Publishing Co. has contracted with *The Onion* for two books.

Monthlies and Bimonthlies

Badgerland Sports For Youth
2564 Branch St., Ste. B13, Middleton
• (608) 831-2110

This new monthly publication is geared to young athletes, both boys and girls, ages 5 to 15 living throughout South-Central Wisconsin. It's available free from a variety of locations in Dane County, including schools.

Dane County Kids
2564 Branch St., Ste. B13, Middleton
• (608) 831-2131

This free monthly parenting guide is distributed the first of every month through 200 locations in Dane County including libraries, daycare centers and some restaurants and stores. It specializes in health and other news of special interest to parents. Each month the publication prints a listing of local, family-oriented things to do and see. The press run is 22,000.

Feminist Voices
(608) 251-9268

A bimonthly publication written by women for women, *Feminist Voices* acts as an open forum for the discussion of timely issues affecting women. It openly supports the right of women to "shape their own lives." The free publication is distributed at Downtown coffee shops, libraries, some specialty stores and around the UW-Madison campus.

Freethought Today
(608) 256-5800

Started in 1984, this tabloid-size newspaper, the only one of its kind still being published in North America, is published 10 times a year. The house organ of the Freedom From Religion Foundation, a national association of free thinkers, it carries news of interest to atheists and agnostics who are especially concerned with issues of separation of church and state. Circulation is about 4,500.

La Nacion
2 S. Pinckney St., Ste. GL26
• (608) 256-8641

Founded in 1989, *La Nacion* is a local newspaper printed in Spanish to serve the Hispanic community in Dane County. It has a circulation of about 5,000 and is distributed free on the second Friday of the month at various locations throughout Madison, including Mexican restaurants, Centro Hispano and the Main and South branches of the Madison Public Library.

Mature Lifestyles
2984 Triverton Pike Dr., Madison
• (608) 274-5200

This free, monthly publication, distributed on the Friday closest to the beginning of each month, was started in 1986 and is primarily targeted to people ages 55 to 75. Stories center around retirement and a variety of issues — legal, health, lifestyle and financial — of interest to people in that age category. *Mature Lifestyles* is distributed throughout Dane County, primarily through major food stores. It has two sister publications in outlying counties.

Now Hiring Employment Guide
2564 Branch St., Ste. B13, Middleton
• (608) 831-4303

Published bimonthly, *Now Hiring* is a free guide listing employment opportunities in South-Central Wisconsin. A good place to find it is at area libraries.

The Soccer Scoop
3 S. Pinckney St., Ste. GL26
• (608) 256-8641

The Soccer Scoop is published by Viscarra Communications, a multimedia company that also publishes *La Nacion* (see previous entry). Distributed free on the third Friday of the month, the newspaper promotes soccer as a family sport and contains information about local soccer news and events. It's available at many sites in and around Madison including soccer stores, indoor centers, bookstores, high schools and the UW-Madison Athletic Department.

Wheels For You
2013 Fish Hatchery Rd., Madison
• (608) 250-4154

If you're in the market for a good used car, *Wheels For You*, published biweekly by Madison Newspapers Inc., is a good place to start. The newspaper exclusively carries ads for "anything that moves on wheels." Distributed free throughout Dane County and beyond, the publication is available through racks positioned at major grocery stores.

Community Newspapers

Deerfield Independent
7 S. Main St., Deerfield • (608) 255-1041

Started in 1887, *Deerfield Independent* is a weekly newspaper that, in addition to covering Deerfield, reports news from Cottage Grove and the Monona Grove School District. Publication day is Thursday. Circulation is about 1,500. *Deerfield Independent* is a sister paper to *The Sun Prairie Star*.

DeForest Times Tribune
108 Market St., DeForest
• (608) 846-5576

Founded in 1895, this community weekly hasn't missed a week of publication in more than 100 years. With a circulation of 2,500, it's published on Thursdays and primarily covers the news of DeForest, Windsor and Morrisonville.

The Edgerton Reporter
21 N. Henry St., Edgerton
• (608) 884-3367

This community weekly covering Albion, Edgerton and rural parts of Dane and Rock counties is published on Wednesday and has a circulation of about 3,200. It is also noted for its annual "Lakes Edition," a recreational guide published just before Memorial Day weekend with features and calendars of events for tourist hotspots including lakes Ripley, Koshkonong, Kegonsa and Waubesa and the Rock River. It's available for free throughout the summer months at area businesses.

INSIDERS' TIP

With a doctorate in animal behavior, veterinarian Patricia McConnell has a popular following for her radio and television shows, "Calling All Pets," which airs at 11:30 AM Saturday on WHA AM; and "Petline," aired nationally on Animal Planet (Cable Channel 35 in Madison) twice a day (noon and 4:30 PM weekdays) and three times on Saturday (2 AM, 1 PM and 4 PM.). She lives near Madison in Black Earth.

Middleton Times Tribune
7507 Hubbard St., Middleton
• (608) 836-1601

Owned by News Publishing Inc., *Middleton Times Tribune* has a history dating back to 1893. It's published on Thursdays and has a paid circulation of 3,200. News Publishing also owns several other small weeklies in outlying Dane County.

Fitchburg Star
2934 Fish Hatchery Rd., Ste. 226, Fitchburg
• (608) 273-3576

Monona Community Herald
6041 Monona Dr., Monona
• (608) 221-1544

McFarland Community Life
6041 Monona Dr., Monona
• (608) 221-1544

Oregon Observer
845 Market St., Oregon • (608) 251-3252

Verona Press
120 W. Verona Ave., Verona
• (608) 845 9559

These five weekly newspapers are owned by Schroeder Publications, with main offices in Monona. Combined paid subscription for the five is 6,100. All are published on Thursday. In operation for 31 years, Schroeder Publications, headed by Henry Schroeder, also publishes free shoppers with a combined circulation of 31,000 in the same communities.

The Star
114 Columbus St., Sun Prairie
• (608) 837-2521

Part of the Hometown News Group, *The Star* is published every Thursday and covers news of interest to Sun Prairie and outlying areas. It has a paid circulation of about 5,000. Hometown News also publishes two shoppers, including *The Advertiser* which reaches into the East Side of Madison. Additional community newspapers are *The Independent*, based in Deerfield, and *The Courier*, with offices in Waterloo.

Stoughton Courier-Hub
301 W. Main St., Stoughton
• (608) 873-6671

One of the oldest community newspapers in the area, *Stoughton Courier-Hub* has a colorful history dating back to 1880. Published every Thursday, the tabloid newspaper has a circulation of about 4,300 and specializes in covering the news of Stoughton and the townships of Rutland, Dunn, Pleasant Springs and Dunkirk. Stoughton originally had two rival newspapers — the *Hub* and the *Courier*. In the early 1900s, they were combined into one newspaper, the *Courier-Hub*. It operated as a daily until after World War II. Today, Woodward Communications, based in Dubuque, Iowa, owns the paper as well as three radio stations in Madison.

The Sun Prairie News
104 N. Bristol St., Sun Prairie
• (608) 825-2649

This tabloid-size newspaper published by Madison Newspapers Inc. is an insert appearing every Wednesday in both the *Wisconsin State Journal* and *The Capital Times*. It concentrates on the news of Sun Prairie, of course, but also Windsor, DeForest, Marshall and Cottage Grove. Call (608) 825-4608 to reach the editorial department.

Waunakee Tribune
105 South St., Waunakee
• (608) 849-5227

Dating back to 1920, *Waunakee Tribune* is a weekly newspaper, emphasizing the news in Waunakee for 3,500 subscribers. The newspaper also publishes a shopper, *Prairie Valley*, each Monday.

Magazines

The following magazines are all published in Madison, although some have a following far beyond county and even state boundaries.

InBusiness
611 N. Sherman Ave., Madison
• (608) 246-3599

What started out in the late '70s as little more than a newsletter has become a slick business magazine delivered primarily to executives working in Madison and Dane County. The monthly magazine has a controlled circulation of 15,000 and is published by Magna Publications in Madison, which

MEDIA • 421

Photo: Wisconsin Public Television

Dave Iverson and Patty Loew are co-anchors of *Weekend*, WHA-TV's award - winning news program focusing on Wisconsin issues. WHA-TV is one of the first non-commercial stations in the country.

also publishes nationally distributed newsletters on a variety of subjects. The object of *InBusiness* is to "provide business leaders with an opportunity to learn from the experiences of their peers and provide information vital to success." The January issue listing Dane County's top-100 businesses in terms of gross revenues is always popular.

Madison Magazine
625 Williamson St., Madison
• **(608) 255-9982**

Madison Magazine is just as it sounds — a monthly city magazine emphasizing events, people and activities, including dining, in and around the Capital City. Visitors can get a little better feel for the pulse of the city by perusing a copy. Circulation, including newsstand sales, is about 19,000. Especially popular is the magazine's "Best of Madison" reader poll usually published in July or August. Started in 1980, the magazine is now owned by Morgan Murphy Stations, which also owns WISC-TV in Madison.

Madison Pet Gazette
402 Starling Ln., Madison
• **(608) 249-8707**

Begun in the spring of 1997, this monthly magazine printed on newsprint is distributed free in about 400 locations throughout Madison and Dane County. Meant to be "fun, relevant and informative," it includes news of local interests about all kinds of pets.

The Progressive
409 E. Main St., Madison
• (608) 257-4626

What started in 1909 as the La Follette weekly newspaper for the Progressive movement has turned into an influential, outspoken, liberal political magazine with 35,000 paid subscribers from around the world. Filled with scrappy investigative reporting and social commentary, *The Progressive* made national headlines in '79 when the U.S. Government tried and failed to stop the magazine from publishing the story: "The H-bomb Secret: How We Got It and Why We're Telling It." The story turned out to be not nearly as dangerous as the government had thought.

Umoja
533 S. Shore Dr., Madison
• (608) 255-9600

Umoja (oo-mow-ja) means "unity in the family, community, nation and race" in Swahili. As the first of seven principles of Kwanzaa, it is the driving force behind *Umoja*, a monthly magazine dedicated to printing only positive news and achievements of the African-American community in and around Madison. The magazine evolved from a calendar of events first published in 1989. It continues to promote activities of special interest to African-Americans and sponsors the Kwanzaa Holiday Fair each winter (see the November section of our Festivals and Annual Events chapter).

Wisconsin Academy Review
1922 University Ave., Madison
• (608) 263-1692

You must become a member of the Wisconsin Academy of Sciences, Arts and Letters to receive this quarterly magazine filled with both fiction and nonfiction, poetry, photography and cultural reviews.

Wisconsin Agriculturist
2820 Walton Commons W., Ste. 136
• (608) 224-1030

Published 15 times a year, *Wisconsin Agriculturist* is filled with farming production information of specific interest to farmers within the state.

Wisconsin Golf
2317 International Ln., Madison
• (608) 244-2600

This bimonthly magazine is exclusively devoted to golfing in Wisconsin. The magazine includes player profiles, PGA instruction tips and information about golf courses in the state. It has a paid circulation of about 10,000.

Wisconsin Trails
6225 University Ave., Madison
• (608) 231-2444

Wisconsin Trails is Wisconsin's answer to *Midwest Living*, although actually that statement could be easily reversed since *Wisconsin Trails* came first. The bimonthly began in 1960 and today has a combined circulation, paid and newsstand, of about 50,000. The magazine primarily showcases the diversity of leisure and travel in Wisconsin but also often includes historical and personality profiles of people and places. Another sideline business is contract publishing.

Midwest Sport Horse Journal
1214 Fish Hatchery Rd., Madison
• (608) 257-1567

Teamed with a growing regional interest in equestrian events, this bimonthly magazine contains stories about all breeds of sport horses and the disciplines in which they participate, including dressage, driving and jumping. Circulation is about 400.

Radio

Madison radio is no different than many businesses today that must rely on paid adver-

---

INSIDERS' TIP

The first issue of the first newspaper in Madison, the Wisconsin Enquirer, was published on November 8, 1838. The Wisconsin State Journal traces its roots back to a weekly Whig newspaper, Madison Express, first published on December 2, 1839.

tising for their livelihood. Instead of appealing to a wide audience, individual stations are targeting niche markets. Thus, even within the realm of rock music, you'll find a variety of possibilities, from light and classic to progressive and alternative.

Though sometimes it's difficult to ascertain the differences, stations know exactly what kind of listeners they're attempting to attract. And with 14 FM stations alone in operation, the public has plenty of choices even if almost all of the stations are owned by three companies. The majority of adolescents will opt for WZEE (Z-104), just as their baby-boomer parents are likely to go with WOLX, unless they have a yen for crooners Frank Sinatra, Tony Bennett and Nat King Cole. Then, the obvious choice is a mellow, soothing mixture presented by WTSO. Of the two country-music stations, WWQM is more traditional, with WYZM aimed at the younger, crossover listener.

Spend very much time listening to Madison radio and you'll discover that the city has its share of vibrant, sometimes even outrageous radio personalities, most of whom duke it out in the popular early morning drive-time slot, from about 5:30 to 10 AM. For those who like outlandish pranks and prattle, tune into Johnny Danger of WJJO, the caustic Sly on WTDY, Marc Anthony and Vicki McKenna on Z-104 or the "Fletch (Fletcher Keyes) and Sara (James) Show" on WOLX. The only local female duo is made up of Boo Henderson and Petie Rudy, whose one-hour talk show is carried on WTDY AM beginning at 10 AM on Saturday.

Often radio personalities try hard to make a name for themselves to move into a larger metropolitan market, but quite content here in Madison are J.D. Barker at WWQM (Q-106) and Dave Anthony with WIBA AM.

No one has a bigger national following than talk-show host Michael Feldman, whose popular comedy quiz show, "Whad'ya Know?," is hosted from the Monona Terrace Convention Center from 10 AM to noon on Saturdays. Tickets to attend the show are $5; call (608) 263-4141 for information.

If you happen to be driving in your car while the Green Bay Packers are playing, tune in to either WIBA FM or AM. The latter is also good for Brewers baseball and UW Badger basketball, football and hockey.

In a Class By Itself

WORT 89.9 FM is an alternative radio station sponsored and primarily operated by a staff of 200 volunteer listeners. Its programming is eclectic. News programs and even speeches are interspersed with a wide range of music, from classical, folk and country to jazz, blues and alternative rock.

Christian
WNWC 102.5 FM

Classical
WERN 88.7 FM (Wisconsin Public Radio)

Country
WYZM 105.1 FM (hot country)
WWQM 106.3 FM (contemporary country)

Contemporary
WMLI 96.3 FM (adult, light hits)
WMGN 98.1 FM (adult contemporary, some light jazz)
WZEE 104 FM (Top-40 hits)

Easy-listening
WSJY 107.3 FM

INSIDERS' TIP

To "reconnect" citizens with local government and important community issues, a civic journalism project was launched in 1992 by the Wisconsin State Journal, Wisconsin Pulbic Television, Wisconsin Public Radio, WISC-TV and Wood Communications Group in the form of old-fashioned town hall meetings and other forums. "We the People" has been very successful in spurring people to speak out and make a difference.

Oldies
WMAD 1190 AM (1940s through the '60s)
WOLX 94.9 FM (1950s through the '70s)
WTSO 1070 AM (adult standards from the 1950s through the '70s)

Rock
WIBA 101.5 FM (album-oriented rock)
WMMM 105.5 FM (progressive rock)
WJJO 94.1 FM (active rock)
WMAD 92 FM (new rock, alternative)

Sports
WHIT 1550 AM (news and commentary)

Talk and News
WIBA 1310 AM
WTDY 1480 AM (carries Rush Limbaugh Monday through Friday, Boo and Petie on Saturday, 10 to 11 AM)
WHA 970 AM "The Ideas Network," as 970 AM, Wisconsin Public Radio, is referred to, is home to Michael Feldman's show described previously.

Television

Madison's white-collar, educated demographic profile bodes well for many area businesses. That includes television broadcasting. It's a strong, healthy market — the 88th-largest in the United States out of 212 markets (New York City is the largest).

Madison is home to three network television stations, a Fox affiliate, a government-access station and both community and statewide public stations.

With the advent of cable television, which arrived in Madison in the early '70s and is currently serviced by either TCI Cablevision of Wisconsin Inc. or Marcus Cable (Fitchburg and Waunakee), viewers in and around Madison can flick through dozens of channels — for a price, of course. For cable hookup, call TCI at (608) 274-3511 or Marcus at (800) 652-9456. If you're interested in installing a dish or wireless antenna system, contact Sky Cable TV Of Madison, (608) 271-6999.

WKOW-TV Channel 27 (Cable Channel 7) was Madison's first station to go on the air (in 1954). Shortly thereafter, WMTV Channel 15 (Cable Channel 5) and WHA-TV Channel 21 (Cable Channel 11), the third-oldest noncommercial television station in the country, came on the scene, followed by WISC-TV Channel 3 (Cable Channel 9). The latter, which now is the CBS affiliate, created a controversy within Madison broadcasting by procuring the only VHF channel, thus giving the station what at the time was considered "unfair advantage." VHF carried far greater distances than ordinary UHF. The tempest abruptly died out in the late '50s when federal broadcasting policy enabled all stations in Madison to switch to VHF. But it is a chapter in Madison broadcasting history that is still talked about.

Competition from cable has spurred Madison stations to do what they do best even better: cover local news, sports and weather. Local newscasts are broadcast at 6 and 10 PM nightly. For a weekly roundup of television programming, make sure you get "TV Week," which appears every Sunday in the *Wisconsin State Journal*.

WHA-TV reaches viewers throughout the state, except for Milwaukee. Among its strengths are educational and statewide programming (including public-affairs shows such as *Weekend*, every Friday at 7 PM) and widespread community support. To become a member of WHA-TV and receive its monthly programming guide, *Airwaves*, call (800) 422-9707.

The Federal Cable Act of 1984 helped to launch three local cable channels in Madison: WYOU Channel 4, Madison City Channel 12 and Madison Metropolitan School District Channel 10.

INSIDERS' TIP

To place a classified ad in either the *Wisconsin State Journal* or *The Capital Times*, call (608) 252-7723. For delivery information, call (608) 252-6363.

Local Stations

WISC Channel 3 (CBS)
WMTV Channel 15 (NBC)
WHA Channel 21 (Wisconsin Public Television)
WKOW Channel 27 (ABC)
WMSN Channel 47 (FOX)
WYOU Channel 4 (Public Access Television)

CitiCable 12

City of Madison government-access television broadcasts Madison School Board meetings live on Monday nights, City Council meetings on Tuesdays and Dane County Board meetings on Thursdays.

MMSD Cable Channel 10

Madison Metropolitan School District's cable channel carries educational programming supervised by the district. Current events and arts programs occurring in public schools often are taped and shown on television, as are Madison School Board meetings.

WYOU Cable Channel 4

This public-access station is best described as an "electronic soapbox." The public is invited to submit tapes or provide live programming to foster intelligent debate on important issues. There are guidelines, of course, that must be followed. For instance, no form of advertising is allowed. WYOU is on the air from 3 PM to 8 AM daily and coordinates 49 hours of original community programming weekly.

Outlying Stations

KSUN Cable Channel 12
KIDS 4 TV Cable Channel 4

These are community-access channels for Sun Prairie. The latter specializes in shows taped, produced and directed by children for children.

Based on the area's ethnic heritage — Norwegian, Irish, German and Italian — it is no surprise that Lutherans (predominately Norwegian) and Catholics make up the largest share of area churchgoers.

Worship

The cosmopolitan atmosphere that is driven by the university, permeating so much of Madison life, blows full gale through the city's religious community.

Based on the area's ethnic heritage — Norwegian, Irish, German and Italian — it is no surprise that Lutherans (predominately Norwegian) and Roman Catholics make up the largest share of area churchgoers, although they no longer dominate the religious scene. Madison is home to a wide variety of faiths and denominations, including Nature Spirituality, Baha'i, Muslim and Buddhism. (His Holiness the Dalai Lama made his third visit to Madison in May 1998.)

To find out the time of weekend worship services for many Madison-area churches, refer to the "Saturday Worship Directory" that appears weekly in *The Capital Times* and *Wisconsin State Journal*.

It wasn't too many years ago that church leaders stood at the forefront, championing or condemning a multitude of controversial issues, school prayer and desegregation notwithstanding. That hardly happens anymore, though conservative views, when voiced, automatically attract more attention for daring to buck Madison's liberal climate. Have we mentioned how political correctness rules the roost in Madison? We thought so. (See our Politics and Perspectives chapter for details.)

One atheist group that isn't afraid to speak out — and does so often — is The Freedom From Religion Foundation, a Madison-based organization that guards the First Amendment (separation of church and state) with unremitting zeal. Everything from community-sponsored nativity scenes to UW Christian coaches who lead their players in prayer has come under attack in recent years by this organization.

Uniting for Good Causes

The religious scene in Madison is and always has been healthy, diverse and very independent. The Wisconsin Conference of Churches serving the entire state just happens to be based in Sun Prairie. But Madison has no local ministerial society or association of churches. For the most part, individual denominations go their separate ways except in the support of local, humanitarian causes. These include providing shelter and food to the poor and homeless and assisting other community organizations like Habitat for Humanity in building low-cost housing.

Members of many congregations, for instance, actively volunteer at the homeless shelter operated by Transitional Housing out of one of Madison's most historical and architecturally significant churches, Grace Episcopal, 6 N. Carroll Street, on the Square. (See the Attractions chapter for more information.) The church was completed in 1858 and today has about 400 members. Grace Episcopal is the only remaining church of four on the Square. That is no indication, however, as to the health of Downtown churches. Unlike most cities, many have continued to thrive even after housing moved farther out.

One of these is Holy Redeemer Church, 120 W. Johnson Street, the second-oldest Catholic church in Madison and the first German Catholic church built in the city. The parish was founded by 80 families in 1857, and the church was dedicated in 1869. Holy Redeemer now serves a mix of descendants from the original parishioners, university students and those who are attracted to the church's time-honored traditions and preserved old-world charm.

Withstanding the Test of Time

The biggest congregation is at Bethel Lutheran, 312 Wisconsin Avenue, just three blocks off the Square and originally established in 1855 as the Norwegian Lutheran Church. It has about 6,300 members. Using as its motto, "A citywide church with a worldwide ministry," Bethel Lutheran measures its progress not by the size of its congregation but rather by the number of people it serves. Church outreach programs include a camp for disadvantaged youth in Iowa County and housing for men with chronic mental illness.

The congregations of several churches in Madison are more than 150 years old. The First United Methodist Church, 203 Wisconsin Avenue, traces its roots back to 1837, to a service preached by an itinerant minister in the bar room of the American House, then a hotel on the Square. The Methodist congregation, which numbers 1,300 today, built its first church building, which no longer exists, in 1848.

The First Congregational Church, 1609 University Avenue, goes all the way back to 1840. Its present home — a distinguished, block-long Georgian Revival-style building on the edge of campus — was dedicated in 1930 and is described as "Wrenaissance" for its resemblance to many London church buildings designed by Sir Christopher Wren.

Another "old timer" is Madison's First Baptist Church, 518 N. Franklin Street, which celebrated its 150th anniversary in '98. Madison's population was only 632 when the congregation began worshipping.

The Growth of Catholicism

The first Catholic Mass in Madison was performed in 1842. A short time later, a small wood church was built on W. Main Street, which was later replaced by what is considered to be the oldest Catholic church building in Madison, St. Raphael's Cathedral, 222 W. Main, which opened its doors in 1862. Built on a high plot of land one block off the Square, St. Raphael's lofty 235-foot-high steeple (added in 1882) sets off the landmark early Romanesque Revival cathedral that is attended often by Catholics visiting Madison.

It was the Irish Catholic immigrants living nearby who supported St. Raphael's. The Germans, as previously mentioned, built Holy Redeemer. But soon, there would be too many Irish for St. Raphael's to accommodate, so a third church, St. Patrick's, was erected on the other side of the Square, 404 E. Main Street, by John Nader, a Madison architect who considered the Romanesque Revival-style building among his best works. Nader also added the steeple to St. Raphael's. St. Patrick's was appropriately dedicated on St. Patrick's Day, 1889.

The Madison diocese, which incorporates 137 parishes in 11 counties, including Dane, has grown appreciably since breaking off from the Milwaukee diocese in 1946. Offices are located at the new Bishop O'Connor Pastoral Center on the far West Side, former home to Holy Name Seminary. William Bullock is the third bishop to serve here. For information about the diocese, call (608) 821-3000.

The largest congregation — 2,500 strong — worships at St. Dennis Catholic Church, 313 Dempsey Road on the East Side. On the near West Side, Our Lady Queen of Peace, 401 S. Owen Drive, is almost equally as large.

Synagogues

The two main synagogues in Madison are Beth Israel Center, 1406 Mound Street on the corner of Mound and Randall streets, and Temple Beth El, 2702 Arbor Drive, just off Monroe Street. Both are on the near West Side, within a couple of miles of one another. The latter is the sole Reform congregation in Madison, representing the liberal tradition of Judaism. Beth Israel Center is the more conservative of the two.

B'nai B'rith Hillel Foundation, 611 Langdon Street, is a center that coordinates Jewish activities on the UW-Madison campus. Call (608) 256-8361 for information.

The first synagogue in Madison, Gates of Heaven, was built in 1863 at 214 W. Washington Avenue and is considered to be one of the oldest synagogues in the nation, although the building was only used as a synagogue for a short time. Gates of Heaven was moved to James Madison Park and is now owned by the city. (See the Attractions chapter.)

African-American Influences

The first church serving primarily African-Americans in Madison was founded in 1902 by John Turner, described by David Mollenhoff in *Madison, A History of the Formative Years* as a "brilliant but illiterate former Kentucky slave." The church was the Free African Methodist, and although it was described as the center of black community life for a number of years, it no longer exists today.

But the oldest remaining black church (c. 1911), Mount Zion Baptist, 2019 Fisher Street on the South Side, remains an important cornerstone of the African-American community in Madison. Mount Zion is the largest African-American church in the city with a congregation of about 625. If you like gospel music, this is a great church to attend. As minister of music, Leothea Stanley, a noted Madison musician who conducts many high-spirited workshops for Madison school children, oversees four choirs for the church. These include a children's choir with more than 100 voices and the Chancel Choir, the oldest and best known of the four, which presents a mixture of traditional and contemporary gospel. If you decide to attend, be forewarned that Mount Zion is also noted for having one of the longest Sunday morning church services — sometimes lasting two hours.

If Mount Zion is increasingly singled out for more contemporary gospel music, the Second Baptist Church, 4303 Britta Parkway, an offshoot of Mount Zion that is nearly a half-century old itself, is equally notable for wonderful, more traditional gospel. Altogether there are at least a dozen African-American churches in Madison, most of which are on the South Side; all are very active and growing. One of the newest is Faith Community Baptist Church, which meets at St. Mark's Lutheran Church, 605 Spruce Street.

Diverse Places to Worship

While Lutheran churches outnumber every other kind in Madison, many different denominations and faiths call the city and surrounding area home. These include the Islamic Centre of Madison, 21 N. Orchard Street, near the UW-Madison campus; the Society of Friends Quaker Meeting House, 1704 Roberts Court; a major Buddhist monastery serving the entire Midwestern region, Deer Park Center in Oregon; and the Assumption Greek Orthodox Church, the only one of its kind in Madison, at 11 N. Seventh Street.

With walls and ceilings decorated in traditional Byzantine style, the latter is one of the most artistically decorated and treasured churches in the Midwest. Renowned Madison artist David Giffey, who studied in Greece to master the iconic-style of painting, has been working on the church since 1979.

Another visually celebrated church is the First Unitarian Society of Madison, 900 University Bay Drive, because it was designed by Frank Lloyd Wright. (See our Attractions chapter.)

Circle Sanctuary, also known as Circle, is an international Nature Spirituality resource center and Shamanic Wiccan church head-

---

INSIDERS' TIP

Bethel Lutheran's church service at 7:55 AM Sunday is signed for the deaf and televised live on WKOW-TV (Channel 27). A signed service for the hearing-impaired is also available at 11 AM Sunday at the First Unitarian Society of Madison, 900 University Bay Drive. The Madison Catholic Diocese offers a signed Mass at 7:30 AM Sunday on WISC-TV (Channel 3).

quartered on a 200-acre sacred nature preserve near Mount Horeb. Contrary to popular belief, the center has nothing to do with evil spells or devil worship. Founded in 1974, Circle's ministry is multifaceted, incorporating research, networking, publishing, counseling, interfaith and multicultural dialogue, education and spiritual healing. Circle operates Circle Network, an information exchange linking individuals and Nature spirituality groups to centers throughout the United States and more than 50 foreign countries. Seasonal festivals, nature meditations, workshops and other activities often are held on Circle Sanctuary's land. For more information contact The Rev. Selena Fox at P.O. Box 219, Mount Horeb, WI 53572.

William Wineke, columnist and religious writer for the *Wisconsin State Journal* and also an ordained minister, preaches every Sunday at an independent, nondenominational church for the down-and-out, the Rescue Mission, 2540 E. Mifflin Street. Rescue Mission was founded in 1962 by the late John Henrickson, once a street bum who managed to turn his life around and open a church for alcoholics. Wineke became chaplain in '77. Food is available throughout the week at the Rescue Mission, although its main meal is served following the Sunday service. While Wineke preaches great sermons, he welcomes all the homeless to dinner, whether they come to listen to him or not.

Interfaith Opportunities

In 1953, a group of Benedictine Sisters moved from Iowa to Middleton to establish a monastery and open a girls' college prep school. In 1966, the school was converted into a retreat and conference center providing hospitality and meeting space to religious groups, nonprofit organizations and individuals. Saint Benedict Center is at 4200 County Highway M in Middleton. The community reaps the benefits of the monastery and the retreat and conference center. Situated on a beautiful 130-acre tract of land, 50 acres of which the sisters are actively restoring to prairie, the center represents a very affordable oasis from the harried demands of everyday life. Everyone is welcome, although the facility mostly serves religious and nonprofit groups.

Saint Benedict's is the only ecumenical monastery in the United States and welcomes women from all Christian faiths as well as individuals seeking space for a personal retreat. For information about Saint Benedict Center, call (608) 836-1631. Dial extension 158 to inquire about the ecumenical monastery, extension 101 if you're interested in a personal retreat or extension 121 for groups.

The Interfaith Dialog Group was formed in 1987 by George Hinger, former program director at Saint Benedict Center, for people of various world religions to communicate better among themselves within an atmosphere of mutual trust and understanding. Set up primarily as a religious networking organization, the Interfaith Dialog Group is most interested in sharing faiths, scriptures, ideas and rituals. It usually meets in the morning the second Wednesday of the month at Saint Benedict Center. For information, call Hinger at (608) 271-8559.

Madison Urban Ministry

A nonprofit, nondenominational charitable agency, Madison Urban Ministry, 1127 University Avenue, is supported by as many

---

INSIDERS' TIP

In the 1880s, more women than men were at the forefront in establishing churches in Madison, according to research compiled by David V. Mollenhoff in his book, *Madison, A History of the Formative Years*. That's because of the heavy emphasis placed on temperance by churches. Generally, women championed it and men tried to avoid it.

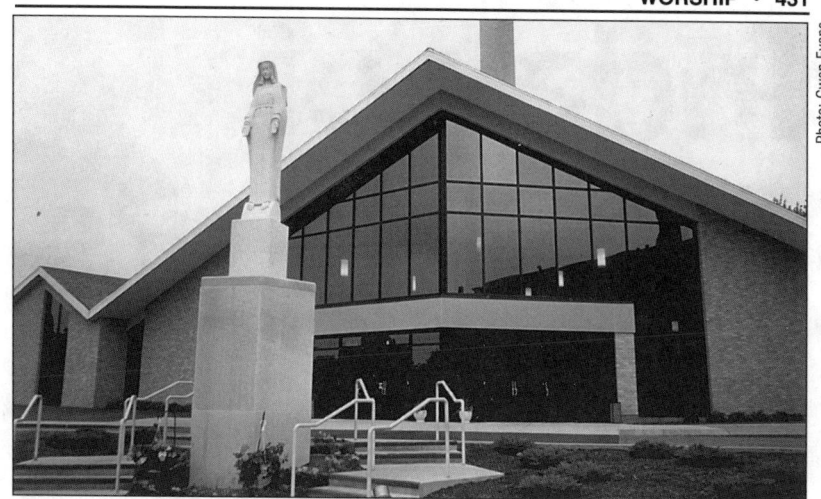

Our Lady Queen of Peace is part of the Madison Diocese.

as 50 congregations in a variety of civic-minded causes from helping to stock area food pantries to building houses for the poor.

Two of the better-known programs initiated by the Madison Urban Ministry are the Madison Community Health Center and Madison Transitional Housing. A current program, "Safe Night," seeks to eradicate violence and drugs among youth. Tutoring and mentoring of Madison's urban school population is also a focus of the agency.

Established in 1973, Madison Urban Ministry also conducts community forums to promote meaningful dialogue between churches of varying faiths and political beliefs.

Jericho Project

Founded in 1993 by a group of men inspired by a Promise Keepers retreat in Boulder, Colorado, to establish more and better Christian outreach, the Jericho Project is a nonprofit organization dedicated to renewing and revitalizing the roles churches play to better serve the Christian faith and humanitarian needs of the community.

Through a survey of 158 senior pastors conducted in '96 to help churches better understand themselves and work together, two issues arose. The majority of pastors expressed both a need to better lead the "unchurched" to the Christian faith and a concern for serving the increasing population of poor.

With the latter in mind, the Jericho Project launched Project HOPE, in which people lend emotional support to families caught up in federal and state welfare reform. It is also hoping to organize a March For Jesus in Madison in 1999 and, if funding is procured, offer a course that will aid area churches in teaching the basics of Christianity.

Dave Konkol is executive director of The Jericho Project, P.O. Box 46045, Madison, WI 53744. Call (608) 277-5765 for further information.

Index of Advertisers

Annie's Bed & Breakfast 129
Arbor House 129
Beat Road Farm
    Bed & Breakfast 131
Canterbury Booksellers
    Cafe Inn 229
Canterbury Inn 129
Captain Bill's .... Inside Front Cover
Collins House 129
Edgewood College 379
Edgewood High School 367
Flower Shop, The 236
Gray Line Madison 29
Happy Pastime
    Collectibles .... Inside Front Cover
Herzing College of Technology 383
Hilldale Shopping Center .... Insert
Home Savings 345
Indigo Moon 236
Jan Byce's .... Insert
Katy's American Indian Arts 236
Little Luxuries 229
Livingston, The 133
Lousianne's Etc. .... Inside Back Cover
Madison Concourse Hotel, The 112
Madison Gas & Electric 336
Madison Inn, The 121
Madison's Small Inn and Bed &
    Breakfast Association 129
Mansion Hill Inn 115, 129
Marriott Madison
    West .... Inside Back Cover
Meriter Hospital 386
Meriter Retirement Services 403

Middleton Antique
    Mall .... Inside Back Cover
Middleton Chamber of
    Commerce ..... Inside Front, Back Cover
Orange Tree Imports 236
Orchids by the
    Ackers .... Inside Front Cover
Patrick's Look of the Isles .... Insert
Pepperberry, The .... Inside Front Cover
Playthings .... Insert
Pleasant View
    Golf Club .... Inside Front Cover
Puzzlebox, The 229
Quivey's Grove 38
Ramada Inn I-90 Capitol
    Conference Center 117
Rowe Pottery Works 237
Soap Opera, The 229
Spring Green Chamber of
    Commerce 299
St. Mary's Care Center 407
St. Mary's Hospital 389
Stamm House at Pheasant
    Branch .... Inside Front Cover
Stark Company Realtors 324
Studio You 237
U.W. Health 393
University Coin, Stamp
    & Jewelry .... Inside Back Cover
University Heights
    Bed & Breakfast 129
Wehrmann's of Madison .... Insert
Wisconsin Education
    Association Council 364

Index

Symbols

20th Century Books 221
"400" Trail Depot 275
55 Alive Driver Training Program 409

A

A Room of One's Own 216
Aardvark's Bookstore 221
AARP 403
Abercrombie & Fitch 228
Abraxas Press 225
Abundant Life Christian School 373
Access to Independence 394
Active Endeavors of Madison 239
Admiralty Room 56, 114
Adolescent Alcohol/Drug Abuse Intervention Program 398
After School Inc. 170, 362
Agri-View 417
AIDS Network 394
Aikido of Madison 288
Airports 32
Alco-VanGalder Bus Lines 33
Aldo Leopold Nature Center 162
Alex Jordan Creative Center 303
Alexander Company 330
All Star Lanes 276
Allen Centennial Gardens 205, 272
Allen, Oscar and Ethel 205
Alley Oops! 162, 164
Alliance for the Mentally Ill 398
Allied-Dunn's Marsh 352
Alphabet Soup 240
Alternative Medicine 399
Alt'n Bach's Town Tap 295
Alzheimer Association 394
American Calliope Center 301
American Cancer Society, Dane County Unit 396
American Diabetes Association, Madison Chapter 394
American Eagle 228
American Heart Association of Wisconsin 394
American Players Theatre 301
American Red Cross, Badger Chapter 394
American TV Appliance & Furniture 254
Amphitheater in the Plaza 205
Amtrak 35
Anchor Inn 85
Angelic Brewing Company 40, 106
Angelic Rabbit, The 238
Angels For All Reasons 248
Ann Taylor 228
Annie's Bed and Breakfast 129
Annual Events 135
Antique Gallery 189
Antiques and Collectibles 235, 298
Antiques Mall of Madison 237
Antonio's 61, 68
Apartment Guide & Renters Handbook 330
Apartment Living 327
Apocalypse Paintball Inc. 289
Appalachian Ridge 342
Apparel, Women's 250
Apps, Jerry 219
Arbor Hills 351
Arbor House, an Environmental Inn 129
Arboretum 197
Archery 272
Archery Center 272
Area Overview 9
Argus Food & Spirits, The 40, 88
Art Fair 200
Art Fair off the Square 149
Art Fair on the Square 149
Art Galleries 188
Art Museums 187
Art Partners 187
Arthritis Foundation, Wisconsin Chapter 394
Artisan Gallery 190, 306
Artisan Gift Shop 249
Arts Consortium 174
Artschwager, Richard 209
Assumption Greek Orthodox Church 429
Atelier — Art To Wear 252
Athlete's Foot 228
Athleticwear 239
Atlas Delicatessen 55, 80, 232
Atomic Interiors 235
Attic Angel House and Garden Tour 147
Attic Angel Retirement Tower 408
Attractions 193
Atwood, David 416
Avenue Bar, The 49, 97
Avol's Bookstore 216

B

Babcock Dairy Plant 203
Babcock Park 269
Babes at the Depot 261.
Babe's Grill & Bar 76, 94
Back Porch Concerts 148
Badger Bowl 276

INDEX

Badger Bus Depot 34
Badger Cab 35
Badger Coaches 34
Badger Dolphins Swim Club 293
Badger Gymnastics 162
Badger Herald 415
Badger Kennel Club Dog Show 143
Badger Prairie Park 274, 285
Badger State Spelling Bee 142
Badger State Summer Games 147
Badger Store, The 202
Badgerland Sports For Youth 418
Bahn Thai 72
Bailiwick's 46
Ballooning 273
Ballrooms 91
Baptist Churches 429
Bar, The 86
Baraboo 322
Bardeen, John 213
Barrymore Theatre 85, 178
Bartlett, Tommy 314
Bartlett's Robot World & Exploratory 314
Bascom Hall 380
Baseball 257
Bashford House 210
Basketball 258
Basketball Girls and Boys Tournaments 141
Bassett Neighborhood 337
Bath & Body Works 228
Bauman, Sue 19
Bavaria Sausage Kitchen Inc. 110
Bay Creek 351
Bayview 340
BBB Farm 130
Be My Nanny 362
Beaches 160, 291
Beanie Babies 250, 254
Beat Road Farm Bed and Breakfast 130
Beckman, Sylvia 209
Bed and Breakfast Inns 127
Beijing Restaurant 261
Belleville Senior Citizen Center 403
Bennett House Bed and Breakfast 317
Bennett Museum 317
Best Buy 228, 230
Best Western Inn on the Park 114
Best Western Inntowner 115
Best Western West Towne Suites 116
Beth Israel Center 428
Bethany United Methodist Nutrition Site 404
Bethel Horizons 171
Bethel Lutheran 427
Bicycle Federation of Wisconsin 275
Bicycling 274
Big Chief Go-Kart World 316
Big Mama & Uncle Fats' 74
Big Ten Pub 95
Bike Clubs 36
Bike Rentals 36
Bike Ride 144
Bike Trails 274, 298

Biking 35
Bill Paul LTD Studio 232
Billiards 275
Biotron 379
Bishop O'Connor Pastoral Center 428
Bishops Bay 325
Bishop's Bay 325, 356
Bistro, The 56
Black Bear Inn 98, 295
Black Earth 300
Black Earth Creek 268
Black Hawk War 298
Black History Month 137
Black Wolf Lodge 318
Blackhawk Country Club 344
Blessed Sacrament School 371
Blooming Grove Historical
  Society Museum 202
Blue Bus Clinic 394
Blue Marlin 78
Blue Moon Bar and Grill 90
Blue Mound State Park 271, 277
Blue Mounds 305, 306
Bluephies 46, 232
Blum, Martha 182
Blum, Raymond 219
Blum, Richard 182
B'nai B'rith Hillel Foundation 428
Boat Rides 313
Bol Weavils 93
Bolz Conservatory 198
Bombay Bicycle Club 36
Bon Appetit 59
Book Clubs 215
Book Fair on the Square 215
Book Rack, The 220
Booked for Murder Ltd. 220
Bookstores 215, 228, 230
Bookworks 216
Boot Barn 228
Borders Book Shop 215, 220
Borders Books Music & Cafe 220
Bormann's Apparel 233
Boston Store 228, 230
Botanical Gardens 198
Botham Vineyards and Winery 305
Boulders Rock Gym 162, 168, 279
Bowl-A-Vard 276
Bowling 166, 168, 275
Bowling Green Recreation Center 276
BR Diamond Suite 243
Bram's Addition 351
Brave Hearts Theatre 178
Breadsmith 232
Break Away Sports Center 162, 287
Brentwood Village-Bruns 346
Brewpubs 105
Briarpatch 394
Brigham, Ebenezer 213
Brigham Park 270
Brittingham Apartments 404
Brittingham House 343

Brittingham-Vilas 340
Broadway Antiques Mall 238
Broadway-Simpson 351
Broom Street Theater 183
Brothers 98
Brown, Frank 206
Buck's 70
Bucky's Locker Rooms 234
Buddhist Monastery 429
Budget Bicycle Center 36, 274
Budget Cinemas 103
Budget Host Aloha Inn 118
Budgetel Inn — BudgetDome 116
Buffalo Wild Wings & Weck 74
Builders 333
Bull Feathers 99
Bullock, William 428
Bullwinkle's Pub 99
Burke Heights 346
Burlington Coat Factory 230
Burnie's Rock Shop 254
Burr Oaks 351
Bus Service, Commuter 33
Buy and Sell Shop Inc. 237
By the Light of the Moon 216, 248

C

Cafe Assisi 100
Cafe Continental 68
Cafe Montmartre 42, 108
Cajun/Creole Restaurants 53
Calabash Gifts 189
Calvary Christian Academy 373
Cam-Rock Park 271, 274, 285
Cambridge 297
Cambridge Antique Mall 298
Cambridge Chamber of Commerce 298
Cambridge Country Inn & Pub 50
Cambridge House Bedand Breakfast 131
Cambridge Woodfired Pottery 297
Cameo Rose Bed & Breakfast 131
Camille's 250
Camp Black Hawk 171
Camp Gray 171
Camp Randall 5, 380
Camp Randall Sports Center 164
Camp Randall Stadium 5
Camping 268, 277
Camps 169
Camps Wawbeek and Pioneer 171
Campus Assistance Center 328, 382
Cancer Information and Support Groups 396
Candinas Chocolatier 305
Canoeing 279
Canterbury Bookseller 215
Canterbury Booksellers Coffeehouse 101, 216
Canterbury Cafe 81
Canterbury Inn 127
Cantor, Joanne 377
Capital Brewery and Beer Garden 107
Capital City Jazz Festival 142

Capital Columns 242
Capital Times, The 415
Capitol Centre Foods 404
Capitol Christmas Pageant 155
Capitol City Band 180
Capitol Sports Center 162
Capitol Theatre 194
Captain Bill's 78
Cardinal Bar and Dance Club 84
Cardinal Stritch University 382
Career Fair 142, 151
Caribbean Club Bar and Grill 90
Caribou Tavern 97
Carillon Tower 380
Carl's Paddlin' Canoe and
    Kayak Center 240, 279
Carmike Cinemas University Square Four 102
Carousel Collectibles & Antiques 304
Carousel Inn & Suites 317
Carriage Rides 35
Casa De Lara Authentic Mexican Restaurant 65
Cascade Mountain 291
Caspian Cafe 66
Casual Corner 228, 230
Catholic Herald 417
Catholicism 428
Cats of Wisconsin 145
Cattails to Clouds Hot Air Balloon Rides 273
Cave of the Mounds 306
Cay's Comic Strip 97
Century 21 Advantage Gold 331
Century 21 Affiliated 331
Century 21 City Wide 332
Century House Inc. 242
Chadbourne Hall 2
Chadbourne, Paul 2
Chalet of the Golden Fleece Museum 307
Challenger's Pub 86
Champs 228, 230
Charlie's Charters 34
Charming Tales 249
CHAT 396
Cheap At Any Price Poets' Collective 224
Cheese Country Recreational Trail 309
Cheese Factory The Restaurant 319
Cherokee Park 348
Cherokee-South 290
Cherry, Kelly 218
Chihuly, Dale 203, 209
Child Care 359
Child-care Assistance for Low-income
    Families 361
Child-care Referral Services 360
Child-care Support Groups 363
Children's Arts 185
Children's Clothing 240
Children's Museum 200
Children's Zoo 159
Chili Cook-off 152
Chili's 228
China International Gourmet 72
China Moon 71

436 • INDEX

Chose Family Inn 124
Chosy Gallery 189
Chris Kerwin Antiques & Interiors 235
Christmas Mountain Village 315
Chula Vista 315
Chula Vista Resort 318
Churches 427
Cigar Bars 105, 110
Cinema 4 Pizza Cafe 51
Cinema Cafe 103
Cinemas 101
Circle Sanctuary 429
Circuit City 228
Circus World Museum 322
CitiCable 12 425
Clarenbach, Kathryn 20
Clasen Bakery 43
Clay Market Cafe 51
Climbing 279
Clock Tower Crafts 250
Clothing, Men's 243
Clothing, Women's 250
Club Tavern 295
Club Tavern & Grille, The 97
Coaches Sports Bar & Grill 76, 96
Coalition of Wisconsin Aging Groups 402
Cobblestone Carriages 35
Coburn, Jean P. Miner 206
Coffee Mill Antique Mall 238
Col. Hans Christian Heg 206
Coldwater Canyon Golf Club 315
Coldwell Banker Sveum Realtors 332
Collectibles 235
College Library 223
Collins House Bed & Breakfast 127
Colonial Acres Apartments 408
Colonial Motel 124
Colonial View Apartments 409
Come Back In 97
Comedy Clubs 84
ComedySportz 84
Comfort Inn 118
Comfort Suites 116
Commercial Art Galleries 188
Community Action Coalition 405
Community Coordinated
       Childcare Inc. (4-C) 360
Community Newspapers 419
Community Thrift Store 246
Concentra Occupational Medical Center 392
Concerts in the Gardens 145
Concerts on the Square 148
Concordia University Madison Center 382
Concourse Hotel, The 114
Cooperative Children's Book Center 223
Copper Grid 95
Cornblooms 228
Cost Plus World Market 228
Cottage Grove 356
Cottage Grove Company Store 250
Council for Wisconsin Writers 224
Country Corners 91

Country Day School 374
Country Inn & Pub 297
Country Inn and Suites 124
Cover Story 417
Cows on the Concourse 146
Coyote Capers 59
Crabtree Room, The 51
Crazy King Ludwig's Adventure Park 316
Crazy Legs Run 142
Creole Cafe 53
Crescent Bear & Bath Boutique 250
Crestwood-Glen Oak Hills-Merrill Crest 353
Criminal Justice Reference and Information
       Center 224
Crosby, David 183
Cross Plains 300, 354
Cross-Country Skiing 290
Crowne Plaza Madison 119
Crystal Corner Bar 85
Crystal Grand Music Theatre 316
CTM Productions 184
Cue-Nique Billiards 275
Curtis Effigy Mounds 342
Curtis, John 197
Curtis Prairie 197
Curve, The 42
Curveball Sports Bar & Grill 295

D

D. Royal Limousine 35
D.W. Zemke Traditional Clothiers 244
Daily Cardinal, The 416
Dairy Cattle Center 158
Dance Clubs 84
Dance Organizations 179
Dane County Breakfast on the Farm 146
Dane County Commission on Aging 404
Dane County Cooperative Extension Office 411
Dane County Cultural Affairs Commission 174
Dane County Fair 149
Dane County Farmers' Market 194
Dane County Humane Society Dog Jog 152
Dane County Job Service 410
Dane County Kids 418
Dane County Kids Expo 140
Dane County Law Library 223
Dane County Memorial Coliseum 175
Dane County Parks 280
Dane County Parks and Campgrounds 278
Dane County Regional Airport 32
Dane County RV Dealers Show 137
Dane County Senior Olympic Games 412
Dane County SOS Senior Council 404
Dardanelles, The 67
David's Restaurant 59
Day and Night Limo Service 35
Day Camps and Classes 169
Days Inn 122
Dayton Street Cafe and Bakery 42, 57
Daytrips 297
Dean Urgent Care Center 392

Deb & Lola's Restaurant & Lounge 57
Deerfield Independent 419
DeForest 354
DeForest Area School District 367
DeForest Area Senior Center 403
DeForest Times Tribune 419
DeHaven, Doc 92
Del-Bar Steak House 319
Delaney's Charcoal Steaks 79
Delicatessens 55
Delitalia 55, 69
Dells Boat Tours 314
Dells Duck Tours 313
DeRicci Gallery 188
Derleth, August 215
Design Shelters 334
Devil's Head Lodge And
    Convention Center 316
Devil's Head Resort 291
Devil's Lake State Park 322
Dimaggio's Euro Design 242
Dimension 2 242
Discovery Zone 161, 164, 166
Disney Store, The 228
"Doctor For You" 388
Dodgeville 300, 304
Don Q Inn 304
Don Simon Homes 334
Donnel, Samuel Hunter 210
Door Creek Country Club 282
Dotty Dumpling's Dowry 42
Douglass China and Gifts
    & Dimension 242
Downhill Skiing 290
Dream Lanes 162, 168, 276
Dream Lanes Bowling Center 164
Driver Escort Program, RSVP 409
Drums on Parade 148
Dry Bean Saloon & Smokehouse 75, 91, 287
Dudgeon-Monroe 340
Dwight Foster House 298

E

Eagle Heights 342
Eagle School 371
Eagle's Nest Ice Arena 165
East Bluff 347
East Buckeye-Droster 349
East Emerson 350
East Madison/Monona Coalition 401
East Side YMCA 363
East Towne Mall 230
East Towne Suites 119
Easter Seal Society 395
Eastgate Cinema 103
Eastman Recital Hall 177
Eastside Evangelical Lutheran School 373
Econo Lodge 120
Eddie Bauer 228, 230
Edenfred 343
Edgefest 151

Edgerton Reporter, The 419
Edgewater Hotel, The 114
Edgewood Campus Grade School 372
Edgewood College 382
Edgewood High School 372
Edgewood Motel 122
Ehlenbach's Cheese Chalet 110
Ehlers Construction Inc. 334
El Dorado Grill 65
Elder Care of Dane County 404
Electric Power Farm Equipment Show 141
Elite Repeat Of Madison 246
Ella's Deli 161
Ella's Kosher Deli &
    Ice Cream Parlor 55, 56
Elvehjem 349
Elvehjem, Conrad A. 199
Elvehjem Museum of Art 188, 199 380
Elver Park 165, 266, 290
Emergency Clinic For Animals 399
Employment Options Inc. 410
Enchanted Valley Bed & Breakfast 131
Epilepsy Center South Central 395
ERA Krause Real Estate and Builders 332
Esquire Theatre 175
Essen Haus 61, 100, 106
Ethan Allen 242
Eva Ruxton's Shop 298
Evinrude, Ole 298
Evjue, William T. 415
Evora Pool and Health Club 412
Exclusive Co. 231
Executive Residence 198
Exel Grand Hotel 122
Exel Inn 120
Extended Day Care Project 361
Extreme Pizza 70

F

Faircrest 342
Fairfield Inn 124
Fairfield Inn by Marriott 120
Faith Community Baptist Church 429
Falk, Kathleen 19
Fall Flower Show 153
Family Land 313
Fanny Garver Gallery 189
Far West Neighborhoods 344
Farm Tavern 88
Farmers' Market 139, 142
Farwell, Leonard 3
Fassett, Norman 197
Fast Forward 161, 166, 287
Fat Jack's Barbecue 75
Feeney, Mike 305
Feldman, Michael 423
Feminist Voices 418
Festa Italia 145
Festge Park 268
Festival Choir, The 180
Festivals and Annual Events 135

438 • INDEX

Fiddleheads 209
Field House 380
Field's 227
Field's Steak 'n Stein 321
Fine Dining 56
Fireside Restaurant & Playhouse 298
First Baptist Church 428
First Call For Help 395
First Congregational Church 428
First, Neal 377
First Unitarian Society of Madison 429
First United Methodist Church 428
First Weber Group Inc. 327, 332
Firstar Eve 155
Fish Camp Launch 280
Fish Lake Park 268, 280
Fishing 280
Fitchburg 354
Fitchburg Senior Center 403
Fitchburg Star 420
Fitness Training 280
Fjelde, Paul 206
Flags of Freedom 147
Flashback Denim 'n' More 247
Flashbacks 85
Florilegium 238
Flower Shop, The 248
Flower Show 198
Fluno Center 378
Flying Dutchman Bar 300
Fontana Sports Specialities 231
Fontana Sports Specialties 239
Food Fair 405
Football 259
Football, Indoor 263
Forbes-Meager Music Center 412
Forest Hill Cemetery 5, 213
Fort Atkinson 297, 298
Fox, the Rev. Selena 430
Foxboro Golf Club 283
Fraboni's Italian Specialities & Delicatessen 64
Fraboni's Italian Specialties 80
Francie's Casual Cafe 46
Francie's Restaurant 115
Frank Lloyd Wright Visitor Center 302
Fredric March Play Circle 177
Free Entertainment for Kids 169
Free-Meal Sites 405
Freethought Today 418
Frostiball 136
Frugal Muse Books, Music & Video 220
Funny Business Comedy Club 78, 84
Fyfe's Corner Bistro 79, 87

G

Gallant Knight 35
Gallery 323 242
Gallery Night 187
Gallery of Design 188
Gallery Shop, The 187
Galvano Golf Academy 316

Galway Bay 252
Gap 228, 230
Gap Kids 228
Garden Expo 138
Gardens, Botanical 198
Gardner Marsh Boardwalk 164
Garver Gallery 189
Gary's Art & Frame Shop 191
Gates of Heaven 428
Gates of Heaven Synagogue 210
Gazelle 239
Gear Up Madison Bike Ride 144
General Motors 299
General Pediatric Urgent Care 392
Generations 209
Geology Museum 158, 201
George Vitense Golfland 167, 283
German/Swiss Restaurants 61
Gersmann, Joel 183
Giffey, David 429
Gift Shops 248
Gilmore, E.A. Residence 213
Gino's 62
Gino's Italian Deli 69, 80
Gino's Restaurant 69
Glacial Drumlin Bike Trail 298
Glacial Drumlin Trail 274
Glen Oak Hills 343
Glendale 350
Glenway Municipal Golf Course 285
Gloria Jean's 228
Glorious Woman, The 252, 298
Golden Care 404
Gold's Gym Health Fitness & Beyond 280
Golf 281, 315
Golf, Miniature 167, 168
Goodland Park 160, 269
Goodman-Rotary Senior Fitness 412
Goodman's Jewelers 243
Goodwill Industries 411
Gorman and Company Inc. 330
Governor Dodge State Park 304
Governor Nelson State Park 271, 285
Grace Chosy Gallery 189
Grace Episcopal Church 210, 427
Grainger Hall 378
Granita Italian Restaurant 63, 69
Grape Stomp Festival 322
Gray Line Madison 34, 300
Great Dane Pub and Brewing Co. 42, 106, 111
Greater Madison Apartment Showcase 331
Greek Orthodox Church 429
Greek Restaurants 61
Green Bay Packers 259
Green Bay Packers' 257
Green County Courthouse 309
Green County Historical Museum 309
Green County Tourism Bureau 306
Green County Tourist Bureau 308
Green Earth 399
Green Golf Center 168
Green Room, The 275

INDEX

Green Tree 352
Greenbush Bakery 44
Greenbush Bar 62, 69, 261, 97
Greyhound Bus Lines 34
Grianan Bris Caife 52
Grocery Stores 228
Groundhog Day Community Breakfast 137
Gymboree 228

H

H.H. Bennett Museum 317
Haas, Richard 208
Haen Real Estate 330
Half-Price Books, Records
  and Magazines 222
Halloween At the Zoo 153
Hampton Inn 118
Hampton Inn Madison East 120
Hamrol, Lloyd 208
Handcrafts 298
Hanna's 77 88
Happy Pastime Hummels & Collectibles 250
Harbor Athletic Club 281
Harmony Bar & Grill 49, 85
Hartmeyer Arena 165
Hartmeyer Ice Arena 286
Hatcher, L. Brower 205
Hawks View Bed & Breakfast 131
Hawthorne 347
Health-Maintenance Organizations 387
Healthcare 387
Heartland Grill 42, 123
Heg, Col. Hans Christian 206
Heidi Festival 308
Heinemann's...Too 44
Helen Louise Allen Textile Collection 188
Henkes, Kevin 218
Henry Vilas Zoo 30, 159, 160, 196
Heritage Heights 350
Herreman's 52
Herzing College of Technology 383
Hieroglyph 206
Hiestand 350
High Point Christian School 372
High Point Estates 352
High Point Swim Club 293
Higher Education 377
Highlands of Seminole 354
Highlands, The 343
Highsmith Education Station 230, 254
Hiking 285
Hill Farms 343
Hill Farms State Office Building 343
Hilldale Shopping Center 227
Hilldale Theatre 102
Hillside Home School 302
Hinger, George 430
Historic Bennett House 132
Historic Bennett House B&B 319
Historic Blooming Grove Historical
  Society Museum 202

Historical Buildings 210
Historical Museum 200
Historical Society Archives Division 223
Historical Society Library 223
History 1
Ho-Chunk Casino & Bingo Parlor 312
Hoard Museum and Dairy Shrine 298
Hockey 262
Holiday Art Fair 154
Holiday Fantasy In Lights 155
Holiday Flower and Train Show 155
Holiday Home Tour 155
Holiday Inn 318
Holiday Inn-Madison East 121
Holle Mackerl Southern Style
  Fish & Seafood 75
Holy Cross Lutheran School 373
Holy Redeemer Church 427
Home Decor 242
Home Goods Store 230
Home Health United 396
Home Healthcare 396
Home Products Show 140
Home-Buying Assistance 326
Home-Delivered Meals 404
Hometown USA Festival 146
Hong Kong Cafe 72
Hoofbeat Ridge Resident Camp 171
Hopkins and Crocker Inc. Art and Antique
  Gallery 238
Horizon Management Properties
  Senior Division 407
Horse Fair 142
Horseback Riding 286
HospiceCare Inc. 396
Hospitals 388
Hotel Docs Inc. 392
Hotels 113
House of Wisconsin 110
House on the Rock 300, 303
Howard Johnson Plaza Hotel 115, 388
Hoyt Park 341
Humanities Building 177
Husnu's 66

I

I Can Cope 396
Ice Skating 164, 286
Icehouse Antiques 239
Imhoff, Loren Homebuilder 334
Immaculate Heart of Mary School 374
Immediate-care Facilities 392
Impala Custom Homes 334
Imperial Garden 73
Imperial Palace 73
In-Line Skating 286
InBusiness 420
Independent Living 401
Indian Hills 344
Indian Lake Park 269, 285
Indian Restaurants 65

252
...tball 263
...ygrounds 164
...ools 292
...The 85
... for Environmental Studies
...(IES) Library 224
...rfaith Dialog Group 430
...iterlaken 171
International Children's Film Festival 138
International Crane Foundation 322
International Holiday Festival 154
Iowa County Historical Museum 304
Irish Waters 89
Irish Waters Restaurant and Tavern 47
Irishman's Bay 89
Ishnala Supper Club 321
Islamic Centre of Madison 429
Isthmus 337, 417
Isthmus Jazz Festival 153
Isthmus Playhouse 175, 195
Italian Restaurants 61
Italian Workmen's Club 62
Ivy Inn 116
Ivy Inn Restaurant 48

J

J.T. Whitney's Brewpub and Eatery 107
Jacobs, Herbert I Residence 213
James Madison Beach 160
Jamieson House Inn 132
Jan Byce's 227, 252
Janesville 297, 299
Janesville Convention & Visitors Bureau 300
Janet's Antiques 235
Jazz Festival 142
Jazzman Isthmus, The 243
Jazzworks 179
JCPenney 228, 230
Jericho Project 431
Jewelry 243
Jingle Bell Run 155
Jingle's Coliseum Bar and Restaurant 94
John Powless Tennis Center 294
Johnson, J. Seward Jr. 209
Jolly Bob's 91
Jones, Dick 417
Jordan, Alex 303
Jordan Creative Center 303
Josie's Restaurant (3 Sisters) 62
Josie's Spaghetti House 69, 261
JT Puffin's 253
JT Whitney's Brewpub 48
Juju & Moxie 244
June Jam 146
Jungle Gyms 163
Jura Silverman Gallery 301

K

Kabul Afghanistan and Mediterranean Restaurant 67
Kanopy Dance Theatre 179
Kappel's Clock Shop 238
Karaoke Clubs 87
Karate America 288
Karen & Co. 251
Katy's American Indian Arts 232, 249
Kay-Bee Toy & Hobby Shop 228
Kayaking 279
Keenan House 211
Kendall House 211
Kennedy Heights 347
Kennedy Manor Dining Room & Bar 57
Ken's Bar and Grill 88
Kerwin Antiques & Interiors 235
Keyes House 211
Kid E-Corner 247
Kid World Inc. 161, 168
Kids Day 150
Kids in the Crossroads 169
Kidstuff 157
Kilbourn Dam 311
Kinderhaus 375
King, William 209
Kitakuni Noodle House 71
Kitchen Hearth 80
Kites On Ice 135
Knapp Memorial Graduate Center 212
Knickerbocker Place 232
Kohl Center 177, 202, 257, 337
Kohl, Herb 261
Kohler Art Library 199
Kohler, Walter 21
Kohl's Department Store 228
Kollege Klub, The 99
Konkol, Dave 431
Koshkonong Creek 298
Kosta's Restaurant 78
Kutzbock, August 210, 212
Kwanzaa Holiday Fair 154

L

La Follette, Belle 20
La Follette, Phillip 21
La Follette, Robert "Fighting Bob" 20, 213, 417
La Leche League of Madison 363
La Nacion 418
La Paella 60, 110
La Provenzale 87
Laidlaw Transit Inc. 34
Lake Delton 310, 311
Lake Edge 350
Lake Farm Park 269, 286
Lake Kegonsa 280
Lake Kegonsa State Park 271, 278
Lake Ripley 298
Lake Shore Path 204
Lake Waubesa 280
Lake Windsor Country Club 282
Lakeview Hills 347
Lamp, Robert M. Residence 212

INDEX • 441

Lands' End 304
Lane's Bakery 43
Langdon Street 338
Lao Laan-Xang 72
Laredo's 65
Laser-Beam Tag 167
Last Square, The 189
Lathrop Hall 177, 378
Laurel Tavern 89
Law Enforcement Memorial 208
Lazzaro Signature Gallery of Fine Art 191
Le Tigre Lounge 90
League Sports 288
Learning Shop, The 253
Lechayim Lunchtime Plus 404
Leckrone, Mike 94
Leitch House 339
Leopold, Aldo 197, 215
Lerner New York 230
L'Etoile 57
Libraries 222
Library Branches 224
Library Service for the Blind and Visually Handica 413
Light Sculpture 208
Lighten Up 249
Lighthouse Nautical Gifts 250
Limited 228, 230
Limousines 35
Lincoln 209
Lincoln, Abraham 298
Lincoln-Tallman House 299
Line Dancing 287
Linen Closet 234
Linen Closet Gallery and Gift Shop 234
Literary Organizations 224
Literary Scene 215
Little Luxuries 231, 248
Little Norway 306
Living Room, The 99
Living The Dream 206
Livingston Bed and Breakfast Inn 339
Livingston, The 128
Llama Market 145
Local TV Stations 425
Lombardino's 63, 69
Longnecker, G. William 197
Longnecker Garden 197
Lost Canyon Carriage Rides 317
Lotus Chinese Restaurant 73
Louisianne's Etc. 55, 60
Lower Wisconsin River 301
Luigi's Diner 61
Lulu's Restaurant 67
Lutheran Church 427

M

M.Y. (Monona Youth) Dream Park 163
Mad-City Ski Team 169
Mad-Town Aquatics Swim Team 293
Madhatter's 99

Madison Aquatic Club 293
Madison Area Builders Association 326, 333
Madison Area Doll Club Show and Sale 141
Madison Area Technical College
   166, 292, 383, 411
Madison Art Center 187, 200
Madison Art League 200
Madison Athletic Club 280
Madison Black Wolf 257
Madison Boat and Sportsmen's Show 136
Madison Book Fair 152
Madison Boychoir 186
Madison Brass 180
Madison Business College 384
Madison Business First 417
Madison Central Montessori School 372
Madison Children's Choir 186
Madison Children's Museum 157, 162, 200
Madison Church Supply 221
Madison Cigar Bar, The 111
Madison CitiARTS 174
Madison Civic Center 175, 194
Madison Civics Club 413
Madison College 384
Madison Community Health Center 431
Madison Concourse Hotel 114
Madison Department of Public Health 395
Madison Drum and Bugle Corps
   Association 186
Madison Equal Opportunity Commission 328
Madison Fishing Expo 138
Madison Folk Dance 180
Madison Gas and Electric 328
Madison Holiday Parade 154
Madison Ice Arena 165, 286
Madison Inn 116
Madison Jazz Society 180
Madison KOA Campground 278
Madison Literacy Council 413
Madison Mad Dogs 263
Madison Magazine 421
Madison Marathon 144
Madison Marriott West 124
Madison Media Institute 385
Madison Monsters 262
Madison Municipal Band 181
Madison Opera Inc. 181
Madison Pet Gazette 421
Madison Public Central Library 222
Madison Public Library — Central
   Branch 157, 195
Madison Repertory Theater 184
Madison Savoyards 184
Madison School-Community
   Recreation 288, 292, 295, 413
Madison Schools 2000 366
Madison Senior Center 402
Madison Spelling Bee 138
Madison Storytellers' Guild 225
Madison Symphony Chorus 181
Madison Symphony Orchestra 181
Madison Taxi 35

442 • INDEX

Madison Theater Guild 184
Madison Times, The 418
Madison Transitional Housing 431
Madison Ultimate 294
Madison Urban Ministry 430
Madison Veterinary Clinic 399
Madison's Demographics 9
Madtown Twisters 162
Maduro 90
Magazines 420
Majestic Theater 102
Mall-Concourse Office 174
Mallatt Pharmacy 232, 399
Mama Digdown's Brass Junction 93
Mandt Ice Arena 165
Mango Grill 84, 261
Mansion Hill District 210
Mansion Hill Inn 128, 212
Maple Bluff 353
Mapletree Antique Mall 238
Maquina 209
Marathon 144
March of Dimes Birth Defects Foundation 395
Mardi O'Brien Real Estate 332
Margaret H'Doubler Performance Space 177
Mariner's Inn 79
Market Square Theatres 102
Marquette 338
Marsh Shapiro's Nitty Gritty 45, 88
Marshall Field's 227
Martial Arts 288
Martin, Vicki 325
Mass Transit 33
MATC Jazz Ensemble 181
Mature Lifestyles 418
Maxwell Street Days 150, 231
Mazomanie 300
McCarthy, Sen. Joseph 24
McDermott Books 216
McDonald's 164, 228
McDonnell-Pierce House 211
McFarland 354
McFarland Community Life 420
McFarland School District 368
McGettigan Company 332
McGovern's Motel 124
McKay Visitor Center 197
McMillan Gallery 189
Meadowood 352
Meadows of Sixmile Creek, The 283
Media 415
Memorial Carillon 176, 204
Memorial Union 203, 379
Memorial Union Terrace and Rathskeller 98
Mendota Beach Heights 343
Mendota Park 160, 270
Mendota Rowing Club 279
Mendota Wall, The 209
Mental Health Center of Dane County 398
Mental Health Services 398
Mercury Players Theater Company 184
Meriter Home Health 398

Meriter Hospital 388
Meriter Hospital Women's Center 395
Meriter Nurses Run 143
Meriter Retirement Services Inc.
    Retirement Center 407
Merrimac Ferry 321
Metro Dance 180
Metro Ride of Wisconsin Inc. 34
Metro Transit System 33
Metropolitan Art 304
MetroRide of Wisconsin 409
Mexican/Southwestern Restaurants 65
Mickies Dairy Bar 45
Microbrewies 307
Mid-Continent Railway Museum 323
Middle Eastern/Mediterranean Restaurants 66
Middleton 354
Middleton Antiques Mall 239
Middleton Area Historical Museum 201
Middleton Cycle and Fitness 240
Middleton Glen 409
Middleton Good Neighbor Festival 151
Middleton Health Sciences Library 224
Middleton Hills 356
Middleton Memorial Veterans Hospital 391
Middleton Players Theater 185
Middleton Senior Center 403
Middleton Times Tribune 420
Middleton-Cross Plains Area
    School District 368
Midland Builders 334
Midvale Heights-Tokay 343
Midway Farm 302
Midwest Horse Fair 142
Midwest Sport Horse Journal 422
Military Ridge State Park Trail 274
Military Ridge Trail 306
Miller & Sons Super Market 405
Mills Concert Hall 177
Millstone 344
Milwaukee Brewers 258
Milwaukee Bucks 258
Mimosa Community Bookstore 217
Mineral Point 304
Mineral Point Visitors Bureau 305
Miniature Golf 167, 168, 288
MIR Russian Space Station 314
Miracle, the White Buffalo 299
Mitby Theater 178
Mitchard, Jackie 218
Mobile Meals 398
Model Railroad Association Show 138
Monkeyshines 89
Monk's Bar & Grill 321
Monona 356
Monona Bait & Ice Cream 255
Monona Community Festival 148
Monona Community Herald 420
Monona Golf Course 290
Monona Grove School District 368
Monona Municipal Golf Course 285
Monona Pool 163, 292

Monona Senior Center 403
Monona Terrace Community and Convention Center 195
Monona Terrace Convention Center 337
Monona Youth Dream Park 265
Monroe 306, 308
Monroe Welcome Center 309
Monroe Welcome Center-Historic Cheesemaking Center 309
Monson Construction Co. Inc. 335
Montage 297
Monty's Blue Plate Diner 50, 69
Moorland-Rimrock Road 351
More Books! On State Street 217
Morey Airplane Co. 32
Morgan Shoes 228
Morphy Recital Hall 177
Motel 6 121, 123
Motels 113
Mother Fool's Coffeehouse 101
Mother's Day Concert 144
Mothers of Multiples (Moms) 363
Mount Horeb 305
Mount Horeb Area Chamber of Commerce 305
Mount Horeb Mustard Museum 306
Mount Zion Baptist 429
Mountain Biking 274
Mountain Jack's 228
Movie Theaters 101
Movin' Shoes 239, 289
Moze's Gourmet Specialities 234
Mr. Bulky 228
Munz Corporation 330
Museums 199
Music and Memories 298
Music Go Round 246
Music Hall 177
Music Organizations 180
Music Stores 231
Mystic Waters Aqua Dome 318

N

Naeset-Roe Bed and Breakfast 132
Nakoma 340
Name of the Game 233
Nanny Services 362
Narodno International Dancers 180
National Academy of Early Childhood Programs 361
National Association for the Remodeling Industry 326
National Association of Buyer Representatives 331
Native American Archaeological Trail 286
Nature Spirituality 429
Nature's Gallery 189
Nau-Ti-Gal 50, 279
Neighborhoods 337
Neilsen Tennis Stadium 294
Nelson Industries 357
Nesaule, Agate 219

New Century School 370
New Glarus 306, 307
New Glarus Bakery & Tea Room 307
New Glarus Brewery 307
New Glarus Hotel 307
New Glarus Maennerchor 308
New Loft 169
New Orleans Take-Out 55, 81
Newell Gallery & Fine Wine 191
Newspapers 415
NewStart 398
Nichols Design and Construction LLC 335
Nicks, Diane 19
Nielsen Tennis Stadium 379
Night at the Zoo Benefit Dance 149
Night Heron Bed & Breakfast 132
Nightlife 83
Nine Springs Golf Course 285
Nissedahle 306
Nitty Gritty Restaurant and Bar 261
Noah's Ark 313
Nolen, John 25
Noodles & Co. 81
Norman Acres 347
North Lake Mendota 347
North, Sterlling 215
North. Jessica Nelson 215
North/Eastside Senior Coalition 401
Northwoods Bar and Grill 121
Norwegian Pavilion 306
Now Hiring Employment Guide 419
Now Hiring Job Fair 144

O

Oakbrook Corporation 330
Oakcrest Tavern 45
Oakcrest Tavern at the Stadium 95
Oakwood Theater 178
Oakwood Village Retirement and Health Care Community 408
Observatory Drive 2
O'Cayz Corral 85
Odana Golf Course 166, 290
Odana Hills Municipal Golf Course 282
Odana Road 30
Office of Community Services 361
Olbrich Botanical Gardens 160, 198
Olbrich Gardens 339
Olbrich Home Garden Tour 149
Olbrich, Michael 198
Olbrich Park 266
Olbrich Park-Cottage Grove Road 349
Old Feed Mill 52, 300
Old Governor's Residence 212
Old Market Place Neighborhood 339
Old Post House 300
Old Town Pub 48
Olde Time Grocery Delivery 404
Olin House 342
Olin, John 25
Olin-Turville Park 290

444 • INDEX

Olive Garden 228
O'Malley's & O'Malley's Sports Pub 52, 76
Omega School 373
Once Upon A Child 246
Onion, The 418
Open House Imports 305
Opera for the Young 186
Opera House, The 108
Opera House Wine Bar and Restaurant 57
Operation Fresh Start 374
Orange Tree Imports 232, 249
Orchard Ridge 352
Orchids by the Ackers 255
Oregon 356
Oregon Observer 420
Oregon School District 369
Oregon Senior Center 403
Oriental Restaurants 71
Oriental Specialties 249
Original Wisconsin Ducks 314
Orpheum Theatre 101
Oscar Mayer 5
Oscar Mayer Theater 175, 194
Otis Redding Memorial 206
Otto's Restaurant & Bar 67
Our Lady Queen of Peace 372, 428
Our Redeemer Lutheran School 372
Outdoor Pools 292
Outdoor Public Art 205
Outreach 395
Ovens of Brittany, Shorewood 48
Over 55 Employment Service Inc. 411
Owen Conservatory 290

P

Packer Inn 97
Paddle & Portage 146
Pail and Shovel Party 24
Paintball 289
Paisan's 62, 69, 261
Pantry, The 51, 297
Paoli Creamery 307
Paoli Creamery Cafe 191
Parade of Condominiums 151
Parade of Homes 145
Parental Stress Center 363
Park Ponderosa Ballroom and Supper Club 91
Parkcrest Swim and Tennis Club 293
Parking 31
Parks 265
Parkwood Hills 344
Parman's Service Station 232
Parthenon Gyros Restaurant 61
Pasqual's Salsaria 66
Pasqual's Southwestern Deli 232
Past and Present Inn 132
Pasta Per Tutti 64, 69
Patrick's Look of the Isles 249
Paul's Book Store 217
Peace Lutheran School 375
Peacock, The 251

Pearl's Nightclub 86
Pearson, Dennis 195
Pecatonica River 309
Peck, Rosaline and Eben 416
Pedro's 66
Pendarvis 305
Pepperberry, The 250
Performing Arts 179
Performing Arts For Children 186
Perfume Shop, The 249
Period Garden Park 211
Peter's Briar Patch 307
Pew, John C. Residence 213
Phantom Lake YMCA Camp 171
Phoenix Garden Chinese Restaurant 73
Pic-A-Book 217
PICADA 398
Pick More Daisies 232, 249
Picnic Point 25, 204
Pier 1 Imports 228
Pine Bluff Observatory 380
Pioneer Log Village and Museum 323
Pitcher's Pub 96
Pizza Pit 70
Pizzeria Uno 70
Play It Again Sports 246, 287
Playgrounds 163
Playgrounds, Indoor 168
Playthings 254
Playtime Productions 187
Plaza Tavern and Grill 44
Pleasant View Golf Course 283
Plough Inn 340
Point Cinemas 102
Politics and Perspectives 19
Polynesian Resort Hotel & Suites 318
Pooh Corner Bookstore 254
Pooh Corner-East 222
Pooley's 76, 96, 295
Porta Bella 62, 69
Porta's Wine Cellar 110
Powless Tennis Center 294
Prairie Athletic Club 281
Prairie Cafe, The 123
Prairie Garden Bed & Breakfast 132
Prairie Hills 353
Prairie Lanes 277
Prairie Towne Shopping Center 346
PRESENTing WISCONSIN 234
Princeton Club 120, 281
Princeton Custom Homes Inc. 335
Private Campgrounds 278
Private Schools 371
Pro Arte Quartet 182
Progressive Movement 20, 21
Progressive, The 422
Project Home Inc. 405
Project HOPE 431
Property-Management Firms 330
Public Art 205
Public Beaches 291
Public Health Nursing Services 395

INDEX • 445

Public Schools 365
Pubs 97
Puttin' On The Ritz 248
Puzzlebox, The 231, 253

Q

Quaker Services 429
Quality Inn South 123
Quarry Park 274
Quiet Woods Bed & Breakfast 133
Quivey's Grove Stable Grill 52, 89
Quivey's Grove Stone House 60

R

Race For The Cure 144
Racquetball 289
Radio 422
Radio Park 341
Radisson Inn 118
Ragstock 246
Rainbow Bookstore Cooperative 217
Rainbow Play Systems 161
Ramada Inn Capital Conference Center 124
Ramada Inn RainTree Resort 318
Rathskeller 203
Razzmatazz 251
RE/MAX Preferred 327, 332
Real Estate 325
Real Estate Firms 331
Reality Check 232
Recreation 265, 272
Recreation Equipment Inc. (REI) 228
Red Deer Gallery 189
Red Gym 2
Red Lobster 228
Red Pepper Chinese Restaurant & Bar 73
Red Shed, The 100
Redding, Otis Memorial 206
Reedsburg 323
References to Madison and Dane County in National Magazines 9
Regent 341
Regent Street Retreat 95
REI 165
Reindahl Park 347
Relocation Experts 326
Remodeling Expo 136
Rent-Search 328
Rental Cars 33
Rental-Information Publications 330
Reprise Theatre Inc. 184
Reptile Palace Orchestra 94
Resale Shops 244
Rescue Mission 430
Residence Inn by Marriott 118, 121
Resident Camps 170
Restaino Bunbury & Associates 327, 332
Restaurant Magnus 58, 87
Restaurant Ton-Ton 71

Restaurants 39
Retired Senior Volunteer Program (RSVP) 411
Retirement and Senior Services 401
Rhapsody in Bloom 146
Rhythm & Booms 148
Rick's Olde Gold 234
Ride Services 35
Ridgewood Country Club Apartments 330
Ridgewood Pool 294
Ring's All-American Karate 288
Ristow, Charmaine 180
Riverview Park & Waterworld 313
Road Star 118
Roberts Drug Store 307
Rock Climbing Gym 168
Rocky Rococo's 70, 162
Rocky's Party Pizzeria 70
Roller Skating 166, 168, 286
Rollerdrome 168, 287
Ronald E. Mitchell Theatre 177
Ronald McDonald House 363, 388
Rossario's 64, 69
Rotary Gardens 299
Roughing It In Style 307
Rowe, Jim 297
Rowe's Pottery Works 243, 297
Rowing 279
Rubin's Furniture 242
Rude's Lanes 169
Run/Walk Events 143, 144, 155
Rundell's Menswear 244
Running/Walking 289
Rupert Cornelius 227
Rupert Cornelius — The Women's Store 253
Russian House 74
Russian Restaurants 74
Rusty's Bar 98
Rutabaga 240, 279
Rutabaga's Canoecopia 140

S

Sa-Bai Thong 72
Sacred Heart Catholic School 375
Saigon Restaurant 72
Sailboarding 289
Sailing 289
Saint Benedict Center 430
Salmo Pond 268
Sal's Pizzeria 69
Sapphire Ballroom 91
Sassafras Ltd. 251
Satellite Family Child Care Inc. 361
Sauk Creek 346
Sauk-Prairie 321
Saukborough-Woodland Hills 344
Saz 67
Schoolhouse Shops 307
Schools 365
Schwoegler Park Towne Lanes 166, 276
Science Hall 2
Scoshi 252

446 • INDEX

Seafood Restaurants 78
Sears 228, 230
Second Baptist Church 429
Second Story 90
Sedona 252
Select Day Care Personnel Services Inc. 362
Select Inn 122
Seminole Hills 354
Senior Centers 402
Senior Nutrition Sites 404
Senior Olympic Games 412
Senior Services 401
Sentry Foods 228
Sepp Sport Inc. 240
Sergio's Niteclub 86
Seth Peterson Cottage 319
Seven Hills Skydivers 291
Seventh Day Adventist School 374
Severson, William Conrad 209
Shakespeare's Books 217
Shakti Book Shop 217
Shalala, Donna 20
Shamanic Wiccan Church 429
Shelf & Dining Furniture Ltd. 242
Sheraton Madison Hotel 122
Sherman 348
Sherman Village 348
Sherry J's Curve Cafe 297
Shish Cafe, The 71
Shoe Box 300
Shoe Gallery 227
Shoe Stores 227
Shoppers Express 404
Shopping 227
Shopping Malls 227
Shorewood Hills 353
Short Story Cafe, The 304
Sidran, Ben 92
Sienna River Gallery 297
Silver Buckle Press 225
Simon and Voss 333
Simon, Michael F. Builders 334
Simple Gifts Gallery 307
Sinykin, Sheri Cooper 219
Sir Michael's 35
Ski, Sky and Stage 314
Skiing 165, 290
Sky Aces Inc. 273
Skydiving 291
Skyview Meadows 353
Skyview Park 343
Skyview Terrace 343
Sledding and Tobogganing 165
Smarty Pants Resale Shop 248
Smoky Jon's No. 1 BBQ 75
Smoky's Club 79
Soap Opera 231, 248
Soccer 291
Soccer Scoop, The 419
Soccer World Inc. 162, 287, 291
Social Work Library 224
Society of Friends Quaker Meeting House 429
Sophia's Bakery and Cafe 50
South Madison Coalition of the Elderly 401
South Towne Cinemas 103
Southern/Southwestern Barbecue Restaurants 74
Space Place 197
Spaightwood Galleries 190
Spare Time 206
Special Services and Support Groups 394
Sporting Goods Stores 231
Sports 257
Sports Bars 76
Sports Savers 239, 287
Spring Flower Show 141, 198
Spring Green 300
Spring Green Arts and Crafts Fair 301
Spring Harbor-Indian Hills 344
Spring Tavern 340
Springs, The 300
Sproat, Christopher 208
Square One 227
Square One Outfitters 253
St. Dennis Catholic Church 428
St. John The Baptist School 375
St. Maria Goretti School 373
St. Marys Health Works 412
St. Marys Hospital 390
St. Patrick's Catholic Church 428
St. Paul's Lutheran Church 404
St. Peter Catholic School 375
St. Raphael's Cathedral 428
Stadium Bar, The 95
Stadium House 128
Stagecoach Players 187
Stamm House At Pheasant Branch 53
Stand Rock 313
Stanley, Leothea 429
Star, The 420
Stark Company 333
Stark Company Relocation Division 327
Start Renting Inc. 331
State Capitol 193
State Historical Museum and Gift Shop 200, 219
State Medical Society of Wisconsin 387
State Parks 271
State Spelling Bee 142
State Street Brats 99
State Trunk Highway Act 24
Steak and Seafood Restaurants 78
Steenbock Memorial Library 224
Steep and Brew 100
Steinhafels 242
Stewart Park 270
Stillwaters 44, 99
Stonefield Woods-Ridge 344
Stoney Oaks 130
Stony Hill Antiques 235
Storybook Gardens 317
Stoughton 356
Stoughton Antique Mall 239
Stoughton Area School District 369

INDEX • 447

Stoughton City Hall Theater 178
Stoughton Community Hospital 391
Stoughton Courier-Hub 420
Stoughton Historical Museum 202
Stoughton Hospital Urgent Care 392
Stoughton Senior Center 403
Stoughton Trailers 357
Stoughton Village Players 185
Stoughton's Mainstreet Market 405
Strollers Theater 184
Stubblefield, Clyde 93
Studio You 162, 232
Studt, Teddy 187
Substance-Abuse Treatment Centers 398
Sugar Bakers 298
Sugar River State Trail 308
Suiter's Limited 244
Sun Prairie 357
Sun Prairie Aquatic Center 163, 292
Sun Prairie Area School District 370
Sun Prairie Civic Theatre 185
Sun Prairie Country Club 283
Sun Prairie Historical Library and Museum 202
Sun Prairie Ice Arena 165
Sun Prairie News, The 420
Sun Prairie Sweet Corn Festival 150
Sundae in the Gardens 150
Sunlife "Cloud 9" Limousine 35
Sunporch Cafe and Art Gallery 49
Sunprint Cafe 49
Sunset Hills 341
Sunset Village 341
Super 8 123
Supreme Pizza 70
Survivors Of Suicide (SOS) 395
Susan's Closet Resale Boutique 246
Sushi Bars 71
Suzen Sez 253, 298
Swim Clubs 293
Swimming 160, 166, 291
Swimming Pools 292
SwimWest Family Fitness Center 162, 292
Swiss Historical Village Museum 307
Sycamore Park 346
Synagogues 428
Synergy! Jazz 183
Syttende Mai Folk Festival 144

T

Taco Bell 228
Takeout Taxi 80
Taliesin 300, 302
Tallman House 299
Tan-y-deri House 302
Tandem Press 190
TAP-IT New Works 183
Taqueria Gila Monster 65
Taste Of India 65
Taste of Madison 151
Taverns and Lounges 90
Taxis 35

Taylor Conservation Park 350
Television 424
Tellurian UCAN 399
Temple Beth El 428
Tenant Resource Center 328
Tenney Beach 160
Tenney Park 164, 267, 286
Tenney-Lapham 339
Tennis 294
Theater 183
Theater Bus Inc. 173, 413
Thistle Hill Tabletop Company 304
Thompson, Gov. Tommy 198
Thurow, Nancy 184
Timekeeper 206
Tobogganing 165
Token Creek Hot Air Balloons Inc. 273
Token Creek Park 270
Tommy Bartlett's Amusements 314
Tony Frank's Tavern 89
Tony's 64
Top of the Park 59, 114
Tornado Steak House 78
Tower Hill State Park 300, 301
Town and Country Antiques
    Show and Sale 152
Toy Stores 231
Transportation Services 409
Trapper's Turn 316
Triangle Ethnic Fest 150
Trollway 305
Tropic Jewel 231
Truax 348
Tuesday Noon Concerts 145
Tumbledown Trails Golf Course 283
Turner, John 429
Tutto Pasta Trattoria Bar & Caffe 63
Tyrol Basin 166, 291, 306

U

UBS for Kids 221, 234
Ultimate Frisbee 294
Ultra Zone 161, 167
Umoja 422
Unbridaled Wedding Alternatives Party 153
Union Cab Cooperative 35
Union South 203
Unitarian Meeting House 212
Unitarian Society 429
United Cerebral Palsy 396
United Refugee Services of Wisconsin 411
United Way of Dane County
    Volunteer Center 411
Unity Chapel 302
University Book Store, The 219, 221, 234
University Book Store's Digital Outpost 219
University Cab 35
University Coin Stamp & Jewelry 243
University Heights 342
University Heights Bed and Breakfast 128
University Inn Hotel 116

448 • INDEX

University of Wisconsin Arboretum 290
University of Wisconsin Hospital and
  Clinics 390
University of Wisconsin-Madison 2, 377
University Ridge Golf Course 282
University Theater 185
Upper Iowa University Madison Center 385
Upstairs, Downstairs Restaurant and
  Deli 56, 228
Urban Ministry 430
Urban Outfitters 231
Urban Pizza Co., The 69
UW Arboretum 164, 197
UW Babcock Dairy Plant 203
UW Children's Hospital 391
UW Clinic Research Park Aquatic Center 293
UW Dance Program 180
UW Doctors/Physicians Plus Urgent Care 392
UW Geology Museum 201
UW Memorial Carillon 204
UW Space Place 158, 197
UW-Madison Arts Outreach Program 181
UW-Madison School of Music 183

V

Valperine Gallery 190
Vegetarian Restaurants 81
Verona 357
Verona Area School District 370
Verona Area Senior Center 403
Verona Bus Service 34
Verona Core Knowledge School 370
Verona Press 420
Veterans Hospital 391
Veterans Museum 201
Veterinary Care 399
Veterinary Medical Teaching Hospital 399
Victor Allen's Coffee & Tea 100
Victorian Treasure B&B Inn 133
Victoria's Secret 228, 230
Viking Lanes 277
Viking Village 278
Vilas Beach 160
Vilas Communications Hall 177
Vilas, Henry 196
Vilas Park 163, 164
Vilas Park and Beach 266
Vilas, William F. 213
Vilas, William S. and Anna 196
Vilas Zoo 196
Vilas-Edgewood Avenue 342
Village Cohousing Community 408
Village Green 53
Village Inn Restaurant & Catering 53
Village Peddler 165
Vin Santo 64
Vintage Door 243
Vintage Interiors 238
Visions Night Club 88
Visiting Nurse Service Inc. 398
Visual Arts 187

Vitense Golfland 288
Volksfest 308
Volleyball 263, 294
Volunteer Opportunities 411

W

W Club 234
Wagonfactory Mercantile 298
Walbridge Academy 373
Waldenbooks 228, 230
Walgreen's 228
WalkAmerica 143
Walking 37, 289
Walking Events 143
Walking Iron Park 269
Wallace, Ron 215
Walnut Grove 346
Walnut Grove Shopping Center 228
Walnut Hollow Woodcraft Outlet 304
Walter R. Bauman Outdoor Aquatic Center 163
Walters Swim & Sun 240
Wando's Tavern 96
Wanuakee 357
Warner Park 267, 286, 290
Wasabi Japanese Restaurant and Sushi Bar 71
Washburn Observatory 2, 204, 380
Water Aerobics 295
Water Parks 312
Water Tower Pub 96
WaunaFest 150
Waunakee Senior Center 403
Waunakee Tribune 420
Waunona Way 351
Wear It Again 247
Weather 14
Wedding Planner and Guide Bridal Show 136
Weekly Newspapers 417
Weinman, Adolph A. 209
Wells Clay Works 297
West Side Bill Paul LTD Studio 244
West Side Swim Club 294
West Towne Cinemas 102
West Towne Mall 228
Western Koshkonong Lutheran School 375
Westgate Cinemas 102
Westhaven 353
Westmorland 340
Westside Senior Center 403
Wexford Ridge 346
Wheelchair Basketball 295
Wheelchair Recycling Program 396
Wheels For You 419
White Horse Inn 59
Whitehouse Tavern, The 295
Whitney Way 30
Whole Foods Market 399
Whoops! & Co. 254
Wicca 429
Wick Homes 335
Wil-Mar 338
Wild At Heart Studios and Gallery 190

Wild Child 232, 240
Wild Hog in the Woods Coffeehouse 101
Wild Iris Cafe 46, 69
Wilder, Amos P. 416
Wilderness Hotel and Golf Resort 316, 318
Wilhelm Tell Festival 308
Willalby's Cafe 50
William S. Middleton Memorial Veterans Hospital 391
Williams Sonoma 228
Williamson Bicycle Works 36, 275
Williamson Street Co-op 339, 405
Willy Street Fair 152
Wilson Street Grill 45
Wilson's Bar 97
Wine & Hop Shop 110
Wine Bars 105, 108
Wineke, William 430
Wingate Inn 123
Wingra Park 340
Wingra Quintet 182
Wingra School 373
Winter Art Festival 154
Winter Concerts in the Gardens 136
Winter Horse-drawn Vehicle Rally and Display 135
Wintersilks 255
Wisconsiana 208
Wisconsin Academy Review 422
Wisconsin Agriculturist 422
Wisconsin Badgers 262, 263
Wisconsin Badgers — Men 259
Wisconsin Badgers — Women 259
Wisconsin Center For Paper Arts 190
Wisconsin Chamber Orchestra 183
Wisconsin Dance Ensemble 186
Wisconsin Deer & Turkey Expo 141
Wisconsin Dells 311
Wisconsin Dells Visitor & Convention Bureau 316
Wisconsin Dells/Lake Delton Chamber of Commerce 316
Wisconsin Dental Association 387
Wisconsin Dept. of Transportation 410
Wisconsin Elder Law Center 402
Wisconsin Film Festival 135
Wisconsin First Step 363
Wisconsin Fury 263
Wisconsin Golf 422
Wisconsin Homecare Organization 398
Wisconsin Hoofers 286
Wisconsin Law Enforcement Memorial 208
Wisconsin Off-Road Bicycling Association 275
Wisconsin Screenwriters Forum Inc. 225
Wisconsin Singers 183
Wisconsin State Capitol 1
Wisconsin State Journal 416
Wisconsin Trails 422
Wisconsin Union Art Collection and Theater Galleries 188
Wisconsin Union Theater 177
Wisconsin Veterans Museum 158, 201
Wisconsin Youth Symphony Orchestras 187
Wizenheimers, The 93
Woldenberg's 227
Woldenberg's Men's Apparel 244
Woldenberg's Women's Apparel 253
Wolff Kubly 228
Wollersheim Winery 322
Women and Kidstore Resale 247
Women's Store, The 253
Women's Transit Authority 35
Wonder's Pub 100
Wooden Voices 234
Woodworks 242
World Dairy Expo 153
World Famous Buckeye Inn 96
Worship 427
Wright, Frank Lloyd 212, 429
Writers' Place, The 225

Y

Yahara Builders Inc. 335
Yahara Hills Municipal Golf Course 282
Yellow Jersey 36, 275
YMCA 166, 289, 291, 293, 295
YMCA Camp 171
YMCA of Metropolitan Madison 170
Yost's 228, 252
Younkers 228, 230

Z

Zeier, Joan 219
Zemke Traditional Clothiers 244
Zoo 159, 196
Zor Shrine Circus 138

FALCONGUIDES® leading the way

Travel the great outdoors with
A FALCONGUIDE®

- Comprehensive information on essential outdoor skills, trails, trips, and the best places to go in each state.

- Detailed descriptions, maps, access information, photos, and safety tips.

- Easy-to-use, written by expert, and regularly

To locate your nearest bookseller or to order call

1-800-582-2665.

Ask for a FREE catalog featuring books on nature, outdoor recreation, travel, and the legendary American West.

FALCON®

Going Somewhere?

Insiders' Publishing presents 51 current and upcoming titles to popular destinations all over the country (including the titles below) — and we're planning on adding many more. To order a title, go to your local bookstore or call (800) 582-2665 and we'll direct you to one.

Adirondacks	Michigan's Traverse Bay Region
Atlanta, GA	Minneapolis/St. Paul, MN
Bermuda	Mississippi
Boca Raton and the Palm Beaches, FL	Monterey Peninsula
Boulder, CO, and Rocky Mountain National Park	Myrtle Beach, SC
Bradenton/Sarasota, FL	Nashville, TN
Branson, MO, and the Ozark Mountains	New Hampshire
California's Wine Country	North Carolina's Central Coast and New Bern
Cape Cod, Nantucket and Martha's Vineyard, MA	North Carolina's Mountains
Charleston, SC	Outer Banks of North Carolina
Cincinnati, OH	The Pocono Mountains
Civil War Sites in the Eastern Theater	Relocation
Colorado's Mountains	Richmond, VA
Denver, CO	Salt Lake City
Florida Keys and Key West	Santa Fe
Florida's Great Northwest	Savannah
Golf in the Carolinas	Southwestern Utah
Indianapolis, IN	Tampa/St. Petersburg, FL
The Lake Superior Region	Tucson
Las Vegas	Virginia's Blue Ridge
Lexington, KY	Virginia's Chesapeake Bay
Louisville, KY	Washington, D.C.
Madison, WI	Wichita, KS
Maine's Mid-Coast	Williamsburg, VA
Maine's Southern Coast	Wilmington, NC
	Yellowstone

THE INSIDERS' GUIDE®

Insiders' Publishing • P.O. Box 2057 • Manteo, NC 27954
Phone (252) 473-6100 • Fax (252) 473-5869 • www.insiders.com